24.95
CM Vanier

D0948374

CONTAINER SYSTEMS

MATERIALS HANDLING AND PACKAGING SERIES
James R. Bright, Advisory Editor

MARINE CARGO OPERATIONS
Charles L. Sauebier

PACKAGE DESIGN ENGINEERING
Kenneth Brown

INDUSTRIAL PACKAGING
Walter F. Friedman and Jerome J. Kipnees

WAREHOUSE OPERATIONS PLANNING AND MANAGEMENT
Andrew J. Briggs

GRAVITY FLOW OF BULK SOLIDS AND TRANSPORTATION OF SOLIDS IN SUSPENSION
Alexey J. Stepanoff

PNEUMATIC CONVEYING
H. A. Stoess

CONTAINER SYSTEMS
Eric Rath

CONTAINER SYSTEMS

ERIC RATH

TRANSPORTATION ENGINEER
PRESIDENT, TRC DEVELOPMENT, INC.

A Wiley-Interscience Publication

John Wiley & Sons

NEW YORK • LONDON • SYDNEY • TORONTO

Library of Congress Cataloging in Publication Data:

Rath, Eric, 1911–
Container systems.

(Materials handling and packaging series)
"A Wiley-Interscience publication"
Bibliography: p.
1. Containerization. I. Title.

TA1215.R38   380.5'2   72-13139
ISBN 0-471-70921-2

Printed in the United States of America

10 9 8 7 6 5 4 3 2 1

Foreword

Eric Rath once described himself as a "transportation entrepreneur." He is more than that. If Malcolm McLean, the trucker who founded Sea-Land Service in 1956, can be called the Father of the Container Revolution, Eric Rath is truly the "Grandfather" of this phenomenon.

It is true, as Mr. Rath points out in Chapter One, that techniques for handling large containerized cargo units date back almost 2,000 years to the transportation of wild beasts in cages from Africa to Rome. When wheels were attached to the cages, the possibility of intermodal transportation was created.

It is also true that Seatrain Lines started taking railroad cars to sea in 1927, and that such vessels as car ferries were in operation for many years before that event. The marriage of the highway and the sea really began in 1953, however, when Eric Rath formed Trailer Marine Transportation, later known as TMT Trailer Ferry. This company was the first to take truck trailers to sea on roll-on, roll-off trailerships.

Eric Rath uses a very interesting analytical process to systematize containerization and coordinated transportation. This process was developed over the last twenty years for the design and management of large-scale, complex military and space systems, and has been variously identified as systems analysis, systems engineering, operations research, operations analysis and systems science. Basically, the process consists of applying the scientific method to operational objectives. The operational objective in this case is to minimize the total economic and social cost of the movement of goods from point to point.

The total cost (supply price) of a product is composed of two major cost categories. The first is the production cost of creating the product. The second cost is associated with the distribution of the product. Since the advent of mass production, the ratio of production cost to supply price has been steadily declining. At the present time, it is below fifty percent. However, the distribution phase of our economy has not experienced the same economies that have taken place in the production phase. Increases in economic efficiencies generally come from two sources: economies of scale and technological change. Containerization provides an opportunity for increased economic efficiency from both sources in the distribution phase. In this book, Eric Rath examines the transportation system impacts of containerization and its implication for reducing distribution costs. This distribution phase of domestic and international economy needs increased productivity of service.

Mr. Rath is particularly fitted to write about container systems because he has been in the transportation field for nearly forty years. From 1933 to 1935, Mr. Rath was coordinator of less-than-carload container service between railroads, motor carriers, and steamships for the International Container Bureau in Paris. He was Coordinator of Transportation for the Government of Colombia from 1936 to 1939. From 1940 to 1942, he was Superintendent of Transportation for the Texas Company in Colombia. After a two-year service in the United States Army, where he was in the Motor Transport Corps at Fort Knox, Kentucky, Mr. Rath opened his own air transport business, handling cargo and operating an air charter service in Europe.

Thereafter, he joined the Acme Air Cargo Company and became Vice President in charge of its Latin American operations. In 1953, he founded TMT and was its President for several years.

After leaving TMT, Eric Rath was successively consultant to United States Lines in setting up their North Atlantic container service, President and founder of Cool-Chain, Inc., consultant to Litton Industries on the Fast Deployment Logistics Ship (FDLS) Project, transportation consultant to the Department of Defense, and President of The Rath Company, a marine and coordinated transportation design and servicing organization. In this book, Eric Rath is sharing with the reader the fruits of a lifetime of rich and varied transportation experience. We consider it vital reading for students of economics, management, and marine transportation.

William Sembler, M.B.A., Master Mariner
Professor of Marine Transportation
State University of New York, Maritime College
Fort Schuyler, New York

Professor Joseph D. Carrabino, Ph.D., P.E.
Graduate School of Management
University of California, Los Angeles
Board Chairman, EMSCO (Engineering &
    Management Sciences Corporation)

Preface

After thousands of years, ocean shipping changed radically during the last three decades. Marine operations, with its diverse related activities, are now a part of total transportation, reduced to a single component of the overall physical distribution chain of goods. With the solution of the intermodal transfer problem between shipping points, various carrier modes and final consumer facilities, this new total transportation became so closely aligned with the production of the goods to be shipped, that the resulting containerization appears to be little more than the extension of the production facility itself. The container creates a "bulk" unit out of the individual pieces of freight. It not only moves shipments in standardized, unitized, uniform, outer shells (the container itself), but also combines in-transit protection with cost-effective bulk handling. This opens new, unknown fields of endeavor to the farmer, the manufacturer and the consumer alike. A new day in these capabilities widens the work cycle of life.

Of the many problems which accompany this development, three are especially difficult to solve. The first problem deals with the need to continually assess the long-term effects of the innovative changes. It is the nature of this technology that further improvements must be expected to effect the gains and force even further changes. Secondly, the co-existence of the modern methods with the remnants of the older technology of conventional shipping produces problems to the application and timing of a quick, uniform changeover. Since the new system supersedes existing habits and customs, the resistance to change by the human sector calls for solutions never before applied or even tried. Finally, the third problem in our growing world is that containerization shows greatest results in its most complete application with the expenditure of giant-sized investments. This field is reserved today to the highly-technologically developed nations. In countries with fewer resources, these effects produce rising expectations looking toward benefits to affect them also; but at the same time, produce a gap between the segments of the transport world which could widen out of proportion. In November 1972 the United Nations organized the world's first conference on international container traffic to which more than 120 nations and organizations sent their representatives to the meeting in Geneva, Switzerland. I attended as a representative of one of the non-governmental technical organizations. Never before in transportation history had people from as many parts of government and industry of the world assembled to discuss the problems of combined transportation. The three problems described in this Preface were clearly evident as the representatives of the developed nations faced a majority of some 90 developing nations.

Dealing with transport policy options with respect to containerization in international, intermodal transport related to the developing nations the inevitability of containerization in one form or the other was generally accepted by the developing nations. However, the assembly estimated that it would require at least a decade to implement this. The developing nations must give consideration to the systematic interfacing of the new transport technology with the employment of their natural resources, their large human labor pools, their shortness of capital and their economic and political independence. It is the mission of transportation systems science to close the gap between nations and allow the people to benefit from the ultimate opportunities of intermodal transport.

I have written this book, placing emphasis on the essential structure of the discipline as a typical application of systems science. The teachings related to cross-fertilization from fields related to the basic subject matter will guide the reader through the maze of novel techniques. I have concentrated on the key elements of the discipline and the unique magnetism which developed as the different phases of intermodalism attract each other to form an integrated systems structure. In theory, this same cause-and-effect relationship demonstrated here should apply to the systems technology of many other problem areas in our modern science. Containerization as a system is the result of the inseparability of subsystems and components, like the parts of the Chinese symbol of the Yin and the Yang.

ACKNOWLEDGMENTS

The author would like to extend thanks to his many friends to whom he is deeply indebted. This is an acknowledgement of his gratitude to them. Much time and help in formulating, reviewing, correcting and improving has been given by a group of friends, each of whom is well known in his own professional field. Words can hardly express my thanks for their cooperation, to make this work possible.

Professor Harald Burmeister	Lee Ross
Charles Cushing	Jerome Schwarzbach
Russell Hinds	Robert Stoessel
Peter Hunter	Colonel Vancel Beck
Frank Richter	James Warwick

Particular thanks are also due to Josephine Ann Siegle for her indefatigable secretarial assistance and to Ada Stough for her galley proof reading.

Eric Rath

Contents

Section IV   INTERFACE SERVICES

Section V   COMMAND AND CONTROL

Section VI   INTERDISCIPLINARY ENVIRONMENT

CONTAINER SYSTEMS

SYSTEMS AND RULES

I am a part of all I have met
yet all experience is an arch
where through gleams the untraveled world
beyond the utmost margin of known thought.
Alfred, Lord Tennyson, 1853

Container Systems

PRAGMATIC ERA

In over 40 years of worldwide personal experience in integrated transportation, I have dealt with a variety of problems in many lands, under changing conditions, in various undertakings and levels of skill. I have found, however, some general rules of practice in the container industry hold true in most situations. Yes, during the ten development years, containerization has taken off in many directions; yet the principles of the basic system have not fundamentally changed. This knowledge of the tenets of component integration and interface systems produced some denominators for the cargo systems science.

Containerization consists of the simple application of temporary portable storage facilities loaded with cargo made mobile as a unit for intermodal unified transport. The tridimensional coordination problem of the system resides in the relationship between the three base elements: man, machine mobility, and the box united in global motion.

Unitization, therefore, brings the transport engineer, the equipment designer, and the port operator face to face with unusual problems which are new and not common to their own customary fields of endeavor.

3

Marine managers are faced with determinations which affect areas outside the normal marine field, such as surface transportation by truck, railroad car, and possibly by aircraft. The magnitude of the novel problem increases with the extension of the service areas. Containers must move without restriction. This includes operations in technically advanced countries as well as developing nations. This freedom of motion provides internal and specific constraints of each mode, which must be overcome and adjusted to avoid costly friction in an international, intermodal container community.

Container technology requires a community of interests; to reduce the complexity of such a program to a minimum, interface and friction require common behavior in the segments. This system affects the transfer of containers in dissimilar fields of application. It requires a system of mutuality, where the acceptance of the other medium's container must be adjusted to international cooperative interests and must be planned to carry one product without rehandling over several systems of transportation mobility.

Containerization is a systems approach to transport service. It represents the dawn of an era, in which all modes of transportation will be subjected to integration into a single, worldwide system.

John Griffith, Chairman of Norton Lilly, Inc., summarized the position of the entire steamship industry on containerization by stating, "We're realizing as an industry that we are no longer just in the steamship business. We are beginning to realize that we are in the transportation business and the means of transportation is the container. The container, only incidentally, is carried by a ship."

BOX PASSING

"Passing the buck" in colloquial terms refers to a tendency to avoid accepting responsibility for a solution. Yet "buck passing," historically, was the first communal system devised by city dwellers to extinguish fires. Forming an effective chain of men handling buckets of water still is often the only solution to smother flames. In effect, modern containerization is a technology devised to improve transportation methods by systematically passing a cargo from carrier to carrier, in the same container, without touching the cargo placed in the container by the original shipper for the consignee.

A "bucket brigade" is indeed very similar to the "box passing" system of today's container world. Members are faced with the need of handling containers passed to them by other transport media. It is, therefore, understandable that the size, shape, form, and condition of the container—if considered in these terms—requires more thought than any single mode of transportation equipment to permit the formation and maintenance of an effective chain system.

To fulfill this mission of integrated transportation, the container requires a synthesis of all the resources and facilities of the systems components in order to form a well-linked chain. This means that the parochialism which in the past has dominated the transportation industry in each country, as well as in international trade, must change or disappear. In its place, world transportation everywhere must become a communal affair. The consideration which affects each one of the members of the transportation community becomes the container issue of all.

BURDEN ON PLANNING

Unfortunately, this throws a heavy burden on the planner and organizer. There is an insufficient backlog of precedent and experience available on which to form judgments. Instead, a flood of unrelated facts and information come to mind. The container decision maker is faced with the requirement to know and understand what is happening worldwide. What adds to the difficulty of broad comprehension is the frequent appearance and disappearance of innovative concepts. To gain a full overview of the container community requires a systematic approach to the situation. This can be done in historical retrospect, but the container community is an expression of modern times and creates relationships which are changing frequently.

My approach to the problem is to summarize developments into understandable systems elements. At the risk of being too brief, I had to limit the discussion to what I feel are the most significant facts.

Many periodicals and some yearbooks should be consulted, not as a scientific source, but rather for additional information. The container community is a combination of facts, figures, elements, and systems related to each other and to the resource performance, like a large, imaginary assembly of world production.

HISTORY OF THE CONTAINER

For almost 2,000 years, man developed techniques to move goods on the land; these were primarily in single dimensions. The wheel served as the basis for land transportation; the sail for water transportation.

Whatever improvement in the efficiency of movement could have been gained as a result of innovations and machinery had still to be limited to the speed with which each piece of cargo could be placed onto or unloaded from the basic transport mode.

Since the days of the Roman Empire, man has been faced with the need to handle large cargo units onto the transport vehicle. The first such pieces were the cages in which wild beasts were transported from Africa to the circus in Rome. The nature of the cargo made it imperative to find a way to load the animal within its cage. Blocks and tackle attached to the ship's mast were used to transfer the unit load from land to ship and vice versa. Wheels were attached to the four corner posts of the cargo for continued land transportation. This created the possibility of intermodal transportation. But the idea faced difficulties. Man had first to find mechanical means to transfer large loads from vehicle to terminal. With the improvement of locomotion, the intermodal relationships provided systems of land transportation from shoreline to shoreline.

Progress in water transportation had to deal with the cargo transfer problems. The handling of cargo onto a ship was restricted to a system of laboriously moving cargo up from shore, across to the ship, and down into the hold. Improved, large-scale cargo transfer could be effected only within sheltered ports, where the ship would be alongside the pier, protected from the dangers of the breaking surf.

About 50 years ago, the monodimensional limitation of man in the movement of goods was overcome by the introduction of mechanized lifting facilities capable of handling the large, heavy cargo units and swinging them from place to place while being suspended. While improved overhead lifting equipment became available for ships and ports, the weight capacity remained small for a long period. World War II and postwar rehabilitation of Europe provided the first incentive for change. After World War II, it became apparent that port techniques adversely affected the economy of many nations. A long line of ships anchored in the harbor for days, idly awaiting their turn to berth was an all-too-familiar scene in many ports in the world. When this occurs, the ship is idle while its overhead expenses, including the wages and maintenance costs of ship and crew and the interest on capital invested, keep mounting. The delivery of goods is delayed, the goods themselves are even sometimes diverted, freight rates are increased, and trade is hampered. Even when delays in port do not evidence themselves in such a striking manner, nevertheless, they frequently arise; and they are very costly to the shipowners, the owners of the cargo, and the community as a whole.

PORT CONGESTION

Many factors account for port congestion. Sometimes, and fairly often, it occurs because of industrial disputes affecting port workers, and on other occasions because of the relatively low productivity of labor in handling the goods. Slow turnaround of ships became one of the main preoccupations of shipowners in all maritime countries in 1950. In 1951, the Council of the Organization for European Economic Cooperation recommended that member countries "take all possible steps to improve the turnaround of ships in the ports within their territories as a means of ensuring increased carrying capacity of world shipping and the more efficient use of ships" and "instruct their representatives in the appropriate agencies of the United Nations to draw the attention of non-member countries to the necessity of action with the object of eliminating the causes of the slow turnaround of ships." The International Cargo Handling Coordination Association (I.C.H.C.A.) was set up largely to carry out investigations into shipping and to develop a cargo systems science. A methodical and rational approach to handling large, compartmentlike containers was made, turning away from the one-man lifts.

Monomodal tradition, objection by labor to the technology devised to supplant capital investment for labor, and conventional international shipping methods produced an era in which containerization could progress only at a very slow pace. It took pioneers with personal incentive to implement the newly rediscovered container idea. Makeshift adaptation of tankers to containerships followed the tradition of World War II when airplanes were ferried to Europe on top deck. Landing ships designed for tanks were used for roll-on methods, using conventional road truck trailers instead of containers. Truck bodies, commonly sized to a 17-foot length in the eastern United States, set the pattern for the design of containerships to serve in international trade with Venezuela. The offshore islands of the United States, with their restricted protection to American-flag vessels, offered opportunities for the beginning of integrated services. In like manner, such trade developed containerization between England and the European mainland at the same time.

CONSOLIDATION OF CARGO

Containerization has been defined by The Containerization Institute as "The utilizing, grouping or consolidating of multiple units into a larger container for more efficient movement."

Almost parallel with development of the transportation container came cargo unitization in two similar forms of transport. The use of pallets provides a simple medium to carry and haul individual cargo grouped together. The pallet became an accepted system for cargo transfer in the distribution process since 1945, when fork-lift trucks, adapted for the handling of pallets, became generally used in the transportation industry. The use of large, highway-truck trailers with their own wheels, on top of flat railroad freight cars, just as on ships, became common practice in the U.S. in 1950. The size of the trailer as cargo container produces approximately the same available loading space and weight capacity as the unwheeled cargo container. This system became commonly known as "piggyback" if by rail; and "RO-RO" (short for roll-on, roll-off) if by water.

Containerization spread, during the 1960s, to far more than sea and land transportation. The innovative action, once started, soon affected all modes of transportation and human life. The apparent simplicity of the idea was expected to automatically produce a single, universally acceptable planned system. This, however, did not happen. Rather than creating one, single, world-wide, universally standardized container system, variations of the basic idea by several pioneers have formed competing systems, so that presently several container systems are in use all over the world. Only about half of these systems are compatible with each other to some extent. Others, although similar in concept, are quite different in application. Therefore, the hoped-for unified world transportation system as devised by the planners and systems engineers is, in reality, a combination of uncoordinated systems and subsystems. With existing transportation tradition requiring changes to accept containerization, containerization has become an intricate web of complexity, albeit the variations stem from the same basic idea. Attempts to produce unification in containerization have produced merely regulation and control, not integration.

IMPACT ON STEAMSHIP INDUSTRY

After prolonged stagnation in the development of better ocean shipping methods, containerization came initially to the steamship line business. Prior to this technological breakthrough, the thinking in the steamship industry first emphasized physical hardware. Ships, equipment, speed, and operation were the essence of scheduled sailings. Now emphasis is laid on systems, systems engineering, coordination, and integration. This has had a tremendous impact on the steamship industry, and subsequently, due to extension of the steamship container systems, the rest of the transportation industry became involved. There are new goals not only for those in the industry, but also for those who plan their relationship with the transportation system. As far as steamships are concerned, the first impact is a change in the internal organization of the company. In a typical steamship company there were departments dealing with marine operations, piers, finance, administration, and freight traffic. In all these departments, involvement in some facets of marine transportation is always present and encompasses a great many marine-oriented matters. Now, with the advent of containerization, the old methodology is disappearing. Ship operation is relatively simple, and can be handled by computer operators. The ship itself is sophisticated, but again can be programmed since it deals almost exclusively with time-experienced transactions. Compared to a normal liner operation, container ship turnaround and operations are relatively simple.

The impact of containerization on cost and profit of a steamship business comes from the substitution of labor by intensive capital operation. In the conventional liner operation, a mass of people handled tens of thousands of pieces of cargo, leading to an ever-rising labor cost, which forced the industry to change over. As Griffith put it, "By investing a large amount of capital in the system, which decreases the dependence of the system on hand labor, we have a chance to resist the terrible squeeze between cost and profit." At the very beginning of containerization, the cargo loading rate in the simplest form rose from 15 tons per gang-hour to 200 tons per gang-hour. The savings through cost effective utilization of the ship space amounted to $6–$10 per ton. How could the industry resist that?

If you accept the theory that steamship companies are going to continue being in the container systems business, it follows that new people entering the industry must have a basic understanding of the multifaceted systems components and realities of containerization.

EDUCATION IN THE BOARD ROOM

After a few years in which the negative aspects of the cost of transfer and delay exploded, management had to become interested in the qualifications of containerization. This required education in the board rooms to guide the undertaking through the problems and uncertainties of the new industrial revolution. In trying to achieve this capital-intensive transport system with a low human labor content, the industry experienced traumatic misgivings due to failures and successes. Actually these were caused by the lack of professional guidance in the face of the phenomena of the changing technology. The steep price in the cost of labor as well as in the cost of capital investments through errors and omissions caused the destruction or demise of many well-established concerns. Axel Johnson, President of Johnson Line, states, "Understanding and acceptance of this situation is not only fundamental to full professional competence, but is also the first and necessary step towards a successful commercial and social response to the sudden impact of rapid change which one expects to continue and quicken." While up to now the naval architect alone had the leading role in the development of the steamship system, today it is up to the new container systems designer to develop the functional factors and design the parameters around the system. Creating and solving the optimum transportation system requires broad experience beyond the conventional role of the naval architect. To develop the owner's functional needs requires, first, a conceptual systems design in which the ship has its place in the overall picture.

From here, in the preliminary design phase, the systems engineers would have to follow a three-step approach:

- The design philosophy;
- Major systems definitions;
- Subsystems optimization.

Intuition, the faculty to attain direct knowledge without going through the process of rational thought, is the key to creativity. The benefit of such intuition, however, can apply only with simultaneous understanding of the three areas which produce decision bases for containerization to follow:

1. Understanding of the mission which containerization will serve;
2. Overview of technical limitations based on experience;
3. Sensitivity to the polarity of human resources and systems integration.

Container systems are, of course, born of dreams, just as ships and other devices were born of dreams in the past. But the successful dreams will come only from the minds of men armed with the prerequisites of scientific education, training in analysis, practical experience, and intuition. To fully realize the potential of containerization as overall integration of media requires an approach from a wide circumference in the fields of both human and physical relationships.

The development of a design is a spiral which systematically, in progress, evaluates and ties into the development process all facts known to be pertinent. Forecasting the future of a container system of rapid changes is a precarious exercise in the evaluation of past experiences in transportation. The lights and shadows which will provide the basis for forecasting as the sun provides light for a sundial, come from regions until now considered very remote to transportation. Typically, they contain elements of geography, history, political science, meteorology, agriculture, and physics. Of course, such a field description quickly establishes the fact that every systems design must reflect that today's transportation is finite. There comes a moment when the values in world transportation will change, and the particular system will no longer be valid. Provision for such contingencies must be made. It is in the light of these ramifications of containerization that one must analyze, also, such seemingly far-fetched matters as environmental protection, national security, industrial employment, and world food problems.

The present years are crucial for the transportation industry. Decline of the number of ships on main trade routes and realignment of world trade carriers make change imperative, while the unrelenting influence of containerization growth becomes inevitable.

SUBSYSTEMS

The problems involved in coordinating several noncompatible containerization systems are very complex. The solutions are to be found, most likely, in a comparative analysis of the systems components.

Much has been talked about coordination between the five primary modes of transportation and the development of interrelationships between these modes and the container. The five modes are sea transportation, rail service, highway trucking, air cargo transportation, and coastal and inland waterway transportation. All these five modes are involved in containerization, as the major systems create interface between the modes for the economical through service.

The subsystems fall into four categories, as they relate to equipment (hardware), installations (interface), operations, and control (software) relationships.

Four subsystems are also involved in the hardware phase itself: dealing with the container, the containership, the land mode conveyance, and the interchange system.

Further operational subsystems must be considered. First, the movement of goods into the containers, commonly called the "stuffing system." Another phase is a system dealing with the gathering and distribution of empty and loaded containers, including the intermodal transportation, from the waterfront to the shipper or vice versa. Stuffing in the operation at the container freight stations is another important subsystem.

In the area of software, we deal with the growing complexity of restrictions set forth by rules, regulations, and voluntary agreements among the carriers. Service planning and updating appears to have unique systems characteristics, which lead to conclusions of the impact of planning and updating on capital investments, format changes, labor and human resources adjustment, and the protection of the system against obsolescence. Finally, a special subsystem deals with the evaluation of the technical equipment, capital efforts, and operation subsystems, as related to the fulfillment of the mission in the interest of the operator, as well as the container community at large.

Containerization has, in its short history, stimulated inventiveness. New fabrication of materials, new specialized container types, new automation devices on the ship and ashore, and new computer applications become apparent frequently. What impact, if any, this or any particular device will have, not only on the individual system to which it has been introduced, but also on the competitive position this system holds within the industry, has to be determined by the intrasystem relationship. Many second- and third-generation approaches to an individual subsystem must be held back temporarily, in order not to destroy the overall systems effectiveness. However, as each of these progressive methods is developed, it must be evaluated constantly. It is quite possible that with the growth of the cargo volume or the growth of the population, a new subsystem can become valid within a short span of years. No other technology has ever been subjected to so many radical and sudden changes in its life. This tendency must be expected to continue.

The next chapter will provide the reader with an overview of the framework of the regulations which govern containers as a transport system.

Rules of the Game

FUNCTIONS OF RULES

Before the advent of the modern container, the advantages of coordination of transport media were well known. Over the years, accommodations between all kinds of carriers were established mostly on a bilateral basis. Many of these understandings were effective and economical and still remain in effect. Often these accommodations, however, did not deal with the physical transport of the cargo from one area to the other. Instead, interline services were established for the benefit of the users and the carriers.

The need to expand the benefits of transportation for the nation was pressing, as the economy of the nations grew and placed further demands on the physical distribution machinery. It was then generally agreed that the best way to promote continuous and expanded transportation integration would be by developing a special common denominator. In September 1928, Senator Silvio Crespi of Italy proposed to the International Road Transport Congress in Rome the expansion of the use of the container as a common denominator. It is worth noting that the arguments on containerization in those days were exactly as they are today, but that the development has now taken the aspect of a combined effort to develop a new technique. This technique contains physical elements, as well as functional elements. Relationships with the container and its system deal with both organizational functions and institutional functions.

The organizational functions of the container are directed toward creating a relationship which is simple, efficient and enduring between the transportation media, the transfer facilities, and the public agency having supervisory powers over the field. The institutional functions are those which provide for the deployment of the idea conceived by the implementers of containerization that the van or container is a transportation vehicle lacking its own facilities for movement. This concept provides the basis to separate the legal functions of the container from the packing box protecting the cargo. Although both may look alike, the container is dedicated by rules of transportation and, as such, enjoys privileges and benefits designed for this type of medium.

A SYSTEM IN THE MAKING

The previous chapter describes the container system as a whole. The formation of the system follows conventional methodology in bringing together a host of interests in transportation and uniting them for a common purpose. The interdependent relationships between many participants in a container system require precision tooling. Most of the participants never meet each other face to face, do not have common interests other than the container, and, so to speak, understand each other only in the language of the container. Therefore, the development of rules is to the container as grammar is to a language.

Containerization is the methodic result of systems engineering. Rule making is the first basic requirement to develop such a system. The basic principles used in forming containerization deal with methods for improving transportation. This means that certain changes must be accepted in order to develop a streamlined physical distribution technique. Agreement to accommodate the new system must be without destroying the unique characteristics of each existing transportation mode. The goal is to create something better, not something new.

STAGE IDENTIFICATION

The proper arrangement of job distribution creates a primary demand for the identification of each stage developed in the new process. In the first stage, improvement must be introduced in the systematic relationship which is created between the transportation links. Simultaneous allocation of new interface facilities on the nodes where the links meet permits a division of labor. This leads to the next step, the replacement of man by machine. The intensification of capital provides mechanized equipment, and this produces an upswing in capacity. The interface, therefore, affects each participating medium. This scaled-up combination of links and nodes provides for the economy of scale introduced by the container.

Alfred Marshall singled out the effects of economy of scale in his book, *Principles of Economics*. Through specialization of tasks, a close relationship has been produced between formerly competing modes of transport. The result is many times more efficient and more economical than each of the former segments could be by itself. The unique advantages of containerization must be developed and protected by a body of rules among interrelated media.

DIVISION OF LABOR

Carlos Fallon, in his book, *Value Analysis to Improve Productivity*, describes physical distribution as an aspect of production that increases the value of goods by moving them through space and time, by carrying them from where they are not needed to where they are needed, and by storing them when they are surplus and releasing them when and where required. The elimination of physical handling of the cargo affects the cost of the commodity. To implement this system, containerization had to develop its own code made up of three vast segments:

1. The public segment is made up of laws and regulations issued by local or national governments or international authorities at the governmental level;

2. The private segment is made up of rules developed by the professional and technical organizations which are intent on eliminating friction in the division of labor;

3. The conflict segment is the interface between rules developed under procedures of public and private segments and the outdated remaining regulations and jurisprudence.

Often this segment is circumvented by a free-wheeling pioneer who develops a new method using old existing rules to implement his own method of transportation without consideration for the other modes.

Once it was established that the container is not part of the commodity in the transportation chain, but the ipso facto carrier, then rules could be established to separate the control and/or supervision of the container from the cargo. Then to avoid physical inspection of the contents of the container, rules were developed to reflect the data on the contents on documents which must accompany the container. In effect, then, the container has a dual personality. It is a physical device accompanied by a host of papers. Only by properly arranging the movement of both document and container in compliance with the body of rules is the container system capable of fulfilling its mission. In the days of electronic data processing, a transaction must be precisely in conformity with the rules developed to provide the advantages of speed and economy.

PAPER POWER

Most regulations result in paperwork. The extent of this documentation work far exceeds many real requirements. The only explanation that can be given is that the effect of containerization is slowly noticeable in improved understanding among the three segments. How tremendously important the streamlining of this paperwork is can be seen from the following 12 highlights of the report. "Paperwork or Profits," prepared by the Department of Transportation (DOT) and the National Committee of International Trade Documentation (NCITD). The highlights are:

1. A total of 46 different types of firms and government agencies regularly are involved in international trade.
2. As many as 28 of these parties may participate in an export shipment.
3. A total of 125 different types of documents are in regular and special use.
4. The 125 types of documents represent more than 1,000 separate forms.
5. A total of 80 types of documents are in regular use, and the remaining 45 types of documents in special use.
6. Average shipments involve 46 separate documents, with an average of over 360 copies of documents in special use.
7. U.S. international trade annually creates an estimated 828 million documents and these generate an estimated $6\frac{1}{2}$ billion copies.
8. Average export and import shipments require 64 man-hours to prepare and process ($36\frac{1}{2}$ man-hours for an export shipment and $27\frac{1}{2}$ man-hours for an import shipment).
9. Total U.S. international trade documentation annually consumes more than a billion man-hours, equivalent to more than 144 million days of work, and equal to 600,000 work years.
10. Average documentation cost per international shipment amounts to $351.04.
11. On the basis of current shipping volumes, total documentation costs

aggregate almost $6½ billion a year and represent 7½ percent of the value of total U.S. export and import shipments.

12. The report recommends the elimination of 85 documents. If achieved, this would eliminate over 400 million separate papers (and almost 4 billion copies per year), with an aggregate saving of an estimated $3 billion per year.

THE SPIRIT OF RULE DEVELOPMENT

To streamline the system requires very careful planning of the interface. The ideal method of cargo transfer in physical distribution can best be imagined as an assembly-line procedure in industry. In other words, the container will move relentlessly over an imaginary conveyor belt from the shipper to the end of the line.

This imaginary conveyor belt is made up of independently operated links related to each other by the acceptance of the container standards. Precise timing is necessary to provide capacity and efficiency. How such a highly sophisticated system can be made to work in a forest of laws, regulations, constraints, and institutional lethargy is hard to understand. But containerization is moving forward and the job of improving the body of rules shows signs of eventual accomplishment. The system which leads to success provides six steps:

1. Initiative—suggestions for improvement;
2. Concurrence—two or more industry members agree;
3. Accommodations—other industry members willing to go along;
4. Consensus—majority of industry accepts standards;
5. Convention—all industry with few exceptions proposes new rules;
6. Regulation—publication of the modifications of existing rules or new rules to become industry norms.

CONTAINER BODY POLITICS

The unique relationship between the container and the data-document system provides for specific regulations. This institutional code for the container operations is produced by the three segments mentioned heretofore. The political structure which creates or changes the code is made up of five different types of organizations developing de jure or de facto authority over the systems technology:

1. Governments dealing with the legislative branch; the administration, regulatory and enforcement agency, and the judicial system;

2. International bodies made up by intergovernmental and semigovernmental organizations, composed of experts in the various fields of transportation, trade, law, and related areas;

3. Social interest groups having a membership made up of individuals or firms having a proprietary interest in certain phases of containerization;

4. Trade organizations formed to further the interest of one particular mode and frequently engaged in the development of interface regulations in the interest of its members;

5. Professional societies made up of engineers, economists, scientists, and other qualified individuals having a professional standing which warrants their opinions to be used as guidelines.

PARTICIPATION IN CODIFICATION

A number of organizations in many related fields have influenced the development of the codification of the container rules. This is the place to mention an organization such as The Containerization Institute, which is composed of both corporate and individual members. During its meetings, which are held several times a year in different parts of the United States and Canada, the members present their points of view. Discussions ensue and an agenda is developed for the activities to be brought before the other organizations, in order to obtain new container rules. The development of these guidelines often are a result of an encounter between different interest groups, such as shippers and carriers.

In the railroad industry, the Railroad Piggyback Association is a specialized group made up of only railroad members and deals with the experience made in this field. Containerization is closely related to the movement on flat cars (TOFC) and, therefore, the voice of the Piggyback. Association contributes to the orchestration in the field of regulations from the railroad experience.

The International Cargo Handling Coordination Association (ICHCA) was the first private organization developed by the European community to dedicate itself to the scientific study of the efficient movement of goods. Made up of both corporate and private members of 75 nations, it is the sounding board of many ideas, not confined to containerization but very much concerned with it. Cargo systems engineering, which is the prime interest of the organization, of course, considers containerization as the greatest advance in economy of scale. Through its members and their local government connections, ICHCA remains active in the creation of the container code.

Of the professional societies, the Society of Naval Architects and Marine Engineers has expressed the greatest systematic interest in containerization. As part of the ship operation technical committee, the Panel 0-31 is dedicated to cargo handling and again, of course, does much analytical and deep thinking preparatory to changes required by the industry.

UNITED STATES GOVERNMENT ACTIVITIES

The interest in developing the rules for containerization is widespread in the United States government. Here we find the Department of Defense dealing with the development of structural analysis leading to establishing factors for Army purchase of containers. But unwittingly, these studies also influence the code work by the standard organizations. On the other hand, the U.S. Department of Agriculture (USDA) wishes to develop improved methods for the handling of U.S.-grown perishable cargoes. The inherent desire of the government is to effect the balance of trade by exporting commodities which would not be able to be handled overseas except in containers. The USDA maintains field offices in such places as Rotterdam, Holland, to check on the actual outturn of the container shipments. Another office is planned for Japan soon. The Department of Transportation (DOT) has very actively helped further codification of streamlined container handling systems. The DOT's Office of Facilitation exercises its efforts to study the container rules of practice in depth and help improve the lagging covenants. The Maritime Administration, part of the Department of Commerce at this time, provides mostly regulations dealing with the design and construction of containers and containerships. All regulatory agencies, such as the Interstate Commerce Commission, Civil Aeronautics Board, and the Federal Maritime Commission, establish the law by ruling on decisions. These form part of the lore of the container, just as any other court would deal with these matters.

USCG — IMCO

Of all agencies, the United States Coast Guard (USCG), under the DOT, has the most international enforcement power relating to the container. The Coast Guard steamboat inspection service was formed in the days of the steamer Savannah. Eventually, it became the Coast Guard Office of Merchant Marine Safety. Now the USCG is looking at containerization to identify safety problems involved with that marine phase of container movement. This is how the Coast Guard got involved with the Intergovernmental Maritime Consultative Organization (IMCO).

IMCO is the specialized agency of the United Nations having about 64 member governments. Since its formation in 1958, the tangible results of its work are several international conventions, the most notable ones being the "Safety of Life at Sea" (SOLAS) Convention of 1960 and the "Loadline" Convention of 1966. These conventions set safety standards for the safe design and operations of ships in international service. IMCO gives much attention to the safety of cargo carried in ships and, therefore, it is interested in intermodal container transport by ships.

ECE FORERUNNER

ECE, the Economic Commission for Europe, is also a United Nations body, organized for the purpose of regional development and coordination of economic activities. ECE fostered the first international convention on container transport covering European service. This convention helped set the stage for our current generation of containers by providing for the movement of goods in a sealed reusable van across several national borders without customs check, except in the country of origin and the country of destination.

Today, the same convention applies to containers moving by sea. The signatory governments include several outside Europe; namely, Australia, the United States, and Japan. Obviously, the ECE has had a very vital influence since this customs treatment of containers is the key element in the current concept of containerization.

INTERNATIONAL STANDARDS

ISO, the International Organization for Standardization, is a private non-governmental body that has been working to describe a family of containers in recommendations that eventually become national standards by U.S. adoption. The Container Committee of ISO is called the Technical Committee 104 (TC 104). In the United States, the standards organization is the American National Standards Institute (ANSI). The purpose of the recommendations and the eventual standards which would result from them is to facilitate the interchange of equipment by setting common dimensions and by specifying certain minimum abilities expected of the container to withstand normal conditions of transport. Although the work of shaping the recommendations is still in process, tens of thousands of containers have been built to conform to the draft recommendation. Compliance with the ISO recommendation is voluntary; and, therefore, the developments have not hindered the growth of such other nonstandard container fleets as Sea-Land, Matson, and Seatrain, all U.S.-flagship lines.

IMCO, whose members are governments with maritime interests, has a concern for container transport. Maritime transport is a common experience of every container in intercontinental trade. The marine mode is the interface between nations. A second reason for IMCO's interest is the container carriage on board ship which presents concern with problems and, conceivably, threats to safety. For instance, there were spectacular cargo losses when dozens of containers were lost over the side of containerships while at sea in 1969–1970. These events raised many questions in the minds of experts as to the possible consequences to the ship and its crew, if the stability of the ship became suddenly impaired by such losses.

There are problems of procedure, too, and these are being addressed by the expert group on facilitation, an adjunct to IMCO. The United States participates in this work as well.

MARITIME SAFETY

The Maritime Safety Committee is only a small body within IMCO. Sixteen nations represent the eight largest shipping fleets, in terms of gross tonnage, plus eight other nations who are elected to the committee on the basis of interest in maritime affairs. The detailed work of the Maritime Safety Committee (MSC) is done in ten subcommittees, each of which deals with some specific aspect of marine transport. MSC developed a list of all the factors which might influence the safety of ships carrying containers and then relegated these to its subcommittees for detailed investigation. They were then to report back with recommendations for rule making, where these were warranted. Subcommittees deal with problems of subdivision and stability, fire protection, ship design and equipment, and containers and cargo.

DANGEROUS CARGOES

In a separate but parallel effort, a subcommittee is looking at the special problems related to hazardous materials in containers while at sea. MSC had in mind to design an international convention on carriage of containers, which would be accepted by all nations in a fashion similar to the SOLAS Convention. One alternative would be to develop an "international code for recommended practice." A government convention would be more binding, but an industry code of practice would be a more flexible instrument. This is an important consideration in the rules and regulations in the developing technology. In both events, the end product could be worked out at an international convention, if MSC can accomplish the necessary preliminaries and convince the council that such a conference would develop not only a practical rule, but also a valid precedent for rule making.

TENETS OF CODE

One of the basic tenets of IMCO is that it does not duplicate the work done by other organizations. In its considerations on container structure, it has shown a willingness to adopt the ISO recommendation as a suitable description of the container safe for marine transport. IMCO will coordinate its own work with ECE and other organizations having a similar interest in codification of all aspects of container transport.

The subcommittees have decided that containerships are a special cargo vessel. The rules must, therefore, adequately cover the containerships. The subcommittee on Containers and Cargoes is proceeding on the assumption that "internationally acceptable certification of containers, to meet safety, health and other requirements, is desirable." There is a container certification scheme for customs purposes. It is assumed that safety and health requirements can be worked into a combined multipurpose certification arrangement, which is a basic part of the container code at large.

Safety requirements are viewed as creating perimeters within which containers can be designed and built. Appropriate methods of testing are included. Acceptable behavior under an appropriate test will enable governments to certify containers as meeting the official obligations for the safety of life and property. The signatory governments to the customs conventions on containers have accepted the fact that the proof testing on each new container would be an extremely onerous requirement. It is assumed that the objective of the testing program could be met by thoroughly testing one or more representative containers. If the manufacturer has a creditable quality control program, this scheme is called "type testing." It has been authorized by the International Agreement for Customs Purposes.

MAKE-UP OF WORK GROUP

Container fleet owners and operators are concerned with the possible effect which all official developments might have on acceptability of containers in areas they serve. Safety certifications of containers appear likely to become a prerequisite to the free interchange of containers in international commerce. Such requirements will have significance for all container owners. There is an implication of even greater significance for the U.S. innovators in ocean container movement. In IMCO, there is a bias toward ISO recommendations for container design. Innovators often use containers that do not conform to the ISO recommendation. The U.S. Coast Guard agrees that there is no evidence that these containers are less safe. Now the industry shares significantly in the formation of the U.S. delegation for sessions of IMCO. U.S. delegates and spokesmen are at sessions of the MSC and the subcommittees, with USCG experts in maritime safety supplementing them. The Coast Guard has also tapped the extensive resources of industry for technical assistance in specialized fields. In keeping with past practice, the Commandant of the Coast Guard has formed a working group on container operations. This provides the resources needed for framing positions for sessions of IMCO work dealing with containers. This working group includes representatives of the leading containership operators, marine underwriters, container manufacturers (through their trade association), the American Bureau of Shipping, the National Cargo Bureau, the Maritime Administration, the Department of Labor, the Department of Transportation, and the Coast Guard. The meetings of this working group are basically technical, informal in nature, and held as often as the group feels necessary.

Industry has a voice at a higher level also, as in the preparation of the more formal position papers carried by the U.S. delegation to higher-level sessions of IMCO, such as the MSC and the IMCO Council. Each position paper is discussed in the U.S. Department of State Shipping Coordinating Committee, which again includes representatives of the Marine Transportation Industry.

Another way in which the industry has an impact in these international discussions is by furnishing technical advisors in the delegation. The industry has made available and has paid the expenses for some very valuable experts to assist in the work of the delegation at the IMCO session. The delegation puts them to work and they share in the technical discussion.

INTERNATIONAL CONTAINER CODE

Herman Tabak devotes a large portion of his book, *Cargo Containers,* to the existing regulations and laws. His very excellent description will make good reading in addition to our relatively brief suggestion of the depth and dimension of the rules of the game.

With the progress of time and expansion of the container idea, a world container code becomes a vital element in systems engineering. Much of the original work was accomplished by the International Container Bureau (BIC) of Paris, which was created by Paul Wohl, then a Director of the International Chamber of Commerce. On July 3, 1969, after almost 40 years of the BIC's foundation, the idea had acquired prominence in international shipping. As the first step toward international cooperation, the BIC has created a code for international marking and identification of containers. To serve the purpose, identifying marks must be unique and duplication must be avoided. This requires a centrally coordinated registration. In contrast to motor vehicles, containers need not be registered individually, unless the laws of a particular country or a carrier so require. Therefore, the BIC adopted a simple identification alpha code under which the owner registers a prefixed code only and places his own serial numbers on the container. This procedure is very similar to the system used in the United States by the Official Intermodal Equipment Register; this identification leads to recognition by the carriers for purposes of payment of per diem charges for use of the container.

Many of the rules will have to be learned by those active in the field. The only method recommended is a suggestion of rote learning of the basic regulations. Then participation in the trade organization and professional program will allow participation in the continuing code formation.

Next, we will direct attention to the hardware and tools governed by the rules. This is the unique interrelationship of the container system.

Parametric Overview

SIGNIFICANCE OF HISTORY

Information in the foregoing chapters has shown the extension of the container community and its institutional framework structure. It would be incorrect to consider that the world-wide development obeyed any predetermined plan or scheme. Singular local conditions and international relationships have produced the incentive for the present arrangement. Technical, economical, and political developments have contributed toward an apparently confusing and uneven extension of containerization. No wonder that the world of containers today may look like a patchwork quilt. On reconnaissance, the bits and pieces all have their particular reason in transportation history. Designed with economy of scale in mind, the togetherness of the developments has radically changed the institution, the capital structure, the facilities, and the competitive lineup in world transportation.

There was no plan or overall design. Many services have grown unrelated to each other. In order to give the reader the full understanding, I would need more space than allowed in this book.

But since I believe that from the history of transportation lessons can be drawn, I will undertake to give an abbreviated overview of the status quo. Empirical assimilation of experiences, if properly analyzed, provides an insight for the reasons for their success or failure. Since all container pioneers were motivated by one common thought, namely, to improve transportation by coordination, the reader can learn from their mistakes as well as from their successes. To the cargo systems science, the particular facility, equipment, or system is significant only when it produces a rule for further application. Therefore, I will attempt to emphasize the real significance of the events rather than details which I consider less important. For the purpose of this book, any number of ships, number of containers, or size of a facility is not as important as the systems function which they fulfill. More and better facilities can be added easily. The outmoded or obsolete will be replaced, but the container system in its unique coordinating capacity will remain for the foreseeable future as the interface of many systems.

INTERNATIONAL ORIGINS

I concede to transport historians like Paul Wohl that containerization was known hundreds of years ago. It is debatable whether the effort to promote containerization at the International Road Transport Congress in September 1928, or the presentation of a movie at the International Chamber of Commerce in May 1929 at the same time covering rail transport, had any significant influence on the overall development of containerization. The film was prepared by Acme Fast Freight, Inc., and showed their system, as well as the developments of the L.C.L. Corporation, an offspring of the New York Central Railroad. I was present at the latter occasion and received the distinct impression that containerization was used widely in the United States.

The next historic benchmark was the decision of the British government at the end of World War II to expand containerization in Great Britain as an efficient, speedy supply medium for England's depleted inventory of box cars.

In the ensuing decade of the mid-fifties, containerization for marine transport made its first significant showing in the United States. A stevedore contractor who, because his German-sounding name was too difficult to pronounce, called himself "Tiny DeLong" developed the use of 40-ft. containers for cargo on barges to Alaska. He experimented with double decking and with stacking, and he first proved that containerization could be so effective that the quality of the vessels themselves would be overshadowed by the economy obtained. Alaska was the first part of the United States to take full advantage of containerization.

DEEP SEA EXPERIMENTS

Shortly after World War I, Charles Brasch organized Seatrain Lines to provide railroad car service by water to Cuba and the United States coast. His system used specially designed shoreside cranes equipped with trays with railroad tracks installed on them. A loaded boxcar would be placed on a tray and the tray would be lifted onto the ship through a permanently opened hold. Within the ship, a device called a "moose" would move the car off the tray into position on a track installed on one of several decks where the car would be carefully stowed in place. Like any innovation, Seatrain had to fight opposition for many years. The lack of cooperation of the railroads eventually developed into an all-out hostility. As a result, in 1968, Seatrain Lines abandoned the use of railroad equipment and reequipped its ships for containerization. By that time, the company had been taken over by a group of bulk shipowners.

We can trace the cross-fertilization of the Alaska idea described above and the Seatrain forerunner to the development of containerization by Matson. Here the novel ship design developed by Leslie A. Harlander, Chief Engineer of American President Lines today, led to the conversion of the first conventional cargo ships into containerships. The selection of the 24-ft. container by Matson came after an extensive study. Two 24-ft. vans loaded on chassis could be moved by one tractor under California highway laws. Harlander developed the use of stacking in cell guides which became the standard practice for deep sea containerships.

A follow-up to the Matson idea was undertaken by Grace Lines to enter the United States-Venezuela trade with two specially designed containerships. Opposition by Venezuelan port labor, however, never did allow the system to go into service.

DEVELOPMENT OF ROLL-ON

Just as the concept transplant led from the railroad car ships to the cellular containerships, we can find the beginnings of the other containerization methods in the railroad car ferries. For sixty years, railroad cars were driven onto ferry steamers on the Baltic Sea, on the Inland Sea of Japan, on the Great Lakes of this country, and between Italy and Sicily and Florida and Cuba. Notable was the success of the West Indies Fruit and Steamship Company. Daniel Taylor took former Great Lake car ferries, established a service between Palm Beach, Florida, and Havana, Cuba, and, eventually, moved a large portion of the merchandise traffic between the mainland and the island of Cuba.

During World War II, the military developed the landing ship, the largest of which is the LST (Landing Ship Tank), which would carry heavy, loaded vehicles. The major difference between the railroad car ships and the military LST's was the hull opening. All railroad car ferries were designed with a single-piece, closed bow while the military ships aimed at landing procedures at the beach. This led to the development of the bow door opening, and a host of technological consequences followed. But while the military, of course, considered all their equipment expendable and proved over the past 25 years that bow doors can form a solid strength element in a ship, the classification societies who have the final say on commercial ship design would not go along with it. The naval architectural idea behind their resistance deals with the fear that on impact with oncoming waves, the ship may split open from bow to stern. Such an accident did occur with a ferry boat between Crete and Italy in 1970. This was not an LST but a specially built automobile, trailer, and passenger ferry.

The design constraints on the LST's led to the systems development of roll-on, roll-off (RO-RO) by TMT Trailer Ferry. The unique condition that the LST's could be used only as unmanned vessels and with certain modifications of the bow framing produced the economic incentive for towing by ocean-going tugs, instead of by self-power of the vessel. The writer had started TMT on August 7, 1951, with the shipment of a converted 20-ft. truck trailer body whose wheels had been removed. This container, the first American 20-ft. unit, was placed on the bulk cement transporter, the *M/V Ponce,* for transportation from Fort Lauderdale to Ponce, Puerto Rico. It was followed by the use of truck bodies made into containers as the demand grew. The remaining two berth line services which were giving irregular and infrequent service between Florida and Puerto Rico withdrew from the South Atlantic as a result of TMT's competition. The first large-scale container service in the Atlantic started between the mainland and Puerto Rico. The withdrawal of the Bull Line and Alcoa Steamship Companies, after 50 years of continuous service, opened the way for Sea-Land, followed by Seatrain and TTT (Trans-America Trailer Transport), to institute the service on the Atlantic, with TMT and Carib-Hydro on the southern routes.

Why did the lines have to withdraw? Several reasons are still significant in the containerization development. With three LST's in service as towed barges and about 700 used highway trailers as containers, TMT provided slow but consistent service and convenient door-to-door transport. The new breed of traffic managers who came to Puerto Rico to serve the industrial development program was accustomed to American truck operations for their shipments on highways in the United States.

The difficulties of pierside accumulation of break-bulk cargo and infrequent shipments, coupled with the requirement for better packing, made TMT's service desirable.

THE NEW ASPECT

What was much more significant was the diminishing cost of operations by TMT in contrast to the rest of the American shipping industry. Fifty-five trailers and 60 automobiles would be loaded and unloaded by a standard gang of longshoremen in one day. This compared favorably with 7 to 10 days loading and unloading time for a conventional 13,000 ton ship. This result in cost saving induced the National Academy of Sciences and the National Research Council to promote this type of shipping as an answer to the problems of the American Merchant Marine.

TMT has proven to be a good revenue earner compared to the American Merchant Marine, in general. Its example has been followed by improvement in the process. In 1971, the Crowley interest established the same type of service between Miami and Puerto Rico. Instead of using LST's, Crowley employed powerful tugs and two barges, each of which was 400 ft. by 100 ft. These barges were originally designed to transport pipe for the Alaska pipeline which, at this writing, is still delayed. The container capacity of these two barges is double that of TMT, yet does not require more towing power. This operation also uses trailers in the Ro-Ro method, a corollary to the sagacity of the original concept. If anything, TMT was the birthplace of cargo systems science.

SHIFT IN SHIPPING

In the half-century prior to containerization, shipowners and operators could be grouped into five very clearly defined sectors:

1. Bulk carriers;
2. Liner trade;
3. Tramps;
4. Ferry services;
5. Meat/fruit carriers.

The bulk carriers engaged in the transportation of bulk liquids, iron ore, grain, and similar large-quantity commodities with a target of moving as large a lot at one time as the consignment would permit. Their ships have grown so much that IMCO is considering placing limits on the ship size, to provide for greater safety of the sea lanes. It is technically possible today to design and to build oil tankers carrying one million tons of oil.

The liner trade was the main servant of international economic interchange. The best principle applied is to have vessels available all over the world and in constant circulation, so that the shipper could find frequent incentives to make use of this service. The world's largest liner company today is NYK Lines (Nippon, Yusen, Kaisha Lines) of Japan. This company, too, is turning toward containerization, following the example of America's largest liner companies, such as Lykes Lines and United States Lines.

While the liner trade developed extensive networks of agents all over the territories, tramp carriers offered ships of opportunity wherever a consignment incentive existed. Tonnagewise, the tramp segment carried more cargo than the liner trade, because anytime a shipper had a large enough consignment, he would seek a lower rate and turn to the free-wheeling, unregulated tramp group. This created normal checks and balances between the growth of these two segments. The ships very frequently were built in such a form that they could be interchanged as trampers or in the liner trade.

The ferry services as well as the fifth category, the meat/fruit carriers, were customarily established in routes between two or three terminals. This allowed them to function on a fixed-schedule basis or on demand; but in any event, there was little, if any, competitive friction between the liner and tramp segments and the ferry and food carriers.

MANAGEMENT RECOGNITION

The major impact of the recognition of containerization's effect on shipping occurred in the liner trade and tramp segments. Analysis of the advent of unitized transportation provoked a basic management review of the functions of the new services compared to the existing trampers and liners. The conclusions were simple and straightforward:

1. The report of pyramiding costs became alarming.
2. The effects of reversing heretofore-accepted productivity standards became disastrous.
3. Unitization appeared simple and easy to handle and, therefore, a more generalized solution, in line with the desire of the shipper.
4. A top-to-bottom follow-through of the changeover would require the use of new, large, and costly ships and facilities and would require mustering of more resources than each of the shipping companies could afford.

These four thoughts took almost a decade to materialize into the greatest changeover which has occurred in any industry since hand weaving was replaced by the mills.

SEA-LAND SERVICE

Sea-Land Service is unique because its system was the first to be designed to begin to fulfill complete door-to-door physical distribution measures. The founder of Sea-Land, Malcolm McLean, had obtained years of experience in his own growth from a gas station operator to the owner of one of the country's largest truck fleets. The advantage of combining the flexibility of trucks, gathering relatively small lots of freight, with the efficiency of large ships for long-distance hauls, was a creed of the new enterprise. In January 1955, McLean formed the first company to operate both trucks and ships under one control. Under pressure of the Interstate Commerce Commission, he divested himself from trucking ownership and purchased the Waterman Steamship Company and its wholly owned subsidiary, Pan-Atlantic Steamship Corporation. This gave McLean Industries a fleet of 37 medium-size cargo vessels.

McLean worked with me analyzing the TMT experience. As a result, before testing out the Pan-Atlantic ships in container service, he installed stringer decks on two modified tankers, each carrying 60 trailer bodies between New York and Houston. By 1959, Pan-Atlantic became Sea-Land Service, Inc.

The military application of containerization to the war zone in Viet Nam materialized in spite of opposition, due to the personal activities of Malcolm McLean. He personally traveled to Viet Nam, where he arranged for terminals, cranes, and trucking services. The largest shipping contract the United States government ever entered into was the well-deserved prize for Sea-Land. The logistic ability of this service was, no doubt, a surprise and of great concern to political adversaries of the United States.

In 1966, Sea-Land started weekly service to Europe by signing agreements with 325 European truckers. Today, Sea-Land has developed foreign-flag feedership services connecting with its mainline runs to many shipping points in the world.

One significant lesson again deals with the obsolescence of one component. When Malcolm McLean started with highway trucks in eastern United States, they had a maximum length of 35 ft. and were 8 ft. 6 in. high. This, therefore, was McLean's original selection. Being stuck with this size for the underdeck slots of the cellular containerships, it is only now that competition on the North Atlantic and North Pacific forces him to make preparations to be able to carry 40-ft. containers as well. These units will be carried on deck where there is better flexibility and capacity. Regardless of the fact that the 35-ft. container had retained only a limited life-cycle effectiveness in 1965, Sea-Land did not change its cellular ships. Rather, they expanded regionally where the 35-ft. container would have a long expected life. This allows Sea-Land time to deal gradually with the problems of the 40 footers.

SUBSIDIES AS DETERRENT

Influences that forced or attracted Matson and Sea-Land into the container business were not present, however, with other American subsidized lines. Under the long-standing overaged subsidy legislation, the United States government picked up the tab for inefficiency. This took the form of about half of the cost of building the ships and considerably more than half of the cost of operating a subsidized American-flag vessel on a competitive international trade route. The failure of the industry to innovate and institute economy of scale can be attributed to this coddling of the owners. Lack of competition between certificated trade route operators or other incentives to improve productivity began to be looked at during the Kennedy administration. In the mid-60's, maritime critics inside and outside the government began to attack the alarming rise in the cost of government shipping supports. While foreign operators were beginning to automate their ships, and while the first signs of containerization's effectiveness became visible, the American steamship operators appeared to become less competitive and more dependent on government support. Therefore, with continued analysis and prompting by the Maritime Cargo Transportation Conference of the National Academy of Sciences, the container issue was broadened. A top-level study team and an interagency Maritime Task Force were called in to find ways and means to equip the American fleet for the coming age in shipping. It was understood by the public that this meant, as *Fortune* magazine put it, "to give the subsidy program the well-deserved heave-ho."

RAILROAD CONTRIBUTION

Parallel with the offshore development in containerization, three unique rail-based container systems were activated. The Southern Railway System found its growth stymied in the early sixties. Rather than blame this on the unfair truck competition, the management hired Mr. William Burke, a former truck executive himself, and the company embarked on a two-pronged program to use containerization to their advantage.

The two problems which Burke had to face were that the Southern started only in Washington, D.C., while its main shippers were located in the eastern corridor from New York to Boston. While other railroads could institute so-called piggyback service, placing trailers on flat cars (TOFC), the Southern found obstacles in the many tunnels that the railroad traversed. For both of these problems, containerization was the optimal answer. The introduction of containers instead of trailers allowed piggyback on the Southern; and by turning its containers over to truckers, just as the steamship lines were doing, the Southern would be able to serve the northeastern traffic area on an interline basis by coordinating transportation services. The Southern implemented container control and real-time inventory analysis, as well as other subsystems, to its benefit. When United States Lines started its test program for containerization in Europe, it used a Southern container for the experiment.

FLEXI-VAN SYSTEM

To solve similar tunnel clearance problems, the New York Central Railroad worked in cooperation with Strick Trailer Company. The resultant design became known as the "Flexi-Van System," which is a patented integrated, intermodal container system in itself. The equipment consists of special freight cars equipped with turn tables. The truck trailer consists of the container itself and a sliding undercarriage, which is slipped onto a rail attached to the rear of the container on both outer sides. The method of operation is simple in that the truck trailer is backed up against the freight car at a 90° angle. The container then slips from the undercarriage onto the turntable which is attached to the railroad car. The tractor keeps pushing until at least half of the container is engaged and balanced onto the tracks of the turntable affixed to the railroad car. Then a special fifth wheel, which is mounted on the front of the tractor across the hood, is released. This fifth wheel proceeds to direct the tractor parallel to the freight car. Since the container is still engaged on the tractor's kingpin, this movement turns the container sideways until it rests almost completely fore and aft on the freight car. The tractor now disengages itself from the container, and thereafter uses a hydraulic ramp which enters the corner casting of the inside right forward corner of the container, and by doing so, pushes the container until it is fully loaded onto the freight car. The unloading procedure is done exactly in reverse of the loading procedure.

The New York Central has expanded its Flexi-Van container service in cooperation with other railroads and some steamship lines. On its own network, the Flexi-Van has been used very effectively in containerizing mail in New York State. Flexi-Van containers are loaded at the main post offices for destination along the Flexi-Van train system. Loaded at the central point on the unit train, the containers are often pulled off from the boxcar at railroad level crossings by the trains merely stopping to exchange one or two containers with the local truck service.

INTERPOOL TRANSFER

Interpool, Inc. has developed another application of significant impact on rail containerization. Using the Steadman side-transfer system, which is described in Chapters 7 and 12, Interpool has simplified the transfer method by using rack-and-pinion systems engaging into the bottom corner casting of the container. This allows transfer by using a specially equipped trailer which can be used either as delivery vehicle itself or as a transfer tool. The Interpool system has developed great acceptance in Canada and among midwestern railroads. Its practicality is greater than the Flexi-Van System, since it can handle the Flexi-Van container as well.

FORWARDER CONTRIBUTION

The three railroad container systems which developed physical links for intermodal service during the pioneering decade were all somehow captive systems primarily designed to improve competitive traffic positions of railroads in their own struggle against highway competition. With the advent of the container impact, the three railroad systems each conformed with the container standards, and they may have, in this respect, provided viable contributions to the overall transportation industry.

Under other circumstances, forwarders have provided an institutional rather than a physical link in the past. The American forwarding industry grew as a result of the need of the traffic to interconnect the numerous rail and transportation services of this country. Intermodality requires a combination of businesses and dealings with as many carriers as are required to handle freight from origin to destination. While forwarders in international fields act more as agents of steamship carriers and port representatives of the shippers in the United States domestic picture, freight forwarders assume the role of carriers. This development came from the institution of the first American Railway Express service which would take care of the shippers' door-to-door needs by whatever means of transportation required. While this was done in the past by couriers traveling with the shipments, the organization of the forwarding industry grew to the extent that a fixed establishment of facilities at key points would fulfill the functions of the couriers.

I can clearly remember how I traveled in the role of courier on the *M/V Ponce* with the first three containers of TMT Trailer Ferry. With the growth of the traffic, organizational agents handled the transfer and, thus, the system began to emerge. The American forwarding industry learned from the European forwarders that there is better remuneration for its service in taking advantage of tariff rate differentials for volume shipments. The loading of individual shipments into one railroad car, truck, or airplane is known world-wide as "groupage." Under the consolidation system, the forwarder, of course, charges his shipper the individual package rate; but he pays the carrier the lower rate which applies to a fully loaded car, truck, or airplane. The steamship industry never wanted any part of the groupage consolidators.

FORGASH AND BRADLEY

The status of the American freight forwarding industry as carriers themselves was an institutional victory for the late Morris Forgash, organizer of the world's largest freight forwarding organization, United States Freight Company. Assisted by his competitor, Thomas A. Bradley, who got into freight forwarding after the railroads failed to accept his container idea, he and Forgash were able to convince Congress that the freight forwarding industry has as much significance as the other regulated transportation industries. There is no doubt that the coordinated services of the American forwarding industry have made an outstanding contribution to the transportation coordination which exists today.

Morris Forgash, in particular, set the stage for container standards by originating the geometry of the ISO standards. He was the one to propose the 8-ft. height by 8-ft. width dimensions with the length variations of 10 ft., 20 ft., 30 ft., and 40 ft. It is quite interesting to note that while Forgash was a firm believer in intermodal interchangeability and containerization, his own most successful entry into the marine container business does not apply these standards. United States Freight purchased the Marine Run operation which was started in May 1960 with one converted Landing Ship Medium Rocket (LSMR) operating between Miami, Florida, and Guatemala. The operation was renamed "Coordinated Caribbean Transport" (CCT); and under the management of Hector Calderon, it serves all of Central America with 35-ft. and 40-ft. refrigerated trailers. This service has opened international transportation between the Central American Republic and has efficiently connected Florida with all of Central America. If there is a lesson to be learned from this, it deals with the "greening flow pattern" described in Chapter 6. Prior to this Central American service, most traffic between the United States and Central America moved through New Orleans.

INTERMODAL EFFECTIVENESS

The effectiveness of intermodal operation attracted the shipping interests to the "switch to Miami." Conventional ship traffic analysis, which was used as a planning tool for the development of this container service, proved useless because there were no records of available tonnage. By methods of cargo systems analysis, we reached the conclusion that the service would develop a new flow pattern; and this recognition proved to be significantly correct.

Forwarding became effective in coordination of through shipments under the control of the Interstate Commerce Commission. By institutional constraints, however, this system remained within the limits of the continental United States. Even forwarders of Puerto Rico and Hawaii operated in more of an express-company style than as a true intermodal link. The rate advantage implied in the forwarder tariff differentials also constrained forwarding to the relatively small shipments of less-than-carload size. The pressing need for economy of scale demands further cost effectiveness—obtainable, it appears, only through intermodal linkage with the transfer of the vehicle body from carrier to carrier. The result is containerization, and it allows the shipper to participate directly in the volume discounts previously reserved to the forwarder. European interests have been strongly in favor of developing a new forwarder type called the Combined Transport Operator (CTO). An international convention for this purpose would give the CTO similar positions in international containerization as the ICC-certificated forwarder enjoys under the Interstate Commerce Act Part IV. Thus, there has been little support for this convention among the intermodal interests in the United States.

FOUR FORCES

The overview over the developments in the first container decade in the United States indicates the presence of four forces bringing about standardization. These groups were:

1. Equipment manufacturers interested in producing standard sizes of containers and handling equipment of what appeared to be a growing market;
2. Railroads and forwarders interested in partaking in the potential marine through-traffic market;

3. Steamship lines who had watched Sea-Land, Matson, and TMT grow into economy of scale and full effectiveness;

4. The United States government agencies interested in taking the new tools into consideration for the benefit of defense, agriculture, reduced shipping subsidies, and increased export traffic potentials.

The international standardization efforts by ISO (see Chapter 2) and its TC-104 became reflected in the American National Standards Institute (ANSI) MH-5 Committee. The Truck Trailer Manufacturing Association (TTMA) and, singularly, Fred Muller, U.S. delegate to the TC-104 Committee, displayed an outstanding effort to bring about a standard size guide for containers. The latest standards are described in Chapter 13. Since there are constant changes, the reader should consult the latest developments by contacting ANSI or ISO before using any present size as an ultimate in container geometry.

CLASHING INTERESTS

The developments were delayed and almost frustrated by the conflict arising out of the standardization moves intersecting with the developments by the pioneers mentioned in this chapter. The efforts by the advocates of rigid standardization found opposition from Sea-Land (with its 8 ft. × 35 ft. × 8 ft. 6 in. containers), Matson (with 8 ft. × 24 ft. × 8 ft. 6 in. containers) and Grace Lines (here the problem dealt mostly with a nonstandard corner casting). The opposition resulted in a law under which Congress ordered equal treatment in the use of all container sizes, standard and special. This setback for the move to standardization was only the first of many changes.

Much more about these forces of tolerance vs. rigidity in container acceptance is developed later in the book, but the simple conclusion is that containers will serve many purposes. The owner or designer must consider the commercial life and possible shift in trade (see Miami/New Orleans cargo shift). Standards are very desirable, since they establish a simplified application. However, acceptance of all containers, including nonstandard sizes, should be the preferred design criterion for transfer facilities.

THE SWEDISH IDEA

While Americans worried about the tooling-up of containerization, Olof Wallenius, the late world leader in automobile shipping, worried about how to finance the economy of scale. The recognition of the size of ship investments required to be effective in containerships led Wallenius in the mid-'60s to offer the idea of his "Consortium" to many shipowners. The idea of pooling shipowners' resources was new. Any such move crossing national borders was bold, but the combination between trampers and line tradesmen was unheard of. The "Cunning Swede," as he came to be known, offered his idea of a single transatlantic pool to all who showed any interest. His offer to United States Lines had to be rejected because of the subsidy nationality issue clouding the minds of most people in the United States. But Cunard (Great Britain), French Lines (France), Holland-America Lines (Netherlands), and two more Swedish concerns, Swedish-Transatlantic and Swedish Lines, formed the world's first consortium with the Wallenius Lines.

The consortium idea had originally been considered by Arnold Bernstein who, after World War I, entered the transatlantic trade with a number of old ships. Facing stiff competition from the Conference Line, Bernstein was permitted to carry vehicles only. Containers were included in this category by consent of the conference carriers. Bernstein realized shortly that his Hamburg-based A. B. Line would not be able to develop a trade large enough to fill containerships. These were the days before the Volkswagen had changed the automobile habits in this country. Bernstein, therefore, purchased an interest in the Belgian "Red Star Line," but World War II forced Arnold Bernstein to seek refuge in the United States. Matson entered into a container pool agreement with two Japanese Lines, NYK and Showa. This agreement provided for the furnishing of two modern containerships by Matson, while the two Japanese lines would each furnish one ship. Unfortunately, this single experiment of American international consortium failed. Matson, without certification to Japan, and without subsidies, had much higher operating costs than its two Japanese consortium partners. This resulted in retrenching by Matson's management in the summer of 1970, and also resulted in their abandoning the first and only international experiment of the United States Merchant Marine.

EXPANSION OF THE CONSORTIUM IDEA

The Wallenius idea of amalgamation of shipping interests has proven to be the greatest institutional change in world shipping. Joint services became most significant in areas where the largest ships and most containers would be required. Therefore, several new consortia arose all over the world. Most of them were motivated by recognition of the implications of economy of scale in the construction and operating stages and the

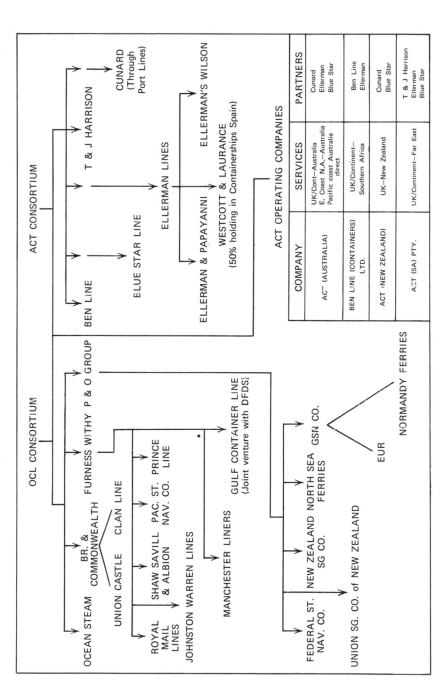

FIGURE 3-1. MAKE-UP OF THE BRITISH CONSORTIUM FOR THE AUSTRALIA TRADE, KNOWN AS THE OCL/ACT GROUP (AS OF JANUARY 1, 1971).

identification of the massive capital investment this would call for. Japanese interests, on the other hand, were guided by the paternal system prevailing in the rapid growth of Japan's gross national product (GNP). Here the purest form of coordination was used to strengthen and modernize integrated containerization. The leading international consortium groups at this time do not include any Americans:

1. OCL/ACT (Overseas Container Lines and Associated Container Transport), providing service between Europe and Australia and between the United States and Australia (Fig. 3-1);
2. Japanese group comprising several consortia by destination targets:
    a. Japan-West Coast Line, made up of K (Kawaski) Line, YS (Yamashito Shinon) Line, Mitsui-OSK Line, and Japan Line (formerly Daido);
    b. West Coast pool: NYK and Showa Lines;
    c. The six companies comprising all of the above in joint service to Seattle and eventually to the United States East Coast;
3. Dart Lines, a consortium made up of Belgian Lines, the British Manchester Lines, and a Canadian Company, Clarke Traffic Services;
4. Atlantica Line, a consortium of German Hansa Line and Italian Fassio Line cooperating with the French Fabre Line;
5. Johnson Line together with Blue Star Line of England and East Asiatic Company of Denmark has formed the ScanStar service with weekly service between Scandinavia, England, and the West Coast of the United States;
6. Combi Line, a consortium of Dutch and German steamship companies giving service between the Gulf and North Sea ports.

UNCERTAINTY PREVAILS

The parametric overview thus far may have appeared as glowing success stories. Nevertheless, now at the end of its first decade, the advance of containerization has entered a new phase of problems. This is a time of crisis for most of the world's transportation services. More than ever, transportation is faced with an increasing number of obstacles in the development of a functional, integrated, and profitable container system.

Every major nation during the last decade has seen large amounts of capital invested toward the formation of increased transport efficiency. But while technology resulting from these investments has increased, the profitability and the return on investment have been very disappointing.

INCREASED CAPACITY

The capacity to meet many of the present-day transport needs has been increased so substantially that in some areas there is greater capacity than there is need. More and more giant containerships are locked into heavy competition across the Atlantic and Pacific.

This new capacity has developed at a time of many economic uncertainties, decline in trade, and business recessions. The carriers who had been counting on reduced operating costs which led them to pour massive sums into equipment for expanding operations have seen the opposite come true. Many find themselves committed to further expansion to meet increased competition for the lagging traffic, while the revenue thus far has not indicated sufficient margin to insure profitability.

Container services committed large capital investments, hoping for an increase in end-productivity to be translated eventually into a diminishing operating expense pattern. This would then have allowed the carriers to hold the line on pricing, even in the face of inflationary pressures. However, the opposite has happened. Operating expenses have gone up. Work rules, labor demands and, of course, the rise in equipment prices have turned each rate increase into a new round of problems. Each time new carriers specifically raise their rates, they must face the danger of pricing themselves out of the market or causing traffic to be diverted.

SWITCH IN THINKING

The old techniques of boosting revenue have begun to lose popularity in the transportation community. Ocean shipping on the main routes has been subject to rate disagreements stemming from overtonnage. The diminishing shares of cargo have produced an increase in interline rivalry. Ship lines which have made large investments in new containerships are faced with the prospect of sailing short-loaded. A number of lines have reportedly cut rates and have indicated their dissatisfaction with the existing rate-making conference. Thus, the present apparent consequence of economy of scale amounts to an imbalance and crisis on the ocean.

The railroads of the world, on the other hand, suffer from the opposite effect. The lack of modern freight and up-to-date facilities coupled with overage work rules make the railroad industry a victim of the transportation crisis, too. Here economy of scale is possibly the only solution of the ills, but the concurrent investments required have been avoided. Development, thus, has been retarded to the detriment of the community.

A number of nations have attacked their problems on a national basis. But no matter how much funding is poured into the facilities, transportation continues to operate in a deficit.

Problems affecting the transport industry have produced certain unlikely results in the field of coordination. First, in the transportation field not affected by containerization, the truckers, water carriers, and rail-roads of the United States have joined together to support a new legis-lative action, called the "Surface Transportation Act." It calls for reforms in transport financing, rate setting, regulation of service rights, allocation of funds, and taxation. In the field of American waterfront container ser-vices, the lines serving the United States have also shown two signs of beginning to work toward integration.

REVENUE POOLS AND SOIC

Twenty-three steamship companies have formed an organization dealing with the intermodal services between themselves, the trucks, and rail-roads. This organization is the Steamship Operators Intermodal Com-mittee (SOIC), which could pave the way to better relationship and service parameters when marine containers are handled on land segments.

In the traffic field, the ocean carriers of the Atlantic have formed the first international revenue pool. The four American carriers, Sea-Land, Seatrain, U.S. Lines, and AMEX (American Export Isbrandtsen Lines), have entered into a revenue pool with their two European competitors on the North Atlantic route. The share of the American carriers in this revenue pool is 55 percent of the tonnage at this time. Although the U.S. government has still to give approval to this idea, the pool would allo-cate shipping quotas to its members and set each participant's port of call by geographic area, as well as by service frequency.

All three institutional events, the Surface Transport Act (if passed), the SOIC, and the Revenue Pool (if approved), indicate a new direction to be followed. As in the wild days of railroading, all of transportation today feels the crunch of the unfulfilled promise of total transport inte-gration.

In the August 1971 issue of the magazine, *Container News,* editor Marc Felice asks the pertinent question, "We wonder whether the present malaise could not have been avoided if prudent planning would have prevailed?"

SYSTEMS ENGINEERING

The panorama of containerization indicates the urgent need for inter-face planning. Up to this era, transportation has grown in empirical fashion based on segmented modal experiences only. Any further step in technology has separated the modes further from each other and has enlarged the rift between them. Just the opposite is needed if transportation is to survive as a cost-effective industry. If this is not brought about, transportation will develop into a social service of the community which would have to be maintained at growing cost to the taxpayer and at a loss or retardation of the gross national product.

If interface integration is not implemented in transportation, I foresee two unfavorable consequences for the national economy:

1. The taxpayer will be called upon to subsidize the deficit in modal transportation with the final result of overall nationalization of the services.
2. The gross national product (GNP) will show loss or retardation of growth which eventually will lead to the diminishing importance of a nation.

PATTERN RECOGNITION

The need for accommodation of coordination requires a recognition of the pattern and an integrated approach to implementation. The broad approach to complex situations demands thinking in terms of the whole rather than of operational parts. To cope with complexity, we must initiate systems cybernetics. Norbert Wiener, in his book, *Cybernetics,* developed the requirements for the systems design in 1947. He speaks of the need for information and feedback. Since that time, industrial engineering has developed a characteristic type of scientific approach to solve the complex difficult problems. Most interesting among the tools for systems design is the "Design Work Study" technique developed for the United States Navy by the Stanwick Corporation. This type of planning demands careful critical analysis and the identification of the stages at which the interface must occur.

Since transportation first became a matter of management engineering in the '40s in the United States and Europe, all learning was in a segmented, sectionalized manner. Each student dealt with a particular field: railway management, air, truck, ship, or pipeline transportation. The time had not come for the integrated approach to the transport system. But with the advent of the container and the interface implementation, we note the developing science of the cargo systems.

AEROSPACE APPROACH

The aerospace industry owes much of its accomplishment to the systems of industrial engineering. Having attained many of its primary goals, the aerospace industry has entered a noticeable decline. It is more than a coincidence that many of the great corporations of the aerospace world have entered into activities and investments in some phases of transportation. Lockheed, General Dynamics, and Litton have gone into the shipbuilding business; Aerojet General and Bell Aerospace have interest in surface effect craft; and Rohr and others have begun to build railcars.

While we are not interested in corporate shifts, the transfer of the system of planning and the technique of coordination used by the aerospace industry, undoubtedly, provide important tools for the approach to containerization. Each system has its own integrity. Here, as there, all subsystems contribute to the appropriate effectiveness of optimal outputs from given inputs. The scientific approach to cargo engineering requires a detailed review of many parts, tools, steps, and phases which make up the system. In the following parts, the book will try to develop from this parametric overview a basic understanding of the cargo systems elements which affect the total integrated structure.

HARDWARE AND TOOLS

*Those who cannot remember
the past are condemned to
repeat it.*
George Santayana
The Life of Reason, *1905*

Container Basics

DRIVING FORCES

The first section of this text was dedicated to the definition of the institutional overview and logical implementation of the container into coordinated transportation. Our approach method is to using systems engineering, which in the framework of containerization deals with three basic elements: physical components, human elements, and institutional organization patterns. The container establishes the common denominator for the systems. The understanding of the basics and the technology of this systems tool, therefore, is the task of this present section. Hardware and how it will fit into the traffic stream will be discussed in sequence.

THE MASTER PATTERN

The container is the master element of the system named after it. At first, a large shipping crate, a square highway trailer, and the cargo container look very much alike. But these outside looks are really the only similarity. Each one of these pieces of equipment is specifically designed to fulfill a mission in a particular system. The shipping crate normally provides protection from weather and undesired human interference. The shipping crate's strength lies in the connection between the cargo and the crate; and, therefore, it is very often fastened to the cargo.

The truck trailer is a monocoque shell intended to provide both a lightweight protection for transit and the bridge support structure on which cargo can be carried with proper distribution of weight on the tractor and the undercarriage of the trailer. Its box shape occupies the maximum cubic space allowed by various constraints, such as highway regulations and underpasses, and in the metamorphosis of development, has borrowed from the experience of lightweight aircraft structure design.

Undoubtedly, the highway trailer or the truck body provided the initial input to the design of the cargo container of today. Behind the thin skin of the container, however, hides the carefully designed compromise structure which will serve as master element to the new transportation synthesis. To accomplish this, the structure must comply with a large variety of conditions. Since, unfortunately, the dream of a single compatible transportation system has given way to a manifold mesh of subsystems, the requirements and the state of the art of the container are important to many systems. The general-purpose freight container takes many forms and a great variety of shapes. Generally speaking, all have in common a rectangular outer shape; a relatively weatherproof outer skin over a strong inner structure that protects it while separated from underlying transportation; and the fact that the contents are handled as a unit load, being transshipped as a whole without rehandling.

THE BASIC VARIETY

We recognize three basic types of container in accordance with the type of cargo carried in them:

1. Dry cargoes;
2. Liquid cargoes and bulk commodities;
3. Special cargoes requiring protection from the environment.

The dry-cargo container group consists of a large fleet of the rectangular boxes protected on all six sides by the container shell, and usually equipped with one door in the rear. The loading of single large pieces often requires the removal of the roof. This can be done by maintaining the corner posts and replacing the roof structure by a canvas cover. Thus, these containers are commonly known as "rag tops." The canvas is specially treated for resistance to water and tearing and is attached to the four container sides by a system of loops with a chain or cable passing through them, in compliance with the international CCC regulations. Another type is built with the removable upper rail at the door side, so that loading can be accomplished either from overhead or from the rear, as the needs may dictate. To give this container rigidity, the upper rail beam must be replaced for shipment, and removed only for loading and unloading.

Other types of dry cargo containers have built-up ends and small built-up sides, and may or may not have doors. These containers are called "trays." They are used for the shipment of precut lumber, pipes, steel products, or automobiles. The corner structure is also either permanently attached or removable for loading purposes. One similar type of tray consists of only two components; namely, the flat bottom deck and the front wall. These containers are very common in Europe and are referred to as "tilts." They constitute the minimum unitized equipment.

SYSTEM KEY

On August 3, 1953, the first American self-propelled ship engaged in container transportation sailed from Port Everglades, Florida, to Puerto Rico with a load of truck bodies doing the job of cargo containers. The ship line that operated the container service, TMT Trailer Ferry, collected all kinds of truck bodies and retired truck trailers and converted them into useful containers for their service. However, the difference between this example of a pioneer undertaking in the container field, and the large-scale new systems which were to be implemented (based on the experiences of TMT) is the fact that the large ships require cellular structure for the quantities of containers that can be stowed in the hold, as well as on deck. The system key or the basic need for standards was and is intermodal and intercarrier exchange of containers. Once standards were established, any container would fit any ship, railcar, or chassis; and ports, shipyards, terminals, and manufacturers had common-denominator dimensions and weights to work with in designing equipment, yard layouts, etc. This called for standardization; and five years after TMT's beginning, in July 1958, the committee for "Standardization of Freight Containers," presently known as the MH-5 Committee, was established by the American National Standards Institute.

It took another ten years of international discussions to come up with the first meaningful agreement in container systems integration. Only after the International Standards Organization (ISO) Meeting in Moscow in 1967, did the uniform corner fitting become the sole firmly-accepted international norm. Only three systems—Sea-Land, Matson, and Grace Line, who had been in business before the acceptance of the corner-fitting standard—retained their own fitting, since their own intrasystem equipment would have required a costly conversion.

The container sizes are so varied that detailed description would not serve a purpose. Certain dimensions are presently contained in existing ISO standards. In addition, there is constant pressure from a number of sources to construct an even greater variety of sizes. Planning container systems must allow for the trend toward larger sizes. At this time, the overwhelming majority of containers are 20 ft. to 40 ft. long and 4 ft. to 9 ft. 6 in. high. The height variety is the result of the consideration that the stacking of half-size-high containers within the cellular ship structures allows an increase in density and, consequently, revenue. The 40 ft. by 4 ft. 6 in. tray can be used in many bulk commodity shipments, such as grain, barbed wire, lumber, or steel. Therefore, it is very likely that the next phase of containerization development will bring into being more of the "special cargo" containers, and proportionally fewer of the dry cargo boxes.

The width of the containers has remained almost constant. The original 8 ft. width is still equivalent to the space occupied by two horses pulling a Roman chariot with a whiffletree. Recently, for internal use, the rail carriers in Europe began to change from 8 ft. to 8 ft. 6 in. This is in response to the needs of improved cube utilization by the German railroads, since this new width dimension fills the clearance diagram better than the 8 ft. container. In the United States, the 8 ft. width is the limit that is permitted on the highways in all 50 states, and changes would require major legal confrontation. These are only a few examples of the state of flux in which the container transportation industry finds itself.

DIMENSIONS AND RATINGS

Draft ISO Recommendation No. 804, drawn up by the Technical Committee ISO/TC 104, has been an accepted ISO Recommendation since February 1968.

Containers of standard dimensions have special corner fittings which meet the recommendation of the ISO. These permit ready handling, stacking up to six high, secure fixing in transit, and ready transfer between different modes of transport.

ISO Recommendation No. 804 defines a container as an article of transport equipment that is:

1. Of permanent character and, accordingly, strong enough to be suitable for repeated use;
2. Specially designed to facilitate the carriage of goods by one or more modes of transport without intermediate reloading;
3. Fitted with devices permitting its ready handling, particularly its transfer from one mode of transport to another;
4. So designed as to be easily filled and emptied;
5. Constructed to have an internal volume of 1 m³ one cubic meter (35.3 ft.³) or more.

SWING AWAY FROM STANDARD

There has been a marked swing away from standard height, a trend gaining in popularity to go to 8-ft. 6-in.-high containers. Cunard, Sea-Land, U.S. Lines, and Matson have been operating units at this height for some time. The latest operator of importance to go to the 8 ft. 6 in. height is container leaser, Integrated Container Transport, who has decided to order all future equipment at 8 ft. 6 in. The 8 ft. 6 in.-high, 40 ft. container was approved by the ISO in late 1969.

Statistics compiled by the U.S. Maritime Administration during the second quarter of 1969 revealed the growing popularity of the use of the larger container sizes in the North Atlantic and in the Pacific.

World-wide, over 350,000 twenty-foot or larger containers are in use today. A comparison of steamship line equipment is shown in Table 4-1.

Typical equipment of steamship companies using 20-ft. and 40-ft. containers consists of eight types of containers shown in Table 4-2.

TABLE 4-1. TYPICAL STEAMSHIP CONTAINER DIMENSIONS

Inside Dimensions	Compatible System	Sea-Land	Matson
Length	39'6"	34'7-1/2"	23'6"
Width	7'9"	7'8-1/2"	7'9"
Height	7'10"	7'10-1/2"	7'10-1/4"
Max. cargo weight	60,950 lbs.	45,000 lbs.	44,200 lbs.
Tare weight	6,940 lbs.	10,500 lbs.	3,800 lbs.
Cubic capacity	2,398 cu. ft.	2,088 cu. ft.	1,415 cu. ft.
Outside Dimensions			
Overall length	40'	35'	24'
Overall width	8'	8'	8'
Overall height	8'6"	8'6"	8'6-1/2"

Table 4-2. Typical long-line steamship company container equipment

	40-ft. Dry Cargo	40-ft. Dry Cargo Hi-Cube	40-ft. Reefer	40-ft. Tank	40-ft. Open Top	40-ft. Half-High Open Top	(AL) 20-ft. Dry Cargo	(FRP) 20-ft. Dry Cargo
Outside Dimensions								
Length	40'	40'	40'	40'	40'	40'	20'	20'
Width	8'	8'	8'	8'	8'	8'	8'	8'
Height	8'	8'6"	8'6"	4'3"	8'6"	4'3"	8'	8'
Inside Dimensions								
Length	39'7"	39'6"	37'10"		39'6"	39'6"	19'6"	19'7"
Width	7'9"	7'9"	7'4"		6'8"	7'9"	7'8"	7'10"
Height	7'4"	7'10"	7'1/2"		7'6"	3'4"	7'4"	7'6"
Door Opening								
Width	7'5-3/4"	7'6"	7'6"		7'6"	7'6"	7'5-3/4"	7'5-3/4"
Height	6'11-3/4"	7'5-1/2"	7'5-3/4"		6'11"	3'4"	6'11-3/4"	6'11-3/4"
Construction	aluminum	aluminum	aluminum	st. steel AISI 304	aluminum	aluminum	aluminum	plastic plywood
Internal cu. cap.	2,250 cu. ft.	2,398 cu. ft.	1,988 cu. ft.	6,020 gals.	2,296 cu. ft.	1,020 cu. ft.	1,096 cu. ft.	1,151 cu. ft.
Max. load cap.	60,260 lbs.	60,950 lbs.	50,000 lbs.	51,600 lbs.	59,280 lbs.	45,000 lbs.	44,800 lbs.	40,650 lbs.
Tare weight	6,400 lbs.	6,940 lbs.	10,700 lbs.	9,260 lbs.	7,750 lbs.	6,660 lbs.	4,500 lbs.	4,500 lbs.
Special features	end door opening	end door opening	temp. control; meat rails	bulk liq.; loading equip.; supplied	end door opening; open top loading; swinging roof bows	end door opening; open top loading; swinging roof bows	end door opening	end door opening

ECONOMIC EFFECTIVENESS

The value of the container as a transport vehicle must take into consideration the relationship between the available cube space and the overall tare weight of the container. Construction methods of containers vary according to the intended use, environment, relative costs of materials, state of the art in manufacturing, and the imagination of the engineers who provide the design idea. Internal dimensions are not included in any international standard, and are rather left to the ingenuity of the container designer, since the restriction on inland used by truck depends largely on the deadweight ratio. Table 4-3 identifies the leeway of the container builder, as he relates to the same piece of equipment. These dimensions must be valued again as related to the payload capacity, maximum payload, and tare weight, before a figure of merit can be established. Such a figure of merit would come up with the Maximum payload $\times$ Maximum cube $\times$ Minimum weight.

COST/MAINTENANCE FACTORS

All containers depend on durability of the front panel and the door panel. Container sides, floor, and roof are usually damaged only by accident and, as such, are designed to different criteria. Such accidents should be locally repairable.

TABLE 4-3.   MANUFACTURERS' VARIATIONS IN
CONTAINER EQUIPMENT

Manu-facturer	Internal Dimensions			Door Dimensions	
	Length	Height	Width	Height	Width
A	19'3-13/32"	7'15/64"	7'7-9/64"	6'10-13/64"	7'5-11/64"
B	19'5-1/2"	7'4-1/2"	7'8-1/2"	7'1"	7'6"
C	19'4-1/2"	7'3-15/16"	7'8"	7'1-1/16"	7'6"
D	19'4-1/2"	7'5-1/4"	7'7-1/4"	7'-7/8"	7'5-5/8"
E	19'5-1/2"	7'5"	7'9"	—	—
F	19'4-1/2"	7'3-3/4"	7'9"	7'0"	7'6"
G	19'5-3/4"	7'4-1/2"	7'8-1/4"	7'-5/16"	7'5-1/4"
H	19'3-15/16"	7'4-7/16"	7'8-3/4"	7'0"	7'5"
I	19'5"	7'4-1/2"	7'8-3/4"	7'1"	7'6"

N. B. Widths given are for unlined containers. Normal lining material is 1/4 in. plywood.

Under these conditions, a renewal program has been developed for these two panels. If the front panel is built with increased panel strength, such as the corrugated front and rear ends of a railroad boxcar, the renewal would require only replacement. However, all standard containers with an integrated panel strength depend not only on the resiliency of the sheet, but also on the fastening method and the deterioration of welding seams. A recommended practice is to replace the entire corner frame at least every ten years. This corner frame takes in the two corner posts, and the four corner castings at the upper and lower rails. The same principle applies to updating the rear door panel. Here, additionally, the door panels themselves and all the hardware should be renewed. Retesting of refurbished containers is required by the CSC Convention.

One of the best recommended practices to improve sealing of marine containers is to develop a hatch-cover-type door fitting in which the closing is not obtained, as in present conventional containers, by hardware attached to the outside of the door, but rather by recessed jams which will be fastened inside the door frame and which can be tightened, as the conditions may require.

MODE CONTROL

The highway weight restrictions, as well as underpass clearances and turning radius of vehicles, provide the neck of the bottle, if containerization can use this parable. Highway laws have had the greatest influence on container geometry, basically, since American standards were made the common denominator in the first modular development era. The decision of the German railroads to increase containers for European transportation from 8 ft. to 8 ft. 6 in. provides the indication that, increasingly, railroads may desire to obtain a better utilization of their profile and car capacity in years to come. In November 1970, the Truck Trailer Manufacturers Association, which represents the builders of most of the original shipboard containers, announced a survey covering details of construction among the manufacturers in 1969.

The TTMA survey shows that 84.2 percent of the containers were general-purpose dry vans, 6.9 percent were refrigerated vans, and 1.5 percent were insulated vans. The remaining types were: open tops, 2.7 percent; platforms, 1.2 percent; open-side gondolas, 0.7 percent; tanks, 0.6 percent; car haul, 0.2 percent, and others, 2.0 percent.

In light of this, the visible trend development shown in the aforementioned statistics covering van trailer length, overall height, interior loading width, and interior loading height is very significant, since it shows that for the controlling highway mode, van trailers developed from an average length of 24 to 26 ft. in 1946 to 49 ft. in 1970. It indicates the relinquishing of capacity between the terminal transfer points and inland terminals with the 20-ft. and 40-ft. containers, which have become customary standard equipment in the container industry. In October 1970, at The Containerization Institute's Symposium in New York, Eugene Hinden of Gindy Manufacturing Corporation suggested that the 30-ft. container become the new industry standard, since it would allow operation of two trailers of 30 ft. length, each carrying 30-ft.-long containers over the highway. This would be an almost 50 percent improvement in the truck capacity based on the 40-ft. maximum container. The 30-ft. container is preferred by the British container operators, since it is the standard element used by the British Rail Liner Trains. The 30-ft. container would provide two axles under each container. It is likely that such a modification of standards may occur. The container height may go to 9 ft. 6 in., and the width in Europe for inland and short sea trade may advance to 8 ft. 6 in.

PATTERN ON INTEGRATION

The corner fitting allows the integration into the system of any container so equipped. The composition and structure of the corner fitting will determine the performance of the systems integration. Rather than to install a fitting in the corner post of the container itself, as it is done by Sea-Land, the system provides 3 in. × 5 in. uniform blocks of casting to which other container structural elements are attached. The castings are made of steel or aluminum. Welding produces better joint strengths with steel than with any other material. Not only must the corner casting be perfectly fitted in three directions, corner post and two rails, but the welding must also have good resistance to continuous use of the fitting. Many overhead factors must be considered. For example, in overhead handling, the container may be lowered at considerable speed onto a nonparallel surface, impacting one corner before the other three can contact. Therefore, the strength of the composition and welding must be carefully tested in the design process.

Commonly, the top corner fittings have top, end, and side openings to take hooks, shackles, slings, or other engaging pickup devices mounted on spreaders or on other containers. When the containers are carried under deck, the corner fitting provides the contact between the cell guide structure and the container unit. Rolling, pitching, heaving, and other motions transfer the sea impact significantly from the ship's structure through the corner fitting to the container. Racking, like impact, is transferred through the weld joints and resolved by the structural rigidity of the container frame. If the corner fitting is not properly aligned, failures will occur, which eventually will produce major damage to the container. When containers are carried on the deck of a ship at sea, the restraining of containers against the ship's motions is accomplished entirely through the corner fitting to the restrained system. The exposure can be excessive at a given moment; and damage to the securing of the container can be anticipated. A combination system, in which the exterior restraint system is further supported by a buttress or cellular deck guide system, supports the lashed type under heavy-duty conditions.

The following considerations are of particular importance, and especially significant where containers may be handled infrequently:

1. Containers (20 ft. or larger) must be lifted vertically from the top corners, requiring a spreader frame or the equivalent. Lifting a loaded container with slings leading at an angle from the corner fittings may buckle the container.

2. Containers may be lifted with fork lifts or straddle trucks ONLY when they are designed and built for such handling, fitted with such special devices as fork-lift pockets, recesses for straddle carriers, or grapple holds.

3. When containers are set down or stacked, their weight must be carried entirely on the corner fittings. Support at any other points will damage the container.

When the container is carried on a chassis or railroad car, the corner fitting will slip over a conical male connector. Commonly known as a "dog," this conical element is rotated inside the corner fitting and provides a large internal bearing surface for vertical restraint. Lateral restraint is provided by the vertical sides of the cone base, which fits closely within holes in the base of the corner fitting. Four simple fittings, therefore, constitute a self-aligning and self-locking system which best resists motions from railroad or road transportation. With this type of dog system, containers can also be moved on flat-bed trucks or railroad cars or by conveyor systems. Conveyors use an expandable, hydraulically operated, conical dog, instead of the exterior movement from the supporting deck, rail car, or platform trailer.

DESIGN PARAMETERS

The guiding consideration for the design deals with the static and dynamic loads which the container may be exposed to. They are as follows:

1. Floor load—static and dynamic loads imposed on the floor by the payload and the wheels of handling equipment when used;
2. End load—static and dynamic loads imposed by the payload on the freight container walls and doors which are perpendicular to the longitudinal axis of the freight container;
3. Side load—static and dynamic loads imposed by the payload on the freight container walls and doors which are parallel to the longitudinal axis of the freight container;
4. Roof load—external static and dynamic loads imposed on the roof of a freight container;
5. Superimposed load—external static and dynamic loads imposed vertically downwards on the structure of the freight container.

As a result of this, we must analyze the five design elements, each of which has to correspond to one or a combination of the static and dynamic loads. These elements are:

1. Floor base;
2. Corner structure, including fittings and rails;
3. Bulkhead, front and rear;
4. Roof structure and support;
5. Lateral sides.

As is true with critical unit construction of airplane fuselages, submarine hulls, or other pressure vessels, the container is integrated into a unique cellular geometry and rectangular shape. This means that any opening, even in the side, top, or bottom, detracts and diminishes from the precalculated unit strength. Analysis must be very carefully made of the conditions created by this change in stress, in order to identify reinforcing structure required to restore structural integrity to unit standards. This is quite different from a single supported bridge structure used to build a railroad boxcar. There the strength is primarily integrated into the floor. But the design integration of the container is based on a five-element synthesis.

CONSTRAINT ANALYSIS

The different forces which work on the five-design elements can also, in a given moment, complement each other. Such an overpowering energy combination may produce excessive stress and collapsed containers. The analysis of this constraint spectrum requires an individual consideration of each of the container components:

1. Corner structures—vertical frame components located at the corners of the freight container, integral with the corner fittings, and connecting the roof and floor structures;

2. Corner fittings—fittings located at the corners of the freight container which normally provide means for handling, stacking, and securing the container;

3. End frame—each of the structures of the container perpendicular to its longitudinal axis consisting of the corner structures and the end members of the base and of the roof;

4. End wall—assembly surrounded by the end frame which encloses either end of the container;

5. Side frame—each of the structures parallel to the longitudinal axis of the container consisting of the corner structures and of the bottom side rails and roof rails;

6. Side wall—assembly surrounded by the side frame either side of the container;

7. Roof rails—longitudinal structural members situated at the top edge on either side of the freight container;

8. Bottom side rails—structural members situated on the longitudinal sides of the base;

9. End door—door located in an end wall;

10. Side door—door located in a side wall;

11. Roof—assembly forming the top closure of the container limited by the end frames and the roof rails;

12. Base—assembly of which the principal components are the two bottom longitudinal members, the two bottom end members, the floor, and possibly the cross members;

13. Cross members—traverse components attached to the bottom side rails and supporting the floor.

Without special doors, the design of the door end frame and the connections between the horizontal members and the corner posts must provide the strength to resist the racking effect caused by ship motion or when stacked eccentrically. This is particularly important for stowage above deck, where lashings are used for support against racking instead of cell guides. Corner fittings are located at the top and bottom of each corner post for lifting and securing. The high-load-bearing corner-post construction is the principal feature of the container which makes it different from normal over-the-road vans. ISO Series 1 containers have sufficient corner strength to allow containers to be stacked six high; ISO Series 2 containers can be stacked only three high.

RACKING DEFORMATION

Container deformation caused by racking has been a problem for containers stowed above deck, where they do not have the support provided by the cell guide structure below deck. Unless the container is able to resist all of the racking stresses, the diagonal lashings must provide this resistance.

Presently, the ISO recommendations do not include container racking strength criteria. However, Lloyd's, American Bureau of Shipping (ABS), and other regulatory bodies have established racking-test load requirements for certification of 20-ft. and 40-ft. containers. Containers built during the period from 1958 to 1968 approximate the established racking strength requirements of the 20-ft. container, but fall short of the 40-ft. container requirements, in fact, as much as 40 percent. Steel, aluminum, plywood, fiberglass, and combinations of these materials are used in container construction. Each type of container has its advantages and disadvantages, so that use depends upon the type of operation. Some of the differences and relative advantages are discussed later in this chapter.

CONNECTORS AND FITTINGS

The outside of the container does not lend itself to the use of nonstandardized connecting and lashing fittings. The very often reproduced picture of a cargo hook used in the bottom corner castings will work principally due to the angular position of the cargo hook in the corner casting during the lifting process. However, for other uses, anything that does not fit exactly the purpose of container corner fittings is not recommended.

With the growth of containerization, the desire to develop more versatility in the use of containers has also grown. One area of interest to users of freight containers of ANSI/ISO modular sizes is the ability to take two units of one length and connect them end-to-end to form a composite unit of twice the individual unit length. The most likely candidates for this form of handling are two 10-ft. containers connected to form a 20-ft. unit, and two 20-ft. units connected to form a 40-ft. unit.

There are several reasons for wanting to join units together. One of the most important is the ability to take two 20-ft. containers and connect them for shipment in the 40-ft. cells of a containership. Another is the necessity to move two 20-ft. units over the road as a single 40-ft. unit in states where "doubles" are not allowed. However, many other economies of handling can be achieved in utilizing the connectors, so that the two smaller units can be moved as a larger unit.

All containers conforming to ANSI/ISO sizes have corner castings with openings on the exposed faces to receive various types of handling or restraint hardware (Fig. 4-1). The connecting device must be com-

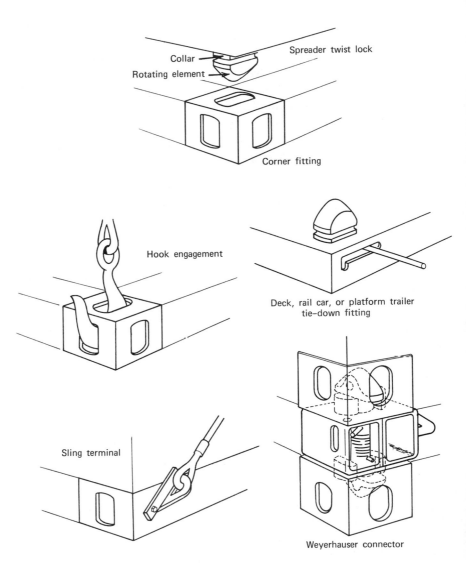

FIGURE 4-1. FIVE WAYS TO CONNECT OR ENGAGE INTO CORNER CASTINGS OF STANDARD ISO SYSTEM.

patible with the end openings in both the top and bottom castings, in order to make one design work in both types of fittings. The device must be capable of resisting high compressive and tensile forces, as well as transmitting shear forces between units. It should be simple, rugged, and easy to install and remove. Typically, the Weyerhaeuser Company's (Tacoma, Washington) connector is made from two pieces of low-alloy, high-strength steel which can be opened or closed by means of a bolt passing through one piece and threaded into the other. The closed connector is installed through the mating casting end holes, as the containers are brought together. The lugs on the ends of the connector engage the inside face of the castings when the bolt is turned, separating the two halves of the device. The heavy central portion acts as a spacer between the connected containers to keep the overall length to that specified for the equivalent longer unit.

BRIDGE LASHINGS

Swedish equipment manufacturers have produced a new deck lashing aid which should eliminate many of the problems in weatherdeck transportation of containers. Similar in size to the normal corner casting and weighing 15 kilos, it is officially described as an automatic self-engaging, self-locking lashing fitting. Key to the design is a double-acting twistlock fabricated from a single shaft of solid steel, spring-operated in a square housing of cast steel.

For loading operations, the fitting is secured in the lower corner casting to automatically engage when lowered into the stack, thus dispensing with the need for stevedores working in exposed positions to place bridge and top fittings. A bridge fitting is a spacing element between two containers. Similarly, it becomes unnecessary for stevedores to release such fittings for off-loading, as this fitting can be released from the deck or at short-ladder level.

SEA SERVICE

Ship service routine requires container restraint systems permanently installed with portable fittings designed for the size and weight of containers. Lashing assemblies for securing containers on deck must include provisions for ready tensioning of lashings to remove all slack after loading. At the same time, excessive pre-tension in the assembly must not distort the container. All stacking fittings used between tiers of containers lashed on deck must fit well at each corner to prevent horizontal movement. Also, bridge fittings should be used to provide horizontal support between rows of containers within a stack, and should prevent tipping.

Number and application of lashings in the securing system of containers must be determined from calculations based on predicted sea conditions. The weight and stiffness characteristics of the containers must be integrated in the calculations. Required strength of container tie-down must be based on maximum loads determined from system calculations. A factor of two or more on the breaking strength for lashing assemblies and corner fittings is available, but a safety factor of three on the ultimate strength of supporting structure is a basic requirement.

Corner fitting lashings must be tested for proof of adequacy. Samples should be tested to failure to verify designed performance. To maintain the tightness and structural integrity of containers, procedures for inspections must be set up. Container door frames must be inspected for tightness after and during each use.

CONSTRAINT FACTORS

Constraint analysis must deal with many service conditions and outside effects in considering the life-cycle prediction for the container. Two of these factors deal with the cargo itself. Some cargoes are incompatible with the type of container they are stowed in. Many container organizations, such as the Japan Container Association, the International Cargo Handling Coordination Association (ICHCA), the Swedish Commission for Transportation and Research, and the National Cargo Bureau of the United States, have issued guide booklets of instructions for the shipper which should be analyzed, if cargoes are loaded which have a great weight impact enabling the cargo to pressure the sidewalls of the container. The condition called "stow impact" results from improper stowage and inadequate unit packing, or from tie-down, bracing, wedging, nailing, or securing of cargo within the container to withstand the lateral or force-and-aft movements. Shock forces caused by road bounce on railroad car humping, as well as by the heave of the ship, require firm attachment of the cargo to the floor to prevent stow impact.

Other factors appear frequently, as a result of container overhead lift operations presently used. The roof is designed to carry two longshoremen on the roof while working. Frequent depositing of spreader bars, cargo tools, and ship's gear on the roof has become an occurrence with semicontainerships and caused considerable damage to the container roof and the cargo inside.

When containers are lifted without a snug-fitting spreader frame from the top corners, the lifting load frequently exceeds the design strength of the container rail structure. The designed "column strength" of side rails can be exceeded when slings are used at improper angles from top or bottom corner fittings. The lifting of loaded containers by fork lift from the bottom provides for unequal distribution on the floor weight which, in turn, produces a tendency of drooping of the unsupported ends of the container outward from the lift-truck forks. "Fork drooping," as this problem is called, produces excessive strain on the entire container. When containers are set down or stacked, the weight must be uniformly and simultaneously distributed to the entire corner-fitting structure.

The missed-stack damage is equivalent to the list damage encountered by containers in cell guides when the ship lists 6° or more. This condition is very frequent and found during reloading of a loaded container-ship where the ballasting position of the ship is not carefully being watched.

ENVIRONMENTAL CONDITIONS

Twelve environmental conditions provide additional sea service constraint. They are:

1. Water damage;
2. Solar absorption;
3. Infrared penetration;
4. Fungi growth;
5. Ultraviolet absorption;
6. Loss of elasticity and waterproofness;
7. Chemical effect of sea-water absorption;
8. Corrosion;
9. Expansion and contraction of metal parts;
10. Joint distortion;
11. External temperature differential;
12. Condensation and sweating.

The greatest harm comes from the environmental effects of the rise in temperature. This can impose stresses upon the container structure for which the unit is not designed. Evaluation of the properties of the material must include a consideration of the rigidity in heat and the brittleness on temperature drops. Finally, as the air temperature inside the container is lowered due to weather changes in transit, the ability of the air inside the structure to hold moisture is reduced. Condensation may form on cold surfaces, and this sweating, which has been found to produce over seven gallons of water within 24 hours in a 20-ft. container exposed to a 20° temperature change, is important to the design specification.

CARGO ACCOMMODATION

Certain special requirements of the cargo itself or of the method of customary stowing of cargo in a vehicle lead to the special requirements on the design specifications. One very customary requirement is an additional opening. Where 40-ft. containers are concerned, the shipper will like to effect delivery through a side door. Other openings have been known to be placed in the roof for loading bulk commodities by conveyor belts or elevator nozzles. The installation of trap doors in the floor for bulk discharge or in the back door has been frequent in Europe.

If the floor of the container is not made out of wood, but rather of aluminum or other metal, the installation of nailing boards between the corrugations of the floor aids in the bracing of the cargo. Tie-down rings are frequently installed along the sidewalls to allow passing of ropes through them to secure the cargo. Another device frequently incorporated is the "logistic track," wherein rails are installed either dividing the entire container into fore and aft sections, or into upper and lower sections by installation of an additional floor deck. Individual rope ties may also be installed at intervals along the track. Another application of logistic tracks deals with fastening of a bulkhead or bulkhead bars at three or four levels inside of the rear door of the container to prevent the entire load from shifting against the door, as a result of ship or rail humping motions.

Fresh meat in sectionalized carcasses is shipped suspended from hooks. The support of the metal rail structure from which these hooks are loaded requires additional strength in the sidewall of the container, since the entire load is now supported from the roof. This, in turn, requires the provision of supporting bars or elements on which the master rail runs along each one of the inner sides of the container. The same master rails may also be used for loading internal cargo units attached from the rail rather than loaded piece by piece on the floor. The design of these meat-rail structures must be such as to support the entire weight, under all critical conditions, on the container floor rather than on other parts of the structures.

ALUMINUM CONTAINERS

The advantages of aluminum construction are numerous. A few are listed below:

1. It is lightweight.
2. Extruded corner posts can be made in one piece.
3. Wide sheets available permit one-piece roof, sides, or ends.

STEEL CONTAINERS

Weight and corrosion have been the disadvantages to the use of steel for container construction. Several companies, through new lightweight designs, have greatly reduced the weight of steel containers. The inherent strength of steel, minimizing damage from collisions or puncturing by fork-lift trucks, is a definite advantage.

PLYWOOD/FIBERGLASS CONTAINERS

FRP/Plywood containers, generally, have steel frames with $3/4$ in. fiberglass-reinforced plywood; smooth thinner walls; no ribs, bracing, or other members that reduce the internal space; and, consequently, greater cube efficiency, allowing for a greater payload as high as 10 percent.

PART TRUCK AND PART SHIP

Container equipment design today is in a great dilemma. It is being specified by marine designers accustomed to technology of conventional ocean transportation. Containers, however, are being built for the most part by truck and trailer body builders most familiar with highway conditions. Containers, therefore, have the peculiar problem of having to focus in four directions at the same time to find compatibility with the four underlying transportation media.

This interface problem is real and significant. It shows up today with big loss ratios on cargoes. This was not experienced by the pioneers during the 15 previous years. The lack of interface coordination also affects insurance rates, ship and cargo safety, and investment in ports and equipment; and most importantly, it spells success or failure for the shipper who pays for the new services. Today a "hermaphrodite" container

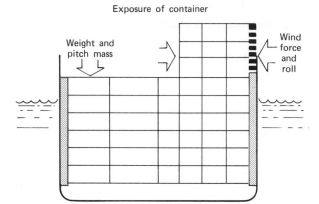

FIGURE 4-2.   THE CONTAINERSHIP PROBLEMS.

sails the oceans, part truck and part ship. This helter-skelter design effort will end quickly when systems analyses and cost effectiveness are utilized. Sobering days of recognition usually follow in the wake of the first enthusiasm. To guide the industry to a solid future requires systematic analysis, a practical exchange of experiences made, and cooperative planning for the future.

Presently, the most significant container problems have to do with the carriage of containers on the decks of ships. The American Bureau of Shipping, the United States Coast Guard, the American Institute of Marine Underwriters, the National Cargo Bureau, the Interstate Commerce Commission, and the Department of Labor, to name a few, all have some influence on the design of containers. Their positions vary, and both shipowners and container builders are still faced with uncertainty at many points. On-deck carriage is the part of the overall problem the marine industry is studying. This is only the beginning of the task.

STRESS PROBLEMS

Many of the container design problems become quite evident when pictorially represented in sketches. They deal with typical overhead lifting, as presently applied to containerships. Also included are the forces developed when a 40-ft. container is picked up with slings and stowed in a conventional manner on one of the hundreds of conventional cargo ships which now begin to carry these units. The indignation of the builder of container bodies will be provoked by merely comparing these exposures with his normal design ideas.

Another group of sketches deals with the exposure of containers in the ship. The impact of weight and pitch, wind force, and roll are continuous (Fig. 4-2). They are really to be feared more than the sudden exposure of a container to green seas. But this, too, will be well understood if one realizes that the forces in the wave are so strong as to break up dams built from boulders on the shoreline. It is a fact that the same forces are contained in the wave that were encountered by the ship at sea; and it is, therefore, questionable if anything other than the ship plate, which has a minimum of $\frac{1}{2}$ in. steel cross section, can resist such impact. But who would like to have containers made of $\frac{1}{2}$ in. steel and to transport them in competition with containers made of thin 6060 aluminum sheet? The weight difference is significant.

The overall container details have now been discussed and allow me to present the factors and critical elements for design decision making.

As the result of the International Convention for Safe Containers (CSC) and the Customs Convention on Containers (CCC) agreed to by the UN/IMCO conference of December 1, 1972, both a safety approval plate and a customs origin registration plate shall be permanently affixed to every container.

Decision Elements

PRIME DECISION MAKING

Once investigations and evaluation have been conducted, identifying a container unit system as the preferred choice, it becomes necessary to understand the variety of conditions imposed on the van unit itself, as well as consequent mechanical, structural, cost, and weight compromises required and the available trade-offs. No one construction method can serve all conditions equally well, so I will describe some of the more satisfactory configurations with the rationale and refinements that have produced them.

Although container construction varies as widely to the type of materials and design as to the cargoes it is destined to carry, four critical decision points will determine the construction decisively:

1. Mode compatibility;
2. Functional design;
3. Cargo accommodation;
4. Economic effectiveness.

CONFIGURATION STANDARDS

Since the governing mode of container movement deals with the transfer of the cargo in intermodal service, the lifting standards have become the most important mode compatibility criteria. Again, we must point out that there is a tendency toward developing linear motions of containers either fore or aft or sideways by the use of conveyor belts or similar horizontal movement devices. But at this time, the vertical movements which are incurred as the containers are lifted from one transport media to the other, provide the rules of the design and governing decision, especially for marine containers.

Generally, the International Standards Organization has recognized four types of lifting systems by the corner fittings. Top-lift, by use of automatic spreader equipment fitted with twist locks, or a manual top-lift using cargo hooks or clevises, are two current and coexisting means. The semiautomatic, top-lift equipment using spreader twist locks, or the bottom-lift system using slings hooked through or attached to the bottom corner fittings are more common for the transition stage when general cargo ships provide on-deck transportation.

CONTAINER BRIEFING

Containers are produced mostly by the companies of the truck-trailer industry. Their existing product line and manufacturing techniques put them in an advantageous position to move into container production. Nevertheless, there are some vital differences between containers and trailers. The most obvious difference is the demountable character of a container. When in the separated condition, the container loses the strengthening and rigidizing contribution of the chassis.

The loading conditions encountered in the various operating modes impose severe structural requirements on containers. Most of these conditions are not experienced by trailers. Several loading conditions which govern the design of containers are discussed below.

Stacking: Containers may be stacked six high in cells of containerships. Lateral restraint is provided by the vertical cell guides of the ship. The load force is applied at the corner fittings.

Lifting: Lifting may be performed by attaching lifting devices to the top corner fittings (most often the case) or the bottom corner fittings.

Fork-lift pockets in the lower members of certain containers are also provided. Lifting a container at twice its rated capacity in order to account for dynamic amplification of stress response is a structural requirement.

Racking: Side forces are applied to the upper end-frame members and resisted at the lower end-frame members of the container due to inertia forces of stacked containers on ships' weather decks where guide rails do not provide continuous lateral restraint. In this connection, it may be noted that in nearly all stowage arrangements of containers aboard ship, the long axis of the container is aligned with the ship's longitudinal axis.

Restraint: Forces are applied in both directions through the container's bottom structure as a consequence of transient motions of the transport vehicle and the inertial reaction of the loaded container.

Wall pressure: Forces are applied to the sidewalls and both ends of the container due to the bearing of the contents on the walls as the loaded container is accelerated under ship motion, retardation of rail cars, or the like.

Floor pressure: Forces are applied to the container floor and its supporting structure due to the entry of a loaded warehouse lift truck.

Roof pressure: During transfer and lashing operations aboard ship, there are times when the container roof must be used as a platform. This has led to a requirement that the roof be capable of supporting the weight of two men. In the few cases where a loading condition is common to both container and trailer operating modes (for example, wall pressure), the container can be expected to experience a greater amount of stress. In short, the conditions of container service are more rigorous, and any tendency to regard intermodal demountable containers as mere packing boxes is not justified when the details of the operational environment have been examined carefully. With this background, it is possible to appreciate some of the features of the conventional design practice of the container manufacturing industry.

End frames: End frames (Fig. 5-1) are provided at both the front (A) and rear (B). These generally are welded assemblies of steel members incorporating corner castings (C) with a standardized pattern of handling sockets. The stacking and racking requirements lead to fairly husky material thickness in end frames, and $\frac{1}{4}$-inch material formed into a box section is a common design solution.

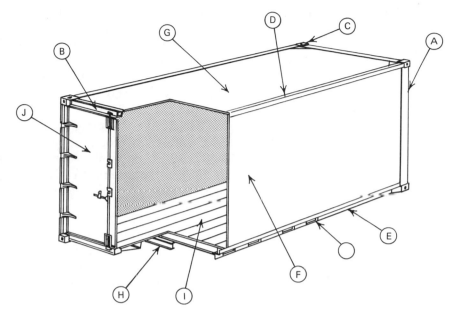

FIGURE 5-1. CONTAINER STRUCTURAL FEATURES.

Longitudinal rails: Side rails (D, E) running longitudinally along the top and bottom of the container join the two end frames together and, additionally, mount the side panels (F). These members are either steel or aluminum, with the latter currently being the preferred material in the industry. Most of the rail-to-frame joints are by bolting. Figure 5-1 also shows a typical section of an extruded aluminum type of rail.

Side panels: The end frames and rails provide a support for the attachment of panels (F), basically sheet material. In the case of aluminum side panels, sheet-post construction is used, with the posts being of a hat-section type, as shown in Fig. 5-1. Posts are spaced between one and two feet apart and may be either exterior or interior, depending on where the operator desires to have the flush surface. Sheet material thickness of 0.062 inch is common, with the weight being 0.89 lb./sq. ft. The weight of stiffeners is quite variable, but a value of 0.92 lb./running ft. has been computed for a representative extruded section. With posts spaced two feet apart, the weight of panel material is 1.8 lbs./sq. ft. Aluminum panels are often augmented by a plywood interior liner which may be either half- or full-height. With a half-height liner, the average panel weight is approximately 2.2 lbs./sq. ft.

FRP/plywood panels consist of a plywood core with a fiberglass-reinforced plastic overlay on each face of the panel. Most often, the fibers are in a woven roving form; for example, untwisted in a fabric within a polyester matrix. Common thickness of plywood stock is ¾ inch. Total panel thickness is usually in the range of 0.84 to 0.88 inch. The weight of such a sandwich panel is in the range of 3.0 to 3.2 lbs./sq. ft., depending on the proportion of glass fiber in the overlay and the thickness. The panels are joined to the frame by riveting.

Steel panels are also used, primarily on containers from foreign sources. Steel-container sheet material is usually rigidized by corrugation, and separate posts are not added. Welding is used as the joining means. A typical design employs 18-gauge (.049-inch) sheet stock with corrugations of about 1.5 inches depth. Such a panel fabrication weighs about 2.6 lbs./sq. ft.

Roofs: The roof (G) is generally of the same material and construction as the side panels, with only a few exceptions. Roof bows of aluminum units are often joined with adhesives. One-piece sheet material is preferred in order to maximize resistance to water entry from above.

Bottom structure: The understructure and flooring transfer loads induced by deadweight and inertial reactions of the contents to the side rails. The cross members (H) are formed channels or extruded shapes with a depth on the order of 5 inches and a thickness of about 0.188 inch, if aluminum. Steel is also used for these members, generally when the side rails are of steel. The deck surface (I) is usually of oak or softwood floorboard, shiplap jointed, and between 1⅛ and 1⅜ inches thick. Plywood is also used for flooring, in which case an FRP overlay with a silica sand finish may be applied.

Doors: Doors (J) are most frequently of heavy plywood clad with metal faces, referred to as plymetal. The thickness of the composite is in the range of 0.75 to 1.0 inch, with the face material being about 22 gauge (0.031 inch) if steel and .040 inch if aluminum. Sandwich fabrications for doors may also have an aluminum exterior and a steel interior, where the steel is not exposed to a highly corrosive atmosphere and at the same time resists the forces and abrasion of cargo impacting the end wall. Doors are generously proportioned for the further reason that when firmly engaged to the end frame, they significantly contribute to the container's resistance to racking forces. Thus, locking bars, either one or two per door half, are securely anchored in keepers on the door and in camming locks on the end frame. In so-called anti-rack hardware, these locks restrain the bar end from play in all directions. Hinges complete the assembly.

Handling provisions: Standardized corner fittings (C) may be seen in Fig. 5-1. These fittings have elongated sockets on top to which are engaged connecting fittings of the spreader of a crane or mobile handling unit. It may be noted in the detail in this figure that there are protective plates in proximity to the top corner handling fittings to guard against damage when a spreader drops on a container top misaligned with the fittings. Similar sockets are on the under surface of the bottom corner fittings to provide restraint when containers are on deck or on a land vehicle. Locking is performed by twisting of the male element either manually or by remote actuation. The container's corner fittings also have openings on their sides to enable hoisting by hooks and slings at both the top and bottom corners. Additionally, fork-lift pockets (K) are provided to permit handling from the bottom by the tines of lift trucks. This mode of handling is losing favor, and as a consequence pockets in the understructure of containers are becoming relatively rare. Note on this figure that four pockets are shown in the typical design. Usually the outer pockets are aligned with the fork-lift tines of a high-capacity lift truck capable of handling a loaded container. The two inner pockets are used by lift trucks capable of handling only an empty container.

SPECIAL-PURPOSE CONTAINER TYPES

The most frequently used container type is the general dry, cargo container as described in the previous section. These comprise over 95 percent of all containers in use, excluding refrigerator types. There are variations from the design of this type to make containers more suitable to some cargoes, which do not adapt well to the standard van. The alternate types comply generally with standardization requirements on dimensions, handling provisions, and load-carrying capability.

Open-top containers: These containers differ from the standard vans by using a canvas closure over the top to protect the contents from the elements. The advantage of open-top containers is that cargoes which are unsuited to loading into the container by fork-lift can be lowered in by hook from overhead. Long lengths of lumber are an example. Specially designed containers for the transport of automobiles have structural similarities to open-top units and are related in function to highway automobile transporters.

Racks and half-height containers: These containers are inherently open-top since they would not have adequate clearance for loading otherwise. Their advantage is that, in the case of very heavy cargoes—for example, structural steel shapes—they avoid the loss of cube that would result from the use of full-height containers. They fully conform to dimensional standards when two half-height units are stacked.

Tank-type containers: These containers enable the efficient transport of liquids in small quantities. Typically, 5,000-gallon-capacity tanks are mounted within a framework which satisfies the dimensional and load-carrying capacity of the standard twenty-foot container. Provisions are included in most designs to enable flammable liquids and various chemicals to be transported safely. Most tank-type containers are suitable for transporting some bulk solids, a typical example being plastic pellets.

THE CUP CONCEPT

The overhead container-handling system had to develop an automatic hookup system not requiring hand labor. This, in turn, called for outfitting the cranes with an automatic spreader frame which would fit snugly and safely over the container section closest to the crane. The design consideration resembles the principle of lifting a cup by four points installed in the upper rim. The excessive strength requirements could be avoided since a calculation of the forces transmitted during the temporary connection between the crane and the container shell are easily predictable. Yet the container has maintained its main strength in the bottom plate, which is comparable to the bottom of the cup. This has led to the design of an additional lip on the bottom from which the container can be lifted with clamps reaching under the lip, in a relatively loose fit. Since the bottom-lift fit is not as secure as the upper lift, and not possible in the cells of a containership, the system is applied mostly to motions from an overhead stacker which does not have the exposure of the long reach of the overhead ship crane. In many cases, especially as far as 20-ft. containers are concerned, fork pockets have been installed in the base frame to allow lifting and mobility within container yards. This feature reveals the importance of the rim integrity of the cup.

MATERIAL SELECTION

Virtually all commonly available structure materials have been employed in container construction at one time or another. Carbon steel and high-tensile steel are the most commonly available and lowest-cost materials. Easy to fabricate and weld, steel is especially popular with steel-oriented shipowners and with leasing companies who must obtain large numbers of containers at the least possible cost. Low-carbon steel is most susceptible to corrosion in marine environments, requiring elaborate protective coatings to extend a relatively short life of 5 to 10 years.

Aluminum, three to four times as expensive as low-carbon steel, is easy to fabricate; but welding is more difficult and produces strength-deficient joints in the as-welded condition. Aluminum surfaces do not offer wear resistance and high local strength required for corner castings and corner posts. Aluminum sheets do not offer the puncture resistance afforded by either steel or FRP plywood. Two important characteristics of the material, however, have made it popular: light weight and good resistance to corrosion in marine environment, even when untreated.

A relative newcomer to container construction, fiberglass-reinforced plywood is steadily increasing in popularity for several reasons. With a cost/weight ratio between steel and aluminum, it is the least affected by salt water. Properly designed, large one-piece panels may be fabricated without posts, bows, corrugations, or seams. This method reduces costs and eliminates many potential points of leakage. Also the panels have low thermal transmissibility, marking the material a logical choice for insulated containers.

Material selection is the largest single factor in acquisition costs, a major factor in life-cycle costing, and a function of environmental and operational conditions.

MATERIAL COMPARISONS

The difficulties of evaluating materials when the options include composites with particular orientation of fibers and laminations have been stated by the Air Force Materials Laboratory. In the case of evaluating candidate materials for application to containers, numerous complexities become apparent through the examination of the properties of the individual materials. Noteworthy points to consider when bringing the individual materials into a unified comparison are:

1. Effectiveness of the final product is dependent, to a degree, on low tare weight, so the strength/weight parameter is important.

2. Cost of the final product is critical, so the *cost/strength* parameter must enter into comparative rankings.

3. The marine atmosphere to which containers are habitually exposed is

highly corrosive, thus the materials must be corrosion resistant—inadequate capability leads to shortened service life and continual application of surface protection, both of which affect cost.

4. Mechanical properties in addition to strength affect the serviceability of the end product and the manufacturing processes which may be employed.

5. The several materials are unequal in their progression from raw materials to a finished product—the particular case in point is the supply of FRP plywood stock in large enough sizes to be used directly as panels whereas metal sheet stock needs further fabrication.

6. The materials have properties which affect their design efficiency and fabrication processes—one obvious case is the supply of aluminum alloy sheet stock in the hardened condition, thus limiting its formability.

A simple single-valued merit ranking for the candidate materials is not feasible. Comparisons performed must, therefore, include attention to the critical parameters with maximum use of graphical displays to enable the application of engineering judgments.

STRENGTH-TO-WEIGHT RATIOS

In weight-critical structural applications, the strength/weight ratio parameter displays the relative efficiency of the available materials. Reference to the values used in ratio calculation show the density and the ultimate tensile strength for a broad range of materials. FRP has several different values, depending on the form of the reinforcing glass fibers, even though average values are taken for each form of the fibers. Aluminum alloys and steels are intermixed in the range from 4,000 psi upward. Both wound-filament-type constructions and titanium alloys are included for reference purposes. On both charts, the composite sandwich materials A and B are as follows:

A—FRP/plywood, 3/4 in. core, 24 oz. woven roving, polyester overlay, total thickness—7/8 in., weight—3.2 lbs./sq. ft.

B—FRP/urethane, 7/8 in. core, 24 oz. woven roving, polyester overlay, total thickness—1.15 in., weight—1.15 lbs./sq. ft.

These compositions were selected as representatives of composite sandwich types. Their strength is a synthetic value based on the tensile strength of each in proportion to the amount by volume in the composite.

PROPERTIES OF ALUMINUM

Strength/weight ratios are shown on Table 5-1. It may be seen that two aluminum alloys rank highest. These alloys are widely used in aeronautical structure applications but not in marine structures, being deficient in corrosion resistance due primarily to their copper content. The aluminum alloys in container construction are in the upper middle of the spectrum. These aluminum alloys are in the hardened state.

PROPERTIES OF STEEL

Steels cover a wide range from the ultrahigh-tensile alloys down to mild steel (1020) at the lower end of the rankings. Note that, at best, steel does not have the strength/weight ratios of aluminum alloys as presently used in container construction. The consequence of this observation is profound. The widely circulated claim that steel produces the strongest container structure can be true only if the weight of the end product exceeds that of the comparable aluminum structure in proportion to the strength/weight ratios. The result of current design practices is, however, that steel containers are quite close in tare weight to aluminum. The weight penalty of current steel containers is not sufficient to compensate for its unfavorable ranking in strength/weight ratio even when the possible design advantages offered by steel are exploited.

TABLE 5-1. STRENGTH-TO-WEIGHT RATIOS
OF SELECTED ALLOYS

Alloy*	Density, lbs./cu. in.	Spec. Gr.	UTS, ksi	S/W	YS, ksi	S/W
7075-T6	.101	2.80	86	30.6	73	26.1
X5090-H38	.095	2.60	69	26.6	53	20.4
2014-T6	.101	2.80	70	25.0	60	21.4
5052-H38	.097	2.68	42	15.6	37	13.8
6061-T6	.098	2.70	45	16.7	40	14.8
3003-H14	.099	2.73	22	8.1	21	7.7
ALCLAD						
7075-T6	.101	2.80	76	27.1	67	23.9
6061-T6	.098	2.70	42	15.6	37	13.7

Source: U.S. Govt. I.
* Refers to Std. Mfr's Code.

PROPERTIES OF FRP

FRP materials fall in the mid-range on strength/weight ratio, generally, behind the aluminum alloys. It would be possible to select an FRP with a highly unidirectional characteristic to its reinforcing fabric and show FRP superior to aluminum. However, with a reasonably balanced fabric-and-polyester matrix, FRP ranks just ahead of aluminum alloy 5052-T6. Even with a balanced fabric such as 181, which loses only 10 percent of its strength in the transverse direction, there is a loss of approximately 50 percent in the 45° direction. For a composition with chopped strand glass mat, FRP falls behind the common aluminum alloys.

PROPERTIES OF COMPOSITES

When FRP is put into a composite sandwich construction with either a plywood core or a low-density urethane core, the resulting strength/weight ratio ranks it behind aluminum.

STRENGTH/WEIGHT PARAMETER

The differences between the materials on the basis of strength-to-weight are not so great so as to lead to any immediate eliminations. Mild steel could possibly be eliminated in view of the superior steels just ahead of it. It should be realized that steels which rank high in strength/weight will lead to designs which have thin sections and are, therefore, more vulnerable to corrosion. However, ABS plastic, which is even lower, leads to useful sandwich constructions that meet certain specific requirements in an advantageous way.

COST/STRENGTH PARAMETER

The introduction of a cost parameter in material performance comparisons is essential, since the application of engineering materials invariably includes economy as a decision factor. In the several previous discussions on materials properties, some key items of cost data were noted. There is an element of uncertainty in the prices. The suppliers will quote only approximate levels when no firm order is contemplated. Additionally, it is well known that discounting of posted prices occurs in industry under the influence of supply and demand.

The cost/strength parameter is derived from the cost of a quantity of the material to resist a unit tensile load. The cost per pound is converted to cost per cubic inch for each material and to the cost of a volume which is of unit length and of sufficient cross section to fully utilize its UTS (unit tensile strength) to resist the unit load.

POSITION OF STEEL

The advantage to steel is immediately obvious. Most of the low-ranking (favorable) positions are occupied by steel. The higher-strength steels are in the most favorable positions showing that, in general, costs do not rise in proportion to the gain in strength. It is also apparent that no cost penalty must be paid for the improved corrosion resistance of COR-TEN. However, the fully stainless group of steels is not in this favorable position. Structural (muffler) grade of stainless is above the important alloys of aluminum and an austenitic stainless, type 302, despite its high strength, is near the top on cost/strength. This is obviously the price to be paid for the total combination of properties offered by this type of stainless steel.

POSITION OF ALLOYS

Aluminum alloys are in the mid-range positions. There is a sharp increase from steels to aluminums. Then the aluminum alloys increase from the stronger alloys upward, similar to the behavior noted for the steels. Thus, economy considerations would lead to selection of the higher-strength alloys.

POSITION OF FRP

Some interesting shifts appear in Fig. 5-2. The typical FRP compositions are high on the scale, ranking above 20 on the cost/strength parameter. FRP with mat reinforcing is highest, but it is free from a highly directional character to its strength. In a composite sandwich with Douglas Fir plywood, the new material has an excellent position in cost/strength. The beneficial shift is due to the favorable position of wood on the cost/strength scale. On the strength/weight scale, the result was

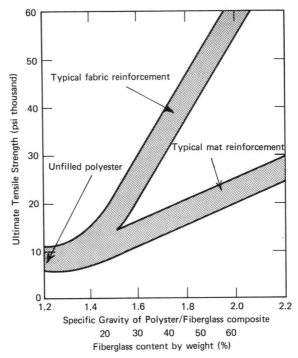

FIGURE 5-2. VARIATION OF AVERAGE STRENGTH OF FRP WITH FIBERGLASS CONTENT (SOURCE: U.S. GOVT. I).

the opposite where the position of FRP was degraded when it was in the composite sandwich. Had more variations in the composition of FRP been plotted, it is possible that the trend of steel and aluminum showing better cost/strength for higher-strength materials would have repeated.

POLYESTER SUITABILITY

The suitability of polyester as a vehicle for fiberglass reinforcement is indicated on a cost/strength basis. While only a few representative plastic products are shown, polyester has a 2:1 advantage over the nearest alternative plastic. Additionally, it offers the advantages of a thermoset over a thermoplastic in temperature resistance.

OVERALL RANKINGS

Despite all the previous remarks on the pitfalls which must be faced in comparing materials which have inherent dissimilarities, an attempt is made in this chapter to perform a ranking. The first step is an aid to assimilating the major results. A cross-plot of strength/weight against cost/strength should be made by the decision maker. This will enable a simultaneous comparison of many materials on the basis of these two very important performance parameters for materials of engineering.

RANKING ALUMINUM ALLOYS

The alloys of aluminum are in the most favorable position overall. Their region on the cross-plot is low and extends well to the right. The most frequently used alloys in structural applications, such as freight containers (5052-H38 for sheet and 6061-T6 for extrusions), are medium in their ranking with respect to the other alloys. Their elongation, in the range of 6 to 10 percent, enhances their use where high-intensity loads may lead to overstress. Their corrosion resistance rating is excellent in industrial atmospheres and good to very good in marine atmospheres. Their workability and formability limitations in the hardened states (hard states are implicit in their strength levels) do not prevent the evolution of reasonably satisfactory designs for stiffened panels. (The inefficiencies found in present aluminum panel designs are not believed to be an essential consequence of the properties of the alloys.)

Aluminum alloys are available with superior properties as compared to the two alloys most used in containers. Despite the higher unit cost of alloy 7075-T6, it is in the most favorable position of the aluminum region on the cross-plot. It, thus, offers opportunities for both weight and cost savings. Its relative corrosion resistance is lower than the two alloys identified above, but is, nevertheless, fair in marine atmospheres and still comparable to FRP. It appears more applicable to extrusions than to sheet stock in view of the lower corrosion resistance. An experimental alloy under development at Olin Aluminum, designated X5090, is expected to offer a 60 percent gain in strength, as compared to 5052, with a lesser increase in cost.

COMPARISON — FRP/ALUMINUM

By comparison with FRP as a face material for sandwich constructions, aluminum alloys are preferred by their position on the cross-plot. The aluminum alloy region is clearly lower than the FRP region. While the FRP region does extend well to the right, the apparent benefit is sacrificed to directionality in the properties of FRP.

COMPARISON — ALUMINUM/STEEL

By comparison with steels, the aluminum region is unfavorably higher. However, the clear advantage to aluminum alloys in corrosion resistance cancels the apparent cost benefit of steel.

FRP AND COMPOSITE SANDWICH

Fiberglass-reinforced plastics occupy an unfavorably high region on the cross-plot. However, they do extend well to their right and can thus lead to lightweight structures. As their strength/weight ratio improves, they also become more attractive on a cost/strength basis. The associated disadvantage is an increasing unidirectional characteristic of their strength properties. In the extreme case, which is the filament-wound type of FRP structure, their strength/weight ratio is about twice the value of the next nearest competitor among the metals. Whether or not filament-wound structures could be adapted to a workable container design is a question that awaits further development effort.

When FRP is combined with a core material to produce a composite sandwich, the resultant products occupy a region which is well down on the cross-plot. FRP/plywood benefits substantially from low cost/ strength position of Douglas Fir plywood. However, the composite sandwich is a material adapted to special applications. The plotted position contains a bias in that the plywood strength has been credited to the sandwich material in proportion to its volume in the composite. In a panel application, where bending governs the design, much of the core material is lightly stressed and the favorable plywood strength/weight ratio does not lead to efficient structural design. The additional problem of a proper match of moduli between face and core material in a composite sandwich has been identified and, since it limits the utilization of the FRP strength, there is a further disadvantage to FRP/plywood. When FRP is used as a face material with alternative core materials—for example, foamed urethane—the cross-plot indicates that a gain in strength/weight is accompanied by a loss in cost/strength, as compared to the case of the plywood core.

FAVORABLE SANDWICHES

On the positive side, FRP/plywood and similar sandwich constructions have favorable properties which do not appear on the cross-plot. It was noted above that the mass of material in the core leads to structural inefficiency in bending applications. All metal structures can be put into a form which will resist bending by judiciously locating the material into flange and web members, thereby producing lightweight products. However, in a container panel application, the mass of material in the core of a composite sandwich provides a useful insulating property. Service experience with FRP/plywood containers has shown that many commodities are carried which do not require the controlled temperature of a refrigerated unit, but which are harmed by extremes of temperature encountered during shipment. There is sufficient insulating effect in an FRP/plywood panel to smooth the extremes in the daily temperature excursions and to thereby safeguard those commodities.

COMPOSITION PARAMETERS

By comparison with aluminum alloys, FRP must be ranked lower overall. As a material for general use, it suffers from a high range of its cost/strength parameter. It can be a useful material when the directionality characteristics of the high strength/weight compositions are adapted to specific applications. In composite sandwich constructions with a plywood core (recall that the plotted point has two favorable elements of bias), there is a great gain in cost/strength, but there is also some loss in strength/weight. In corrosion resistance, the use of a polyester matrix leads to materials which are rated good-fair under long-term exposure in the marine environment, not quite the equal of aluminum alloy 5052. Corrosion resistance could be improved by the use of epoxy resins as the matrix, but then the resulting product would be more than twice as high on the cost/strength scale.

STEEL

The great advantage of steel is its low position on the cost/strength scale. This indicates that the least cost structure to meet a given strength requirement is most probably steel. However, it frequently turns out that corrosive conditions lead to high maintenance cost for surface protection and reduce the life of a steel product, clearly the case with steel containers. Thus, the potential advantage of steel becomes lost. Improvements in strength/weight—for example, martensite—while seeming to make steel a stronger candidate material to the transportation industries, appear to worsen the position of steel, at least for applications of sheet stock. Consider that higher-strength steels will lead to thinner sheet gauges that are vulnerable to the loss of a few mils of material.

Several steels which have received relatively low interest in the container industry appear, on the basis of the cross-plot, to warrant further investigation. In particular, COR-TEN clearly surpasses plain carbon steel (1020) on a comparison of strength/weight without any penalty on

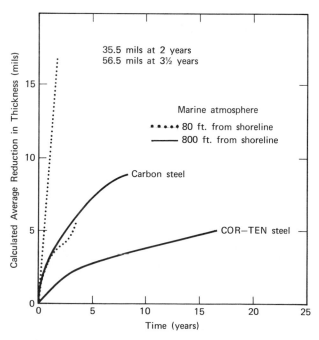

FIGURE 5-3. CORROSION RESISTANCE OF STEELS TO MARINE ATMOSPHERE (SOURCE: U.S. GOVT. I).

cost/strength. The improved corrosion resistance, thus, comes along as an extra benefit. See Fig. 5-3. The extent of this benefit is uncertain. Bridges have been built of COR-TEN, and the maintenance savings from no periodic painting have been substantial. U.S. Steel Corporation makes no claim for the corrosion resistance of COR-TEN in a marine environment. However, the tests of Inland Steel Corporation show a benefit in terms of lost material on unpainted surfaces exposed to the marine atmosphere which ranges generally between 3:1 and 8:1, depending on the test conditions.

CROSS-PLOT DATA

The data on the cross-plot contain an advantage for steel which is not obvious. The strength values which underly both strength/weight and cost/strength are not the maximum values attainable by fully hardening each of the steels (except the case of martensite), whereas strength values quoted for aluminum alloys are the maximum hardness values. Thus, the steels are readily workable and each could be put into nearly any desired corrugation geometry.

DOWNWARD TREND

The downward trend of cost/strength and the improved strength/weight for higher-strength materials that were observed for aluminum alloys recur in the case of steels. In short, the price differential for the higher-quality materials is less than the proportion of improvement in the properties of the material. An interesting case in point is the chromium-nickel-molybdenum alloy (4340) in the right-hand side of the steel region on the cross-plot.

DESIGN ACCOMMODATION

The findings presented up to this point lead to an enigma. On the one hand, the FRP/plywood-paneled containers are shown by the damage statistics to be the least prone to damage. The influence of damage carries through to maintenance costs and full life-cycle costs in subsequent chapters, and it may be seen that FRP/plywood containers benefit in the final comparisons from their superior damage resistance. On the other hand, the aluminum alloys used in container construction have properties which make it appear to be superior as a structural material. Similarly, steel has structural efficiency properties which are relatively better than its performance when it becomes a container material.

The obvious possibility exists that the designs which transform the materials into useful end products are not all equally efficient. It is necessary to examine some of the design characteristics of containers. This chapter will examine the main design features. There will be no attempt to obtain the precision of results usually associated with detailed stress analysis. Rather, it is intended to develop enough information to perform an overall assessment of the state of the art in design.

DESIGN CRITERIA

The manufacturing industry is under a number of influences as it prepares designs. No evidence was uncovered in research to show that a formalized and rational set of criteria are promulgated in the manner followed by project offices of the military departments. Nevertheless, these influences can be examined to determine their validity and completeness. The term "influences" is used to connote a situation in which some design criteria are firmly applied and others are loosely applied.

LEAST LIFE CYCLE

The steamship lines and other transportation companies must give some recognition to life-cycle costs because the domestic operators do not purchase the lowest-cost containers—all-steel units. However, it is also apparent that no full-scale attempt is made to ascertain what design criteria would lead to a least life-cycle cost. Cost analyses suggest the possibility that an additional expenditure in initial cost could reduce a container's susceptibility to damage and bring maintenance down to a point where the investment increment would be more than offset.

TARE WEIGHT

There is undue emphasis on tare weight, although the field survey shows it to be losing importance in decision making. A number of shipping operators in responding to questions on preferred attributes ranked tare weight behind ruggedness, maintainability, cost, and usable cube.

Nevertheless, two important containership operators are very weight conscious, and the others do not disregard weight altogether in their procurement actions. There are times when highway weight restrictions are the limiting factor on the load being hauled, and least tare weight is clearly advantageous.

Low tare is obviously desirable from the manufacturer's viewpoint. Containers have a material cost which is an unusually high proportion of final cost. Thus, the designer is under pressure to use material in the most efficient way. See Table 5-2 for a sampling of container tare weights taken from the equipment register and other published container characteristics.

USABLE INTERIOR CUBE

The revenue-producing capability of a container is directly proportional to the usable interior space that can be loaded with cargo. Where stiffened panels, whether corrugated or with attached posts, are used, they detract from cube. Very little design effort appears to have been put on maximization of cube other than the specification of FRP/plywood panels and the new aluminum plate design which are obviously superior to thin-gauge metal panels which are stiffened and strengthened by deepening the section. The range of values encountered in the field can be seen in Table 5-2.

TABLE 5-2. TARE WEIGHT AND USABLE CUBE FOR
STANDARD 20-FT. CONTAINERS

Tare Weight	Cube	Tare Weight	Cube
3,133	1,090	4,030	1,101
3,200	1,130	4,100	1,077
3,500	1,130	4,450	1,130
3,530	1,091	4,500	1,093
3,530	1,112	4,500	1,118
3,570	1,098	4,660	1,100
3,640	1,098	4,870	1,116
3,660	1,095	4,900	1,118
3,710	1,098	4,980	1,119
3,750	1,113	5,070	1,123
3,800	1,112	5,071	1,098
3,970	1,090	5,200	1,112

STRUCTURAL LOADS

In the course of pointing out the differences between trailers and containers, the several ways of engaging a container for transfer of restraint were noted. The ANSI-MH5 document places quantitative values on handling loads. These loads are taken literally by the manufacturing industry and are used in proportioning members.

The loads as specified in the standards are the result of committee deliberations. They are not loads that can be assigned any probability of occurrence. Furthermore, they are not a complete description of all loads which will act on a container during its service life. No dynamic loads are included in the standards except that static lifting (for example, nonaccelerated) is required with twice the normal load of the contents to approximate the effect of highly accelerated lifting.

The transportation companies are obviously aware of the shortcomings of the standardization documents. It appears that instead of attempting to define the handling and natural environments more comprehensively and precisely, they simply add design-type requirements. For example, the problem of misalignment of spreaders as a crane operator attempts to engage a container's top corner fittings is well known. Instead of requiring that a container be able to resist the load due to mishandling and specifying the magnitude of the load, the purchaser simply specifies that a protective plate be placed at the top four corners.

Side panels are another case in point. Various loads during handling and transportation cause damage to the panels. Instead of specifying that loads of a particular description and magnitude be resisted, the purchaser simply specifies that the panel material be of a particular composition of materials that he believes will stand up better in service.

End wall construction could be included as another example. It was determined during field survey work that a railroad requires reinforcing plates at the end wall in its containers. By specifying this feature, they are recognizing that the end wall load requirement due to railroad humping does not come up to loads that are actually experienced, and often enough to create a repair problem.

STRUCTURAL EFFICIENCY ASSESSMENT

This critique of the structural efficiency of some of the vital members of a shipping container will consider not only the design condition as actually established in the industry, but also the full range of criteria as discussed above. The approximate analytical techniques used are considered by the authors to be suitable for the purpose of the efficiency assessment.

SIDE PANELS

For the purposes of considering panel efficiency, it is assumed that the frame is relatively rigid and capable of providing a foundation for the panel. The possible loading conditions are:

1. Normal static load on panel, uniformly distributed, due to contents which fill container solidly bearing on panel under steady lateral acceleration;
2. Normal impulsively applied load, uniformly distributed, similar to above except that contents may have clearance with respect to walls and may impact panel with an initial velocity; or well-packed container may be subject to acceleration pulse;
3. Normal concentrated loads, similar to above either static or impulsive, due to nonuniform bearing of contents on wall;
4. Normal highly concentrated impulsive load applied by hard object, different from above in that this type of loading would not induce bending or membrane tension but rather tearing or crushing types of stress;
5. Distributed shear, due to joint action with longitudinal upper and lower rails to form built-up girder and resist box bending as container is lifted at its ends or in the center on the bottom;
6. Edge compression, due to transfer of load from end frame under stacking condition in which case the condition is localized at either end, or due to application of handling gear which grasps container near center and produces a crushing tendency on box.

The first item in the listing is contained in the standards at a value of 0.6 times the weight of the contents. This amounts to 24,000 pounds against a panel for a nominal container tare weight of 4,800 pounds. The uniform pressure is:

$$P/A = 24,000/146 \times 144 = 1.14 \,\text{psi.}$$

Nominal inside dimensions of 19 ft. 6 in. by 7 ft. 6 in. are used in the area computation. This being the sole design condition used in the industry, the emphasis in panel efficiency examination will be centered on pressure loading.

A "beam strip" or two-dimensional type of analysis is sufficiently accurate. The justification follows. The maximum stress (s) and deflection (y) of a plate are given by the following expressions (taken from Roark's widely used volume), for the case of all edges fixed and a uniform load over the entire surface:

$$s = \beta \, \frac{wb^2}{t^2} \quad \text{and} \quad y = \alpha \, \frac{wb^4}{Et^3},$$

where w = the pressure load in lbs./sq. in.;

  a = the length of the long edge;

  b = the length of the short edge;

  t = plate thickness;

  E = Young's modulus;

and α and β are from the table below.

a/b	1	1.2	1.6	2.0	∞
β	0.3078	0.3834	0.4680	0.4974	0.500
α	0.0138	0.0188	0.0251	0.0277	0.0284

The a/b ratio for a container panel is 2.5. The table shows that for this value the coefficients β and α are very close to their asymptotic values. Thus, the long dimension of the panel is insignificant and the load is, in effect, resisted by elements of the plate supported across the short dimension.

SIDE RAILS

The most conventional designs incorporate longitudinal rails. The section designs which were examined show basically flat geometry. Since the rails are the members which give a container much of its resistance to bending—as, for example, when lifted at the corners—they may be either in tension or compression. The top rail is more likely to be in compression than in tension, in which case it is a slender column, even though engaged by the side panels and roofs. A column design would normally attempt to locate the material of a section so as to produce a maximum value of the least radius of gyration of the section. Flat sections are poor in this regard. (Surveys indicated that buckled sections can be frequently observed.) There appears to be an opportunity to develop a section design which will maximize resistance to buckling. A closed section extrusion which would have suitable surfaces for attaching panels and other structure would appear to offer a gain in design efficiency.

Designs of sections for some rails contain a characteristic which must be rated as deficient. There are instances when protruding flanges are torn. This kind of damage is more serious than it appears on cursory inspection since the members are vital when lifting maximum gross weight. A design goal for rail cross sections might include beveling or even some degree of rounding.

There is an interrelation between resistance to denting, bending, and tearing, and resistance to buckling. A deformation in a slender column can lead to eccentric load paths which accelerate buckling. Thus, a section design which will best resist localized abuse can enhance buckling resistance of rails.

Whether welding would be a preferred means of joining panels, roofs, and cross members to rails is a moot question. There are reasons of manufacturing interest, which appear elsewhere in this book, why welding is avoided. From the structural point of view it is also not favored in the industry because of potential loss of strength in the heat-affected part of the member. During this investigation, it was noted that rail failures in some cases went through bolt holes and it is believed that the stress concentration at that location contributed to the failure. In short, the structural efficiency of welded joints may be sufficient to accommodate the detrimental effect of the heat on materials properties and result in a gain in efficiency as compared to joints producing stress concentration. Obviously, whichever joining means is preferred should be provided for in any attempt to develop a section with superior buckling resistance.

BOTTOM STRUCTURE

This area in the conventional design practices in the container industry appears to offer the greatest potential for weight saving. The attention of a critic is first drawn to the load paths when a cargo is subjected to inertial loading. The forces of the cargo bear on floor boards which distribute and transfer the loads to cross members. There is no direct load transfer to rails when flooring is aligned longitudinally. Cross members transmit loads to rails which, in turn, transmit loads to end frames. Thus, the load path due to hoisting or ship heave and pitch follows a tortuous path from its origin to its points of resistance. The possibility is attractive that all bottom structure could be put into an integrated structure which would stress the material up to efficient levels under nonredundant load paths.

The use of oak flooring is worthy of special note. It is efficient for its purpose. It enables the use of nailed-down chocking lumber. With the general absence of any means for cargo restraint, this is an important feature. It resists the wear of warehouse trucks and cargo movements. Nevertheless, flooring is typically in the range of 500–600 pounds. Without going into a major development as described in the previous paragraph, there may be an opportunity to develop another suitable wearing surface which would probably not be nailable and then to build in nailing sections at convenient locations.

CONCEPT IMPROVEMENT

Concentrating on panels, the potential of aluminum as a structural material appears to be unexploited to the maximum degree. Stiffening of panels by the sheet and post approach is not efficient. Consideration could be given to corrugation patterns which balance the material about the centroid and offer the opportunity to further optimize the balance of material between flange and web, as beam strips. If the required formability of the material leads to a lower-strength temper, this should not be regarded as unacceptable but rather as a trade-off with the gain in design efficiency.

Panel sections which have continuous outer skins and corrugated cores have been under development in the aluminum producing industry. Additionally, the role bonding process by which such panels can be produced in efficient cross sections may require additional development. This type of process is capable of producing high-strength joints, as demonstrated by its use in the aircraft industry, where a highly stressed helicopter hub was produced by diffusion bonding of several titanium sections.

The continuing effort to produce a minimum weight design without any sacrifice of strength, cube, general ruggedness, and the like, might be served by the maximum integration of all structural members. This is, of course, not a novel proposal. The matter of potential gains in the bottom structure has been noted. It has also been noted that heavier panels might enable lighter rails. The point being made here is that this approach does not appear to have been applied to the total container design.

NO END TO ANALYSIS

The deeper one goes into the evaluation of materials for the planned construction of new containers, the more difficult it becomes to make a systems engineering decision valid under all circumstances. The spectrum of application is so diverse and large that the computer analysis program will have to use so many variables that it may become worthless as a decision-making tool. This, of course, does not hold true if we feed the parameters of a restricted service range and constraint scenario into the program. So the systems engineers' principal duty here is to restrict the decision factors to those probably having technical or economical bearing on the selection procedure, and eliminate excess demands on the decision making. My reader is referred to a very complete study made by Control Systems Research, Inc. for the United States Army Mobility Equipment Research and Development Center at Fort Belvoir in 1970 entitled "A Critical Analysis of the State of the Art in Containerization." Much of the present material has been taken from this study. Another good analysis was prepared by the American Plywood Association showing the favorable factors involved in their material. But the author of that study, Jo Bonney, dealt with many facts summarily and not in as much depth as the Belvoir study.

FUTURE MATERIALS

The future in container construction is rather difficult to assess because the factors of corrosion, maintenance, and weight at various times are subjugated to economic factors. In Europe and Japan, most of the van containers are made of steel. In the USA, conventional highway van trailer construction principles were applied to freight containers as they were made by the same manufacturers and, therefore, the relationship of steel to other materials was a natural carry-over. When a company buying containers intends to use them in leasing service, economy tends to push down the other factors so that the lowest-priced container is often purchased. This is usually a steel container. For situations where a high capitalization is involved, a greater emphasis is placed on life-cycle costs, and here it is presently found that aluminum and plywood skins are placed on a steel frame.

Looking ahead, we may find that entirely new steels or new steel shapes will be used in the construction of containers. The major effort in steel now is being placed in the area of reduced corrosion damage. This effort involves the use of metalic coatings such as zinc, preprimed or prepainted steel, and chemical-type coatings.

CONSTRAINT SPECTRUM

Any intermodal container must be designed to carry and, while carrying to protect itself and its contents, when severe conditions could affect its survival. The wide range of requirements which establish the world constraint scene is impossible to limit to a few instances. Anyone could prove that I have overlooked some. In several parts of this book, while dealing with conveyances and transfer systems, I, therefore, have pointed out some of the container construction and maintenance features which may be involved in a specific decision-making procedure. Without any claim to completeness, some considerations are given here because of the general interest in arriving at a selection for container design and construction.

SOURCES OF CONTAINER DAMAGE

The causes of container damage will be identified at this point. The types of damage to the individual parts of the container originate from several sources. The sources of damage can be related to the transport modes, handling equipment, and natural environment which constitute the total container life.

SEA TRANSPORT MODE

Damage due to "racking" of the end frame on containers stacked on deck is reported. End-frame deformation causes the buckling of doors, breaking of hinges, and crumpling of the end wall panel. Aluminum end wall panels were observed with diagonal ripples formed across the entire face, requiring replacement. Container damage to the panels, doors, and other structural members due to cargo broken loose by ship pitch-and-roll motions has also been experienced.

External restraint systems used to lash containers on deck have failed, resulting in damage to the unit and sometimes its cargo. The reported frequency of occurrence has not been high, but the damage costs can be extremely high. A single loose container in a rough sea can cause havoc among the rest of the lashed units, even though they themselves have been properly secured. A study by twelve member carriers of the American Institute of Merchant Shipping reported that of 55 casualty incidents involving container cargo loss or damage:

1. In 47 of the incidents, the containers were stowed on deck.
2. Some 38 of the cases involved more than one container.
3. In 51 incidents, the method of restraint was by wire lashing.
4. In 26 cases, a contributing factor or secondary cause was the failure of securing devices.

One operator reported damage caused by the tie-down cable for securing deck-loaded units. Most of the damage was confined to the upper rails and rain gutters. It should be noted that no damage due to the vertical force loads incurred under stacking conditions in cells or on deck was reported by the ship operators. However, the result of stacking units on deck contributed to the racking damage mentioned above.

TRANSFER MODE

According to findings from the steamship lines, the ship-to-shore transfer of containers represents an operation where a high frequency of damage to the container occurs. This is due both to equipment operator error and the use of marginally suitable equipment for the transfer, such as a single fall boom with slings. Operator error may be caused by inexperience with new types of handling equipment. Port operators report that as experience with the new equipment increases, the occurrence of damage decreases. However, this has not eliminated all damage to the container, even in the most sophisticated of operations. Human carelessness and the pressures of handling to meet a sailing schedule lead to additional incidents of damage.

The most frequent damage to the container during transfer operations occurs when the spreader frame is dropped on the container roof, missing the corner fittings. This action causes roof punctures in the near vicinity of the corner castings. Not much of a force is necessary to accomplish a puncture of this type since the roof panel is one of the weakest of the container components. Since the crane operator does not necessarily have a clear view of all four corners, roof puncture damage is commonplace. Recurring experience of this kind has led to the placement of protective plates at the top corners adjacent to the fittings.

Some operators have reported that the use of slings in lifting has damaged the top rails. A great amount of damage to the external ribs or stiffeners during sling operations has been found. Over a period of repeated use of slings, rivets may loosen due to bending of the top rail.

CELL SLIDE

Some damage during the placement or lifting of containers into cells was reported. The most severe cases included the ripping off of side panels. Minor damage consisted of cell-guide abrasions to the end frame; however, this abrasion damage does not necessitate the removal of the units from operation for repair. It does not affect the structural strength. Original containers purchased with aluminum corner castings deform quite readily. The source of the damage apparently cannot be associated with any particular condition, but rather consists of a series of occurrences which gradually deform the fittings.

SINGLE FALL

Lifting a container by single fall can also lead to damage. When lifting this way and encountering an eccentric center of gravity, a shifting of the cargo can damage the side panels. The tilting of the container or sway due to wind can cause it to hit the ship's deckhouse bulkheads. In addition, the use of a single fall can lead to a dropped container—a force which the unit is not designed to withstand. In fact, no standard drop test for containers at even small heights exists at present.

RAIL TRANSPORT MODE

The severe deceleration forces experienced by containers on railcars in classification yards (rail humping) is the primary cause of damage for the rail transport mode. The transient motion on the railcar platform causes the loosely stowed cargo to shift against the end wall panel or doors resulting in damage ranging from minor to major in nature. Some amount of rail humping damage is often experienced when transporting units by rail.

DRAFT GEAR

One of the variables influencing the degree of damage suffered by containers on railcars is the effectiveness of the car's draft gear and suspension resilience. There is a distinct difference in the environment provided by recently manufactured cars with well-designed cushioning devices as compared to older cars without such devices. The problem experienced is the inability to assure shippers that the better railcars would be available for through shipment of their containers. Cushioned cars are available for movement of containers from the port city. Containers, however, are often being transferred to unsatisfactory cars for the final leg of the shipment to remote locations. The consequence is that an extra handling operation is introduced into the cargo shipment cycle and that the harsh environment of humping and railcar motions are difficult, if not impossible, to avoid. Thus, damage of all sorts continues to accumulate during rail transport.

TOFC VS. COFC

I have found that when both container-on-flatcar and trailer-on-flatcar (including a container coupled to its chassis) modes are used, damage is less in the latter case. Both modes suffer some damage from continued humping, but the suspension of the chassis cushions the loads as they are transmitted from the deck of the flatcar to the frame of the container.

GANTRY

The use of gantry cranes in rail transfer operations can cause damage, depending on the manner of lift employed. A top-lift device with spreader is responsible for roof puncture. In addition, if a bottom-lift attachment with grapplers is used, bottom rail damage is possible. One of the contributing factors for this damage is the lack of specified standard lift points on the various sizes of containers. Similarly, many units are not fitted with lifting hard points which would protect the rails.

ROAD TRANSPORT

I have found in the transportation field, and especially with steamship lines, that reports have been varied and uncertain on the subject of damage sustained when containers move over the road. The problem is due to the transfer of responsibility for the shipment to the highway common carrier when he moves the container/chassis unit out of the port terminal, with his own truck tractor. The highway carrier is responsible to deliver the container/chassis back to the terminal in the same condition in which it left, and all claims for cargo damage sustained after leaving the terminal go against him. Thus, records on repairs of highway damage are necessarily incomplete.

ROAD RANGE

The type of damage sustained on the road ranges from minor to catastrophic. In the first category, there are many light collisions with obstructions in which side panels tear, posts crumple, and rails are lightly bent. Major damage includes such accidents as "low-bridging" a container, which may put the frame into such a condition that it is not repairable. In less severe cases, the top rails may be torn and bent and the roof taken off completely. Rolling over of a container/chassis unit is another possibility. The frequency of occurrence of major damage is relatively rare, but the value of individual losses is high.

MARSHALLING

I have found that the marshalling yard is the place where damage to the container most frequently occurs. Handling operations are frequent as specific containers are moved to ships or on to inland destinations. Generally, maneuver space for handling equipment is limited. Fork lifts and straddle carriers constitute the major handling-equipment types used in yard operations. They transport the units from the yard to piers or rail sidings, lift them onto and off of chassis, and maneuver them around the yard, as required.

FORK LIFT

I have found a significant amount of fork-lift puncture damage to the container, especially to the bottom rail and side panels. This damage usually occurs when the fork-lift operator tries to pick up off the ground a container which does not have fork pockets. However, even units with fork pockets experience frequent damage because the operator often misses the pockets with the fork tines. Cross-member damage can also occur when lifting a container that does not have fork pockets. When larger units (35–40 feet) are lifted by a fork lift, a bow in the bottom rail can result which could prevent the unit from seating properly in a ship cell, on a chassis, or on railcar bolsters.

CLAMP CARRIERS

Straddle carriers were introduced into transfer operations to help reduce fork-lift damage. However, some ship operators report that they have not experienced any significant change. Carriers with top-lift devices still produce punctures when hard contact is made with the roof. When stopping quickly, straddle carriers allow the container frame to rock and possibly to bend. External panel stiffeners are often ripped off when an improperly aligned straddle carrier approaches a unit. Also, when a straddle carrier employs a bottom-lifting device (grappler), bottom-rail damage due to the squeezing action can result, as previously mentioned.

CHASSIS ENVIRONMENT

Damage usually associated with chassis operations in the yard occurs to the bottom rail, side panel, and side posts when one container on a chassis hits another which is parked. One reason for this is the lack of chassis standards (especially a height standard), which results in several sizes of chassis being used for one standard container. If, in addition, yard space is insufficient, the parking of the units next to one another can result in damage to both the container and the chassis.

NATURAL ENVIRONMENT

The natural environment includes elements which are damaging due to cumulative effects over a long period of time, or which strike abruptly, as in the case of a storm at sea. The question of whether large-amplitude ship motions are natural environment or induced environment is a moot point and does not warrant any lengthy discussion. One point is clear: the forces applied to containers on ships passing through storms can exceed standard design loads which do not cover the worst of ship motions.

TEMPERATURES

The hostile environmental conditions which deteriorate containers to the point where damage can be identified are the atmosphere with its moisture and salt content, sea water over the deck, and temperature extremes. The first two act as a catalyst for corrosion and can deteriorate metal parts to the point of failure.

COLD CLIMATE

Under extreme cold conditions, the freezing of water with its related expansive properties in forming ice, can spring the door hinges on containers. This is especially true of North Atlantic winter conditions where the sea spray hitting the deck-stowed units freezes on contact. Extreme cold has also been reported to make some of the sealants used in the construction of the container brittle, such that the sealant breaks away, rendering the unit subject to leaking.

TROPICAL HEAT

Under severe thermal excursions (especially due to the high temperatures of the tropics), containers constructed of dissimilar metals with different coefficients of expansion experience thermal stresses leading to loosening of rivets and joints. I have found that the loosening of mechanical joints is primarily due to stress cycling, but there is no reason to neglect the contribution of thermal cycling.

RAIN AND SALT

Rain and salt water both represent secondary sources of damage to the container. They both are involved as agents in the corrosion processes which result in container damage.

GREEN SEAS

Heavy seas, especially in the North Atlantic during winter months and the Pacific during typhoon season, are a source of severe if infrequent damage to deck-stowed containers. Indirectly, the energy of a heavy sea is translated into extreme ship pitch-and-roll motions, which result in racking damage to units on the bottom of the pile. Deck-stowed containers are also exposed to boarding seas. The tremendous power of a wave hitting the exposed units may result in severe, if not total, damage to one or more of them.

CARGO ITSELF

Container damage can be attributed to the cargo for two reasons:

1. Improper weight distribution;
2. Improper dunnaging.

The weight of the cargo should be distributed evenly throughout the unit. The center of gravity of the load should be within two feet of the center of the container in the fore-and-aft direction, and within one foot in the transverse direction. If the load is concentrated in a small area, the unit could deform upon lifting or even break in half, depending on the weight distribution.

Both minor and major damage to the container can result if the blocking and bracing of cargo is insufficient or improperly applied. The omnidirectional forces experienced during intramodal transport and handling are much more severe than those encountered in ordinary rail and highway transport. If the cargo has not been braced tightly, shifting of the cargo results, which can lead to the cargo's breaking loose. This loose cargo can then damage the container walls, and possibly even break through containers.

G FORCE

The fundamental cause for most of the exposure of the container structure and skin damage comes from motion. All transportation involves motion. Objects in uniform motion in a straight line are kinetically identical with objects at rest, but this offers no protection since all four modes conveying the container have numerous changes in rate and direction of the motion. The single, most powerful element is the rapid acceleration force. The damage occurs quite similarly to the impact of a hammer blow on the material. Kinetic forces are transferred as the container is dropped or as it is moved on the ship, on the road, by rail, or by the crane. There are, of course, other types of damage not involving energy, such as direct sea-water immersion, corrosion, atmospheric pressure, humidity, moisture, and wind. These factors have to be considered secondary, however, to the kinetic control of the g force.

The force of gravity provides a common measure of energy transfer. In a freely falling body at the Earth's surface, the magnitude of force is such that the body accelerates at the rate which can be taken to be 32.2 feet per second, per second, equivalent to 980 cm per second, per second. This force is purely acceleration and has no relationship to the weight. This acceleration of any object of any weight is expressed as one g.

Acceleration is controllable and produces the impact on the equipment expressed as the change of velocity in a unit of time. Velocity is a quotient; namely, space traveled divided by the unit of time:

$$a = \frac{V_t - V_o}{T_t - T_o} = \frac{dV}{dT},$$

$$a = \frac{V_t^2 - V_o^2}{2(S_t - S_o)}, \quad a = \frac{d^2S}{dT^2},$$

$$g = \frac{a}{32.2},$$

where

V_o = initial velocity, and V_t = final velocity in any change of speed in time, T;

T_o = initial time reading, and T_t = final time reading in any change of speed;

S_o and S_t = initial and final space coordinates;

a = acceleration, equal to 32.2 ft./sec.^{2};

g = a unit of acceleration;

dV, dS, and dT = changes in velocity, distance traveled, and lapse of time.

As a typical example, we may consider the drop of a steel drum 4 feet from the door of the container to the concrete floor. The drum will tend to dent a little, bounce a little, bend elastically a little, and most probably come to rest in 1/100 of a second. Under these conditions, a in the above formula has a value of 100 × 8, or 25 g's. The rate of damage could have been reduced by putting a rubber pad on the concrete. This would have reduced the energy transfer by increasing T to 1/50 of a second and lowering the g value from 25 to 12½.

Vibration produces a complex set of damaging forces. It is a law of natural frequency similar to the vibration of a tuning fork which continues the oscillation at a constant frequency unless external restraint prevents it from doing so.

Even a small vibration in transport can impart damaging energy to a container and eventually to the cargo. It automatically forces the build-up to damaging proportions when the natural frequency of the container is the same as that of the vibration. This requires a careful planning of countermeasures. These measures have been established by tests conducted by shipowners, railroad equipment manufacturers, and the clarification societies. The limit of the required g protection depends on the exposure plan for the container.

The entire stress spectrum deals with 16 conditions which can produce g forces in almost unpredictable directions. Ship motions provide for rolling, pitching, slamming, yaw, and heave. Road conditions produce continuous small vibrations, side rolling, acceleration, and deceleration. Rail conditions produce rail pounding, quarter rolling, acceleration, and deceleration, especially during humping. Transfer systems produce corner lifting stress, compression strains, and bending.

CLASSIFICATION REQUIREMENTS

All major ship classification societies have responded to a need of the container operation by establishing procedures for testing, inspection, and certification of containers, container repairs, and maintenance conditions. The published requirements generally cover containers over 10 ft. long. These requirements relate standards of strength, integrity, and quality of construction or repair to the certification. The eight organizations currently developing these standards are:

1. American Bureau of Shipping;
2. Lloyd's Register of Shipping;
3. Germanischer Lloyds;
4. Norske Veritas;
5. Bureau Veritas;
6. Nippon Kaiji Kyoka;
7. British Standards Institution;
8. Department of Shipping and Transport (Australia).

The requirements and the loading and test criteria of the various authorities are generally similar to the ISO Draft Recommendation 1496 with the exception of:

1. End wall loading, for which the tests vary from a uniform loading of $0.2 \times$ payload to $0.5 \times$ payload;
2. Racking loads, for which ISO carries no criteria and representative requirements are shown in Table 5-3.

Stacking-test loads are generally $9 \times$ gross weight, a static equivalent to a six-high stack plus an $0.8g$ acceleration force on top of the bottom (loaded) container in a ship's cell.

The considerations that result from the requirements must be incorporated into a design stress analysis for any new container program. Since the quantities of equipment involved require large outlays of funds, and since the life cycle of this equipment will be a major determining factor to the success of the enterprise, the systems engineer engaged in container system design must have an understanding of the problem. Heretofore, frequent arguments set forth by salesmen of truck body manufacturers have prevailed in equipment selection.

TABLE 5-3. COMPARISON OF RACKING-TEST REQUIREMENTS

| | Total Typical Racking-Test Load (one end) | | | |
| | 20-ft. Container | | 40-ft. Container | |
Authority	lbs.	kg.	lbs.	kg.
American Bureau of Shipping	22,404	(10,160)	33,605	(15,242)
Lloyd's Register of Shipping	25,813	(11,710)	39,250	(17,804)
Germanischer Lloyds	22,000	(10,000)	33,000	(14,970)
British Standards Inst.	28,000	(12,700)	42,000	(19,050)
Dept. of Shipping & Transport (Australia)	27,500	(12,475)	41,300	(18,720)

ADEQUACY TESTING

In addition to the inspection and certification of the equipment by the classification societies, the container soundness should be ascertained in a comprehensive testing procedure. During the last year, numerous facilities have been organized in the U.S. and in many other nations, where the structural investigations and the functional testing of the container as assembled can be accomplished. Such testing procedure normally includes an oscillographic system for use with strain gauges and transducers for pressure, acceleration, shock velocity, and displacement. Fatigue testing will determine the life endurance expectancy of the container and the structural components. Static testing of structural proof loads will confirm the design data. This is especially important for containers destined to be used on decks of ocean liners, where they will be exposed frequently to the impact of high sudden winds and sometimes to green seas. Adequacy testing, therefore, can simulate those conditions and predict the outcome in service. Also, environmental testing will indicate the true intermodal geography of the container, which may be exposed to tropical roof temperatures exceeding 120°F, as well as freeze conditions exceeding −10°F.

The testing procedure is designed to align the four constraints shown heretofore with the material selection. In particular, the economic weight limit of the container for intermodal transportation puts a premium on light weight, highly resistant containers. Were it not for this, it stands to reason that a container could be made out of the same plate size and thickness as the ship itself. And, of course, under these conditions, there could be no doubt as to its performance at sea. Creative application of new materials will become most desirable when a weight increase becomes the determining factor of the validity of containerization in face of increased demands on the system.

FLOOR DETAILS

The design of the container floor must meet the requirements expected of the most severe service conditions. The specification, therefore, must be determined by two questions; namely, what is going to be hauled; and how is this cargo to be loaded and unloaded into the container? Much of this will depend on the location of the cross members which stretch from sidewall to sidewall. Cross-member strength and dimension are important. The floor of a 40-ft. van should be capable of supporting an approximate load of 110,000 pounds, since 2,750 pounds per square foot of running length has been found to be the most satisfactory concentrated load impact. How much load the floor will carry without damage will depend on many factors. There are three basic types of floor: oakwood, aluminum, or a combination of the two. Aluminum reefer floors are primarily designed to allow air circulation through the floor, but they are not recommended for carrying pallets or other load units that may get jammed in the openings of the floor surface. Operators who haul barrels, kegs, or similar containers usually drop them on their side in loading, so that they can be easily rolled. This requires a wood floor. Concentrated loads, such as rolled newsprint, stacked steel sheets, steel castings, steel coils, and machinery on small bases, should have the load distributed so that the weight can be carried by the greatest number of cross members in the floor. For example, a 1-1/16-in. laminated hardwood floor with 4-in.-deep steel or aluminum cross members on 12-in. spacing will provide the 2,750-pound floor mentioned above, which should be satisfactory to withstand normal loads and even reasonable abuse.

The rear cross members and the rear area of any floor of a standard container should be constructed to support the impact loads of lift trucks entering from the dock. Table 5-4 shows the typical concentrated load per square foot and per linear foot encountered when a lift truck enters the container from an even dock height. If the same fork truck would drop down from a dock higher than the container floor, the impact could easily double.

DOOR DETAILS

Standard doors are located at the rear end of the container and form the fourth wall of the unit. As a functional bulkhead, doors are subjected to more impacts, strains, and stress forces than the front wall. While

TABLE 5-4.   LIFT TRUCK CONCENTRATED LOADS

Typical Floor	Cross Members & Spacing		Lift Truck Front Axle Cap.	Concentrated Loads	
				Per Sq. Ft.	Per Lin. Ft.
1-1/16″ Laminated	aluminum	12″	11,000	2,750	2,750
or T & G hardwood	steel	12″	12,300	2,750	2,750
1-1/8″ Composite	aluminum	12″	14,000	2,750	2,750
	steel	12″	14,900	2,750	2,750
1-1/16″ Aluminum	aluminum	12″	8,900	2,750	2,750
	steel	12″	11,000	2,750	2,750
1-5/16″ Laminated	aluminum	12″	14,000	2,750	2,750
or T & G hardwood	steel	12″	15,900	2,750	2,750
1-3/8″ Composite	aluminum	12″	15,500	2,750	2,750
	steel	12″	16,400	2,750	2,750
1-1/16″ fir	aluminum	12″	10,500	2,750	2,750
	steel	12″	11,700	2,750	2,750
1-1/8″ Composite-laminated yellow pine	steel	18″	13,000	2,750	2,750
1-1/8″ Composite-laminated hardwood	steel	18″	13,000	2,750	2,750
1-1/16″ Laminated or T & G hardwood	steel	18″	9,800	2,750	2,750
1-5/16″ Laminated or T & G hardwood	steel	18″	12,000	2,750	2,750
1-1/4″ Laminated	aluminum	18″	9,700	2,050	2,050
	steel	18″		3,050	3,050
1-1/4″ Composite	aluminum	18″	13,000	2,050	2,050
	steel	18″	14,000	3,050	3,050
1-1/4″ Aluminum	aluminum	18″	10,000	2,050	2,050
	steel	18″	12,000	3,050	3,050
1-5/16″ T & G pine	aluminum	18″	9,000	2,050	2,050
	steel	18″	11,000	3,050	3,050
1-5/16″ T & G hardwood	aluminum	18″	10,000	2,050	2,050
	steel	18″	12,000	3,050	3,050

the front can be designed to have an inherent diaphragm strength, the separation of the outer door frame from the door wings requires subjecting this entire assembly to the transfer of forces from one section to the other. The doors have to open; and when closed, the container end wall must endure the entire spectrum of service stress. Therefore, the doors under these conditions must contribute to the strength of the entire container. The example of a cardboard box with one end removed will point out the weakness inherent in the necessary multipanel door opening. The doors—just as panels to which separate items, such as fastening gear, hinges, and other components, often referred to as the "hardware," are fitted—consist of units combining to form a complete door assembly. Many components have to fulfill separate and important individual functions, but are all closely interrelated. The design of any one of the components, therefore, cannot easily be changed without having an effect on all other components.

The complete door assembly helps to withstand the racking forces to which the container might be subjected when the ship is rolling considerably. To provide maximum resistance, the doors should be located within the confines of the end frame, like a hatch coaming of a ship. Doors must satisfy a number of operational requirements. They should be capable of being opened, closed, fastened, and unfastened with ease under normal conditions by one man, and also under adverse conditions, particularly in cold weather when the seals may be frozen or the load has moved and exerts pressure on the inside. For unobstructed access in loading and unloading, doors should be capable of being opened through an arc of nearly 270 degrees, and fastened against the side of the container. Provisions should be made to prevent the doors from being damaged when open. The door assembly must be designed to resist pilferage. Customs authorities prescribed design of closures in the CCC rules. To prevent damage to other containers, no part of the door fittings should protrude further than the outside surface of the end frame.

The door panels are made of plywood, metal, or a combination sandwich called plymetal which is weatherproof and boilproof. It is faced on one side with sheet aluminum or with galvanized steel. Alternatively, for all-steel containers, it is faced with galvanized steel on both surfaces.

The plywood is usually composed of Douglas Fir, because of its great strength, and the normal thickness is 1 in., with sheets of metal of suitable gauge, usually 20-gauge aluminum and 24-gauge galvanized steel, to provide suitable stiffness combined with resilience of the whole door assembly. The adhesive used to bond the plies is of particular importance. It must continue to provide an unimpaired bond under the conditions mentioned earlier, so that it must withstand test temperatures up to 180°F and must remain unaffected by immersion in water for at least 16 hours. Another requirement is that the adhesive should be insect resistant. It should neither attract them nor be of food value to them. This is necessary if the container is to be used in Australia or New Zealand, when the plywood will have to be specially treated. The Department of

Health in both countries demands that the timber be impregnated against insect infestation.

The door hinge assembly consists of a hinge arm which is fixed by bolts to the door, a bracket which is fixed to the end frame of the container, and a pin. The pin passes through the open hole of the bracket, through the hole in the hinge arm, and then through the bottom hole of the bracket. This holds the door in place, yet allows it to be smoothly opened through an arc of nearly 270 degrees. To provide adequate strength and to insure alignment, four hinge assemblies are used for each door, each being mounted at intervals of approximately 22 inches and spaced equidistant about the horizontal center line of the door.

The hinge arm is of weldable forged steel, with a bushing of stainless steel or plastic to resist corrosion and to insure that the action operates freely and smoothly in all climates. The hinge pin is preferably also made of stainless steel. A special type of "lock open" hinge is produced, which eliminates the need to fit the conventional hook-and-eye fastening to the side of the container to hold the door open.

The hinges have to be made extremely rugged, due to the important part that the fastening gear plays in resisting racking movements. The hinges form the points of attachment of the door to the end-frame columns, and the top and bottom of the door are held to the end-frame cross members. Any movement between them will be transmitted to the hinges. To resist such relative movements, the hinges must be considerably more robust than if their sole duty was to bear the weight of the doors when open.

It might be thought that the door fastening gear of containers could be similar to that used in the larger types of van; but, in fact, the door fastening gear for containers should add substantially to the rigidity of the end frame and assist in resisting racking. The amount of skill required in design, the thoroughness in selecting the most suitable materials, and their utilization to fullest effect in evolving fastening gear specially suited to its purpose, can be impressive.

The fastening gear consists of a steel tube which is contained in tube guides fastened to the door, to the ends of which are welded cam assemblies. A tube is used instead of a solid rod for several reasons. For instance, when the container is rapidly accelerated and the load moves sharply backwards, causing the door to budge, the tube will bend, but only temporarily. Also, a tube can be rotated in the bent condition, so that the doors can be opened when there is a pressure from the inside of the container. Furthermore, a tube is lighter in weight than a solid rod of comparable strength, and has greater torsional rigidity. Plastic seals around the edges of doors accommodate tolerances and flexure without leaking.

PREDICTABLE DETERIORATION

Regardless of the adequacy testing made with the prototype container, and the service checks as described heretofore, during the life of the container a certain amount of deterioration must be predicted. To compensate for the elements which affect container life once it has gone into service, certain methods of treatment must be applied to steel containers and should also be taken into consideration for containers of other materials. The recommended practice for the treatment of the interior and exterior of steel containers is detailed next.

STEEL CONTAINER TREATMENT

Treatment of steel containers consists of sandblasting or steel brushing, and coating. The applications and the specifications for the coatings are described in Tables 5-5 to 5-9.

EXTERNAL FINISHES

The outer surface finish has two purposes: to provide resistance to weather and marine conditions, and to improve the appearance. Protective finishes have an effect on the service life of a container. The rigorous conditions to which a container may be subjected can reduce drastically the life of a container that is ill-protected. Unsuitable or insufficient protective measures initially, or impairment of such protection due to deterioration, produce damage by abrasion.

Metals, in particular, are susceptible to corrosion. All that is required is a protective coating extending all over the surface and along the edges of the material. Some metals and alloys, such as aluminum, aluminum alloys, and stainless steel, provide their own resistant coating, affected by the oxygen of the atmosphere, which combines with the metal on the surfaces to form a thin but very resistant, stable, and tenacious coating of oxide. The formation of the oxide is self-limiting, so that only an extremely thin film develops. The film remains transparent, so that the surface of the metal beneath is seen through it. Because of the presence

TABLE 5-5.   EXTERIOR TREATMENT OF CONTAINERS

Process	Paint & Treating Agent	Treatment
Pretreatment by deoiling and rust-cleaning	deoiler—aromatic neutral solvent of emulsion type, including boundary activator 15–18% (V) rust cleaner—phosphoric solvent, inclusive inhibitor, boundary activator, and rust preventive	deoiling and rust-cleaning done by spray coating at a normal temperature with use of the acid emulsion of deoiler and rust cleaner (spray pressure: 50 kg/cm²)
Cleaning of strong rust	rust cleaner of phosphoric paste, inclusive rust preventives and boundary activator	brush coating; leave untouched about five minutes (Wire brush is used in case chemicals cannot be used.)
Washing down	water	spray washing at a normal temperature
Rust-preventing film	phosphoric soda solvent, inclusive amino rust preventive 1–3% (V)	spray coating at a normal temperature
Anticorrosive coating—first application	epoxy, zinc-rich primer (three-liquid epoxy, zinc-dust primer); mixing ratio (by weight); primer—100%; (main component: hardener: zinc dust, 29: 11: 60); thinner—15–20%; spreading rate and film (one coating) 150–200 g/m², 20–25	airless-spray coating; drying at a normal temperature
Second application	epoxy, zinc-rich primer	same as first
Finishing—first application	chlorinated rubber paint (color specified); mixing ratio (by weight); chlorinated rubber—100%; thinner—15–20%; spreading rate and film (one coating) 170–200 g/m², 20–25	air-spray coating; infrared ray drying
Second application	chlorinated rubber paint	same as first

TABLE 5-6. INTERIOR COATING OF CONTAINER

Process	Paint & Treating Agent	Treatment
Pretreatment	In accordance with Process 1 of Table 5-5.	
Anticorrosive coating—first application	In accordance with Process 2 of Table 5-5.	drying at a normal temperature
Second application	In accordance with Process 3 of Table 5-5.	drying at a normal temperature

TABLE 5-7. FLOOR COATING OF CONTAINER

Process Steel	Paint & Treating Agent	Treatment
Pretreatment	In accordance with Process 1 of Table 5-6.	
Anticorrosive coating	epoxy resin, denaturated-tar enamel (two-liquid epoxy resin, coal-tar enamel); mixing ratio (by weight); enamel—100% (main component: hardener 93: 7); thinner—5%; spreading rate and film (one coating) 200–250 g/m2, 80	air-spray coating; drying at a normal temperature
Wood Finishing	quick-dry bituminous anticorrosive insulating paint (under seal) black; spreading rate and film (one coating) 0.8–1.0 kg/m2, more than 600	drying at a normal temperature

TABLE 5-8. DILUTION RATIO AND VISCOSITY

Paint	Mixing Ratio (Paint/Thinner)	Viscosity Photo (Cup No. 4)
Epoxy, zinc-rich primer	100/15–20%	12–15 seconds
Chlorinated rubber	100/15–20%	45–65 seconds
Epoxy resin, denaturated-tar enamel	100/5%	
Quick-dry bituminous anticorrosive insulating paint (under seal)		density 345 (JIS-K-2560 indicated value of penetrometer)

TABLE 5-9. DRYING TIME AND COATING INTERVAL

Paint		Application Temperature			
		41°	68°	86°	140°
Set to touch	epoxy, zinc-rich primer;	10 min.	5 min.	5 min.	
	chlorinated rubber;	1 hr.	0.5 hr.	0.5 hr.	
	epoxy resin, denaturated-tar enamel;	1 hr.	2 hr.	1 hr.	
	under seal	1 hr.	0.5 hr.	0.5 hr.	
Hardening	epoxy, zinc-rich primer;	1.5 hr.	1 hr.	1 hr.	20 min.
	chlorinated rubber;	5 hr.	3 hr.	3 hr.	1 hr.
	epoxy resin, denaturated-tar enamel;	72 hr.	24 hr.	15 hr.	—
	under seal	24 hr.	24 hr.	24 hr.	—
Finishing (time in which to be finished)	epoxy, zinc-rich primer;	48 hr.	24 hr.	24 hr.	1 hr.
	chlorinated rubber;	16 hr.	14 hr.	14 hr.	1 hr.
	epoxy resin, denaturated-tar enamel;	96 hr.	24 hr.	16 hr.	—
	under seal	—	—	—	—

of this highly resistant film of oxide on aluminum and stainless steel, the surfaces need little further attention.

Iron and steels are also affected by the oxygen of the atmosphere under humid conditions, so that a layer of hydrated oxide of iron, commonly known as rust, is formed on the surface. However, iron oxide takes longer to form and is not a stable coating; and in time, it flakes or rubs off, leaving a fresh metallic surface underneath to be affected similarly, until finally severe corrosion has taken place. Therefore, since ordinary steel does not produce its own protective layer, a resistant material of some kind must be applied to it—such as zinc (as in galvanizing), a phosphate coating, paint, or a combination of these.

The treatments applied to the types of containers are dealt with in Table 5-10. Stainless steel has an inherent surface condition obtained by the rolling or polishing of the steel and not by the application of a protective coating layer.

PASSIVE OXIDE FILM

The passive oxide film which forms on the surface of stainless steel in contact with air is extremely thin, transparent, and tenacious and is immediately self-repairing when damaged by abrasion. This film resists not

TABLE 5-10. COMPARISON OF COATING MATERIALS

Performance Factor	Alkyds	Chlorinated Rubber	Epoxies	Vinyls	Inorganic
Moisture and ion holdout	poor	good	good	very good	good moisture holdout
Resistance to corrosion products (caustic)	not resistant; film attacked	good	very good	peels; film not attacked	prevents corrosion
Adhesion to steel	good	good but critical	good but critical	good but critical	excellent but critical
Sensitivity to contamination (adhesion loss)	not sensitive	very sensitive	very sensitive	very sensitive	sensitive
Type of coating failure in corrosive atmosphere	film degraded to soap	peeling and blistering	blistering	peeling and blistering	none
Chemical resistance	poor	good	very good (selective)	very good	poor
Water resistance	fair	good	fair–good	excellent	excellent
Film thickness and continuity	moderately thick film	thin films per coat	thick films common	varies with product; 7–8 mils	medium
Physical properties	soft initial; harden on weathering	hard	tough and hard; some types brittle	excellent; tough	outstanding; hard, tough, and abrasion resistant
Weathering resistance	good; chalks	fair–good; chalks	durable but chalks; color change	very good	excellent
Solvent resistance	very poor	not good	varies, depending on epoxy; can be excellent	resist certain hydrocarbons, alcohols; not ketones or esters	excellent
Ease of application	applies easily	requires care	requires care	requires care	requires care
Temperature resistance	fair–good	good but limited	excellent	good but limited	outstanding

only corrosion and staining, but also penetration of dirt and grime, so that it is easily cleaned with a soap-and-water solution. By reason of its permanently "clean" and hygienic appearance, stainless steel is especially suitable for containers where long-term maintenance costs are of importance, and for foodstuffs. The fact that it is highly resistant to most chemicals may be an advantage under some circumstances. This is especially so in the case of containers for bulk liquids, where spillage of corrosive liquids and solvents may damage the protective paint coating on the framework and cladding of other container materials.

Most finishes are imparted to stainless steel in the rolling mill. The finishing rolls may have a highly polished surface, so that the sheet produced has a very smooth and bright surface with high reflectivity, which is retained by "bright" annealing in inert atmospheres. Other finishes may be produced by fine grinding with abrasives or scratch brushing, but these are generally for decorative purposes.

However, most stainless steel is produced with a matte appearance. It is frequently used, for example, for the cladding of container rear doors for safety reasons, as a highly reflective surface at the rear of a container might present a hazard when the container is being transported by road, especially at night. The finish is produced by a descaling process during the rolling operations.

TEXTURED FINISH

Increased stiffness and a textured finish can be given to stainless steel sheets by a "rigidizing" process, in which a pattern of embossed squares or other figures is pressed into the sheet.

Since the coating of oxide formed on the surface of aluminum is stable and tenacious, and covers all the surface, the sheets do not require an applied coating for protective purposes. However, the appearance of aluminum under severe conditions changes with the passage of time, the brightness disappearing and grey patches forming; but this does not indicate any deterioration of the metal or any lowering of its resistance to corrosive influences. So the decision has to be made as to the value of appearance of the container, and whether paint should be applied merely to provide a good appearance.

If a container spends practically all its time at sea and little time being hauled on a trailer along roads in view of the public, painting for the sake of appearance may be questionable. But if the container will spend a higher proportion of its time on the road, and it is desirable for the container to conform to the established livery of the owner, or for the sake of prestige or the possible value of the container as a mobile advertisement, it may be well justified. See Table 5-11 for application data on marine coatings and Table 5-12 for cost elements.

ALUMINUM PAINTING

Aluminum sheet can be painted by the container manufacturer; but is often, and possibly preferably, done by the producer of the metal, so

TABLE 5-11. COMMON MARINE COATINGS APPLICATION DATA

Item	Primers			Metal Coatings		Paints			
	Inorganic Zinc Steel Primer	Weldable Inorganic Zinc Steel Primer	Alkyd Inhibitive Primer	Inorganic Zinc-rich Coating	Aluminum Paint	Vinyl Copolymer Paint	Vinyl Acrylic Paint	Amine Epoxy Paint	Isophthalic Alkyd Paint
Recommended Dry Film Thickness per Coat (mil)	3/4	3/4	2	3	2	1 1/2	1 1/4	5	2
No. of Coats Required	1	1	1	1	2	2	2	1	2
Theoretical Coverage per Coat (ft.²/gal.)	565	750	915	332	250	235	240	185	665
Applicable Surfaces	Abrasive Blasted Steel	Abrasive Blasted Steel	Blasted Steel or Mechanically Cleaned Metal*	Abrasive Blasted Steel or Zinc Primer	Blasted Steel or Aluminum	Inorganic Zinc or Alkyd Primer	Inorganic Zinc or Alkyd Primer	Inorganic Zinc or Alkyd Primer	Alkyd Primer Only

* Alkyd inhibitive primers are incompatible with zinc primers and galvanizing.

TABLE 5-11. (Continued)

Item	Primers			Metal Coatings		Paints			
	Inorganic Zinc Steel Primer	Weldable Inorganic Zinc Steel Primer	Alkyd Inhibitive Primer	Inorganic Zinc-Rich Coating	Aluminum Paint	Vinyl Copolymer Paint	Vinyl Acrylic Paint	Amine Epoxy Paint	Isophthalic Alkyd Paint
Application Method	Airless or Conventional Spray	Conventional Spray	Airless or Conventional Spray, Brush	Conventional Spray	Airless or Conventional Spray, Brush, Roller	Conventional Spray, Brush, Roller	Conventional Spray or Brush	Airless or Conventional Spray	Conventional Spray, Brush, Roller
Drying Time	30 Min. To Topcoat 24 Hrs.	30 Min. To Topcoat 24 Hrs.	4 Hrs.	30 Min.	2 Hrs. Each Coat	1st Coat 2 Hrs., Top-coat 2–8 Hrs.	1st Coat 2 Hrs., Top-coat 4 Hrs.	8 Hrs.	Between Coats 8 Hrs. For Service 24–48 Hrs.
Topcoat	Inorganic Zinc Vinyls, Epoxys	Inorganic Zinc Vinyls, Epoxys	Isophthalic Alkyds, Epoxys	None or Recommended Topcoat	None Required	—	—	—	—
Weight per Coat per ft.²	.30 oz.	.38 oz.	.50 oz.	1.50 oz.	.40 oz.	.23 oz.	.16 oz.	.75 oz.	.20 oz.

Source: U.S. Govt. I.

TABLE 5-12.   COST ELEMENTS OF CONTAINER COATINGS

Item	Zinc-rich Primer/Epoxy Paint	Zinc-rich Inorganic Coating	Aluminum Paint	Alkyd Primer and Paint
Surface preparation, cents/sq.ft.	26.0	26.0	20.0	20.0
Material, cents/sq. ft.	12.8	5.6	5.2	6.8
Application, cents/sq. ft.	6.2	3.1	6.2	9.3
Miscellaneous	5.5	5.5	5.5	5.5
Coating total, cents/sq. ft.	50.5	40.2	36.9	41.6
Coating job cost, $ (885 sq. ft.)	446	356	325	378
Probably service life, years	7	5	3	3
Annualized coating cost, $	64	71	108	126

Source: U.S. Govt. I.

that the sheet is supplied already painted and ready for fabrication. Prior to painting, it is important that the surface is thoroughly cleaned and that either an etch primer is used as a first coat or that the surface has been pretreated chemically to insure adequate adhesion of the whole paint system. One of the most satisfactory paints from several points of view is considered to be one of the stoving type, one coat of which will produce a hard and durable finish equivalent to several coats of a non-stoved paint. Paints of the alkyd or acrylic types are often used. Paints of various types are considered in greater detail later.

When carried out by the suppliers of the aluminum, all processes relating to painting will be performed under the most suitable and controlled conditions, which are necessary for the most successful results.

The appearance of an unpainted aluminum container can be enhanced by efficient cleaning from time to time to remove dirt and all surface contamination. For this purpose, a proprietary cleaning solution can be used, which has an acid base. This solution is applied, left for a short time, and then washed off.

As mild steel does not provide its own protection against atmospheric corrosion, applied forms of protection are not optional, as in the case of other materials, but vitally necessary.

USING PRE-GALVANIZED SHEET STEEL

Some manufacturers of sheet-steel containers are now using pregalvanized sheet steel; that is, steel clad with zinc. The reason is, of course, that zinc simply oxidizes and, therefore, corrodes faster than steel and, thus, sacrifices itself more rapidly than steel. In the event of removal of some of the paint resulting from scratching or impact, the surface of the steel is protected by the "sacrificial" protection afforded by the surrounding layers of zinc. New methods of applying the zinc are being used, to insure complete and uniform coverage and near-perfect adhesion on the steel. A matte finish of zinc is usually considered more suitable than the traditional "spangle" finish, as the finer-grained surface insures better keying of the paint system. Paint is usually applied on the top of galvanized steel or on the bare metal. It is essential that the surface of the sheet mild steel be prepared suitably to receive the paint and insure its adhesion. There are several methods of doing this.

Shot-blasting is a cleaning process for removing oxide scale and is achieved by directing a stream of shot or grit under pressure at the surface to be cleaned. Phosphating is carried out usually by a proprietary process, the purpose of which is to convert the surface layers of metal into strongly adherent insoluble metal phosphates. They are not only rustproofing processes, but also provide a good key for the application of paint. Galvanized steel sheets cost slightly more than mild steel sheets, but the paint films last much longer, as there is no rusting at scratches and less maintenance.

ACQUISITION COSTS

Containers that are being produced today differ very little from those manufactured ten years ago. Minor design changes were introduced to prove durability based on sea experiences of the user. The development of the hardware, therefore, reached a temporary plateau in which it will remain unless automation places more emphasis on a different ship loading system. In this case, the container sizes may change more easily both in width and height. The present base plate or pallet, however, is very adequate in design to take care of handling systems changes, if and when they occur in the next generation of container equipment.

The most important movement now is to reduce the cost of the capital outlays required. One of the factors driving the manufacturers to search for new methods of cost reduction is the market fluctuation in available container units for lease. Leasing companies which have sprung up all over the world have searched more than the manufacturers for the lowest acquisition costs, as related to the maintenance and per diem obtainable as a lease. See Tables 5-13 to 5-15 for comparisons of maintenance costs. This has produced a movement away from the fancy, costly equipment to a solid second-generation container with a price cut of almost

TABLE 5-13. COMPARISON OF REPORTED AND CALCULATED
ANNUAL UNIT MAINTENANCE COSTS

Ship Line	T Reported	T Calculated	T Minimum	T Maximum
A	287,500	275,500	165,000	382,000
B	1,105,000	1,134,100	945,000	1,314,500
C	1,000,000	1,054,200	871,100	1,230,000
D	717,000	523,300	446,100	590,000
E	1,256,500	1,275,600	1,135,600	1,416,600
F	138,500	125,700	113,500	138,100

Source: U.S. Govt. I.

TABLE 5-14. ANNUAL UNIT MAINTENANCE COSTS
BY OPERATOR DATA

Type of Container	Annual Cost Per Unit	Range
Aluminum	$113.47/yr.	$102.34–$124.60/yr.
Steel	$301.65/yr.	$231.89–$371.41/yr.
FRP/Plywood	$ 69.39/yr.	$ 40.63–$ 94.35/yr.

Source: U.S. Govt. I.

TABLE 5-15. COMPARISON OF ANNUAL UNIT
MAINTENANCE COSTS

Source	Aluminum	Steel	FRP/Plywood
1. Operator Reports	$113	$302	$69
2. Damage Survey	138	287	78
3. Ratios—Line 1	1.6	4.4	1.0
4. Ratios—Line 2	1.8	3.7	1.0

Source: U.S. Govt. I.

50 percent compared to the prices charged four years ago. Highly sophisticated systems trying to protect the container against wear and tear
were found to be more costly than the preventive maintenance program,
which can be implemented through the use of independent contractors
after the end of each voyage. It is now standard procedure in the leasing
industry to use container maintenance yards as receiving and delivery
agents. These yards are able to recondition the container at the expense
of the last user and deliver it in good condition to the next user. In this
respect, a control of the conditions becomes very important.

COMPONENT COMBINATION

Ten components make up the freight container. All ten are required,
and three basic materials or their combinations are utilized in the components. The three basic materials are steel, aluminum, and wood. The
first three components are usually of only one material, while the next
six components can be quite different in materials, weights, costs, and

TABLE 5-16. MATERIALS USED FOR CONTAINER COMPONENTS

Component	Steel	Aluminum	Wood
Corner castings and connections	casting	—	—
Flooring	—	—	lumber
Door hardware	steel castings, forgings, or stampings	—	—
End frame	carbon or stain-less formed post	aluminum extrusions	—
Upper rail	carbon or stain-less formed rail	aluminum extrusions	—
Lower rail, sills, and fork pockets	carbon or stain-less formed or rolled sheet	aluminum extrusions or bent plate	—
Side and front panels	formed sheet	reinforced aluminum sheet	FRP/plywood
Roof panel	sheet (formed or reinforced)	reinforced aluminum sheet	FRP/plywood
Doors	formed sheet or combination of steel or aluminum on plywood		
Miscellaneous	all basic materials and many others		

performance. The tenth component consists of minor parts, such as welding rod, fasteners, door tiebacks, and coatings, and is not detailed here. Table 5-16 shows the components and the materials in popular use today to serve those particular functions.

Related to containerization, carbon steel's basic characteristics include high strength and stiffness, low cost/pound, and ease of assembly or repair. In thin sheet form, it is reasonably resistant to impact damage but extremely subject to corrosion. Both carbon and stainless are relatively heavy materials for strengths achieved. Stainless solves the corrosion problem, but only small quantities of stainless steel are used because of cost per pound.

ALUMINUM

Aluminum, in appropriate alloys, provides high strength and stiffness at low weights for framing needs. In sheet form, it is very easy to puncture, and in its basic forms of extrusions or sheet it is about four times the cost per pound of steel. It, however, does not have the corrosion problems of carbon steel, and is lower in cost than most stainless steels.

WOOD

Wood, in itself, does not have the strength per shape to serve as container framing. Its strength per pound and its shock- and impact-absorbing qualities make it a very suitable flooring. In plywood form, it is commonly used as an inside liner for aluminum skin containers, and covered with fiberglass reinforced plastic, makes an excellent impact-resistant sidewall at competitive costs on a square-foot or pound basis. Metal-covered plywood is a popular door material, utilizing the metal skin to achieve higher stiffness and environmental protection, while the plywood core soaks up impact. Untreated wood is subject to rot, swelling, infestation, etc. in most marine and humid exposures.

It is interesting to note that hardwoods are commonly used for flooring, following the example from the trailer industry. Hardwoods have superior abrasion-resistance characteristics which are important when the unit is loaded and unloaded four to five times a day. Containers with a weekly load/unload cycle can often use a softwood which, while providing equal strength, can be lighter in weight and lower in cost.

TODAY'S DRY-CARGO CONTAINERS

Almost all of today's dry-cargo containers fall into three general types. One is a basic steel unit with steel sidewalls, roof, framing, and fork pockets and with lumber flooring.

A second basic type is a steel-and-aluminum frame with aluminum skin sidewalls reinforced with steel and plywood lined, aluminum skin roof with steel or aluminum roof bows, steel fork pockets, and lumber floors.

The third general type utilizes metal framing, metal fork pockets, and FRP/plywood walls and roof, with lumber deck.

Six variations of these three types with components by weight are listed in Table 5-17. All six of these units are designed and built as ISO-style 20-ft. units built to meet ABS and Lloyd's requirements, and include four fork pockets. They all utilize steel corner castings, lumber floor, and plymetal doors, but vary in framing metals and in sidewall and roof construction.

TABLE 5-17. COMPONENT WEIGHT IN POUNDS OF SIX
DIFFERENT TYPES OF 20-FT. CONTAINERS

Component	Basic Steel Unit	Aluminum Frame, Al. Skin Unit	Steel Frame, Aluminum Skin Unit	Steel Frame, FRP Unit	Aluminum Frame, FRP Unit	Steel & Al. Frame, FRP Unit
	(A)	(B)	(C)	(D)	(E)	(F)
Corner castings (steel)	180	180	180	180	180	180
Connections	—	60	60	—	60	60
Door hardware (steel)	110	110	110	110	110	110
Flooring	575	575	575	575	575	575
End frames	700	360	700	720	360	720
Upper rail	125	75	75	125	75	75
Lower rail, sills & fork pockets	940	650	800	1,000	650	800
Side & front panels	1,250	700	900	795	795	795
Roof panel	700	200	300	350	350	350
Doors (plymetal)	320	275	275	320	275	300
Misc.	100	200	200	200	200	200
TOTAL	5,000	3,385	4,175	4,375	3,630	4,165

Source: Weyerhauser Co.

TARE WEIGHTS

Tare weights of these six units vary from a low of 3,385 lbs. to a high of 5,000 lbs. Some container operators, in their evaluation procedures to select containers, consider that every pound of weight above the minimum required will cost them almost one dollar per pound in additional operating costs over the life of the unit.

Two variations of the aluminum-skin unit are shown with the lighter unit utilizing aluminum framing. Three variations of FRP-sidewall units are included with variations in metal framing between steel and aluminum.

When the basic materials in each component group are separated out and regrouped by basic material, the results are shown in Table 5-18.

Two of the three basic materials are usually priced on a per pound basis, while the third material is normally priced on a volume or cube basis. To facilitate the comparison processes, the wood products' prices have been translated from their volume basis to a price per pound. Table 5-19 shows representative prices for the basic materials.

OTHER DECISION KEYS

We have defined the factors influencing the size, shape, strength, configuration, and building materials that comprise today's container. A

TABLE 5-18. POUNDS OF BASIC MATERIALS IN SIX
DIFFERENT TYPES OF 20-FT. CONTAINERS

Basic Material	Basic Steel Unit	Aluminum Frame, Al. Skin Unit	Steel Frame, Aluminum Skin Unit	Steel Frame, FRP Unit	Aluminum Frame, FRP Unit	Steel & Al. Frame, FRP Unit
	(A)	(B)	(C)	(D)	(E)	(F)
Steel (basic)	3,715	—	1,870	1,845	—	1,245
Steel hardware	290	350	350	290	350	350
Aluminum (basic)	—	1,835	755	—	1,085	350
Wood flooring	575	575	575	575	575	575
Plywood	—	150	150	—	—	—
FRP/plywood	—	—	—	1,145	1,145	1,145
Doors	320	275	275	320	275	300
Misc.	100	200	200	200	200	200
TOTAL	5,000	3,385	4,175	4,375	3,630	4,165

Source: Weyerhauser Co.

TABLE 5-19. COST PER POUND OF BASIC MATERIALS

Item	Price/lb.
Carbon steel standard shapes	10¢
Stainless steel standard shapes (depends on grade)	40¢–65¢
Steel hardware	50¢
Aluminum extrusions or coiled sheets	40¢
Plymetal doors (depends on facing)	30¢–40¢
Wood flooring	20¢
Plywood (depends on grade)	5¢–11¢
FRP/plywood	40¢

breakdown describing the quantities and types of containers in operation throughout the world will show frequent changes.

Figure 5-4 illustrates damage rates as a function of container operating systems. The newer ships with wide flared bows and forward pilot houses, reduce the incidence of green-water damage. New cranes with anti-sway mechanisms and automatic deceleration controls are not only faster, but also reduce damage from impact and accident. Some proposed ship cell systems even eliminate the necessity for six-high stacking strength. Keeping abreast of these decision points and forecasting tomorrow's is the job of a full-time systems specialist.

Next, we will show how the consequences are usually rewarding for both the shipper and the carrier, when a properly designed container system is put to work in the environment for which it is planned. The trend is toward more and larger container fleets, as carriers, ports, and handling facilities throughout the world gear to this more profitable means of moving goods.

BURDEN OF SERVICE

There is progressive validation of the critical importance of maintenance from operator reports and by data from all other sources. With the high frequency of damage occurrence in service, the problem of container availability arises which bears directly on the operator's ability to provide revenue-producing equipment to shippers. Additionally, the cost of maintenance directly affects the operator's economics to a significant degree. Accordingly, this chapter covers the essential details of the container maintenance burden in sufficient detail to justify cost estimates.

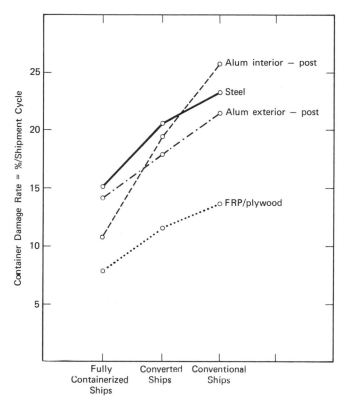

FIGURE 5-4. DAMAGE RATES AS A FUNCTION OF CONTAINER SYSTEMS (SOURCE: U.S. GOVT. I).

MAINTAINABILITY FUNDAMENTALS

The U.S. military has formalized the terminology, the techniques for quantification of the maintenance burden, and the practices of assurance. "Military Standard Definitions of Effectiveness" (MIL-STD-721B) is the basis for some of the usages.

The fact that the containers and their associated systems are operated by commercial enterprises is no detriment to the carryover of the military approaches to maintainability.

MAINTAINABILITY AND MAINTENANCE

The characteristics of design and installation which affect the performance of maintenance, specifically the time required, are related to maintainability. By definition, *maintainability* is the probability that an item will be retained in or restored to a specified condition within a given period of time when maintenance is performed in accordance with prescribed procedures and resources. Thus, it may be seen that maintainability attempts to measure the inherent quality of design and assumes, for the purpose, that the maintenance environment is standardized. The concept is most useful in evaluating alternatives during a development-and-design phase for a new system or equipment item.

One of the more important characteristics of maintainability is accessibility—a measure of the relative ease of admission to the various areas of an item where work is to be performed. An example where the several different container types can be distinguished on the basis of accessibility is the case of plywood liners used with aluminum panels. Reports by operators and independent maintenance facilities indicate that the necessity to remove these liners increases the job cost and complexity in many instances of repairs to panels. All containers encounter an accessibility problem when the cargo is present. The Truck/Trailer Manufacturers Association (TTMA) Maintenance Manual recommends removal of all cargo before maintenance is performed. Obviously, the operator will avoid this if at all possible, since the cost is substantial, even exceeding many repair jobs.

Maintenance is the aggregate of all actions necessary for retaining an item in or restoring it to a *specified condition*. This includes both corrective and preventive maintenance. The former is the result of a *failure* and the item must be restored. The latter attempts to avoid failure by a sequence of inspection, detection, and prevention of incipient failure. Note that two terms have been introduced which have specialized usage in maintenance work: specified condition and failure. The essentials of specified conditions are obviously those covered by the standardizing specifications, such as watertightness, load-resisting capability, and dimensional correctness. Each operator may amplify these conditions to meet his own needs. Failures will be discussed in more detail under the next heading.

Maintenance engineering analysis must be included in container systems projects. The analysis task identifies specific maintenance actions that will be performed at each level of activity. A determination must be made of the necessary tools, test equipment, facilities, personnel, and technical data. Support needs must be planned. Personnel requirements are expanded to include skills and numbers of men.

RELIABILITY AND FAILURES

By definition, *reliability* is the probability that an item will perform its intended function for a specified interval under stated conditions. If an item is unable to perform within specified limits it is, by definition, in a failed state. Thus, the notions of reliability and failure are intimately related.

While the container industry tends to use other terminology, two concepts do apply. There is clearly some probability that a container will perform its intended function for a specified interval under stated conditions. The conditions of service are not precisely defined, but this situation is also encountered in military systems applications.

Of the several terms which may be used as analogous to reliability, *ruggedness* probably fits best. It implies both strength and durability. In the industry, there are no difficulties of understanding with this term. For example, this term is used by the steamship operators when describing the qualities they seek in their container procurements. It should be noted that ruggedness ranked ahead of low tare weight, usable cubic space, and other attributes.

The matter of reliability, in the general sense of ruggedness, bears on the total maintenance burden. It governs the frequency of occurrence of failures. The frequency of occurrence of failures, in turn, governs the amount of maintenance to be performed. Thus, during the evolution of an item's characteristics and ultimately during its design, it often is a trade-off of reliability and maintainability.

If maintainability is good and reliability gains lead to high cost, the optimum design may be reached by sacrificing some built-in reliability in exchange for planned obsolescence.

AVAILABILITY

The combined effect of maintainability and reliability is described by the concept of availability. By definition, *availability* is the measure of the degree to which an item is in an operable and committable state at the start of a mission, when the mission is called at an unknown (random) point in time. It is a direct and logical step from the definition to an expression of the measure of availability in the form of a ratio of the percentage of time available (in an *up* state) to total time. The way in which reliability and maintainability enter can be seen in the expression below:

$$\text{Availability} = \frac{\text{Up Time}}{\text{Total Time}} = \frac{\text{MTBF}}{\text{MTBF} + \text{MTTR}},$$

where MTBF = Mean time between failures,

MTTR = Mean time to restore.

Note that MTBF and MTTR taken together must equal the total time. Thus, the various elements of delay during which no actual maintenance is being performed are included in MTTR. Maintenance operations certainly share in common, at one time or another, several delay components shown. Transport delay time might include the movement of a container to a maintenance contractor's facility. A further delay from the time of arrival until work is scheduled and actually starts might be chargeable to administrative time. Supply delay time covers periods during which work cannot be performed for lack of materials. Note that uptime includes periods when an equipment item is actively in use for mission-oriented purposes and when it is on standby. There is an additional category designated inactive time, when the item is not in service at all and the elapsed time is not chargeable at all against any standby or delay periods.

QUANTIFICATION INDICES

Several unique parameters are useful to quantify the burden due to maintenance. The first is MTTR, which has been introduced above. It is a measure of time during which the system or equipment item is unavailable for service. If MTTR is being analyzed to examine work distribution, the corrective maintenance time might exclude delays. This parameter specifically does not indicate the amount of maintenance work done. It is determined by the expression:

$$\text{MTTR} = \frac{\text{Total Corrective Maintenance Time}}{\text{Number of Maintenance Actions}}.$$

The amount of maintenance effort is given by the Maintenance Support Index (MSI), which relates the maintenance hours to the operating time:

$$\text{MSI} = \frac{\text{Total Maintenance Man-hours}}{\text{Total Operating Time}}.$$

TABLE 5-20. DAMAGE BREAKDOWN BY
AFFECTED CONTAINER PARTS

Repair Cost Code	Aluminum Exterior Container Part	FRP/Plywood Container Part	Steel Container Part	Aluminum Interior Container Part
1	Bottom Rails	Panels	Roof	Roof
	Stiffener/Sheet	Roof	Bottom Rails	Frame
	Roof	Bottom Rails	Panels	Panels
	Floor/Cross Mem.			
2	Frame	Panels	Bottom Rails	Floor/Cross Mem.
	Floor/Cross Mem.	Floor/Cross Mem.	Floor/Cross Mem.	Frame
	Stiffener/Sheet	Main Frame	Panels	Panels
	Roof			
3	Stiffener/Sheet	Panels	Bottom Rails	Frame
	Frame	Doors	Panels	Roof
	Floor/Cross Mem.	Floor/Cross Mem.	Floor/Cross Mem.	Doors

Source: U.S. Govt. I.

MAINTENANCE PROCEDURES

A survey of maintenance procedures is reported here. This is part of the background essential to an understanding of what goes into an operator's maintenance budget. Obviously, the damage situation must be noted while considering the repair work. Table 5-21 indicates damage breakdown by parts. In accordance with the established concepts, maintenance in both categories, preventive and corrective, is included. Costs for damage repair are shown in Tables 5-21 and 5-22.

TABLE 5-21. TYPICAL BID BREAKDOWN FOR
MAJOR CONTAINER DAMAGE

Cost Element	Parts	Man-Hours	Labor Cost
Replace doors	$345	17	$ 68
Replace two plywood liner sections	15	1	4
Replace five posts—one side	50	10	40
Replace three panel sections	63	9	36
Replace door sill	24	7	28
Wash and paint	15	5	20
Transport to facility	—	—	20
Totals	512	49	216
		TOTALS FOR PARTS AND LABOR	$728

Source: U.S. Govt. I.

TABLE 5-22.   MAINTENANCE COSTS FOR DAMAGE REPAIR
(PER CARGO SHIPMENT CYCLE)

Handling Environment	Aluminum (External Posts)	Aluminum (Internal Posts)	Steel	FRP/ Plywood
Average for All Systems	$11.61	$11.34	$13.40	$5.91
Fully Containerized Systems	9.11	6.08	8.95	4.59
Converted Ships—Deck Gantry Cranes	11.26	11.67	14.35	6.52
Partially Converted Ships— Conventional Deck Gear	14.49	16.21	16.90	6.58

Source: U.S. Govt. I.

INSPECTIONS

The transportation companies, steamship lines in particular, make maximum use of their opportunities to perform inspections. The port terminals of the lines invariably include an adequate, covered facility for performing the inspection. Empty containers are passed through the inspection facility and cleaned prior to their dispatch to a commodity shipper. Upon the return of a loaded container to the port terminal prior to transfer aboard ship, another inspection is performed. Loaded containers coming off an inbound ship are inspected prior to their dispatch to the consignee. Containers which move primarily from the port terminal to another port, and which are stowed at the port with less than full lot goods, are subjected to similar inspections, although the total number will be less in this type of operation.

Weathertightness: One objective in these frequent inspections is to assure watertightness. The exteriors are examined for evidence of tears or any penetration of the panels which would admit water. If the container is empty, a search is made for entering light rays in the closed and darkened interior. Water spray may be applied and then a check made for leakage from the outside to the inside. Some operators use smoke bombs which are set off in the closed interior and then provide visual evidence of a leak path by the passage of smoke to the outside. Doors are checked for distortion and proper locking. Obviously, many of these inspections are applicable only to empty containers.

Structural soundness: The inspection opportunities are further used to determine that no serious structural damage exists on the container and that it will continue its transit safely. Framing is checked for cracks and dents. Old repairs are examined to determine their present serviceability. Corner castings are examined for evidence of cracks and general soundness.

PREVENTIVE MAINTENANCE

In the industry as a whole, preventive maintenance, other than the essential checks, is neglected. For example, the only opportunity one line had to do anything about preventive maintenance was during a strike of longshoremen when no cargo was moving. This situation arises due to the inadequate maintenance float in most of the container fleets. Much of the preventive maintenance that does get performed is close to the border with corrective maintenance. Nevertheless, a number of items of work do fall in the category of preventive maintenance and are sometimes performed.

REPAIR ANALYSIS

Patching of aluminum panels: A cutout around the damaged material is made of rectangular or square shape, using electric or manual shears. The edges are smoothed by filing. Ready-made aluminum patches are available from material suppliers with predrilled holes and rubber adhesive sealing. Alternatively, a patch may be cut from the same sheet stock as the original, normally alloy 5052–H38. In either case, the patch overlaps the cutout by about two inches. The holes in the patch are used as a template to drill holes in the parent material of the panel. Spacing of the rivet holes is determined by the need to compress the sealant in order to obtain a watertight joint. For patches prepared on site, the sealant might be a nondrying, latex-base caulking or a self-adhering rubber tape. *Pop rivets* are used to avoid bucking from the inside, especially if a field patch is being applied to a loaded container.

The problem of applying patches expeditiously is often complicated by the presence of a plywood liner as commonly used with aluminum panels. Most liners extend only up half the height of the side wall, so that patching at locations above halfway avoid the liner. The general rule is that the liner section must be removed and replaced when the patch job is performed.

This has a noticeable effect in increasing maintenance costs for aluminum-paneled containers.

TABLE 5-23. TYPICAL COSTS ON REPAIR JOBS

Job Description	Aluminum		Steel		FRP/Plywood	
	Material	Labor	Material	Labor	Material	Labor
Replace Post	$ 15	$ 21	—	—	—	—
Replace Panel Section						
Plain Sheet	20	45	$ 10	$ 80	—	—
With rivet holes						
predrilled	25	30	—	—	—	—
Replace Side	—	—	—	—	$180	$200
Replace Rail						
Lower	55	90	25	130	55	90
Upper	55	60	25	150	55	60
Splice Rail						
4-ft. section	12	50	—	—	12	50
10-ft. section	30	80	—	—	30	80
Replace Crossmembers	20	25	10	25	20	25
Replace Floor	200	210	200	210	200	210
Replace Roof	100	200	50	275	180	200
Replace Corner Post	90	100	90	100	90	100
Replace Castings	30	45	30	45	30	45
Replace Door Sill	20	50	20	70	20	50
Replace Door	180	120	180	120	180	120
Patch Small Holes	1	7	1	15	1	7

Source: U.S. Govt. I.

Replacing sections of aluminum panels: When damage is extensive, say extending over more than 8–10 inches in any direction, the entire panel section is replaced. The old section is removed by drilling or knocking out the old rivets. The replacement section, of the same alloy as the original, is fitted with the overlapping exposed edge toward the rear. Drilling of the replacement section is performed in place, but over-size rivets (as compared to the original) are used to allow for reaming out the old holes.

Typical rivet sizes are 3/16 inch for the vertical joint, which includes the attachment of the side posts, and $\frac{1}{4}$ inch for the horizontal joints between the panel and the rails. All joints are sealed with material as described at the patching job.

Repairs to steel panels: Minor puncture damage in steel panels can be, and frequently is, repaired by riveting a sealed patch over the cleaned-up cutout in a way similar to what was described for aluminum jobs. In many cases, especially where extensive straightening is required along with patching, an entire section of panel from top to bottom is cut out. One of the difficulties in performing these repairs is the necessity of stocking replacement panel sections to match the rigidizing corrugation pattern of the original panel. The cutout is carefully performed to enable the patterns to be matched up when the replacement material is welded into position. After welding is completed, the area of damage is prepared for and refinished with a protective coating.

Patching of FRP/plywood panels: Large damaged areas can be repaired by the patch method. An area 50 inches by 33 inches has been patched and then successfully tested for minimum ANSI–ISO requirements. This is near the limiting size. Larger damaged areas require panel replacement.

Damage to FRP/plywood panels is repaired by cutting away an area, usually rectangular in shape, and sufficiently large to reach sound wood. A powered hand saber saw is used. The edges of this cut are beveled at a 45-degree angle with the smaller surface area outward. If the damaged area is small, say less than six inches across, the edges may be normal to the container walls.

A patch of the same thickness FRP/plywood is then cut to fit. A bead of polyester resin is applied to the edges of the hole and the resin is allowed to dry and set. The original gel coat is then sanded off down to the reinforcing glass to a width of 2–4 inches each side of the joint between patch and existing wall. This is done on both the interior and exterior sides. A coat of polyester resin is brushed onto the sanded area and a 4-inch width of woven roving in tape form is rolled on to cover the joint. Then polyester resin is brushed on, thoroughly saturating the woven roving tape. When it has dried and set, another coat of polyester resin is applied and allowed to dry.

If the damage is extensive, an entire vertical section of the side wall from upper to lower side rail may have to be replaced. The width depends on the size of the area damaged. Vertical cuts are made with the edges of the cut beveled at a 45-degree angle as in the case of a large patch. The damaged section is then unbolted from the side rails. Caulking compound is laid on all surfaces where metal and wood will be joined. A replacement section is cut to fit, bolted to the rails, and the joints between the repair section and existing wall treated in the same manner as a patch repair.

FRP/plywood panels may suffer damage of a type which results in delamination but no surface rupture. Successful repairs can be completed by drilling small holes through the panel material and forcing catalyzed resin through the holes into the delaminated areas. Pressure is then applied and the resin cured.

The surface of a panel may develop small cracks through service usage. These are repaired by removing the damaged area of the overlay down to a feathered edge. Then the catalyzed resin with impregnated chopped strands of fiberglass is applied. The composition usually includes sufficient filler to prevent the wet resin from running down a vertical surface.

Repairs to side rails: If the damaged section extends over a substantial length of the rail, say about one-third or more, it is replaced. This is a major job which involves dismantling the entire side of the container. The rail must be disconnected from the panels and end frames and, if an upper rail, from the roof or, if a lower rail, from the cross members. Therefore, splicing of rails is frequently the means to restore these members to serviceable condition. The splice may be a channel section. Here again, the material should be disposed to provide an equally strong section as the original and the alloy should be the same. The splice is joined by rivets or bolts but never by welding, presumably because of the heat treatment problem. If forklift pockets are provided in the side rails, the job becomes extremely difficult and the cost is up accordingly.

Repairs of roof damage: Breaks and holes in the roof are promptly and effectively repaired to prevent entry of water and consequent damage to the contents. In general, small penetrations are repaired in a manner similar to that by which side panels are patched. However, the tendency to replace the entire roof surface is greater than in the case of side panels. Aluminum roof stock provides a one-piece surface which, after the application of sealant, is riveted at one end, stretched taut, and riveted at the other. Riveting along the sides is then performed. In the case of steel, the old surface is removed by torch cutting and the one-piece replacement surface welded into place. FRP/plywood roofs are relatively simply replaced. After removal of the damaged roof panel, surfaces are prepared for sealing and the new stock is bolted to framing members.

The Greening Flow Pattern

RANKING SCORE

While the preceding parts of this book dealt with the technology of the container and its institutions, the present part will show how the container fits into the distribution environment for which it has been designed. This requires examination of mission fulfillment of the container as related to:

1.   Container service interface with shipping and portal facilities;
2.   Management of containers and loading process;
3.   Restraint of through movements by customs authorities.

From the Industrial Revolution to the postindustrial era, the carriers and shippers developed a whole framework which came to be known as the "Physical Distribution System." Relationships were established prior to containerization; the system, therefore, requires determination for container utility. Five forces press for growth of containerization:

1.   General growth of the economy to supply world demands;
2.   Expansion of mass production methods;

3. A new network of distribution channels directly related to overseas production;

4. Diminishing availability of conventional ships and the catering to the specific wishes of the shipper;

5. Limitations on the willingness of labor to handle certain cargo, weights, sizes, and commodities in less-than-unit loads.

THE SEED FUNCTION

The effects of the changeover to containerization are gradually being felt by the shipper. With few exceptions, the changeover acquires impetus only because the owners of the containerships are now forced to concentrate on this method and no longer have any alternative but to accommodate the shippers. At first, readily available tonnage came from former conventional shipping. Little expansion followed this traffic in the second instance, because the effect of the container growth was slowly noticeable. This has led to the use of the container as the seed to develop newer, greener "pastures," more directly related to the new process. The understanding of this stage is important for the cargo flow pattern developed in the relationship between the conveyance systems and the containerports. The final goal of the "greening flow" is to move all cargo, or as much as possible, in uniform, standard, single-size units. This would allow optimal interface handling systems, greater economy of scale, and greater efficiency. But the many restraints and obstacles in the way permit only partial solutions at a time.

SIMULATION AND MARKET ANALYSIS

Since the early sixties, the Division of Engineering and Industrial Research of the National Academy of Sciences and the National Research Council undertook a program of comparative analysis of inland and maritime transportation of unitized cargo. This program by the Maritime Cargo Transportation Conference (MCTC), organized by the Division, undertook the program at the request of the Departments of Defense and Commerce. Parallel with this, many companies, such as Matson and United States Lines, developed data to help what steps their own companies would take to develop containerization. The collection of data was costly and not very useful, because while the data were collected, changes occurred which could not be taken into account.

During this period, many research economists tried to develop network models to produce computer estimating bases for corporate planning and relationships. At one time, it was hoped that the simulation process could be used to update decision networks. The simulation program is the executive routine intended to render pragmatic results from available sample elements.

SEA-LAND STRATEGY

Sea-Land's main approach to traffic development was and still is "to serve the shipper." To provide for this, Sea-Land used the marketing-analysis method of the American trucking industry. Hundreds of freight salesmen contacted thousands of shippers. They inspected the shipper's premises, and learned about his commodities and markets and how containers could best fit into the shipper's picture. Thereafter, the salesman would bring the idea back to the company for a study of the equipment accommodation and rate-structure analysis. The result of the study had to be an attractive service to the shipper, with load incentive rates and with a good revenue per container to the operator. This type of market analysis has proven to be a better system than simulation, based on analysis data.

To provide a staff large enough to handle this market analysis, Sea-Land first enlisted the cooperation of hundreds of truckers. The trucker still obtains Sea-Land's container and chassis free or at a very low per diem rate. This makes it attractive for the trucker to use the equipment in his own service and have it on hand when the shipper would have a container for a marine shipment. The fact that Sea-Land's container is only 35 ft. long, against the standard highway trailer sizes now ranging between 40 and 45 ft., did not affect this strategy. The weight regulations make it desirable to have heavier loads move shorter distances on the road, and heavier loads require less cube. Simultaneously, Sea-Land developed a good interline relationship and induced the trucker to turn the container over to him for the long haul. The result, in addition to producing traffic, produced an automatic marketing analysis better than any simulation program could have done.

GRIFFITH'S ANALYSIS

Sea-Land had containers and trailers available, each of which would cost them under $2.00 a day, according to age and condition. This tool gave Sea-Land a position to approach the market, as described in the preceding chapter. The reaction of the conventional steamship industry was presented by John H. Griffith, then General Freight Traffic Manager for United States Lines, at the Cargo Systems Symposium held at Fort Schuyler in 1968.

We're realizing as an industry that we're no longer just in the steamship business. We're beginning to realize that we're in transportation business. What we're selling is transportation, and the means of transportation is the container. The container only incidentally, is carried by a ship. In order to get this point across, however, we've really got to start looking at the customer in quite a different way than we've done heretofore. We've got to break down our customers. We have to use the tools, for example, that have been developed in the manufacturing industries of segmenting our market—to know who we're selling to and how to sell to him in the right way. We've got to separate the forwarders out, as one distinctive group of customers. We've got to separate out the LCL cargo business and set up consolidation systems to take care of them. We've got to examine the needs of the full-carload shippers and establish adequate systems of providing them with trailers to move the cargo from point to point. In short, we have to amend our thinking and stop worrying about the techniques—the mystics of the Merchant Marine Industry—and worry more about what the customer wants and how we're going to give it to him.

This is often called a market-oriented business philosophy, as opposed to a product-oriented philosophy. There's no question that steamship lines are traditionally product-oriented. We worry about the product, the product being the ship up to this point. Everything is designed around the ship. If you look at a typical organization scheme of a liner company, you'll find that in most cases, the emphasis in the organization table itself is on the technical end—the marine end. We have a product—it's the ship. What do you do with a product? You sell it. It's the same as if you manufactured toothpaste. You say, "We're going to make a lot of money." We've been trying to sell ships' space to people who want something else. That's not what we have to do. We have to determine what the customer wants. If the customer has a need for a certain type of transportation system, we can make money by filling that need. And his need in 1975 is going to be different than his need was in 1955.

MOVEMENT VARIABLES

The operation of transporting the container from and to the customer's loading (or unloading) point has reached a certain degree of accuracy and reliability. Trucking and rail transportation are used according to the selection criteria of the traffic man who analyzes the alternative routes that are available. But the degree of effectiveness of this intermodal service depends upon a number of variables which call for examination:

1. Condition of empty journey;
2. Load type (commodity and package);
3. Container sizes used;
4. Modal distance and transfer facility;
5. Degree of container utilization;
6. Facilities at shipper/consignee portal.

CONDITION OF EMPTY JOURNEY

The extent to which the container can travel empty without cost to the shipper or container operator limits the range of through-container movements. This has been a difficult problem to solve in the United States. When the container moves on a truck for distances not exceeding 300 miles, a one-way empty haul is assumed to be normal for this type of operation. The one-way loaded rate for the container will include a compensation for the trucker for the empty haul. Railroads in certain areas have acceded to steamship companies' requests for empty load journeys, in particular from the Port of New York to Florida and between New Orleans and Chicago. As R. H. Wiersema, Director of Service Planning and Analysis for the Illinois Central, stated at the San Diego Container Age Systems Conference, "The Illinois Central Railroad, for example, moves containers both empty and loaded both north and south. We have yet to move a container loaded in both directions. The steamship lines insist that this container deadheading is one of the necessary evils of containerization and that given existing cargo patterns, nothing can be done about it." Only in the United States is the container always treated as a piece of transportation equipment assimilated to railroad cars. Railroads pay each other, by law, a per diem for the use of cars and move them empty without charge. The rest of the world treats the container as a piece of steamship equipment. Consequently, the inland carriers of other nations do not pay per diem under any circumstances, and the container pays the charge each time it moves, whether loaded or empty. Whether this charge is absorbed by the container operator or by the shipping interest depends on local customs. There is a tendency now among American railroads to charge for the movement of any piece of equipment not owned by a railroad. Even private railroad cars are beginning to pay. Strangely enough, this may provide Seatrain Lines with a unique advantage. From the past, Seatrain operations owned certain small railroad lines connecting with their train ships. Under this new type of rail arrangement, Seatrain Lines may be able to take advantage of the situation as a railroad owner and develop rail and land bridge services with cost-free empty return equipment. Other steamship lines have also been considering the purchase of minor unimportant railroad lines for this reason.

LOAD TYPE

Originally, the container was a closed, standard-size box. This appeared as an oversimplification to the traffic manager. The box would not attract as many shippers as the "tailor-made" variety offered by the railroads. Looking at a railroad train, one finds a great variety of cars dedicated to special services. These cars have advantages for the shipper, since they can better serve their variety of commodities. The inside dimension of the container varies with the wall composition, as shown in Chapter 4. Therefore, the shipper may lose a complete row of boxes if the container's inside varies, as is frequently the case. As an example, refrigerated containers will have a maximum clear width of 86 in. inside. If the shipper wants to load a certain quantity of boxes, he must design his boxes accordingly to obtain a snug fit; otherwise, a wrong fit may endanger the entire success of the container's mission.

SPECIAL EQUIPMENT

On the other hand, we have the reverse or the use of a piece of equipment for a special type of load. For example, the rates which govern transportation in piggyback trailers of refrigerated commodities have originally been established to serve as a deterrent to truck competition. The container on a chassis, of course, is equal to a trailer for railroad rating purposes. This rate differential makes the refrigerated container undesirable for many railroads in its present condition. An approach for the domestic use of containers on a special container railroad car is the development of the "Van-Car." This container is equipped with both side and rear doors and can, therefore, be loaded like a boxcar and unloaded like a container or trailer. The railroads are hoping to qualify this container as part of the railroad car on which it is moved. Van-Car containers would be assessed railroad-car rates, which are more favorable to railroads. Under these conditions, the railroads would be more interested in containerization of the Van-Car variety, than in piggyback of containers on chassis. Of course, the Van-Car container would be 9 ft. high and more productive than the ISO standard container.

An entirely different concept is involved when the container service cannot be duplicated by anything known previously. For example, tank containers have been developed for many types of liquids. Frame containers have been designed to carry wrought iron and specially low-rated heavy commodities, such as barbed wire, nails, and spikes. The American National Standard Institute (ANSI) has had to increase its standards by continuously adding new types of intermodal containers. The latest list of standards is shown in Chapter 13.

OVERSEAS AT MINUS 452°F

High-purity liquid helium is now being shipped in specially designed tank containers from the United States to Japan and Europe. Containerization has helped to make these exports possible. Over-the-road tankers, which were generally employed before, were for inland deliveries only. They did not have the ability of holding liquid helium for periods longer than 7 to 10 days and, therefore, could not be used for overseas movements. Liquid helium is the coldest of all liquids. It has a normal boiling point of $-452°F$. At this normal boiling point and 14.7 PSIA (Pounds/Sq. In. Atmosphere), one volume of liquid will produce about 754 volumes of gas.

The unit, which has been developed by Air Products' Cryogenic Systems and Industrial Gas Divisions, consists of a cryogenic inner vessel that will hold 4,000 gallons of liquid helium (the equivalent of more than 400,000 cu. ft. of helium gas) at a temperature of $-452°F$ for 30 days, and possibly longer, without any specific surveillance and control. This inner vessel, which is completely enveloped by a radiation shield, a liquid nitrogen shield, a vacuum jacket, and layers of super insulation, is set in a standard 8 ft. × 8 ft. × 20 ft. container frame. The weight of the unit is approximately 20,000 pounds loaded and 23,000 pounds empty. The container's great tare weight is due to the complex insulation and refrigeration systems required to maintain the helium in a liquid state.

BEER BARRELS

Take draft beer, for instance. To maintain its freshness and best taste, it must be shipped at a temperature that remains constantly around

38°F. This was always an almost impossible task. With the exception of stowage in ship's chilled holds, there was virtually no protection from heat or cold for beer in barrels moving over land to and from ports. Very often, too, the barrels had to await shipment for several days at pier warehouses that were not equipped for storage at specific temperatures. And even when stowed in the chilled hold of a ship, the beer was often put next to other perishable commodities that required chilling or refrigeration, or a controlled atmosphere which was different from that needed for the brew and in themselves at variance. Frequently, the beer arrived solidly frozen. The result was that, after having been subject to so many temperature changes, it became cloudy and flat, sometimes to the point where it was unfit for consumption.

Refrigerated containers put an end to all the difficulties. Now the barrels are loaded into 40 footers at the breweries in Europe, at the required temperature, which in the sealed units remains unchanged until arrival at the distributor's warehouse in New York. This, of course, is

TABLE 6-1. BASIS FOR INLAND CALCULATIONS

Line-Haul Mode and Distance	Unitizing Location	Load Type	Van Size	Stowage Factor (cu. ft./LT)*
1. Truck, 220 miles	Shipper portal	Container	40′ × 8′ × 8′	112
2. Truck, 220 miles	Shipper portal	Container	40′ × 8′ × 8′	76
3. Truck, 220 miles	Shipper portal	Container	40′ × 8′ × 8′	56
4. Truck, 220 miles	Shipper portal	Container	20′ × 8′ × 8′	112
5. Truck, 220 miles	Shipper portal	Container	20′ × 8′ × 8′	76
6. Truck, 220 miles	Shipper portal	Container	20′ × 8′ × 8′	56
7. Truck, 220 miles	Pier facility	Container	40′ × 8′ × 8′	112
8. Truck, 220 miles	Pier facility	Container	40′ × 8′ × 8′	76
9. Truck, 220 miles	Pier facility	Container	40′ × 8′ × 8′	56
10. Truck, 220 miles	Pier facility	Container	20′ × 8′ × 8′	112
11. Truck, 220 miles	Pier facility	Container	20′ × 8′ × 8′	76
12. Truck, 220 miles	Pier facility	Container	20′ × 8′ × 8′	56
13. Truck, 220 miles	Container frt. sta.	Container	40′ × 8′ × 8′	112
14. Truck, 220 miles	Container frt. sta.	Container	40′ × 8′ × 8′	76
15. Truck, 220 miles	Container frt. sta.	Container	40′ × 8′ × 8′	56
16. Truck, 220 miles	Container frt. sta.	Container	20′ × 8′ × 8′	112
17. Truck, 220 miles	Container frt. sta.	Container	20′ × 8′ × 8′	76
18. Truck, 220 miles	Container frt. sta.	Container	20′ × 8′ × 8′	56

* Cargo stowage factors of 112, 76, and 56 cu. ft. per long ton (LT) correspond to cargo densities of 20, 29.5, and 40 lb. per cu. ft., respectively.

equipped to maintain it still further at the required level, until the barrels reach the customer, sometimes still in the original container or, if it is a smaller order, by truck.

CONTAINER SIZE AND FLOW RESTRICTIONS

The previously cited MCTC study dealt in detail with the advantage of using the 40-ft. container rather than any smaller sizes. Cost data developed on the basis of the stowage factor of the cargo are shown in Tables 6-1 and 6-2, as a comparison.

TABLE 6-2.   U.S. INLAND COSTS FOR EXPORT CARGO,
ASSUMING 220-MILE TRUCK LINE HAUL
(Dollars per Measurement Ton)

Load Type, Container Size, Unitizing Location,[a] and Cargo Stowage Factor[b]	Inland Costs ($ per MT)				Container or Pallet Ownership	Total
	Unitizing	Other Handling	Drayage	Line Haul		
40′ Vans, SP, 112	$0.38	$0.19	$ —	$1.77	$0.10	$2.44
20′ Vans, SP, 112	0.38	0.19	—	1.82	0.14	2.53
40′ Vans, CFS, 112	0.38	0.95	0.42	1.77	0.10	3.62
20′ Vans, CFS, 112	0.38	0.95	0.42	1.82	0.14	3.71
40′ Vans, CP, 112	0.50	0.61	—	1.75	0.10	2.96
20′ Vans, CP, 112	0.50	0.69	—	1.75	0.14	3.08
40′ Vans, SP, 76	0.38	0.20	—	2.62	0.10	3.30
20′ Vans, SP, 76	0.38	0.20	—	2.69	0.14	3.41
40′ Vans, CFS, 76	0.38	0.96	0.60	2.62	0.10	4.66
20′ Vans, CFS, 76	0.38	0.96	0.60	2.69	0.14	4.77
40′ Vans, CP, 76	0.50	0.65	—	2.53	0.10	3.78
20′ Vans, CP, 76	0.50	0.77	—	2.53	0.14	3.94
40′ Vans, SP, 56	0.38	0.22	—	3.56	0.10	4.26
20′ Vans, SP, 56	0.38	0.22	—	3.63	0.14	4.37
40′ Vans, CFS, 56	0.38	0.98	0.82	3.56	0.10	5.84
20′ Vans, CFS, 56	0.38	0.98	0.82	3.63	0.14	5.95
40′ Vans, CP, 56	0.50	0.69	—	3.43	0.10	4.72
20′ Vans, CP, 56	0.50	0.87	—	3.43	0.14	4.94

[a] Where unitized: SP = Shipper Portal, CFS = Container Freight Station, CP = Container Port.

[b] Cargo stowage factors of 112, 76, and 56 cu. ft. per long ton (LT) correspond to cargo densities of 20, 29.5, and 40 lb. per cu. ft., respectively.

The second of this set of tables shows the extrapolation of the combination used in the first table, as related to the data collected. The actual cost figures have almost doubled since that data collection period; however, the general ratio still remains valid.

ROAD TRANSPORT RESTRAINTS

Highway length and weight laws control the access to most industrial and agricultural areas of production and limit the type of service that can be given (Fig. 6-1). The use of a container and chassis always results in higher empty weights than the light weight truck trailer designed for highway effectiveness. The basic reason is that the containers carry a heavy structure in the corner posts and side rails (top and bottom) which are necessary for use on ships, but excess weights for road transport. If

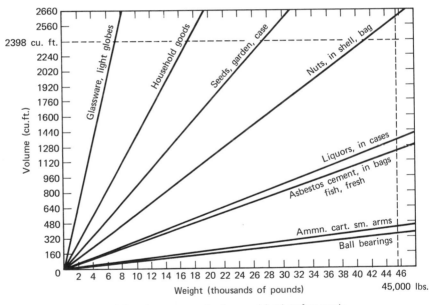

Max. Highway Load Capacity _ _ _ _ for improved hard surface roads

FIGURE 6-1. WEIGHT/VOLUME CHARACTERISTICS OF CARGO OFTEN DETERMINE INTERMODAL USE DUE TO HIGHWAY WEIGHT RESTRICTIONS. CHART SHOWS CERTAIN COMMODITIES AS APPLIED TO CONTAINER CUBE AVERAGING 2398 CU. FT. FOR A 40-FT. ISO-STANDARD VAN.

the container is refrigerated and is for shipboard use, the refrigeration unit requires recession of the unit into the front section of the container. This is equivalent to a loss of usable cubic space for road transport, because the laws allow the refrigeration unit to stick out of the trailer in the upper front panel without penalty. This space for the outer portion of the cooling unit covers the upper region over the tractor cab, which otherwise would be empty. Tractor wheels themselves reach about 8 ft. to 16 ft. under the chassis or the trailer, to conform to length laws.

Similarly, the problems of the container size must conform to the area usage in road transport. This is how Matson decided on the 24-ft.-size container and Sea-Land decided on the 35-ft. container, complying with the regulations which were in effect at the time of decision making. In the western United States, the law is based on the overall length of the rig. This leads to the possibility of using double-bottoms or a chain of two 4-wheeled trailers behind one tractor. Since each of these trailers can carry one container, the trucker from the western United States can accommodate more than the truckers from the East Coast and Gulf areas. With the increase in permissible length, Seatrain chose the 29-ft. container, which is also 9 ft. high. By using double-bottoms here, one tractor can transport 58 ft. of usable container length plus the added height advantage. To produce a new traffic pattern in competition with Matson, Seatrain designed their ships to accept the 29 ft. × 8 ft. × 9 ft. containers. This new size also affects the use on rails. The use of three 29 ft. containers on a flatcar required the design of a special car for the purpose, equipped with specially spaced corner fittings for safe attachment to the railcars.

MODAL DISTANCE EFFECTS

Containerization plans must include route analyses between the place of cargo origin and the containerport (CP), the hub of all land/sea interchange. Such an analysis must typically resolve not only the technical restraints which might develop, but also certain unique rate structure systems which will, of course, affect the overall cost picture of container use.

In California, on the freeway system, truckers can legally move three 20-ft. empty containers on a combination truck/trailer-bed system. These are the same type of flat trucks and trailers available in large quantities in all western states. We cannot recommend this practice as being particularly safe. We have seen such containers on the side of the road many times, having fallen off the trailer beds where they were attached by chains only. The reason for this type of movement is that the empty weight of the containers conforms with weight laws. The only difficulty consists in the bulky size of the containers.

Sometimes careful analysis can develop a good system by combining the best of two services. Ocean container services are limited in size and weight capacity, while domestic cargo by truck van takes advantage of a more carefully designed use of highway weight limits. Such an example may be cited for the southern California area between Los Angeles and San Diego. Flatbed trucks carry loads of construction material southbound from Los Angeles to San Diego, but have no return cargo. On the other hand, the export shippers in San Diego require three or four times as many containers for their loadings. These containers are then trucked full to Los Angeles and shipped from there. Consequently, a number of truckers have developed an interesting combination. On the southbound trip, they carry two flat trailers with their normal domestic load and one tractor-trailer combination loaded with three empty 20-ft. containers. This can be done by overhanging two containers from one trailer with a long tow bar. Approximately 10 ft. of each container rides supported by the rest of the structure which is loaded onto the flatbed of the trailer. On the return trip to Los Angeles, each one of the three trailers carries one outbound loaded container.

OPTIMIZATION FOR COORDINATION

Simulation studies can provide very valid guidance on the ranking of each of the conveyance systems and their interrelationships. It may be too costly for all but major container users to apply such a deep-study method complete with collection of data and computer analysis. The advantage of the use of each transport mode in the sector where it benefits the overall system to the greatest extent has brought about a search for available transfer methods. There is no problem of transfer at the major railheads. Most centers are equipped with adequate transfer facilities; this will be discussed in detail later. There are 35,000 traffic origin locations in small towns in the United States. To service some of these locations often requires costly long-haul by truck.

The search for simple railroad transfer methods has led to the idea of use of containers by surface transport. A very interesting system has been developed by Hans Gerzymisch, a German trucker. He installed two elevated rails at a height of 4 ft. from the ground. One end of these rails slopes up gradually, so that one end is approximately 2 in. higher than the other. By installing steel members equipped with railroad wheels (approximately 6 in. in diameter) on each lower-corner casting, the container lifts off automatically when the wheels on the outer rail rise.

SIDE TRANSFER FLEXIBILITY

A more flexible system is the Interpool Transfer System. Interpool's system provides a trailer specifically equipped to handle both 20-ft. and 40-ft. containers by pulling them sideways from the railroad car to a trailer chassis or vice versa. The same unit can be used for transfer from the side puller to another road trailer or to a storage rack. One unit will handle all ISO standard containers between 20 ft. and 40 ft. This unit is already in use in England and in Canada. Details of this interesting device are shown in Fig. 6-2.

Dimensions:	Overall length—38'9" minimum (20' units) to 56' maximum (40' units) Overall width—96" Height to sliding surface of bolsters (light)—51"
Frame:	Telescoping main rails, with special fabricated, tandem gooseneck, all-welded construction. Front section slides in rear half of frame and locks at various positions to accommodate specific intermediate container sizes (e.g., 24'3", 27', 30' ISO, 35'). Standard spacing for 20' and 40' ISO containers, other positions to be specified as optional extra. (King pin to front jacks—84")
Bolsters:	Hydraulic, extending bolsters, front and rear, provide continuous slide "bridge" for container corners during transfer. Individually controlled, extend 15" each side. Built-in lock assemblies provided at each end.
Landing Gear:	Front lift jacks replace conventional landing gear, have built-in lock valves to prevent "run-back" under prolonged loading.
Suspension & Axles:	44,000 lbs. underslung tandem suspension, 5" dia. axles, 12¼" × 7½" air brakes, cast spoke wheels, 15" × 7.5" demountable rims, 10.00 × 15 tires (8).
Electrical:	12-volt, 7-way plug, with lighting to comply with Provincial and ICC Regulations.
Power Unit:	Wisconsin VH4 air-cooled gasoline engine (26 hp at 2100 rpm), with direct-drive 16-gpm gear pump;

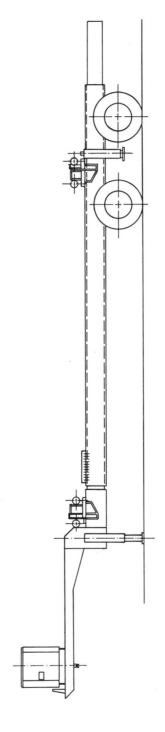

FIGURE 6-2. 20′–40′ SELF-POWERED, CORNER PULL, UNIVERSAL TRANSFER UNIT.

	25-gal. oil reservoir; mounted at front of trailer over kingpin.
Controls:	Mounted behind front bolster, may be operated from either side.
Leveling:	Four 7″-dia. jacks, two at front, two at rear, individually controlled (Max. ht. rear bolster with jacks extended—63″).
Transfer Mechanism:	Pivoted, spring-loaded hooks are built into sliding housing mounted to sliding hydraulic bolsters. Total hook travel—23″ either way from central position. Full-power control operates hook retraction, permitting instant reversal of direction of transfer as required. Hooks engage in sequence in base hole of standard ISO lower-corner casting. First pull off railcar is with portable adaptors which engage in side hole of corner castings, providing an extension to the container for engagement of transfer hooks. Through-transfer from railcar to delivery trailer, or vice versa, is possible. Hydraulic supply to transfer bolsters is synchronized for even movement, but individual operational control is also retained.
Rated Capacity:	Container plus load—70,000 lbs.

DEGREE OF CONTAINER UTILIZATION

The MCTC study has pointed out the importance of container utilization. The assumptions and round-trip utilization factors are shown in Table 6-3. This table gives an indication of the analysis applied to outbound shipments only. Again, the differences which occur in each particular shipment require marketing analysis which, in turn, produces a routing system for the carrier and a marketing system for the shipper.

UNIT UTILIZATION

To understand the problems resulting from unit size and utilization factors, one must consider the application of lot sizes to modern production. This is where the physical distribution system interfaces with the planned production process. Package size with certain quantities of unit

TABLE 6-3. SYSTEM COST ALLOCATION

| Load Type | Van Utilization Factors | | (Assumed) Ratio of Inbound to Outbound Tonnage[a] | Van Round-Trip Utilization Factor[b] |
	Unitizing Location	Ownership of Vans		
1. Break-bulk	—	—	2/3	—
2. Strapped pallets	Shipper portal	Ship operator	2/3	5/6
3. 40-ft. vans	Shipper portal	Ship operator	2/3	5/6
4. 40-ft. vans	Shipper portal	Trucking co.	2/3	5/6
5. 40-ft. vans	Shipper portal	Van-Leasing co.	5/6	11/12
6. 40-ft. vans	Shipper portal	Shipper	0	1/2
7. 40-ft. vans	Container port	Ship operator	2/3	5/6
8. 40-ft. vans	Container port	Van leasing co.	5/6	11/12

[a] Computed on a measurement ton (MT) basis, Ratio = (Inbound MT/Outbound MT).
[b] Eighty-five (85) percent of the van's inner cube is assumed usable, allowing for 15 percent broken stowage inside the van. Thus, maximum van utilization (an entry of "1" in column 5) would indicate that each van is 85 percent full on both the outbound and return trips. An unbalanced trade is assumed, in which all vans are fully utilized on the outbound trip. Since, in each case, the outbound utilization factor equals 1, the ratio of inbound to outbound tonnages (column 4) also equals the inbound utilization factor. Hence, the average round-trip utilization factor (column 5) equals 1 plus the value given in column 4, divided by 2. Where the ship operator owns the vans or pallets, 64 percent are assumed to be full on the inbound trip. This results in a round-trip utilization factor of 5/6.

components have led to trade usages based on previously available vehicle dimensions. For this reason, for example, a container not capable of handling a load of California citrus consisting of 1,036 cases requires that the shipper establish and introduce new standards. The results of this relationship affect the application of containers. Delay in changeover will depend on how fast the trade accepts the container sizes as measures of effectiveness, and this, in turn, reflects the result of the vector of the accommodation environment. The accommodation environment typically is affected by:

1. Through-rate combination from door to door;
2. Shipper's traffic procedures to cope with his physical arrangement at his shipping platform;
3. Production changes affecting production process;
4. Cost of operating at the shipper's facilities;

5. Trade usage lot sizes;
6. Resistance to change.

PORTAL FACILITIES

The sixth and last of the movement variables which must be considered is the facilities at the customer's door. If the container remains at the shipper's plant or the consignee's distribution warehouse for a period of time, there must be enough platform space at the warehouse or there must be special parking facilities. If the containers are to be parked away from the building, arrangements have to be made with the trucker, and/or a shuttle tractor must be available. It has become customary for container operators to make such arrangements with large shippers.

FROM THE GROUND UP

Containers are usually presented at shipper's premises on a chassis. Loading takes place either at level from a raised 4-ft. loading platform, or the goods must be lifted up from ground level. If the container itself is on the ground, all operations will be carried out at ground level. This presents a problem of lifting the loaded container for transportation. The U.S. Army developed a new self-loading, self-unloading semitrailer which expedites handling of containers in the field. The prototype is capable of handling a variety of containerized cargo up to 8 ft. × 8 ft. × 20 ft. and 44,600 pounds, as well as palletized supplies. The twin-hoist, tilt-deck system picks up containers over the end of the trailer instead of over the sides, as do most other existing systems. It is expected to be particularly useful in military over-the-beach landing operation. Containerized cargo dropped on the beach by helicopter or landing barge will be picked up quickly and loaded for transport inland. The new rig is expected to find applications in other branches of the military, as well as in commercial shipping, trucking, materials handling, and other related industries.

FROM GROUND LEVEL TO DOOR

Fork trucks are used to lift goods up to tailboards of the container floor level. When loading a chassis-mounted container from ground level, the actual stowage of the goods inside the container generally has to be executed by hand, although a light weight fork lift may be placed inside the container. Care must be exercised to insure that undue strain is not imposed upon the container floor. The ISO Standards require container floors to withstand a maximum wheel loading of 6,000 lbs. with a minimum contact area of 22 sq. in. per wheel. The operation of fork trucks inside the container raises considerable questions of floor strength.

UPSTREAM-DOWNSTREAM

There are substantial capital and operating costs involved in running a container flow pattern. It becomes clear that the operating costs of container handling equipment can be optimized only through an even flow of containers at the interchange, as well as at origin and destination points. Thus, it is critical that container equipment be distributed logistically to all points of interchange, where its operating cost is at least at even trade-off with the cost benefits of efficient container flow.

Finding the points where containers will do the most good per dollar is no simple task. It involves thousands of sophisticated decisions, each with a staggering number of variables. The wrong decisions will result in expensive duplication of both containers and handling equipment, with boxes and equipment in the wrong places at the wrong times.

The analysis of our first examination of container application can be concluded with comparing the container service pattern and interfaces with log transportation. The best service is from the upstream starting point to the downstream destination in the lumbermill pond. The "upstream-downstream" process requires continuous perfection and removal of obstacles.

The second group of management techniques deals with the activities to be deployed when and where the cargo itself meets with the containers. As stated previously, this can be either at the containerport, at a container freight station, at a shipper's load facility, or at the portal of the shipper's own inland distribution premises.

PREPARATION OF CONTAINERS

Before commencing packing operations, the container must be properly prepared, and the stowage of the contents must be preplanned as far as possible. The container operators will supply a container in clean condition, but this should not be assumed. A careful check should be made before loading is commenced. The container should be clean and dry; it should be free of loose dust and dirt; and it should also be free from any smell. If it is necessary to wash out a container, strong-smelling detergents or disinfectants should not be used, and loading should not start until the container is quite dry.

STUFFING RULES

The use of freight containers has been acclaimed as the panacea for improved delivery, but success depends upon efficient stuffing and proper securing of contents. The goods have to be stowed in a manner which will withstand the rigors of a sea voyage. Many specialized cellular containerships are fitted with stabilizers; but at best, these only reduce the worst effects of pitching and rolling. The contents can still be subject to wild lurching movements such as would never be experienced in any inland movement.

Shippers faced with the task of stowing containers for intermodal voyages must acquire new skills. Not only must they learn to use efficient loading techniques; but they must also learn to follow those basic principles of stowage which are second nature to the experienced longshoreman. Always bear in mind the very worst conditions at sea. The contents must be secured to withstand extreme conditions when the ship may roll up to 30° or 40° each way, or pitch up to 10° or 15°. Although cargo handling techniques have changed, the sea in its worst moods has not changed since the beginning of time.

COMPATIBILITY OF CARGO

It is of vital importance that goods should be compatible with one another. Many commodities are easily tainted by strong-smelling goods, such as soap, copra, and fertilizers. Such goods must not be stowed together in the same container. Similarly, hygroscopic goods may give off moisture and damage nonhygroscopic goods. As an example of the latter, one should never stow fresh-sawn timber, vegetables, or wet hides in a container together with steel, which would rust, or flour, which would compact and become moldy. The contents of a container must be compatible chemically, physically, hygroscopically, and thermally.

AMBIENT ATMOSPHERE AND ENVIRONMENT

Wide temperature variations can also result in the formation of condensation inside a container, resulting in damage to anhydrous chemicals, steel, canned goods, and a wide range of other susceptible commodities. As a typical example, a container packed in the South on a mild, humid day in winter can, within seven or eight days, be subjected to subzero temperatures inland in the United States. Moisture-laden air trapped inside the container will then be cooled below the dew point, and condensation will form on the sides and top of the container interior, subsequently dripping onto the cargo with harmful results. Cargo must, therefore, be suitably protected against this risk.

Cellular containerships carry one-third of the containers on deck. Apart from the obvious risk of damage by heavy waves, and possible ingress of sea water and salt-laden moisture, containers may be subject to temperature extremes which can cause damage to certain types of cargo. In general, there is always a chance of shipment on deck with most ocean container services and precautions must, therefore, be taken as if this were to be the case. Direct exposure to hot sun introduces risk of damage to goods with a low melting point, such as chocolate, photographic materials, and canned goods. Alternatively, certain goods, such as fruit or vegetables, can be damaged by frost.

STOWAGE PRINCIPLES

Stowage must be planned in accordance with well-defined principles. First, the weight must be evenly distributed. There is a strong temptation to load heavy goods first. The weight must be spread evenly, so that the container is not heavy at any one end or along any one side. All container-lifting equipment is built on the assumption that containers will be evenly loaded and not overloaded. Any departure from this could result in lifting gear failing to engage. Lifting gear can be strained beyond breaking point and a serious accident can occur, possibly causing fatal injuries.

It is suggested that the center of gravity should never be displaced from the center of the container by more than 2 ft. in a fore-and-aft direction, and not more than 1 ft. in a transverse direction. In all containers, the center of gravity should not be above half the height of the container. Containership stability calculations are based on the assumption that the center of gravity of each container will be at the geometric center.

Light weight packages must be overstowed by heavier packages. Precautions must be taken to prevent crushing; and for this reason alone, common sense demands that light goods should always be given top stowage or overlay. Liquids should never be stowed above solids, and solid packages with sharp corners and protrusions must obviously not be in contact with soft packages which could be torn, crushed, or otherwise damaged.

HAND PACKING RULES

When containers are packed by hand, great care must be exercised to avoid damage by crushing and chaffing, and packages should be interlocked wherever possible, in order to give a tight compact stow which will not collapse with movement at sea. It is particularly important that goods stowed in the doorway are tightly interlocked or secured. Often, after a container has undergone a rough sea voyage, the contents cascade down upon the unfortunate individual who has opened the doors, sometimes causing injury. Also, it is important that the container be equipped with defensive devices to protect movement of the cargo within the container, when the entire container is subject to the g force at sea or by rail. Customarily, the two best solutions are:

1. Nailing strips integrated into the floor, where cargo can be anchored by nailing it down or even bolting it into wood;
2. Cargo load-control devices which consist of three or four longitudinal tracks on both sides of the container near the door. Wooden duct boards are interlocked on both sides to prevent the cargo from sliding against the door.

There are many variations of these two themes, but one must remember that the doors of a container are not designed to withstand the pressure of 20 tons or more of solid load pushed against them by the g force transmitted from the conveyance.

SWEDISH PUBLICATION

The Swedish Transport Research Committee has established rules for stowing of containers. This operation of packing containers demands care and planning. Container packers must apply the skill of the longshoremen. It is unfortunate that the word "stuffing" has come into common use. Goods must never be *stuffed* into containers; this suggests a careless, haphazard operation. Containers must be stowed carefully and scientifically; otherwise, the shipper will lose the opportunity of insuring arrival of goods factory fresh. This opportunity has never previously existed, and it should not be wasted. Finally, never allow anyone to smoke inside a container. Apart from the risk of damaged goods due to a carelessly discarded cigarette end, containerships only have limited firefighting facilities, and a serious fire in a container could result in loss of ship and loss of life.

The United States National Cargo Bureau has also published valid loading guides. Posters with pictures are available, too.

PACKING EFFICIENCY ANALYSIS

Stuffing commodities in containers would appear to be the ultimate link in the production line. Analytical stow plans may spell the success of best cube and weight use. A typical example is given.

A rational method to efficiently pack boxes into a container that was not specifically designed for the boxes must follow analysis of the cube relation. Let a, b, and c be the dimensions of the box and let X, Y, and Z be the dimensions of the container. If X is an exact multiple of one of a, b, or c; if Y is an exact multiple of another one of a, b, or c; and if Z is an exact multiple of the remaining box dimension, then we can pack all the boxes parallel to each other and without any wasted space. For example, Fig. 6-3 shows boxes 2 in. × 3 in. × 5 in. packed into a container 9 in. × 10 in. × 16 in. Sixteen is a multiple of two 8 times, ten is a multiple of five 2 times, and nine is a multiple of three 3 times. Therefore, $8 \times 2 \times 3 = 48$ boxes that may be packed in parallel fashion without wasted space.

Suppose now that one of the dimensions of the container is not an exact multiple of any one of the three box dimensions. For example, consider boxes 2 in. × 3 in. × 5 in. to be placed inside a container 6 in. × 10 in. × 11 in., where 11 is not an exact multiple of 2, 3 or 5. In this case, it may still be possible to pack the boxes without any wasted space, but not with all the boxes parallel.

In general, a box may be placed with its sides parallel to the sides of the container in six different orientations as shown in Fig. 6-4 and Table 6-4. To determine efficient packing, first examine how well each of the six orientations will pack, paying less attention to the number of boxes packed than to the shape of the unfilled space. Table 6-4 does this for the example of a 2 in. × 3 in. × 5 in. box to be packed into a 6 in. × 10 in. × 11 in. container.

The lower the capacity as given in Table 6-4, the larger the remaining space and this, in turn, allows for more maneuverability in the utilization of that remaining space for the packing of boxes which are not parallel to the basic orientation. Of course, it is good to see a zero in any of the last three columns of Table 6-4 because this indicates that the

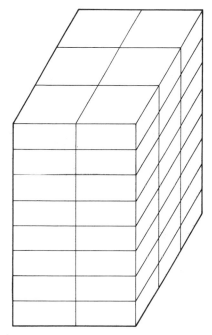

FIGURE 6-3. FORTY-EIGHT BOXES, EACH 2 BY 3 BY 5 INCHES, PACKED INTO A CONTAINER 9 BY 10 BY 16 INCHES IN PARALLEL FASHION WITHOUT WASTED SPACE (SOURCE: *Design News*).

dimension is completely filled; but the 1-in. number on any line is bad because there is no way in which a box 2 in. × 3 in. × 4 in. can be packed into a space which is 1 in. thick. Line b, with its 2-in.-thick empty space along the 11-in. dimension is thus seen to offer the best possibilities for packing additional boxes. In fact, four more boxes, not parallel to the original orientation of the first 18, may be packed to completely fill the container.

In a last example, consider boxes 2 in. × 3 in. × 4 in., each with a volume of 24 cu. in., to be packed into a container 17 in. × 19 in. × 22 in. with a volume of 7,106 cu. in. This is sufficient volume for 296 boxes with 2 cu. in. remaining. However, we will succeed in packing only 292 boxes. Perhaps some reader can improve on this.

Table 6-4 shows the capacity and remaining space for the six basic orientations in this example. The final three columns of residuals show 1 in. left over on all lines except line b. As stated earlier, this box cannot utilize a space 1 in. thick. We, therefore, examine the L-shaped space

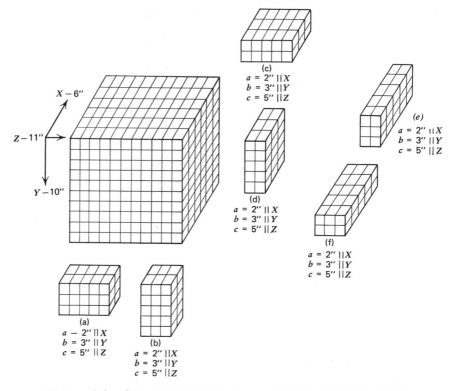

FIGURE 6-4.   SIX ORIENTATIONS OF A BOX WITH RESPECT TO THE CONTAINER.

TABLE 6-4

Orienta-tion Shown in Figure 6-4	Dimension of Box Parallel to (inches)			Number of Times Box Fits Along This Dimension (inches)			Capacity (number of boxes)	Empty Space Along This Dimension (inches)		
	X = 6	Y = 10	Z = 11	X = 6	Y = 10	Z = 11		X = 6	Y = 10	Z = 11
a	2	3	5	3	3	2	18	0	1	1
b	2	5	3	3	2	3	18	0	0	2
c	3	2	5	2	5	2	20	0	0	1
d	3	5	2	2	2	5	20	0	0	1
e	5	3	2	1	3	5	15	1	1	1
f	5	2	3	1	5	3	15	1	0	2

Note: The capacity is the product of the numbers in the three columns preceding it. It does not include the number of boxes which may possibly be packed into the remaining empty space.

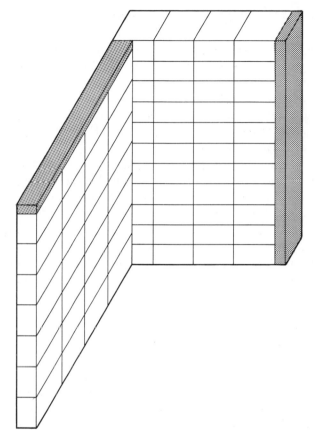

FIGURE 6-5.   AN EXAMPLE IN FILLING AN L-SHAPED SPACE. THE
SHADED AREA INDICATES WASTED SPACE (SOURCE: *Design News*).

indicated by arrangement b and shown in Figure 6-5. Here we see that
28 additional boxes may be packed into the 2-in.-thick leg of the L and
that 44 additional boxes may be packed into the 3-in.-thick leg of the L,
making a total of 220 + 28 + 44 = 292 boxes.

In summary, to pack boxes efficiently, first examine the packing to be
obtained from each of the six basic orientations shown in Figure 6-4 and
Table 6-4. Then endeavor to utilize the leftover space, if any, as efficiently as possible.

SPECIAL COMMODITY PLANNING

Several lines loading containers in transpacific service have begun to use cotton in bales in containers. The average load capacity of a container is about 18 bales per 20 ft. Care must be taken that the cotton is dry enough and properly compressed. Wet cotton may develop into a fire hazard under the influence of changing ambient temperatures. Another damage danger consists in swelling of the baled cotton. This can damage the container severely.

Even with the growth of bulk transportation for large quantities of cargo, there is often an opportunity to use small bulk quantities for container shipments. Grain loading gates installed in the rear door before closing the outer door prevent cargo from deforming the closure. This also allows loading of the tilted container by means of a gravity belt shooting the load into the container.

Installation of special roof hatches facilitates the bulk loading procedures. Such "bulk-hatches" can be installed in a routine manner between the roof bows of the container.

CONTAINER FREIGHT STATIONS

Developing standards for container freight stations (CFS) deals with the origin where the actual pieces of freight are moved into or out of the container. Upstream-downstream services provide for the most "greening" because they really give the shipper the means to extend his own production line to the premises of his buyer or consumer. Yet, while this is desirable, the developments of container service must count on the consolidation of cargo at the CFS to handle a large portion of the traffic.

The container carrier must provide terminal facilities for this service, where the transfer of the individual shipment from the pickup-and-delivery system to the line-haul container system takes place. Located on a container chassis and backed up to a CFS, the container can be handled like a truck trailer.

PLATFORM ENGINEERING

Train terminal platform engineering is not new to the trucking industry nor to the rail industry. "Freight houses," in the freight-forwarding business of the United States, are facilities for the transfer of cargo from truck to railroad cars. Truck terminals effect transfer only between two types of trucks, local and long-haul. In both cases, the similarity of the system has developed certain terminal-procedure standards. Based on linear mobility of the transferred cargo, a multiple choice of assembly and distribution systems is used at the juncture of the routing. In the local pickup-and-delivery sector, small individual shipments are being picked up from the production lines of the shipper and brought to the transfer platform. Here the cargo is divided according to destination (or origins, as the case may be) and then consolidated with portions of other pickup-and-delivery loads to form the new bulk for the line-haul transport medium. The trucking industry has an outstanding performance record in developing platform services for efficient consolidation and redistribution of individual shipments. Of course, highway shipments do not require the same care in stowing as the containers for overseas shipments. Due to the intermodal connecting service, containerization follows the trucking load pattern. This often departs from the careful stow methods practiced by the longshoremen on the pier and described hereafter.

The physical operation between pickup or delivery trucks and the fleet of line-haul containers consists of eight customary maneuvers:

1. Stripping cargo from pickup truck;
2. Stacking cargo in lot sizes;
3. Movement of this cargo to place of rest or link transfer system;
4. Stacking preparatory to loading of container;
5. Measurement for bill-of-lading purposes (weight–cube);
6. Document data checking (origin or interline);
7. Movement into line-haul containers;
8. Stacking and securing in line-haul containers.

Implications of these steps are the similar in reverse for inbound cargo. The added restraint of customs clearance, if international trade is involved, is also discussed in the latter part of this chapter.

SPACE SENSING

The CAPROCON System was developed by the air cargo industry for quickly and accurately obtaining package weight, dimensions, volume, and density data. All dimensions and weight are gathered and processed while the packages are in motion and conveyed through a material handling system. This system is now in use at United Airlines in Los Angeles.

The physical characteristics of a package must be combined with related data to identify packages or cartons on both an individual and lot-shipment basis. Information is then fed to a computer for statistical data analysis and transmission to other locations. The information is also used to produce properly identified shipping labels and develop permanent records. The CAPROCON System was developed by Fairbanks-Morse. It is intended for integration into a material handling system where data is used for accurate billing of shipments by weight and/or volume, optimum loading of transport vehicles, and improved control of material movement.

Most cargo processed through any container-handling facility is conveyor borne at some period. Inserting a system in the conveyor line provides the optimal means of obtaining dimension, volume, and weight information for each piece of cargo without interrupting the line of movement.

The CAPROCON line conveyor, scale, and dimension-sensing unit are mounted on a common subbase which is easily inserted into the conveyor line. The dimension-sensing unit is mounted on the subbase, between the approach conveyor and the weigh conveyor, so that the sensing place is at a right angle to the direction of travel. The approach and weight conveyors are arranged to provide a smooth transfer of packages through the dimension-sensing unit, thus insuring accurate dimension and weight data. CAPROCON is capable of processing, at a belt speed of 60 ft. per minute, packages having a maximum height and width of 3 ft. and a length of 4.5 ft. and weighing up to 500 lbs. To be accurately processed, an item must be no less than 2 in. in height and width, 8 in. in length, and 0.5 lb. in weight. Height and width are limited by the width of the conveyors and the size of the dimension-sensing unit. Maximum length is governed by the length of the weighing conveyor, which is 4.5 ft.

The capabilities of the present CAPROCON System are being expanded to increase its measuring and weighing capacity. Since the maximum length which can be measured is a function of the length of the weigh conveyor, a longer weigh conveyor will increase the capacity of the system to measure longer packages. A weigh conveyor exceeding 4.5 ft. in length will be available shortly.

DIMENSION SENSING

The dimension-sensing structure consists primarily of two identical photoelectric systems for measuring the height and width of the container as it moves through the sensing structure. Each photoelectric system consists of a group of light emitters and an associated lens or photoreceiver. One group of emitters produces horizontally oriented parallel beams used to obtain the height measurement; the other group provides vertically oriented parallel beams used to obtain the width measurement. The photoreceivers are mounted on the opposite side of the sensing frame to receive the beams of light produced by the corresponding emitter. Therefore, one emitter and one receiver (located on opposite sides of the sensing frame) control the light beam.

The parallel light beams produced by each emitter are approximately $\frac{1}{4}$ in. apart to produce an accurate measuring system. Special precautions were taken to prevent adjacent beams of light and ambient light from causing inaccuracies. The photoreceivers for obtaining width measurements are mounted across the top of the sensing frame with their corresponding emitters across the bottom to prevent overhead ambient light from causing errors in the sensing system.

HEIGHT AND WIDTH

The electronic circuits convert the large number of signals produced by the photoreceivers into a condensed digital code. This action reduces the number of signals between the dimension-sensing unit and the data processing controller to a minimum. These electronic circuits (mounted within the sensing unit adjacent to the photoreceivers) are arranged so that objects may be accurately measured when interrupting the light beams of either dimension in any position. It is not required to guide the units to one side in order to establish a zero reference. Obviously, the height measurement in most cases will have the bed of the conveyors as a zero reference. Should odd-shaped items with extensions, such as motor shafts, be processed, they, too, will be accurately measured.

The electronic circuits combine the signals from the photoreceivers in a manner that holes, such as the slot spacings in a crate or the center opening in a tire passing through the measuring system, are ignored. This design provides an accurate measurement of the volume. When items with holes are processed, the dimensions used in the measurement are the outside dimensions of the containers.

LENGTH

The length of the item passing through the dimension-sensing frame is obtained from pulses generated by an electromagnetic pulser mounted on the drive motor of the weigh conveyor. Since the rotor of the pulser is attached to the shaft of the drive motor, the interval between pulses represents a discreet incremental distance on the belt of the conveyor. Therefore, any change in speed of the conveyors, which nominally move at a speed of 60 ft. per minute, will not affect the accuracy of the length measurement. Such speed changes may be caused by frequency fluctuations and loading of the motor.

VOLUME IS CALCULATED

After the container has passed through the dimension-sensing unit, the *maximum* height, width, and length which were stored into the data processing unit's memory, are multiplied to obtain the "cubed volume." Since these dimensions are measured and stored in hundredths of cubic feet, the "cubed volume" will be calculated to the nearest hundredth of a cubic foot.

"Cubing" is only one method of obtaining volume. This method is suitable for rectangular or square items. When measuring irregularly shaped objects, such as logs or cylinders, "cubing" is no longer effective. To calculate the volume of these odd-shaped objects, the dimension-sensing unit slices the object into minute increments and sums each increment over the length of the object. Volume obtained using this method is known as "summation volume." Basically, this method is a very-high-speed addition made possible by integrated circuits used in the data processing unit.

The maximum dimensions of height, width, and length (for both "cubed" and "summation" volume methods) are also individually placed into memory to be interfaced to the desired output devices.

Immediately upon passing the measuring frame "light curtain," the package is completely supported by the weigh conveyor. The output of the load cells supporting the weigh conveyor is converted to a digital count proportional to the conveyor live load in a micrologic adaptation of a well-known weighing method.

Since items are frequently accumulated prior to processing through the CAPROCON System, an automatic spacing control is provided to space the containers so that no two containers will be scale-borne at the same time during the weighing cycle. This allows print-out of the data before another container enters the dimension-sensing unit.

For billing purposes in the air cargo industry, to determine whether a container should be charged on a volume or weight basis, the CAPRO-CON System produces an "equivalent weight" or "volume weight" by multiplying cubed volume or summation volume by a predetermined, manually selected factor. Examples of typical factors are:

1. 250 cu. in./lb. or 6.9 lbs./cu. ft.—the domestic density factor for miscellaneous air cargo;
2. 266 cu. in./lb. or 6.5 lbs./cu. ft.—the density factor used for flower shipments;
3. 194 cu. in./lb. or 8.9 lbs./cu. ft.—the international density factor.

Multiplying the volume by these factors will provide an "equivalent weight" in pounds which is compared to the actual weight of the container in pounds. Generally, the larger of these two "weights" is used for billing purposes.

In many instances, the values of volume and weight which are obtained for individual items may be required on a total basis for a predetermined number of such items. Generally, these totals are required on a shipment basis, but may be totalized for pallets, aircraft, or aircraft sections for center-of-gravity determination or simply on a fixed-time basis for statistical purposes.

A second set of counters and memories is provided in CAPROCON to accumulate and store:

1. Accumulated summation volume;
2. Cubed volume total;
3. Accumulated weight in pounds or kilos;
4. Accumulated equivalent weight in pounds.

The automated sensing system has been given a detailed analysis because it is the first valid attempt to automate cargo stowage in containers. This system, together with "Equipment Inventory Cybernetics" described in Chapter 15, presents the possibility of further economy of scale. The CAPROCON System of United Airlines may be ahead of its time for use in air cargo containerization.

LONG-DISTANCE MOBILITY

*The evil which was suffered
patiently as inevitable, seems
unendurable as soon as the idea
of escaping from it crosses
men's minds.*
Alexis de Tocqueville, 1835

Railroad Transport Systems

ECONOMY OF SCALE

Cybernetics and systems engineering found a natural field in the railroads. The ratio between the extent of efficiency and the size of operation, commonly referred to as "economy of scale," applies primarily to railroad service. All other conveyances, such as ships, aircraft, and highway trucks, require major technological changes to attain the economy of scale. The railroads, in effect, could just increase their train size by adding more cars to make longer trains, and also by integrating modified cars into the mix of different types of cars, thereby producing unit trains of larger capacity.

Railroading is, therefore, the first industry where containerization was studied in depth. Labor cost in railroad operations is directly related to terminal efficiency and container size. (See Table 7-1.) Breaking and remaking of trains in switch yards accumulate most of the cost, while the line-haul produces most of the profit. This may be an oversimplification, but it has led to the idea of the unit train as the latest movement in the direction of reducing terminal costs at origin and destination and eliminating intermediate terminal costs.

TABLE 7-1. RAIL TERMINAL COSTS
(CENTS PER LOADED CUBIC FOOT)

Percent ER	Container Size				
	20-ft.	24-ft.	27-ft.	35-ft.	40-ft.
TOFC—Ramp					
0	4.04	3.22	2.91	2.49	2.21
50	4.42	3.52	3.17	2.68	2.47
100	4.70	3.82	3.43	3.08	2.70
TOFC—Top					
0	3.50	2.80	2.54	2.20	1.96
50	3.88	3.10	2.80	2.49	2.22
100	4.26	3.40	3.06	2.69	2.48
COFC—Top					
0	3.30	2.77	2.50	2.13	1.90
50	3.52	3.00	2.70	2.37	2.11
100	3.74	3.23	2.91	2.60	2.31

Source: U.S. Govt. Report V.

Railroads, of course, consider the boxcar as their own "container." While American boxcars went early to the 40-foot length with high inside cube, European boxcars—for example, in Great Britain—stayed at or under 20 feet. American bogies were designed for high-speed running and greater axle or carrying loads, while Europe stayed behind.

It looked as though the American boxcar itself would play an important role in international shipping, too. Ocean services by car between the United States and Cuba and between the United States and Alaska were as efficient as the train ferries of the Baltic Sea and Japan. These ocean services were conducted by West Indies Fruit and Steamship Company of West Palm Beach, Florida, and by Alaska Hydrotrain from Seattle, both using the roll-on, roll-off method. Seatrain Lines came up with a revolutionary design of the early '20s, which was *lifting* of full standard-size boxcars onto ships. These railroad ships originally operated between the East Coast ports of New York and Savannah, Georgia, and the Gulf ports of Belle Chase, Louisiana, and Texas City, Texas. An attempt to introduce this same lift-on service to Cuba was ruled out by a political maneuver of the competing West Indies Fruit and Steamship Company. The Seatrain ships eventually came to a capacity of about 100 railroad cars on several decks, until the company decided to containerize these ships in 1968. Thus, Seatrain Lines, which recently built the fastest gas turbine containerships for the Atlantic trade, is actually the offshoot of the pioneer in railroad containerization. Today on the American scene, the only successful roll-on rail–ship operation remaining connects the Canadian rail belt with Whittier, Alaska.

UNITIZATION ATTEMPTS

American railroads, going as large as the 89-ft. high-cube boxcar, for a long time considered themselves capable of the further "economy of scale" increase without having to go to the technology of true container-ization. An attempt was made by the N.Y. Central Railroad in the late '20s to create a container service, and this resulted in the formation of the L.C.L. (Less than Carload Lot) Corporation for merchandise traffic in the highly populated Eastern United States. However, this was never successful for more than the containerization of bulk cement. With the arrival of the Depression, the reduction of the volume of shipments led to a new look at the large carload shipments. The company produced the first viable method of transferring containers from a freight car to a truck chassis by pulling them off at the two ends of the railroad car by cable. Acme Fast Freight's first container attempt in 1929 did not survive, because the introduction of the L.C.L. rate structure by the railroad al-

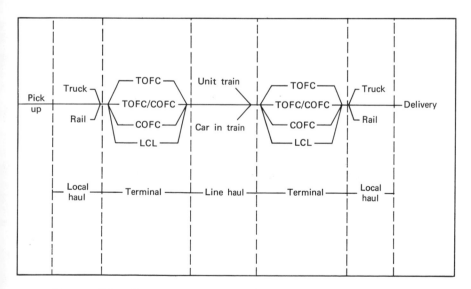

FIGURE 7-1. REPRESENTATIVE CONTAINER RAIL-FLOW ALTERNA-TIVES (SOURCE: U.S. GOVT. III).

lowed the freight forwarder (see discussion—Chapter 2) the possibility of earning his revenue by receiving L.C.L. shipments and consolidating them manually into a carload lot (Fig. 7-1).

PIGGYBACK

The most noteworthy step of railroading is the development of the so-called "piggyback" service. In this service, the railroads accept freight loaded in a highway vehicle by rolling the highway vehicle over a stern ramp onto the car. Since circus trains were customarily loaded this way, ramps were available at many locations and the type of train loading was called "circus fashion." Originally, this system had been used by the Paris-Lyon Mediterranean (PLM) Railroad, now a division of the French State Railroads, to bring fresh vegetables overnight to the market in Paris. The New Haven Railroad first copied this system in the '30s, and it was later expanded to give service between Boston and New York.

TOFC-COFC

Noting the development of the "piggyback" service, the New York Central Railroad, excluded from this method by clearance of height, reached back again for a container idea. Leo Mellam, Director of Transportation for the New York Central Railroad, developed, with the cooperation of Strick Trailer Company, a highway van which could be pushed against the railroad car. This railroad car is equipped with a turntable which receives the container, while the wheels remain on the ground. All that is necessary is to equip the loading tractor with one fifth wheel in front of the front axle. This wheel allows the tractor to push the container from the right angular position, where it started out, to the longitudinal position on the freight car for loading or unloading. This system became known as the "Flexi-Van" system. It is still used, with emphasis being placed on that of distributing mail in containers. To load and unload Flexi-Vans filled with mail, the trains have to stop merely at grade crossings.

Many ideas were developed during the '60s. The C & O Railroad spent a considerable amount of time developing a highway trailer equipped with a dual wheel system. This trailer could run on rails by lowering its railroad wheels and it could also run on the highway on its rubber tires. The B & O and the Missouri Pacific Railroads tried containerization with 17-foot containers. The Southern Railroad, too, was plagued by low tunnel structures in its territory. To participate in the ever-growing rail–highway traffic, the Southern Railway decided to go the route of 40-foot containers on flat cars. The system was so similar to the shipboard 40-foot containers, that in 1963, United States Lines leased a Southern Railway container to use in Europe for a period of two months, to determine container sizes and road conditions on the Continent. In effect, therefore, American railroads helped introduce shipboard containerization on the North Atlantic.

Table 7-2 compares the results for hauling containers in unit trains by using containers on chassis (TOFC) vs. containers without chassis (COFC) according to container size, number of cars and mileage. Table 7-3 compares the train line haul costs (TOFC vs. COFC) by size and by return distance.

START UP

Also during the '60s, railroads all over the world began to look at containerization itself to improve their own services. I recall having used

TABLE 7-2.   UNIT TRAIN LINE-HAUL COSTS
(CENTS PER CUBIC FOOT)

Ctr Size (ft.)	TOFC					
	1,000 Miles			3,000 Miles		
	45 Cars	60 Cars	90 Cars	45 Cars	60 Cars	90 Cars
20	8.47	8.20	6.30	25.4	24.6	19.6
24	8.62	8.42	6.56	24.8	24.2	18.8
27	7.68	7.48	5.83	22.2	21.5	16.8
35	8.73	8.46	5.96	26.2	25.5	19.9
40	7.71	7.47	5.29	23.0	22.4	18.9

Ctr Size (ft.)	COFC					
	1,000 Miles			3,000 Miles		
	45 Cars	60 Cars	90 Cars	45 Cars	60 Cars	90 Cars
20	7.09	6.49	4.92	19.2	19.0	14.9
24	7.27	6.66	5.30	20.3	20.0	15.8
27	6.56	6.01	4.81	19.1	18.0	14.2
35	7.60	6.96	4.82	20.8	20.6	16.3
40	6.66	6.10	4.04	18.3	19.3	14.2

Source: U.S. Govt. V.

TABLE 7-3.   TRAIN LINE-HAUL COSTS
(CENTS PER CUBIC FOOT)

Container Size	Empty Return	400 Miles		2000 Miles	
		TOFC	COFC	TOFC	COFC
20	50	7.70	5.28	36.3	26.2
	70	8.56	5.86	40.3	27.9
	100	9.85	6.73	46.3	32.0
24	50	6.11	5.50	28.8	26.7
	70	6.79	6.28	32.0	29.6
	100	7.81	7.12	36.7	33.9
27	50	5.49	5.03	25.8	24.0
	70	6.11	5.80	28.7	26.6
	100	7.03	6.41	32.9	30.5
35	0	4.38	4.09	20.0	19.5
	19	5.00	4.67	23.5	22.3
	50	6.01	5.63	28.4	26.9
40	0	3.83	3.61	18.2	17.2
	19	4.39	4.12	20.7	19.6
	50	5.30	4.97	25.0	23.7

Source: U.S. Govt. Report V.

the piggyback method on the Honduran Railroads, to overcome about 140 miles of bad highways. Also in 1965, we demonstrated for the Mexican National Railroads that trailer-on-flatcar service of 40-foot highway trailers could put them in the container business between Central America and the United States. How did it start? This era was the culmination of a trend which began with all the railroads around 1935. During that period, the International Chamber of Commerce Transport Committee came to the conclusion that in the interest of trade and for the benefit of the railroads, containerization should be implemented. When the International Container Bureau was organized as a section of the International Chamber of Commerce, its members were almost exclusively engaged in rail transportation, or in one form or the other of surface transport. During those days, only one steamship company, the Red Star Line of Arnold Bernstein, was the sole ocean conference carrier with the exclusive rights of transporting general cargo and automobile parts in containers in the transatlantic trade. Therefore, in 1970, when the International Railway Congress in London assembled 500 delegates from 40 different countries to discuss containerization and railroad involvement, it was after almost 35 years of a varied container history.

BIMODAL VS. INTERMODAL

Most railroads today are engaged in containerization in one form or another, particularly if you consider piggybacking a container on chassis or running gear. The breakthrough in *not* transporting the chassis and running gear is yet to come in the U.S. Almost all major railroads simultaneously operate two different types of containerization on their network. These two different types are:

1. Bimodal containerization to attract a larger share of the freight market or to handle it more economically;
2. Intermodal containerization, using shipboard containers to accommodate ocean carriers and to participate in international trade.

Bimodal containerization uses truck trailers or other highway vehicles or special containers either of the ISO or special system. This service uses the rail network as the main artery and as prime source of railroad revenue. The off-line service is given as an accommodation to the freight market. On the contrary, the intermodal container participation of the railroads is plugged into ocean services. In this phase, the railroads use mostly the steamship companies' ocean container equipment. However, when forced to cooperate, in order to obtain a share of well-paying traffic, the railroads have, in many instances, purchased intermodal ocean-type container equipment to qualify for interchange with ocean carriers.

Even though the railroad may handle both types of containerization with the same facilities and staff, there is a marked difference in the equipment and in the rules which govern this service. For example, deadheading of ocean containers is a practice which the railroads try to do away with. The container is a valuable element in the distribution chain only when it is at the right place at the right time. Otherwise, it turns into a costly and detrimental liability. In this respect, the railroads consider ocean containers as special equipment. They would rather let them sit empty at one spot or move them empty, than to use them in their own service. It is true, nevertheless, that a single carload of ocean containers would be of little or no value in a mass transportation system using boxcars and road trailers. However, the distinction is not so much in the physical dimension or specification, but in a conceptual difference of systems technology. The container is not something that can simply be plugged into the present system of rail transportation. It demands and deserves changes in the technology of distribution, in the relationship of carrier–consignee interest, and in the major segments of the shipping industry itself. It is not enough that the container approach embraces all the factors of distribution, supply, and demand inherent in the idea of door-to-door shipments. The container offers the railroads more than they presently have, if total systems integration is developed; but only then.

Boxcars have a greater cubic and weight-carrying capacity than containers. For example, Union Pacific's 40-foot boxcars vary in capacity from 3,180 to 5,028 cubic feet with lading capacity from 80,000 to 110,000 pounds. Its 50-foot boxcars vary in capacity from 3,505 to 6,051 cubic feet with lading capacity from 100,000 to 182,000 pounds. To aid in making a comparison, it should be stated that a container of the 8′ × 8′ standard size produces a cubic space of approximately 50 cubic feet per each foot of running length. In other words, a 20′ dry-cargo container usually has about 1,000 cubic feet.

PER DIEM

Railcar per diem is higher than that applicable to containers. Since railcar per diem is based on a combination of four factors—valuation, age of car, line-haul mileage charge, and daily time charge—all four factors go into the building of the total charge applicable to each individual car. The Railway Equipment Register contains a car hire rate table applicable to all cars in the United States. The daily time charge is applicable per calendar day.

There are no uniform per diem rates applicable to marine containers in railroad service. Rates applicable on days the equipment is in revenue service are as follows:

1. 20-foot containers—$2.50 with or without chassis;
2. 40-foot containers—$5.00 with or without chassis.

PROCESS EXTENSION

Railroads can use containerization to improve their own service. The motivating forces of the production industry are imposting the impact of containerization on surface transportation, as well as on marine transportation. Some of the industries have reduced production cost at a low level but further reductions must be achieved. Fig. 7-2 shows the annual unit cost for the facilities required for gantry crane operation of containers, as related to the number of lifts per day. For one, in our production work rules, duplication and terminal process require urgent reformation to improve rail transportation service. This emphasizes the need to search for possibilities to improve functions other than manufacturing. Such a search deals with the stages prior to and after production and deals mostly with handling, storage, and distribution. The adaptability of the container allows it to become part of the production stage. Elimination of costly packing and crating represents for the manufacturer a very important advantage of time, cost, and damage prevention. The intermodal container, at the same time, can serve as a storage facility. A large soap company in the United States first explored "open-air" storage of their soap products in closed 40-foot standard intermodal containers at almost half the cost of warehousing. Containerization is so much more cost-effective than palletization and other forms of unitization, that a substantial impact of the system would be felt if pressure were brought by industry on the railroads.

By far the largest containerization system for railroads is the use of highway trailers on top of flat cars. This service is commonly known as "Trailer-on-Flatcar (TOFC) Service" or by its popular name of "piggyback." Originally, this service used any of the existing available standard flat cars, but during the last twenty years, the American railroads have developed a preference for a car that can accommodate two 40-foot highway trailers. The two trailers are separated by a space averaging three feet in the center of the car. There are several types of connecting

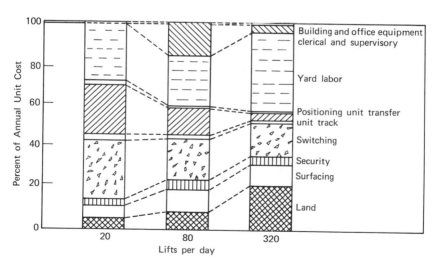

FIGURE 7-2. COMPARATIVE ANALYSIS OF ANNUAL UNIT COSTS FOR A GANTRY CRANE (SOURCE: LITTON INDUSTRIES).

fifth wheel plates—some reset and some hydraulically elevated, while others are installed mechanically by the tractor moving across the car. There is also a special screw-type tool used in small stations.

THE PLANS

TOFC service has been developed into five plans (Table 7-4) which are defined as follows:

Plan I: Railroad–Motor Carrier Joint Intermodal Service

Railroads transport trailers of motor common carriers in substituted rail-for-highway service, the traffic moving at all-motor rates on motor carrier bills of

TABLE 7-4.   U.S. RAIL TOFC PLANS

Plan	Equipment Ownership	Service	Pricing
1	Rail carrier supplies car, motor carrier supplies trailer or container.	Rail carrier hauls between rail terminals, motor carrier performs pickup and delivery.	Motor carrier tariff (motor carrier and rail carrier negotiate nonpublished price for rail haul).
2	Rail carrier supplies both car and trailer or container.	Door-to-door, including pickup, delivery, pickup and delivery, or neither.	Rail tariff.
3	Rail carrier supplies car, shipper supplies trailer or container.	Same as Plan 2.	Rail tariff.
4	Shipper supplies both car and trailer or container.	Same as Plan 2.	Rail tariff per car.
5	Rail carrier supplies car, motor carrier or rail carrier supplies trailer or container.	Door-to-door.	Joint rail–motor carrier tariff.

Source: U.S. Govt. Report III.

lading. The motor carrier takes trailers to and picks them up at railroad TOFC terminals, and performs any required road-haul before or after the rail movement. The railroad has no direct contact with the shipper. When the rail carrier furnishes the trailer, a per-trip fee is assessed for use of that equipment.

Plan II: Railroad Operation, Door-to-Door

The railroads carry their own trailers at rail rates on railroad billing, performing a complete service, including pickup and delivery. Rail rates are competitive with those published by motor carriers.

Plan II-A: Railroad Operation, Ramp-to-Ramp

The railroads perform the same type of service as described under Plan II, except patrons may elect or may be required to perform pickup and/or delivery service between their places of business and point adjacent to rail carriers' ramps. For performing such service, they receive (when authorized by tariff) a per-trailer allowance and pay user charges (when applicable) named in carriers' tariffs.

Plan III: Shippers' Trailers, Rail Carriers' Railcars, Ramp-to-Ramp

The railroads carry the shippers' trailers and the shipper delivers the trailers to the rail ramp. The rail carrier places them on flat cars, secures them, transports them to the destination ramp, and grounds them. The shipper then picks them up at the destination rail terminal.

Plan IV: Shippers' Trailers, Shippers' Rail Cars, Ramp-to-Ramp

The railroads carry two shippers' trailers on shippers' flat car at a published charge per flat car. The railroads perform terminal-to-terminal line-haul movement only. When the rail carrier supplies the trailer and/or railcar to the shipper, a per-trip fee named in the tariff is assessed for use of that equipment.

Plan V: Railroad–Motor Carrier Joint Intermodal Service

The railroads carry their own trailers or highway carriers' trailers under joint rail–truck rates on an end-to-end basis. Plan V is physically similar to Plan I, but is a true joint operation which, in effect, extends the territory of each participating carrier into that served by the other, permitting each participant to handle shipments originating in or destined to the other's territory, and allows each to sell for the other. This plan involves a motor carrier road-haul on one or both ends of the rail movement.

TERMINAL LINK TIMES

Piggyback operation has shown an almost continuous growth of nearly 10 percent per year. As a result of that, the railroads have seen themselves forced to develop a higher capacity of container-handling systems. For the time being, there are eight systems being employed, each of which has certain advantages and disadvantages.

Conventional End Loading (circus fashion): Requires least amount of land and minimum initial investment but also requires much shunting of cars. Transfer times are long due to the fact that each trailer has to be moved to the end of the train. Maximum length of the loading track is approximately eight 85-foot cars, longer tracks being difficult to load. The crew consists of a hitch man and driver—remainder of crew ranging from 1 to 4, depending on volume.

Rubber-Tire Gantry: Requires large investment cost of crane and concrete paving. Very flexible for both trailer and containers. Crew consists of a train man, hitch man, and two tractor drivers. Average loading time:

Unload from cars	2.31 minutes/trailer or container
Load to cars	2.39 minutes/trailer or container
Average	2.35 minutes/trailer or container.

Rail Gantry: Initial investment is less than half of the cost of the rubber-tire gantry. No hitch man is needed. Crane has same flexibility as rubber-tire gantry. Usual crew consists of train operator and two tractor drivers. Observed actual crane cycle time, including travel:

Trailer—2.80 minutes; Container—3.82 minutes.

See Fig. 7-3 for a cost comparison between ramp and gantry crane systems.

Wheeled Side Loaders: The investment is less than in gantries, but speed and flexibility are similar. Crew consists of operator, hitch man, and two tractor drivers. Requires more paved land area than gantry crane. Because of fast loading cycle, trailer delivery often exceeds loader time, thereby setting pace for transfer time.

Tractor Side Loader: Flexi-Van system restricted to container handling of special containers and special railroad cars. Requires large paved areas.

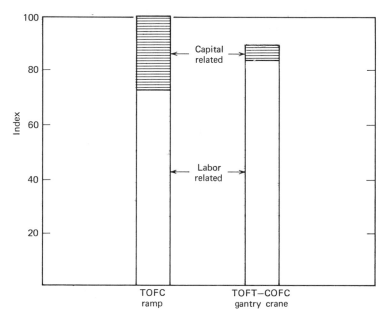

Figure 7-3.   Rail terminal cost per transfer (Source: Litton Industries).

Mechanical Truck Unit Side Loader: Interpool or Steadman system. Transfer procedure consists in unloading of container via side loader and reloading of delivery unit. On occasion, transfer unit delivers container. Observed actual transfer time with delivery is:

Unload to side loader	.99 minutes/container
Reload to delivery unit	.88 minutes/container
Related travel	.68 minutes/container
Total	2.55 minutes/container.

Land area requirements are small. Initial investment for container chassis at the terminal far exceeds cost of truck side unit. Not capable of handling trailers.

Hydraulic Truck Unit Side Loader: Physically, this is almost identical to mechanical truck, except purchase price is less. This system can also use detachable legs for "set down." The observed actual average transfer time without delivery is:

Unload to side loader	1.45 minutes/container
Reload to delivery unit	1.23 minutes/container
Related travel	.68 minutes/container
Total	3.36 minutes/container.

Self-Powered Trailer Side Loader: This system tops all loading methods for minimum personnel requirement and transfer cycle time. Trailer side loader is also delivery unit. The average actual transfer cycle time observed is 2.02 minutes per container. Minimum labor cost offset by huge initial investment in self-powered trailers: high cost of license tags and insurance to be paid by owner of transfer trailers due to state laws. Consequently, this best transfer-cycle-time loader has penalty of requiring the largest original equipment investment and related licensing and insurance.

Few of these gantry straddle front-end loader systems handle both containers and trailers. In order to obtain this equal treatment, additional capital investment is required, which indicates the need to analyze the value of a limited system in view of the capabilities of a more general commonly adaptable containerization system.

As indicated above, the limited piggyback system requires high investments in equipment and facility to become cost-effective. There are, of course, means to improve the labor/investment ratio. Piggyback yards can be automated for computerized handling. This would require overhead rail-operated gantrys to pick up and load containers or trailers on the railroad car. The great advantage of an automated computerized piggyback yard would be the fact that the railroad could then operate with a true unit train and save the cost of train make-up. If automation is to become the selected method, then the overall system should be designed around the container and its most cost-effective employment. Figure 7-4 shows an economic evaluation of various transfer systems.

INTERCHANGE RULES

The Association of American Railroads has set up interchange rules which govern the interchange of, repairs to, and settlement for the use of trailers and containers in this type of service. Containers of steamship services are considered as "foreign" equipment. To accept this equipment, most railroads require the trailer to be equipped with 8-wheel container chassis. Therefore, these rules are usually referred to as "rubber rules," where the main line service is given by the railroads providing flat cars for rubber-tire-equipped trailers or containers. Also, delivery and

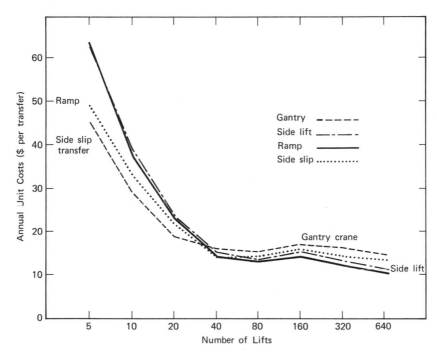

FIGURE 7-4. ECONOMIC EVALUATION OF VARIOUS TERMINAL TRANSFER SYSTEMS—UNIT COST VERSUS VOLUME (SOURCE: LITTON INDUSTRIES).

pickup are made as road vehicles. These rules also deal with the inspection of equipment, particularly in the case of damage to the equipment.

RAIL CONTAINERS

Two railroads in the United States operate container systems, as mentioned before. The New York Central Railroad uses the Flexi-Van system. Several connecting railroads also place this type of equipment in their service, more or less, to allow through-movements originated by the New York Central Railroad. Since the transfer components on the Flexi-Van are located on the bottom rail, they do not interfere with the standard ISO corner casting and pickup system. Therefore, the Flexi-Van system has been extended to destinations in Europe and Japan. But basically, this system is restricted to the owner of the Flexi-Van-equipped railroad cars. Typical container trainload services are illustrated in Table 7-5.

TABLE 7-5. TYPICAL CONTAINER TRAINLOAD SERVICES CAN
BE ILLUSTRATED BY THE FOLLOWING THREE PLANS

Plan	Source	Service	Rate
1	Union Pacific, Norfolk and Western, Western Pacific.	Coast–Coast, F.A.K. between foreign points only.	$1,020 per car in trains of more than 30 cars, carrier supplies car.
2	AT&SF, Penn-Central.	Coast–Coast, F.A.K. between foreign points only.	$72,000 per 80-car train, shipper supplies car.
3	Northern Lines.	Pacific Coast–Midwest, F.A.K. imports only.	$48,900 per 60-car train, carrier supplies car.

The Southern Railway has developed containers of all sizes, in addition to their 40-footers. The Southern Railway was forced into this business by its reduced tunnel clearances. Since the Containerized captive system was developed by the Southern, it became successful. Then, in addition to this, the Southern increased its tunnel clearances, usually by lowering the roadbeds in the tunnel. Hence, the Southern now operates in both piggyback and container services. The Southern system is based on picking up containers with a clamp from the two leading edges at the bottom of the container.

The great depth of the development of bimodal container systems comes from Great Britain, France, Germany, and Japan. The European group was led by the British in the development of the "Liner Train." These are trains designed for maximum speeds of 75 miles per hour and axle loads between $17\frac{1}{2}$ and 25 tons. The Liner Train is operated like a steamship operation between fixed terminals. Generally speaking, the facilities are made available to the trucking companies in Great Britain. However, in 1968, a National Freight Corporation was established in cooperation with the British Railways Board and the British Road Service, to give integrated service to the shipping public. The "Freightliner" container was begun in 1963. See Fig. 7-5. At this time, although the ISO recommendations relative to overall length, width, and height were reasonably well established, the design of corner fittings and handling procedures was not finalized.

The British Railways were interested, essentially, in their domestic container projects; and their containers were, therefore, built for the requirements of the internal system. The container selected was 30 feet long. However, in making provisions for the transfer equipment, British Railways were able to convert their domestic system into one which is fully capable of handling both their own internal 30-foot containers and

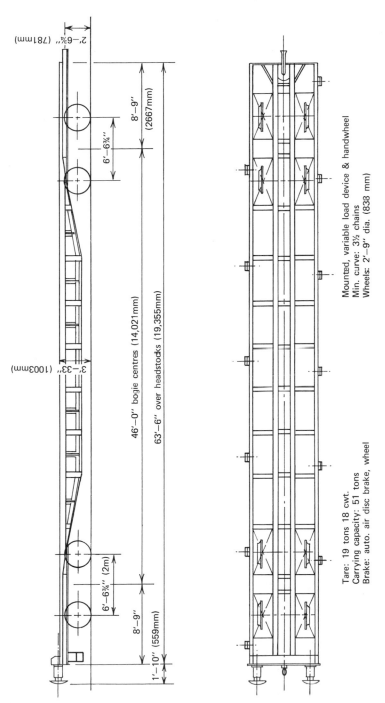

2'-6⅞" (781mm)

8'-9" (2667mm)

6'-6¾"

46'-0" bogie centres (14,021mm)

63'-6" over headstocks (19,355mm)

3'-33" (1003mm)

6'-6¾" (2m)

8'-9"

1'-10" (559mm)

Tare: 19 tons 18 cwt.
Carrying capacity: 51 tons
Brake: auto. air disc brake, wheel

Mounted, variable load device & handwheel
Min. curve: 3½ chains
Wheels: 2'-9" dia. (838 mm)

FIGURE 7-5. FREIGHTLINER CONTAINER CAR (SOURCE: BRITISH RAIL).

standard ISO equipment. This led to very interesting railroad-car features. But the British pioneering spirit did not stop there; in order to accommodate domestic cargo, they also designed an open-flat container with an overall body width of 8'6" (2590 mm). Thereafter, a box container was designed 1 millimeter wider (2591 mm.), and all of this equipment is being handled concurrently. This confirms the rule that man's ingenuity can cope with coordination problems, if necessary.

THE FREIGHTLINERS

Recently, the German and French railroads have joined with the British railroads in the European rail container system. Now, therefore, the railroads in Europe are dealing with all kinds of containers; not only on their transfer equipment, but also on their cars. Basically, European railroads consider containers in four main categories:

1. The ISO standard, including the 35-foot, Sea-Land containers;
2. The Transcontainer for European service with a length from 10 to 40 feet, specified in weight groups: 10t/10 ft., 20t/20 ft., 25t/30 ft., 30t/40 ft., as specified in UIC Memorandum No. 592-1 (See Fig. 7-6 and 7-7);
3. The Overland containers, also known as T-Containers, also 10 to 40 feet long, but whose roof area matches the dome-shaped loading gauge of European railroads, per UIC Memorandum No. 592-2;
4. The railroad containers. which are now basically 2.5 m wide and, therefore, not interchangeable with an ISO system.

European railroads also accept within their system, three other groups of containers:

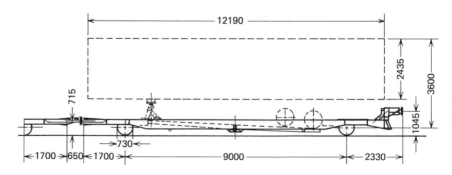

FIGURE 7-6. EUROPEAN TRANS-CONTAINER MULTIPLE-USE CAR (SOURCE: TRANS-CONTAINER).

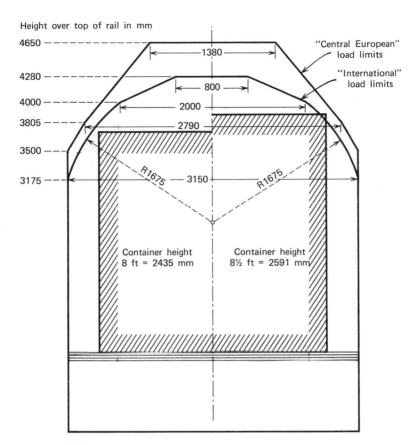

Height over top of rail in mm

4650 — — — — — — — — — — — "Central European" load limits

"International" load limits

4280 — — — — — — — —

4000 — — — — — —

3805 — — — —

3500 — — —

3175 — —

1380

800

2000

2790

R1675 — 3150 — R1675

Container height
8 ft = 2435 mm

Container height
8½ ft = 2591 mm

FIGURE 7-7.   EUROPEAN   TRANS-CONTAINER   LOAD   LIMITS
(SOURCE: TRANS-CONTAINER).

1. "Flats"—These are large pallets with or without side panels. They must be handled by grab claws and are equipped with "grip edges." Flats with folding side panels can be stacked in great numbers for empty return.

2. "Swap Bodies"—This is any container to use in continuous land transport, and may be transferred by roll-on or lift-on method. Bodies differ from containers, in that they are built of lighter materials and more like a packing box. The width always is 2.5 m, but the length varies from 6 to 12 m.

3. Air Freight Containers—Standard belly containers for airplanes are acceptable to European railroads.

TOLERANT SYSTEM

The spectrum of container systems in Europe had emerged already in 1930 from the long stagnation of the railroad operating methods. We classify the existing coordinated containerization as a "tolerant system." In the market that is open to the modes of containerization, the acceptance of all kinds of containers, in addition to the handling of railroad monomodal services, is a significant systems approach. The German railroads since 1930 have accepted "small containers" (Klein-Rehalter), which are really large packing boxes equipped with casters and pallet openings for ease of handling within other containers on flats or in boxcars. This facility was developed to attract traffic from small manufacturers to assembly plants, since it saves the cost of intermediate product packing, and otherwise would have gone to trucks providing direct service. This is very much like the very special small containers in the U.S. used prior to the advent of interline piggybacking, which really gave the U.S. railroads their thrust when some decided that they could work with truckers by hauling semitrailers on flat cars.

At the time when piggybacking got its major thrust in the early '50s, Gene Ryan and Paul Turner, who were then General Sales Managers for the Electro-Motive Division of General Motors, felt that railroads had a great opportunity to be the mode of moving many of the trailers that were traveling between cities on highways. They interested General Motors, through the Electro-Motive Division, to the extent where General Motors did some design work as an industry effort comparable to the work they had done on the Train of Tomorrow and to how much goodwill and favorable image reaction they had obtained. They went so far as to build a ramp at LaGrange and showed a large-scale model of the same thing at the railroad exhibit at Atlantic City. This was a system wherein either the rail tracks were depressed or the loading platforms were elevated so that the trailers could ride on and off flatcars, because both flatcars and the loading and unloading area were at the same level.

Unfortunately, no railroads were imaginative enough to see how piggybacking could grow to make that initial investment for such a terminal. Building stub-end ramps or inclines at a terminal or team track cost so much less that they started with the circus loading method.

From that time on, there have been a number of special designs of that nature that the Japanese have developed. Notable amongst these are some designs of Alan Cripe, who also worked with Ken Brown of the C & O combination rail/highway car and also that version of Talgo-Aero-Train X scheme that became the United Aircraft train design built for the C & O and the Department of Transportation as Turbotrains.

THE JAPANESE WAY

Not all railroad container systems, however, accept the large variety of container sizes within their operating structure. The outstanding example of a different standpoint is the one operated by the Japanese National Railways. According to M. Hashimoto, Chief of Container Services of the Japanese National Railways, it was the government direction to provide the most rational means of instituting integrated freight traffic which led to the present Japanese system. Japanese rail containerization uses only two types of containers; these are 8' × 8' × 10' with a capacity of 5 tons and 8' × 8' × 20' with a capacity of 10 tons. Of the 200,000,000 tons of freight hauled by JNR in a year, 4 percent is now containerized in these containers, but it is expected that the tonnage will increase to 50,000,000 tons. Commodities moving in Japan in containers include many commodities that are handled in other countries by conventional means of transportation. This unique container is integrated into an area distribution system. All container stations are considered according to their freight traffic as Class A, B, or C bases. The service between 22 Class A stations is provided by Freightliner-type trains similar to the Liner trains in Great Britain. Space on these trains is fixed in advance, with the location of all the containers to be loaded on the trains for a period of 7 to 10 days set on a magnetic disc on the central railroad computer. As the central computer has terminal sets in every base station, city terminal, and depot, the entire container system is operated on real-time on-line. When a client or his forwarding agent applies for space reservation for a certain number of containers on a designated train for shipment, on a designated day between designated stations, the data are transmitted from the terminal set to the central computer. All the shipper has to do is to bring his container in time for the train. If no space were to be available on a designated train, the best alternative is sought by the computer. The same happens if the shipper misses his start-up time.

THE ITRAN SYSTEM

Since growth in piggyback traffic is vital to both the railroad and the economy, General Electric's Locomotive Operation Planning Section has conceived a new concept, appropriately named ITRAN, for quickening the pace of intermodal transfer. Phil Noble, GE's developer, is responsible for the design of and economic studies on the system; and he describes ITRAN as an automated approach to the interchange of trailers and containers between rail, highway, and ship transportation modes.

By integrating automated handling with automated processing documents, ITRAN is said to reduce the time, manpower, and land required for trailer interchange, thus dramatically improving service while lowering the total cost per transfer. These reduced cost and improved service factors may very well hold the key to the future of TOFC/COFC operation.

Since ITRAN performs all transfers on an elevated guideway which does not interfere with the rail right-of-way or with ground traffic, it eliminates ground congestion and allows trains to run through the yard with minimum delay. The system doesn't impose any restrictions on train length or require breaking up the train and switching cars. Actual transfers are accomplished by automated cars electrically powered from a third rail built into the guideway. These cars take a trailer or container from the incoming tractor through storage and load it on the train. Each car receives its instructions from the yard computer which generates and continually updates the loading/unloading schedule. These instructions are communicated to wayside signal stations which, in turn, transmit them to the car control system.

The overhead guideway, which can be designed in any configuration from a simple loop to a complex network, not only eliminates interference of highways and rails with the transfer cars, but also allows high-density ground storage of trailers and containers. A basic system for handling approximately 100 trailers per day with storage for 100 trailers in transit and 200 empties would measure 1,440 ft. long and 270 ft. wide, and would cover about nine acres. The guideway would consist of a primary running loop and a switch with a short spur as a maintenance area. To provide the interface, 1,200 ft. of the guideway would run over a rail siding.

In this particular yard, the rail interface is designed to handle 13 TOFC cars at a time. Size of the trains which can be accommodated is limited only by the length of the rail siding. The truck interface consists of a row of stalls under the guideway. Trailers are positioned by their drivers and left for pickup by the transfer car.

The design advantage of this system is that it combines the overhead gantry system used in many manufacturing plants for conveying materials and components with the automated material-storing system in some very advanced warehouse and stores facilities in industry. With respect to the latter, for example, Union Tank Car, at its new Chicago Tank Car plant, has compressed its stores area very greatly and at the same time draws specific materials from the area merely by inserting a programmed card into a palletizing unit that goes to the storage bin, as instructed by the programmer.

What's significant about these approaches is that they consider handling of the container at the interface as a materials handling problem. The General Electric and Japanese approaches, in particular, come very close to more sophisticated automated material-handling systems or highly mechanized production-line systems that have been put into manufacturing plants for the purpose of increasing productivity.

AUTOMATIC RELOADING

The container reloading device is made up of sheath-like arms, similar to the telescopic arms of a stacker crane ordinarily used in a multilevel warehouse, that can be elongated or shortened in three stages, and a device that moves the arms up and down.

The arms extend like the fork of a fork lift to scoop up the container at spot #1 of the "A" train, and when shortened, they bring the container to where the reloading bogie is located. Then the reloading machine runs, on its own guide rails, and stops at the #2 spot of the "B" train, where the machine stretches out its arms to place the container on the indicated spot. In order to make the reloading machine automatically stop accurately at #1 or #2 spot, steel pieces on the side of the freight car underframe indicate the center spot of the containers. The reloader is equipped with a metal-approach switch which can detect the steel pieces. When the position of the foremost container on the train is made the basic point, the reloading machine counts the steel pieces while running on the rail, and can easily remove whichever container is desired to be taken off the train. If this number is recorded in advance on the tape and put into the computer of the reloading machine, container loading and unloading operations can be automated.

The time required for one cycle operation; that is, the reloading machine running from the midpoint of 1 and 2, to point 1 where the container is lifted off the wagon, and returning to the original point after placing the container at point 2; is 140 seconds for the distance of 17 m between points 1 and 2. Simulation with a computer revealed that reloading of 10 containers takes 9 minutes and 25 seconds.

If it becomes possible to unload containers in a short time from a container train that has come to a stop at a class C base station, and then have the train leave from the same spot, it might be said that great progress has been made. The conventional method of having to pull a train from the main line onto a side track with no overhead wiring, using a shunting locomotive, and then to do the unloading with fork lifts, has surely been costly.

Generally speaking, a greater part of the traffic moves along trunk lines.

According to investigations conducted at several junctions on the Sanyo Main Line of JNR, only 5 percent or fewer of the freight cars of each train were taken off to branch lines or to local lines. Adding those cars coupled or uncoupled at the junction stations, the maximum reached only about 25 percent. Most cars ran on in the same direction. This goes to show how wasteful it is to break up and make up whole trains in yards, as has been the practice.

Besides the transferring of containers from one train to another, the reloading machine is capable of unloading containers onto the ground, as well as transferring containers among more than two trains, using the lifters in combination, though this requires an underground passage set up at a right angle to the track group.

The only difficulty is that it is not easy to reload containers from or onto trucks; that is to say, for the truck to stop at the right spot in parallel to the reloading machine, keeping a specified space in between.

SUBSYSTEM BASICS

All rail containerization deals with the five basic subsystems which determine the effectiveness of the rail-container operation:

1. Rolling stock adapted for the intended use;
2. Container handling yards with terminals designed for the types of containers and cars;
3. Unit trains or "block trains" made up of container cars;
4. Container train schedules;
5. Tariff structure for container marketing.

ROLLING STOCK

Trailer Train Company, which supplies piggyback cars for both trailers and containers on flatcars to all railroad members, has four all-purpose cars:

1. TTX 101—*Cushioning:* 15-in. hydraulic draft gear. *Hitch:* noncushioned, tractor-operated. *Pedestals:* noncushioned, adjustable for 20-, 24-, 35-, and 40-foot containers, fold into car deck. *Hand brake:* fold down.
2. TTX 102—*Cushioning:* Cushioned pedestals and hitch. *Hitch:* tractor-operated. *Pedestals:* nonadjustable, fold into car deck. *Hand brake:* fold down.

3. TTX 103—*Cushioning:* Cushioned pedestals and hitch. *Hitch:* tractor-operated. *Pedestals:* nonadjustable, fold into car deck. *Hand brake:* does not fold down.

4. TTX 104—*Cushioning:* Cushioned rub rail and hitch. *Hitch:* tractor-operated. *Bolsters:* adjustable to any length resting on 5½"-high raised center sill (storage space in center sill for four bolsters). *Hand brake:* fold down.

There are also, among the railroads, three cars which are experimental at this stage but which have significance as future components of the container system:

1. The Eugene Ryan Conback Car—This is a well car which can accommodate either two piggyback trailers or six 20-foot containers;

2. North American Car Company's Portager Car—This is a skeleton car designed for one 40-foot or two 20-foot containers, but has the possibility of being extended to cope with the new 45-foot trailers permitted in highway transportation in certain states;

3. McClasky Car Adapters—These adapters convert a standard flatcar into a container by applying certain attachment devices in the car's stake pockets.

Most railroad cars used in Europe are the four-wheel, two-axle wagons with two bogies. The axle loading is limited; therefore, the permissible axle load on European cars seldom exceeds 20 tons per axle. Generally, the weight ratio per axle for the same wagon is limited to 2 for a two-axle car and 3 for a car with two bogies.

If one evaluates the savings in dead weight between containers and trailers, it appears that there is a 4-ton saving for each 40-foot container. A 55-vehicle train could save 220 tons of trailing weight. An additional 195 tons per train could be saved by the possible use of lighter-weight cars, according to Frank Richter of *Progressive Railroading* magazine. With a lowered center of gravity and reduced wind resistance, a trailer train could easily run at speeds of 90 to 100 miles per hour.

Many European cars have the tolerance of the system built into them. In other words, they will allow transportation of containers of almost any system on the same car and still provide for speedy loading and unloading. Safety in transit and protection of the containers against shock during the hauling have been thoroughly developed, and two types of measure have been adopted:

1. Installing powerful shock absorbers or other devices capable of absorbing kinetic energy developed during the shock;

2. Avoiding passage of container or trailer cars through marshaling yards where large numbers of switches would produce shock.

In both cases, the container, in principle, must be made solid with parts of the underframe of the railroad car by means of adequate securing devices. A minimum of resistance required by European railroads for all container equipment tie-down is 2 g, which equals a gravity acceleration of 19.62 m/sec. The length of the cars for container or trailer service is as follows:

1. Europe/Japan—two axles = 40 feet;
2. Europe/Japan—two axled bogies = 60 feet;
3. United States/Mexico/Canada—two bogies = 86 feet.

CONYARDS

The new systems have brought about complete changes in classical freight yards. Sidings, ramps, and freight houses are now replaced by two yards. In the container-handling yard (Conyard), containers are kept between the rail–highway interface. In the container terminal, these containers are physically exchanged between railcars and other conveyances. Each terminal installation must be developed according to the task it is to perform, and the conditions under which these functions must be performed. The methods used by the railroads influence the arrangement of the container yard. There are two basic possibilities:

1. Railcars are moved individually or in groups at the origin and destination through the marshaling yards to a piggyback facility;
2. Unit trains or groups of cars remain unchanged between journeys and require no marshaling.

Since the American railroads handle "rubber" delivery for the piggyback trains, most other railroads follow this example rather than to operate rail feeders with their connected and related costs. Therefore, the handling-yard system becomes really a link between either of two rail services—a rail service and a highway service, or a rail service and a ship service. Of course, the faster the equipment is transferred, the less cost in labor is involved. On the other hand, transit without waiting requires availability of a great number of vehicles in the next link to reduce the subsystem time of the transfer. Therefore, the transport chain system must determine which delay time and which scheduling of subsystems functions most economically and in the interest of the freight market. Of course, the Japanese system, with its monolithic preplanning and storage, provides possibly the optimal service; but is possible only under economic conditions prevailing in Japan.

AUTOMATION OF TRANSFER LINK

The automation of the transfer link is the major task of rail transportation in the generation to come. There is no other technological obstacle of magnitude to be overcome. The problems will be just like those with containerships—the risk taking of new and large investments. A typical automated container yard is able to handle both storage of containers and loading of railroad cars without human hands. In this system, both containers and trailers can be used; and it is a tolerant system, impervious to container size and dimensions. This is the chance for railroad automation. As the growth of traffic volume proceeds and the cost of highly technical labor advances, railroading must search for the ultimate productivity.

All yard links of railroads are designed to handle both containers and piggyback. Therefore, railroad yards must be adapted to efficient transfer of both the containers and trailers, which are components of bimodal rail systems, as well as all ocean and intermodal container systems.

This is a multifacet inlet–outlet problem, in which there are three key systems components:

1. Temporary land site storage;
2. Physical transfers at entry, exit, and internal relocation;
3. Search and identification of the constant inventory.

The major constraints occur in the interface of the handling and storage systems at entry into the yard link, at exit from the yard link, and upon moving about within the yard from vehicular mode to storage and vice versa. Railroads have been troubled by the almost unavoidable delay of train make-up in the marshaling yard. As combined container systems terminals become congested, more emphasis is placed on stacking containers as a means of solving the land problem. Apparently, advance container terminals are experiencing major difficulties when combined with port terminals. Experience has shown that purposely designed separation of functions provides better results than integration of the dual functions in one yard. A typical functioning separated terminal is the Freightliner terminal at Parkeston Quay near Harwich, 25 miles outside of London. In this yard, "rubber delivery" is used between the dockside gantry area, the storage area, and the secondary rail-gantry system. Transfer systems have been described in this context, as connected with American piggyback operation (see Terminal Link). These can be augmented by a conveyor system presently being developed for Rijn Port, the new integrated terminal facility for Europort at Rotterdam.

Since the location of each container or trailer must be systematized, so that each unit's whereabouts can be accurately and quickly established, the time and labor expenditures definitely justify three automation features which lend themselves very well to the use of conveyor belts between subsystem areas. These three elements are:

1. Identification of all movable equipment, such as containers, trailers, railcars, and chassis, in the area;
2. Centralized, computerized inventory control;
3. Efficient command/control teleprinter network.

With these three elements, the efficient yard can expedite not only its internal economic transfer systems, but also the loading cycle of ships and the effective planning of train movements, which are the critical dimensions in intermodal systems.

SCANNING

Scanning is automated speed reading, popular in all phases of computerization today. In the railroad terminal, there must be scanners keeping an eye on all inventories, as well as access and exit links. The scanners, which are described in connection with container-yard operation in Chapter 15, are set up to identify labels affixed to the side of a vehicle or container. The essential theory is that freight containers and railroad cars should not be treated as storage warehouses, but instead be kept moving as much as possible, so that they can approximate closely the idea of a moving pipeline of goods. This, as far as railroads are concerned, leads to the unit train proposed at the 11th Pan American Railroad Congress by William B. Saunders in 1963, and now commonly accepted. When a train operates continuously in a given service, it forms a shuttle; but when a train moves solidly without breaking up, it is called the "unit train," even if it does not operate between the same points. "Block trains" are a development for smaller railway operations. The block of cars can be shunted from a unit train at the final terminal to a conventional train if, for example, a large section of the unit train should go to a secondary destination. Block trains are, therefore, subsystems at the ship–rail interface, which provide further systems integration between the two elements.

Unit trains have been used in the United States as single-commodity trains carrying such products as ore, grain, liquid bulk, and coal. However, the greatest application of the unit train is the dramatic importance of its utilization in railroad containerization. Utilization of the equipment is the key factor in determining the relative value of replacing the old conventional system by containerization. The example of the Japanese railroads, described heretofore, is self-evident.

An experiment conducted in Europe, named "Terre" (Trans-European Railroad Express), operated for several years as a private container service. Eventually, it has led to the formation of the European specialized railroad container train unit called "Inter-container," which handles all international container traffic with European railroads.

A good example of a container unit train is the Sante Fe "Super C" which operates between Chicago and Los Angeles in 40 hours. Sante Fe has thrown down a bold challenge to trucking and air with this premium Super C service a 2,200-mile run, but does so at a price higher than normal rail rates.

Super C service, for piggyback and containers only, is available every day except Sunday from both Chicago and Los Angeles. At present, the train runs straight through with no intermediate pickups or setoffs, although consideration is being given to adding a stop at Kansas City. The Super C is the world's fastest freight train, but it is more significant than that. Heretofore, most railroads have stressed competing in terms of price, with services that are often slower or otherwise inferior to those of other modes. With the Super C, Sante Fe is taking exactly the opposite approach; it is charging a high price and bidding for high-rated traffic entirely on the basis of service.

The Super C evolved from studies by Sante Fe's market research group, an arm of the traffic department. These studies showed that a significant and growing volume of "premium" freight was moving by truck and air freight between the midwest and the west coast. This premium freight consists of truck, air, air freight forwarder, REA, and parcel post traffic that Sante Fe believes is more service sensitive than price sensitive.

The Scandinavians have been well aware of the Super C service. They contend that they would like to do the same thing, but lacking the potential for full-train business in their countries, particularly in Sweden, they are working on giving special service for container movements in their "mixed consist" high speed freight trains. The most outstanding container unit trains are the Canadian CN and CP between Atlantic ports such as Halifax and St. John and the interior and U.S. midwest.

Unit train and containerization integration was shown to have return effect in the distribution of both fresh and conserved foodstuffs in the U.S. Frank Macomber and James Benjamin of A. T. Kearney developed a special mini-piggy train which would allow low-cost handling of unit trains at many stations equipped only with a portable trailer handler. In effect, this system would be quite similar to the system developed by Leo Mellam and Sol Katz of Strick Trailers.

The cost of owning, maintaining, and depreciating containers and railroad cars is a function of time. Car-mile costs are a function of miles. By making a separation of costing into these two categories, the difference becomes very obvious. By the elimination of switching, less damage is done to the equipment which, in turn, further reduces the general operating expenses. The unit train and its subsystem, the block train, represent the logical application of container systems technology to railroading and, in effect, apply assembly-line techniques spread out over greater distances.

To achieve the unit train optimum design, the four basic constraint factors must be analyzed first:

1. Container on–off systems;
2. Train scheduling;
3. Storage–intermodal interface;
4. Advance planning capabilities of the system.

Unit trains which are responsive to design decision of these four criteria are the desirable method of container handling. This was the consensus of the railroads represented at the International Railway Congress in London in 1971. Such trains can be established at passenger-train speeds or better, which, in turn, would be the telling factor in generating the desirable long-haul business. This would allow the design of special cars with cushioning train shocks, rubber friction stabilizers, and disc brakes. The train would also allow the use of the skeleton car without the car floor where the containers are carried and secured on the center sill with bolsters and special strength (see Portager car). The end-of-car or sliding sill mechanism designed in the United States will joint with the disc brake system for constant service mileage designed by the Freight-liner Group.

SCHEDULING

Equally critical in the development of containerized train service is the factor of train movements through terminals. In our era of fluidity of the economic process, delay times become a major systems constraint. It takes two days for a container to go on a chassis from London to Rome by highway and six days by rail, the world's best example of such inefficiency of rail containerization. On the other hand, the Sante Fe Railroad operates the Super C freight trains between Los Angeles and Chicago by avoiding terminal through-put with conventional means, and is the world's fastest, fully containerized train movement. The 2,000 miles are covered in 40 hours, by merely systematizing the train movements. The advantages of such service affect industrial production and allow geographical separation of two sections of an assembly line nearer their optimal location.

The Super C service indicates the importance of systems integration in the unit train operation. Most time in the United States is lost in interlinking freight between railroad systems. Even the speeding up of transfer of trains must be optimized to the extent that the Liner system is applied to one run even if equipment, roadbed, terminals, and information systems are owned by more than one road. Joint documentation services which share the information will aid the railroads in the development of such services.

This points to the direction of the major container problems the railroads face. The container must go quickly from origin to destination. The problem in the United States is that the railroads in the East are overloaded by operational traffic and environmental problems. As long as this prevails, the full advantage of containerization's effectiveness does not accrue to any railroad's participation, even the one who does best on his particular segment. Typically, the perishable transportation industry of the United States is built on through movement from California to New York or from Florida to New York and other Eastern markets. In the Florida–New York movement, the control of the traffic from Florida to Virginia rests with the Seaboard Coast Line. The service has been effective, because in the congested upper East area the rail distances are short. On the other hand, the Western roads—specifically, the Sante Fe's efficient transcontinental service—are lost in the area of Chicago/St. Louis. Therefore, it loses most of its impact as an East-West service facility. Unless the integration is complete, the neck of the bottle deters from the system's effectiveness.

All the major railroads outside of the United States are either owned or controlled by the government. A modified policy of nationalization is being pursued by all railroads so owned. Attempts to get the government out of railroad operations, control, and policy making are restricted to these phases. Whether the railroads are privately owned and operated, as presently in the United States, or are government owned, the technology applying to containerization finds the same internationally favorable response. Everywhere railroad men must work on detailed plans of keeping up with the growing world population and economy. Costing of services becomes the decision-making junction of railroad practices. Higher-capacity railroading is a significant leap from archaic conventional methods, and containerization holds the promise for application by railroads. At this stage, the problem with railroads is mostly their frame of mind. As the publisher of *Container World* stated in June of 1971, "The greatest deterrent to intermodality is in the 'state of mind' of the carriers themselves. In other words, most carriers seem to talk intermodal; but think modal." Motivation of railroads comes from the challenge of the national economy directed by the political entities of each nation; ocean containerization is, however, motivated by trade interests and the trends of world trade. The patterns that emerge from the meeting of both are similar and far too comparable to be coincidental. It is the container challenge of economic integration of transportation into distribution. (See Fig. 7-8.)

THE LAND BRIDGE

A good example of the new application of container systems technology to the rail industry can be developed out of the mystique and the practice of land bridges. The definition of land bridge is a container through-route in which one major part involves transportation via a rail link. True or pure land bridges are those where vans are shunted by railroad from one ocean steamer to the other. When one inland rail leg is tightly plugged into an ocean service "sui generis," we talk of "mini-bridges." If there is any difference between the normal intermodal rail–water link and the true or mini-bridge, it consists in the perfection of pragmatic interline relationship between carriers, not the provision of certain physical facilities. The outward deployment of container intermodes in land bridges is not appreciably different from the higher grade of intermodalism or transmodalism that should be applied to all rail–water container connections. So one might say that the entire land bridge idea was a promotional stunt at first, but developed into a well-defined service pattern, as container lines had to search for more paying cargoes.

During the administration of President Kennedy, when the Republic of Panama gave signs of objection to enlargement of the Panama Canal, the United States' attention was directed to the existing facilities in the Isthmus of Tehuantepec. I participated in a study tour for a group including Commissioner John W. Bush of the Interstate Commerce Commission, representatives of the Mexican National Railroads, and others, during the Pan American Railroad Congress then taking place in Mexico City. The Panama crisis never came off, and the interest in the now-feasible land bridge 200 miles between the Atlantic and Pacific remains in the "study and investigation" files of the Mexicans, the United Nations, and Sea-Land Service, Inc.

THE EFFECTS OF SUEZ

But when the Suez Canal really was closed, the land bridge idea became a possibility. The world map shown in Fig. 7-8 designates the forerunner land bridges which are now or have been discussed seriously. The Kedem Land Bridge (12) from Ashdod to Eilat, two ports in Israel, is the only such land bridge which actually runs parallel to the Suez Canal and is presently used by some container cargoes from Europe to East Africa. The distance is only 200 miles long, but there is no rail line. Containers are moved by truck. The service pattern between the Atlantic and the Pacific remains similar to the service started years before by my former company, now CCT, between Guatemala and the other Central American republics facing the Pacific shores.

The contenders for the long-famed land bridges (the two rail-bridges possible through the United States, plus the rail service through Canada) compete with the trans-Siberian land bridge (13) of the Soviet railroads connecting Europe with Japan via Vladivostok, thence by ship to Yokohama. Many economists and transportation engineers have studied these land bridges. Their thoughts have been reflected in many reports and in much conversation. But the practical application of the service has lagged behind. As a matter of fact, only the trans-Siberian railroad has produced an appreciable amount of unique traffic, due to the close cooperation between the Soviet railroads and Trans-Containers, the container group of the European railroads. Sporadic container movement to Vancouver from the east has not allowed the Canadian land bridge (1) to acquire any significance. As a result of this development, container systems experts have come to the conclusion that only small land bridges or mini-bridges would be cost-effective.

SEATRAIN MAKES IT WORK

Then in 1972, Seatrain Lines came up with the idea of negotiating special rates and service conditions with the Santa Fe Railroad for traffic from the U.S. Pacific Coast to Europe and vice versa. At some time, Seatrain had considered shorter land bridges between the Pacific and Galveston or other points on the Gulf. But the final analysis led to the California-to-New York land bridge service.

Thus, the land bridge application became a practical idea for the carrier who, as a true transmodalist, applied his own ideas to attract more

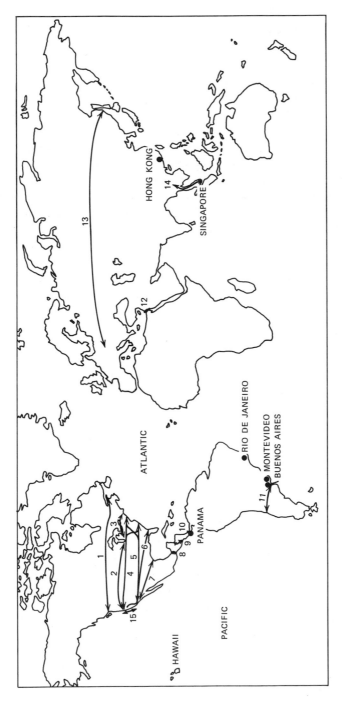

FIGURE 7-8. CONTAINER LAND BRIDGES: (1) TRANS-CANADA, (2) SEATTLE–CHICAGO MINI-BRIDGE, (3) NEW YORK–CHICAGO MINI-BRIDGE, (4) SAN FRANCISCO–U.S. EAST COAST, (5) LOS ANGELES–U.S. EAST COAST, (6) LOS ANGELES–JACKSONVILLE, (7) CALIFORNIA–GALVESTON, (8) TRANS-MEXICO, (9) GUATEMALA–SALVADOR, (10) PANAMA AND OTHER CENTRAL AMERICAN ROUTES, (11) CHILE–ARGENTINA, (12) ASHDOD–EILAT, (13) TRANS-SIBERIA, (14) SINGAPORE–BANGKOK, (15) LONG BEACH, CALIF.–OAKLAND, CALIF.

traffic to his main routes at the expense of true intermodal service. It is certain that the cost of equipment and some of the cost of the unit train transfer must be discounted from the route revenue by containers eventually moved on the ship. But even so, these containers contribute something to the overall rentability of the North Atlantic route; and they do this without affecting the revenue pool share from the United States Northeast area where Seatrain competes with all other transatlantic carriers.

LAND BRIDGE VS. LONG-LINE

The fight for rentability is the struggle to keep the ships full with high-paying containers. In direct opposition to the land bridge system applied by Seatrain, and to a certain extent by Sea-Land, is the "Long-Line" service operated by U.S. Lines and ZIM Lines. These two lines apparently calculate their rentability on the per day use of the container slots on the ship. It allows them to build up certain long lines with little long-line traffic, but with much intermediate traffic. Against this, the principle of the land bridge remains to attract most traffic to the short haul by sea at the expense of giving more costly, yet often faster, service by inland means. The mentality of intermodal cooperation between the sea carriers so engaged, and the rail carriers who work with them, may mean the future for transmodal cooperation which can become more significant than today's rail-container operations, as it is being applied to the marine field.

NEW RAIL SERVICES

Any improvement in any segment of rail container systems requires careful analysis as to its value as a component part of the entire transportation market. Only those improvements which can provide adequate economic justification and service benefits to the entire system will be deserving to be plugged into the effective terminal link system.

But any exotic system will demand an entire logistic structure by itself; therefore, in effect, it will create a new railroad system as such. With the horrendous increase in the cost of building, we would wonder if this would be feasible by any private carrier. In light of this, the evaluation of the desirable features may indicate a small degree of practicality. Santa Fe Railroad is active in the development of advanced railroad concepts—to wit, the Super C train—and has proposed a new coaxial train.

This concept developed from a method of hauling 50 welded rails on 14 railroad cars with a train length of 1,400 feet, which proved no problem around curves for train travel. This led to the design of a central beam bending around curves laterally, yet having sufficient strength to carry heavy loads. Actual tests indicate speeds in excess of 100 miles to be possible with the existing road bed of the Santa Fe. There would be four times as many wheels on this train as on the conventional train. Each wheel would have its own suspension system and drive motor. The existence of the bullet train in Japan shows that service can be maintained with great frequency, as well as high speed.

IMPLICIT EVALUATION

Implicit in the evaluation of the trend of continued unit growth per ship conveyances is the tendency of other conveyances to research for their own continued economy of scaling two systems, both calling for new automated highways or railways. Even the application of the hovertrain principle developed by Berlin and Kaplan of France has been considered a linkable candidate for the increase of speed and unit size of inland trains. Obviously, the planners were trying to look off into the far future. Experience makes me feel that new land systems have to overcome so many physical, logistic, and financial disadvantages that their introduction would be far down the line.

Ship Systems

THE STRANGE MARRIAGE

Containership design and development should be the result of the analysis of the entire container system rather than the traditional suboptimization of vessel parameters. It has been stated that the compromise between marine requirements, systems demands, and container capability can well be summed up by the old adage dealing with wedding gifts, "Something old, something new, something borrowed, and something blue." Containerships were not invented; they were developed. They have evolved over the years as the advancing container technology produces new solutions to old problems.

Before the age of unitization, the proponents of new ship programs would bring their problems first to the ship designer. Experienced naval architects and marine engineers were the beneficiaries of a long line of professional scientific background accumulated through research and information exchange. The great value of a professional organization such as the Society of Naval Architects and Marine Engineers (SNAME) consists in its updating such information of technology.

But the ship is no longer the only key element in the transportation program designed for intermodal communication between producer and consumer. It is one of several key elements which the systems designer must consider. First, however, he must think through-transport and only thereafter can he devise the links which make up the door-to-door chain. Without doubt, the ship is one of the most important links. But before a decision can be made on ship configuration, all systems design elements must be carefully planned, interfaced, related to each other, and weighed. Many naval architects today have recognized the expanded role of their profession. Some have acquired intermodal experience themselves and others form teams with systems engineers. Those who customarily want to tell their clients what they want to hear may not do as good a job for the service proponent as those who are outspoken and will point out the problems in the coordinated line-up.

PRELIMINARY PROPOSAL

The preliminary proposal which the client wants from his systems engineer and naval architect must plug into the traffic picture the proposed cargo handling technology. Three diagrams typically develop the interrelationship between preliminary analysis requirements, design studies, and systems engineering proposals. These three diagrams will illustrate the order of events (Fig. 8-1).

Early development in the ship–shore cargo methodology created certain concepts in the state of the art. Although the early system as such did not survive because of matters outside the concept area, the validity of the basic idea has remained. Pioneering failures cannot always be ascribed to concept validity. These failures are often results of weak financing, lack of intermodal cooperation, or institutional resistance.

A very typical example of such early concept validity in the face of enterprise failure was a transatlantic roll-on, roll-off ship service instituted by TMT Trailer Ferry in 1957. Lloyd's *Gazette of London* called the original voyage of the TMT *Carib Queen* across the North Atlantic then, "the coffin nail of conventional shipping." This prognosis proved to be right. Although TMT failed on this trade route due to an inefficient and poorly adapted boiler system, three lessons were learned from that experience:

1. The intermodal transfer of cargo inland to inland would constitute the parameters of the container world.
2. Trailers which are vehicular containers can be stowed in multiples in several forms of ship hulls.

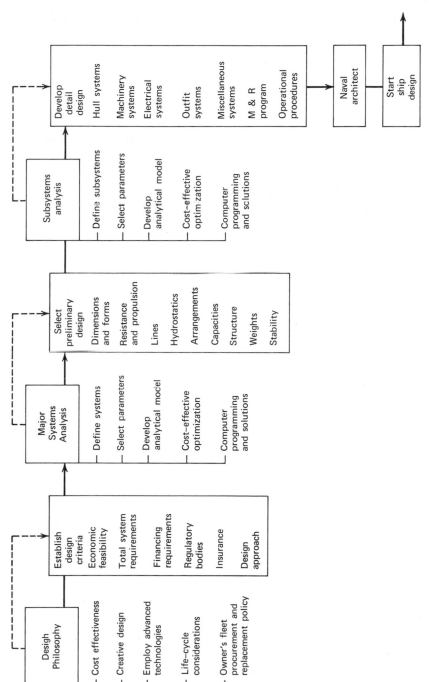

FIGURE 8-1. CARGO SYSTEMS STAGE IDENTIFICATION AS RELATED TO THE DESIGN AND DEVELOPMENT OF A CONTAINER-SHIP AND INTERMODAL SYSTEM.

3. The key element in novel ship design is the speed of interface for ships with ports.

The ascendency of the containership proves that the vision of the designer must be coupled with a thorough knowledge of the state of the systems economics to maintain a steady advance. Ship capability is the backbone of container transportation. An effective design process must be fully aware of the technologically sophisticated systems analysis. Otherwise, it will overlook the benefits in terms of future possibilities.

ESTABLISHING REQUIREMENTS

Containerships are both instruments of commerce and components of the transportation system. Consequently, the relentless growth of the economy coupled with advances in transportation technology dictated the need for analysis relating to the design, construction, and operation of the ocean conveyance which will operate together with land-based container systems. To shape the policy for a design effort requires as much practical knowledge of the constraints as of the output from operations research and mathematical simulation. Eight basic factors must be fully considered prior to making any design effort:

1. Traffic;
2. Geographical considerations;
3. Analysis of the particular containership service for which the ship is being designed;
4. Effect of competitors on the new service;
5. Labor;
6. Intermodal interface operators;
7. Life-cycle economic evaluation;
8. Consideration of obsolescence due to technology.

SHIP CATEGORIES

At the present time, the hundreds of ships which can carry containers of one kind or another comprise five major groups:

1. Cellular containerships carrying intermodal van-type container units (no wheels);
2. Roll-on, roll-off ships having large deck areas and internal ramps and carrying vehicular-type trailers (with wheels);

FIGURE 8-2.   TYPICAL BARGE AND CONTAINER CARRYING VESSEL.

3. Barge carriers carrying a floating, barge-size container so that the container is simultaneously both barge and container (LASH and SEABEE); see typical barge carrying vessel in Fig. 8-2.

4. Combination roll-on containerships—two types of this category allow either simultaneous handling of roll-on cargoes and cellular stowage or loading of the ship in a roll-on method and cellular stowage, using a shipboard container crane (TARROS ship type); see Fig. 8-3.

5. The conventional-type cargo ship capable of carrying a large number of containers on the hatch covers (semi-containership).

Most containerships presently use the cellular construction and the lift-on, lift-off method. A shoreside or shipboard crane locates or removes a container from a horizontal corner-guide system. The roll-on ships lend themselves well to carrying all sizes of containers which are driven on and off, over or through the bow or stern ramps and side ports. In the case of refrigerated containers, the roll-on ships have the advantage of being able to use the space under the container for the installation of a diesel generator and or fuel tanks. This provides great flexibility in picking up fresh fruits, vegetables, and meats from widespread agricultural areas without the need to transfer the product and thus run the risk of

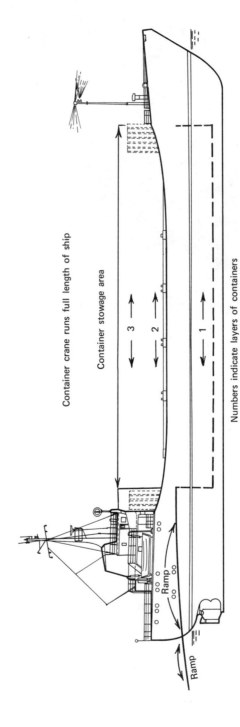

Container crane runs full length of ship

Container stowage area

3 →

2 →

1 →

Numbers indicate layers of containers

Ramp

Ramp

FIGURE 8-3. COMBINATION FEEDER ROLL-ON/CONTAINERSHIP.

damage or spoilage to the product. While on shipboard, the trailer reefer machinery can be plugged into the ship's electrical system.

The barge carriers serve mostly as conveyances to countries where there are large inland waterway networks with pickup and delivery points in areas served by waterways. The large dimensions of the container-barge unit over the intermodal container or trailer serve better for the handling of the large quantities of cargo usually involved in bulk transportation where 8–10 containers might have to be used instead of just one container barge.

The variety of designs incorporating some features of the container transportation system is so great that it is not possible to describe all the varieties and possibilities. For the systems engineer it is important to point out the major key features which will influence decision making from a technical, operational, and economical point of view. The analysis of the cellular containership is the most important.

CELLULAR CONTAINERSHIPS

The role of cell guides is critical. They enable the containers to be lowered to stowage positions when the crane is not precisely centered over the hold or if the ship is listing. In the process of stacking successive containers one over the other, cell guides assure that eccentric loading does not exceed a controlled amount due to misalignment. The function performed by the guides is to resist the horizontal loads exerted by the containers under the influence of ship motions. Both analysis and actual experience have shown that the functions are performed best when the guides taper inward toward the bottom. This assures that eccentric loading is at a minimum at the bottom of a stack where the imposed loading is highest.

CELL GUIDES

The standardizing ISO documents relative to containers contribute to the design of cell guides by specifying tolerances on the envelope dimensions of the containers. With a known variation of plus zero, minus $1/4$ inch on the outside container dimensions, it is possible to assign dimensions to guide spacing which will result in a satisfactory interface, or clearance between the container and its guiding rails. A clearance space of $1/2$ inch all around has proven to be satisfactory. Excessive clearance permits tilting to take place, with the result that binding is possible. If the clearance is too small, then jamming may result.

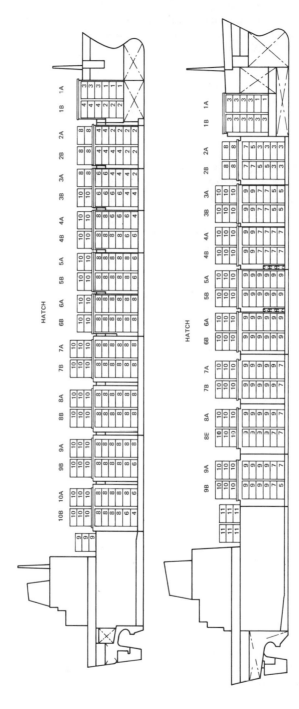

FIGURE 8-4. TWO TYPICAL 20-FT. CONTAINERSHIPS WITH SUPERSTRUCTURE AFT (SOURCE: OCL/ACT AND HAMBURG-SUD).

CONTAINER ALIGNMENT

The general situation on *container alignment* is that the long dimension is along the longitudinal axis of the ship. Some designs have been proposed in which the containers would go into stowage spaces in the athwartship direction, but they are relatively rare and have not been pursued into actual construction. The effect of conventional alignment is that forces due to ship motion, which are greater as a consequence of roll than due to the other motion components, will lead to greater forces on the sides of the container than on the ends.

VARIABLE DIMENSION

It must be pointed out that the cell guides on each ship are of fixed dimensions so that only a particular length of container can be accommodated by a cell. Matson has designed into its containerships an adjustable cell-guide structure so that different-size containers can be accommodated concurrently. Leslie Harlander reports that some of the details of this changeover method can accommodate various patterns of container mixes. The transverse framing which mounts the cell guides consumes about 30 feet of hold length, leaving 120 feet free for payload. This can be divided into five bays for the 24-foot special Matson containers or six bays for the standard 20-foot units. The transverse frames can also be positioned for a mix such as two bays of 40-foot units and one each of 24- and 20-foot units. A changeover from one cell geometry to another can be performed during the annual overhaul of the ship. In this design, the transverse members within each 150-foot length are not required as strength members of the ship's hull girder and are essentially floating with only bolted connections.

LATERAL CELLS

A number of containerships are conversions in which the main deck, being a primary strength member of the ship's hull girder, is not cut out for vertical access to each cell. Seatrain Lines is the main proponent of this approach. Containers are lowered through existing hatch openings to form a stack on a skidway at the longitudinal centerline of the ship. After the stacks are loaded, a 50-ton hydraulic power unit (Moose) applies a force to position the stack at its outboard location. Container han-

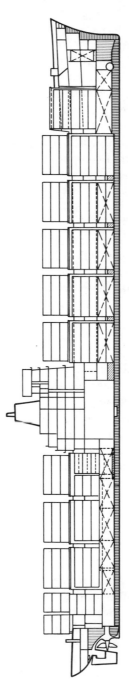

FIGURE 8-5. COMBINATION 20-FT. AND 40-FT. CONTAINERSHIP WITH MIDSHIP SUPERSTRUCTURE (SOURCE: AMERICAN MAIL LINE).

dling in each hold is remotely actuated and no personnel are required below decks.

SEMI-CONTAINERSHIPS

We also do not think that the term "semi-containerships" has any systems significance. Any ship with good-size deck space created either by the hull or by the hatch covers can carry all types of containers, as well as other cargo, on the exposed deck area. As a matter of fact, for some time, the development of container shipping seemed to go along a slow curve of volume increase. It was soon found, however, that this change toward integrated transportation required a realistic decision on behalf of the shipowners as to what capacity, speed, and cargo system could do to reduce operating cost. It was the appearance of Sea-Land in the North Atlantic that hastened this decision, even before Sea-Land's own case was proven. It became quite clear that in competition with a fully containerized ship, especially one with shoreside crane systems, which are so cost-effective, there would be a move to deter any combination ships from operating. Where combination ships are still in use today—for example, in the transpacific and Asian trade—they are decidedly on the way out, as their cost of operation is excessive. In order to handle these ships, they must go to a container berth for their on-deck cargo, and then to a conventional berth for the break-bulk cargo. The same occurred with Sea-Land's original two tankers which carried a load of containers on deck. These ships served well to familiarize the trade with the idea that containers could be carried on ships, but they lacked the cost effectiveness for survival.

DESIGN SPIRAL—START

Regardless of the possible variations in ship-design approaches, all are iterative processes which may be conceived of as moving in a spiral fashion to a balanced conclusion with all features compatible. In the containership development, the spokes of the spiral are naval architectural features, as well as considerations of both the containers and the cargo in containers. The systems designer, therefore, will start with a rough general idea of the volumetric requirement of the proposed containership. It is with the selection of the type of machinery that he must deal next. There are four basic power plants available, but only three are in the stage of economic development as to be available to the ship designer at this time. The four potential power plants are as follows:

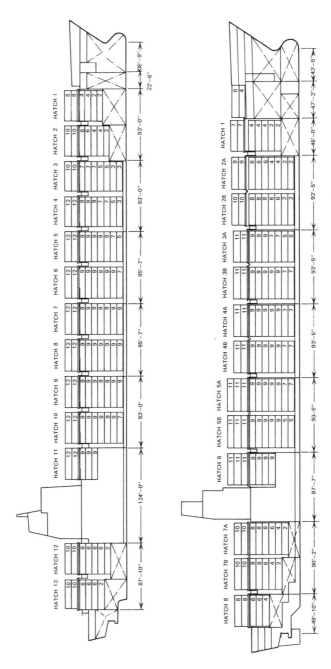

FIGURE 8-6. TYPICAL 20-FT. CONTAINERSHIPS WITH STEAM PROPULSION AND THREE-QUARTER SUPERSTRUCTURE LOCA-
TION (SOURCE: *Marine Technology*).

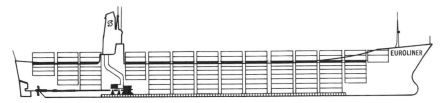

FIGURE 8-7.   TYPICAL 40-FT. GAS-TURBINE CONTAINERSHIP WITH
MIDSHIP SUPERSTRUCTURE (SOURCE: SEATRAIN LINES).

1. Steam turbine; (see Fig. 8-6)
2. Diesel;
3. Gas turbine; (see Fig. 8-7)
4. Nuclear power (under development).

With each power plant goes considerations of the space required to install the power plant, weight, quantity of the fuel, maintainability, as
well as the vessel speed. Containerships are being built for speeds in excess of 22 knots, during the last year or two; and in the foreseeable future, a design speed in excess of 30 knots will become commonplace.

With the initial estimates of the vessel capacity and speed, the overall
length and beam of the ship then begin to develop. Containerships on
major routes are over 700 feet long and frequently exceed 900 feet. The
beam and length are limited by the possibility of the ship's having to
clear the Panama Canal, which restricts the ship beam generally to 104
feet maximum, which gives this type of ship the name of "Panamax."
In reality, ships of larger beam may transit through the Canal, but only
with certain costly and detailed preparations.

TABLE 8-1.   CHARACTERISTICS OF LARGE CONTAINERSHIP
DESIGNS (1966–1970)

	Ship A	Ship B	Ship C	Ship D	Ship E	Ship F
LENGTH, O.A.	523'-6"	544'-0"	942'-0"	941'-0"	719'-9"	712'-8"
BEAM, MLD.	68'-0"	75'-0"	105'-6"	105'-0"	95'-0"	95'-0"
DRAFT, MLD.	23'-¾"	31'-8½"	30'-0"	32'-0"	30'-6"	32'-0"
DISPLACEMENT	16,240	20,809	50,200	59,500	38,742	40,048
FIXED BALLAST,						
TONS	1,328	0	0	5,735	0	0
S.W. BALLAST						
CAPACITY, TONS	—	—	10,417	6,087	5,014	5,903
TOTAL CONTAINERS	196	160	1,968	2,294	1,222	1,223
SEA SPEED, KNOTS	16	21	33.5	28.5	23.9	22.1

DESIGN PROCEDURE

The design procedure for a containership is in many ways identical to that of any other ship type. However, there are certain problems peculiar to this design. As long as the vessel operates in deep-sea spaces, the depth of the hull is limited only by stability considerations. Actually, a deep hull has great structural advantages since the deeper the hull, the greater the section modules. Canal passages and harbor channel depths may strongly constrain the deep hull design. The economy of scale under the pressure of growth may therefore lead to land transfer alternates. In other words, where the maximum-size deep-sea vessel cannot pass loaded, the cargo must be transferred from one body of water to another. The importance of land bridges and automated conveyorized container transfers will increase under these conditions. Details of this analysis are discussed in Chapter 20.

As the saying goes, "There is more than one way to skin a cat." When the Southern Railway planned to enter piggyback service, they were prevented by their tunnel height limitations from loading trailers on flatcars. The company then went two ways. First, they advocated containerization which allowed the cargo to be carried in containers on flatcars, eliminating the height of the chassis. When the traffic grew, the Southern Railway lowered the track bed in their key tunnels, such as Baltimore, and then allowed the use of piggyback trailers. Sooner or later this type of decision making must be used in ocean transportation.

HULL BENDING STRENGTH

The structural resistance to bending forces by the hull of the containership is difficult to achieve. In longitudinal bending, a tanker presents an evenly balanced hull girder with a full, solid deck and equivalent bottom shell. The containership has a stiff double bottom for the bottom flange of the hull girder, and this must be balanced as much as possible by two compact longitudinal box girders, with open hatchways totaling often more than 80 percent of the beam.

STRUCTURE TORSION

The containership, due to its requirement for large hatch openings, is at a disadvantage in torsion. Not only does it have to resist the same torsional moments as the tanker, but the open box-like structure results in greater angular difficulties which, in turn, set up high local stress. The axial stresses due to warping cause a relative movement between the port and starboard sides which, except for the closed ends forward and aft, is resisted only by the transverse deck girders supporting the hatches. High stress concentrations may be expected at the connections of the transverse deck girder to the longitudinal box girder.

SEA LOADS

The determination of sea loads and stresses follows the calculation of the still-water bending moments and poising the ship at a heading of 180 degrees on a wave equal to the ship's length. Due to the fineness of the ship, one finds that the maximum allowable longitudinal bending stresses, instead of reaching a peak amidships, as on a tanker, are difficult to keep from exceeding the maximum over the midship half-length. This is one of the reasons that this procedure of determining wave-induced stresses is not sufficient for a containership. (See Figs. 8-8 and 8-9.)

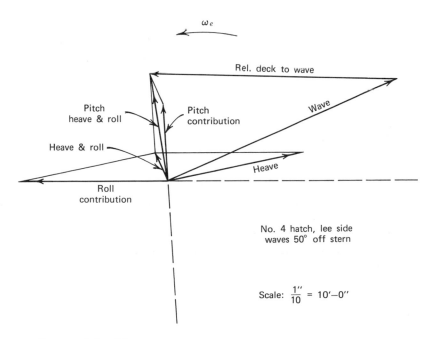

FIGURE 8-8. VECTOR DIAGRAM OF MOTIONS AT DECK EDGE (SOURCE: U.S. GOVT. VII).

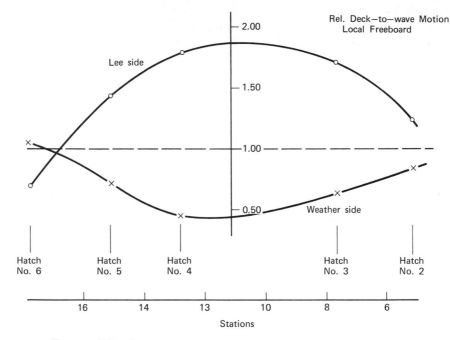

FIGURE 8-9. RATIO OF RELATIVE MOTION BETWEEN DECK EDGE AND WAVE TO LOCAL FREEBOARD (BASED ON SERIES 60 SHIP C_B = 0.60, 19 KNOTS, 26° ROLL REGULAR WAVES 57 FT. HIGH WITH 12-¾-SEC. PERIOD QUARTERING FROM 50° OFF STERN) (SOURCE: U.S. GOVT. VII).

HORIZONTAL BENDING

Although the longitudinal bending moments do not change appreciably due to a change of heading of, say 20–30 degrees, the horizontal bending and torsion moments increase considerably and may cause stresses reaching a maximum at about the quarter-length of the ship, superimposing some of their components on the longitudinal bending stress. So far, only static stresses have been considered.

SPECTRA POWER

It is also possible to determine, with a fair degree of accuracy, the dynamic and hydrodynamic forces acting on the hull. By calculating these forces due to waves of varying direction and length, the short-term distribution of stresses may be determined by superposition.

FATIGUE

The short-term distributions obtained are superimposed with the aid of seaway statistics to a singular, long-term frequency distribution. On the basis thereof is then determined the stress value that is, on an average, exceeded once during a given number of load cycles.

STRESS ANALYSIS

In addition to the stresses so analyzed, the high-speed containership may be subject to stress magnification due to wave-excited hull vibration. Although the ship speeds are still low enough so that the frequency of encounter of resonance occurs at the low-energy part of the sea spectrum, the magnification still could be considerable.

STABILITY

The large, fast containership has many inherent trim and stability problems. The large wind area presented by the high freeboard of a high deckload of containers has a profound effect on the required metacentric height. The result is a ship with requirement for a low metacentric height or low center of gravity. Except for ballast conditions, the metacentric height for various loading conditions varies in a rather narrow range since the weight of the fuel consumed is compensated for by taking on ballast water. Maximum flexibility dictates minimum use of fixed ballast. High speeds require large bunker capacity and the desirability of a clean ballast system usually makes it difficult to find adequate space for liquid ballast.

Another aspect of the metacentric height is the large heel angle experienced by the ship when traveling at high speed, caused by sudden large rudder angles changes. These maneuvers are quite dangerous, especially if the helmsman tries to correct the situation by giving opposite rudder. Even greater problems exist if the GM is this low. The lower the GM of the loaded ship is, the more violent sudden conditions may endanger the consistent maintenance of stability under heeling and rudder angle changes.

VIBRATIONS

Aside from any mechanical unbalance of the propulsion system, the propeller is one of the major sources of vibrations. The fact that, due to high power and low draft, most high-speed containerships are twin-screw is a blessing and at least reduces the propeller excitations.

Horizontal vibrations are more difficult to endure by the human body than vertical vibrations. Unfortunately, the containership response is susceptible to high horizontal vibrations due to its low torsional rigidity and considerable coupling of horizontal and torsional vibrations.

The high powers of modern containerships make it necessary to investigate these phenomena. The constant increase in power makes it necessary to perform a more detailed vibration analysis.

CONTAINER FRAME STRENGTH

The depth of the ship determines the number of tiers of containers that can be stacked below deck. Current container design standards are based on the assumption that they are stacked to a maximum of six high. Increasing the number of tiers decreases the need for a high deck load and, therefore, affords better container protection and simplifies the lashing problem. However, it decreases the initial stability due to a rise in the

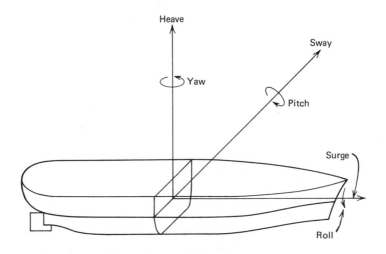

FIGURE 8-10.   AXES OF MOTION ON CONTAINERSHIPS.

height of the center of gravity of the light ship and also increases the loading cycle time.

An increase in ship's capacity will require the stacking of containers more than six high in the holds. The use of reinforced containers for certain locations would appear the obvious answer. However, this places an additional constraint on the loading operation which may well render this economically not feasible.

CARGO PROTECTION AT SEA

Winter sailings on the North Pacific and North Atlantic and other oceans have led to a large number of damaged deck containers and cargoes. Proper stowing and special ship design can overcome these problems.

When the ship sails, the cargo is subjected to a new and continuing set of motions. There are six ship motions: rolling, pitching, yawing, heaving, swaying, and surging. The ship may move in any one of these motions or in any combination of them at one time. The vessel will pitch, slam, and roll without ceasing; and if the weather is moderate, the cargo will be moving forward at the speed of the ship, up and down with the pitching, and side to side with the rolling. Of these motions, more damage can be attributed to the rolling than any other. It is interesting to note that acceleration forces bear a direct relationship to the vertical position of the cargo in the vessel relative to the rolling center. The top on-deck container is subject to far more severe motion than that in containers stowed near the rolling center, for example, the lower 'tween deck.

On-deck cargo is subject to sea, wind, and weather. See Fig. 8-11. It may start in 90°F temperature, possibly experience subzero conditions, and then be discharged in hot weather again. First, the cargo must be properly packed for the intended voyage, so that it won't move in its package and won't crust when stowed up to 8 feet high or tossed about as previously described. Second, the package must be properly stowed in the container, so that it won't move, crush, or damage itself or other cargo.

RULES FOR STOWAGE

The procedures for proper stowage of ships are also applicable to stowing a container. The proper container for the job must be selected. The cargo weight must be distributed evenly, so the bottom of the container

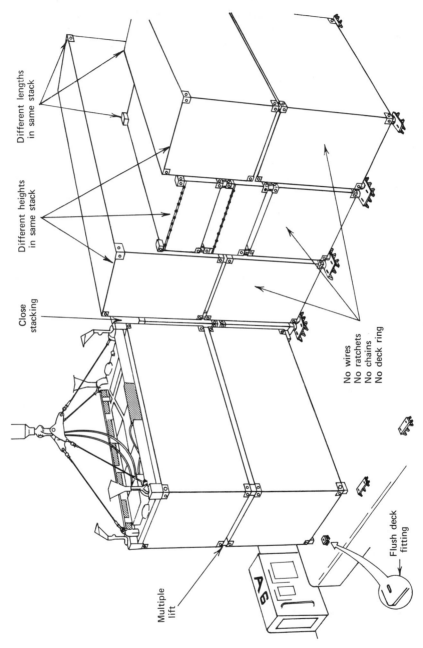

Different lengths in same stack

Different heights in same stack

Close stacking

Multiple lift

No wires
No ratchets
No chains
No deck ring

Flush deck fitting

FIGURE 8-11. TYPICAL CONTAINER DECK ARRANGEMENT (SOURCE: MIDLAND-ROSS).

won't drop out or the container won't sag, hog, or rack, and also to prevent tilting when lifting. It must be stowed so that no part of the contents will shift and thus damage itself or other cargo in the container or go through the side and damage adjacent containers. The cargo must be compatible, so that it will not contaminate or be contaminated by other cargo in the container. The problem of compatibility covers a wide range of possibilities, including wet with dry and poisons with foodstuffs, as well as the various combinations of hazardous-labeled cargoes. For stability purposes and that of protecting lower tiers, the dense cargo shall be stowed beneath the lighter cargo.

A container is subjected to the same conditions as any other type of cargo. See Fig. 8-12. Its movement on board the vessel must be eliminated by the use of proper lashings or securing devices. Various methods

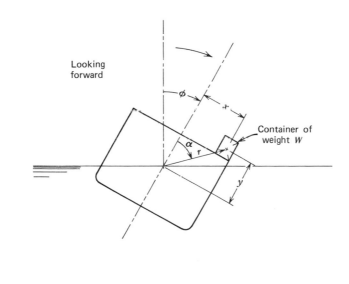

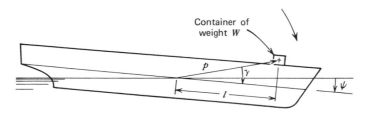

FIGURE 8-12. CONTAINER LOCATION CONSEQUENCES (SOURCE: U.S. GOVT. VII).

have been employed for this purpose, including cells, locking arrangements, and lashings. These for the most part have proven effective in immobilizing the containers and have not constituted a major problem.

THE TOP-SIDE THIRD

The problem with most containerships stems from the fact that one-third of the containers must be carried topside. This means that the container is exposed to the wind, sea atmosphere, and the boarding seas, in addition to the ship movements described heretofore. Three solutions have been discussed to alleviate the considerable loss and damage problems:

1. Stow all containers below deck;
2. Strengthen the container to resist the sea;
3. Develop guidelines for on-deck containers by reducing ship motions, by proper securing of containers on deck, and by locating the containers on certain deck areas only.

Solution #1 would make the containerships uneconomical, although Manchester Lines, which operates in the very stormy part of the North Atlantic between western England and Canada, felt otherwise and designed ships accordingly. Other operators calculated that the damage

TABLE 8-2. SUMMARY OF CONTAINER DAMAGE SURVEY

Type of Ship	Damage	Aluminum Exterior	FRP/ Ply- wood	Steel	Aluminum Interior
All Ship Types	Units Observed	2819	4987	1668	1227
	Units Damaged	499	495	322	233
	% Damaged	17.7	9.9	19.3	19.0
Fully Containerized	Units Observed	872	2792	575	317
Ships	Units Damaged	124	219	88	34
	% Damaged	14.2	7.9	15.3	10.9
Conversion Con-	Units Observed	1189	1316	767	577
tainer Ships Deck	Units Damaged	213	152	158	113
Gantry Cranes	% Damaged	17.9	11.6	20.6	19.6
Partially Converted	Units Observed	758	909	326	333
Conventional Ships	Units Damaged	162	124	76	86
	% Damaged	21.4	13.6	23.3	25.8

Source: U.S. Govt. Report I.

possibility for on-deck containers is primarily concentrated during the winter period, and they decided to take a chance rather than to forego this cargo potential.

The second solution is excluded, because it would make the container economically too heavy. Heavy empty weight restricts the intermodality factor.

Table 8-2 shows the effect of sea damage to containers of different materials. Table 8-3 evaluates the cost of repairs to these damaged containers and Fig. 8-13 reports the locations where these incidents occur.

MARITIME GUIDELINES

Therefore, guidelines developed by the Maritime Administration were recommended as the key, with the cooperative effort of the industry by

TABLE 8-3. CONTAINER DAMAGE ANALYSIS
RELATED TO VESSEL TYPES[a]

	Aluminum Exterior	Fiber-glass	Steel	Aluminum Interior	Totals
TOTAL CONTAINERS OBSERVED	2819	4987	1668	1227	10,701
Code 1	366	413	233	185	1,197
Code 2	127	79	82	45	333
Code 3	6	3	7	3	19
TOTAL	499	495	322	233	1,549
PERCENT DAMAGED					
Code 1	13	8	14	15	11
Code 2	6	2	5	4	3
Code 3	0	0	0	0	0
TOTAL PERCENT DAMAGED	18	10	19	19	14
PERCENT OF DAMAGES BY CODE					
Code 1	73	83	72	79	
Code 2	25	16	25	19	
Code 3	1	1	3	1	
TOTAL	99	100	100	99	

[a] Code 1 cost of repairs $0.00 to $50.00, Code 2 cost of repairs $51.00 to $199.00, Code 3 cost of repairs exceeding $200.00.

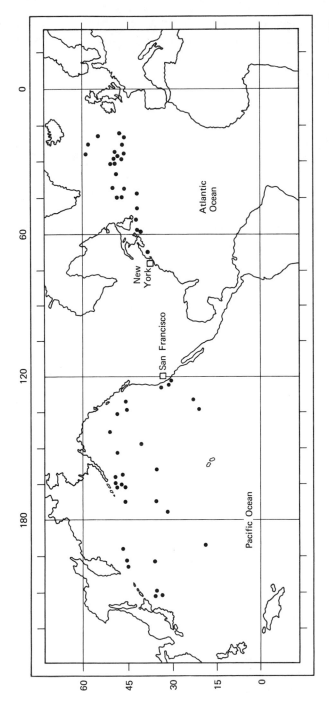

FIGURE 8-13.   LOCATION OF REPORTED OCEAN INCIDENTS OF CONTAINER DAMAGE (1969–70) (SOURCE: U.S. GOVT. VII).

the Technical and Research Panel 0-31 of the Society of Naval Architects and Marine Engineers. This decision received full industry support at a Maritime Research Symposium held at Woods Hole, Massachusetts, in 1969.

A summary of the guidelines is as follows:

1. To minimize susceptibility to severe rolling, a containership should have a small bilge radius, carried well forward and aft, in conjunction with bilge keels.

2. To minimize susceptibility to severe pitching, a containership should have a low displacement/length ratio.

3. Containerships should be fitted with bilge keels to minimize susceptibility to rolling.

4. Bilge keels should be located right at the turn of the bilge for maximum effectiveness and should be greater than 18 inches in depth, to insure that they extend beyond the boundary layer.

5. Model tests should be made to determine optimum trace of bilge keels for minimum resistance, and to determine resistance and effectiveness trade-off data for establishing optimum depth.

6. If a passive-tank roll-damping system is used, it should be thoroughly model tested before installation to assure effectiveness over the full range of the sea conditions expected in service.

7. Activated stabilization systems on containerships should include safeguards in the system to prevent induced or aggravated rolling in the event of derangement of the normal control system.

8. For the development of intact trim and stability calculations, the following criteria should be applied:
    a. Container weights should be based on data from the operator's experience on the particular trade involved. Where there are no data, according to Maritime Administration Guidelines, weight should be assumed as 60 percent of the rated maximum.
    b. Permeabilities should be assumed 0.60 for volume occupied by containers and 0.95 for remainder of hold.

9. Permanent ballast should be installed in the minimum amounts necessary to satisfy the U.S. Coast Guard stability standards.

10. Permanent ballast required because of possible deck cranes or other installations to be made in the future should not be fitted until the future installation is actually made.

11. Freeboard of a containership midbody should be at least 60 percent greater than the minimum required by the regulations.

12. Freeboard at the bow of a containership should be at least 6 percent of the overall length of the ship.

13. Investigations for adequacy of freeboard in severe ocean conditions on

the routine contemplated should be made in the preliminary design of a containership.

14. Flare on the order of at least 25 to 35 degrees should be incorporated into the forward sections of a containership to reduce the possibilities of boarding seas at the bow.

15. Model tests should be made of any new containership design to determine optimum flare.

16. A containership should have a substantial breakwater as secondary protection for the forwardmost deck-stowed containers against green water shipped over the bow.

17. Bulwarks for protection of containers stowed on deck from boarding seas should be provided on ships operating with freeboards less than about 25 percent of the beam.

18. Any ship which routinely carries containers on deck should have a container restraint system with permanently installed and portable fittings specifically designed for the size and weight of containers being carried and for the particular ship involved.

19. Selection of the type of securing system for deck-stowed containers on a containership should be based on trade-off studies of structural, lashed, and locked systems, considering life-cycle costs and degree of security afforded.

20. On-deck containers should be positioned on restraint fittings.

21. Positioning and restraint fittings for on-deck containers should be located within specified tolerances so as to fit the containers to be carried.

22. Ship structure under decks supporting containers should have sufficient local strength to support the container weight concentrated at the container corner fittings.

23. Where containers are carried over hatches, the strength of the hatch covers should be sufficient to carry the load of the containers, or supports of sufficient strength should be fitted across the hatch openings.

24. The supports for containers on deck should be adequate to carry the longitudinal and transverse loads from ship motions into the ship's primary hull structure.

25. The design of structural supports for on-deck containers should be based on the combined gravity and maximum dynamic loads from ship motions, and on a factor of safety of three on the ultimate strength of the material.

26. Lashing assemblies for securing containers on deck should include provisions for readily tensioning the lashing when installed to remove all slack and avoid excessive pretension in the assembly. (See Fig. 8-14 for typical lashing systems.)

27. Stacking fittings should be used between tiers of containers lashed on deck, at each corner fitting, to prevent horizontal movement.

28. Bridge fittings should be used to provide horizontal support between

rows of containers within a stack, and should be of a type to also resist tipping.

29. The number and arrangement of lashings in a lashed securing system for containers should be determined from calculations based on predicted sea conditions and the weight and stiffness characteristics of the containers to be carried.

30. The required strength of container lashings should be based on maximum loads determined from lashing calculations, a factor of safety of two on the breaking strength for lashing assemblies and attachment fittings, and a factor of safety of three on the ultimate strength of supporting structure.

31. Lashing assemblies should be proof tested and samples should be tested to failure to verify designed performance.

32. The arrangement of a buttress securing system for on-deck containers should provide for minimum interference of the structural posts with container handling and stowage, and for ready handling of the stowing frames by container-lifting equipment.

33. The strength of a buttress system should be based on maximum combined gravity and dynamic loads for expected extreme sea conditions and a factor of safety of three on the ultimate strength of the material of the structure.

34. In selection of arrangements for on-deck stowage of containers, athwartships arrangements should be included in the alternatives for consideration and evaluation.

35. Arrangements for container stowage on deck should include fore and aft access for personnel between container stowages and the deck edge with clear passageways a minimum of about three feet in width.

36. Where container stowages on deck require access to make up and inspect the restraint system, the arrangement should provide for a minimum of 30 inches of spacing between the ends of containers in adjacent rows.

37. Where reefer containers are carried on deck, the arrangement should provide a minimum of 30 inches' clearance for the container ends in which the reefer units are mounted.

38. Where ventilated containers with covers required to be opened and closed at sea are carried on deck, the arrangement should provide a minimum of 30 inches' clearance between the ends of containers for access to the covers and to permit the covers to swing open.

39. Fire stations, sounding tubes, and other features on deck requiring access at sea should be located clear of container stowages.

40. Where containers are carried directly on deck outboard of a hatch, stowage fittings should be provided under the container corners to hold the containers securely in position and to elevate them clear of a wet deck.

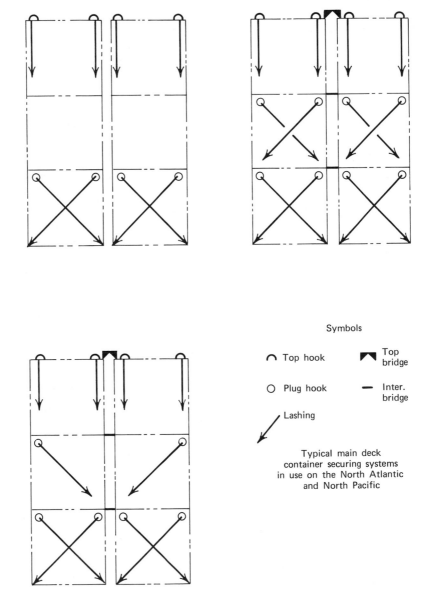

Symbols

⌒ Top hook   ◤ Top bridge

○ Plug hook   — Inter. bridge

↙ Lashing

Typical main deck
container securing systems
in use on the North Atlantic
and North Pacific

FIGURE 8-14. TYPICAL LASHING SYSTEMS FOR SECURING CON-
TAINERS ON DECK (SOURCE: U.S. GOVT. VII).

RO-RO SHIPS

Many of the sophisticated design and systems analysis problems described heretofore for the cellular containerships are avoided by the roll-on, roll-off ships. These ships have been in ocean-going service since 1950. They are basically a development stemming from the deep-sea ferry boats, which have carried railroad cars and highway trailers for the last 60 years. The two outstanding deep-sea, roll-on container services are:

1. In the transatlantic trade: Atlantic Container Lines;
2. In the Australian–Pacific trade: PAD (Pacific Australia Direct) Line owned by Rederiaktiebolaget, Trans-Atlantic Gothenburg, Sweden.

The largest impact of the roll-on, roll-off ships is in the feeder service. The two pioneers are still operating: namely, TMT Trailer Ferry in the Caribbean and Transport Ferry System (formerly Atlantic Steam Navigation) in the North Sea and cross-channel trade. The international directory of roll-on, roll-off services shows over 100 operations in Europe, Asia, Australia, the Caribbean, and the short-sea trade of the Mediterranean and Alaska. All these services use combinations of container systems with a variety of loading devices. One of the interesting features is the transfer of containers on board the roll-on ships, such as the Italian vessel *Vento di Tramontana*, which consists of the stowage by means of crane and cellular location, while port discharge is by means of roll-on, roll-off. Also, there are many passenger ferry boats which have a bow opening and use their main decks for the transportation of containers. Since most of these services are designed for specific weather and sea conditions, there is no general doctrine for their use.

FEEDER SHIPS

Cargo, in moving from origin to destination, can move the entire way on one vehicle, or it can be transferred from one mode to another. Charles Cushing, President of Cushing and Nordstrom, gives four distinct reasons for this intermodal or transfer method of transporting cargo:

1. To take advantage of vehicles or conveyances which are more efficient on each route;
2. To overcome physical obstructions on the various routes;

3. To consolidate or collect cargo in larger, more efficiently transportable units;

4. To split or group shipments for different routes.

These last two reasons give rise to the feeder concept of transportation. The governing principles apply equally to airline, trucking, railroad, and marine operations, and, for that matter, to any network flow system. I will confine myself here, however, to marine feeder operations and, more specifically, container feederships.

A feedership may be defined as a vessel which transports cargo from one of a number of ports or origins to a consolidation point where it is transshipped in larger carriers. More generally, a feeder may be described as a branch-line vehicle.

The size of a feedership is independent of its basic definition. Obviously, the feedership is smaller than the trunk-line carrier, which carries cargo from several feeders together with cargo that originates in the consolidation port. It is not a feeder operation, if a vessel transfers cargo to another vessel of equal capacity, but of different characteristics, more suitable to the second route—such as from a river vessel to an equal-sized ocean vessel. This would be better defined as an intermodal operation, rather than a feeder operation. While most of the feeder vessels today are comparatively small, the observer is cautioned against assuming that feeders are only small vessels.

Feederships in marine operations are as old as shipping and trading. Many examples are familiar to all: coastal and harbor tank vessels, harbor and river barges, and coasting freighters. Many modern steamship companies, such as Farrell Lines in West Africa and Grace Lines in South America, have employed feeder vessels in their break-bulk operations.

While feederships are not new, containerships are, comparatively. It is interesting to note that containerships were around for seven years before the first container feedership was put into service. This was the German-flag ship, *M. V. Adda,* which was built in 1965 and put into service for Sea-Land.

CONTAINER FEED SERVICE

The importance of feeder vessels is magnified by the nature of modern containership operations, and their attendant high capital costs. Formerly, it was practical and economic for a cargo vessel to serve several (say anywhere from three to seven) ports on each end of its ocean route.

Today, two factors in container operations mitigate against this. The first is that container cargo, usually high-value finished products, demands the fastest possible deliveries. Quick delivery is not possible if the line-haul vessel performs the pickup-and-delivery-type service.

Second, due to the very high speed and attendant high capital cost of modern containerships, it is uneconomical to have the expensive large vessels serving small ports. It is suggested that a large, high-speed transoceanic containership should serve only one terminus on each side of an ocean. The addition of a second port at each end should be considered carefully. A third port at either end is a step which the planner should treat very skeptically. The size and speed of container feeder vessels should be determined as a result of a careful study of the entire system. It is possible that one feeder may serve two or more out-ports, in a chain-like distribution. Alternatively, the feeder service may permit the feeder to carry cargo to one or more ports, and then return to the consolidation port for cargo to be distributed to a second series of ports. In planning the operation, and especially the characteristics of the feeder, the entire system and the interrelationship between the line-haul vessels and the feeder, and even possibly the contribution that inland distribution methods can bring, must be evaluated. The feeder design characteristics also must be compatible with local physical restrictions, such as harbor depths and ice conditions.

In order that the correct number of feeders and line-haul vessels be selected, all possible combinations of feeder and line-haul vessels serving all different combinations of ports must be evaluated. In the trivial case, with one out-port and one consolidation port, the optimum solution can be achieved almost by inspection. However, with the addition of a few more ports, the problem becomes so complex that only the use of sophisticated operations research techniques will guarantee that the optimum has been found.

SEA-GOING BARGE UNITS

For many years, containers have been moved on deck of barges within the inland waterway systems of Hong Kong, Holland, the United States, and Japan. The first outstanding ocean-barge system with wide impact was TMT Trailer Ferry, as previously explained. Now the idea has been developed further with special ocean-going barges being used.

Most "transocean barges" are unmanned and controlled by a towing vessel. A tug-barge operation is characterized by:

1. Fleet configuration;

2. Number of tugs and barges;

3. Size of tugs and barges;

4. Route and barge interchange pattern.

Several concepts exist for moving a barge or flotillas of barges in trans-ocean service:

1. Tug-barge push systems have certain cost advantages over systems in which the tugs pull the barges. Pulling system costs per ton mile, including capital costs, can be as much as 10 percent higher than pushing system costs.

2. Under existing conditions, particularly manning scales, the tug-barge system cost advantage over self-propelled ships for trades which can accept a lower level of service can be as great as 35 percent in break-bulk services. It is smaller in container and still smaller in bulk. Even tug-barge systems, which do not take advantage of their ability to detach their propulsion and cargo units, can be cost competitive with self-propelled ships.

3. Tug-barge systems can take advantage of their ability to detach from one another in services with a high ratio of port time to sea time and an even distribution of cargo among the ports. Under ideal conditions, a detach mode of operation can realize cost savings up to 40 percent over tug-barge systems which do not detach.

4. The capital required for tug-barge systems in break-bulk services can be as low as 40 percent of the capital required for a comparable ship system. The capital savings of tug-barge systems in container services are not as great, and the capital requirements for tug-barge systems in bulk services tend to be about the same as for ships.

5. Construction costs of tug-barge systems are significantly lower than ships of comparable dead weight at low speeds but increase more rapidly as speed increases because of the hydrodynamic inefficiency of the closely coupled units.

6. The lowest-cost tug-barge systems are larger and slower than comparable ship systems, and hence, have poorer service frequencies and transit time.

7. Current tug-manning scales have been approved for at least one pushing transocean system. Transocean tug-manning scales, however, are subject to negotiation with the Coast Guard and the unions; they will probably increase as tug-barge systems increase in size and use.

8. Insurance rates for tug-barge systems in liner service will continue to be higher than ship rates until tug-barge systems develop claim records as low as ship systems.

9. Technology: The critical force acting on barges in multiple-barge flotillas is caused by the lateral bending moment. This force could reach sufficient magnitude to cause a failure in the barge structure if normally propor-

tioned barges with normal scantlings were used. The most economical corrective measure is to change barge proportions.

10. Physical research and engineering development are required in the following areas:
    a. Hydrodynamic inefficiency of closely coupled units. If hydrodynamic efficiency can be increased through improved hull design, faster tug-barge systems could be used to reduce the disadvantage of poor service frequency and transit time. Simultaneously, the existing cost advantages of multiple-barge flotillas would be increased.
    b. Forces and motions acting on flotillas of barges. Tests should be performed on linkages which allow limited relative yaw (to reduce the critical lateral bending moment) and on flotillas with barges abreast as well as ahead. These data will be required if designers are to develop linkages for flotillas with a large number of barges (more than two or three).
    c. Specific linkage designs with particular attention to safety and reliability. Tests are currently being carried out.

SHIP-SIZE RATIONALE

The selection of vessel size as measured by cargo capacity is one of the most important decisions affecting the overall economics of a proposed ship. This decision is often a difficult one because the predicted availability of cargo has long-term trends upwards or downwards. The selection of ship size has, in the past, been rather arbitrary simply because the complexities of the problem precluded any sort of rational approach. However, some problems of this nature can be solved by using computers. This chapter shows how ship size may be selected in such a way as to provide the most economical design for a given forecast of cargo availability.

PROFITABILITY RANKING

In designing a containership, the selection of size ranks among the most important decisions affecting the overall profitability of the ship as an investment. How one should approach the problems of size depends on circumstances. Bulk carriers, for example, usually find their cargo available in practically unlimited amounts. General break-and-bulk cargo is limited in availability, and ships in those trades are denied the economic benefits that come with too great a size. This explains why general cargo liners seldom exceed 13,000 dead weight tons, whereas tankers have grown to 15 times that capacity.

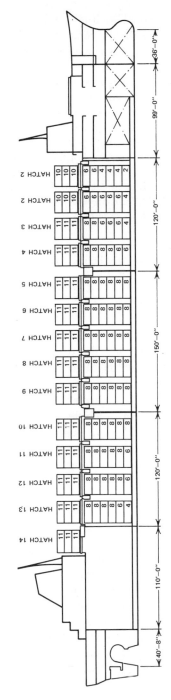

FIGURE 8-15. TYPICAL 20-FT. CONTAINERSHIP WITH FORWARD SUPERSTRUCTURE.

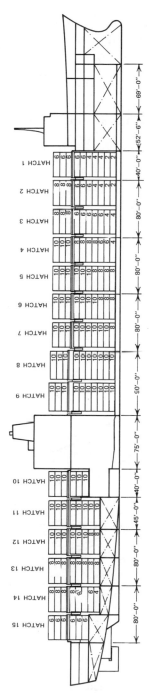

Figure 8-16. Typical 40-ft. containership with midship superstructure and forward navigating house.

A typical cargo forecast for a containership in the trade must be considered. (See Fig. 8-17.) In addition to expected long-range upward trends, the cargo available per voyage will probably have large seasonal fluctuations and will differ greatly between the two legs of the round trip. Furthermore, the average freight rate per ton of cargo may be appreciably different inbound and outbound. The optimum vessel size must fall between the extremes; it can be found only by analyzing the potential economics of several arbitrary designs representing the continuum of all intermediate sizes.

Many factors in addition to those already mentioned influence the op-

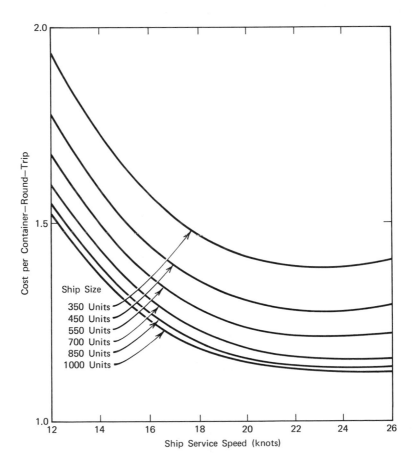

FIGURE 8-17. PROPORTIONATE COST PER CONTAINER-ROUND-TRIP
VERSUS SHIP SIZE AND SPEED, IN PERCENTILE (SOURCE: U.S. GOVT. III).

timum size for a containership: length of voyage, fuel costs, port turn-around time, and bunkering schedule, to name a few. As is usually the case with system analysis, there are too many factors to allow a complete study of every conceivable combination. Typical variable factors are summarized:

1. Displacement;
2. Cubic number;
3. Shaft horsepower;
4. Sea distance;
5. Sea speed;
6. Bunker schedule: one way or round trip;
7. Relative freight rates inbound and outbound;
8. Economic life or planning horizon;
9. Port days per round trip;
10. Forecast cargo availability inbound and outbound year by year.

A problem common to all optimization studies is the selection of a measure of merit. One presumably wants to find the most economical ship, but may have trouble deciding on what is meant by "most economical." Ships in the liner trade normally charge for their services according to conference agreements. The revenue per ton, then, would presumably be the same for every alternative design. The advantage of one ship over another would not be an ability to offer lower rates, but a greater return on the investment. After considering various alternative measures of merit, the required freight rate (RFR) was selected as being the best of an imperfect lot. RFR, briefly, is the freight rate a shipowner would have to charge, if he wants to earn a reasonable after-tax return of about 10 percent on his investment. The optimum ship is defined as the one that has the lowest RFR; and, to keep our calculations under control, a constant freight rate for the life of the ship was assumed. As a general approximation, an arbitrary 20-percent interest rate of return before tax was selected for discounting future amounts.

REQUIRED FREIGHT RATE EQUATION

The required freight rate is derived from an equation of the nature:

$$\text{RFR} = \frac{\text{investment} + \text{present worth of operating costs}}{\text{present worth of cargo transported in tons}}.$$

The actual relationship is slightly more complicated because of differing freight rates inbound and outbound.

The computer results are plotted to find the optimum ship size and minimum RFR for each set of assumptions. One can also find the range of sizes that are within some minimal departure from the optimum. In these studies, the reasonable range is defined as being an arbitrary 2.5 percent of the minimum required freight rate.

The following general conclusions can be drawn:

1. Reasonably large departures from the exact optimum size are permissible. As a rule of thumb, if one can keep ship size (for example, cargo capacity) within $\pm$ 20 percent of the optimum, overall profitability will be within 2.5 percent of the maximum. Considering such intangibles as customer satisfaction, ease of cargo handling, and maintenance of sea speed, most owners might prefer a ship that is 15 to 20 percent larger than the optimum.

2. The most unexpected result is the qualitative influence of return cargo on optimum size. I find that the availability of return cargoes actually reduces the optimum size.

3. Cargo capacity is selected appropriate to the assumed conditions of the forecast. The important exception to this is the case of extreme seasonal fluctuations in cargo availability.

4. The relative insensitivity of the foregoing results is probably justified. It is highly debatable whether we would find any significant change in optimum size as a result of switching to a different power.

5. Analyzing the outcome of a range of cargo forecasts hardly seems worthwhile unless there are large seasonal fluctuations. The reliability of predicting the magnitude of the fluctuations should not influence examining the effects on the ship design.

CONTAINERSHIP BUILDING

The bulk of the output of commercial shipyards has consisted of tankers, bulk carriers and general cargo ships. From the production point of view, these differences pose a number of challenges for shipyards in their efforts to increase their efficiency. Most containerships will become larger than the general cargo ships they replace. Among existing yards, strenuous efforts are being made to overcome restrictions by enlarging the building ways or by constructing new building locations. The advent of super mammoth tankers and bulk carriers has fostered the construction of large building docks in many shipyards, particularly abroad. Very few, if any, containerships are built in these facilities. A tanker is about five-eighths structural work and only three-eighths outfitting. In a general-cargo ship we deal mostly with arrangement of decks and gear in the hull. In a containership the interior work is simple. A tanker is about 83 percent flat and the rest is curved. A general-cargo ship is about 75 percent flat plate, and on a containership only one-third of the plate is curved. This makes a significant difference in the way one approaches the building of a ship.

CONSTRUCTION COST CONSIDERATIONS

For many years ship construction costs were based on the cost per dead weight ton. This was particularly true when the comparison dealt with tankers or bulk carriers. As far as containerships are concerned, the application of the dead weight basis would be the worst way to measure a ship. It would be much better to use cubic capacity or light ship weights for cost parameters. There are so many variations that the systems engineer is best guided by applying the principles commonly known as "comparing oranges with oranges" and not "oranges with apples." Compared to tankers and bulk carriers, containerships have thinner plating and a more irregular structure. The hull form is finer, leaning to a greater proportion of curved panels, as compared to flat panels. Containerships have a great deal of wing and double-bottom tankage of cellular construction; while tankers, bulk carriers, and general-cargo ships have large tanks or several decks and, therefore, more of a flat or panel type of construction. The modular nature of containerships and their function of accommodating standard-size containers leads to a type of component standardization. Hull lengths, spacing of container stowage guides, hatch sizes, and many other elements are uniform all over the hull. Deck shear and camber are either absent or minimized as they are not compatible with the rectangular container configuration. They adversely affect the container arrangement, causing waste space. By proper attention to details of standardization, substantial parts of the ship can be standardized or made fairly identical. Among the facilities that are used for containership production, modern shipyards are installing flat-panel shops where these important components of the ship are fabricated on assembly lines. This is different from the conventional practice, which was developed during World War II, of piecemeal fabrication at fixed positions of these panels on subassembly flats. The movement of the work to the machines in the shop enables highly mechanized equipment to perform fitting and welding operations of plates and stiffeners. In some cases, a tenfold increase in productivity has been achieved over the previous fixed-position methods.

FABRICATION OF MODULES

Curved panels on the containership are quite important. To fabricate curved panels efficiently, some shipyards are using special adjustable devices on which such panels can be properly supported. A curved panel has to be built on a form that maintains the shape of the panel while it is being constructed. These devices are adjusted to the contour, prior to the fabrication of each panel. Each curved panel has a different shape. This is in contrast to the fixed mock-up of conventional shipbuilding, which has to be assembled and dismantled each time it is used. The adjustable devices enable a specially equipped area to be set aside for curved-panel fabrication. Because of the greater proportion of curved panels on a containership, a shipyard building containerships has more reason to install a curved-panel shop than one that does not build containerships.

The modern trend in shipbuilding is toward the installation of outfit material on the completed structural panels, as early as possible in the production process. The advantages of the modern trend are several. The work, being more accessible, is easier to perform. Sometimes the cost of installation labor is as little as one-third that of conventional procedure. In conventional practice, the hull is generally built on the ways. The ship is closed in, and it is difficult to get the outfit material to the place where it is to be installed. In the subassembly area, a panel lies on the ground or in the shop, and it is conveniently accessible to cranes. As a matter of fact, you can get up and walk on it. The work is in the down-hand position. For this reason, you get savings in labor of up to two-thirds for the installation work. The time required at the building berth is drastically reduced, and fewer people have to work under crowded conditions in inaccessible areas aboard the ship. This is because the work is open; and by reducing the time on the building berth, you can actually turn out more ships in a given facility.

PRODUCTION PLANNING

The required extent of production planning in material control is greatly increased, and the sequence of operation is different. You have to do a much more thorough job of production planning and control and identifying where material is to be used. It is a much more thorough job than is generally thought of in conventional shipbuilding. The results are that lower-skilled employees are required for normal production work and more draftsmen and planners are required in proportion to direct production workers. You need also greater dimensional control over the work which creates the need for the computer techniques in lofting the ships and defining the shape of all the parts. The total construction time of the ship is greatly reduced. In Japan, where this system is widely adopted, it is common to deliver a ship within 8 to 10 months after the start of fabrication, compared to the 14 to 18 months it used to take. An older Japanese shipyard, having five building ways and 5,300 total employees, regularly delivers 15 to 18 ships every year. The preoutfitting which makes all this possible, requires extensive space for spreading out panels, so that the work can be performed efficiently. The panels, sometimes weighing over 100 tons, must be positioned and transferred to the building locations. This movement is often by special rubber transporters equipped with hydraulic lifting jacks. The panels are placed on racks under which the transporters can position themselves. The racks with the panels on them are picked up in the fabrication shop and moved to the subassembly location where they are spotted. On completion of preoutfitting, they are moved to the ship erection area where they can be lifted off and positioned for erection. This modern concept is ideally suited for containership production.

TASK SHIP SYSTEM

In view of the problem that results from size limitations in cellular holds of container ships, a design has been developed to accommodate a variety of lengths, widths, heights, and types of containers. The word TASK, therefore, stands for the expression "takes all sizes and kinds." This ship is capable of carrying containers, trailers, and other unitized cargo on master pallets or skids.

It is interesting to note that while we developed this idea in the United States mostly to cope with the desire to have large intermodal ship capability at the same time with modern cargo handling techniques, a similar independent design process went forward in Europe spearheaded by Meeusen, who calls the ship "The MECO ship" (Fig. 8-18). Both TASK and MECO have one thing in common: both use the level-load, continuous, automated cargo motion during the loading and unloading process (Fig. 8-19).

The key feature to this technology is the dual-level deck where the functions of cargo handling are operationally separated but functionally

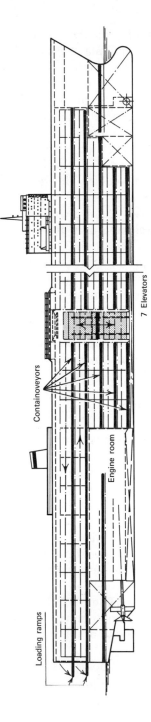

FIGURE 8-18. LONGITUDINAL CONTAINER-LOADING SYSTEM ON THE MECO SHIP (SOURCE: MEEUSEN CONSULTANTS).

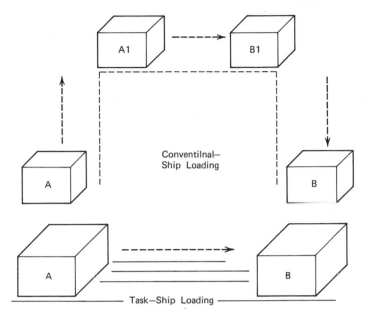

FIGURE 8-19.   THE TWO BASIC SHIP-LOADING PRINCIPLES.

integrated. The baseline decking provides for mobility of both wheeled and skid cargo on one level, and propulsion of all cargo recessed in grooves in the deck.

This decking has many functions integrated into it. While serving as a cargo handling facility, the grooves created by the double-decking serve as prefabricated ducting for environmental control, humidity and air conditioning, as well. Electric circuitry, gas, water, and air lines are stowed in this system and are, therefore, cheaper to install, repair, maintain, and control. The baseboard decking provides for directional mobility of the entire range of parcels of cargo, including such things as trucks, logs, steel rods, container boxes, bales, and barrels, in longitudinal lanes and transversing avenues. The ship's interior resembles a "pigeon-hole" garage.

This roll-on method of containerization can be made very simply. Selective handling is possible with winch lines. It can also, however, be highly mechanized by using the "Magnet-Move" method which moves containers like slot cars in miniature race tracks.

The TASK Ship System provides the mechanics to fully computerize and automate a ship's cargo system. Selective loading, stowing, discharge, and readjustment for intermediate port stow could be done by computer.

Such selectomatic handling will improve considerably on present cellular containership loading and unloading. Not only will it permit reduction of turnaround and port time, but also freedom from restriction to certain, preequipped berths.

The TASK Ship System stays entirely within the present state of the art. Model cost analysis shows superior performance against any other system under any given scenario. Use of high-powered gas turbines, bow and stern thrusters, and superior crewing with caretaker manpower would allow two vessels of 4 million cubic feet cargo capacity to serve the North Atlantic or North Pacific, replacing four or five less cost-effective ships.

TASK is the latest result of the roll-on, roll-off technology applied to containerization and unitization. It will undergo many refinements and improvements, and it can place the Merchant Marine in a more competitive position again over the older, slot containership. The infinite possibilities of combining subsystems in containerization are shown in Fig. 8-20, which shows a TASK type ship using an underdeveloped port with a simple portable piece of equipment on an unprepared key.

FIGURE 8-20. SUPER-SIZE HORIZONTAL-STOW SHIPS (MECO AND TASK TYPES) CAN USE SIDEPORT UNLOADING OF CONTAINERS WITH EXISTING PORT AND PIER FACILITIES.

RADICAL DESIGN CHANGES

Instead of cellular containerships with open decks, the new designs like TASK have again closed decks. The TASK ship will have no vertical cells, but horizontal, longitudinal lanes beside and above each other from the bow to the stern. The containers from the lower lanes are moved to the higher lanes and vice versa, by means of elevators. Two lanes of the higher levels are used for loading and unloading the containers in continuous streams to and from the terminal.

All lanes are provided with heavy-duty conveyor belts which will have met special requirements due to the heavy loads, different bottom constructions of the containers, the protruding corner castings, etc. The existing types of belts do not meet these requirements, so specially designed conveyor belts are to be constructed. A possible solution for this problem is the so-called containoveyor. It is a conveyor provided with rubber pads and is suited for any type of container, regardless of its bottom construction. Its energy losses due to friction are extremely low. Each lane inside the ship has two containoveyors beside each other, upon which travel containers stacked two-high, in order to save space. On the containoveyor, the containers can travel with practically no interspace in the longitudinal direction.

Between the containers, in crosswise direction, there is sufficient space for the guide rails and the clamping arrangement. All containers are clamped simultaneously by eccentric rails controlled from a central position, saving considerable manhours.

Since the ships are the heart and soul of today's containerization, a very exacting study has been required of the subsystems which come together within these parameters. We have attempted only to point out the key features both of present ships in use and those being considered. The most important consideration is that the ship which serves both as ocean transporter and carrier of the individual containers must defend both the container device and the cargo stowed in it from the adverse conditions of the sea. Yet the special conditions imposed on the containers must be held to a minimum since the ship system is only one of the conveyances which will provide the door-to-door movement of the container. Having reviewed the situation of containers in railroad service and on ships, the third important component in surface containerization deals with the adjustment of containers in the road transport system.

Road Haulage and Cartage Systems

TIDEWATER TRUCKING

In 1955, Lee Ross estimated that between 50 and 81 percent of all cargo was hauled to or removed from world ports by motor vehicles. Since then, containers have come into the picture, and this share has increased even further. Few ports are now wholly dependent on rail or waterway connections. Even in the planning of the barge-carrying ships, the waterway operation is designed to be a terminal area intramove, not an intermodal connection. Thus, the opposition of European container operators to consider the application of TCM or for CTO's to barge-carriers, stems from their own interest in competition with waterways. Although motor trucks were first used during the siege of Paris in 1870–71 to carry ammunition containers, the technology of this mode has remained simple and unsophisticated to date. Constraints imposed on trucking by governments and road regulations limiting the size, length, weight, and often the height of vehicles, leave a narrow restricted field for future developments. Therefore, the incentive to the truck operator lies in attempting to obtain economies of scale. More cargo should be moved per man-hour of driver or terminal employee.

SERVICE PATTERNS

The key element of trucking is the motor-driven, driver-controlled, self-propelled traction. Innumerable variations of this vehicular idea have been built, used, and changed, to create combinations. Since 1921, the Fruehauf Company, builders of trucks, developed wagons to be pulled by motorized tractors of road size and automobile speeds, realizing that the pulling power of the tractor is a multiple of the carrying capacity of the motor truck chassis itself. The only idea which has never been possible to implement is the replacement of the driver by an automated device. This is a function of a speed-direction movement. In the Rohr Automove and many other mechanized warehouses, electrically directed tractors of the intraplant variety are being used, following computerized service instructions. This is possible because there are prescribed paths with a multiple choice of intersections only. This requires a large investment in prescribed route with underground guide systems, switches, and similar appliances, thus making this type of transportation a rubber-wheeled railroad, rather than a motorized truck. Thus, the great flexibility that the motor truck provides is given at the price of growth limitation. Certainly, more use can be made of motor-truck driver and power arrangements. During the Italian military in Ethiopia, a thought was advanced by designer Pavesi to create a concrete road system with middle-of-the-track elevated guide rails for automated steering. Again, the track idea of the railroad was used.

TRUCKING FUNCTIONS

True trucking is limited to one, two, or at most, three large trailers to be attached to and follow in the track of the motorized tractor.

With the system limitation of the motor–man relationship, let us analyze the areas where trucking really is the complete bracket of all intermodal exchange and the true interface facilitator:

1. Intraterminal transfer operating between two or more systems points in ports, yards, and interline facilities;
2. Pickup-delivery drayage operating in a medium range between points of origin or destination and other intermodal services;
3. Long-haul, where the trucking assumes the role of line service.

Figure 9-1 shows the variety of alternatives when the container becomes a truck in local haul, line haul, and terminal operation.

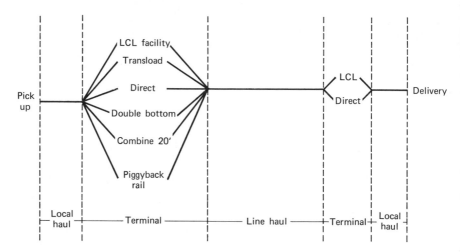

FIGURE 9-1. REPRESENTATIVE CONTAINER TRUCK-FLOW ALTERNATIVES.

It is apparent that there is much overlapping between these service groups. But the main characteristics which separate the three types consist of the use of terminals, the man–truck relationship, and the characteristics of the vehicles deployed. The length of the service distance depends very much on local conditions. Usually, though, the intraterminal distances would be limited to the port or yard areas, and the movement between them. Here is where we encounter the first man–machine conflict. As long as there is a separation in the unions between those working in the ports or railyards, and those driving the truck between them, the rational employment of the same traction equipment may not be within a single labor jurisdictional area. While pickup-delivery distances usually are considered to lie within the economic area of the terminal (such as city and suburbs, or commercial zones, as defined by the U.S. Interstate Commerce Commission), this concept is often related to the port limitations principles. Since the "cargo follows the ship" and many former import-export areas are now without container facilities, PU/D systems (Pickup/Delivery) may include medium-range trucking up to 350 miles. There are no hard and fast rules anywhere. Europe handles intercontinental (which also means arriving by ship from overseas) containers at a distance of 75 miles and more by rail as economically as by truck. Local road characteristics, receiving platform facilities of shippers/consignees, location of container stations inland, and the range of the commodities all require specific systems analysis before a conclusion can be reached.

FACILITATING INTEGRATION?

Truck container handling is a materials handling system built around the container itself. Everything involved, including terminals, rolling stock, vessels, etc., has one primary objective: facilitating container movement.

As one looks at the container as a part of the truck movement system, it is important to consider various subsystems and the flexibility which may be secured in various areas. The economics involved in this area are often misunderstood.

The container is designed for transport without wheels and will always be handled in this fashion aboard containerships. There is no need to handle them without wheels for inland movement. As we have seen, there is no one "right" container size for all commodities and all trade routes. The attempt to standardize on one size would ignore the laws of transport economics. Standardization is essential, but not to the point of forcing everything into one inflexible mold. Management's problem is how to fit these varying requirements into a single total system.

TRAILER EXCHANGE

When trucks were initially presented with requests to accommodate containers for inland movement, the handling of trucklines' interchange trailers was already a well-established system. The hardware was on hand, a pricing structure had been developed and with little change was readily available for container movement. The container represented nothing more than a trailer body. Likewise, the first of the big container operators, Sea-Land, found that inland movement was greatly facilitated if containers were placed on rubber tires and handled as trailers everywhere, except on the ship itself. The trucking industry, noting Sea-Land's experience, could see no reason why the container should not be mounted on rubber tires and handled within the existing system. Rather than recognizing the container as a system unto itself, it was forced into an already existing national transport system. As long as container movements remained small, this posed no problem. The motor carrier accepted the container on conventional terms, furnished by the steamship, on wheels, then moved it through his normal system. This was satisfactory until:

1. The steamship lines largely standardized on a 20-foot container;
2. These boxes began to move out of the immediate port area.

As hauls became longer, the difficulties of securing return loads for trailers half the standard size of the motor carriers and the difficulties of moving under rates intended for a much larger vehicle became evident. Again, the container was being forced into a system intended for radically different use.

In adopting the 20-foot containers, the steamship lines failed to regard the effect of this type of unit on inland transportation systems. The 20-footer was adopted because this was an optimum size from the steamship lines' standpoint. Effects of this unit on inland transportation systems apparently were not considered. That there are some rather serious economic disadvantages from this size container from the standpoint of inland movement has become evident in the attempts of various carriers, both motor and rail, to apply penalty charges for container movement. Although the steamship lines were fortunate in not having a preexisting system, they nevertheless failed to develop a system from a total distribution point of view.

CONTAINER LINK

Let us examine what is required to develop a fully integrated truck transportation system which the container demands.

A fully utilized and efficient system has not developed because of the failure to regard container movement as a system built around the container itself. The first obstacle which must be overcome if integration is to succeed is the thought of resignation. Traditionally, the transportation mode thought only of itself without considering its part of a through movement as an entity unto itself. With traditional methods of cargo handling, this was satisfactory, since the cargo changed vehicles several times during the course of its movement. Therefore, little coordination was required between modes.

Further, each carrier thought of its own terminals just as ends of its line haul. The terminal represents the beginning and the end of the movement. The container, however, does not stop at the water– or rail–highway interface, but moves right on through. The terminal is an interchange designed to facilitate through movement of vehicles.

Inland transportation has tended to regard carriers of other modes strictly as competitors and consequently has made no real effort to cooperate or integrate their operations. This attitude cannot survive in an era when the most economic and efficient transportation requires use of several modes in coordination to provide a truly efficient service package for the customer. This tendency to regard other modes as competitors carried over, in many cases, to relations between inland truck carriers and the water carriers. This is difficult to understand since most water carriers would seem to have considerable difficulty in reaching the majority of inland destinations by themselves.

SUBSYSTEM LIMITATIONS

In addition to the reluctant acceptance of the container by the medium-range and long-haul trucking interest, the variety of road weight, length, and other restrictive regulations vary from state to state in the United States. Since changes occur frequently, the concerned reader would have to consult the latest report of the truck trailer size limitations issued in table form by the Truck Trailer Manufacturers Association in Washington, D.C. Concurrently, the developments overseas are changing. It is surprising that thinking in the developing nations progresses faster than in the major industrial countries. The reason is that less institutional tradition has to be overcome. Therefore, economy of scale can be transferred easier to new nations than to old ones. In the report presented at the British Transport Docks Board in 1967, McKinsey, the British consultants to the Government Dock Board, summarized the truck interface problems for England. Since the same analysis holds true for many of the port situations faced by containerization world-wide, we cite them as examples.

The cost of road transport is less sensitive to these developments than other modes. The cost advantages to road transport of a standardized container are limited with regard to improved utilization. While utilization could improve significantly by operating directly between standardized locations, such as a port and an inland depot, there are practical limits to how far this can go, even on motorways. The main problem is lack of control over the public highway, so that container movements become slow and irregular due to road congestion resulting from a highly variable traffic density. For example, containers moving to and from Sea-Land's Port Elizabeth terminal add to and are hindered by congestion on the New Jersey turnpike.

ECONOMY OF SCALE FLEXIBILITY

Neither can road transport take advantage of economies of scale. There are practical limits to the size of vehicles that can be used on public roads. The obvious physical and safety restrictions on roads contrast with the high degree of flexibility possible at sea. This limitation on size restricts the productivity of both labor and capital. The necessity of a driver to control a relatively small load means that road transport must continue to be labor-intensive compared to rail and sea transport. Similarly, the need for an individual traction unit to haul relatively low cargo volume limits the productivity of capital.

The key advantage of road transport is its flexibility to operate on any route. While this is of prime importance when many routes must be used, it is of reduced importance when standardized routes are utilized. Synthesized road transport costs for moving containers between ports and inland depots in Great Britain are shown in Fig. 9-5. These costs are in broad agreement with other studies made by road haulers.

LINE-HAUL ANALYSIS

Intermodal container standards were related to domestic highway standards as they existed several years ago and further related to foreign highway and railroad standards. Domestic truckers have maintained their growth largely through increasing the total size of their "standard" unit

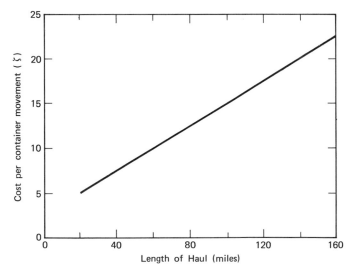

FIGURE 9-2.   COST OF TRANSPORTING CONTAINERS BY ROAD BE-
TWEEN PORTS AND INLAND DEPOTS (SOURCE: U.S. GOVT. III).

as rapidly as highway laws allowed. Now the earlier close relationship between maritime container sizes and truck operations is no longer valid.

The primary breakthrough in motor carrier line-haul transportation has been in the increased payload behind the driver. This increase has been accomplished by using large trailers, and by operating trailers in double and, in a few isolated cases, even triple bottoms. The use of the larger 35- and 40-foot trailers in tandem involves some modification of a single-bottom operation. Normally, the units are assembled at a station adjacent to a turnpike or interstate highway exit after being drayed one at a time from the motor carrier's terminal. The station or terminal hookup of trailers is reflected as an additional cost of about $4.00.

BALANCE OF EQUIPMENT

For the trucker, the balance of equipment and drivers is crucial. The balancing of equipment and drivers implies a balanced flow of traffic. It also implies an ability to reload any kind of equipment introduced into the system, an attribute not common to maritime containers.

International container freight is generally heavily imbalanced in the import direction. This traffic imbalance often adds to an existing directional imbalance in domestic cargo. The truckers maintain that this imbalance places an overabundance of nonstandard equipment inland that costs him more in lease costs than the ownership costs of his standard equipment and costs him more in weight and cube penalties to operate.

Some truckers look askance at the interchange of marine units. East Coast truckers, in particular, complain bitterly about the equipment they receive in interchange. One carrier estimated that 85 percent of the units received were unfit for over-the-road haul due to defective tires, lights, or other running gear.

INTERCHANGE STANDARDS

Added to this is the fact that most interchange agreements call for a per diem payment to the steamship carrier of $8.50, on the average, for one 40-foot or two 20-foot units. Most truckers calculate that domestic 40-foot vans cost them $3.00 per day to own. An adjustment of 30 percent to reflect free days (Saturdays, Sundays, and holidays) on international containers yields a cost difference between domestic trailers and international containers of roughly $3.00 per day in extra cost for the container.

Assume that a trucker has the use of standard 27-foot and 40-foot

TABLE 9-1. USABLE CUBE & PAYLOAD

	40-ft. Trailer	27-ft. Trailer	40-ft. Container	40-ft. (8½) Hi Container	20-ft. Container
Cube (cu. ft.)	2,420	1,760	2,280	2,400	1,130
Tare wt. (lbs.)	11,000	7,000	13,900	14,100	7,600
Usable cube (cu. ft.)	2,060	1,500	1,930	2,040	960
Payload (lbs.) (@ 14 lbs./cu. ft.)	28,800	20,900	27,000	28,600	13,400
RT payload (lbs.)	57,600	83,600*	54,000	57,200	53,600*

* Doubles.

trailers, a standard 8 × 8 × 40-foot container, an 8 × 8½ × 40-foot container, and an 8 × 8 × 20-foot container with the specifications shown in Table 9-1. Assuming a fairly long haul inland, with 20- or 40-foot containers, a West Coast trucker would be giving up the round-trip payloads and revenues (at $0.75/cwt) shown in Table 9-2 by not using domestic 27-foot doubles.

CONTAINER DEFICIT

In this example, the cube penalty has virtually disappeared with the introduction of the hi-cube, 40-foot container. Since the option to stuff domestic trailers has been economically ruled out in the east by the

TABLE 9-2. LINE-HAUL TRUCK COSTS
(CENTS PER CUBIC FOOT)

Ctr. Size (ft.)	400 Miles	1,000 Miles
35	10.60	23.70
40	9.30	20.80
Twin 20	10.00	22.50
Double 24	10.60	24.50
Double 27	9.45	21.90
Double 35	7.32	17.00
Double 40	6.94	14.90

Source: Cost of Transporting Freight by Class I and Class II Motor Common Carriers of General Commodities 1968—"Transcontinental" (U.S. Govt. Report III).

50-mile rule, the trucker is faced with the following balance of the round-trip costs versus a domestic load:

	40-ft. Hi-Cube	40-ft. Standard	20-ft.
Container Deficit	$24	$48	$70

In terms of weight problems, it is generally conceded by highway carriers that the additional line-haul costs for a container are negligible. The argument is that weight cuts into backhaul revenue. Using our previous example, most states allow roughly 73,000 pounds in gross weight for single semi-vans. Allowing 12,000 pounds for the tractor and 11,000 tare for the trailer, a potential payload of 50,000 pounds remains. With a usable cube of 2,057 cubic feet in a 2,420-cubic foot van, a product density of 24 pounds per cubic foot would be required to "weight out" the van. Even at 100 percent cube utilization (a rare occurrence) a product density of 20.7 pounds per cubic foot would be required. The average freight density of major highway carriers is 14 pounds per cubic foot, and it has been reported that 85 percent of the motor freight is less than 22 pounds per cubic foot. Generally, as the length of haul increases, the average operating speed increases, and unit line-haul costs decline (Table 9-2). In the United States, the motor carrier haul begins to pay off when it is more than 400 miles long. Yet, since fuel and labor costs, as well as traffic conditions vary from region to region, cost differences up

TABLE 9-3.   ROUND-TRIP EXTRA COSTS
(WEST COAST)

	40-ft. Hi-Cube Container	40-ft. Standard Container	20-ft. Container
Payload penalty	26,576 lbs.	29,776 lbs.	30,016 lbs.
Revenue loss on cube	$199	$224	$225
Plus per diem difference (7 days)*	7 $206	7 $331	7 $232
Less cost to transload	40 $166	40 $191	40 $192
Plus coupling costs (2)	—	—	20
Total RT average excess cost	$166	$191	$212

* Adjusted unit cost for 40-foot or two 20-foot containers versus two 27-foot trailers.

TABLE 9-4.   ROUND-TRIP EXTRA COSTS
(EAST COAST)

	40-ft. Hi-Cube Container	40-ft. Standard Container	20-ft. Container
Revenue loss on cube	$ 3	$27	$29
Plus per diem difference (7 days)*	21	21	21
	$24	$48	$50
Less cost to transload	25	25	25
	−$1	$23	$25
Plus coupling costs (2)	—	—	20
Total RT average excess cost	−$1	$23	$45

* Adjusted unit cost for 40-foot or two 20-foot containers versus a 40-foot trailer.

to 39% have been found to exist among carriers operations in the various areas, which makes it difficult to draw general conclusions as to transport economics from any given example.

It is readily apparent that it is uneconomic for a West Coast trucker to move container freight very far inland without shifting to domestic equipment. The issue of containers versus the domestic 40-foot trailers used by East Coast truckers is not so clear-cut, as shown in Table 9-4.

The addition of such elements as platform handling costs, identified with LCL operations, widens the gap. These variations confirm the conclusion that, at best, ICC statistics provide only general indicators and are inadequate for specific traffic moves.

VAN TERMINAL COSTS

ICC origin and destination terminal costs reflect domestic operations. Truckers indicate that pickup and delivery at port terminals constitute a difficult situation. The additional coordination of scheduling and paper work demands that specialists at the terminal assume these operations or that outside drayage be used. For this reason, we have developed costs for an inland terminal operation and for a port terminal operation.

Ocean containers are often transloaded by long-haul truckers; although not publicly acknowledged, the procedure is also practiced on the East Coast. Under the transloading system, the containers are off-loaded at the port and drayed to the truck terminal, where the cargo, even if destined

TABLE 9-5.   TRUCK TERMINAL COSTS
(CENTS PER CUBIC FOOT)

Container Size (ft.)	Inland Terminal	Port Area Terminal	For Double Bottoms Add
20	1.32	2.52	0.40
24	1.04	1.98	0.31
27	0.92	1.76	0.21
35	0.71	1.35	0.95
40	0.62	1.18	0.83

Source: U.S. Govt. Report III.

for a single consignee, is transferred directly to a standard highway trailer. The cost of this operation is $25 to $40 for a 40-foot van. The truckers feel that this cost is easily offset by foregoing per diem payments on the container and by improved equipment utilization.

Truck terminal costs are shown in Table 9-5 for an inland terminal, for a port terminal, and for double bottoms, by container size.

BOX SHORT HAUL

Within a 300-mile radius of the port, short-haul trucking of containers predominates. In terms of both size and method of operation, it is distinct from long-haul trucking. Even in cases where a long-haul trucker carries local container traffic, he often finds it best to operate a separate organization.

Competition for local container traffic tends to be very keen, as the capital investment required to enter the business is, at the least, limited to a tractor. Even large operations require only a small service area for parking and office facilities. Table 9-6 shows total short-haul truck costs.

TABLE 9-6.   SHORT-HAUL TRUCKING
(CENTS PER CUBIC FOOT)

Container	100 Miles	200 Miles	300 Miles
20	.077	.133	.187
24	.061	.105	.147
27	.054	.093	.130
35	.041	.071	.100
40	.036	.062	.088

Source: U.S. Govt. Report III.

Terminal costs are included in the total cost, since this practice is consistent with the nature of the short-haul trucking operation. These costs reflect a 30 percent backhaul.

INLAND MILEAGE BLOCKS

Each inland mode, because of traffic balance, container size, etc., has a cost advantage over other inland modes for a particular mileage block. Using typical empty return ratios (100 percent for 20-foot and 19 percent for 40-foot containers), Figure 9-3 illustrates the relative advantages for each mode with 40-foot containers. Up to about 300 miles, local trucking tends to have an advantage. Beyond 300 and up to about 500 miles, the long-haul trucking has an advantage. For longer distances, piggyback (TOFC) operation tends to have the advantage. For comparative purposes, the cost of a unit container train is shown; as miles increase, the advantages of unit-train operation over piggyback operation increases.

This, however, is not always possible. When the 20-foot container is used, the relative advantages of the various inland modes are transformed, as shown in Fig. 9-3. When the long-haul trucker is able to handle two 20-foot containers together, his advantage is greatly increased relative to the piggyback operation. The steeper slope of the piggyback operation using 20-foot containers versus 40-foot containers reflects the higher empty-return ratio associated with the 20-foot containers, too.

SIZE PROBLEMS

Eugene Hindin, President of Gindy Corp., has developed the reasoning of the container–truck interface logically to the conclusion that the ISO-sized 30-foot container is really the optimal intermodal container.

The container size presents a perfect example of the impossibility of attempting to impose standards which ignore the economic growth of scale. The adoption of the 8 ft. × 8 ft. × 10-ft., 20-ft., 30-ft., and 40-ft. sizes by the ISO, while apparently settling the controversy, actually settled very little. The American National Standards Institute has been realistic enough to include the 8½-ft. height, and the 24-ft. and 35-ft. lengths, since containers of these sizes still represent about 10 to 15 percent of the world's container population moving in intermodal traffic.

Containers being produced today differ very little from those produced 10 years ago. Minor design changes were made to improve durability, as manufacturers realized that containers did, in fact, encounter some ser-

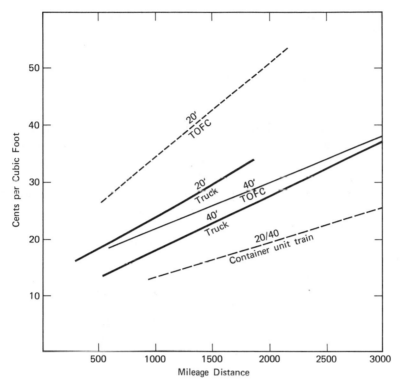

FIGURE 9-3.   INLAND-MODE COST COMPARISON OF 20-FT. AND 40-
FT. CONTAINERS IN USA (COSTS = I.C.C. OUT-OF-POCKET WITH
10 PERCENT RETURN ON INVESTMENT OF EQUIPMENT EMPLOYED).

vice conditions that were different from those encountered in over-the-road traffic.

THE CHEAP VAN

Apparently, while container operators are attempting to weather stormy economic seas, and while existing patterns of freight movement are being shaken down, the emphasis on economical hardware is to be expected. While there is no point in designing hardware which is needlessly expensive, and while reduced capital outlays can certainly reduce maintenance costs and are desirable in their own right, the overall cost of transportation, which is really the name of the game in containerization, is affected very little by even substantial differences in the cost of hardware.

PROGRESSIVE PATTERN OF GROWTH

The next thrust for transportation progress will come, not from technology, but from legislation through the liberalization of overall length limitations to permit the operation of 30-ft. doubles over the highway.

For the highway mode, the manufacturer could finally design a combination which could give the trucker a vehicle as much at home in his own operation as when hauling ocean freight. The weight and cube possibilities which would result from these sizes could be made very attractive, from an economic standpoint. This would permit the more economical positioning of containers, since they would be useful for hauling typical trucker-type cargo.

The truck conveyance could be the greatest beneficiary, although fairly wide acceptance of the 30-ft. size would be necessary before the benefits would become attainable. The design of automated or semiautomated handling equipment to handle 20-ft., 24-ft., 27-ft., 35-ft., and 40-ft. sizes is tremendously difficult and costly. A system to handle 30-ft. containers might be accomplished quite readily.

The attainment of a very attractive weight also benefits the ports and terminals. Many designers of the terminal equipment are plagued by the design of road-to-rail transfer equipment. With the rising cost and virtual scarcity of land in the dock areas, many operators have considered the possibility of pigeon-hole parking in areas where the land prices are cheap and where the environmental conditions will not adversely affect the presence of a high-rise freight terminal (see Chapter 11). Simplification of the size problem would help not only this facet of the terminal problems, but all the handling between ship's hook and road chassis.

VAN SIMPLICITY

The every-box-on-a-chassis system provides that the container does not have to ever be rehandled on land. Eventually, however, the areas required become enormous; for example, trailer parks are approaching sizes of up to 100 acres, if the land is available. It seems that the possibility of getting a container size that would present an opportunity for some economics is worth exploring.

At the moment in the United States, there are virtually no 30-ft. containers in use. Internationally, the only large body of 30-ft. containers is in Great Britain, where the 30 ft. is standard on their liner train operation. If the 30-ft. container were adopted, what would the weight and load limitation of cargo be for foreign-to-inland shippers? The weight limitations would be based on present axle load limitation; currently in most of the United States, that is 18,000 or 20,000 pounds per single axle. Basically, the 30-ft. container would wind up as part of the doubles train, in which case it would essentially have two axles under each container. Working within the existing legislation, we should be able to handle around 76,000 pounds gross combination weight for the train.

Since all of the containers today are structurally capable of carrying more load than they are legally all ed to carry over the highway, the l requires an extended wheelbase quirements and axle loading re- 40-ft. container at 30 long tons it very few containers are loaded diverse cargoes are carried, par- carrying LCL (less-than-container increasing. Therefore, it is clear n a more favorable weight-cube

e 20-ft. size in the early days of erations that led to the modular ft. containers and combine them it is obvious that if each con- acity, you would have an over- aldn't go anywhere. The ability lationship is the purpose of the

a year after Hindin made his velded, all-aluminum bulk resin on was awarded to Dorsey Trail- tensively in transporting resins rsey, a subsidiary of The Dorsey t its manufacturing facilities in the 30 ft. × 8 ft. × 8 ft. boxes will be of exterior post construction to provide smooth interior surfaces. Specifications call for baffles in all corners to prevent trapping bulk materials. Another set of baffles between two 8-inch-diameter discharge chutes on one end, facilitate unloading by tilting. Net usable cargo volume will be 1,630 cubic feet. The roof of each container will have a 20-inch loading hatch and an 8-inch inspection port.

LATIN AMERICA TRUCKING

Presently, Latin America has a retarded development as related to containerization. Since much of the American foreign trade is with Latin America, we must review the parameters in this part of the world, and the effects these conditions may have on U.S. containerization. Except for the use of pallets, the concept of unitized cargo is not yet generally employed to a significant extent in Latin America. Container service has been in operation in most Latin American ports, but the containers are usually handled and transported like any other conventionally packed cargo. Therefore, this method of transportation loses the basic characteristics of efficiency, both in concept and in practice.

The desire to employ as many people as possible to spread the incoming payroll contradicts the principle of work saving through mechanization.

The use of containers in Latin America has been confined to the transport of valuable cargo subject to loss or damage, such as cigarettes and electric batteries. The few Latin American countries where containers are more extensively used are Venezuela, Ecuador, Colombia, Uruguay, Brazil, and Argentina. The only countries which have signed an agreement to facilitate highway transport of containers are Argentina, Brazil, and Uruguay.

Brazil is the only country of Latin America where the law allows simplification of customs formalities for the entry of containers. Brazilian law has established that containers in international transit are exempt from import duties and other federal taxes. Likewise, this legislation facilitates the export of the containers by permitting containers with export merchandise to be sent directly from a location in the interior of the country to the port of embarkation. Brazil also is a good example of road/rail transport integration under one CTO.

There is general agreement in Latin America regarding permissible maximum width. With the exception of Paraguay, which allows only 2.40 m (7.9 ft.) because of its underdeveloped road system, and Colombia, which sets 2.45 m (8 ft.), the remaining countries permit a width of 2.50 m (8.2 ft.). Only Brazil and Venezuela exceed this limit, allowing 2.60 m (8.5 ft.).

International traffic of containers under current regulations will be hindered in Paraguay, since the 2.40 m (7.9 ft.)-limit is less than the standard sizes of the containers. The other countries offer no serious problem in the matter of permissible width, although it should be clearly pointed out that the chassis for vehicles for this type of transport should be specially fitted and equipped with tie-downs and other special accessories, so that the container forms a part of the chassis. This is required because the existing limits leave little allowance for placing apparatus or lateral outside support on the container.

Seven countries of the area set the permissible maximum height at 3.80 m (12.5 ft.) under the strictest regulation. The remaining countries exceed this limit, with Mexico having the most liberal regulation—4.15 m (13.6 ft.) for its Class A highways.

Consequently, in the counrties where 3.80 m (12.5 ft.) is in force for the maximum height of vehicles, the upper part of the chassis of any vehicle for container use must have 1.36 m (4.5 ft.) maximum height above ground level.

TURNING RADIUS VS. KINGPIN SETTING

Flatbed trucks arc used to handle containers in any of the two trucking phases (Terminal Area-TA and Pickup/Delivery-PU/D). In long haul (LH) operations, the container becomes an object of the existing trailer methods of the truckers. When the importance of weight, height, and length of the tractor-trailer unit affects marketing of container handling services in competition with other transport methods, the size and type of container chassis begin to matter.

Originally introduced by Sea-Land for shipping, and by Southern Railway for trucking, the best fit of container versus trailer chassis consists in the design of a tunnel in the forward 6 feet to 8 feet of the container understructure. This allows the container to fit on the chassis like a foot in the shoe. The raised chassis portion acts as a retaining device. Sea-Land later added a safety clamp to the rear end; Southern never did.

This system is fine when the steamship operator, like Sea-Land, furnishes the container chassis. However, when the operator relies on the truckers' ability to interchange, flat-bottom container chassis with corner locking provisions become the optimal solution. The change of a container from one type to another costs about one-third the cost of a new container. Thus, the economics make the changeover undesirable.

Container chassis today can best handle one 40-ft. or two 20-ft. boxes. Local custom in every country gives preference to certain types of chassis which are shown in Figs. 9-4, 9-5, and 9-6. The inclusion of one 30-ft. unit per chassis (instead of a 40-ft.) makes the chassis versatile, yet loses economic value in competitive service.

There are two more important interfaces with the container trailer chassis. West German law, contrary to all other nations, restricts the use of container chassis to the one that complies with the short turning radius prescribed. Depending on the setting of the king-pin, articulation

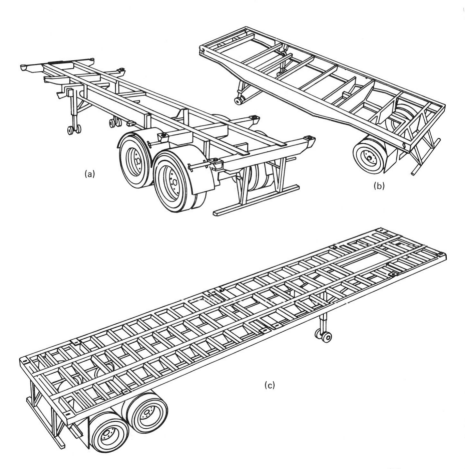

FIGURE 9-4. TYPICAL EUROPEAN CONTAINER CHASSIS FOR 20-FT. TO 40-FT. CONTAINERS COMMONLY USED IN SHORT-SEA TRADE (SOURCE: IRU).

of the total unit is needed for the use of 40-ft. containers. In the United States, the state laws differ according to the bridge-weight formula, as previously described.

In other words, the entire truck unit is considered as a bridge, with the tractor wheels being considered as one support, and the trailer wheels as another support. This system led to two systems of attaching the rear wheels to the trailer chassis which carries the container; namely,

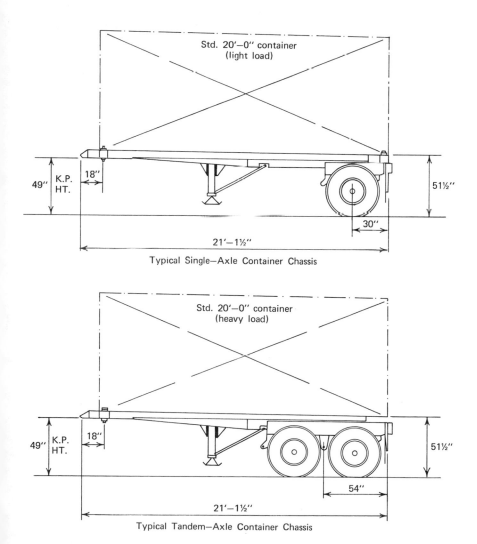

FIGURE 9-5. TYPICAL U.S. CHASSIS FOR 20-FT. CONTAINERS.

1. East Coast setting;
2. West Coast setting.

In the West Coast area, the 8-wheel-equipped undercarriage is attached to the rear section of the chassis, just ending in profile with the tail section. In the Eastern United States, the shorter turning radius is required, and this is obtained by setting the rear axle to a point about 10 ft. forward from the end. Thus, in Germany, the axle set must be able to turn like the rear wheel of a large fire engine. The systems impact of these rules again resides in the facilities which this system provides to bring the trucked container into the distribution chain.

To do just this takes initiative and invention. Gerzymisch, a German trucker, developed a very low-cost interchange system to lift containers from a chassis and transfer them to a railroad car. By attaching wheel-equipped arms to the four lower corner castings, the wheel rides up one

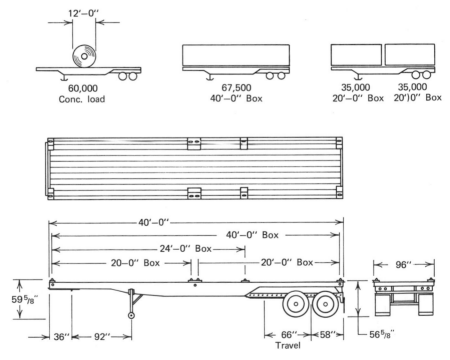

Figure 9-6.   Typical U.S. 40-ft. chassis for 20-ft. to 40-ft. containers.

ramp made out of rails and installed along both sides of the interchange facility. As the tractor pulls forward, the wheel climbs onto the rail which gently lifts the container from the chassis, one side first and the other side later. This system allows the interchange of containers loaded on railroad cars well and gives a low-cost interchange system.

Much of systems engineering will have to be applied to improve the economics of the truck conveyance interface. Due to the legal constraints of the road system, this is a tedious process in the developed nations. But in a country planning for new and modern distribution without having to throw over existing systems, such as China, the systems engineering of the three truck phases may hold the key to a leap ahead in containerization.

DE-BULKING

The first principle of containerization, as we have shown before, is to create bulked shipments out of single consignments. Therefore, since trucking is the general common denominator of the intermodal phases of containerization, we must study the ways in which the three trucking services (TA, PU/D, and LH) interface with the bulking and de-bulking systems on one side and the modal conveyances (ship, inland water, rail, and air) on the other side. The flexibility of the simplest, most generally used truck equipment, flatbed trucks and flat trailers, can be used, providing weight limitations are not critically enforced by heavy container load excess to a certain degree. Faced with container trucking, California has closed its enforcement eyes at looking at the overall length of tractor-trailer combinations hauling containers. It has become customary to handle three 20-ft. containers with one moving unit, two containers being loaded on a 35-ft. trailer with overhang front and back, and another 20-ft. container loaded directly on the tractor chassis. This operation is not desirable, because these containers are not locked onto the chassis with standard corner locking devices, but are usually attached with chains slung over the container; and the container, basically, rides by its own weight. In the event of a collision, two or three containers may be thrown across the road, thus causing excessive hazards. With the container systems slowly moving toward 40-ft. sizes, this practice, which is now used for empty containers only, will not be used much in the future. The constant pressure of cost limitations will have to find new ways to handle more than one 40-ft. unit in the three trucking services. This would also be beneficial to the rail–truck interface, because it will allow a coordination between a TOFC/COFC carload and the PU/D systems, where the traffic and road size allows it. Many systems have been studied to improve the truck phase.

PICKUP/DELIVERY

Better product protection, less damage due to fewer rehandlings, less exposure to transfer, a considerably smaller number of distribution mistakes because of containerization on a regional basis, and, most important, a shorter time cycle from the plant to the customer's store are the advantages of a novel system of transporting in PU/D container systems.

One system consists of using railroad services for longer hauls, instead of the trucks employed in short-haul set up. This system thoroughly embraces containerization's door-to-door concept. This is an important breakthrough in a trade where the customer is often without any container-handling facilities. The need for special equipment to handle containers by the consignee has been eliminated. The container itself is taking the role of a delivery truck at the customer's door.

Initiated and operated by Armour Foods, the system features a container with retractable legs. These containers lock on a trailer bed. An electric motor, operated by the batteries of the pulling tractor, lift each container high enough for the set of retractable legs to be withdrawn. When the legs are set down, the trailer is pulled out. The individual container is then picked up by a smaller truck for delivery to the consignee.

Each container is loaded in delivery sequence. This is a load that one man can handle. It is also a load that usually satisfies the requirements of one single area. The size of the shipment, if handled this way, also eliminates the burdensome chore of unloading by hand from a trailer and putting it on a local delivery truck. This means that the cargo will not be exposed to the weather, nor will it suffer possible damage because of extra handling.

Another valid solution is the use of coupable chassis, originally developed by such trailer manufacturers as Dorsey, Strick, and Fruehauf.

COUPLING PROCEDURES

The procedure for coupling is done by locking the brakes on the load chassis and moving the tractor forward while the sliding subchassis is extended to receive the kingpin section of rear chassis. (Either chassis may be operated individually in an extended position for hauling extremely heavy loads.) When the lead unit is backed under the rear chassis, the kingpin and locking guides engage automatically. The landing gear must then be swung upward. With the front axle slider released and brakes set, the entire unit must move forward until two suspensions automatically unite into a load-equalizing tandem.

BALANCING PU/D SYSTEMS

The 20-ft. container size gave rise to speculations that a door-to-door delivery truck body had entered the intermodal distribution field. Yet the economics of the container operation quickly led to the increased use of the 40-ft. instead of the 20-ft. container. The container has greatest value when moving a "bulked" full load from point to point. An analysis of PU/D truck systems shows that the container has no value in the phase of the system.

A way to increase pickup and delivery size is to reduce pickup and delivery frequency through a controlled PU/D system. The system must consider the geographic location of customers, the work content, the capacity of vehicles, and restrictions on pickup and delivery times; then through computer logic, an optimum network is developed. CARD (Computer Assisted Route Development) networks have been developed for Chicago, Pittsburgh, Philadelphia, Baltimore, Washington, and Houston by several system-engineering firms, and are available to all truck lines. This program provides a grid of an entire city, with time and distances computed for driving between points in the city. The program also accepts customer information, such as volumes picked up and delivered and the amount of time to make various-sized pickups and deliveries. It will also accept codes for time-of-day pickup-and-delivery restrictions, days of the week each customer is to be served, vehicle capacities, and route-day restrictions; then the computer decides how this total mix of situations can best be arranged in a routing system.

It makes sense to combine all distribution activities under a single control. This control has equal standing in management with sales and production. It, in effect, should become an independent factor in management. Suppose a PU/D plan is developed that states if a customer purchases less than seven gallons each week, on the average, he should be served every other week. If a customer buys between seven and 20 gallons each week, he should receive a delivery each week; and if he averages over 20 gallons a week, he qualifies for twice-a-week service.

Whatever the choice, the guidelines should reflect an equitable balance between reasonable delivery service to customers and the costs associated with those services.

If less than 20 routes are operated in any one location, you can reroute just as effectively on a manual basis as you can by computer. Rerouting is simply trying to reduce the total number of driving miles to an absolute minimum, based upon the locations of customers and the frequencies at which you serve them. Certainly, if you operate large networks, 50 or 60 in one territory, the computer may be the way to go.

TRUCK CONTAINER SERVICE

Many motor carriers participate reluctantly in the container trade. One specialized trucking firm, however, is developing rapidly as a hauler of intermodal containers to and from steamship terminals of the New York–New Jersey metropolitan area, and serving New England and the Middle Atlantic States. The company conceived the idea of establishing a trucking firm that would specialize exclusively in the carriage of containers. With competent advice and support from the U.S. Department of Commerce and financial help from the New York Urban Coalition, True Transport, Inc. started operations in August 1969. Four months later, in December, the company had already handled close to one thousand containers. What has happened proves beyond any doubt the urgent need for a specialized Terminal Area container carrier.

Knowing from experience about the feelings between ocean container carriers and truckers about the handling of containers convinced the company of the need. In implementing the container transport concept, the TA trucker has to undergo other changes, which are innovations for a trucking firm. Personnel with steamship background and experience in handling ocean freight and customs documentation have to be hired. New equipment has to be bought, and specialized supporting facilities have to be established.

To guard against pilferage and hijacking, a radar-type burglary alarm system was installed which protects the containers held overnight in the company's storage yard, as well as freight stored in its warehouse.

An efficient alarm system is especially important since part of the new operation requires pulling containers from container yards at night, or in the later afternoon, when the yards are less busy, and holding them overnight for delivery the next morning.

Therefore, container freight stations are the inland facilities now taking the place of the shoreside docks of conventional shipping. Freedom to develop neutral internal container freight stations, as well as container depots, is almost a must in the future development of expanded containerization. Eventually, this will find reflection in the transportation laws of the country.

PORTS OF CALL VS. TRUCKS

Trucking is without doubt the area of containerization least attempted by the new methodology. Typically, Pacific Motor Trucking, one of the largest container haulers in California, describes its activities like this. The containers and chassis are owned and controlled by the steamship companies, and PMT furnishes the drivers and power equipment. The type of power equipment is conventional, two- and three-axle units, depending upon the weight to be handled. The service provided is pickup and delivery or line-haul in nature and is governed by published tariff rates.

The legal weight, height, and length laws differ from state to state, and from country to country, international conventions notwithstanding. The principles of "Port Limitation" for containerships, and the desire of railroads to engage only in remunerative traffic affect the truck conveyance development.

The economics achieved by containerships is such that their operators sometimes find it cheaper to absorb the cost of transporting the freight from one port to another in the same coastal range by truck or rail than to provide facilities in both ports. They will concentrate on one major port, and defray the cost of transporting the freight to the other port. This has been the case with Japanese lines servicing Seattle and Portland, and other companies serving New York and Philadelphia.

If the system works over an extended period of time, as it is supposed to work, exporters and importers in one major port area will fare alike insofar as rates are concerned. The rate on freight to an address in the Philadelphia area will be no greater if imported and forwarded via New York than if shipped via Philadelphia. If there is any difference at all, it may be in the delivery time which could, though it wouldn't necessarily, favor business in the New York area.

THE PHILADELPHIA CASE

Philadelphia, like Portland and in some respects San Diego, has a great deal of money and effort expended in the development of its port. If that port is by-passed by containerships, because of the greater volume flowing through New York, those who have worked so hard and spent so much to create a modern port area will find themselves left behind. By by-passing these ports, trucks will intermodally handle more cargo over those distances from inland points in Philadelphia or Portland to New York or Seattle. The people who have worked so hard to develop these ports at great expense to the community decided to take this case to court. One could think that this is similar to the historical fight against machine weaving in England. Here, as there, economy of scale will injure a large segment of the population. It means that the courts must eventually evaluate what is more important from the legal point of view.

Economy of scale at least means by-pass of ports at first. That the ports might have a chance to develop with genuine new trades later is a question. On the other hand, the export trade would benefit more from the economy of scale. Such a decision is hard to make. Many ports find themselves within the same apprehensive situation. Along the New England coast, a score of ports, including Salem and Marblehead, found their positions as shipping centers eroding many years ago, as trucks began to concentrate freight movements on Boston, which now finds itself in pretty much the same threatening situation as Philadelphia. The larger steamships become, the more they tend to concentrate on relatively few ports where their earnings prospects are best.

Philadelphia maritime interests have won agreements from ocean carriers to end the controversial practice of diverting cargoes from movement through competing New York. More discussion of this problem will be covered in Chapter 20.

Containership companies maintain that such practices are legal and amount to nothing more than a substitute of service for freight shippers in the diverted seaport area. Basically, the containership companies want to limit the port calls of their expensive vessels, and they would like to use the diversion practice as a means of serving shippers in the ports not served directly by the vessels.

There is much to be said on both sides. The matter is not simple. It is doubtful if any long-range solution can be found until the issue of container inland service is solved.

SERVICE PLAN

A five-point terminal and equipment pooling program to bring about a more economical operation by motor carriers has been proposed.

R. S. Tarsitano, Traffic Manager of the Wall Rope Works of Beverly,

N.J., made his proposal in a letter sent to the Interstate Commerce Commission. He complained that recent truck rate increases have been accompanied by very little improvement in service and proposed:

1. Common motor carriers should be made to combine their operations in cities served by more than one carrier by operating from separate terminal facilities. Large cities would naturally require from two to four terminals, depending on their size.

2. Carriers operating from the same terminal facilities should be made to pool their vehicles under control of the participating carriers for the performance of pickup and delivery service.

3. Carriers having an imbalance problem to terminals with insufficient tonnage . . . should be permitted to joint load with each other in moving freight between terminal areas served by a group of carriers operating from and to the same terminal.

4. The cost of operating the terminals and vehicles (thus pooled) . . . would be prorated among the carriers.

5. Existing terminal buildings situated in areas that can be enlarged to accommodate all carriers serving a particular area should be expanded. All other terminals not required would be disposed of through sale.

In asking the ICC to use its regulatory authority to impose such a pooling program on the carriers, Mr. Tarsitano said he is "confident that a program of this nature will contribute to a more economical operation." He added that another result would be substantial reduction in the vehicular congestion that clogs urban thoroughfares.

Airlift Conveyance Systems

AIR CONTAINERS

The importance of containers to air transportation is immeasurably great. The high cost of aircraft requires fast loading, since the investment in the flying equipment can be utilized economically only if the full technical utilization is attained. Containers, in the larger sense of the word, are the simplest loading device for many small parcels into the fuselage of the airplane.

But the airplane as a cargo carrier is not yet a true systems component of the intermodal chain. The high cost factor per ton-mile associated with air transportation requires coordinated and integrated delivery and pickup systems for the benefit of the air cargo market, just as piggyback is an adjunct to the rail transport system. Therefore, air cargo has developed into a unique bimodal system connecting airplanes with trucking. True examples of interface relationship between air cargo, rail, and ship container systems are infrequent, although much of it has been used to widely promote this idea.

The reason that air cargo had to develop its own system is that the intermodal container concept, developed around the ISO standards, has required the design of heavy corner castings, corner posts, and structure into the container for integrated transportation by ship. The carriage of this excess weight demands an excessive effort of energy, as far as the airplane is concerned, against the value of some intermodal savings. Air freight at this stage is a rather unique isolated method of high-speed, long-distance hauling of commodities. It is important and effective, when related to products which are time-conditioned. These time-price-related commodities represent approximately one percent (or even less) of the total volume of goods moved in the world, and are mostly in two categories.

1. Consumer products;
2. Industrial components needed urgently.

AIR CARGO DEVELOPMENT

Air freight, in general, is a postwar development which grew out of the need for fast transportation of supplies on a world-wide basis during World War II. The Air Transport Command (ATC) and the Naval Air Transport Service, now the Military Air Transport Service (MATS), handled 1.8 billion ton-miles to 1945. After the war, some veterans picked up surplus planes and started freight lines. They were aided in getting established by the fact that the certified carriers were preoccupied with increased passenger growth. Many of these nonscheduled air freight operators in the United States went out of business, but small national air cargo carriers appeared as "flag lines" of some developing nations. This trend provided for continuance of the acquired air cargo idea and contributed to further development of international viable services. Only four of these early nonskeds were certificated by the Civil Acronautics Board (CAB).

Aircraft manufacturers predicted in 1950 that air freight carried at 15¢ per ton-mile would be 500 million to 4 billion ton-miles. These estimates proved to be overly optimistic.

In spite of more rapid growth in air cargo volume, the air freight share is still only basically a system by itself, not enmeshed in the overall transport containerization. With the economic recession of 1970, the search for more economic ways to distribute cargo has brought many shippers and receivers back to ground containerization. This move has nothing to do with technology, but is a result of economic conditions and cost. We must, however, analyze aircraft as a conveyance using containers with all its limitations and benefits, to formulate conceptual ideas for further development and the contributions both systems can make to each other.

MODE INTERFACE

Our analysis deals with the key precepts and significant elements in this relationship between the air mode and the interface using containers. To dwell on the important issues requires elimination of the euphoria created by a glamorous new industry in promoting their often untested plans. Validity results from incorporation of several novel ideas of containerization to further cost reduction and service improvement in air cargo and at this junction, eventually, the two systems will interface and produce economy of scale for air.

AIR INTERFACE FACTORS

The review of the important factors deals, therefore, with:

1. Weight-cube relation constraints;
2. Present ATA and IATA container standards;
3. Terminal systems;
4. Road/air bimodality technique;
5. Perishable commodity service;
6. Stuffing/forwarding procedures;
7. Contribution of V/STOL technology.

Air freight transportation will probably not reach its state of maturity until 1990. In the meantime, we are living in an age of experimentation and expansion on every frontier of a rapid-growth industry. Aircraft development has been, and will continue to be, the major field of exploration. For it is advances in the power technology that formulate the lifeblood of air cargo.

The aircraft, more than any other transportation vehicle, must be carefully evaluated as to its cubic ratio weight-carrying capacity. We measure the cost of carrying a pound of weight or a cubic foot of loadable volume in all of our aircraft evaluation programs. Its significance extends beyond the area of aircraft evaluation, for considered from this standpoint we can envision new concepts of rate-making being entirely feasible. In addition, we can better understand the elements that control the degree of material handling system implementation that can be introduced into the aircraft subsystem to offset ground-handling, terminal, and distribution costs.

USABLE VOLUME ANALYZED

The determination of the maximum usable volume in a circular fuselage envelope represents one element in the process of optimizing the aircraft design. It must be kept in mind that one can suboptimize a portion of the system or several portions of the system and yet arrive at a design which is less than optimum for the whole system. For example, if a fuselage configuration were selected which was only slightly larger than that of the containers which are to be carried—and which is, therefore, perhaps longitudinal in cross section—this design might prove to be very high when measured in terms of the usable volume compared to the total internal volume. However, the weight penalties involved in constructing a noncircular cross section fuselage capable of withstanding pressurization loads might be such that the resulting design would not be optimum in terms of weight-carrying ability.

The analysis of the maximum volume in a circular hull envelope provides the basic understanding. The maximum useful area (volume) within a circular segment envelope is of interest in the design of cargo containers for aircraft compartments. The dimensions of the container for maximum volume should be determined. Referring to Fig. 10-1, we have:

$$A = 2(ab + ac); \tag{1}$$

$$b = \sqrt{R^2 - a^2}. \tag{2}$$

Substituting the value of b in Equation 2 into Equation 1, we obtain:

$$A = 2(a\sqrt{R^2 - a^2} + ac). \tag{3}$$

In order to determine the value of a which yields maximum area, Equation 3 is differentiated with respect to a and set equal to zero:

$$\frac{dA}{da} = 2\left[\frac{a(-2a)}{2\sqrt{R^2 - a^2}} + \sqrt{R^2 - a^2} + c\right] = 0.$$

Rearranging terms and squaring:

$$4a^4 + 9c^2 - 4R^2(a^2 + R^4 - c^2R^2 = 0.$$

Solving for a^2,

$$a^2 = \frac{R^2}{8}\left[4 - \left(\frac{c}{R}\right)^2 + \frac{c}{R}\sqrt{\left(\frac{c}{R}\right)^2 + 8}\right] = R^2 f\left(\frac{c}{R}\right), \tag{4}$$

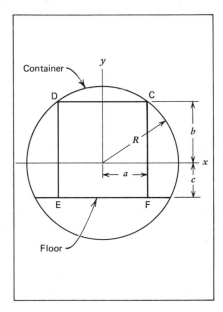

FIGURE 10-1.   MAXIMUM VOLUME IN A CIRCULAR HULL (SOURCE: *Design News*).

and the optimum ratio a/R is then found to be:

$$\frac{a}{R_{opt}} = \frac{\sqrt{4 - \left(\frac{c}{R}\right)^2 + \sqrt{\left(\frac{c}{R}\right)^2 + 8}}}{8} = \sqrt{f\left(\frac{c}{R}\right)}. \qquad (5)$$

The optimum ratio, a/R, is plotted in Fig. 10-2 as a function of c/R. It is noted that a cutoff exists for this ratio and is given by:

$$\frac{a}{R} = \sqrt{1 - \left(\frac{c}{R}\right)^2}. \qquad (6)$$

PAYLOAD REDUCTIONS

Most of the larger commercial jet aircraft use unit load systems in ground operation today. In so doing, the maximum payload will be reduced, sometimes as much as 10 percent. Nevertheless, it is only through use of this degree of mechanization that the ground time can be kept at a low enough value to permit retention of high aircraft utilization. What

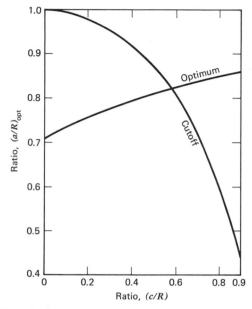

FIGURE 10-2.   OPTIMUM-RATIO DIAGRAM (SOURCE: *Design News*).

is important, therefore, is not necessarily maximum payload per flight, nor maximum aircraft utilization, nor maximum aircraft productivity (ton-miles per day). The overriding criteria are minimum cost per ton-mile or per cubic-foot-mile; in fact, maximum return on investment is even a better criterion.

We can evaluate the changes that will, most likely, evolve in the areas of assembling and distributing of cargo and, certainly, in the area of rate-making.

Let's view, first, the elements of air containerization, which must be considered the basic element of our material-handling systems.

The average weight of shipments today is in the area of 500 to 550 pounds. In projecting the future trend, this figure will not be substantially altered. Furthermore, basic air traffic composition will not vary to any great degree from that shown in Table 10-1.

An industry program has been implemented, which has a twofold objective: (1) to create incentive to shippers to containerize, thus minimizing the total pieces to be handled at the airport terminal, and (2) to pass to the shipper certain discounts for density which will take advantage of the added weight capacity of the jet aircraft, thus increasing their productivity.

TABLE 10-1. PERCENTAGES OF AIR TRAFFIC BY WEIGHT

Weight Bracket	No. of Shipments	Wt. of Shipment
Under 200 lbs.	42%	5%
200 lbs. to 1,000 lbs.	41%	25%
1,000 to 4,000 lbs.	14%	37%
4,000 lbs. and over	3%	33%

TERMINAL COST DETERMINATION

What is still needed is the incorporation into air cargo tariffs of the effect of number of pieces on terminal handling costs, so that this, too, can be accounted for in the container rate structure, thus greatly increasing the incentive to unitize.

The approach to containerization will be expanded as we gain experience. From a sales and operations standpoint, the program has sound, basic logic. It can become a major element in tomorrow's rate-making policy. For the concept can, in the majority of cases, gain the advantages of a density-oriented tariff, yet provide tariff simplification and control. In essence, we are looking at our "cost per cubic-foot-mile." We are gaining experience in converting this knowledge to a rating philosophy; therefore, the emphasis in the future will most likely be in the area of space marketing.

There are several disadvantages of this development. First, only one container type is carrier-owned, because it is specially designed to fit the contour of the individual carrier's aircraft configuration. This container is too cumbersome to handle; it is not compatible with present shippers' dock areas; and it does present some stacking problems. Second, the remainder of the container groups are shipper-owned. If a shipper has a round-trip flow of traffic, there are economic benefits, particularly in the higher-density traffic. But the majority of shippers do not have a round-trip flow. They have two alternatives: (1) disposable containers and (2) return units under normal tariff provisions. Both alternatives have very questionable economic feasibility. The industry is focusing on a container pool as an answer.

SHIPMENT WEIGHT BREAKS

The greatest area of concern lies in shipments whose weight is under 500 pounds, which represents better than 60 percent of the number of shipments received. The container program will not affect this traffic.

While great emphasis has been placed on this very important consideration, the level of efficiency and cost implication does not indicate that we are in an area of profitability. As volume increases, there will be experimentation in areas of carrier-inhouse programs, containerizing further upstream. Implementation of the satellite terminal concept and unitizing devices are now employed.

The general opinion is that the program will follow the American Standard Association's recommendations of 8 ft. × 8 ft. × 10-ft. modules, thus creating greater compatibility with the shippers' dock, as well as the motor carrier haul between that dock and the airport terminal.

The new large jets will provide sufficiently larger fuselage volume to allow carriage of large belly-compartment units and the 8 ft. × 8-ft. cross section van-type containers, in use today, on the main deck.

AIR LAND CONTAINERS

Attempts are being made to achieve as high a degree of standardization as possible. In fact, some of the jets will be able to accommodate containers that are 8½ ft. high. The Society of Automotive Engineers has issued an Aerospace Standard AS 832, "Air-Land Containers," which represents, perhaps, the first serious attempt to standardize on this size of container for the air and land modes.

In the case of the 747 Superjet, Boeing originally established an internal organization specifically to work with and encourage container manufacturers to design and build lower-lobe containers for the belly compartment. The airline operators wanted to include their requirements in the design, and particularly with the advent of the Douglas DC-10 and the Lockheed L-1011, this work was subsequently taken over by a committee under Air Transport Association of America.

INTERCHANGEABILITY

Those airlines who had purchased both the 747 and either the DC-10 or the L-1011 realized that standardization of lower-deck containers would permit them to effect on-line and interline transfers of complete containers between these different types of aircraft. To attain this interchangeability, it became necessary for Douglas and for Lockheed to raise the cabin floors, in order to provide a cargo compartment height equal to that of the 747. All in all, the ATA Committee has issued specifications for three types of these containers, which are as follows:

1. The LD-1 container is designed specifically for the 747; and although it has the same height and longitudinal dimensions of the other containers, it is approximately 15 in. wider. Thus, it achieves maximum volume, but it cannot be loaded into the smaller-diameter fuselages of the DC-10 or L-1011. Moreover, the LD-1 container must be restrained to the cargo compartment floor through its flanges at the base.

2. The LD-2 container is of the size that can be accommodated only in the Boeing 747, but it need not be restrained, and can be considered as of the same nature as any piece of cargo. The upward and sideward restraints are taken by the cargo compartment's ceiling and walls.

3. The LD-3 container can be accommodated in any one of the three wide-body jets and, like the LD-2, need not be restrained in the cargo compartment.

Specifications were design-requirement specifications, and not design specifications per se, so that no given material was listed. The materials being offered in these containers vary from ultraheavy to ultralight, and from ultrafragile to ultrastrong.

A composite of a number of materials was being utilized to take advantage of maximum strength and durability, while offering a minimum weight. The base is fabricated of balsa sandwich panel, the shelves of aluminum honeycomb sandwich; the sides, top, and center partition of skin and frame aluminum; and the doors are of a composite plastic. The manufacturer says this container nets a volume of 173 cubic feet and a weight of 230 pounds. The tare weight, therefore, is 1.32 pounds per cubic foot. Further design refinement and the acceptance of some sophisticated materials may further reduce this figure. Obviously, other manufacturers will produce units that may be heavier but will probably excel in other characteristics.

TRUCKING COMPATIBILITY

The objective is to provide a specification for an airborne container that would primarily be compatible with trucks. The specification provides a container that has the same external cross-sectional and linear dimensions as the USASI-MH5.1 container. It can be carried on and interlined between aircraft, and is intermodal to trucks. It is not intermodal to ships in that it does not retain the capability to be stacked six high and loaded in ships' cells.

The release of the MH5 specification provided that it contain the requirements for an intermodal container. This, of course, did not apply, since the aircraft requirements were, in fact, not covered in that specification. There was an assignment to put into the MH5 specification those requirements necessary to make the container good for air transport, and to do so with a minimum of change to the basic specification.

While only two organizations are working toward provisions of 8 ft. × 8-ft. container specifications, other organizations are interested in the promotion and facilitation of container usage. The Air Transport Association has been very active in providing specifications for the lower compartments. In addition, ATA has a large program of incentives in effect for shippers that are involved with their "A," "B," "C," and "D" size container usage. The "A" container is basically the "Igloo," while the "B," "C," and "D" units are modular nonstructural portions of the "A" unit. This group will, undoubtedly, become involved with refinements and the future of large main-deck containers.

THE IATA SYSTEM

International Air Transport Association (IATA) maintains a container program and an incentive program. While the IATA container program has, for the most part, been relegated to nonstructural containers for use with pallets and nets, this group has, as recently as January 1969, discussed their involvement with the 8 ft. × 8-ft. units.

The U.S. Government, too, has become concerned in what it can do to promote container activities. In the spring of 1968, the Office of Facilitation, Department of Transportation, established a transportation facilitation committee "to identify and to alleviate those impediments in the transportation system that limit full attainment of safe, convenient, and economical transportation." This committee, in turn, established five task forces, among which is the Intermodal Transport Task Force. This task force organized a working group called the "Air Intermodal Container Systems Work Group."

The aim of this group is to "analyze the implications of a total systems application of surface-air container use today and the changes necessary to permit fullest expansion of intermodal transportation and to develop recommendations to improve intermodal transportation." As such, this group has been involved in numerous activities to expedite container approvals through governmental agencies and to expedite container transport in the normal flow of surface and air transportation.

Aircraft cargo systems to date have employed a system of roller trays for conveyance of pallets and containers fore and aft in the fuselage. Except in a few cases, the power has been manual; and it is not uncommon, with heavy loads, to see as many as five or six cargo handlers pushing a load into the airplane.

TARE WEIGHT ALLOWANCES

We would allow $1\frac{1}{2}$ pounds tare weight per cubic foot of volume. With a 100-cubic-foot container, the allowable tare weight would be 150 pounds. I consider this "begging the question," because it means that if a container with 1,000 pounds of payload and with a gross weight of 1,150 pounds is accepted on the airplane, the shipper is paying for 1,000 pounds knowingly. But unknowingly, he still has to pay for the tare weight, because the airplane has to lift the container, as well as the payload. How much better it would be, therefore, if the rate structure were such that there would be zero tare weight allowance, but that the rate per pound would be reduced, so that the shipper with his 1,150-pound chargeable weight is still paying no more than previously. In this way, the shipper who is sending his commodities a short distance with many cycles of use per month could justify a heavier and more maintainable container without being forced to pay for the incremental weight above the tare weight allowance. By the same token, the shipper of only long-distance commodities may wish to have a very expensive and exotic container, since he has very few cycles per month.

With each of the wide-body jets coming into service today—the Boeing 747, the Douglas DC-10, and the Lockheed L-1011—power will be used to move the containers into and out of the airplane, even in the case of the lower-deck LD-series containers.

The 747 can accept any of the following loads: 30 SAE 10-foot containers, 14 of the 20-foot containers, and 5 of the 40-foot containers, 32 commercial or military pallets measuring 88 inches, or random intermix, but not $8\frac{1}{2}$ ft. $\times$ 8-ft. containers.

At the airport, the emphasis must be placed on processing systems and storage capability. While major studies have been made in the area of terminal processing, it must be considered experimental at best. We have, today, the conveyor and the towveyor advocates. Each system implemented has specific advantages over the other.

UNIT LOAD MANUAL

The International Air Transport Association (IATA) has two publications on the subject of containers and pallets. The *IATA Aircraft Unit Load Devices Manual* is a 600-page document containing complete information on aircraft pallets, nets, igloos, and aircraft containers, including temperature-controlled units. There are eleven sections in the manual, which cover general marketing information on IATA incentive programs for bulk unitization; registration and marking requirements; customs clearance; instructions for loading the unit and general handling data; recommended standard load contours; information on all currently operated cargo-carrying aircraft types; IATA Standard Specifications for manufacture of units as well as general technical criteria and serviceability limits; details on individual units presently registered with IATA; and data on equipment used by each airline.

Additionally, the *IATA Register of Containers and Pallets* is a 200-page document which lists all aircraft and nonaircraft unit-load devices presently registered with IATA. It has five sections containing general marketing information on the IATA Container Program, primarily for nonaircraft containers; registration and marking procedures; technical requirements, including minimum design criteria, standard sizes, and test requirements for nonaircraft containers of the present 17 standard sizes; and details of individual units registered with IATA.

Lacking in both approaches is an efficient method of traffic storage, live and/or dead, which is linked to the basic material-handling systems. An efficient system must provide selectivity, multisorting capability, and proper load sequencing. There is unfolding a system approach that combines the advantages of both processing systems—tied effectively to load build-up operation, as well as individual shipment identification in a live and/or dead storage mode. It incorporates a cart-stacking device that can automatically pull the shipments in proper sequences with a high degree of selectivity. Storage capability of unit loads and later intermodal containers must be expanded. While the majority of our terminals today have adequate processing areas, we lack adequate traffic storage capability. The airline strikes have brought this problem into clear focus for those who continued to operate. Our ability to efficiently absorb a surge lay squarely in the area of inadequate storage systems. We are storing on a square-foot basis, rather than a cubic-foot basis. The facility capability is there; but it is not properly utilized. Major emphasis will be placed in this area.

COST BUYS TIME

Air travel is fast and expensive. Speed provides capability for high-priority transport. The additional cost buys time—not additional transport.

Aircraft share with the ships the infinite choice of paths between points, but aircraft can also transit intervening land areas. While the paths are unlimited, the terminal points tend to be very definite. Aircraft operate from terminal facilities that tend generally to be fixed. Excepting for very specialized vehicles, the tendency parallels the need for paths by land vehicles; that is, as heavier and more sophisticated air vehicles are developed, the greater the requirement for terminal facilities from which to operate.

TERMINAL CONSTRAINTS

Any air freight container terminal system must fulfill these requirements:

1. It must offer rapid and reliable service.
2. Its systems, methods, and procedures must be flexible within a standardized framework to permit rapid adaptability to the changing operational need.
3. It should synchronize its operations through a sensitive acceptance and load-assignment organization, with cargo generation, aircraft control, and traffic agencies, so as to secure fullest utilization of available airlift.

Subsidiary benefits that will accrue from the use of the proper air cargo mechanical handling system are:

1. Reduction of cost of ground handling;
2. Increase of tons of cargo handled per man hour;
3. Reduction of damage to cargo;
4. Reduction of lost or astray cargo.

DESIGN PARAMETERS

In arriving at a system for the mechanical handling of air cargo containers, the simultaneous development and adoption of the following are assumed:

1. A single universal document that will serve all purposes—shipping authority, transportation document, and receiving voucher—and is amenable to electronic preparation, computation, and processing;
2. A standardized pallet container module that will give the highest possible cube utilization;
3. A program that will facilitate containers for all shippers.

In the design of a plant layout for an air freight terminal, the exterior shape of the building is not considered until the very last; and then only for what it is—a weatherproofing sheath for the cargo and equipment.

ALL-CARGO AIRPORTS

An all-cargo airport in California has received study. The airport would be at Paso Robles, a small city of some 8,000 population, located near the coast and almost halfway between San Francisco and Los Angeles. Its importance would be its proximity to highways linking the San Francisco and Los Angeles areas, and to the San Joaquin Valley and its produce. Produce could be picked in the early morning hours, loaded into insulated containers, and placed upon trucks which are equipped with refrigeration units that can be quickly coupled to these containers. In a matter of hours these containers could be transported to the airport, disconnected from the trucks, and loaded onto cargo aircraft for departure to the midwest and to the eastern seaboard. Because of the time zone differential, the 1:00 P.M. departure from Paso Robles would result in an arrival, even on the eastern seaboard, at approximately 9:00 P.M. The insulated containers full of produce would then be unloaded and shipped directly to the markets, thus allowing the airplane to be reloaded with similar containers; but, this time, loaded with industrial goods and other commodities which require first-morning delivery in areas as far north as San Francisco and as far south as Los Angeles. Thanks to the time zone differential, a 10:00 P.M. departure from the east coast would result in a 1:00 A.M. arrival in Paso Robles, thus allowing sufficient time for transfer of the containers to trucks and for an up-to-200-mile delivery by truck to the consignee.

PATHS OF OUTBOUND CONTAINERS

Trucks delivering cargo are leveled to the receiving dock by hydraulically lifting the rear wheels of the truck on an "elevator." This is typical of one type of terminal. Cargo is discharged onto an accumulative live-roller platform that can hold the complete load of any over-the-road semitrailer. From these platforms, cargo to be containerized is segregated and put on a package conveyor, where all containerization is done. Cargo to be palletized and cargo that has to travel on its own package are shunted onto live-roller lines. At his control point, determination is made to direct the cargo to a palletization line or directly to storage and load selection lines. Cargo that is to go to a palletization line is moved into the proper line by mechanical means. At the end of each palletization line, trained personnel arrange cargo into a structure (much as a stone mason takes odd-size rectangular blocks and arranges them into a wall or building) so that the cargo does not overhang the modular or the master pallet and with as few voids as possible. The strapped, labeled pallet load is moved onto a live-roller conveyor that takes it to the proper storage and load-selection lines.

At a point close to the receiving section, it meets and joins the line carrying packages directly to the storage and selection lines; and just shortly after this junction, the pallets or container pass over an on-the-fly scale which automatically weighs and cubes and labels the package with the gross weight. At the control point just a little further on, human selectivity is employed to determine shunting to the correct storage and selection line.

In a sampling, it was found that of the total packages handled, 49 percent were 60 pounds or less, and 69 percent were 5 cubic feet or less. It is with these groups that our greatest savings can be accomplished. These packages are routed to the mezzanine floor through a package conveyor and inclined belt, and into one of several spiral chutes. These chutes feed onto a routing table where packages are routed to destination and priority designated. After each consolidation container is filled and closed, it is first routed over an on-the-fly scale which weighs, cubes, and automatically attaches a label showing gross weight, and then routed into the proper storage and selection line.

LOAD PLANNING

As for load planning through the use of computer control, the significance of container loading can be predetermined to accomplish two things:

1. Measuring that the airplane weight and balance will always be within limitation;
2. Getting the "first-off" containers as near to the door as possible. This, in effect, is a system quite similar to the port and ship control system described in Chapter 18.

In the case of a partial off-load, partial on-load operation in connection with certain "milk-run"-type operations, the load planner sets weights onto the beam of the scale to represent thru loads. The facsimile load message that has been sent shows him how many square feet and cube feet he has available. He puts his on-load on that portion of the scale which represents the aircraft floor space available to him and proceeds with determination of the center of gravity, as if all of the cargo were physically being weighed.

Eighty-five to ninety percent of airliftable containers can be handled by the terminal conveyor systems. The remaining 15 to 10 percent constitute either cargo too large to be handled through a special section of the terminal or equipment for their storage and selection line.

All conveyors on the main floor except at work stations should be as close to the floor as possible. This has been done for the following two reasons:

1. In the event of mechanical breakdown or power failure, the terminal can still perform its functions although somewhat limited as to capacity and speed.

2. The growth in tonnage carried by air in the future will necessitate more square feet of storage and selection lines.

GROUND HANDLING

The developments in air cargo, historically, are quite parallel to the elements in ocean shipping. The most costly consequence of the continued growth of air cargo has been the pyramiding connected with labor use at airports. It is realized that if the speed of service is to be maintained with the rapidly increasing throughput, consignments could no longer be handled in the traditional manner.

There are two alternatives. The airline cargo terminals could be automated with mechanical handling and storage systems. Although costly to install, this promises to give overall unit cost savings in the long term. The other alternative is to introduce rating incentives for forwarders to consolidate air cargo into containers for direct loading into aircraft, which would save double handling. Although the second choice is obviously the most beneficial in cost, some of the smaller airlines did not want containers, as they could not carry them on their aircraft.

The airlines have been forced to turn to the obvious solution; that is, if forwarders already handle some 70 to 80 percent of air cargo, they should stuff the containers themselves to avoid double handling. Their mechanical handling systems or their buildup and breakdown areas would become cargo transfer points, not cargo handling docks.

Three-and-a-half-ton freight igloos and pallets are now easily handled by two men, thanks to the introduction of a simple loading platform at Manchester Airport, UK.

The transfer platform is angled and has 850 one-inch stainless steel balls seated in the platform for pallet maneuverability, and a spinning platform which provides universal loading and unloading angles. The success of this equipment in operation can be gauged by the unloading records regularly being achieved—twenty tons in eight minutes by two men.

Whichever side of the fuselage the freight door is located, the new platform can be utilized without the need for the critically accurate positioning when using a transporter system. Complete trains of specially designed side-loading trailers can be brought in a continuous train in close proximity to aircraft without being too close to nose, wings, or steps. All this equipment has a basic height of 20 inches. This unit has proved that side-loading trailer equipment is fast, dependable, and economic.

ROLE OF FORWARDERS

The continuation of investment into air containers will depend upon rate changes which provide an incentive. It is resulting in the formation of far larger companies than have previously been known in the industry. The aim is to gain a large enough share of the market to benefit fully from the container rates as and when they finally appear.

Some countries, and in particular the United States, differentiate between forwarders and agents. In most cases, however, they are regarded as an entity, though the forwarder is only really acting as "forwarder" when he consolidates small shipments into one larger consignment before he delivers it to the airline.

RATE STRUCTURE PHILOSOPHY

The great rate structure philosophy has grown in an erratical and empirical manner, so that there are many areas where the validity of the assumptions leaves something to be desired. The Civil Aeronautics Board has recognized that a full investigation of this rate structure philosophy is required and is encouraging the carriers and the shippers to submit their suggestions for an improvement, which would be of long-term benefit to the entire air cargo industry. Among changes which should be considered are such items as: the effect of number of pieces on terminal costs and, hence, upon rates; the effect of shipment density and aircraft design density upon the cube rules (the value of density below which volume rating is used rather than weight rating); and the allowable tare weights, if any, for containers.

The other types of container will be the wide-body jet belly container and the full-igloo container mentioned previously, but these may well be owned by the airlines as they will really be part of the aircraft equipment.

The larger forwarders have already begun to construct their own pallet and container buildup areas, and this is now being generally accepted by the airlines. However, very few shippers themselves will be able to load the containers. In any case, few shippers have regular traffic of $2\frac{1}{2}$ tons that will exactly fit one of these containers on any one destination with any regularity.

The movement will, therefore, be mainly from forwarders' premises through to forwarders' premises. One additional problem that has to be overcome concerns the customs procedures on arrival in the destination country.

AGRICULTURAL INDUSTRIAL INTERCHANGE

The air container operation can be based on the interchange of agricultural products and manufactured products. An air container system probably could succeed only with difficulty in the movement of either agricultural or manufactured products exclusively. The quantities of cargo interchanged must be fairly constant. The principal movement of commodities probably will be of perishable agricultural products from west to east and south to north, with industrial products on the return haul. There would, of course, be some contrary minor movement of commodities.

It is possible to provide full planeloads of containers filled with agricultural perishables to move by air from extensive agricultural areas to metropolitan centers. New airplanes will make it possible to transport still greater quantities of highly perishable produce efficiently. However, air cargo will not approach its full potential so long as the ground movement time remains such a great portion of the total transit time. This potential will not be reached until methods and equipment for refrigerating perishable air cargo are improved.

With the newer jet cargo airplanes, a typical transcontinental movement of cargo may take about 20 hours from shipper to consignee, with the actual air time only 5 hours of this and the rest consumed in surface transport, ground handling, and waiting on the dock. Obviously, the shorter the trip, the lower the percentage of time that the cargo is airborne.

AIR CONTAINER REFRIGERATION

In designing a refrigeration and/or air conditioning system for a cargo airplane and/or airborne cargo containers, there are conflicting temperature requirements, depending on the type of cargo to be carried, which makes it difficult to use one optimum refrigeration system for all kinds of cargo. For example, frozen foods should have a temperature of 0°F and fresh meat and produce 30° to 45°F, and live animals generally require temperatures in the same comfort range as for humans. Today, many of the commercial jet cargo planes operate with the main cabin divided between cargo compartments and passenger compartments, and are supplied by a single air system controlled to the comfort of the human occupants. In this case, perishable cargo must be packed in containers, insulated, and iced or precooled.

A high strength-to-weight ratio, insulated, air cargo container is now being produced. All materials to be transported must be temperature-conditioned before being placed in the container, the insulation then providing protection for periods up to 24 hours with no refrigeration. An accessory refrigeration unit, inserted through a special door plug, is provided, however, to supply auxiliary protection for preconditioned cargo during extended terminal holding periods. It should be emphasized that these containers are designed specifically for airborne use and careful handling, and are difficult to interchange in some more important aspects than the containerization concept, which will be discussed later.

An important problem affecting the refrigeration of air cargo is the backhaul problem of the air carrier. That is, if an airplane carries a planeload of perishable goods from Los Angeles to New York, it must find some goods to carry on the return trip to Los Angeles, since it is obviously not profitable to fly an empty airplane. Since it would not be practical to build a special all-cargo airplane with built-in refrigeration for the transportation of perishables alone, the flexibility of required temperature differences, humidity, and other environmental conditions must be handled in containers. A portion of the problem resides in the heat affecting the actual shell of the airplane on the ground versus the temperature conditions in higher altitudes. A number of important, but in some ways conflicting, design requirements are:

1. Sufficient capacity for ground cooling when the airplane is on the ground "soaking in the hot sun";
2. The ambient air temperature at the high cruising altitudes;
3. The heat of compression generated, in order to provide a cabin pressure, as required by the commodities being shipped.

THERMAL-TECHNICAL CONSIDERATIONS

All these products that could expand the perishable container air market will depend on the availability of a specific controlled environment.

Agreeing that a controlled environment is needed is easy. Recognizing the variables, compounds the problems.

The commodity mix so often encountered on an airplane creates the first difficulty. Live shipments cannot tolerate a temperature setting much below 40°F. It is recognized immediately that this is not the most desirable temperature for most perishables. Disregarding live shipments for a minute, there are variable temperature settings for fruits and produce.

Refrigerated containers are an extension of the insulated container. In fact, a refrigerating method that can be added or removed as needed would seem highly desirable. Mechanical refrigeration, liquid nitrogen, and dry ice are common methods, and each has its place. Development work is currently underway to determine the most practical way to refrigerate containers for air transportation.

"PORTLESS" TRANSFER

Because perishable commodities are potentially the largest, regular-traffic air cargo that containerization should be planned for, the present terminal procedure constraints require analysis. All dry-cargo air container systems use the same conventional approach:

1. Bulking of package freight into containers or container-size footprint pallets;
2. Mechanized movement of containers/pallets from receiving area to preload storage;
3. Semimanual mechanized plane loading.

When it comes to the perishables, this system results in a system that acts to retard growth of air containerization by reverting to a conventional marine-port type of transfer system. In effect, what happens is:

1. Truck moves air container to field station for loading and returns same to airport facility.
2. Alternatively, perishables in less-than-container-load lots are truck-delivered to airport for consolidation.
3. In both cases, while cargo is being held for plane loading time, it must be refrigerated to remove heat from the perishables.
4. Air carriers have gone to great length to install thermal protection facilities for the containers in the preloading period. This requires considerable amount of specialized terminal labor.
5. Unless such coolants as liquid nitrogen or oxygen are used for refrigeration in transit, a costly and cumbersome refrigeration plant is carried at-

tached to each small air cargo container on the plane with consequence of further cost increase.

6. Upon arrival, there is repetition of the chain of unloading procedure installed as service pattern.

Air cargo containerization has reverted to transfer in ports of the pre-container era. This is an impediment which will nullify many effects of increased productivity and cargo conveyors. An air cargo transfer system without port procedures is without places for the cargo to rest. All traffic based on nonresponsive cargo-handling methods is a source of increased operating costs.

If through-the-load air cooling in transit on the plane is possible, then systems technology can provide for containers which are, in effect, pallets with air circulation capability. These pallets would move inside of bottom-to-top circulation-controlled trucks between the field or packing shed and the airport. The cargo would never be rehandled and would remain in the truck-trailer van until automatically transferred to the plane. There is a possibility of designing the containers as such so that they require no outer shell van and circulation could be provided by contact with the trailer bed directly. This would be a transfer system similar to modern container ports. The containerized cargo must remain on wheels until moved to the airplane.

FORWARD AND UPWARD

Analysis of the current status of air cargo containerization is comparable to the semicontainership. Without doubt, the semicontainership, just as present air cargo containerization, is the entry mode into the container age. However, the boldness of decision making to go the whole route has been made in shipping, but is yet to be done in air. In this case, the same rules of containerization will apply, with some slight modification, to the aircraft, as well as to all other container systems. It must be kept in mind that the airplane, like the ship, like the truck, like the train, is only a tool to move freight in containers in the modern distribution system.

FURTHER WORK ON THE NATURE OF AIR CARGO

The present weight and cube limitation of airplanes require analysis of the nature of the present and potential air cargo to assess the system which may serve this most effectively. The simplest criterion is a study of the cost of service as related to:

- Type of cargo; i.e.,
  Fragility;
  Perishability;
  Need for protection (for and/or from the cargo);
- Shipment size/number of pieces;
  This has a tremendous effect on cost, particularly for Traffic Servicing—or terminal handling costs.
- Cargo density spectrum and its impact on current and possibly future cube rules. This would include additional investigation of the concept of cost per cubic-foot-mile. Unless the aviation industry recognizes the logical relationship between the density spectrum of the cargo it expects to carry (in the 1970s and the early 1980s) and the design density of the aircraft cube rule it expects to utilize, it may well be saddled with apparently unexplainable cost problems. Certainly, whatever changes in rate-structure philosophy emerge from this CAB-ordered investigation, the entire industry will be living with it for the rest of the decade and, possibly, even longer.

INTERFACE SERVICES

*We can learn from each other
and we should; Europeans can
particularly learn from Americans
ingenuity and economy of scale;
Americans can especially learn
from Europeans emphasis on a
total distribution concept arrived
at by continuous and mutual
consultation.*

Jacques Leblanc
A European Perspective, *1971*

Containerports

THE CHALLENGE OF CHANGE

All the conveyance systems discussed up to this point converge at the site of the port. The different modes of transport, carriers, and facilities have related to each other, since the container requires smooth transfer from one mode to the other. With the creation of these hub centers, three trends developed which support the increased significance of the unified hub as the key element:

1. Worldwide physical distribution—More cargo begins to move door-to-door.
2. Port limitation—Container-handling machinery allows larger ports to handle more cargo and concentrate ship calls in these ports.
3. Economy of scale—Reduction of cargo handling costs and ship delays concurrent with larger ships increases cost effectiveness.

PORT PROGRESS

An additional significant advance in handling containerized cargo in ports deals with the speeding up of the time span involved in transferring cargo from mode to mode. Captain Charles Sauerbier, in his book, *Marine Cargo Operations,* describes an engineering analysis conducted at the University of California at Los Angeles in 1953. Sauerbier's conclusions, at that time, can be summed up in his words,

> One should see in this report a clear manifestation of the direction that future events must take to enable port speed to make up its losses to sea speed. There is no question that this is possible. The only question is when will it be done?

Sauerbier's basic premise as to the speed gain still holds true today. The advance of technology has produced so many complexities that the issue of the interfaces today is the key to the containerization issue.

POLYSYSTEMS INTERFACE

The dream of the original designers of containerization to create a single all-embracing activity has never come true. Heretofore, I have explained the coexistence of numerous systems which parallel one another. Regardless of their differences, all these systems and conveyances intersect at a hub.

It has been common practice to call these hubs "terminals." I think this word is somewhat misleading. In intermodalism, where the container is the common denominator, the transport media acquire different roles as subsystems to the overall container dimension. The hub, a combination of mode-terminals, ports, and yards, should rather be called a "containerport."

The chain of events of the first container decade has developed nine problem areas for the port, related to the nature of the polysystems interfaces.

Coexistence of ship types: The first problem is the coexistence of conventional-type break-bulk ships with containerships. Conventional ships need narrow aprons and ship-sized pier warehouses, while containerships need large open areas adjacent to the dock and a multitude of modern service facilities. The coexistence introduces organizational, institutional, and manpower problems. The shift of port facilities from the old to the modern can be implemented only by constructing large new facilities in unused waterfront spaces.

Collision of methods: Previously, ship loading and discharging principles and equipment were rather uniform and flexible. Containerization has produced many variations to the basic theme of container handling.

This applies to such areas as crane location, which can be installed on the ship or on the dock; methods of roll-on, roll-off and lift-on, lift-off; and the LASH method, which loads a barge from the shore.

Contrary to break-bulk shipping, each of these systems is unique in some form and must be rigidly applied to a certain ship type. In other words, the terminal and transfer methods of containerization are less flexible than the break-bulk methods. This collision also brings about a set of difficult circumstances for the participant.

Concentration of modernization: Using the containers or trailers as common denominators in the maritime mode opened the field to the changeover from man-handling to machine systems. The gradual progress of mechanization has produced much of the unrest in labor relations.

Intermix of commodities: All types of commodities in world trade converge at the ports. According to the economy of scale, the form in which these commodities are shipped is in constant change, in order to take advantage of cost effectiveness and distribution. Containerization, of course, transforms all these different commodities into uniform cargo units.

Equipment management: The sophistication of containers has developed a need for specialized equipment. This equipment requires service organizations, maintenance facilities, repair shops, and reconditioning factories. (See Fig. 11-1.) Containerization is a cyclic process. Equipment management requires concentration of container fleets. The containerports are the natural home base for this equipment.

Multiple choice of cargo activities: The passage of the container through the containerport is required because all rehandling activities are concentrated here. In addition to physical throughput, cargo can be inspected, controlled, repackaged, and treated according to the wishes of the shipper. Containerloads can be made-up here or end here, and cargo in less-than-container lots can be reshuffled, consolidated, or distributed. Each of these activities requires special arrangements and specialized areas, where the job must be performed.

Environmental community restraints: The requirements of extensive land areas adjacent to the water plus needed access to airways, highways, and railroads place the need for large territorial demands on the community where the containerport is located.

Geographical and demographical determination: Containerization and the related rail/truck facilities have opened new port areas to new trades. For instance, a shipper who previously used California ports

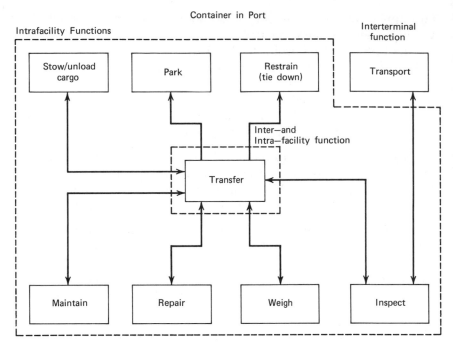

FIGURE 11-1. THIRD-LEVEL FUNCTIONAL DIAGRAM—INTRAFACILITY (SOURCE: U.S. GOVT. I).

might prefer to use Seattle because of certain advantages in inland service. Another example is the recent location of a Sony plant near the residential community of Rancho Bernardo, California, which allows for access to population, as producers of quality electronic products—and the container movement to and from this hinterland makes it possible. The new facility is located about 30 miles from the Port of San Diego and 120 miles from the Port of Los Angeles/Long Beach. After analysis, it was found to be cheaper to ship a number of containers by truck than to divert a containership for a few containers.

Panorama of choices: Since there is no universal standard for containerports, the technology employs a great variety of subsystems, processes, and methods which make the port organization a complicated vector with components such as facilities, water transport, land transport, commodities, and institutional operations.

SIMULTANEOUS ACTIVITIES

Finally, we recognize the fact that many of these activities are proceeding simultaneously. This creates many additional problems at the intersection which require a persistent outlook at the final goals of the planned activity.

At containerports, containerization is less transportation and more industrial processing. The transfer from mode to mode appears like an intraplant conveying system. The design of containerports is the design of an output-oriented industrial complex which has efficient and economical interface as its task. Whether the economics realized are returned to the containership, to the port authority, to the combined transport operator (CTO), to labor, or to the public is a political question. The development of a cost-efficient containerport complex is a condition without which containerization cannot exist. The question of profits will be dealt with in Chapter 18.

The tool required to deal properly with containerization in the containerport areas is container systems engineering. Container systems engineering is a branch of the cargo systems science and will be defined below.

SYSTEMS ENGINEERING

This text has mentioned systems engineering as the preferred tool in dealing with containerization. The detailed discussion for containerport areas is related to the process planning in this polysystems interface. Systems engineering is the only efficient method to deal with the problems, because containerport operation can never get away from forecasting and planning. In the narrow confines of this book dealing with containerization as a whole, there is no possibility to go deep enough into all details.

In the *Systems Engineering Handbook*, Robert E. Machol gives a number of definitions for systems engineering. These imply that the output of the systems engineer is a set of specifications suitable for constructing a real-life system out of hardware.

MIL STD-499 (USAF), *Systems Engineering Management*, July 17, 1969, defines systems engineering in the Air Force sense as:

The application of scientific and engineering efforts to (a) transform an operational need into a description of systems performance parameters and a system configuration through the use of an iterative process of definition, synthesis, analysis, design, test and evaluation; (b) integrate related technical parameters and assume compatibility of all physical, functional and program interface in a manner which optimizes the total system definition and design, and (c) integrate reliability, maintainability, safety, human and other such factors into the total engineering effort.

The approach of Litton Industries, as expressed by John Rubel, Vice President, is:

> The term "systems engineering" is used to describe the integrated approach to the synthesis of entire systems designed to perform varied tasks in what is expected to be the most efficient manner. Thus, the term is used to describe an approach which views an entire system of components as an entity rather than simply as an assembly of individual parts; that is, a system in which each component is designed to fit properly with the other components rather than to function by itself.

SYSTEMS ANALYSIS

The first part of systems engineering is the analytical process. In the *Systems Engineering Handbook,* Machol also defines it: "By systems analysis, I mean the study of a system which does not exist (at least in the modification under study) in an attempt to elucidate its effectiveness or performance, its cost in dollars or other factors, and the effect of parameter variations on these factors."

Alain Enthoven, now Head of Planning and Vice President of Litton Industries, and former Assistant Under-Secretary of Defense for Research and Development, stated in 1965 that he was unable to give what he called a good definition in brief. However, he goes on and indicates that systems analysis, as evolved in the Department of Defense and the aerospace industry, is a "reasoned approach to the problems of decision and quantitative common sense." Enthoven's approach of the scientific method to decision process and its quantitative methods and systems approach was developed for the aerospace science. It can be well applied to containerization at the interface of the many coexistent systems at the containerport. (See Fig. 11-2.)

This complicated polysystems interface at the containerport can use the method of computing specific quantitative measures of effectiveness for container transfer for various configurations of systems and basing many decisions on these measures. Institutional and human attitudes are difficult to quantify, but they are extremely significant, as they act as restraints on possible causes of actions. Container transfer activities must

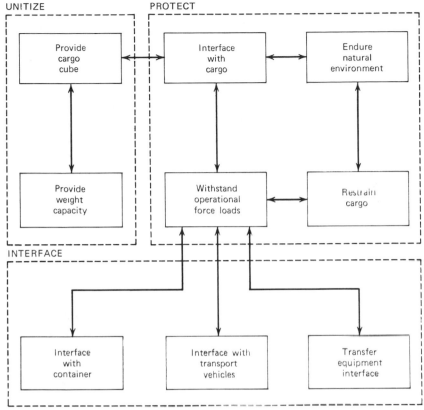

FIGURE 11-2. CONTAINER FUNCTIONAL DIAGRAM (SOURCE: U.S. GOVT. I).

be considered as an integrated set of interacting subsystems, with the overall system interfacing with the environment rather than a group of quasi-independent parts, as even the most efficient port terminals were in the past.

STAGE IDENTIFICATION METHOD

Stage identification is a systems engineering method developed by The Stanwick Corporation for naval ship design procedures. Compliance with this method is described in the book, *Design Work Study,* by The Stanwick Corporation. It has been developed to find a simple form for modification and improvement of existing ship design. There is a great similarity between the complicated subsystems of a ship and those of a containerport. The tools for the identification of these stages are standard methods, conventional to industrial engineering, human factors engineering, and management science. The customary stage identification plan names six steps to solve the problem. For the purpose of understanding the complexities of the containerport, we used the first of the six steps called "select." Select deals with the definition of subsystem problems which are interrelated. It establishes a priority for orderly review in hierarchy arrangement of interrelated subsystems.

We will describe the containerport system around typical container activities from ship to land and land to ship. The path taken by containers reveals the problem areas which must be systematically solved.

APPLICATION OF SELECT

Today, all ports are concerned with containerization. Most ports operate facilities simultaneously for break-bulk cargo, as well as for containerized cargo. This results in complications for the port operation. Finally, of course, there are no two ports alike, whether due to geography, history, or economy of the area. For this reason, it is difficult to develop a clear understanding of port activities. No two ports run in identical lines either. A containerport system can be best described as consisting of facilities, manpower, equipment, processor, and functional organizations which work together, similar to an industrial plant. All components and subsystems must be considered as part of the whole structure and not individually or isolated. It is the overall function that holds the entire system together.

The stage-identification process of systems engineering allows us to present the containerport combination as a multiphasic systems engineering program. The interacting forces and links perform together. All subsystems are presented in a hierarchical arrangement of all functionally related areas. The overall system appears in successive levels containing all major components, subcomponents, processes, and pertinent parts of the system under study. (See Fig. 11-3.)

STAGE I

Men who devote their entire time and effort to one particular kind of problem develop special skills and knowledge, making them expert in their particular area. Without exposure to other subsystems, however,

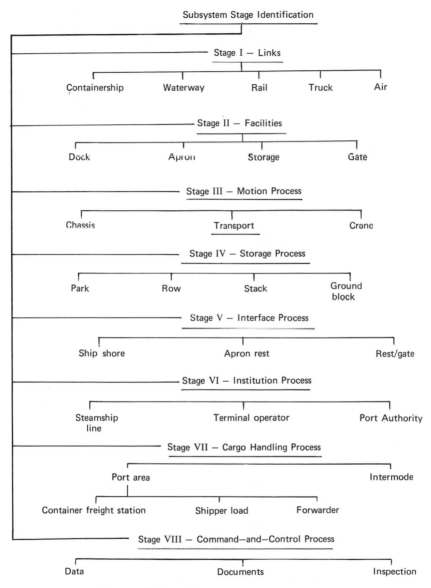

FIGURE 11-3. CONTAINERPORT SYSTEM.

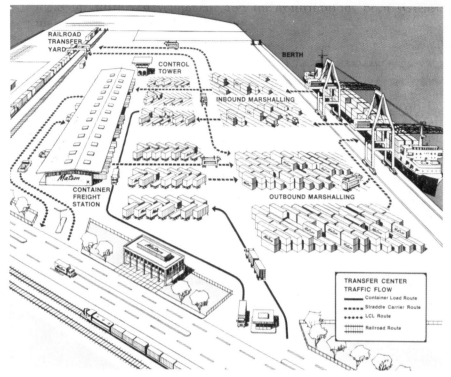

FIGURE 11-4. TRANSFER CENTER TRAFFIC FLOW.

this results in a one-sided, narrow, inflexible view, which the *Wall Street Journal* calls "tunnel vision." Systems engineering uses the opposite approach, since it requires a knowledge of all subsystems at every level. The first phase which must be identified might be called the links subsystem. We deal here with the berth and waterfront marshaling yards (common to all container operations), rail heads, truck terminals, and possibly inland waterway terminals and airports. (See Fig. 11-4.)

Pier Subsystem

In all ports a great deal of the important activities occur in a relatively small area, which is where the land meets the water. The ship berth is the single, most important construction in the modern port. The pier subsystem requires access to deep ocean, turning basins, refueling facilities and, of course, the traditional center of cargo handling. Along the pier, subsystems facilitate making the ship fast to the land, allowing cargo handling protected from the motion of the wave forces of the sea, and yet permitting cargo handling to continue regardless of tidal conditions.

With the change from conventional shipping to containershipping, a pier length averaging 800 feet per berth with a depth of about 40 feet becomes necessary. According to R. B. Oran and C. C. R. Baker, in their book, *The Efficient Port,* the Victorian Convention was to do nothing about new berths until trade demanded new construction. This plan has been completely reversed; and since the pier subsystem is the most important component of the containerport, ports have found that by creating pier facilities in advance of demand, a demand for these have been created.

STAGE II

The second phase of the containerport lineup is made up of cargo flow subsystem components. These are the dock, the apron, the marshaling area, and the reception and delivery interface, where the container is transmitted to the other subsystems, to other carriers, or to temporary storage. The dock, as a subsystem, is a functional component equipped with fuel lines, tie-up facilities, fresh water, gas, and electricity. In addition to tying the ship to the land during discharge, the dock is also the area for certain services to the ship. To hasten the time in port, Sea-Land, for example, has a special crew of maintenance men swarming over the ship, each with a different function, working around the clock until their jobs are completed. Most ships require port power connection and access to telephone systems for their functioning in port.

Apron Subsystem

The apron is the interlink between the land subsystem and the containership. The major component operating between the apron and the ship is the container crane. Most containerships are designed to rely on shoreside or pier cranes. These cranes must be high enough to provide clearance for the loaded container stack on deck when operating. Some containerships, notably the Columbus Line ships and Sea-Land's remaining self-sustaining ships, have shipboard cranes to do the same job as the shoreside crane. Shipboard cranes are cumbersome, more costly to operate and maintain, and generally not as fast as shoreside cranes. But the shipboard crane does give the so-equipped containership the capacity to operate in ports which do not have shoreside cranes. In the event that a crane-carrying ship calls at a port with shoreside cranes, the cranes double up, if the ship length permits it.

Hook Cycle

The crane is a major subsystem. Its importance in the interlink functions in the containerport is unique. Whether the crane is attached to the ship or installed on shore, the operation process is the same. The container crane performs a cyclic maneuver. The movements are those of the "hook" which is used in conventional shipping and is installed at the end of the ship's cargo gear or the shoreside crane. To carry cargo, this hook is physically attached to the pallet, box, or container to be moved and released at the other end. The speed of this hook operation determines the efficiency of the overall process in the port. This process has come to be known as the "hook cycle," in port work-study procedures (National Academy of Sciences). Hook cycle, thus, has become a generic term and is used even when we refer to today's container "spreader system."

Whether loading or unloading, the hook cycle consists of:

1. Positioning of the container frame over the container;
2. Linking up the frame with the container (in some instances, two 20-ft. containers can be picked up at the same time);
3. Lifting the container from the dock, out of the hold, or from the deck, as the case may be;
4. Moving the container suspended from the frame in the direction of the operation (dock to ship or ship to dock);
5. Stopping the container in a "well" position over the location where the container is supposed to be discharged (cell guide, deck structure, other containers, chassis, or on the ground);
6. Lowering the container into the desired position (see 5 above);
7. Connecting the container with the cell guides or chassis or merely depositing it on the ground;
8. Releasing the container frame from the container;
9. Positioning the container frame for the next cycle.

Crane Subsystem

Most modern container cranes complete this cycle in a time average of 2 to 4 minutes per container (see Tables 11-1 and 11-2). As can be seen, there is a relationship between the man, operator and/or the equipment itself. Electronic sensitizing is costly, but if volumes of containers are to

FIGURE 11-5. CONTAINER BERTH WITH ONE CRANE IN OPERATION.

be moved with regularity, it is the preferred subsystem. This completes our review of the container crane subsystem. Expansion on this subject is a function of civil engineering and naval architecture. For three different types of container berths, see Figs. 11-5, 11-6, and 11-7, showing one, two, and three cranes in operation, respectively.

Hoffman Rigging and Crane Service Company, Belleville, New Jersey,

FIGURE 11-6. CONTAINER BERTH WITH TWO CRANES IN OPERATION.

FIGURE 11-7.   CONTAINER BERTH WITH THREE CRANES IN OPERATION.

had a special pioneer crane designed by Harnischfeger of Milwaukee, Wisconsin. This is a mobile truck crane with a lifting arm 400 ft. in length. It can hoist 250 tons in a single pick as high as 70 ft. and move it 36 ft. It can handle 30-plus-ton containers over a 100-ft. radius, which means that it can work to the offshore side of the vessel with containers loaded to highway legal limits. It has application as a subsystem available in the event that the crane is installed on neither ship nor dock. The designers claim that it can handle 19 containers per hour below deck or 25 topside.

Another approach is the Eness "spreading floating crane," which consists of two hulls separated for operation. The crane equipment can also reach over the ship and discharge either to the water or to land. More details on this system are described in Chapter 19.

The following calculations establish the minimum horsepower for the crane drive:

$$\text{Horsepower, HP} = \frac{(\text{Live Load} + \text{Spreader})}{33{,}000 \times .7 \times 2} \times \text{Speed} \quad (\text{Per Motor})$$

$$\text{For Containers: HP} = \frac{54{,}000 \times 115}{33{,}000 \times .7 \times 2} = 135 \text{ HP each Motor}$$

TABLE 11-1.   BREAKDOWN OF IDEAL CYCLE TIME FOR
CONTAINER HANDLING—44,000-LB. WEIGHT
(ONE 20-FT. OR ONE 40-FT. CONTAINER)

Operation	Time (seconds)
Ship to Shore	
Hook On	4
Acceleration (hoist)	3
Hoist	28
Dwell	1
Acceleration (transversing)	3
Travel (transverse)	25
Braking	4
Dwell	1
Acceleration (lower)	1
Lower	26
Brake	2
Unhook	1
TOTAL	99 seconds
Shore to Ship	
Acceleration (hoist)	2
Hoist	7
Dwell	1
Acceleration (transversing)	2
Travel (transverse)	25
Braking	2
Dwell	1
Acceleration (lower)	1
Lower	9
TOTAL	50 seconds

Hook Cycle Time: 2.5 Minutes
Productivity Per Hour: 24 Containers

The Temporary Stop

Stop and go of any conveyor system is detrimental to productivity. Continuous motion is best for conveyor-belt-type systems. Such a continuous process would constitute the best method of operation in the flow pattern of the containerport. However, the attainment of this goal is impossible due to many conditions and restraints. Stop-and-go tactics in port operation require careful analysis. We are familiar with several of them:

TABLE 11-2. BREAKDOWN OF IDEAL CYCLE TIME FOR
CONTAINER HANDLING—70,000-LB. WEIGHT
(ONE 20-FT. OR ONE 40-FT. CONTAINER)

Operation	Time (seconds)
Ship to Shore	
Hook On	20
Acceleration (hoist)	3
Hoist	39
Dwell	1
Acceleration (transversing)	3
Travel (transverse)	37
Braking	5
Dwell	1
Acceleration (lower)	1
Lower	35
Brake	3
Unhook	8
	156 seconds
Shore to Ship (Empty Spreader)	50
	206 seconds

Hook Cycle Time: 3.5 Minutes
Productivity Per Hour: 17 Containers

1. Temporary interlink stop called "dwell";
2. Long-term intralink stop called "marshalling" or "storage";
3. Entry or gate stop for document check and security;
4. Government inspection: United States Customs, Plant Quarantine (Division of the U.S. Department of Agriculture), as well as other agencies.

Therefore, in Phase III, where the motion process is analyzed, the container stop-and-go strategy is an important part of the interface relationship among the port components.

The beginning and end of each "stop" period depends upon other functional subsystems and procedures. For example, the container can be unloaded from the ship directly onto a chassis (Sea-Land system) or onto the ground (Matson system). The chassis has to be moved away by a tractor while the container has to be moved by a straddle carrier or a side carrier or some similar device, which lifts and moves at the same time. At the port entrance, a similar procedure occurs when the container arrives by truck, rail, or barge. It must be equipped with mobility according to the particular port system; namely, either chassis (with tractor) or straddle-lift, truck-type of operation.

Marshalling Subsystem

There usually are two long-term resting areas for the container, one close to the pier and the other further from the pier but more related to the service area. According to the container flow system, the design of the marshaling area must reflect four main features of the storage process operation.

1. Storage on chassis—Container remains in the yard on the same chassis throughout waiting period. Chassis are parked in slots and lanes marked on pavement for identification purposes. Truck lanes must be wide enough for the tractor to back the container chassis into slot, but container chassis can be an average of 9 ft. wide and next to each other.

2. Storage from lift trucks—Containers are stored on the ground. Storage is usually two or three containers high with certain limitations according to straddle-truck equipment. Each container lane must allow space for the penetration of tractor wheels.

3. Side-loader storage—The side-loader trucks pick up a container from the ground, from a chassis, or from the stack by paralleling the container. The lift entails raising and transferring the container onto the bed of the tractor. Storage, consequently, requires lanes for this equipment to approach the containers from the side.

4. Overhead crane storage—A fourth common method employs the use of a single overhead crane which travels back and forth over a determined storage area. Containers can be stored four or six high, with or without cell guides, and the container crane moves them from the place of rest to a dwell location for the link process. This type of storage, of course, requires sufficient support from the soil to maintain stability of the container stack. The average weight of each container should be considered 30 tons, which indicates the floor load required. See Fig. 11-8 for the different types of containerport lifting equipment.

Interline Subsystems

The chain-link process ends on the land side with the delivery (or pickup, as the case may be) of the container to the following:

1. Intermodal carriers—Trucks, rail, or barges usually have their own container interchange facilities and, as common practice, will receive or deliver the container in the specific area of the containerport.

2. Container freight stations—These are stations within the port area, where the cargo is physically loaded into or out of the container. Such places

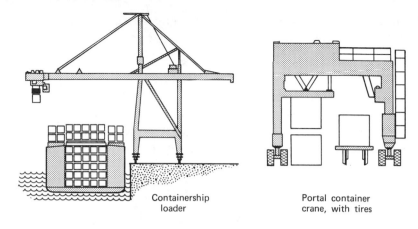

Containership
loader

Portal container
crane, with tires

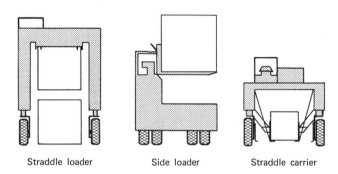

Straddle loader   Side loader   Straddle carrier

FIGURE 11-8.   CONTAINERPORT LIFTING EQUIPMENT.

are usually located off the main premises, and the interline procedure takes place at the containerport gate.

3. Servicing—Containers may move to the container gate for any of the servicing activities, including long-term storage.

STAGE III

In the third phase, we will evaluate the movement of the container through the containerport. In the previous phase dealing with the storage subsystem, we have seen that there are several types of movement which can be applied. The overall concept of the "movement subsystem" in the container terminal tends to approximate the design concept of an industrial production line. The movement systems which can be used are the following:

1. Chassis and tractor;
2. Container transporter (straddle truck, side loader, piggy packer);
3. Overhead crane way (directly connecting links with each other);
4. Special bogies or railroad cars moving on a continuous belt between links;
5. Container conveyor belts (the Nielsen system of Denmark combines container conveyors with overhead cranes and crane ways). (See Fig. 11-9)

The subsystems components of this stage are directly affected by the following factors:

1. Skill of operators;
2. Space requirements;
3. Climatic conditions;
4. Volume of containers to be moved.

Much research has gone into developing standards of operating efficiency. The Maritime Administration, particularly, has concerned itself with the facility planning and design; but until now no accurate, comparative, real-time data control of the movement subsystem for terminal throughput is available. The four factors provide a vector to the subsystem which influences the output efficiency of the containerport.

STAGE IV

Having evaluated the preferred interlink capacity and efficiency of Stage III, we find that the analysis of the storage process is related to:

1. Port space availability;
2. Anticipated volume of containers;
3. Need for in-transit treatment of certain commodities in containers (liquids, chemicals, perishable cargo under refrigeration);
4. Soil strength support regulating the block storage;
5. Frequency of container operation cycles (daily, weekly, frequent or irregular intervals).

The size of the storage or marshaling area must be equivalent to the number of containers which will be loaded onto the ship, unloaded from the ship, and delivered to or received from intermodal connections in a given period of time. As an extreme example of maintaining the effi-

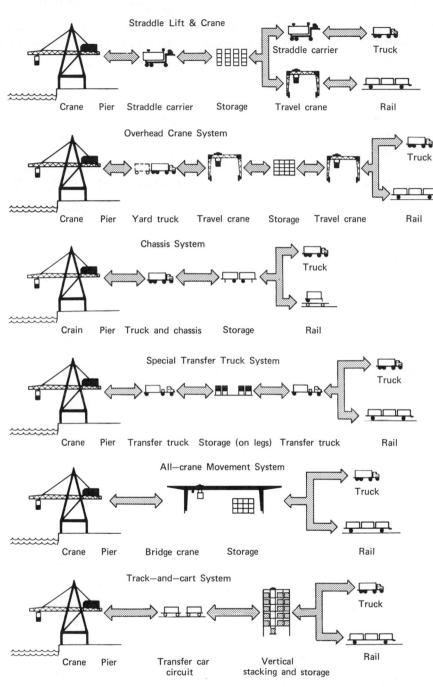

FIGURE 11-9. MAJOR CONTAINERPORT HANDLING ALTERNATIVES.

ciency of a small terminal, we mention the Kowloon Wharf and GoDown Company in Hong Kong, which has a one-shed finger pier and a container storage silo approximately one mile from that pier. This is the operating area for Sea-Land, American President Lines, and several other container operators. Skill of the operating manpower can overcome constraints in this subsystem.

STAGE V

In Stage V, we analyze the productivity performance at the interfaces. There are three major interfaces which we consider subsystems:

1. Ship-to-shore subsystem;
2. Apron-to-marshalling area subsystem;
3. Marshalling area-to-gate subsystem.

The measuring device is the measure of productivity or throughput. This can be measured in cost per ton, cost per container, and cost per ship, all combined into a single figure of productivity merit. Productivity is the ratio between output and input. This arithmetical ratio expresses the overall amount of port resources used as subsystem in providing the container transfer service.

The fact that productivity increases through containerization in the containerport system, as such, does not tell us the reason for this. Since the reason may be due to better interface relationships, the careful study of the work by analytical methods is the permanent indicator of effectiveness. This interface will be fully discussed in the area of the book dealing with control systems.

STAGE VI

The institutional functions of the management of the port are analyzed in this stage. Three types of arrangements are common in this area:

1. Single-user facility—Steamship company owns and/or operates the containerport for its own services, possibly acting as agent for another steamship company. Examples of this are Sea-Land in all their ports in the United States; Matson in handling its own ships and the ships of its former pool partners; NYK; and Showa.
2. Multiple use—Here an independent terminal company owns and/or operates the facilities for a number of steamship companies using the same apron system. The motion and marshaling system may differ ac-

cording to the steamship's operating functions. An example of this is the Marine Terminal Operation in Oakland, California, and the Trans-Ocean Gateway at Long Beach, California.

3. Public use—In some cases, mostly small containerports, the Port Authority provides the land and operates the major facilities. As an example, San Diego is in the planning stage for a public container terminal which would have to be operated either by the port or a contractor acting for the port.

STAGE VII

We now look at actual cargo handling. This is a subsystem of the overall containerport system.

There are several ways in which the cargo can be fed into the containerport (or vice versa, redelivered by the containerport for further physical distribution). Two groups of activities can take place: "port area" activities reaching out to an agreed range, and activities outside the agreed range. All outside activities are considered to be intermodal deliveries and were discussed in Stages I and II of the Stage Identification Plan.

The extent of the port area is generally arrived at by the agreement between labor and the container operators. In New York, this range is a radius of 50 miles from the center of the port. The distance may vary with labor arrangements dealing with jurisdiction between longshore and the labor of interline carriers. Trucking has a particular importance on range setting.

Within the port area, cargo will be loaded into containers or unloaded from containers at several types of locations. The suggested name for this operation, according to the labor agreements, is "stuffing and stripping." Two general types of locations are:

1. Container freight stations—These are facilities at which individual parcels of cargo are delivered, usually by truck, and loaded according to destination into a number of containers available for this purpose. The activity of stuffing and stripping requires certain skills. Also, the steamship company is responsible for the condition of the cargo while at the container freight station. Usually, the stuffing and stripping is done by longshore labor.

2. Shippers' load stations—A number of shippers or freight forwarders located in the port area load the containers at their own premises. Since the steamship company is not liable for the content of the container when it is received sealed, these so-called "shippers' load" containers are usually handled by other than longshore labor. The government also operates shippers' load stations for mail and military cargo.

STAGE VIII

The last stage discussed in this hierarchy deals with the "Command and Control Procedures." In order to provide proper data on the cargo and containers in the port, and in order to handle this by directing movements and storage in the most adequate areas, a command-and-control procedure must be developed for each subsystem. All these data and document systems must be centralized into one containerport control, so that at all times, the operator of the port area knows the state of production and what remains to be done. To develop this control, manual or electronic methods can be used. Such control deals with the entire traffic flow at any given time. Paper work for all terminal activities is usually distributed to the places where the activity occurs and must be correlated into the overall data system. Detailed examples of such operations are presented in Section V of this book. This stage can be summarized into three subsystems:

1. Data and documentation;
2. Equipment cybernetics and inventory control;
3. Ship and port control.

All electronic data processing is normally handled by real-time procedures in which the event is recorded and interpreted almost simultaneously with the occurrence.

PORT SECURITY SYSTEMS

One of the great problems facing modern times is how to keep containerports secured. Originally, it was considered that containerization would eliminate pier theft and robbery. Today, especially in the Port of New York, pilferage has taken on such a sizeable dimension that the Federal Government has started a special security study to find ways and means to prevent further growth of crime. Containers loaded with whiskey, cigarettes, and other valuable items have disappeared. The containers, emptied of their contents, were found many miles from the port areas. We do not consider "security" a subsystem, but it is related to the "control" subsystem. Its function is important due to the great losses which are involved.

CHANGING VARIABLES

We stated originally that one of the problems of containerization is the fluidity with which changes occur. Two examples show both the positive and negative results which have occurred within the operation of containerports during the first decade.

On the positive side, steamship lines have, for the first time, begun to cooperate with each other and have established interline relationships quite similar to railroad services. Such a service has produced interline relationships between Latin America and Europe (United States Lines and Prudential Grace); between Europe and Hawaii (Johnson Line and Matson); and between the San Francisco Bay Area and Micronesia (United States Lines and Dillingham).

On the negative side, changes in container sizes have seriously hampered traffic development for Matson. Originally limited to small container weights and the 24-ft. units only, Matson built container cranes which proved too weak for the later increase to 40-ft. units which would be carried on the second-generation ships. This led to a whole series of change requirements which have affected their growth. Matson was originated by a very inventive group of systems engineers under Foster Weldon of the Research and Development Center of Ford Motor Company. Later, management did not follow up on continued systems analysis and, therefore, fell behind in important growth developments.

FUTURE PORT DEVELOPMENTS

There are three developments of impact which are presently being planned. They deal with:

1. Port islands—If ship size continues to increase in depth and beam, present containerports will not be able to accommodate them. Plans for the possibility of offshore island ports with dual causeways to the main marshaling areas and automated conveyors may accommodate this need.

2. Inland ports—Creation of inland containerports, far removed from the deep-sea waterfront but integrated with all other facilities and components, has been suggested. In effect, these ports could provide better extension of inland container services than the general distribution of containers among many rail and truck carriers. The port design contemplates unification of operation of all container carriers at this location. This would extend the port area considerably.

3. Automated ports—The Dutch designer, Meeusen, has proposed a fully-

automated containerport for the Port of Rotterdam. The system described in another part of this book combines Nielsen conveyors with overhead cranes and automated ship systems.

LASH AND RO-RO

Containerports must anticipate the coming of new ships in the two systems which parallel containerization:

1. LASH barge system—This system and the Seabarge Clipper system accommodate loaded barges, as well as containers. Some ships can alternate between the number of barges and the number of containers (Prudential-Grace, Lykes, Pacific Far East Lines, and Waterman).

2. Ro-Ro (roll-on, roll-off)—This system has been adopted either directly or in combination with containerization (Atlantic Container Lines and PAD—Pacific Australian Direct).

There are advantages accruing to both systems which require a port to facilitate this service. The Port of Oakland and the Port of Long Beach have done this.

EFFECT OF PORTS ON SHIPS

Transport can be compared to a chain belt in motion. The motion begins at the source of the raw materials, proceeds to the factory where manufacture and processing take place, and continues to ultimate destination. The chain comprises numerous links, one of which is the ocean transport, and the other of which is the port. The port consists of a great many actions. All the actions and operations related to container transport together make up the total motion. Any chain is as strong as its weakest link and moves as fast as its slowest section.

The effect of ports on ships must be directed toward turning the ship around with the least possible delay and handling the cargo economically. Port operations, both inward and outward, must function smoothly. Not only the ship reaps the benefit of efficient port operations, but also the shipper, the consignee, and the port worker. In fact, performance affects the entire community.

A port community must recognize the changing trends and support them rather than try to retard them. Changes offer opportunities to be creative. Small and medium-size ports, such as San Diego, have an important and viable role to play in containerization. This role is not to handle large volumes of general cargo. Large volumes will flow into the channels which would include fully containerized ships and specialized container-handling terminals. Small and medium-size ports may find roles as centers to feed containers into and out of the major channels; for example, with LASH barges, truck terminals, and Ro-Ro centers. As the volume of container commerce increases, there will be economic justification for additional major activities at the secondary or smaller ports. Some feeder ports will probably grow into this type; but most will not.

Finally, each port needs to seek its own area of economic specialization or distinctive competence. Ports with prudent and creative managements will grow and prosper.

Logistics Support

PROCESS EXPANSION

The structure of the integrated container systems described in the fore-going parts require structural support by logistic measures and processes. Without these supports, containerization could hardly, if at all, function. These logistics are in four distinct areas, separate from each other, yet discussed together in this chapter, since they relate to our systems technology:

Part I—Equipment use control;
Part II—Rate making;
Part III—Insurance coverage;
Part IV—Customs control procedures.

PART I

CONTAINER USE ENVIRONMENT

The container must be made available for cargo loading to the shipper and must also be available as a unit to the intervening modes, to enable the system to fulfill its door-to-door mission. This results in a complex environment of processes, laws, controls, and services surrounding the container while outside of the hands of the primary container operators. There are two instances only when the owned container is used directly by the owner himself:

1. While the container travels on the ship;
2. While the container is moved or stored in the containerport.

Most of the use is outside of these two areas. All the possibilities of relationships related to ownership, operation, and use of the van present an extreme variety of possibilities.

The box is not necessarily owned by the operator of the ship and port. Equipment sale and leasing systems provide for a great multitude of financial schemes, too numerous to catalog. But it is the control that is important. Primary control of the container as the instrument of the transport mission can be provided through some of the following arrangements:

1. Outright ownership;
2. Long-term lease with or without end purchase;
3. Use of pool as a participant;
4. Use of pool equipment as a lessee;
5. Temporary control as a result of trip leasing;
6. Interchange of units of other concurring carriers.

Two forms of temporary control are often treated similarly to primary control methods:

1. Use of shipper- or forwarder-supplied container;
2. Use of excess fleet pool equipment among participants of a standby system.

Dealing with control over the container leads to the next important issue. The cross-relationship produced by the container creates very demanding conditions for the ways and means of exercising use control and implies specific forms of activities in the interchange of equipment between carriers themselves. The supply functions and the existence of "neutral" (noncarrier-owned) containers must be geared to sufficient supply of vans. These subjects are treated together, since they form part of the functional equipment control per se.

COMPETITION VS. COOPERATION

The effective control, not the legal ownership, is important to establish intermodal transportation. Intermodal combinations form networks to give through service, regardless of ownership of the container, since the service is dedicated to the cargo and derives its revenue from the freight paid.

Cooperative efforts needed to develop international intermodal systems have not existed until recently. The United States public policy, declared by Congress in the legislative acts which cover all forms of transportation, has been historically designed to promote competition between the carrier modes.

The carrier's equipment fleet has traditionally been confined to one single mode, to maximize the inherent advantages of the mode. For example, when trailer-on-flatcar service (TOFC) was developed in the '50s, some railroads designed unique proprietary railroad equipment systems incompatible with all other railroads. The purpose of the existing mode regulatory policy is to foster healthy competition. The evolution to the container use is predicated on the concern with size and inherent line-haul advantage. Containerization is the pioneer system designed to change this basic American transportation philosophy. As a result of this, the regulatory environment in which containers must operate is strongly affected by government.

The interchange of railroad cars among railroads is governed by the Interstate Commerce Commission; and within this mode, all carriers are obligated to interchange with each other. Truck trailers, on the other hand, are only voluntarily exchanged by individual agreement between owners.

There is little, if any, interchange of containers between ship operators who own most of the world's inventory at this time; but operators like to interchange with intermodal roads. Even where container sizes and fittings are standard, ship operators do not often interchange. Institutional arrangements do not exist for carriers collectively to ameliorate the burdens of trade traffic imbalances, seasonable fluctuations, and unanticipated surges in cargo volumes by interchanging containers. This tendency is a great obstacle in the way of systems unification. There are three different ways in which the physical interchange of equipment could be handled among a variety of participators:

1. Open-end interchange—Interchange among all carriers capable of accepting this equipment, similar to the railroad interchange rules;

2. Intermodal pools—Placement of all intermodally standard containers and chassis into national or multinational equipment pools;

3. Leasing systems—Separation of the container ownership from carrier operation by legally placing leasing companies in a position to act as equipment supplier for a number of their clients.

MENTALITY BLOCKS

Containerization endangers its own existence by a mentality among some of the carriers as related to the interchange problems. It is almost as if the intermodality did not exist. Individual carriers try to force out of each other certain advantages to enhance their own marketing picture. The conclusion is that there is little container pooling anywhere in the world, and the future of containerization may well be bogged down until this is resolved.

There are some valid reasons for the reluctance of the carriers to pool their containers:

1. Pride in the marketing appeal of the carrier's own equipment;
2. Uncertainty about the availability of equipment at all times and the possibility of providing marketing advantage to the competitor;
3. Problems of ownership, financing, insurance, and concurrent disadvantages of dealing with other people's containers;
4. Maintenance and repair and condition of containers which may hamper technical use when needed.

Also, in making efforts toward solving the interface among container operators, many problems would appear to be of minor consequence when viewed in the broad perspective. These manifestations of traditional rivalries among carriers are encouraged by ruling philosophies of the United States and foreign government agencies involved and described heretofore. Three stages to break through the problems are needed.

First, consensus is needed for the need of improvement, cooperation, and change. Thereafter, a critical analysis of the obstacles must include the international spectrum. Such an analysis, therefore, must be conducted by organizations with a foothold in many of the key nations which participate in the world container trade. From here on, joint meetings must be organized where all voices within each nation are given a chance to express themselves. Such international machinery would be quite similar to the one used by the International Labor Office (ILO), where governments, management, and labor each hold $1/3$ of the voice when international agreements are being developed. An urgent need for pooling-interchange regulations exists today. Carriers, leasing companies, government, and the shipping public, before long, will forcibly take a stand on the removal of the multinational obstacles.

EIGHTEEN KEY QUESTIONS

What inhibits intermodal containerization today deals with agreements required between the big and small carriers, ocean and intermodal alike. There are more marine container services today than cargo, and fewer inland container services than needed. Here are some, but not all, of the important questions no one today has yet solved:

1. Interchange per diem rates—what are reasonable rates?
2. Who should pay them and to whom?
3. How should repair costs for containers and support equipment moving in intermodal interchange be allocated?
4. Who should pay for the movement of empty containers?
5. What impedes transportation of containers in intermodal interchange?
6. What is a reasonable proportion of empty movement to loaded movement?
7. Is it really economical to have competing carriers holding equal inventories at key loading stations awaiting loads?
8. Is it reasonable to expect shippers to pay for this waste when we produce it?
9. In our individualistic attempts to provide adequate container inventories, will we acquire more containers than are needed to meet real shipper needs?
10. Is there a truly effective way of overcoming historic and varying imbalance in freight movements?
11. Who will bear the cost of maintaining an effective balance of equipment, if there is none?
12. How can we avoid the draining waste of empties passing each other on the rails or highways?
13. Is there an ideal or practical ratio of bogies and chassis needed to support a large container fleet?
14. Where should they be positioned?
15. When traffic patterns change, who should reposition them?
16. Who will be responsible for arranging the repair of a container damaged at an off-line point?
17. Who will pay for the repairs?
18. How will the equipment get back into the system?

FACILITATION

The environment dealing with facilitation of interchange is fractured into many attitudes and positions. There is a split along modal lines and there is a government preoccupation with the concentration of economic power. There is mistrust, jealousy, and uncertainty about the relatively small volume of maritime container traffic compared to the overwhelming volume of the domestic traffic. Everything discourages the true implementation of intermodal interface, yet this is the key decision which this industry must face before it can mature.

All these problems are not technical, nor are they systematic. They are mostly institutional and represent the remnants of old attitudes from conventional transportation. How can this apathy be overcome? Transportation's struggle for containerization is not due to its wish to progress, but rather to certain understanding that the wasteful process of labor-intensive transportation cannot be continued. To escape from the conventional wasteful process, the transportation industry began to share the belief in containerization. It is sharing of the belief that thus far has made the development what it is today. Since this belief continues to be shared, it should lead to a pragmatic solution to the last institutional obstacle in the question of equipment.

EQUIPMENT LEASING

Although steamship companies own the vast majority of the service containers they employ, some additional containers are leased from container leasing companies. The suggestion has been made that container leasing could, in effect, provide pooling and interchange facilities so urgently needed. Leasing companies own their equipment primarily to earn a higher return by temporarily making their equipment available to whoever pays the best revenue. Container leasing, generally, has created a market with rates fluctuating from $0.75 per container per day for a 20-ft. unit to $5.00 per day when there is a shortage.

Some companies in the leasing field specialize in supplying all or almost all of the equipment for one or more carriers. Some leasing companies obtain an assured basic lease for a number of containers for a carrier and then make an overage percentage available to the carrier, when and if needed. Other leasing companies specialize in equipment which is proprietary or specialized.

OBLIGATIONS IN LEASING

Leasing companies must also move empty equipment between depots to balance their inventories, because the carriers will not perform this service. One of the obstacles to extending the leasing companies' services to include pooling is the fear of the carriers that the leasing companies will "get between the carrier and the customer." When the leasing company dispatches containers to shippers for loading, receives requests directly from the shipper, dispatches equipment for pickup, and orders the carrier to provide the long-haul service, he may be engaged in transportation without authority. In any event, he would be gaining a measure of control over the origination of the cargo that is enjoyed by the long-haul carrier. For this and other reasons, many operators are phasing out their leased containers in favor of company-owned containers, particularly, as they complete their fleets. Full-scale pooling and all of its associated services would best be provided by a new neutral organization dedicated to serving all carriers.

CHASSIS POOL SYSTEM

Many steamship companies use trailer chassis for container area handling. The container comes off the ship or out of the marshaling yard, and is loaded onto a trailer chassis. It stays on that chassis, once loaded, until it is returned to the port. A fleet of 1,000 containers might require as many as 300 chassis for container area operation only, assuming even that none of these chassis ever departed from the area. Between sailings (if there is such a time) the container area chassis are used for over-the-road transportation and are brought back to the terminal for the next sailing. However, in a high proportion of container moves, the timing does not work out, and probably another 100 trailer chassis are required to support the 1,000 containers.

LONG-HAUL CHASSIS

Whether containers move on the longer inland hauls via rail TOFC service or truck, they require a trailer chassis under each container at all times. This adds a requirement for probably another 150 chassis to those required to support the same 1,000 containers. In the "pool" system, no chassis whatsoever are required for those traveling inland by rail, since the flatcar-to-chassis transfer is simple and the container on flatcar (COFC) will find "pool" chassis available at inland stations, too. Because the "pool" concept makes rail transportation so much more attractive, it is likely that there will be relatively few long-distance hauls by truck.

The proportions shown heretofore will, of course, vary considerably from fleet to fleet and from port to port. Some fleets use straddle carriers, cranes, or fork lifts and do not need trailers for intraterminal handling. Movements through a port such as New Orleans involve a higher proportion of long-distance inland moves into the hinterland than the movements through the Port of New York, where vans are mainly destined to local points.

By a combination of the many services provided by the leasing pool, trailer-chassis requirements can be drastically reduced in the following areas:

1. No trailer chassis whatsoever are needed for rail movements via COFC.

2. The pool's cartage services include provision of trailer chassis where necessary—inland, in ports, and in port areas.

3. Inland pools of containers are maintained by the pool; chassis are not required for these pools.

4. Empty containers in temporary storage or at shipper's doors may be mounted on low-cost demountable legs, rather than high-cost trailer chassis.

5. At terminal locations, demountable legs can be used for loaded containers as well. Experienced truck drivers can drop a container on legs or pick one up from legs in the same time as a conventional kingpin-and-landing-gear hookup.

6. The pool provides trailer chassis on a per diem basis at ports and at inland points, for peak periods and special requirements.

As indicated above, trailer-chassis requirements may run anywhere from $33\frac{1}{3}$ to 60 percent of the container fleet, depending on a number of variables. The pool can reduce this requirement anywhere from 80 to 50 percent. A conservative value analysis of the savings provided by a pool system in this area can be determined by assuming that a fleet of 1,000 containers which would otherwise require 400 trailer chassis can reduce this requirement to 200 by utilizing pool services.

Trailer chassis for 20-ft. containers may be either tandem-axle, single-axle, or two-container-to-one-tandem chassis. The average daily cost, including interest, depreciation, insurance, licensing, taxes, and maintenance, averages $3.00 per day per trailer chassis. The 200 that are saved would, therefore, be worth $600.00 per day. Applying this to a fleet of 1,000 containers provides a savings of 60¢ per container per day to the user of the pool services.

EXCESS OF FLEET LEASING

In addition to chassis, the pool system can also provide containers. A container pool fleet is maintained with a number of the total container requirement on hand. Each user is, furthermore, assured of the availability of at least some additional units above his mean constant need. By interchanging with other pool members who have temporary overages, a further supply of containers can be made available.

If a container user were to attempt to provide for all temporary or short-term excess requirements by ownership or conventional leasing, he would probably find that 15 to 20 percent of his fleet was utilized only 20 to 25 percent of the time. In terms of a hypothetical fleet of 1,000 containers, this might mean ownership of an additional 15 percent, or 150 containers. Assuming a basic cost of only $1.00 per day, plus an allowance of only 50¢ for maintenance, repair, control, insurance, and chassis to support these containers, the extra 150 containers would cost $225.00 per day, each day of the year.

If, instead of owning these containers, 150 containers were leased from a pool at $2.50 per day, but only for 25 percent of the time, the cost per day on an annual basis would be $93.75, a savings of $131.25 per day. If this $131.25 is distributed over the fleet of 1,000, the savings is 13¢ per day per container.

UTILIZATION OF BASIC CONTAINER FLEET

Many containership operators state that 80-percent utilization of their ships would be optimum, because if the average were any higher, there would be too many periods in which they would be full and unable to provide service to their customers. Realistically, it should be considered that there will be many periods when the ships will be running at 60 percent or less, even under optimum conditions.

In a comparison of ownership cost to leasing cost, it may be argued that the pool's administrative costs could be higher than those of an owner because of interchange. Although interchange provides much higher utilization, the cost of arranging for such interchange is, of course, a charge against the savings. Thus, although interchange in an owned fleet is only for through transportation purposes, the administrative costs of any further interchange would be saved. This is true. The process of interchange between ocean carriers, motor carriers, and railroads is costly. Per diem fees have to be invoiced and collected; containers must be accounted for and traced; containers must be stored for varying periods of time in out-of-the-way locations; trailer chassis attached to the containers get lost and have to be found; interchange agreements have to be entered into with every carrier that ever touches the container.

TRAILER AND CONTAINER INTERCHANGE

Interchange agreements for trailers create different procedures. Some provisions of these agreements are similar because their general content is specified by federal regulations. The Interstate Commerce Commission requires that an interchange agreement between motor carriers, which will apply to containers on chassis, includes these conditions:

1. Specific equipment to be interchanged must be described;
2. Specific terminals for interchange must be designated;
3. The use to be made of equipment interchanged must be stated;
4. The consideration for such usage is defined;
5. Traffic transported in interchange must move on through bills of lading issued by the originating carrier;
6. The transportation of commodities must be by authorized carriers over authorized routes;
7. Equipment must be inspected prior to interchange by the receiving carrier, and found to comply with safety requirements of the Interstate Commerce Act.

While the preceding conditions must be covered by all United States interchange agreements between motor carriers, the detailed manner of coverage will vary. Interchange parties usually specify in the interchange agreement additional operating responsibilities and procedures, to protect the owner from loss or damage to his transportation equipment and to insure prompt return of equipment on completion of its immediate purpose.

UNIFORM MODES

Analysis of agreements to develop uniform container-on-chassis interchange agreements between modes reveals that important procedural differences occur in the following key areas:

1. Prompt equipment return provisions are difficult to establish, and interchanged intermodal equipment may not be promptly returned because of a lack of any specific commitment.

2. Per diem rates are set at various levels but do not provide incentive to keep equipment loaded and moving.

3. Per diem time base may be varied according to prevailing holidays, customs clearance times, and other variables within specific geographic service areas.

4. The legal liabilities for loss or damage to cargo, equipment, and third parties tend to fall upon the operating carrier, with exceptions.

5. The user of equipment generally agrees to keep the equipment in his possession unless he receives written permission from the owner allowing it to go to a third party.

A principal area of carrier concern is the structure and wording of the various indemnity clauses within the interchange agreements. Since each mode has established through legal precedent the meaning and interpretation of certain phrases, it does not want to risk changing them for the purpose of standardization. A result of preserving the differences is that a carrier has one indemnity clause with one meaning in an interchange with a given mode, and different conditions in an interchange with another mode.

VARIATIONS AND OBSTACLES

Agreement variations represent serious operational obstacles to expeditious interchange between modes. Beyond content differences, variations in agreement formats cause confusion and excessive time expenditure by carrier personnel responsible for effecting interchange transactions. A standardized agreement for intramodal interchange of transportation equipment between motor carriers has proven effective and is growing in importance within the motor carrier industry. The Equipment Interchange Agreement was developed by the Equipment Interchange Association. It is particularly effective for containers because of its relative simplicity and wide acceptance as a motor carrier industry standard, but it applies only in the motor carrier's use of containers.

CONTAINERS ON CHASSIS

The agreement between carriers in the Equipment Interchange Association consists only of agreeing to be bound by a common set of contractual provisions and operating rules of the Association. The Interstate Commerce Commission requires each exchange of equipment between regulated carriers to be accompanied by a written receipt and report of inspection. The format of the Equipment Interchange Association's "Trailer Interchange Receipt" (TIR) is a practical matter, and this receipt also incorporates an equipment condition record for damage control purposes, for the benefit of the equipment owner and user.

Recommended guidelines for operational procedures to be used by carrier personnel in completing the Trailer Interchange Receipt are shown in the *Official Intermodal Equipment Register*.

ESSENTIAL STEPS

The essential steps in making a physical interchange, after the requirement for a through service has been established, are outlined as follows:

1. Communications are established between the operating and equipment control groups of two carriers to determine the contractual provisions and operating rules which should govern an interchange.
2. The two parties decide to enter into an interchange agreement to apply at a specified point.
   a. Procedures are set to handle the completion of interchange documentation, principally the trailer interchange receipt.
   b. Other operational procedures, including the completion of the safety inspection report, are established.
   c. Agreement on the return of equipment or movement to other carriers is achieved.
   d. Compensation rates are set.
3. An interchange agreement is established.
4. Interchange takes place.

Increasing numbers of interchange agreements are being patterned after that of the Equipment Interchange Association. The interchange agreement of the Equipment Interchange Association now has 563 signators:

1. 550 motor carriers;
2. Seven steamship carriers;
3. Six railroad carriers.

An increasing number of groups attempting to develop uniform agreements for container interchange are following the Equipment Interchange Association's procedures designed for trailer interchange:

1. Western United States railroads for intermodal container/trailer-on-flatcar services;

2. Steamship Operators' Intermodal Committee for intermodal container/trailer interchange.

PART II

R A T E   M A K I N G — O L D   V S.   N E W

Both shipper and container operators have hopes that the establishment of rates for through service will offer them real tangible profits. Unfortunately, these two tendencies often conflict and the establishment of an equitable, middle-range tariff is needed to grant both sides some compensation adjustment. At the outset, the container is at a disadvantage. Competitive modal services between the production and the use location have placed themselves in a position to attract the most traffic at the best rate. The best rate is one which compensates the carrier and attracts the shipper. The carrier's compensation will often depend upon an innovative approach to the service rather than upon cutting rates. In our regulated traffic world, rate cutting is largely resisted by rules of government agencies, and these are developed by the watchful eye and reaction from competing modes. The better way, therefore, is the improvement in certain conditions of service which could offer the shipper/consignee interest equivalent to rate cutting.

We deal with the stage of containerization in which most systems tend to be marine related. All such cargoes and services are developed to attract freight revenues to fill the ships. Any accommodation for such service by the intermodal connecting services is not coincidental, but designed to help the ship interests. The analysis of market development by containership carriers shown in Chapter 6 provides an insight into this area of development.

The competition between carriers in intermodal through service and those using conventional methods presents a real problem for container users. In the rail-to-port service, railroad cars can carry up to 90,000 lbs. of cargo at a carload rate. The cost of this service is often not more than the cost of shipping a single container on a flatcar. But the single container is limited by regulations not to exceed 62,500 lbs. for a 40-ft. van or 44,000 lbs. for a 20-ft. van. It now must be analyzed if the savings in the rail-to-port rate makes up for the cost of handling all cargo in the port area. Things in the road haulage competition vs. containers are also one-sided. Highway trailers have a 20 to 26 percent greater cubic capacity than vans.

CONSTRUCTIVE THROUGH RATES

In the presence of literally hundreds of thousands of rates and tariff structures applying to the container, none is as yet a true intermodal through-rate. However, rates published by forwarders, such as NVOCC or the rail-sea combination, often called OCP (overseas common point) rates, are through-rates in a certain sense.

There are cases where so-called constructive through-rates exist. They are a combination of rates by the underlying carriers combined in such a fashion that they present the shipper or consignee certain advantages over the existing mode-by-mode rating described in the previous paragraph.

Another area of rate interest to the shipper is the absorption of certain costs by the carrier group. The elimination of transfer charges, forwarding fees, side costs and other incidentals such as lighterage, wharfage, and other special charges amounts to a savings the shipper wants to have as a result of through service. He is not interested in whether it is absorbed by one or the other carrier, or both, or if it is simply eliminated from the tariff. All he knows is it costs less in the container than before it started.

RAISING RATES FOR SHIPPER'S BENEFIT

The above title seems to be pure contradiction per se. It is not. There are some commodities where the shipper has had many production and/ or distribution costs which are now eliminated. In the early days of the TMT Trailer Ferry, lumber and plywood became a very interesting commodity to the shipping public. Container/trailers loaded with plywood were originally rated at conference tariffs, and this appeared to be a great cost benefit for the carrier. The berth-line vessels of the conference had to handle the lumber or plywood piecemeal, while the container carrier handled the entire load as one. TMT then proceeded to raise the rate to about 25 percent above the previous conference rate and found, to its surprise, that more and more wood cargo was offered. The after-the-fact analysis showed that the consignee would use the container/ trailer combination at destination in their own interest. Instead of unloading the load at the lumber yard, the unit would travel around the Island of Puerto Rico as a direct-distribution truck.

Containers occupy the same exterior cube regardless of their contents. But since carriers are subject to weight limitation, they will, more often than not, carry a large portion of their container cube as air. Containers must and will be stuffed to capacity, either by maximum weight or cube. This shows a ratio between cube and weight limit first developed by the International Container Bureau (BIC) in 1931.

The cost factor in transport of containers in door-to-door service is the same regardless of the contents of the van. Under a flat container rate, the shipping costs to be added to ultimate consumer prices should prove out to be less than costs resulting from the current classification and rate structure. This may be seen in conventional ocean traffic which mostly uses weight or measurement ratings at option of the shipowner (W/M/SO). A standard container commodity charge could accomplish the same goal. The proof of this theory may be most readily determined by the percentage of shippers who will utilize containerized cargo at a standard fixed rate per container size, per mile, regardless of contents at a "released" valuation. I can never be fully certain if this theory is valid, unless the government would agree to a project with the ultimate objective of phasing out the current rating and rate structure for a new container service through-rate.

TARIFF RATINGS

Containerization will necessarily modify the pattern of the subordinate transportation activities that make up the intermodal network. All carriers must study the rating system for the new markets. Their study should not be based on a complex conventional rate-making system based on value, handling cost, damage responsibility, and many intangibles. Uncover the function which each carrier contributes most efficiently and economically for the network as a viable basis for competitive rating.

P. P. Geddes, who is affiliated with the New Zealand Government Railroad, presented a most revealing study of the rate structure changeover at the International Railroad Container Conference in London in 1971. He reviewed their tariffs in light of the following points:

1. Efficiency of current tariff structure and ability of maximum revenue results;
2. Extent to which rates correspond with actual cost structure, as applicable to containers;

3. Impact of competition and the extent freight rates can be maneuvered between the floor level set by cost and the ceiling determined by the opportunity of competition.

Geddes' methods of critical analysis are not new. Applicable for container rate consideration, they should be measured by:

1. Correlation of freight rates to the value of commodities;
2. Correspondence of graduated tapered rates to actual cost pattern;
3. Elasticity arising from change in rates and competition.

The three tests presented to the International Railroad Congress in
London are as follows.

THE CORRELATION TEST

This test examined the extent to which the entire range of tariffs measure
up to the values of the various categories of freight hauled. The tariff
system, which was adopted from European railway systems, has been in
operation for over 100 years and has been modified and adjusted from
time to time in accordance with changes in cost and competition. These
adjustments, which were made usually on a percentage increase basis to
certain classes of freight at different rates, have resulted through time in
a change from the original proportions.

The correlation test measured the relationships between freights
charged and the wholesale values of the commodities or their values as
placed on rail. In other words, the test indicated the extent to which the
freight charged corresponds to what the "market will bear"; for example,
an ad valorem basis. The whole range of tariffs was formed into a matrix
of existing rates with the tariff rates indicated for each category for the
various ranges of miles hauled. A similar matrix was formed with wholesale values shown for each category per ton wholesale value. These two
sets of values were then subjected to correlation analysis for:

1. Modal mileage run;
2. Various broad categories of freight at their modal mileages.

If the correlation coefficient were low, then it was assumed that actual
values and rates lacked correspondence. If the total range of coefficients
were high, then it was assumed that generally the principle of "charging
what the traffic would bear" was in operation.

The total correlation for all categories of freight rates at mean mileages
measured against values indicated a coefficient of the order of 0.8. Further

examination revealed that certain categories of goods, manufactured goods of high value involving handling, had a coefficient of 0.9.

THE CORRESPONDENCE TEST

Assuming the correlation tests between rates and values were of a sufficiently high order to substantiate that the principle of "charging what the traffic will bear" is in operation, the next area of scrutiny was the tapering of rates. The main objective of the examination of tapered rates was to ascertain whether the revenue being earned was optimum under competitive conditions and corresponded generally to actual cost criteria. It is well known and understood that, owing to the high percentage of fixed and terminal costs that exist in railway operations, actual costs per ton-mile tend to diminish with the longer distances hauled.

The principle governing tapered rates needs careful scrutiny, however, for it is quite possible that revenue may be at a suboptimum level. We need to be sure that:

1. Tapered rates are, in fact, smooth when plotted graphically and not irregular. This irregularity or uneven character may arise from the successive adjustments that are made to rates from time to time. The smoother the curve, the better, for other things being equal, revenue will be optimized from rates determined from a smooth asymptotic curve.

2. The diagrammatic origin of the rate needs careful examination. The normal pattern of unit cost rate curves, when plotted along a horizontal mileage scale, is an asymptotic curve that tends to approach a horizontal level as it moves away from its origin to the right. Where the point of origin is close to the vertical scale, it is questionable whether out-of-pocket costs are being met. Especially where handling or loading costs are sustained, it is considered that the downward gradient of the cost curve should not begin until the 50-mile level is reached. Where the labor-intensive outlays are high (apart from competitive reasons), these should be allowed for by determining the handling charges for a ton of the given commodity and building these charges into the tapered rate structure. For example, if it takes 30 minutes to load one ton of a given category of goods, then there is a, say 60-cent, charge accruing before the taper begins. If this is spread over the first 10 miles at 6 cents per ton-mile plus out-of-pocket operating costs, then we are corresponding to actual cost patterns. In fact, we need to know much more about wagon loading and unloading patterns before we can "set" the taper curve to correspond with the cost curve.

An examination of the various taper curves suggests that:

1. Actual costs are not being met where mileages are low. This is especially so where handling charges are high or other overhead costs are involved.

2. Costs are being met generally where mileages are high.

3. Some taper curves do not match the calculated cost curves for the same freight categories. Some commence above the cost curves, suggesting that a lower price could attract more in terms of competition; some commence below the actual cost curves, suggesting that pressure from competition, lack of knowledge of true costs, or changes in cost structures (due to increased and more expensive labor loading costs), have caused the diversion; and some taper curves "skew" or cross over the cost curve, indicating surpluses are being made in some mileage ranges and deficits in other.

Considerable research needs to be made into all aspects and categories of tapered costs. Once actual costs have been determined for each main category of freight by applying contoured long-run variable costing, then the asymptotic patterns can be adjusted accordingly with due allowance being made for existing degrees of competition. Otherwise, the general contour or shape of tapered unit rates should conform closely to predetermined unit cost curves.

ELASTICITY TEST

Assuming that correlation and taper correspondence are satisfactory, the final criterion is that of elasticity, which, in a competitive market, is probably the most important of the three. Elasticity is the measure of the relative change in demand induced by a relatively small change in price when other factors are held constant. If a rate increases 5 percent, and the quantity offered falls 5 percent so that the revenue remains constant, then the demand for that class of goods is said to possess unit elasticity. If P = price rate and Q = ton-miles, then $P \times Q$ is the revenue earned. If P increases and Q decreases as a result, then the change in revenue earned can be:

1. Greater than before;
2. The same;
3. Less than before.

If P is lowered and an increase in Q is induced, the converse in revenue may result. Where a rise in price induces an overall increase in revenue, we call the demand for freight inelastic, but if the same rise induces a fall in overall revenue, we call the demand for that freight elastic.

Elasticity can be summarized in Table 12-1.

TABLE 12-1. ELASTICITY

Change in Prices	Inelastic Demand	Unit Elasticity	Elastic Demand
Prices rise	Receipts rise	Receipts unchanged	Receipts fall
Prices fall	Receipts fall	Receipts unchanged	Receipts rise

Note: The above is true when we assume *ceteris paribus.*

Elasticity is often shown in a briefer mathematical form as:

$$E < 1 \qquad E = 1 \qquad E > 1$$

when

$$P_o > P_1 \qquad P_o Q_o > P_1 Q_1 \qquad P_o Q_o = P_1 Q_1 \qquad P_o Q_o < P_1 Q_1$$

when

$$P_o < P_1 \qquad P_o Q_o < P_1 Q_1 \qquad P_o Q_o = P_1 Q_1 \qquad P_o Q_o > P_1 Q_1,$$

where the subscripts $_o$ and 1 refer to the original and subsequent price and quantity changes. Strictly speaking, elasticity is a partial equilibrium phenomenon which applies only to a small change, technically to a change that is infinitely small. As such, it can be measured precisely for elasticity if algebraically shown:

$$E = \frac{\text{a relatively small change in quantity}}{\text{a corresponding relatively small change in price}}$$

or

$$E = \frac{Q_o - Q_1}{Q_o + Q_1} \times \frac{P_o + P_1}{P_o - P_1},$$

where E = elasticity of demand;

P and Q refer to prices and quantities;

o and 1 refer to original and subsequent changes.

Example: Elasticity from an increase in price. In 1952, rates for Classes C and E were increased, and this induced a fall in demand for freight.

Date	Rate	Ton-Miles 000's	
1952	76/10	306 300	Class C
1953	81/0	296 200	
1952	31/4	60 200	Class E
1953	34/8	49 800	

Elasticity for Class C:

$$\frac{306.3 - 296.2}{306.3 + 296.2} \times \frac{76.8 + 81.0}{76.8 - 81.0} = -0.63.$$

Elasticity for Class E:

$$\frac{60.2 - 49.8}{60.2 + 49.8} \times \frac{31.3 + 34.7}{31.3 - 34.7} = -1.83.$$

Note: Elasticity is negative because an increase is generally multiplied by a decrease, for example:

$$(0.0167) \times (-37.57) = -0.63.$$

We can establish our first principle. Any change in freight rates should be governed by elasticity. An increase in freight rates will not alter revenue if the demand has unit elasticity; revenue will fall when demand is elastic but will increase when demand is inelastic. That is, when demand is inelastic, it is safe to increase rates; but if demand is elastic, it might pay even to reduce the rates, for this will induce greater demand and, therefore, revenue.

When the price of eggs or oranges rises suddenly, a person on a meager income will think twice before purchasing the same quantity. However, for a wealthy person, even if the price doubles, he will purchase the same quantity of eggs or oranges—or even cigars! In other words, for people in a low-income bracket, goods tend to be relatively elastic as regards demand, but for people in a high-income bracket, the same goods are relatively inelastic in demand.

This principle is important in setting railway passenger fares. For working people, a small rise in fares may cause a large falling off in demand. Conversely, a reduction in fares may induce a relatively large increase in demand. We cannot say precisely as we cannot (with the data available) disentangle the two effects. But a demand elasticity of the order of 3.0 suggests either a luxury good or an income elasticity, and, in this case, it is probably income elasticity that explains this change.

This point is important, for with freight rates, the problem is more one of price elasticity than income elasticity as the demand for freight on railways generally comes from firms rather than individuals.

Let us state, then, our second principle. Elasticity changes with income. Other things being equal, an increase in income causes demand to be more inelastic, and a fall or loss of income causes demand to be more elastic. That is, in passenger-fare setting, consider income elasticity as of prime importance, but of only secondary importance in freight setting. In fact, income elasticity can be disregarded or held constant for almost all freight-rate changes. Fairly similar to income elasticity is the problem of what is known as the luxury commodity. The demand for luxury commodities tends to be elastic for people on a moderate-to-low income, but inelastic for those on a high income. The point has relevance in railway rate setting, where:

1. A luxury unit is being considered;
2. Some special service rendered is commensurate with the price increase above what is normally paid.

Let us state our third principle. Luxury goods or services are generally elastic as regards demand except for discerning or high-income people. Where price is concerned, not only is income an important factor, but also the price of close substitutes. In rate setting, the price of alternatives is probably the most important aspect or type of elasticity. This type is known as cross-elasticity and measures the extent to which a customer will switch from demand for one brand to another by a small change in price. For example, if the price of one brand of cigarettes or petrol rises by only, say 5 percent, this rise in itself will generate a considerable relative change in demand which will be out of all proportion to the change in price. In fact, a small increase in one brand will cause demand to fall right off, as people swing to the close substitute at a cheaper price.

Fourth principle: Cross-elasticity, or the tendency for an alternative or close substitute to generate a marked change in elasticity, is of prime importance in rate setting. If road or coastal freights rise while rail freights remain constant, then other things remaining equal, this fact of rising prices of a fairly close substitute service will increase the inelasticity of demand for rail freight or cause the demand function for rail freight to increase at the expense of the demand function for road or sea freight. This demand function is also known as competitive elasticity and can be measured precisely by:

$$CE = \frac{\% \text{ change in } Q_b}{\% \text{ change in } P_a},$$

where the subscripts refer to goods (or services) a and b.

This principle, of course, applies in a greater degree with very close substitutes. It is not possible to say that road, rail, and sea freight are very close substitutes—they may be under certain circumstances where a given large quantity of goods of one kind are being conveyed from A to B in a continuous stream. Here a slight price reduction may swing the contract from one mode to another. This illustration suggests the next element in elasticity: that of time.

Fifth principle: Time is having an increasingly important function in choice of modal freight, so much so that time elasticity is playing an important part in change in demand apart from price or competitive functions. Time may be regarded in transport in two dimensions:

1. Where the extent of the time horizon in haulage is of prime importance. Livestock or perishable goods are examples where a higher price will be paid for the element of time;

2. Regularity of time deliveries. Here it is important that the time schedule is firmly adhered to—so that if seven days are quoted for delivery from A to B, the client considers this time span of prime importance.

Time tends to increase elasticity of demand for service. The greater the time taken, or the more irregular the span of time, the higher will be the elasticity quotient. This can be measured pricisely, other things remaining equal:

$$TE = \frac{\% \text{ change in } Q_{tb}}{\% \text{ change in } P_{ta}},$$

where subscripts refer to time associated with services a and b in terms of price and quantity.

Sixth principle: This is service elasticity, which is especially associated with freight haulage. An increase or decrease in associated service with freight causes a change in elasticity of demand for freight. Special added service increases inelasticity relative to a rival mode presuming their service remains constant. This special service can take many forms; i.e., protection from the elements and special protective service including insurance for door-to-door delivery. This form of elasticity can be measured as time was. It plays an important part in what determines a "swing" from one mode to another. In other words, a relatively small change in service added, can induce a relatively larger change in the demand for the mode in question in terms of modal substitution.

The seventh principle is market elasticity. Freight operates in a market condition known in economics as a polyopsonistic oligopoly; that is, many buyers but only a few sellers of freight. Described differently, freight is marketed under imperfect market conditions as distinct from a pure market where there is one price known to all buyers. It is a question of how extensive is the knowledge of the price rates, time, and service functions that rail has to offer. The greater or wider this knowledge is spread to users relative to other modes, the more inelastic will the demand be for freight relative to the other modes.

The application of the elasticity theory to container rate-making was discussed with Professor Harald Burmeister, U.C.-Berkeley, because he voiced objection against its extensive application. There is not, of course, enough space in the text to discuss all rate-making theories and their potential application to containerization. As a result of the London rail containerization meeting, several leading rail men, including Frank Richter, Publisher of *Progressive Railroading*, have voiced opinions in favor of the change in this direction.

PART III

INSURANCE PROTECTION

The meaning of insurance is to supply something corresponding to the shipper's care, while his cargo is being moved by many intervening organizations. In the container system, the organizations are as follows:

1. Shipper;
2. Packer or stower;
3. Inland carrier by road, rail, or waterway;
4. Origin container freight station;
5. Storage in transit;
6. Ports and yards;
7. Interface transfer;
8. Stevedore company;
9. Ocean carrier;
10. Ports and yards;
11. Stevedore company;
12. Customs inspection;
13. Clearance Agent;
14. In-transit storage;
15. Delivering carrier;
16. Road, rail, or inland waterway;
17. Consignee.

By no means is this list to be considered all-inclusive; it is only a typical guideline of the scene in which the container moves.

Should there be loss or damage to cargo shipped by conventional means, it may be possible to pinpoint the particular part of the transit where this has occurred by means of receipts or bills of lading, but the number of parties involved in containerization must lead to arguments, unproductive work, and expense in trying to enforce the liability of one party in the chain for the loss or damage. No one will want to admit liability. Trying to evade or restrict liability often has the reverse of the intended effect as few organizations examine the real cost of staff time in following these procedures. The liability question is complicated by the application or conventions dealing with the international carriage of goods. These conventions vary the liability of carriers from country to country and overrule their printed conditions of carriage. It is quite possible for one of the parties concerned to be liable for a loss which, if the same loss had occurred at a different stage of the transit, would incur no liability. The result, therefore, is that the parties concerned in each segment of the overseas transit of goods are subject to different liabilities and where, as with containerized shipments, the cause and place of loss is difficult to establish, the condition of liability is even more confusing.

Under containerization, individual carrier exposure to large loss and damage tends to be greater than under conventional operations, making it less feasible for carriers to self-insure. Individual containerships are usually larger and faster, and thus more costly, than the conventional ships they replace, increasing the amount of hull and machinery (H&M) insurance on each ship, although not necessarily on an entire fleet. H&M coverage does not extend to containers. Protection and indemnity (P&I) insurance on container contents covers exposure to loss on the ocean voyage and on the inland movement. The value of the cargo in a container often exceeds the limits of a standard P&I policy.

Both underwriters and containership operators have adjusted to the changes in liability inherent in containerization. Underwriters have introduced standard clauses insuring containers against losses from: (a) all risks, (b) war and strike risks only, and (c) the costs of total loss, general average, salvage, salvage charges, and sue and labor expenses (that is, expenses incurred by the carrier to avert or diminish the loss covered by the insurance). "All risks" clauses provide coverage against loss or damage of the container occurring at sea and within territorial limits specified in the schedule. Insurance underwriters have also extended property and indemnity coverage to shipowners who carry containers on through bills of lading to cover (a) loss of or damage to cargo in the container during the land portion of carriage, and (b) third-party liabilities to persons or property arising from the use of the container at any stage of transit.

LIMITATION OF LIABILITY

The limitation upon carrier liability for loss or damage to cargo on a point-to-point land/ocean shipment between the United States and most countries in Europe is different, at the present time, for each of the three segments of the transportation. On the inland U.S. segment, liability generally is unlimited except in the event the carrier had been given permission by the ICC to file a released rate. On the ocean, the limitation of liability is $500 per package or unit. Many ocean conferences have published tariff rules purporting to limit the liability of member ship lines to $500 per container on the theory that a container is a "package or unit" within the meaning of the Carriage of Goods by Sea Act and the Hague Rules. A recent court decision, however, held that the individual units within a container must be treated as packages for purposes of liability under the Carriage of Goods by Sea Act. On land in many overseas countries, the truck limitation is an amount per kilogram that converts to approximately $3.70 per pound, and the rail limitation is an amount per kilogram that converts to $15.00 per pound. The limitation upon air carrier liability for international air cargo is an amount per kilogram which converts to $7.50 per pound.

These diverse limitations of liability present two important problems. First, by insisting that a container is the package, ocean carriers, in the absence of court interference, would virtually insulate themselves from liability and create a different standard of liability for containerized cargo than for other cargo. Second, the limitation of liability of the carrier would depend in every case on a determination of where the loss or damage occurred. While in most cases, it would not be difficult to determine responsibility for the loss of nondelivered cargo simply by referring to carrier receipts, it would be very difficult to determine where damage occurred in a sealed container movement. Yet the carrier's responsibility to the shipper for the damage would depend on whether that damage occurred in the United States, on the ocean, or in a foreign country.

A diplomatic conference was held in Brussels, Belgium, during May 1967, to deal with various maritime conventions, including a proposed protocol for amendment to the Hague Rules. One of the proposals considered was an increase in the limitation of liability under the Hague Rules from $500 to $662 per package or unit. Norway and the United States introduced a counterproposal to eliminate the per package limitation and to substitute a limitation of $3.70 per pound. The purpose of the counterproposal was to establish a limit that was high enough to cover most commodities (though not the extraordinarily valuable merchandise) and, at the same time, to achieve the greatest potential for uniformity on at least two segments of the multisegment international shipment. It was thought that if the ocean limit could be made the same as the truck limit in Europe, changes in the overseas rail convention and in the U.S. land liability provisions would be more readily obtainable, resulting, ultimately, in a single limitation of liability for through transportation in international trade.

Following the first Brussels meeting, vigorous industry opposition to the $3.70-per-pound proposal developed in the United States. Ocean carriers generally advocated a limitation of $828 per package or 60 cents per pound, whichever was higher. On the other hand, the interested agencies and departments of the United States agreed that the limitations advocated by both industry groups were inadequate if a container-load of general cargo was to be deemed a single package. It was finally agreed that the United States would not oppose a limitation of $662 per freight unit or package or 90 cents per pound, provided that packages or units loaded in a container or on a pallet would be considered individually for the purpose of applying the limitation.

At the second meeting of the Conference, held in Brussels in February 1968, it was decided, after lengthy and heated debate, to adopt limitations of liability equivalent to $662 per package or unit or 90 cents per pound, whichever is higher, and to add a container provision.

A question arose immediately as to the interpretation of this provision. The British contended that carriers would be free to charge an additional fee to allow the shipper to enumerate packages in the bill of lading. The United States delegation, which had drafted the container clause, construed it to preclude any additional payment for enumeration. Because shippers could recover up to $662 per package if the number of packages in the container were enumerated, but their recovery would be limited to 90 cents per pound if there were no enumeration, carriers effectively could limit their liability by demanding a high premium for allowing the shipper to enumerate.

The 1968 protocol to the Hague Rules has not been submitted to the Senate for ratification, nor has the State Department requested any Congressional committee to amend the Carriage of Goods by Sea Act to bring it into conformity with the protocol.

It is anticipated that containers will so minimize loss or damage to goods that containership lines, with connecting land carriers, will seek a uniform rule of liability for through transportation and, to obtain this end, will be willing to undertake greater liability than is required under current law. The most likely undertaking seems to be $3.70 per pound, the lowest current land liability limit. Such an undertaking would avoid the red tape, litigation, and shipper dissatisfaction that would accompany different liability rules for each mode.

PART IV

CUSTOMS VS. DOOR-TO-DOOR

Governmental customs authorities are involved in all international trade. Goods exported have to pass through customs in a simple transaction, because the customs authorities exercise various controls to insure that goods in respect of which repayment of duties and taxes is claimed are really exported or that the necessary permission for clearance has been obtained before goods subject to export restrictions are dispatched. When goods pass in transit through third countries, the task of the customs authorities is to satisfy themselves that the goods do, in fact, pass through their territory and do not enter the home market.

When the goods are truly imported into the country of destination, Customs is to collect the appropriate duties and taxes. This might not be the most important task, because Customs is also responsible for the detailed application of a wide variety of measures, the basic policies of which are determined by other government departments. Customs enforces exchange control regulations and import prohibitions, insures compliance with certain public health regulations, compiles overseas trade statistics, and enforces certain agricultural rules.

The idea of the balance between discharge of government regulation in national interest and hindrance to trade has found its expression in establishing the Customs Cooperation Council, which has, at present, 62 member states from all parts of the world. It is the intergovernmental organization concerned with customs technique.

The introduction of containers in door-to-door transport called not only for a revision of existing and often long-established practices, but also for a change of mentality. Customs tried to meet this challenge of containerization and to find solutions to the problems of:

1. Control at the portal;
2. Control during travel from door to door.

CUSTOMS AT PORTAL

Functions of Customs at the doors "upstream" and "downstream" can be carried out with efficiency only if customs controls can be carried out both at the beginning and at the end of the trip, as close as possible to the consignor's and consignee's premises. Bottlenecks can be prevented and authorities can avoid inefficient use of their staff only by sharply reducing the traditional customs controls at the places of exportation and importation. The imposition of additional customs checks at frontiers and ports in transit operations causes considerable interruption of the flow of traffic and also constitutes unacceptable hindrances to international containerization.

To solve these problems, containers should be cleared through the customs at inland centers. In some countries, because of geographical situation, the inland offices may even outnumber border and port offices. The objects of inland customs inspection are:

1. Provision of consolidation gateways;
2. Simultaneous customs control with physical distribution activities.

SIMPLIFICATION PROCESS

Many customs administrations have already reduced their control at exportation to the absolute minimum. A few countries allow shippers to file an export declaration after the goods have left the country. In these countries, some 80 percent of all export consignments benefit from a system of post entry under which Customs accepts documents up to six days after the date of exportation. The remaining 20 percent are subject to the residual export licensing regulations, or are goods which attract repayment of duty (for example, drawback), or are under bond.

Several countries have introduced urgent import cargo clearance procedures. As another means of speeding up clearance, the countries accept entries well in advance of the arrival of the actual goods. Still others accept Telex information in lieu of, or in advance of, certain documents in order to permit quick release of the goods.

There remains the physical examination of goods, which naturally varies according to the nature of the goods and the parties concerned. It is to be expected that in the near future, further simplification will be achieved by the use of internationally standardized documents and of computers and data links; some aspects of the latter are examined in more detail later on.

DOOR-TO-DOOR TRANSIT

The actual transit of goods from door to door involves two problems for Customs:

1. The treatment of security must fulfill legal standards.
2. Goods carried in unit loads must be uniform.

CUSTOMS TREATMENT OF CONTAINERS

In Europe, the size and proximity of most of the countries and the intensive exchange of goods between them created various problems which called for early action at the international level.

The new international instrument is the Customs Convention of Containers, which entered into force in 1973. This Convention provides for the duty-free temporary importation of containers, subject to reexportation within three months, but does not provide for the use of the containers for internal transport during the period of duty-free admission. No standard procedure for benefiting from temporary duty-free admission has been laid down in the Convention, which merely states that such a procedure shall be governed by the regulations in force in the territory of each contracting party.

The Customs Convention also establishes the technical conditions applicable to containers to be accepted for transport under customs seal. An annex to the Convention sets out the structural requirements to be met, the closing systems required for effective customs sealing, and durable marking on such containers. A procedure for approval and identification of containers meeting these technical conditions is contained in another annex. Approval is granted by the competent authorities of the country where the owner resides or is established, or where the container is first used for transport under customs seal.

REVISION OF CONVENTION

The revised text offers the following improvements:

1. The procedure to be applied for the temporary admission of containers;
2. Approval procedure by design type;
3. Attenuate strict cabotage rule prohibiting the use of foreign containers in internal traffic.

The new revised Container Convention has been adopted by the UN/IMCO international conference.

In the long run, further simplifications must be envisaged. The Customs Cooperation Council is considering a proposal for the free listing of containers to exempt containers from all import duties and taxes. The present international practice is to permit only limited internal movements of containers built abroad which have not paid import duties and taxes. This obviously restricts commercial and transport operations and is, moreover, difficult to enforce without cumbersome controls.

GOODS IN TRANSIT

A number of international agreements relate to international carriage of goods in transit. Most of them were drawn up as a result of the commencement of container transport. Road traffic was provided for by the TIR (Transport International Routier) Convention, the Customs Convention on the international transport of goods under cover of TIR carnets, which was signed in 1959 and entered into force in 1960. In 1961, the Customs Cooperation Council drew up the TIR Convention, creating the TIR carnet, a document which may be used for temporary admission operations, but also for customs transit operations. The TIR Convention is already intermodal in its basic concept, the means of transport with which the goods covered by a TIR carnet are carried being irrelevant.

Various other international agreements exist, relating to the customs treatment of international goods traffic with road vehicles within the common market area, and the United States–Canada transit manifest arrangements.

RAIL TRAFFIC

The International Convention to facilitate the crossing of frontiers for goods carried by rail (TIF (Transport International Ferrovier) Convention, January 1952) is intended to reduce to a reasonable minimum the time required for customs and other examinations. An international transit system was designed for goods carried to or from inland stations by use of a standard international customs declaration form (the TIF form). The TIF Convention treats goods under the consignment concept, but basically relates only to rail traffic. In many countries, goods transported under customs control from the frontier office to the place of clearance on importation, or from the place of clearance to the frontier on exportation, partly by rail and partly by other means of transport owned or operated by the railways, may also be transported under cover of its procedure. Containers marked by railroad markings can use this system.

To a very large extent, customs controls during transport are waived or are carried out by the railways on behalf of the customs authorities. The consignment notes relating to accomplished operations are usually kept at a railway document control office, where Customs may carry out post facto spot checks in order to verify whether the conditions under which transit had been allowed were complied with.

BARGE CONSOLIDATION

The LASH container can float virtually upstream to downstream. Legislation is proposed in the U.S. House of Representatives that will permit foreign-flag barge-carrying ships to transfer cargo between barges in the United States for consolidation before ultimate shipment to a U.S. port. This is a new departure. Under the Jones Act, no cargo may be transported between points in the United States in any other vessel than one built in and documented under United States laws and owned by United States citizens. In the interest of efficiency and economy of operations, U.S.-flag operators will find it necessary to reshuffle and consolidate cargoes in the barges. This consolidation of cargo prior to a voyage to a foreign port in a U.S. port will entail transfer of cargo from a ship-carried barge to another ship-carried barge.

The United States Customs restriction on cargo consolidation applies only to foreign lighter-aboard-ship (LASH) operators and not to American LASH operators. It is possible that many foreign governments would retaliate against the United States LASH and Lykes Bros. Steamship Company's barge-carrying SEABEE vessels operating abroad, by following the United States Customs rules and imposing comparable restrictions, and thereby restricting upstream-downstream operations.

NEW CUSTOMS CONVENTION

The Customs Cooperation Council in 1967 decided to prepare a new international customs transit convention to deal with all emerging patterns in international traffic, particularly, the widespread use of intermodal containers.

The aim of this new instrument called the ITI Convention (ITI is a combination of the initial letters of the English words, International Transit and the French words, Transit International) is to reduce costs and delays in international transport. For it to achieve this purpose, it must be constructed on certain basic principles, some of which have called for a considerable departure from traditional customs thinking and methods:

1. Minimize delays at obvious bottlenecks (such as ports and major frontier crossing points) by laying the emphasis on controls at the beginning and end of the journey, only at inland depots instead of frontiers.

2. Permit the movement of unitized loads as quickly as possible to their final destination.

3. Avoid either adding to existing requirements or creating new requirements where none exist at present.

4. Take into account the need to provide for a flexible documentation system without introducing new forms.

5. Reduce administrative costs by providing for a cheap system of prearranged standing guarantees or bonds.

6. Make possible future additional simplification on the basis of administrative arrangements, new transport or communication techniques, etc.

THE UNIT CONCEPT

In a customs transit procedure, there are two quite different concepts under which the goods may be dealt with. They can be dealt with either on a package-by-package basis—the "consignment concept"—or on a unit basis, where they are treated as a single unit regardless of the number of different packages or consignments—the "unit concept." A new ITI Convention will deal with unitized traffic. Under this concept, only one document is required for each unit, regardless of the number of consignments, so that documentary checks by Customs are accordingly simplified, while containers offer greater security for customs purposes.

GUARANTEE SYSTEM

When goods are carried in customs transit, a person or a firm accomplishing the operation is normally required to give security in the form of a cash deposit or a bond for the import duties and taxes which might eventually become payable if the goods are not reexported, or if other obligations under which transit has been allowed have not been complied with. This can be done in various ways.

Under national systems of security, persons are often permitted to give a general security, covering all transactions during a specified period of time, the surety being provided by insurance companies, banks, etc. These systems have the advantage that the security can be arranged in advance of the operations to which they relate and do not, therefore, delay the commencement of those operations. Under existing international transit procedures, the guarantee problem has been overcome by using carnets, examples of which are the TIR carnets. Under such carnet systems, the surety is provided by a guaranteeing association which assumes joint and several liability with the person to whom the carnet is issued. By organizing these guaranteeing associations into chains, surety is provided for the persons to whom the carnets are issued in each of the countries in which the carnets are valid. However, such a carnet system would have certain disadvantages, if it were to be applied to a transit procedure modeled on the door-to-door transport concept, in particular, to customs transit operations with containers.

Firstly, a carnet would have to be issued by a guaranteeing association for each containerload of goods before the operation could begin, and this could hold up the operation. Secondly, containers may be transported by different modes of transport during the course of a single operation, and for certain parts of the journey, no surety might be required. Since a carnet system does not provide the possibility of distinguishing between different means of transport, the guarantee would apply to the whole journey, including those parts where the surety was not required. This could make the scheme expensive.

For the purposes of the new ITI procedure, therefore, a new system had to be developed which combined the best of the two guarantee systems referred to above. General guarantee cover will be provided for the persons who use the scheme by an international chain of guaranteeing associations. Since it is a general system of security and does not relate only to specific loads of goods, the persons (natural or legal) who are responsible to Customs for the accomplishment of ITI operations will have to be provided by their guaranteeing association with evidence that they have obtained guarantee cover. This will be in the form of a guarantee card. Only those persons who are required by Customs to have surety will need to be holders of guarantee cards. In this way, the guarantee will apply only to those parts of an ITI operation for which Customs requires surety to be given; and not, for example, to many rail legs, since already the guarantee requirement has been waived in many countries for railways.

USE OF COMPUTERS

Computers and data links are not yet widely used in Customs administrations in international trade. However, the business of keeping track of the position and state (loaded or empty) of several thousands of containers spread out across oceans and national boundaries is extremely difficult without computers. Like the Association of American Railroads, the Swedish Railways have developed a system which enables information concerning arrival of cars at their destination to be passed virtually directly to clients. As the composition of a train changes during the course of its journey, the facts are notified to a central information center and, with the aid of a computer, the movement of a car from one place to another is registered. By means of Telex communication, it is possible to ascertain within approximately two hours the location of any cars. The center also keeps information about status, weight, and other items.

Keeping track of containers as described in Chapter 15 is only a part of the potential usage of computers in container transport. Examples of broad use of computers and data links for the international movement of cargo are now working in London, in Paris, and in Schiphol. Carriers, agents, and Customs come together in the use of a real-time computer system, to:

1. Control incoming goods;
2. Process information in the customs declaration (entry), including the calculation of import duties and taxes and selection of goods or documents for examination;
3. Prepare invoice for import duties and taxes for agents.

UNIVERSAL COMMODITY CODE

The development of a common international commodity code will make it possible to express complex information in a standard and shortened form, to overcome national and linguistic barriers, and to describe goods and their movements succinctly, yet with sufficient precision for the purpose of the users of the coded information. Thus, international commodity codes will contribute to a more efficient use of EDP techniques. By furnishing speedier and more accurate information on a through basis, they would also contribute to accelerated handling of goods from the customs point of view. Much progress in this direction places the container into the cargo stream. New greening flow patterns are expected to provide the compensation for the new efforts.

Protective and Special Services

SPECIAL COMMODITIES

The basic box-like van contains all the important features for the inter-modal transport linkage. Certain commodities, however, need more than simple walls to survive in the confinement of the container; their ambient requirements are of a specific technological impact. We are talking about heat-respiring, perishable, field-fresh commodities as well as liquids. They are representative of the large field of special commodity groups which would benefit from combining containerization with specific commodity requirements. This produces a novel breakthrough in product distribution.

BOXED-UP ENVIRONMENT

The idea of containing environment within a box, separate and distinct from the ambient environment through which the container travels, is quite simple and pragmatic. The accomplishments in space flights show that man can create and carry with him almost any environment he desires. To do this requires fundamentally two activities:

1. Isolation of the box interior from the ambient environment (as shown in Fig. 13-1);
2. Installed devices to keep the interior environment at a controlled level of purity, temperature, and humidity.

The equipment thus moves one step forward from the mere portable transport warehouse to an actively operated, in-transit, climate-controlled unit.

Geographic distribution of acreage for the planting of fruits and veg-

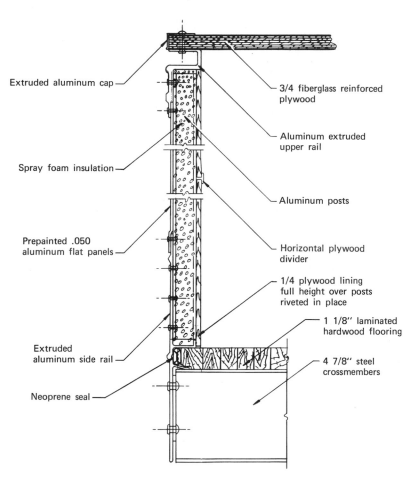

FIGURE 13-1.   TYPICAL CROSS-SECTION OF COMPOSITE SIDEWALL OF INSULATED CONTAINER.

etables and the climate zone varieties which exist around the world provide a cyclic pattern for demand and supply of many foods. Containerization can be of invaluable consequence in the physical distribution for this market.

ENVIRONMENTAL CONTROL

Refrigerated containers thus encompass a complex additional problem area to the already existing problems commonly found in dry-cargo containers. These refrigeration problems are inherent in the very nature of the perishable cargo carried, as well as in the operation of machinery used to protect this cargo. It is not simple to amalgamate various factors, such as insulation, refrigeration, temperature control, humidity maintenance, fresh-air exchange, cargo shoring, internal air handling, reliability, ease of operation, service facility, and maintainability; each one has a complex problem chain which must be analyzed and integrated for mission fulfillment.

The basic design of conventional refrigerated containers (sometimes known as "reefers") currently used by ocean carriers are copied from those used by the trucking industry for highway transportation vehicles designed to hold temperatures for transporting perishables on a normal land trip of 4 to 5 days. In contrast, refrigerated containers in intermodal ocean traffic must be able to transport their cargo door-to-door for periods of 3 to 4 weeks. Therefore, this equipment must be classified according to certain base criteria performance ratings, to meet the individual requirements of the cargo during this long period of time. These criteria are:

1. Commodity characteristics;
2. Through-transport profile;
3. Phyto-sanitary legal requirements resulting from quarantine laws;
4. Delivery inducements to open additional trades for new products.

Fresh fruits and vegetables are living organisms, even though as laymen, we do not usually consider them as such. Fresh meat is in constant transformation. An orange, for instance, is alive and respires just as a human being. To successfully transport such commodities in regrigerated containers on ships over sea distances, one must understand and cope with certain plant physiological and pathological requirements of the orange. A minimum of understanding of plant chemistry is mandatory. Otherwise, it will deteriorate during transit and be of no value when delivered to destination.

PLANT CHEMISTRY

Fresh fruits and vegetables, being organisms in chemical transformation, respire and give off heat and certain gases while using up oxygen in post-harvest confinement. These factors must be taken into consideration in order to provide the right amount of oxygen and humidity (in the form of water vapor) and at the same time remove excess heat. This exchange takes place on the skin of the product. Product preservation depends upon the critical relationship between the skin area exposed to air and the respiration ratio of the product. Simply stated, the conversion of fruit sugars and starches in the particular product in presence of liquids contained both within the cell structure and intercellular spaces is a physio-chemical energy transmission. Heat is generated by this expenditure of energy. Heat, in turn, transforms some of the liquids into vapor. Thus, the vapor pressure rises inside the product and vapor expanding moves some liquids to the skin of the product. Here it is met by the air present and circulating around the product on the inside of the container shell. It is the contact with air that does the job during transit. The larger the contact area, the better the results.

The product has been ripened in the field by solar energy. This heat energy has already been accumulated by the time the product is placed in the transport container. Very few shippers have adequate precooling facilities. Even if they do, at best, fast precooling produces a temporary relief from the heat-up process. To deliver the goods, however, requires product-core stabilization, which takes time.

The enzyme action progresses with the age of the product, so that the precooling effects are not very lasting. Since one can never fully stop the internal energy conversion in the live product, control conditions must be scientifically set up to keep up with the processes of nature between harvest and delivery to the consumer. The requirements for storage temperatures and relative humidity ranges of the most commonly shipped fresh foods are shown in Table 13-1. The table shows the amount of heat produced by various products at different temperature levels. As shown, the biological action of many products is reduced at lower temperature levels, but low-temperature maintenance alone cannot prevent deterioration.

Control of the vapor-pressure balance between the pressure inside the product and the surrounding cooling air stream leads to an optimal relationship between the container temperature range and relative humidity in the air for survival shown in Table 13-2.

Before containerization, only a few critical temperature-controlled car-

Commodity	Temperature (°F)	Heat evolved per ton of fruits or vegetables per 24 hours (B.t.u.)	Commodity	Temperature (°F)	Heat evolved per ton of fruits or vegetables per 24 hours (B.t.u.)
Apples, Winesap	32	300 to 320	Cherries		
	40	590 to 600	Sweet	31	1,249
	60	2,270 to 2,350		36	1,459
Bananas				45	2,811
Green	54	3,300	Sour	32	1,320 to 1,760
	68	8,360		60	11,000 to 13,200
Turning	68	9,240	Corn, sweet (Golden		
Ripe	68	8,360	Bantam cross; not		
Beans, lima, Fordhook	32	2,330	husked)	32	6,560
	40	4,300		40	9,390
	60	21,990		60	38,410
	70	29,220		80	61,950
Beans, snap			Cranberries: Early		
Stringless Green Pod	32	6,160	Black	32	600
	40	10,600		40	870
	60	40,850		50	1,800
	80	49,590	Cucumbers, Producer		
Broccoli (variety			and Wanchula	32	1,690
unknown)	32	7,450		40	2,550
	40	11,000 to 17,600		60	10,460
	60	33,800 to 50,000	Grapefruit, Florida	32	370 to 950
	70	47,340 to 100,000		40	725 to 1,300
Cabbage, Globe	32	1,200		50	1,340 to 2,130
	40	1,670		60	2,200 to 3,980
	60	4,080		70	2,640 to 5,720
	70	6,120		90	5,060 to 6,840
Cantaloups, Turlock	32	1,320	Grapes, Concord	32	602
	40	1,960		40	1,170
	60	8,500		60	3,487
Carrots, topped	32	2,130		80	8,481
	40	3,470	Cornichon and Flame		
	60	8,080	Tokay	36	660 to 1,100
Celery, New York				60	2,200 to 2,640
white	32	1,620		80	5,500 to 6,600
	40	2,420			
	60	8,220			
	70	14,150			

TABLE 13-1. (Continued)

Commodity	Temperature (°F)	Heat evolved per ton of fruits or vegetables per 24 hours (B.t.u.)	Commodity	Temperature (°F)	Heat evolved per ton of fruits or vegetables per 24 hours (B.t.u.)
Lemons, Eureka	32	480 to 900	Peppers, sweet	32	2,720
	40	620 to 1,890		40	4,700
	50	1,610 to 3,670		60	8,470
	60	2,310 to 4,950	Potatoes, Irish		
	70	4,050 to 5,570	Cobbler	32	440 to 880
	80	4,530 to 5,490		40	1,100 to 1,760
Lettuce	32	11,320		70	2,200 to 3,520
	40	15,990	Raspberries	32	3,850 to 5,502
	60	45,980		36	4,400 to 6,600
Mushrooms,				40	6,750 to 8,470
cultivated	32	6,160		60	18,080 to 22,250
	50	22,000	Spinach:		
	70	58,000	Bloomsdale Savoy	32	4,240
Onions, dry,				40	7,850
Yellow Globe	32	660 to 1,100		50	17,940
	50	1,760 to 1,980		60	38,000
	70	3,080 to 4,180	Strawberries	32	2,730 to 3,800
Oranges, Florida	32	420 to 1,030		40	3,610 to 6,750
	40	1,300 to 1,560		50	9,480 to 13,090
	50	2,400 to 4,820		60	15,640 to 20,280
	60	3,650 to 5,170		70	22,510 to 30,160
	90	5,240 to 9,420		80	37,220 to 46,440
Peaches	32	850 to 1,370	Sweetpotatoes,		
	40	1,440 to 2,030	Nancy Hall: Cured	32	1,190
	60	7,260 to 9,310		40	1,710
	80	17,930 to 22,460		60	4,280
Pears, Bartlett	32	660 to 880	Tomatoes:		
	60	8,800 to 13,200	Mature-green	32	580
Peas, Improved Pilot	32	8,160		40	1,070
	40	13,220		60	6,230
	60	39,250			
	80	75,500			

Commodity	Cont. Temp. Range	Relative Humidity Range	Commodity	Cont. Temp. Range	Relative Humidity Range
Apples	30–32	85–90	Fish (fresh)	33–40	90–95
Apricots	31–32	85–90	Mild cured	28–35	75–90
Artichokes (globe)	31–32	90–95	Garlic, dry	32	70–75
Jerusalem	31–32	90–95	Gooseberries	31–32	80–85
Asparagus	32	90–95	Grapefruit	32–50	85–90
Avocados	45–55	85–90	Grapes		
Bananas			American type	31–32	85–90
Gros Michel	54–56	85–95	European type	30–31	85–90
Lacatan	57–58	90	Horseradish	32	90–95
Boxed	53–56	80	Lettuce	32	90–95
Beans (green or snap)	45	85–90	Limes	48–50	85–90
Lima	32–40	85–90	Logan blackberries	31–32	85–90
Beets			Meat		
Bunch	32	90–95	Bacon		
Topped	32	90–95	Cured (fam. style)	60–65	85
Blackberries	31–32	85–90	Cured (packaged		
Broccoli (sprouting)	32	90–95	style)	34–40	85
Brussels (sprouts)	32	90–95	Beef, fresh	29–30	88–92
Butter	32–36	80–85	Hams and		
Cabbage (late)	32	90–95	shoulders (fresh)	30–34	85–90
Carrots			Lamb (fresh)	30–34	85–90
Bunch	32	90–95	Pork (fresh)	30–34	85–90
Prepackaged	32	80–90	Veal	30–34	90–95
Topped	32	90–95	Mushrooms	32–35	85–90
Cauliflower	32	85–90	Onions and onion sets	32	70–75
Celeriac	32	90–95	Oranges Florida	30–32 ⎫	85–90
Celery	31–32	90–95	Calif.	34–36 ⎭	
Cherries	31–32	85–90	Parsnips	32	90–95
Corn, sweet	31–32	85–90	Peaches	31–32	85–90
Cranberries	36–40	85–90	Peas, green	32	85–90
Cucumbers	45–50	90–95	Pepper, sweet	45–50	85–90
Currants	32	80–85	Peppers, chili (ery)	32–40	65–75
Dewberries	31–32	85–90	Persimmons	30	85–90
Dried fruits	32	50–60	Plums (including		
Eggs (shell)	29–31	85–90	fresh)	31–32	80–85
Endive (escarole)	32	90–95	Pomegranates	34–35	85–90
Figs			Poultry, fresh	30–32	85–90

TABLE 13-2.   (Continued)

Commodity	Cont. Temp. Range	Relative Humidity Range	Commodity	Cont. Temp. Range	Relative Humidity Range
Dried	32–40	50–60	Quinces	31–32	90–95
Fresh	20–32	85–90	Rabbits, fresh	32–34	90–95
Radishes	32	90–95	Rhubarb	32	90–95
Raspberries			Spinach	32	90–95
Black	31–32	85–90	Strawberries	31–32	85–90
Red	31–32	85–90			

goes moved by sea. Traffic was largely confined to bananas and some tropical fruits moving north from the tropical farms, either to Europe or North America. New areas now have come in as suppliers of many new commodities in this field. The strength of the American farm economy begins to emerge as supplier of field-packed fresh fruits and vegetables to all parts of the world. Agricultural production in this country is tending even to more specialization in the future.

If the proper cooled containers are available for transportation, the producer will be more interested in getting his commodities to the market in a farm-fresh condition rather than having them canned or frozen for market.

Rapid changes in agricultural production can make importers out of countries which heretofore were producers of perishable foods themselves. For example, in early winter the United States imports some fresh produce from Europe, while at other times, vegetables of the same type are exported to Europe from the United States. Israel produces citrus from November through April and delivers it to Europe, North America, and Japan. South Africa, in turn, produces from May through October. Thus, a shifting in the cooled container fleet (known as COOLTAINER) between both trading areas is possible. This means that the concept of constant container traffic of perishable cargo (with dry cargoes always moving in the opposite direction) is possible between many parts of the world. Taking into consideration the increase in demands for food everywhere, a system of protective containers functionally designed to serve as part of a system will rapidly change demands for fresh cargoes.

SELECTION CRITERIA

The best long-haul cooling equipment for the transportation of perishables had been developed by the railroad-car industry. Numerous designs for adequate air circulation and for mechanical and nonmechanical refrigeration were introduced, and a large fleet of these railroad cars is in use in the United States.

The growth of the American trucking industry has taken a considerable slice of the perishable traffic away from the railroads. Although truck equipment is much less reliable than railroad cars, the truck operator gives:

1. Direct door-to-door service;
2. Greater speed;
3. Driver-care for each machine-equipped vehicle.

HIGH-RATED TRAFFIC

Steamship services are about to face competition from air carriers in the transportation of perishables, just as the railroads had to face competition from the truck operation. It may seem impossible for airlines to carry the large quantities of bananas involved in ocean shipping, but high-paying perishable freight, such as chilled beef, fresh produce, and seafood, already is beginning to take to the air; and if air containers are used in the portless system, this will rapidly increase. During a United States Government bid for the transportation of fresh meat and highly perishable lettuce to Europe for American troops abroad, the air carriers were able to meet the competition of ocean transportation. Experience of the Department of Defense has shown that it would be preferable to fly the products on a day-to-day basis, and that the increase in transport cost could be offset by the reduction of losses normally experienced when using van containers not properly equipped for this service.

The task to develop a reliable, protective, through-service container for ocean and inland transportation which can provide foolproof performance and perfect delivery without increase in the cost of ocean or inland transportation has been completed with the COOLTAINER equipment.

EVEN TEMPERATURES

To find the optimal method for handling quantities of perishable commodities in long-distance, intermodal transportation for periods equaling

15 days or more under variable conditions of ambient container temperatures, COOLTAINER tests were conducted for a period of almost 14 years in the tropics (Haiti, Colombia, El Salvador, Honduras, Mexico, and Florida); in moderate climates in the United States, Canada, the higher regions of Mexico and Central Europe; and in mid-winter cold in the United States, Canada, Europe, and on the decks of vessels crossing the Atlantic Ocean. The products investigated were those which are or will be the main cargoes for international transportation. They range over a variety, such as avocados, watermelons, bananas, plantains, coffee, meat, seafood, citrus, tomatoes, and strawberries, as well as chocolate, photographic paper, plastic wrapping material, typewriters, electrical machinery, compressors, and electronic components.

FACT FINDING

These extensive tests of various products have shown that while each product may have its own protective requirement, many of them can be grouped into behavior patterns. Some products were found to be stable in behavior; others, like bananas, chilled beef, and peaches, go through a condition change while in transit. Products are, in fact, being processed in transit in the COOLTAINER; and their internal organic cycle has not been completed by loading time.

REFRIGERATION/INSULATION RELATIONSHIP

The capability of an environmental system to create and maintain a certain level of temperature in a closed space depends simply on three factors:

1. Refrigeration machinery capable of either consuming the heat inside the space or of changing the internal heat by transferring the calories to the outside of the enclosed space;

2. An insulation, vapor barrier, and moisture barrier capable of preventing the transmission of more heat from the outside to the inside;

3. Machinery to remove the heat generated by commodities stored inside the container. This requires an interface between the cooling coils of the machinery and the heat-generating area of the product, best established by air circulating between the cooling coil and the cargo.

The thickness of insulation and the capacity of the refrigeration machinery must be correlated. In other words, even a large refrigeration machinery capacity is unable to cope with penetrating desert heat of 120° or more, unless the insulation will prevent the penetration of too many calories to the inside. The insulation takes away valuable cargo space for the transportation of merchandise within the container. Therefore, the design and interrelation between the components used in making an adequate intermodal refrigerated container require a detailed optimization process comparable to design methods used in the aerospace technology.

INTERMODAL REQUIREMENTS

The spoilage encountered during the transportation of frozen and fresh fruit and vegetable products in Europe has led to classification of all intermodal containers by the Economic Commission for Europe (ECE) to develop an agreement on the international carriage of perishable foodstuff. This agreement contains test and certification procedures for insulated shells, refrigeration appliances, and heating services. The international containers operating in Europe will have to comply with the requirements. Therefore, the ISO has entered the scene and developed standards for this type of equipment. It is developed in accord with test procedures established by many countries and also by the International Institute of Refrigeration and the American Bureau of Standards. The Convention also deals with the air leakage rate, the refrigeration capacity, and the dimensional rating.

Air leakage rate: A number representing the quantity of air in cubic meters per hour (or cubic feet per hour) necessary to maintain the container interior at a specified pressure.

Refrigerating capacity: The quantity of heat in Btu capacity at $0°F$ or at $35°F$ that a refrigeration appliance is capable of extracting from the inside of the container under a specified set of test conditions.

Ratings: The values of the rating (R), being the maximum gross weight of the container, are those given in ISO/R668:

$$R = P/T,$$

where P = payload and T = tare.

Airtightness test—General: This test is to be carried out after any structural tests have been completed and prior to the Thermal Test. The container should be in its normal operating condition. The temperature inside and outside the container shall be stabilized relative to the ambient temperature, which at the time of test must be recorded.

—Procedure: The container is to be closed in the normal manner.

An air supply through a metering device and a suitable manometer is to be connected to the container by a leakproof connection.

Air is to be admitted to the container to raise the internal pressure to 25 mm (1 in.) ± 10 percent w.g. (water gauge) and the supply then regulated to maintain that pressure. The air flow required to maintain the pressure is to be recorded.

Requirements: See Table 13-3 (Values for maximum air leakage are still to be established.)

Thermal test: This test shall be carried out after successful completion of the airtightness test. It shall be performed with the container in its normal operating condition.

TABLE 13-3. REQUIREMENTS FOR AIRTIGHTNESS TEST

			Temperatures			
		K_{max}	in °C		in °F	
Code	Type	W/m^2 °C	Inside	Outside	Inside	Outside
20	Insulated	0,4	—	—	—	—
21	Open					
22	Heated	0,4	12	−20	54	−4
23	Open					
30	Refrigerated, expandable refrigerant	0,4	−18	38	0	100
31	Mechanically refrigerated	0,4	−18	38	0	100
32	Refrigerated + heated	0,4	−18/21	38/−29	0/10	100/−20
33–39	Open					
40	Refrigerated/ heated with removable equipment, appliance located internally	0,4				
41	Refrigerated/ heated with removable equipment, appliance located externally	0,4				
42	Open					

—**General:** The insulating capacity shall be expressed by the total heat transfer rate (U), which is defined by the following formula:

$$U = \frac{W}{O_e - O_i},$$

where U = Total heat transfer rate, expressed in (W/°C):

$$1 \text{ W/°C} = 0.556 \text{ W/°F}$$
$$= 0.860 \text{ kcal/h°C}$$
$$= 1.895 \text{ BTU/h°F};$$

W = Electrical power consumption by the operation of heater and fan motor (Watt);

O_e = Mean outside temperature of the container;

O_i = Mean inside temperature of the container.

The mean inside temperature shall be the arithmetic mean of the temperatures measured 10 cm. (4 in.) from the walls at the following fourteen points:

a.   the eight inside corners of the container;
b.   the centres of the six inside faces of the container.

The mean outside temperature shall be the arithmetic mean of the temperatures measured 10 cm. from the walls at the following fourteen points:

a.   the eight outside corners of the container;
b.   the centres of the six inside faces of the container.

The mean temperature of the walls is the arithmetic mean of O_e and O_i:

$$O = \frac{O_e + O_i}{2}.$$

—**Continuous operation:** Operation shall be considered to be continuous if after an initial heating (cooling) and soaking period both the following conditions are satisfied: O_e and O_i shall not vary more than ±0.5°C (±0.9°F), and the difference between the average thermal outputs measured over a period of not less than three hours shall be less than 3 percent. All readings are to be recorded at 15-minute intervals.

—**Procedure:** Insulating capacity shall be measured in continuous operation either by the internal cooling method or by the internal heating method. In either case, the empty container shall be placed in an insulated chamber.

Whatever the method employed, the average temperature of the insulated chamber shall throughout the test be kept uniform and constant to within $\pm 0.5°C$ ($\pm 0.9°F$), at a level such that the temperature difference between the inside of the container and the insulated chamber is not less than $20°C$ ($36°F$), the average temperatures of the wall of the container being maintained at about $+20°C$ ($68°F$).

(When the overall coefficient of heat transfer is determined by the internal cooling method, the dew point in the atmosphere of the insulated chamber should be maintained at $+25°C \pm 2°C$ ($77°F \pm 3.6°F$). During the test, whether by the internal cooling method or by the internal heating method, the atmosphere of the chamber shall be made to circulate continuously so that the speed of movement of the air 10 cm. (4 in.) from the walls is maintained at between 1 and 2 metres/second (3.28 and 6.55 ft./sc.).

A. Internal cooling method: Where the internal cooling method is applied, one or more heat exchangers shall be placed inside the body. The surface area of these exchangers shall be such that if a fluid at a temperature not lower than $0°C$ ($32°F$) (to prevent frosting) passes through them, the average inside temperature of the container remains below $+10°C$ ($50°F$) when continuous operation has been established.

B. Internal heating method: Where the internal heating method is applied, electrical heating appliances (resistors and the like) shall be used. The heat exchangers or electrical heating appliance shall be equipped with an air blower having a delivery rate sufficient to ensure that the maximum difference between the temperatures of any two of the fourteen points specified in 4.15.1 does not exceed $3°C$ ($5.4°F$) when continuous operation has been established.

All temperature-measuring instruments placed inside and outside the container shall be protected against radiation.

When continuous operation has been established, the maximum difference between the temperature at the warmest point and the temperature at the coldest point on the outside of the container shall at no time exceed $2°C$ ($3.6°F$).

The mean outside temperature and the mean inside temperature of the container shall each be read not less than four times per hour.

The test shall be continued as long as it is necessary to ensure that operation is continuous. If not all measurements are automatic and recorded, the test shall be continued for a period of eight consecutive hours in order to make sure that operation is continuous and to take the definitive readings.

—**Requirements:** The total heat transfer rate (U) shall comply with the class of thermal container the test container is built for.

SURFACE TEMPERATURE

A problem that the designer of refrigerated container equipment must often resolve is that of determining the surface temperature of the container outside shell subjected to solar radiation.

Consider a plain wall exposed to the environment at temperature T_e, and subject to solar radiation with a solor radiation constant of H_s. The inside wall temperature is T_o. Heat balance considerations indicate that:

$$\varepsilon H_s - \varepsilon\sigma(T_s^4 - T_e^4) - h(T_s - T_e) = U(T_s - T_o). \qquad (1)$$

The convective coefficient of heat transfer h is given by the following expression:

$$h = 0.19(T_s - T_e)/3. \qquad (2)$$

The heat flux is given by the relationship:

$$\frac{q}{A} = U(T_s - T_o). \qquad (3)$$

Substituting Equation 2 into Equation 1 yields an equation from which the surface temperature T_s may be determined. The emissivity $\varepsilon = 0.9$, the solar constant $H_s = 465$ Btu/hr. ft.$^2R^4$ and $\sigma = 7.712 \times 10^{-9}$ Btu/hr. ft.$^2R^4$. In these equations,

ε = Emissivity;

H_s = Solar constant, Btu/ft.^{2};

σ = Boltzmann constant, Btu/hr. ft.$^2R^4$;

h = Convective film coefficient, Btu/hr. ft.^{2}F;

U = Overall coefficient of heat transfer, Btu/hr. ft.^{2}F;

T_s = Surface temperature, deg. F;

T_e = Environment temperature, deg. F;

T_o = Inside temperature, deg. F.

To meet international requirements for perishable cargo, refrigerated containers can be divided into functional groups, depending upon their operating range and special capabilities. Five typical groups are as follows:

Freeze-holding group (FH): Low-temperature unit designed to transport frozen foods only and maintain $-10°F$ in ambients of $100°F$. Unit would provide perimeter air circulation around the cargo to intercept and remove heat that penetrates the insulation before it reaches the cargo. The unit requires no ability to remove heat from the cargo or reduce the cargo temperature in transit.

Heat-removal group (HR):   Medium-temperature units designed to transport fresh perishables and maintain 28° to 55°F in ambients of −20° to 100°F. The unit should supply some perimeter but mostly center-of-the-load air circulation for uniform temperature maintenance within or −1.5°F of the thermostat setting. The unit would also maintain high relative humidity and provide for fresh air exchange during transit.

Combination holding-removing group (CHR):   Multitemperature-range unit designed to comply with all requirements of Group 1 and Group 2. Unit should also have some capacity to reduce the temperature of fresh perishable cargo during transit loaded "warm" at shipping point. This unit should incorporate the facility of using atmosphere-control equipment for certain highly perishable items easily affected by chemical charges, such as strawberries, so as to extend their normal "storage" life. It should also be able to provide an air purification device for the transportation of fresh meat to reduce detrimental bacteria in the air inside the container.

Vented group (V):   Air-ventilated (not refrigerated) unit designed to transport commodities which require continuous or intermittent exchange of air within the container during transit. Outside air is brought into the container to (1) prevent the buildup of undersirable gases, (2) reduce the occurrence of cargo and/or container sweating, and (3) provides limited cooling with outside air during certain periods of the year for non-critical commodities.

Dehumidified, insulated and heated (DIH):   This special group of containers deals essentially with similar problems as the above types, but restricts their thermo-handling to protection from cold, from heat, and from excess moisture and internal sweating.

Classification of refrigerated containers into groups according to their capabilities and certification of their ability to perform specific functions provides both the carrier and the shipper with guidelines, heretofore unknown. These guidelines spell out the proper piece of equipment to do a specific job. They also help eliminate the improper use of equipment, which is causing high losses with certain types of perishable cargo.

Variations in the performance of refrigerated containers are functions of design, and most truck units used today as low-cost refrigeration are designed to transport frozen cargo. Thus, they are not suitable for fresh perishables. Many operators are not aware of this fact and assume that a unit capable of maintaining −10°F for frozen cargo can surely maintain 50°F for fresh tomatoes. Lack of knowledge in this area has led many operators to purchase large fleets of equipment, only to find that they are not suitable to meet their needs for all types of cargo. Because of the mounting pressure by shippers for refrigerated containers, carriers frequently supply unsuitable equipment incapable of providing proper care for the cargo during transit. Losses inevitably occur and claims are filed. As a result, the shipper, receiver, carrier, and insurance company are all dissatisfied.

COMMODITY CHARACTERISTIC ANALYSIS

Food commodities requiring temperature and humidity control can be classified into eight groups. These groups have been established by testing the particular commodity under temperature conditions which allow delivery of these commodities with enough storage life, so that they may be sold in supermarkets for about one week after being removed from the containers. These eight commodity groups are shown in Table 13-4. These commodity groups sometimes require readjustment, because the conditions of different commodities change with the area of production. California oranges, for instance, require a temperature of 35°F, while Florida-grown oranges must be transported at 32°F. The reason for the difference lies in the amount of heat produced during the growing season, as a result of sunlight-radiated heat, reflected heat, photosynthesis, sugar content of the product, and other growing conditions. In the transportation of bananas, a base temperature must be established separately for each growing area, due to inherent differences of each area.

PRETREATMENT FACILITIES

Since the space within the environmental protective container is limited and the energy to move a cumbersome piece of machinery would be detrimental to the economics of container transportation, the preferred method is to establish fixed pretreatment facilities. Here the products gathered from the field are subjected to processes which remove the field heat. This process usually takes the form of treatment in cooled water or cooled air or evaporation in a vacuum tank. Other installations use the pressurized air flow pattern, which we found to be the best cooling

TABLE 13-4. COMMODITY GROUPS AND THEIR
SAFE LOW-TEMPERATURE LIMITS

Group A (−10°F)

All frozen food cargoes

Group B (28°F)

Fresh meat
Dates

Group C (32°F)

Artichokes	Kohlrabi	Apples	Persimmons
Asparagus	Leeks, green	Apricots	Plums
Beets	Lettuce	Blackberries	Quince
Brussels sprouts	Mushrooms	Cherries	Raspberries
Cabbage	Onions	Dewberries	Strawberries
Carrots	Peas, green	Figs	
Cauliflower	Parsnips	Grapes	
Celery	Radishes	Loganberries	
Corn, sweet	Rhubarb	Nectarines	
Endive, escarole	Salsify	Oranges, Florida	
Garlic, dry	Spinach	Peaches	
Horseradish	Turnips	Pears	

Group D (35°F)

		Group G (50°F)	
Coconuts	Tangerines	Grapefruit, Fla.	Pumpkin
Oranges, Calif.		Limes	Squash, winter
Pomegranates		Mangos	Tomatoes, ripe
Squash, summer		Okra	

Group E (40°F)

		Group H (55°F)	
Cranberries	Watermelon	Bananas	Sweet potatoes
Pineapple, ripe		Lemons	Tomatoes, green
Potatoes		Pineapples, green	

Group F (45°F)

Avocados	Melons	Papaya, ripe
Beans, green	Olives, fresh	Peppers, sweet
Cucumbers	Cantaloupe	
Eggplants	Casaba	
	Crenshaw	
	Honeydew	

system for containers. When using air cooling, the packaged product is subjected to the bottom-to-top air stream prior to being loaded in the container. Pretreatment facilities are commonplace in American and Mediterranean agriculture and in the banana industries, where the food is shipped in cartons.

Of course, the stabilization of the heat generation of the product may require a considerable lapse of time in which to obtain the desired results in the stack of product. This has led to an analysis of pretreatment in which blast chilling, hydro-cooling and, eventually, vacuum-cooling have been invented. Certain commodities, such as lettuce, respond very well to vacuum-cooling. But, on the overall, it was found that the pretreatment processes are not as effective as the carriers would desire. The American railroads, at their annual meetings—called the "Agricultural Perishable Commodities Meeting"—at Purdue University, have complained for years about the shipper's failure to properly precool. If this would be the case, the product could be handled more easily with even less efficient transport refrigeration equipment. We have pointed out at two of these conferences that systems analysis would show it to be more effective to improve the environmental protection system of the container, rather than to worry about expensive fixed pretreatment facilities. A better way had to be found to improve transportable cooling facilities for container installations. To do this requires a very thorough analysis of the effects of dry-dehydrated air versus moist air.

MOISTURE IN AIR

"Atmospheric air" is actually a mixture of air and water vapor, often called "moisture." Air itself is a physical mixture, for ordinary dry air and water vapor do not react chemically on one another. To understand the air and water vapor mixtures, one *must* first understand how gases and vapors behave under various conditions of temperature and pressure, either singly or when two or more gases and/or vapors are mixed. There are a few simple facts and laws of nature that govern the action of the gases and vapors.

This information deals with principles of refrigeration. Since ordinary air is a mixture of dry air and water vapor, the law that applies especially to mixtures of gases or gases and vapors is Dalton's Law. Dalton's Law tells us that two gases can occupy the same space at the same time, and that each acts independently of the other and as if the other were not there. Each reacts to changes in volume, temperature, and pressure. Each has its own density (weight per cubic foot), its own pressure (partial pressure), and temperature; but they pay no attention to one another, and each follows the laws that govern it, in its own way.

Dry air without moisture is a mixture of several gases, thus it does not exactly conform to the gas laws, but the gases that comprise air are true gases; so air, the mixture, can be considered as following the gas laws closely. Normal dry air consists mostly of oxygen and nitrogen, with very small amounts of hydrogen, carbon dioxide, argon; and in even smaller amounts, such gases as neon, ozone, and ethylene. Oxygen comprises slightly less than 21 percent of air. Oxygen is necessary to life and yet it is also destructive, as it is the most active agent, causing ripening of fresh fruits and vegetables plus rusting and corrosion of metals.

DENSITY AND PRESSURE OF AIR

Since we can move around so freely in the surrounding air, we might assume that air has no weight. But air does have weight, and is surprisingly heavy. Its density (or weight per cubic foot) varies, being more at sea level, where it is compressed by all of the air above it, than on the top of a high mountain.

The amount of air cooled, heated, and handled in a refrigerated container system is often considered by its weight, as a certain number of pounds of air (including moisture) per hour or per minute. In fact, "standard air" has a weight or "density" of .0749 pound (a little over an ounce) per cubic foot of dry air at 70°F and at sea level.

BLANKET OF AIR

A blanket of air covers the entire load in the container. It is denser at the bottom, and gets thinner and lighter as we go upward. The weight of air causes a pressure of 14.7 pounds per square inch at sea level.

Moisture in the air is water vapor, and air and water vapor exist together in a given space at the same time. The two are independent of each other, and do not respond in the same manner to changes in conditions, especially to changes in temperature.

Water vapor may be in a saturated condition, and if we cool it just a few degrees, we may cause it to condense into a liquid. Two-thirds of the earth's surface is covered with water from which water vapor is being evaporated and to which condensed water (rain or snow) is being returned. The amount of water vapor at any given place or time varies a great deal.

It does not make any difference whether there is any air in that space or not; the water vapor pressure will be the same, for it depends wholly on the temperature of the water. When we commonly refer to atmospheric pressure or barometric pressure, we include the pressure of the air itself and the pressure of the water vapor in it. According to Dalton's Law, the total pressure is the sum of the two partial or component pressures, that of the air and that of the water vapor.

SPECIFIC VOLUME AND DENSITY

If we have a room 10 × 10 × 10 feet, inside measurements, full of this water vapor saturated at 60°, we have 1,000 cubic feet of the vapor. Obviously, there are 1,000 cubic feet of air in the room, just as there are 1,000 cubic feet of water vapor in the room, also. With a total pressure of 29.921 in. Hg (humidity grains) we found that the pressure of the air only is 29.3994 in. Hg. The air is less dense than if there were no water mixed with it. Humid air, however, is not heavy; but is actually lighter per cubic foot than dry air at the same temperature.

Dry air has an actual weight of almost 70 times the weight of the water vapor. Although the amount of water in the atmosphere is very small, as is the variation in that amount from one time to another, it is very important to the conditions of the cargo in the container.

TRADING PROFILE ANALYSIS

Another factor which is of considerable influence in determining the effectiveness of refrigerated containers lies in the ambient conditions surrounding the following:

1. Ambient surrounding product at origin;
2. Environment and duration of transit through different temperature ranges while being transported from origin to tidewater;
3. Oceanic ambient temperature range, especially for containers on deck;
4. Delivery area environment and time used in delivery;
5. Desired minimum shelf life, duration, and temperature;
6. Storage life remaining in final consumer's environment.

For example, products which are shipped from Ecuador to Japan or from Israel to Europe have a very short but violent environment at the beginning. This is followed by sea temperature and environment. The sea ambient is quite steady. Consider the air cooling obtained by the container exposed on deck moving through the sea air by the speed of the vessel. Finally, upon arrival, the environment again requires consideration. If delivery is made in Europe in the fall, spring, or winter, the ambient air is so benign that very little, if any, artificial cooling is required. Yet when a shipment moves inland in the United States, high heat loads can be expected in the spring, summer, or fall, depending on the area in which it moves, requiring the maintenance of the internal environment within the container. A formula can be worked out for each commodity involved, but it is very difficult to evolve one standard for all commodities and all trading profiles. The best answer, therefore, is to have an adequately insulated container that protects the cargo from whatever outside changes occur, while maintaining a balanced internal climate with active product-heat removal.

BASIC SYSTEMS COMPARISON

The refrigerated container is a product of two disciplines. In addition to the cargo systems science dealing with the new intermodality, advanced methods of refrigeration are required to provide the balanced cargo environment. During the first generation of refrigerated containers, the art of refrigeration had been too superficially dealt with. Truck refrigeration units were used mostly to refrigerate containers. But the capability of truck refrigeration equipment is only to provide a protective cargo air system inside the container, preventing penetration of outside heat to affect the cargo. Investigators of the U.S. Department of Agriculture found that removal of heat generated within the closely stacked product on the inside of the container, and its dispersal to the ambient provided the solution for the basic reefer container.

To provide for the machinery installation to do the work of initial cooling requires a larger aggregate for cooling than a truck requires. It was also found that the air circulation system must be ducted, so that the cooling air action is forced through the center of the load, where the heat exchange activity takes place. Truck refrigeration usually short-circuits this area.

Therefore, the sophisticated container refrigeration of both the autonomous and nonautonomous container equipment uses a directed air stream in the container from the bottom to the top.

ASHDOD EXPERIMENTS

The most significant contribution to the development of the art of long-haul perishables was a series of experiments conducted between Decem-

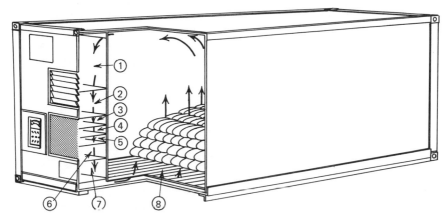

FIGURE 13-2. EXPLANATION OF INTEGRATED COOLTAINER
CLIMATE CONTROL—THE SYSTEM AND THE EFFECTS ON CARGO.
(SOURCE: COOL-CHAIN INC.)

1—Two complete heating/cooling units each capable of maintaining
desired temperature and together capable of precool
2—High-pressure circulation blowers for positive center-of-the-load heat
removal and climate-holding power
3—Narrow-range constant level temperature maintenance ($1\frac{1}{2}°$ plus or
minus of optimal level)
4—Temperature balance modulator prevents chill & freeze damage
5—Programmed gas level and air change administration
6—Electro pure-air field reducing micro-organisms and bacteria
7—Condensate re-vaporizer moisture-level control
8—Moist-aire stream for vapor-pressure balance of product
        Subject to United States and foreign patents

                              Courtesy: Frigitemp Cool-Chain Inc.

ber 1971 and April 1972 in the Port of Ashdod, Israel. Ten containers
were performance-compared in both stationary tests and actual shipping.
The rules of the United States Department of Agriculture, Plant Quarantine Division were applied not only to transport the fresh agricultural
products, but also to perform an additional task, namely, that of disin-
fecting the fruit load and destroying the Mediterranean fruit fly (or other
pests) in transit. This is a case where containerization proves its significance to the physical distribution management. The elimination of several steps, such as precooling or aftercooling or the use of chemicals for
pest control, is accomplished by the use of a door-to-door environmentally controlled container for this purpose. The COOLTAINER, which
had its origin in proprietary development as early as 1958, showed up in

the Ashdod test 14 years after its inception as the tool of this container-ization accomplishment. Not only did the COOLTAINER (Fig. 13-2) become the first to comply with USDA Plant Quarantine regulations presently in the process of being written into law, but it also showed the way of expanding the fresh-food transport and distribution system cover-ing new areas of the world without the fear of transmission of plant pests.

INTEGRATED VS. SHIPBOARD SYSTEMS

As already stated, the maintenance of an adequate uniform transit en-vironment for fresh perishables requires through-the-load cooling. This can be used in either of the two basic refrigerated container systems in use today:

1. The Sabine-Westling, nonautonomous, ship-installed refrigeration system;
2. The integrated, autonomous refrigeration system (e.g., COOLTAINER).

The Sabine-Westling system provides for the ship to produce the cargo air. This air stream is then ducted through the ship to a position where it is introduced into the container through an access hole located ap-proximately 10 inches from the bottom in the front panel. The return air leaves the container through the front panel through a hole about 10 inches from the top. Inside the container, the air is baffled down into the floor.

The system has proven to be very useful and extremely attractive for the transportation of frozen meat from Australia to Europe, as well as to the United States. It has been highly recommended by Ship Owners Research Organization in Great Britain, who made their considerations on the fact that it would be simpler for the shipowner to stay with his conventional, on-board cooling plant.

The shortcomings of the nonautonomous refrigeration system are partly due to the more complicated air ducting in the ship, as a result of the use of containers. The static pressure, which, according to the Ashdod experiment, is required to do the work within the container, is being lost through the duct system which is mandatory for the shipboard system.

Further problems of the system, which was once heralded as the final solution to shipboard containerization, lie in problems of intermodality of the nonautonomous container. To be refrigerated on land, each con-tainer requires another source of refrigeration both in the storage yards and in the truck delivery system. The two systems were developed for truck delivery. The more commonly known one is the clip-on system in which a refrigeration unit is suspended from the front corner posts of the container during truck transit (Fig. 13-3). The slip-on system COOL-TAINER deals with a chassis-installed unit where the container is simply placed on the chassis and the unit automatically takes the place of the shipboard duct system.

The problems of the Sabine-Westling system are in the intermodal application for which the container has been designed. At the intersection of the container technology with the analytical results of a unique storage and inland transport mission, a new characteristic enters into the mission determination. This deals with the relation between ambient temperature profile and cargo characteristics. Transportation of deep-

FIGURE 13-3. CLIP-ON CONTAINER-REFRIGERATION SYSTEM AT-TACHED TO A STANDARD ISO-20 INSULATED CONTAINER. NOTE HOW THE ATTACHMENT CLAMPS ARE SO DESIGNED THAT THEY DO NOT INTERFERE WITH THE NORMAL HANDLING BY SUCH STANDARD EQUIPMENT AS "TWIST-LOCK" SPREADERS, PACECO-TYPE OVERHEAD GANTRY CRANES, STRADDLE TRUCKS, AND SIDE-LIFT VEHICLES. (SOURCE: LUKE SYSTEMS).

frozen goods from the containerport is through a moderate climate zone. In England and in Europe, therefore, nonautonomous containers can be delivered without clip-on units. This, however, cannot be done when sensitive, heat-generating, fresh perishables or fresh meats are involved. Then delivery units are required and the elaborate preparations are costly and intermodally ineffective.

MODIFIED ATMOSPHERE

The inventive spirit has explored the use of modified atmospheres to control the respiration of the product load. This system is very successful in the long-term storage of apples and other products.

Supply of gas additives has shown promise of shelf-life and storage extension, but this still depends on a reliable through-the-load cooling system for the system's effectiveness. I conducted tests keeping a green tomato for one entire year under gas control without oxygen. The tomato stayed green until we broke the seal. Then it ripened within one day to a dark red color. Although it looked fine, when we opened the tomato, we found no structure and pulp, just water. The tomato had "cannibalized" itself.

ELECTRIC POWER

Some containership operators like to use 380–440 v. ac (alternate current) electric power to operate the cooling machinery. Electric power to operate the machinery does affect the system's logistic performance. It restricts intermodal use and calls for systematic intermodal service integration. Most land areas, such as the United States, use 220 v. ac at fixed installations. The containers, therefore, would be best equipped with a 220 v. ac, 3-phase current of 50/60 cycles (also called Hertz). In this event, the 380–440 v. shipboard power can be transformed down to the container voltage of 220 v. On land, at packing sheds, the containers can be plugged into existing currents, not only in the United States, but also overseas. In the event of a failure of the engine, electric power lines from any source would be sufficient to provide emergency power.

POWER STANDARDIZATION

The container-installed electric receptacle has been standardized by ISO, and interchange is possible. However, environmental protective containerization still remains an almost closed system for each carrier, except when the container is self-equipped. A further systems analysis study is required for the location of the diesel standby generators. In most cases, it is best not to install the diesel generators on the container itself in order to provide:

1. More usable cube;
2. Better machinery maintenance.

In this case, generators are installed permanently or temporarily under the chassis that carries the containers on land; while, of course, direct-line plug-in would be used on ships.

KNOWLEDGE LEVEL

A study was conducted by Luigi Fabiano in southern Italy as a result of the FAO Technical Conference on Marketing and Export Trade of Fruit and Vegetables in the Mediterranean area presented in Rome in October 1969. The conclusions reached are summarized as follows:

1. A general lack of knowledge was found among operators in the transportation sector regarding the characteristics of each type of agricultural product and its organic requirements during the transport-and-storage stage. Most carriers generally believe that it is enough to stuff a perishable product in a refrigerated van or container and keep the temperature around 0°C (32°F) to ensure its perfect preservation during transport.
2. They know nothing about the moisture problem, nor do they have the slightest idea about how to stow the various boxes or cartons inside the transportation facility in such a way as to ensure, in all parts of the container, the best humidity and ventilation conditions for each separate product.
3. The same ignorance also applies to heat of respiration; and little importance, if any, is therefore given to this problem.

RESULTS FORMATION

Six basic factors affect the isothermic efficiency of a shell:

1. D = distance air travels within each shell in the circulation cycle in ft.;
2. A = surface area of each particular commodity exposed to heat exchange;
3. P = quantity of air that penetrates stacked cargo;
4. SE = static efficiency rating of the circulation fans;

5. IC = ratio between heat penetrating cargo area and the space left as usable cube of shell after deduction of insulation, Btu;

6. TMI = temperature–moisture index, which is a relationship between water content and heat energy of cargo.

While D can be determined simply by measuring distance, A needs a set of values arrived at for the different commodities in their customary arrangement or packaging while in transit (see Table 13-5).

P was developed by measuring typical stacking patterns of cargo, which produced the following formula:

$$P = \frac{A_e}{A_t} \times 10,$$

where A_e = volume of air moving effectively through the cargo, cfm;

A_t = total amount air produced by circulating fans in shell, cfm.

The value of P varies with the method of packaging and stowing and must be calculated for each individual load.

SE was established by using the standard formula for static efficiency used by The American Society of Heating, Refrigeration and Air Conditioning Engineers:

$$SE = \frac{CFM \times SP}{6356 \times BHP},$$

where CFM = cubic feet of air per minute;

HP   = horsepower used for movement of fan blades;

SP   = static pressure of resistance pressure.

For IC and TMI, the formulations should be

$$IC = \frac{H_p}{C},$$

TABLE 13-5. SAMPLES OF AVERAGE VALUES FOR A IN BASIC IE FORMULA

Apples	6	Grapefruit	8
Bananas	5	Grapes	2
Beans, string	2	Lettuce	8
Cabbage	10	Onions	6
Cantaloupes	10	Oranges	6
Cherries	2	Potatoes	6
Corn	6	Watermelon	12

where H_p = heat penetrating cargo area, in Btu;

C = inside cubic measurement of shell;

$$\text{TMI} = \frac{\text{RF}}{\text{HF}} = \frac{\text{refrigeration factor}}{\text{humidity factor}},$$

where HF = percent relative humidity $\times$ 100;

$$\text{RF} = \frac{12{,}000}{R_e - H_{tl}},$$

where R_e = rated Btu capacity of refrigeration unit;

H_{tl} = total heat load = H (field heat of cargo) + H_b (trailer body heat) + H_r (respiration heat of cargo) + H_l (heat leakage of shell) + H_f (heat of circulation fans).

All these individual factors were then combined into the basic rating formula which permits the comparison of the isothermic transport effectiveness to be calculated for given shell sizes and for particular cargoes. By application of these formulas to 66 products, we reached the design criteria for the isothermic container:

$$\text{IE} = \frac{\left(D \times \dfrac{A}{P}\right)}{\text{SE}} \times \text{TMI} \times \text{IC}.$$

PERFORMANCE REQUIREMENTS

The performance requirements for intermodal service, compared with conventional transport refrigeration units, are as follows:

Intermodal dual electric refrigeration units: Twin-condensor, evaporator, and air circulation systems each capable of independent operation —both units operate during periods of heavy load—each individual unit capable of maintaining desired temperature levels under normal in-transit operating conditions. Dual units provide increased reliability factor against in-transit mechanical failure.

Conventional units employ single-condensor, evaporator, and air circulation system with no built-in backup for mechanical failure.

Intermodal pressurized air circulation: Provides high-volume, positive, center-of-load air distribution for uniform temperature maintenance of heat-generating cargoes. Under-the-floor air flow moves upward through the cargo, following normal gravitational movement of cool air as it absorbs heat.

Conventional units do not have high-volume, pressurized air circulation systems. Many units still use propeller-type fans instead of blowers. The air distribution systems provide perimeter circulation, which has a low capacity for removing heat generated by the cargo in the center of the load. Air discharged from the blower must be forced downward through the cargo against gravity as it absorbs heat.

Intermodal precise uniform cargo temperature maintenance: At any desired level within $\pm 1\frac{1}{2}°F$ of the thermostat setting.

Precise uniform cargo temperature maintenance is impossible with conventional units because of perimeter air circulation and high coil-to-product temperature differential.

Intermodal oversized evaporator coil: Eliminates low-temperature discharge air which frequently causes freeze damage in conventional units when thermostats are set near 32°F.

Conventional units have a smaller evaporator coil than intermodal units and, therefore, must be maintained at a relatively lower temperature to gain capacity. Under these conditions, discharge air temperatures are often 10 to 20°F lower than the thermostat level. As a result, cargo freeze damage often occurs on the perimeter of the load when the thermostat is set near the 32° level.

Intermodal high relative humidity: Can be maintained at the 85- to 95-percent level for fresh perishable products. This is accomplished by maintaining a low temperature differential between coil and product. Dehydration of cargo is reduced by reevaporating condensate water taken from the cargo back into the air stream just before it reaches the cargo.

Even though conventional units may maintain a high relative humidity, the cargo will still dehydrate because moisture from the cargo migrates to the cold evaporator coil and is discharged to the outside of the vehicle as liquid water.

Intermodal air exchange system: Provides a simple means of eliminating the buildup of undesirable respiratory gases that can adversely affect specific products during long trips.

Most conventional units make no provision to exchange the air within the cargo area to eliminate undesirable respiratory gases which can damage fresh perishable commodities during long trips.

The intermodal air purification system: Reduces airborne microorganism population which may cause spoilage of fresh perishable products and fresh carcass meat.

Conventional units do not use an air purification device to reduce airborne microorganisms which can cause spoilage to fresh perishable cargoes.

The intermodal elimination of obsolescence: By integration of technological improvements to present equipment through "updating" engineering.

The design of most conventional units does not provide for updating present equipment to include technological advances.

Intermodal accessability for maintenance and unit replacement: Unit design insures easy access to all components. All drives are direct, eliminating the need for V-belt replacement.

Many conventional units are difficult to service or replace due to poor design. Some use V-belts to drive components, resulting in periodic mechanical failures.

LOADING PATTERN

A good loading pattern is the tool by which the shipper and carrier can obtain maximum performance from the refrigerator unit. The pattern must provide protection for the cargo, allow for air circulation channels when necessary, and be easy to construct by the workers. See Fig. 13-4, which shows a typical "solid stack" pattern which provides safe movement at sea, with good air circulation from the bottom to the top. In conventional van refrigeration units which provide essentially perimeter circulation, it is nearly impossible to obtain center-of-the-load cooling without preplanned air channels. By contrast, the captive air system which directs cold air from under the floor, up through the cargo, is able to reach the critical areas and readily maintain uniform temperatures.

Cargo bracing is another item which is often overlooked by the shipper. He loads the van as if it were a highway truck, not considering it will be subject to many more forces and actions aboard ship than during a domestic trip. Most shippers have little knowledge of the movements experienced by a ship in heavy seas. They are not aware that rolls of 20° to 30° are commonplace on the North Atlantic during the winter months. Such lack of knowledge on the part of a person responsible for loading a van to be shipped overseas is often the cause behind a claim. In general-cargo, break-bulk ships, the cargo officer would never allow the ship to sail unless the cargo was properly stowed and shored. However, when the cargo is out of sight in a van, the ship's officer has no knowledge of the loading and whether or not the cargo has been properly handled. The gap be-

FIGURE 13-4.   TYPICAL "SOLID STACK" LOADING PATTERN. (*Courtesy:* DR. J. BUSSEL)

tween lack of control of loading and responsibility for good arrival is a problem the industry must face with an adequate educational program for shippers.

LOGISTICS AND RELIABILITY

Finally, it must be admitted that the environmentally controlled transportation is the most advanced interface between food technology, agricultural engineering, naval architecture, and transportation design. The resultant interface provides for a very detailed systems integration. It may be complex in design, but it must be extremely simple in operation. The operator must not overlook the fact that men with little skill in many nations of the world, without a community of languages, must be able to handle this equipment.

As mentioned before, the adapted truck refrigeration units, which have appeared as first-generation refrigerated container machinery, have another drawback in their low reliability and high maintenance requirements. In order for this type of equipment to be cost-effective, it must be designed in such a way that it can be foolproof and can operate automatically for at least 30 days without requiring the attendance of mechanics. One of the important factors in Sea-Land ships is the mates' and mechanics' overtime due to the maintainability requirements of the conventional refrigeration equipment used by Sea-Land. The only human contribution to servicing a proper environmental COOLTAINER unit is the pretripping at the point of origin. All other facets have to be intermodally compatible, yet without the requirement of human attendance.

TANK CONTAINERS

The unique requirements of shippers and the system–shipper interface have been related in other parts of this book, where examples of such services are analyzed. Among the special container systems, the most unique system deals with portable tanks, made in the form of containers. Liquid or solid bulk usually is produced and, therefore, shipped in very large quantities. Petroleum products, ores, grains, edible oils, chemicals, and the like constitute the largest percentile, by far, of all cargo moved by sea and on inland waterways. The single-commodity bulker has risen in size from the beginning to almost unlimited size. For years now, designers have been working on the one-million-ton oil tanker. The possibility of moving such a huge quantity of one single commodity presents many theoretical and practical advantages, because the same crew, powerplant, and ship's hull provide for economy of almost unlimited scale. Yet hand in hand with these advances in single-commodity movements goes the expansion of the range of commodities, plus the extension of the distribution network. For both these outgrowths, containerization has some answers in the tank containers. They allow transportation of small quantities of liquids, more costly than in the jumbo bulk ships, yet much more economical than in barrels, bottles, or packaging of this size.

TRIPLE PROBLEM

None of the container fleet has such unique and critical problems as the tank container. The reason is the creation of a large mass made up by the liquid when in motion. Looking at the 20-ft.-high waves of the ocean, created thousands of miles away by pressure of storms, provides an insight into the understanding of the transmission of forces through liquids. Of course, each type of liquid differs from the other in specific gravity and plasma mass behavior. The center of gravity of the liquid load can shift with sudden surges caused by a train stopping, a truck turning a curve, a ship rolling in the sea, or a loaded tank swinging from the crane. Therefore, the body of rules governing tank and bulk containers are tantamount to safety regulations of significance to the systems operation and economy.

INTERMODAL LIQUID CONTAINERS

The use of intermodal tank containers is a recent development. Specifications and technology are still in a relatively fluid stage. The United States' practice is governed by current Department of Transportation regulations. It is necessary to have calculations and drawings for tank containers for handling hazardous products aboard ship submitted to the United States Coast Guard for approval. The carrier must obtain approval for handling each particular type of hazardous commodity in the intended tank containers. It is usually necessary to obtain a special permit for highway service, since the tank container with a removable chassis does not normally meet all requirements of applicable motor carrier regulations.

Intermodal tank containers are those of 500-gallons-or-more capacity used for the transportation of dangerous liquid commodities in "bulk." The definition of an intermodal bulk liquid container is that of transport equipment:

1. Of a permanent character strong enough for repeated use;
2. Designed to facilitate the carriage of bulk liquid commodities, by one or more modes of transport, without reloading;
3. Fitted with devices permitting ready handling and transfer from one mode of transport to another;
4. Having an internal volume of 500 gallons or more.

Each tank container shall comply with dimensional and structural requirements of the particular system with which it is compatible, including, but not limited to:

1. Column strength of corner posts and fittings;
2. Lifting strength of corner posts and fittings;
3. Dimensions of extremities;
4. Location and shape of lifting fittings;
5. Location and shape of anchor fittings;
6. Compressive strength of members withstanding sling lift forces;
7. Lashing loads on corner fittings.

All of these are minimum requirements.

1. The requirements for the safe transport of specific commodities as prescribed in the Code of Federal Regulations, Title 49, Part 173, or in regulations of the United States Coast Guard, are considered an integral part of the specifications.

2. Tank containers, including those having more than one compartment, must be designed and loaded, so that the center of gravity of the product is located near the center of the container from front to rear and side to side.

3. Also, regardless of number of compartments, they may be of multiple-unit construction, providing that adequate free communication of vapor and liquid spaces exist between units, and otherwise structurally connected so as to form one complete container structure.

4. A multipurpose tank container may be divided into compartments of different specification construction. Each such compartment shall conform to specification requirements concerned.

5. A single cargo tank may be physically altered to comply with another cargo tank specification in the regulations in this part; or altered to accommodate a commodity not requiring a specification tank.

While there are no rules for general cargo containers, the material for tank containers is described as follows. All sheet and plate material for shell, heads, bulkheads, and baffles for tank containers which are not required to be constructed in accordance with the ASME Boiler and Pressure Vessel Code shall meet the following minimum applicable requirements:

1. Aluminum alloys (AL)—Only aluminum alloy material suitable for fusion welding and in compliance with one of the following ASTM specifications shall be used:

> ASTM B-209 Alloy 5052
>
> ASTM B-209 Alloy 5086
>
> ASTM B-209 Alloy 5154
>
> ASTM B-209 Alloy 5234
>
> ASTM B-209 Alloy 5454
>
> ASTM B-209 Alloy 5652

All heads, bulkheads, baffles, and ring stiffeners may use 0 temper (annealed) or stronger tempers. All shells shall be made of materials with properties equivalent to H32 or H34 tempers, except that lower-ultimate-strength tempers may be used if the minimum shell thickness for the sections dealing with TC-306, TC-307, and TC-312 are increased in inverse proportion to the lesser ultimate strength.

2.   Steel

	Mild Steel (MS)	High-Strength, Low-Alloy Steel (HSLA)	Austenitic Stainless Steel (SS)
Yield point	25,000 psi	45,000 psi	25,000 psi
Ultimate strength	45,000 psi	60,000 psi	70,000 psi
Elongation, 2-inch samples	20%	25%	30%

Materials used for integral structural framework members or mountings shall have minimum strength values per the above specifications, except that extruded aluminum alloy 6061-T6 may be used for frame members. Materials used for structural framework members not directly attached to the shell or heads may have different strength values for design purposes than materials specified above.

STRUCTURAL INTEGRITY

The maximum calculated stress value in the vessel shall not exceed 20 percent of the minimum ultimate strength of the material as authorized heretofore, except when ASME pressure-vessel design requirements apply (see Section VIII of the American Society of Mechanical Engineers' Boiler and Pressure Vessel Code, 1965 edition).

Cargo tank containers may be provided with additional structural elements as necessary to prevent resulting stresses in excess of those permitted, as stated previously. Consideration shall be given to forces imposed by each of the following loads individually and, where applicable, a vector summation of any combination thereof:

1. Dynamic loading under all product load configurations with minimum dynamic loadings as follows, using the total calculated load as the weight of the cargo tank container, carrying its rated product load times the total g loads as shown in Table 13-6.

The design load factors given in Table 13-6 are mutually exclusive except for the following cases:

 a. For terminal operations and for the highway and rail modes, the downward load due to gravity is assumed to act simultaneously with the longitudinal and lateral loads.
 b. For the marine mode, it is to be assumed that the lateral and downward loads act both simultaneously and separately.
2. Internal pressure;
3. Superimposed loads, such as operating equipment, insulation, linings, hose tubes, cabinets, and piping;

TABLE 13-6. DESIGN LOAD FACTORS

Direction of Load	Terminal Operations	Marine	Highway	Rail
Vertical download, container supported at corner attaching or lifting points	2.0	1.8	1.7	1.5
Vertical lifting upload, container supported at lifting point or points	2.0	2.0	0.0	2.0
Lateral load at center of product weight	0.2	0.6	0.2	0.3
Longitudinal load at center of product weight	0.7	0.2*	0.7	1.8**

* Value shown is based on containers being stowed longitudinally aboard ship; if containers are stowed transversely to the ship's centerline, a Design Load Factor of 0.6 is applicable.

** The previous USA Standard provided for a Design Load Factor of 1.5, which is acceptable for containers constructed prior to July 1, 1970.

4. Reactions of supporting lugs and saddles or other supports;

5. Effect of temperature gradients resulting from product and ambient temperature extremes. Thermal coefficients of dissimilar materials, where used, should be accommodated.

Structural integrity of separate structural framework may be calculated, based on allowable stress values as mentioned heretofore, or based on calculations plus actual full-scale tests of the complete structure, showing its capability to withstand the above g loadings applied individually or in combination as noted.

Materials subject to deterioration during exposure on the high seas shall be suitably protected or an adequate corrosion allowance shall be added to all minimum material thickness values to assure safe operation over the intended life of the tank container.

CERTIFICATION

Certification shall indicate that such cargo tank container has been designed, constructed, and tested in accordance with the applicable specification TC-306, TC-307, TC-312, or TC-331 and, if applicable, the special marine service requirements:

1. A suffix "-M" shall be used to designate CTCs meeting the requirements for marine service. Other markings or permit numbers as required by the U.S. Coast Guard shall also be shown.

2. If a cargo tank container is constructed in accordance with the requirements of one specification and may be physically altered to meet another cargo tank container specification in this part, such alterations shall be clearly indicated on the manufacturer's certificate required.

The body of regulations to cover these specialized liquid, gas, or bulk containers requires specialization exceeding the general interest of the reader of this book. He is referred, therefore, to the further study of the practices recommended by the Truck Trailer Manufacturers Association for further details.

The material shown in this chapter contains apparently many technical details which form the junction of two or more technologies resultant in a single new form of transport technology. These lessons are indicative of the expanded areas of technical cross-fertilization and systems integration which must be expected as a true future of containerization as the consolidated form of world transport. The entire development of enlarged distribution systems within and across the national boundary reaching into remote areas of production and tying together growing consumer regions with the new face of expanded world trade requires the concurrent development of new technological and systems pragmatism.

COMMAND AND CONTROL

*No matter how much information
is collected or how logically
it is arranged, if the ultimate
intuitive element is overlooked
or obscured, the analysis can
create illusions.*

Alice M. Rivlin
Systematic Thinking
for Social Action, *1971*

Chapter

14

Data and Documents

OPERATIONS RESEARCH

Historically, the first problem to receive the name Operations Research
was concerned with how to set the time fuse of a bomb to be dropped
from an aircraft on to a submarine. Professor Blackett solved this problem
for the Royal Air-Force by showing that the fuse should be set to explode
on impact, and not after a period of delay. The real growth of operations
research occurred during World War II, with British scientists' study of
antiaircraft defense. This was followed in the U.S. during the war, in
which the Air Force and the Navy used operations research in many areas.

Operations research as a science would be of little use if another development had not occurred. That was the development of the high-speed
electronic computer. The first known digital device or "computer" was
the abacus, which appeared about 3500–3000 B.C. The abacus is still
in use, and rivals the desk calculator in speed on simple problems.

In 1642, Pascal invented the adding machine. That is the ten-toothed
wheel with carry-over features. Next, a British inventive genius, described
an "analytic engine" (a clearly conceived digital computer, before the

age of electronics) in 1812, but the state of the mechanical arts prevented its successful development.

The ground work for the high-speed computer might be said to have been laid with the invention of the punched card by Hollerith of the Bureau of the Census. It was developed for use in the 1890 census. Then, as you might expect, Hollerith went to IBM. In 1946, ENIAC, the first electronic computer, was developed; and in 1950, the Bureau of Standards developed their SEAL computer. These two machines were used in working up ballistic tables, a type of operations research.

With a high-speed computer that could manipulate numbers in microseconds, the operations research scientists could explore the mathematics of the problems of the military, management, and the government.

MATHEMATICAL SIMULATION

The practical use of mathematical simulation in the maritime industry was started in late 1958 by Foster L. Weldon, then Director of Research for the Matson Navigation Company. Mr. Weldon reported on his work in May 1959. This was followed by the Maritime Administration's work in mathematical simulation. An advisory panel recommended that the Maritime Administration develop and manipulate models for future requirements for ocean transport for predicting numbers and types of commercial cargo movements, and for predicting the influence of technological advances on shipboard and longshore labor.

In August 1960, the Maritime Administration solicited proposals to undertake a broad operations research study of merchant shipping. The proposal selected consisted of three interrelated parts. The first part was a study of selected trade routes to provide characteristics for improved ships, and to provide inputs to the second part of the study. The second part was to develop a mathematical simulation of the operation of merchant ships. The third part was to analyze world-wide maritime and connected inland lengths and to study the mathematical model.

Operations research provides a superior set of tools for fixing our system problems. Without the dynamic detailed analysis provided by the operations research mathematical simulation, one must use extrapolation from information obtained during a single short period, or one must use gross averaging techniques.

THE PAPER MOUNTAIN

As we have demonstrated heretofore, containers did not revolutionize transportation because of a unique invention in technology. In fact, the order of events is rather in reverse. First came the need for integrated transport coordination, and then the container was developed to fulfill this mission. Therefore, the importance of the container lies almost exclusively in the character of common denominator for a multitude of types of cargo. Operations research was required to convert the individual shipments into one almost endless variety of concentrated container loads to be serviced by many conveyance systems. The historic fact is that those who brought about this indication did not know that they were, in effect, engaged in operations research, as such. Since the approach to the problem was not completely scientific, but rather intuitive, a paper mountain was left forgotten when the inventors broke out in joy over the technological advance of containerization. Therefore, it took a second generation of planners to interface in reverse the now-advanced container technology with the left-behind mess in the software area.

As a common denominator, containers permit streamlining of the physical movement of cargoes using different conveyances. However, until now, the streamlining has been confined only to the physical side of transport. The administrative or software side of the container has not yet come of age in supporting this new technology; and to a large extent, the transition from archaic to more sophisticated control is still underway. Figures 14-1 and 14-2 show the movement of containers in the port area from the physical and from the administrative point of view. The separation of cargo from paperwork requires, at this time, multiple, costly, separate operations. To establish a more automated data-cargo relationship is an object of coming research in the container community. Until now, the only really significant changes of administrative practice in transport, as a consequence of containerization, have taken place in the offices of containerized shiplines. The business of stowage planning, cargo tracing, and sorting has been largely integrated with the control of container deployment and facilitated by up-to-date computer systems, described in detail in Chapters 15, 16, and 17.

However, these advances are confined to the field of equipment and are not applied in any organized fashion to the actual movement of cargo itself. Truly integrated transport needs the same or similar systems, but what exists to date does not nearly add up to an integrated transport data system. Little, if anything, has changed in documentation outside the shipline orbit. A common denominator is still to be created or, if it exists, to be applied in the software field. Nineteenth century documentation methods are holding back 20th century transport developments. In many ways, the constraints imposed by this archaic documentation resulting in excessive paperwork, represent a supplement to customs duty tariffs and a unilateral restraint of international trade. The fees assessed for the unnecessary paperwork by the counseling agents of the country

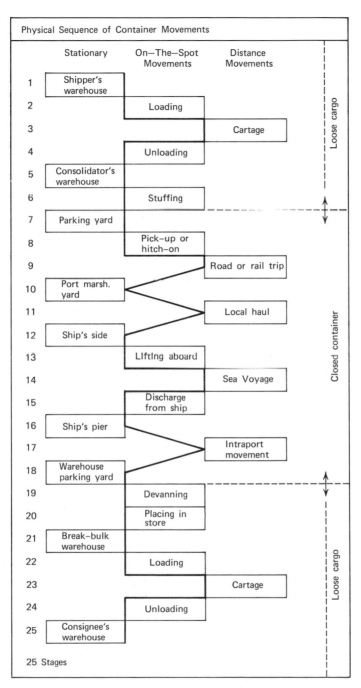

FIGURE 14-1. PHYSICAL SEQUENCE FOR A CONTAINER MOVE-
MENT (SOURCE: JAN F. TEBBE).

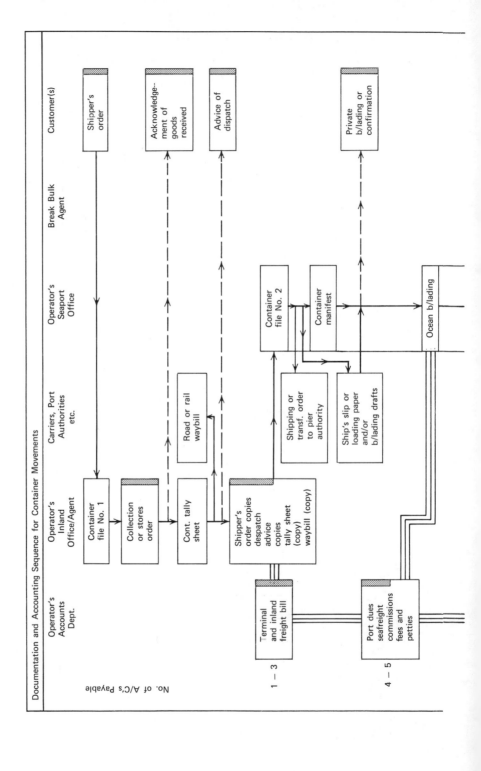

Documentation and Accounting Sequence for Container Movements

Customer(s)

Shipper's order

Acknowledgement of goods received

Advice of dispatch

Private b/lading or confirmation

Break Bulk Agent

Operator's Seaport Office

Container file No. 2

Container manifest

Ocean b/lading

Carriers, Port Authorities etc.

Road or rail waybill

Shipping or transf. order to pier authority

Ship's slip or loading paper and/or b/lading drafts

Operator's Inland Office/Agent

Container file No. 1

Collection or stores order

Cont. tally sheet

Shipper's order copies despatch advice copies tally sheet (copy) waybill (copy)

Operator's Accounts Dept.

Terminal and inland freight bill

Port dues seafreight commissions fees and petties

No. of A/C's Payable

1 – 3

4 – 5

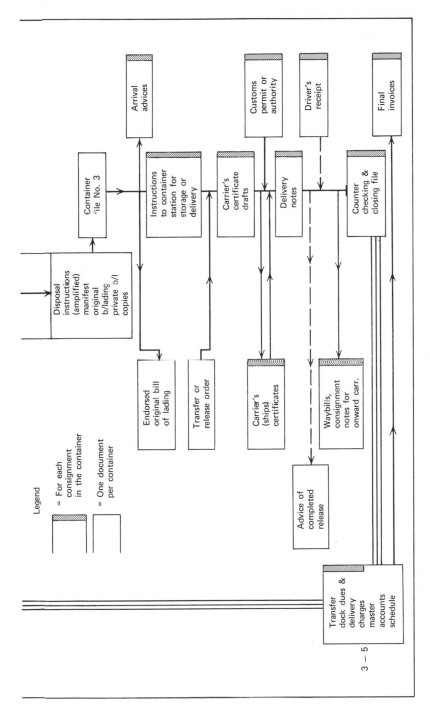

FIGURE 14-2. DOCUMENTATION/ACCOUNT SEQUENCE FOR A CONTAINER MOVEMENT (SOURCE: JAN F. TEBBE).

are often the source of income which smaller nations use to pay for the maintenance of representation abroad.

PROGRESS THROUGH RESEARCH

As shown above, technological improvements in the production of goods and the ability to physically transport cargo expeditiously have exceeded the ability to find simpler and less-costly transport documentation. In many instances, the preparation and processing of documents consume more time and expense than is needed to transport the goods. It has been estimated by the United States government that present transportation documentation costs may amount to ten percent of international trade value. If this estimate is correct, then a major attack must be launched on an international basis to concentrate on the reduction of red tape and replacement of paperwork by a data system.

Many countries have set up organizations to coordinate and develop simplified documentation and procedures for industry.

In the United States, an Office of Facilitation was established in the Department of Transportation, as well as a Transportation Facilitation Committee comprised of government and private members. The purposes of this committee are to locate costly and unproductive systems, to develop more efficient documentation and procedures, and to implement a new system. Industry has established an organization known as the National Committee on International Trade Documentation (NCITD) to work with the government and coordinate private interests to assure greater effectiveness on facilitation projects. This organization has to interface with an amazing number of organizations. The permanent Research Committee structure of the NCITD is divided into five groupings as follows:

Group   I   General Business;
Group   II   Carriers;
Group III   Financial and Insurance;
Group IV   Government and Government Agencies;
Group   V   Exchanges and Associations.

These are the broad, all-inclusive groups around which the specific project committee and the research subcommittees operate.

The current NCITD key functioning subcommittees are:

1. Container Documentation;
2. International Intermodal Shipping Format;

3. Committee on International Through Billing;
4. Committee on Shippers' Export Declaration;
5. Philippine Documentation Committee;
6. Committee on Consular Documentation;
7. Air Cargo Facilitation Committee;
8. Import Documentation Committee;
9. Committee on Customs Drawback;
10. Committee on Elimination and Simplification of AID Forms;
11. Committee on Special AID Forms;
12. Committee on Cargo Liability and Insurance;
13. Committee on Export Expansion and Export Control;
14. Committee on Liaison with United Nations and Foreign Organizations;
    a. Economic Commission for Europe;
    b. International Chamber of Shipping;
    c. International Chamber of Commerce;
    d. National Economic Development Organization—SITPRO;
    e. United Nations Committee on Trade Development;
15. Cooperative Committee on Commodity Codes;
16. Committee on Simplification of Letters of Credit Procedures;
17. Committee on Educational Forums, Seminars and Communications;
18. Financial and Insurance Technical Sub-Committee;
19. Carrier/Shipper Advisory Committee on TCM—Combined Transport;
20. Operators.

Additional working subcommittees are appointed as special research projects warrant.

At present, transportation documentation is separate and distinct for each mode involved in the movement of cargo from origin to destination. Some improvements toward standardization of international shipping documentation format were introduced by a United Nations Working Committee Meeting in Geneva in June 1970. The United Nations Committee voted to support the world-wide usage of the United States Standard Format, around which a great many of the basic international shipping documents can be designed. The format was developed by NCITD and the United States Department of Transportation and would serve the maximum requirements of the United States commercial and governmental interests. This format, at the same time, would fit into the programs being developed by many other countries and shipping groups. The acceptance of the United States Standard Format was preceded by several meetings with the full committee and subcommittees of the Committee of Experts on the Standardization and Simplification of External Trade Documents of the Economic Commission for Europe (ECE), as well as with the International Chamber of Shipping at London (ICS), the International Chamber of Commerce at Paris (ICC), and the Committee on Standardization of International Trade Procedures of the United Kingdom (SITPRO).

THE STANDARD FORMAT

The coming new Standard Format makes it possible, in a single preparation, to produce all of the following data in one document:

1. Bill of lading covering the carriage (ocean or door-to-door);
2. Common dock receipt;
3. Certificate of origin;
4. Arrival notice;
5. Bank transmittal letter;
6. Insurance certificate;
7. U.S. Government bill of lading, and freight warranty;
8. Shipper's export declaration;
9. Drawback form, etc.

By placing the remaining uncommon data content in an "optional area," the maximum use of high-speed duplication and computerization of forms production and processing is assured. Such data are especially important when protective service is required for commodities, such as ventilation, de-humidification, cooling, and treatment in transit.

With the old conventional ocean bill of lading no longer being enough, the combined transport document, or a door-to-door bill is required. It will have to perform three functions, namely:

1. Act as a negotiable document of title to the goods in the container or the barge, transferring the rights in them by the simple handing over of the document itself;
2. Serve as a receipt for the identified goods in the container or barge;
3. Constitute a contract of carriage setting out, amongst other terms and conditions, the liability of the carrier vis-à-vis and toward the holder of the document for any loss of or damage to the goods during transit.

PROCESSING CHARACTERISTICS

Consequently, the characteristics of the new document must be such that it will provide the following services:

1. Since it will be required at the outset of the journey, it will need to be *one* document covering the entire journey from start to finish; although that journey, being a combined transport, is likely to include a combination of road, rail, inland waterway, sea, or even air transport.

2. Since it will be one document, it will need to be issued by one carrier. The so-called *principal carrier* (possibly the first carrier) or the *combined transport operator*, who by issuing the document will become responsible for arranging the entire *through transport*, will also become liable for any loss of or damage to the goods during such through transport, regardless of the stage at which it may have occurred.

3. Since it will be issued at the start of the journey, it will need to be issued at the time the goods enter the through-transport system; for example, at the time when they are received by the principal carrier or the combined transport operator for dispatch, rather than at a later time when they have been shipped on board a named steamer.

4. Since containers may have a full load from one shipper or a combined load from several shippers, the document will need to be equally capable of meeting the needs of the one shipper for one document when the container is filled only with his goods, and the needs of several different shippers, each requiring his own document for his own goods, when the container has been packed with "consolidated cargo," for example, when the container is filled with the combined goods of those different shippers.

LIMITATIONS TO OVERCOME

The present document is subject to certain limitations, yet the new form is being developed. It is not normally possible to state on a combined transport document, issued prior to loading on board ship, whether a specific container has been shipped on deck or under deck, although a high proportion of containers will actually be carried on deck. Having a bill of lading marked "on board" is archaic and is a direct result of the old selling terms where title passed "at ship's tackle." For the use of the combined transport document, the International Chamber of Commerce in Paris has developed new rules. These ICC Rules are used as a base by most of the world's banks, which now state, "an ocean bill of lading," and "on board" will have to change—otherwise, the entire door-to-door container document is useless.

It is also not possible for the combined transport document to vouch for the contents of a container or its condition unless the container has been stowed by a principal carrier or a combined transport operator or by his agent on his behalf. Of course, it is understood that the steamship company cannot vouch to the CTO for the individual shipments in a container for which the CTO issues individual bills of lading, unless the steamship company receives *one* sealed container!

FINANCIAL/LEGAL PROBLEMS

Consequently, the new combined transport document poses problems affecting operators and users and financial and legal interests; and it needs their serious consideration. The principal carrier or combined transport operator is the party issuing the new combined transport document to whom the shipper has entrusted the goods for the purpose of through transport. The combined transport operator, however, does not necessarily need to be an actual provider of transport; for example, a carrier in his own right, whether containership operator or provider of rail, road, inland waterway, or air transport. He may, instead, be a so-called *forwarding agent,* the organizer, but not the actual provider of the necessary transport.

This is a point of importance to shippers, underwriters, and bankers, because of the practical difference between a carrier's document and a forwarding agent's document. A carrier's document would give the holder direct rights against the carrier and would show whether freight had been prepaid or not; for example, whether the carrier had a lien on the goods for unpaid freight. It would show any superimposed clauses ("collect" or "C.O.D.") making it "dirty" and entitling the holder to claim delivery of the goods from the carrier only against payment of freight charges due carrier.

A forwarding agent's document can give the holder rights only against the issuer, never against the actual carrier. For example, the holder of the document can claim delivery from the forwarding agent but not from the actual carrier. The forwarder, in turn, has direct rights against the carrier with whom he had contracted and from whom he would presumably have received a base document in his own favor. When it boils down to actual practice, the lading of the CTO actually acting as an NVO under United States laws and the lading of the foreign freight forwarder are equally useless to a shipper trying to get his cargo released from one of the underlying carriers, such as the steamship company.

There is a difference, however, in the shipper's trying to get his cargo from a subagent of the CTO-type forwarder. The agent is acting only on behalf of his overseas principal, the forwarder. He has the obligation to release no cargo against a receipt held by the shipper, because the lading of the CTO/NVO is a title document and only the signed original proves ownership of the cargo to the CTO agent.

THE FORWARDER'S ROLE

As a consequence, in the event of the documents not "matching," the holder might find that the actual carrier had a lien on the goods for freight, despite the fact that the shipper had prepaid freight to the forwarding agent, because the forwarding agent had not on-paid it to the carrier, or he might find that the apparently "clean" document in his hands was backed by a "claused" document issued by the carrier to the forwarding agent.

This serves to stress both the importance of the business reputation and financial standing of the principal carrier or combined transport operator and the need for future thinking on the subject of documents issued by forwarding agents. The two types of forwarders known in the American Law (I.C.C. Part IV on Ocean) appear to be the best legal and financial risk, since they are both under government supervision. In that respect, shippers and bankers may find comfort in the fact that the economic necessity for a coordinated building of container vessels to avoid over-tonnage is leading to the formation of strong international shipping consortia to operate such container vessels. Also, the need to obtain sufficient cargo to provide full containers for transport is leading to the formation of larger and stronger international "forwarding-agent units," both by mergers and by less formal association in the form of a "consolidator group."

CARRIER'S LIABILITY

As already stated, one characteristic required of the combined transport document is that the principal carrier or combined transport operator shall not only be responsible for arranging the entire through transport, but will also be liable for any loss of or damage to the goods, whether during a stage when he himself is the carrier or whether during the stage when the goods are in the hands of the subcarrier, and the problem is to determine that liability.

The question of liability cannot be oversimplified. This is so, because in the event of loss or damage, a claim is lodged under the cargo insurance; and rights of recovery against the carrier are subrogated to the underwriter. The attitude of shippers is divided. Some are seriously interested in the maximum quantum of a recovery, while others are concerned only with the fact that the carrier is more likely to exercise maximum care in performing the transport service if he has a financial stake in doing his job well. This is a very complex and important area of the relationship. There are many differences not only in liability limitation, but also in the international and national governing areas; and it may take the study of a legal specialist to cope with this complexity. However, many things are being done now to reconcile these differences and lay the groundwork for the successful issuance of door-to-door insurance.

The principal carrier or combined transport operator is, however, definitely interested, since the amount of his liability or exemptions from liability may depend upon the stage of transport during which the loss or damage occurred. This may not be important when it can be proved exactly where the loss or damage occurred, because he will have recourse on his own behalf against the appropriate subcarrier. However, with the carriage of goods prepacked into a locked and sealed container, he is going to have difficulty in proving when and where loss or damage may have occurred. This will result in his being liable without any recourse available to him, even though the loss or damage might have occurred while the goods were with a subcarrier.

The question of amount and conditions of liability is, of course, a legal matter. The method by which the principal carrier or combined transport operator can cover himself is an economic matter. Broadly, he has two alternative methods. He can cover his "risks" with the P. & I. Clubs, which would be the normal and reasonable approach, if the combined transport operator is a shipowning consortium. Otherwise, he can accept full responsibility, subject to being allowed to arrange the necessary cargo insurance document. Although appearing to have superficial attractions, this could be against the best interests of some shippers; and has already led to the temporary withdrawal of the combined document of transport and insurance proposed by OCL/ACT.

BANKING PRACTICES

From the banking angle, the problems of the new combined transport document vary according to whether the bank is acting as the buyer's agent by making a payment under a documentary letter of credit, or on its own behalf concerned with security for advances made to the buyer.

If payment is under a documentary letter of credit, the bank is bound by the terms of such letter of credit dictated by the buyer. In addition, the bank must abide by the terms and conditions of "Uniform Customs and Practice for Documentary Credits," as revised by the International Chamber of Commerce in 1962. This means that in respect to the transport document, unless the letter of credit specifically states otherwise:

1. It must be an on-board document, which means that the goods must be shown specifically to have been shipped on board a named steamer.

2. It must be an under-deck one, which means that the document must not specifically state that the goods have been shipped on deck.

3. It must not be a forwarding agent's document.

The short-term solution is in the buyer's giving instructions for the opening of a documentary letter of credit, specifically naming the type of document to be accepted, if the document can be clearly identified by some description. An alternative solution is to authorize acceptance of whatever is presented by some wording such as, "bills of lading evidencing container shipments acceptable as presented."

The long-term solution is amendment, as appropriate, of certain articles of Uniform Customs and Practice for Documentary Credits. This is something that can be done only when agreement has been reached in shipping and other circles, as to the new combined transport document.

As far as security for advances made to the buyer is concerned, the bank wants an acceptable document giving acceptable rights against a responsible party. Thus, it, too, is interested in the type of document and its user.

USAGE AND COMMERCIAL LAW

Quite obviously, the answers to the problems briefly referred to above demand a legal approach, as well as a practical one. Since the new document will relate to international trade demands, an international solution rather than a national one is needed. The obvious answer is an agreed international convention laying down the nature and basic details of a combined transport document.

This is a course of action which, for a considerable time, has occupied the thoughts of the International Chamber of Commerce, the International Maritime Committee, and the International Institute for the Unification of Private Law (UNIDROIT). A Draft Convention has recently been submitted to and approved by a Congress of the International Maritime Committee in Tokyo.

TOKYO RULES

This Draft Convention briefly provides for:

1. One principal carrier (combined transport operator) to issue one document with the wording, "combined transport bill of lading subject to the Tokyo Rules," covering the entire journey;

2. The principal carrier (combined transport operator) to be responsible for arranging all stages of the transport and to be liable for loss or damage through the entire journey;

3. Certain minimum information to be given in the combined transport bill of lading, identifying the issuer of the document, the journey to which it relates, the point at which liability is assumed and discharged, and the goods and their apparent order and condition, as stated by the party tendering the sealed container;

4. The said document to enjoy the special characteristic of negotiability which is, at present, enjoyed by the traditional bill of lading;

5. The liability of the principal carrier (combined transport operator) to be determined on the basis of the appropriate international convention or mandatory national law, if it can be proved at what stage of transport the loss or damage took place. This would be in accordance with the Hague Rules, where such stage of transport was sea; or with the Tokyo Rules, as to amount and exemption from liability, where there is no international convention or national law or where it cannot be proved where loss or damage occurred;

6. Containers carried on deck to still be covered by the Hague Rules, on the basis that the document does not specifically state that the goods are carried on deck.

Broadly speaking, this Draft Convention seems to cover the essential points. In particular, it provides the all-essential easy identification of the document by requiring it to be headed "combined transport bill of lading subject to the Tokyo Rules." However, there are doubts in certain quarters as to whether negotiability can be conferred by this Convention, or whether it has to be acquired by custom. There are also doubts as to whether the reference to deck cargo, for the purpose of including it within the application of Hague Rules, is adequate. It should be noted that a world-wide uniform software system would make international trade agreements more meaningful and precise.

DATA FREIGHT SYSTEM

Atlantic Container Line (ACL) was one of the first users of computer data and document control systems. Not being hampered by traditional procedures, it was possible for ACL to design a system that is most effective with the use of computer techniques and equipment. The primary problem was how to control approximately 20,000 items of ACL equipment, including containers and associated rolling stock, involving a capital investment of about 50 million dollars. In back of this was the responsibility for an enormous capital investment of around 200 million dollars for a relatively new steamship company. Obviously, the use of computers had to be considered.

Atlantic Container Line put into operation in Europe and North America an electronic freight documentation system which offers a simplified and speedier alternative to the historic bill-of-lading procedures. The new ACL Datafreight Receipt System replaces the bill of lading in the traditional form with a nonnegotiable receipt, which does not have to be sent across the North Atlantic. ACL retains the full liability set out in the company's bill of lading, but processes the relevant data through its communications network linking all the ports served.

ACL will continue to offer the traditional bill of lading for those customers who prefer its use.

ACL studies show that less than 10 percent of cargo shipped across the North Atlantic was financed by documentary credits, requiring the use of a negotiable bill of lading. This means that the majority of ACL shippers could export their goods under a simple, nonnegotiable receipt.

The ACL Datafreight Receipt System is a major overhaul of bill-of-lading procedures which have been virtually unchanged since the 19th century. Since the computer time was available for this equipment control, its use for documentation systems became logical. Datafreight is an example of computer application to obtain real-time control.

REAL-TIME CONTROL

In the computer systems technology, "real-time" can mean both the actual time elapsed in the performance of a computation by a computer and the result of computation being required for continuation of a physical process. If properly programmed, it can mean that the computer responds at exactly the real-world time rate, charting the progress of a container in transit, as it happens. The real-time system lags behind the actual real time in which the series of events takes place. The following explains the real-time application. The computer controlling the launch and docking of a space vehicle must react in milliseconds, with one controlling a factory's output and inventory taking days to respond. Both are "real-time" systems. What they have in common is a computer that is in continuous control of the process and delivers its output to men, machines, or other computers fast enough to maintain that control.

Much of the work of transportation in containers is repetitive or routine. The work assumes emergency status when the repetitive or routine situation is inadequate. It becomes an emergency because just about all the freight which railroads carry is integral with some other economic activity.

Railroading is truly a business of motion. The entire system needs a constant flow and a cross flow of intelligence. It also needs a smoothly flowing and quickly responsive series of actions. It is problematical that any robot ever will be able to impart that intelligence or control these actions. Simulations and models can give a better "feel" for courses of action to take. However, attempts to automate the whole process have met with failure.

The speed and the accuracy of the computer are beginning to break logjams. Computers are beginning to contribute better and faster intelligence, to prevent jams, and to form important cog in the complex of activity that moves containers, plans priorities, and meets emergencies. It is not just in the high-volume and high-speed entry and retrieval capabilities of today's computer systems; these advances are in refining the data equally fast and delivering it "real-time" to on-line and central management systems.

The service can be handled by real-time computer systems and terminals across the network. Three such systems are:

1. CPS (Container Processing System)—This is the system that receives and maintains container inventory records and forecasts movements. Using this input as a base, it provides information for scheduling and helps manage inventory and distribution, as well as generating billing and all accounting records.

2. REDCAP (Real-time Entry Daily Container Activity Program)—REDCAP is a control system for handling the dispatch and movement of containers by all conveyances.

3. Automated WATS/Dataphone System—This is a message-switching service, to transmit information between the various locations in the system. One must also provide interlinkage for the three disparate systems.

Most operators employ two or three modes—many use more. Punched cards still remain common to the greatest number, but use-intensity compared to alternate means within any one company may prove to be lower. Magnetic tape, a strong second, gains increasing acceptance as a primary input as additional "key-tape" units come into use.

The big input news for container traffic management comes from new, sophisticated data terminals. More than a teletype, these units can store information temporarily, perform limited computations, and transmit assembled data at very high speeds, minimizing both transmission time and costs.

Very new cathode ray tube (CRT) units and optical character recognition (OCR) equipment have nonetheless built important bridgeheads in the computer terminal field. The visual display units employing cathode ray tubes permit direct reading of computer stored data on demand, give direct access for revisions of such data, and provide a visual check of input as it is recorded by an operator.

An investigation made by the Association of American Railroads indicated that a real-time system of computer control would best handle the complex railroad problem at this time. Five- to ten- percent increase in utilization could be achieved by a real-time system for controlling equipment.

The reasons for a real-time container system are:

1. Large volumes to be handled;

2. Higher cost of operating alternate semi-mechanical systems;

3. Large geographical input area involved;

4. Reduced necessity to reduce capital investment;

5. Improved service control to the customers.

The details of the first complete real-time container system are shown by John Immer, as they were developed by the system's pioneer, Atlantic Container Lines.

PORT COMPOUND SYSTEM

The British National Ports Council made a study to reduce the paperwork required for export cargoes. The result was a recommendation of these consultants, the E-A Space and Advanced Military Systems Ltd. (EASAMS), for a computer-based central information system to serve all the elements of a port.

The system is suitable for the ten largest ports in the United Kingdom. A further study of the benefits and costs and detailed specifications of the system is being made in cooperation with the ports of London and Liverpool. In both ports, representative groups of shipowners, shipping agents, stevedores, wharfingers, forwarding agents, haulers, and shippers, together with the port and customs authorities, are advising on the specification for a selected section of each port's export trade. If the first trials are successful, most of the cargo management activities of these two ports could be included in such a system within five years.

DESCRIPTION OF THE SYSTEM

The consultants discovered what certainly could not have been a surprise to anybody. That is, that there is a tremendous amount of repetition in the paperwork connected with the export of cargo and that this paperwork is steadily increasing. The problem is complicated by the number of people involved in cargo movements. With faster transit of the goods themselves, more records are involved as less reliance can be placed on memory, as it was in the past.

To deal with the problem, EASAMS proposed a "Compound System" which is sufficiently flexible to handle the documentation requirements of all of the commercial and official port users. The heart of the system is a "Central Data Bank," controlled by computer, from which users may obtain the information they require by Telex, telephone, or direct computer-to-computer links.

The system would provide a high-speed shared filing service; and repetitive information would be read out automatically according to programmed instructions, thus saving clerical effort. Other benefits would include the collection and production of port statistics and their presentation in a form suitable for immediate management decisions, the recording of financial transactions, and possibly the carrying out of transactions between accounts.

COMPOSITION OF THE SYSTEM

The Compound System as proposed would operate by interlocking of a variety of individual users' equipment through a central information interchange facility. The parts of the system are:

1. The individual users' equipment (terminals);
2. The links between them and the central complex (data links);
3. The central complex, made up of the control processor and the data bank;
4. The interfaces between the terminals, the links, and the central complex.

By means of this interlinking, data messages may be interchanged between otherwise incompatible types of equipment, and information which is required by a number of the users can be transmitted automatically to each of them.

On-line interrogation of the central bank facility will not be essential at first. It may be found to be better to devise the system on the basis that a user wishing to make an inquiry enters an inquiry message to the central complex and then goes off the line. Later, the central complex will set up a return call to provide the answer to the inquiry.

In order to allow the central processor to sort and distribute information, it will be necessary to couch messages in standard formats. Users, who for any reason cannot adopt the standard formats or do not know which format to use, can address the system indirectly by calling up an operator at a manual reporting center and putting the message through her.

TERMINALS

The terminals are the devices which individual users of the system have at their own premises by means of which they put information into the system or extract information from it. It is expected that several of these terminals will be peripheral computer systems. The majority, however, will be simple input-output devices, such as teleprinters and data key-sorts.

DATA LINKS

Two classes of data links will connect users to the central data bank, tie lines permanently linking particular users, and exchange lines which any user can employ.

INTERFACES

These are the pieces of equipment which change from one method of expressing data to another, in order to enable machines and men to cooperate. They are of two kinds. The first enables differing types of computers or data processors to work together. The second enables men and machines to communicate with each other.

Within the man–machine interfaces are various methods of data preparation, such as punched paper tape, punched cards, and direct-entry keyboard. The display or output can be in the form of a teleprinter, line printer, cathode ray tube display, in-line read-out, mimic diagram, or a visual or audible annunciator.

For the machine–machine interfaces, the compound system will send to any computer data in the form in which it normally uses or produces it, provided only that it is designed to be connected to a data link of some sort. This is accomplished by data exchange equipment, and it fulfills the purpose of converting the output of each to a form suitable for use by the other.

CENTRAL PROCESSOR

This is the computer which organizes the central data bank. Its functions are as follows:

1. It files data in an orderly manner, so that it can be retrieved on demand, updated by new information, and dumped when of no further interest;
2. It identifies information which is required to be distributed automatically and controls the distribution of it;
3. It verifies that whoever interrogates the data store has a right to receive the information requested before releasing it;
4. It performs certain "housekeeping" functions for the data interchange service, such as keeping a tally of the number of calls by types and preparing charges;
5. It may possibly assist the data exchange equipment to perform its functions by undertaking any complex program control necessary.

CENTRAL DATA BANK

This, the store for information, is envisaged as consisting of three parts. There will be the central processor's ferrite core storage for working space and for programs in continuous use. There will be fast random-access storage (probably disc stores) for data which needs to be available for instant reference, such as the state of processing for each consignment. The majority of the data will be held in magnetic tape stores. As the urgency for retrieval of information in cargo-handling transactions is generally very low, the two minutes or so required to sort information from a tape and transfer it is of negligible consequence. The amount of data involved, even for a large port, will not be intractable.

REPORTING CENTER

The users of the system who cannot communicate directly with the data exchange will be able to call a reporting center. Operators will be on hand to put the data into the system or to interrogate it on behalf of the callers. They would check the identity or authority of the caller before utilizing data or releasing information.

THE FLOW OF INFORMATION

The problem of the flow of information is primarily in the complexity and the interrelationships of the various steps and in the number of agencies or people who are involved in a single transaction. The consultants found that shipping goods for export involved so much paperwork that the labor needed to deal with it often exceeded the labor required for physically handling the goods. As previously noted, the most outstanding characteristic was the duplication of information contained on each form.

Equipment Cybernetics

EQUIPMENT CYBERNETICS

In the previous chapter, we have shown the interrelationship between the data required to move and control the container and the cargo itself, and the system reflection in documentation services. Norbert Wiener, in his book, *Cybernetics,* explains the relationships that lead to a systems development, and he specifically spells out two key elements—"information" and "feedback." The cybernetic rules apply to the triple-interface relationship in the container systems approach: the cargo and the container, the container-terminal operation, and the container-conveyance modes. Information first and feedback later must be developed to enable the operator to control the system. We will deal with these triple relationships in this chapter.

COMMAND AND CONTROL SYSTEMS

The exercise of managerial powers over the movement of freight has a unique combination to cope with. Containerization technology and implementation cannot become effective unless the relationship between the cargo and the related data is integrated into a "command and control" system, because the economic impact of containerization as freight transportation depends on the exercise of these functions.

The "time-value" factor of capital in the capital-intensive operations requires a control over the data of operations as they occur, in order to enable management to exercise its necessary command functions. The concentration in time and space which achieves the fast linking and turn-around of all components of the intermodal system demands a high degree of accuracy, timeliness, and data flow to catch up with the increased speed of the movement. Fig. 15-1 breaks down the time elements related to container availability. It can be stated that the operation of a large modern container system is entirely dependent on the use of modern data processing systems, where computerized information is evaluated on a forward-flow stream. (See Fig. 15-2.)

Equipment control is the major problem confronting container systems. The movements of many thousands of containers owned or operated by their carriers cannot be controlled manually. Manual systems are usually visual. It may take hours to locate a specific container and to ascertain whether it is full or has been emptied and is thus available for further use. In growing and expanding services, the necessary continuous increase of container inventories demands a parallel substantial increase of personnel. Manual control soon reaches the limit of efficiency.

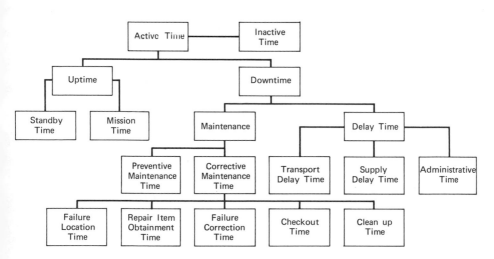

Figure 15-1. Distribution of time elements related to availability (Source: U.S. Govt. I).

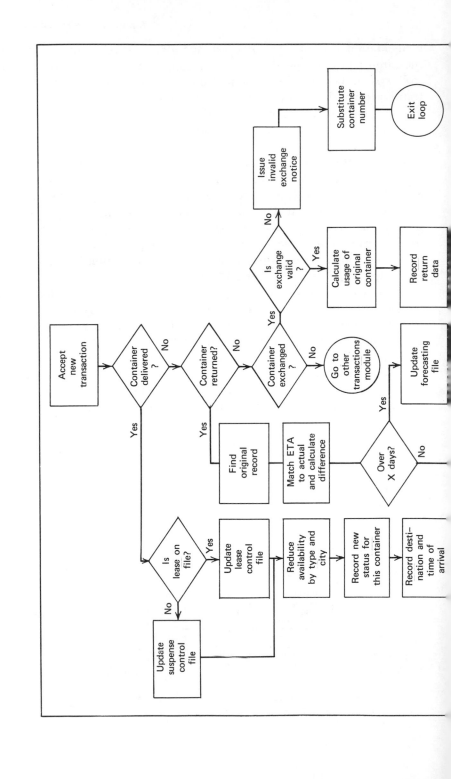

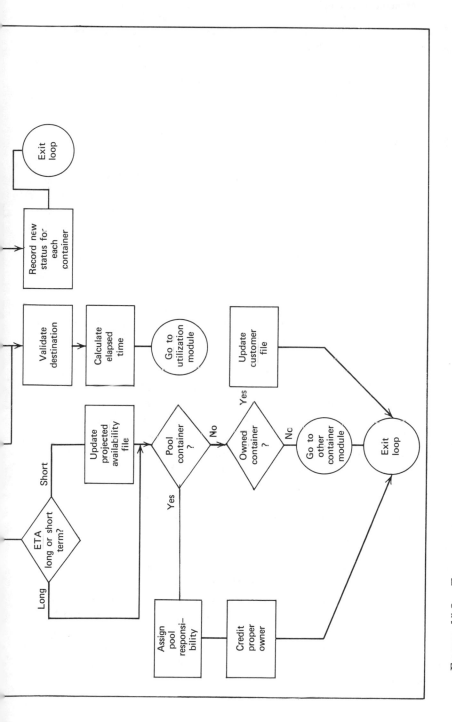

FIGURE 15-2. FLOWCHART OF THE CONTROL OF CONTAINERS BY THE CENTRAL COMPUTER AT CONTAINER TRANSPORT INTERNATIONAL (SOURCE: CTI).

Information derived from it always lags behind the facts. By the time it reaches the decision-making traffic or operations manager, such information is history and does not represent the actual status. The result is uneconomical service, aggravated customers who cannot get their cargo moving, and eventually the loss of business to a more alert competitor.

EMPLOYMENT OF EDP

The solution to this problem can obviously be offered only through the employment of electronic data processing. In fact, most carriers have established a computerized control system. However, electronic data processing for the purpose of control and efficient utilization of equipment is lagging behind the times. Most automatic systems in use today are piecemeal and have been set up merely to complement the manual retrieving of information. Very few operations are integrated and actually computer-controlled.

The shortcomings of the present EDP applications are in operation and responsibility. Electronic data processing is in existence almost everywhere throughout the industry, having been established usually because of the requirements of modern accounting. Use of computers for other than the requirements of accounting departments might, therefore, often be viewed as mere adjuncts, to be performed only when there is no other work to be done. It is established policy in most companies that the vice president in charge of finance or accounting is also the executive to whom the director of the EDP department must report. He makes the decisions about priorities of programing and data processing and he will naturally look to it that the needs of his own departments are satisfied first. This may delay the access to information for traffic and operations managers to a point where it might become irrelevant whether manual or electronic control devices are being used.

The efficient and timely work of computerized container control, as well as all other electronic data processing not related to accounting, can be achieved only if the overall responsibility for company-wide computer operations is invested in an EDP director. This puts him on a level with the mandate to report solely and directly to the president of the company. Another setback seems to be the unfamiliarity of EDP personnel with the industry itself. This is, in fact, a problem which arises in most other industries, too. The education of systems analysts and programmers is still geared to the thinking of their original and almost exclusive employer: Accounting and Finance. With this rather limited background, they sometimes fail to comprehend the urgency of require-ments, the importance and, indeed, the day-by-day management of the very departments that provide the basis for a company's existence.

OPERATING FAMILIARITY

Before setting upon the task of establishing a system and writing a pro-gram, EDP personnel should, therefore, familiarize themselves thor-oughly with the actual operation for which the program must be created. This is not a simple undertaking. It may involve several months of spe-cial schooling, away from the computer—something present-day program-mers are hardly willing to do.

It is a well-known fact that the demand for competent systems analysts and programmers far exceeds the number available. For this reason, too, EDP personnel seldom remain with one company for long periods, but constantly moves on to better-paying jobs. Needless to say, the value and efficiency of a computer program often decreases substantially after its originator has left.

While it may not be possible to achieve a programmer's familiarization with the operational aspects of the industry, a feasible alternative seems to be for the company to discontinue its own programing and seek in-stead the help of professional organizations dedicated to computer pro-graming and employing programers who flock to where the challenges are, that is, in just such organizations. The future trend should, there-fore, be towards time-sharing systems. Computers are being developed continuously to achieve faster and faster outputs. They become bigger and more expensive. The result is that, even in the largest companies, there soon is not enough work for in-house EDP, and time-sharing be-comes a matter of good economics.

COMPUTER SUPPORT ORGANIZATION

The computer is a support element to organization, one that is valuable in checking the validity of data, and in avoidance of the data duplication. However, the computer should not make decisions. These must be made by the inventive human brain. The computer merely provides the infor-mation upon which to base such decisions. In the area of container con-trol and container utilization, the approach that would seem to offer most is simulation. This does not put decision-making burdens on the computer, but rather allows the computer to offer a whole range of data and possibilities which should be evaluated by management before a decision is reached.

The computer must merely supply the information upon which better decisions can be based. Simulation offers the opportunity to make decisions and see their results before money is spent on implementation. It also offers the ability to take more data elements into consideration. Simulation is also closely related to forecasting, without which the container control of the future will be no control at all. (Refer to Chapter 17.) Forecasting is helped by the ability to program daily requirements as they may vary, and to weigh short-term against long-term needs.

It is not enough to have a post-fact control system or to know the exact location and status of a container. EDP must provide information on the basis of which regional needs can be judged and containers can be placed, so as to meet the needs. Container control means, above all, to have the right equipment in the right place at the right time. Container control for internal company purposes is necessary. But of at least equal importance is the control's task to meet the demands of each customer in making equipment available when and where it is needed.

There is the question of whether to centralize or decentralize the control. Any container control, if it is to be really fast-working and efficient, must be rigidly centralized. This does not mean, however, that the system should work only for the benefit of the head office. A centralized computer system must be a two-way street. It should not only demand the feed-in of information, but should also be capable and ready for instant output to other areas, thus enabling regional managers away from the head office to make decisions with the help of the same automatic system as used by top management.

COST OF PROGRESS

Although it had a traumatic beginning, U.S. Line's system features some interesting innovations, as it embraces many facets of the rapidly progressing computer science. It took nearly two years to research, develop, and program, at a cost of over $2 million. The system uses an IBM 360/40 computer with 2 partitions: container control and cargo/container documentation. It keeps a current record on all data pertaining to container movements and vessel bookings, answers all inquiries about equipment or booking status, and updates bills of lading and container historical files.

The nerve center of the control operation is at the company's New

York headquarters, from where there are direct connections to all U.S. Lines offices in the United States, Europe, and the Far East. Once a cargo booking is requested by a shipper, all available information relating to the order is transmitted to the computer by the cargo dispatcher. Based on the booking order information, such as the size and type of the commodity, the computer selects an appropriate box and assigns it to the shipper. The unit so assigned is not necessarily the one that is nearest to the customer geographically, but rather a container that is certain to reach him at the requested date. The container is monitored electronically from terminal to shipper, shipper to pier, aboard ship to port of discharge, and from discharge to delivery. The unit's return, reassignment, or rerouting to the next customer is also recorded. Reassignment of containers is an important function of the control system. For instance, the historical file may show that a container has been dropped at a certain point for unloading. Shortly afterwards, a shipper near that point places a booking. As soon as the computer learns about it, the now-empty unit will be assigned to that shipper, thus saving considerable time, costs, and equipment.

Recognizing that complete control of the movement of containers and their related equipment is essential, Atlantic Container line decided early that a data processing system would be essential to efficiently control the movement of large numbers of containers. Several types of data processing systems can be used to provide the information files and reports necessary for container control. The least expensive in terms of initial cost is the "batch-type" system in which various offices report into a central computer on a fixed time schedule. The computer merely stores this information until all reports are in. Files are updated and reports are issued later, usually during the night.

BATCH SYSTEM VS. REAL-TIME

The difference in systems effectiveness between "batch-type" and "real-time" control systems lies in the time–event factor sequence. Containers are scheduled to arrive at a terminal at a certain time. This will allow processing preparation for loading in the optimal sequence as described in Chapter 16. But events in real life do not conform with programed simulation. Traffic delays, labor procedures, and even the weather often upset such rigidly planned schedules. Therefore, the container procedures cannot start until the van has arrived and is processed. This, in turn, throws the system that is relying on immediate reaction out of kilter. Each delay, in turn, will magnify itself at the next intersection of the system. The transmission of batched data will be much delayed while the real-time computer program reacts instantly. The length of the delay in real-time computerization is the lapse of time it takes to run the operation itself through the computer.

REAL-TIME VS. SIMULATION

The decision was made to install a real-time container control system, on the basis that it would have significant operating advantages and, when fully operational, it would be less costly. It would enable the company to dispatch empty containers arriving at inland pools within hours after their arrival. It would expedite port terminal operations where today, with only one sailing each week, there are already as many as three hundred container movements daily. Three sailings per week are planned, and container movements within the port will multiply.

Having decided on real-time data processing, the next step was to analyze the problem, establish preliminary requirements, and select a computer. The first basic decision was to select a computer, and a Univac 418-II was chosen. The problems involved in establishing real-time systems are well known throughout the data processing industry. Experienced personnel capable of designing, programing, and implementing this type of sophisticated EDP system are exceedingly scarce. In the steamship industry, they were nonexistent. To make matters even worse, the then embryonic Atlantic Container Line had only a handful of employees of any kind in the U.S. Recognizing the lack of experience within the company, it was decided to seek outside help. Two other considerations influenced this decision. First, system design, programing, and implementation are temporary functions, requiring far greater manpower than subsequent operation. Furthermore, this phase of the operation calls for far more experienced and more expensive personnel than needed later merely to operate it.

CONTRACTOR SELECTION

A number of software companies specialize in this type of work. ACL selected a contractor. The initial function of a software firm is to analyze the problem and design a system to solve it. After the system design has been established, its personnel write the programs, apply them to the computer, supervise system start-up, and correct any bugs which occur in initial operations. In the case of ACL freight administration and container control system, the contractor also assumed responsibility, through a subsidiary, for operating the central computer installation.

Despite the fact that very few ACL personnel were involved, the container control system was designed from the ground up and went on the air with a minimum of bugs in slightly over a year's time. The decision to use a Univac 418-II was made in February 1967, and discussions were begun with software organizations. The proposal was submitted in April. System design began in May, and final specifications were completed in September 1967. Programs were completed and phased in during winter and spring, and the system went on the air after Labor Day 1968. (See Chapter 14.)

TERMINAL OPERATIONS AND CONTROL

The portside container terminal is a waterfront interchange facility designed to provide a tidewater transfer service between containerships and other transportation conveyances. The tidewater facility is the result of careful planning with adequate provision made for future expansion. Transocean Gateway Corporation has achieved in Howland Hook, New York, a terminal that provides:

1. Patrons with superior service and unparalleled security;
2. Exceptionally good working conditions for terminal employees.

The yard, located on the northwest corner of Staten Island, encompasses 650 acres—150 acres have been developed during Phase One, with the remainder being set aside for expansion. The berth face is approximately 2,500 feet long and can accommodate up to three containerships. Terminal facilities are divided into the full container load (FCL) and less-than-container-load (LCL) facilities which are completely separated and operate independently of each other.

GATE HOUSE PROCEDURES

A *gate house* provides a land link between the port and the outside world. The gate house consists of 12 check-in lanes and overhead receiving and delivery offices. The check-in lanes are in direct communication with the overhead offices via pneumatic tubes. All the lanes, except those designated for LCL traffic, are equipped with scales. The overhead receiving and delivery offices are in direct communication with the *control tower,* the *customs office,* and the *LCL building* and provide clerical and administrative support for gate processing.

This design of the gate house makes it possible to serve the driver while he remains in his cab and, thus, provides efficient and fast service to the customer. A marshaling area is provided between the gate house and security gates for customers who will not have correct papers and need assistance. A control tower forms the system command and control for activities within the yard and along the berth side. A six-story-high structure, the control tower is centrally located in the yard and is in direct communication with the gate house, LCL building, and, via radio dispatch, with truck and crane drivers in the yard. An LCL shed is entered through the LCL security gates. The building is divided into export and import sections and has a very modern, mechanically controlled, material-handling system between the two sections. Customer service is provided at one of 155 fully equipped doors. The centrally located office controls and oversees all the activities for receiving and delivering at the doors.

The terminal is laid out to provide a clear, smooth, and efficient traffic flow system within the yard. Outside drivers are not permitted to go beyond the pickup and delivery (PU/D) areas. One-way-traffic roads are provided between the gate house and PU/D areas. Sufficient check points are provided en route to insure that drivers do not get lost in the terminal. Security checks are made at the gate house, security gates, and PU/D areas to prevent theft and pilferage.

TERMINAL THROUGHPUT CAPACITY

The Howland Hook terminal is designed to accommodate an efficient maximum throughput of 10,000 containers per week; for example, 5,000 containers for export and 5,000 containers for import. This amounts to, on a straight time basis, 6 full-size containerships per week and approximately 16,000 gate transactions of LCL and FCL traffic. Shipboard containers both for export and import are stored in areas parallel to the berth face that has a combined capacity of 4,740 20-ft. containers, stacked one level high. If all the containers are stored on chassis, the total parking area would amount to 1,120, 40-ft. or 2,200, 20-ft. containers. The entire container storage area is paved.

Ship loading and unloading are accomplished with six shore cranes, each with a lifting capacity of 40 tons below the spreader and each able to handle a maximum of 288 containers during an 8-hour working day.

Twelve check-in lanes at the gate house will, based upon a five-day

week, eight-hour-per-day operation, be able to handle 3,600 FCL transactions per week and 3,200 LCL transactions per week. Ultimately, a
total of 24 check-in lanes may be provided to accommodate expansion
in traffic.

OPERATING CONTROL

Paperwork for all the terminal activities is handled mainly at four locations; they are the:

1. Gate house;
2. Control tower;
3. LCL building;
4. Administrative building.

The functions performed at these locations follows.

Gate House—Receipt of Cargo

The processing starts when the checker makes a *gate pass* for the
driver. The container is checked for seal and damages and is weighed.
The gate pass, along with the truckman's papers, is sent to the *receiving
office* via pneumatic tube. The prime responsibility of the receiving office
is to accept the container and classify the cargo. Prior to acceptance, a
credit check on the shipper is made. The gate pass is returned to the
truckman. The truckman, on his way out, will receive a signed *dock receipt* in return for a properly validated gate pass. Upon the acceptance
of an FCL at the gate, the control tower is given an advanced notice of
container arrival.

The cargo in the LCL operation, unlike the FCL, is checked and verified at the LCL building. The driver is directed to the LCL area.

Gate House—Delivery of Cargo

The *delivery clerk* receiving the gate pass begins with the carrier's
checkout and then verifies the information on the gate pass and *delivery
order*. The prime responsibilities of the delivery clerk are to insure that:

1. The carrier in the check lane is the person authorized to pick up the container and cargo;
2. The carrier's credit rating is satisfactory;
3. Calculation and collection of demurrage charges have been done;
4. The *freight* and *customs releases* have been obtained.

Upon the completion of the checkout, the gate pass is returned to the truckman and the *control tower* is notified of the expected pickup. The appointments for container pickup (loaded or empty) will be made with the delivery clerk.

Customs Control

The *customs office,* located in the gate house, will issue customs releases for cargo after customs requirements, such as viewing and sampling, have been satisfied. A physical inspection, whenever required, will be done at the designated doors in the LCL building. Under no circumstances will the delivery clerk release the cargo without Customs' approval.

Movement Control

All parking and stacking activities are directed from the control tower. It provides (a) shuttle services between pier side and stacking areas and (b) feeder services to and from valet areas and the LCL building. All pierside activities will be supervised from the control tower.

LCL Activities

The LCL building has a subsystem which, in essence, is similar to the FCL operation. The basic difference, however, is in the control of the nonuniform parcels and packages that have to be individually accounted for and require elaborate and time-consuming verifications and checkouts. Requests for loaded or empty containers for unstuffing are made to the control tower. Important functions performed at this building are:

1. Container stuffing and unstuffing;
2. Loose cargo verifications and checkups;
3. Receipt and delivery of LCL cargo from drivers;
4. Paperwork relating to LCL activities.

Administrative Organization

Management control over the terminal is exercised from the administrative building. The *terminal manager* and his office staff are located here.

Following this description of the terminal cybernetics, the treatise of the particular interface developed by the ship in port and at sea follows.

16

Ship and Port Control

SCOPE OF PROBLEM

The previous chapters discussed the physical characteristics and some operations of the elements of multimodal transportation systems which employ containers for the enclosure of cargo, together with a very brief overview of the container system operation. The container transportation system operation consists of loading the cargo into containers and then moving these containers from origin to destination. A significant part of the total trip is to transfer containers (cargo) from one mode to another; for example, to unload a ship onto a dock or marshaling area and then reload onto a truck. The transfer itself is discussed in earlier chapters. Perhaps the most important requirement for efficiency in multimodal operation is efficient intermodal container transfer, and an important requirement for this is adequate planning and control of the transfer. The purpose of this chapter is to describe the essentials of intermodal transfer control. In order to provide proper background, a representative fully multimodal transport system will be described, the functions to be performed will be shown, the kinds of interfaces will be derived, and the detailed operations and functions at these interfaces

437

described. The factors that influence these operations and functions will be shown, and finally, requirements for and means of planning and cost are discussed. Major attention is given to the ship–port–ground transportation node, but the principles are extended to the much less complex airplane–port–ground transportation node.

TRANSPORTATION SYSTEM CONTROL

A container transportation system may be described, in the same manner as any system, as consisting of hardware, personnel, procedures, and facilities, all organized to perform given functions or a given job or to meet specified objectives.

The objective of the container transportation system is to move containerized cargo from originator to final destination with maximum efficiency. The only basic difference between a container transportation system and any other freight transportation system is the use of containers, so that the analysis of the container system follows that of an ordinary system except as changed to maximize the effect of container utilization.

The system may be multimodal, using various kinds of land, sea, and air (and even underground and underwater) transport, or it may use a single mode. The hardware includes the containers which hold the cargo; the cargo itself, which can vary all the way from liquid to small parcels to livestock; the ships, railroad flatcars, tractor axles and wheels, airplanes, and other vehicles used to carry the containers; the equipment needed to operate and support the vehicles and containers, such as cranes, fuel, refrigeration units, and scales; the facilities, such as ports, docks, marshaling areas, and roads; the personnel, ranging through checkers, longshoremen, airplane pilots, union representatives, and port control personnel; and the procedures (and software) which coordinate all these elements into an organized full system and which present the day-to-day instructions to make the system work. Inherent in and central to the functioning of a very complex system such as the one described above is proper planning and control of its operations. The operation of a container transportation system is illustrated by the functional flow diagram shown in Fig. 16-1. This shows the operation of the system from the vantage point of the cargo and container in terms of direct operations that are performed. This is a top-level diagram and does not show the support functions or all of the subfunctions required for system operation. It does show the central position of the airport or ocean port. Another way to think of the system is to consider it as being made up of links, over which cargo is being transported by a given vehicle (ship,

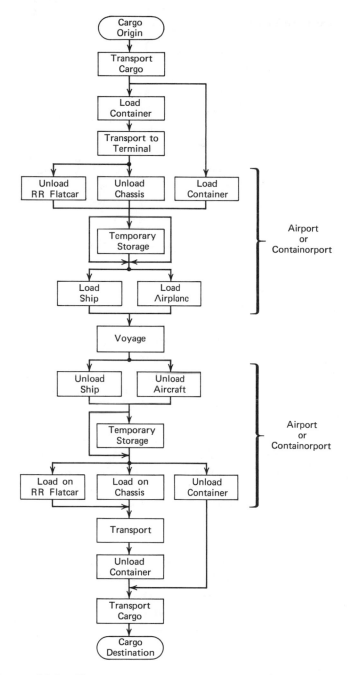

FIGURE 16-1. REPRESENTATIVE TOP-LEVEL FUNCTION FLOW FOR CONTAINER TRANSPORTATION SYSTEM EMPLOYING AIR, SHIP, AND GROUND TRANSPORT.

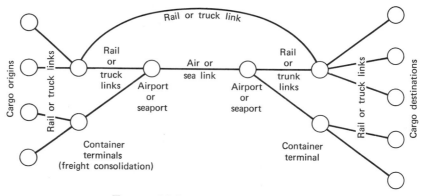

FIGURE 16-2. LINK-NODE DIAGRAM

say), and nodes, where cargo or transport changes mode or form. A representative link–node diagram is shown in Fig. 16-2.

This shows also the central importance of the nodes or transfer locations in the transportation system. These diagrams also imply, and it is true, that the entire system must be considered in obtaining a maximum-efficiency—or lowest-cost—movement of containers. For example, one cannot just design a container terminal at an ocean port without considering its interface and effect on operation of the shipping lines and their schedules.

This flow diagram and link–node diagram are fairly generalized and, in principle, apply to all combinations of transport modes, even though they are not shown. One can examine all transport mode combinations and come up with the following sets of nodes (or interfaces) and the corresponding kinds of loading/unloading that must be performed. These are given in Table 16-1.

TABLE 16-1. TYPES OF LOADING AND UNLOADING AS
RELATED TO TYPES OF TRANSPORT INTERFACES

Interfaces (Nodes)	Container Vehicles Load/Unload
Ship–truck (ocean port)	Truck
Ship–RR (ocean port)	Containership
LASH ship–LASH lighter	LASH lighter
LASH lighter–truck	LASH ship
LASH lighter–RR	Railroad flatcar
Airplane–truck (airport)	Airplane

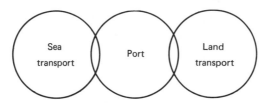

FIGURE 16-3. MULTI-MODAL INTERFACE DIAGRAM

As noted in the flow diagram, there also must be stations where the containers themselves are stuffed and unpacked or, less desirably, where the contents may be redistributed or subdivided.

In spite of the many combinations and permutations, the load/unload process for all kinds of transport is similar and thus, a discussion of one interface and its characteristics applies in many respects to all interfaces.

FUNCTIONAL DESCRIPTION

An ocean port provides the interface between sea and land transport, cargo transfer, temporary storage, limited processing, and support. The ocean port and its operation have been described and analyzed in many places. Herein we provide only so much of a description as is necessary for understanding of the controls required to maintain an efficient operation.

An ocean port is the interface between sea and land transportation. This is illustrated in the sketch below (Fig. 16-3).

The process of the flow of cargo through this port is shown in the sketch below (Fig. 16-4). Each of the functions must be divided into subfunctions in order to understand the process and to be in a position to modify it and improve it. Studies of the process details have shown that the two most complex parts of the operation are ship loading and

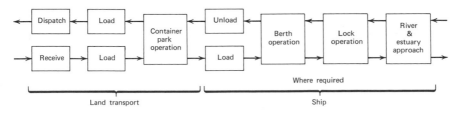

FIGURE 16-4. INTERMODAL CARGO FLOW DIAGRAM

terminal operation. These two operations are the subject of the remainder of this chapter. Each can be divided into two parts:

1. Planning the operation;
2. Means of controlling the operation.

The planning is divided into two kinds:

1. Long-term, which is concerned with planning the future system operation and would be for the purpose of determining such things as route structure, facilities, frequency and kinds of vehicles, manpower, and capital requirements;
2. Short-term, which is for the day-to-day operation of a specific part of the system—say a container terminal or loading of a specific ship.

All planning is done to satisfy, basically, two criteria:

1. That operating and physical constraints and requirements, such as ship stability, are met;
2. That economic requirements are met, to the extent feasible to attain minimum total cost/maximum profit operation.

One of the basic problems in designing and using an efficient control for port operations stems from the requirement that the flow of cargo, both in and out of the port, is a variable and, to a large degree, relatively unpredictable. This requires that planning, including computer programs developed to aid this planning, be able to accept last-minute changes. For example, consider the problem of a shipper of containers of fresh fruit. The fruit is picked and is expected to be packed in containers, mechanically cooled, and transported to be loaded into a ship whose arrival at the port might vary from the specified date by a significant amount of time. The shipper must consider when to pick, whether to load in containers immediately and start cooling or to store in a cooled area, and when to move the containers to the port container park area with or without cooling. All this makes uncertain the exact load of the ship and the facilities required at the port and at the other parts of the transport system.

SHIP LOADING AND UNLOADING

The loading and unloading of a containership involves a large number of items:

1. The ship;
2. Many containers—up to 1,000 or more for a given ship;

3. Cranes to lift the containers to and from the ship;

4. Trucks or lifts to transport the containers from their parking location to shipside and the reverse;

5. The seamen, stevedores, and shipping line personnel required to perform the individual operations.

It is not an easy task to coordinate the people, equipment, and operations into a smooth, efficient process. First, it is necessary to understand what it is that they do, what is required, and even the meaning of efficiency in this context.

A manual system for organizing the loading and unloading already exists and, as a result, certain procedures have evolved either through necessity or prejudice. Improved automated procedures are in the process of being developed. In order to improve the system or, particularly, to automate it, it is necessary to define the process in great detail. This definition must include a description of the job to be done; the system's components; the requirements and constraints imposed by regulatory bodies, unions, safety considerations, and the shipping line; and finally, a set of goals which outline the desirable characteristics of the process.

A scheduled sequence of each individual crane operation during the loading/discharge of a containership is developed, covering the time interval from arrival to departure. The operations can be classified into two types: container movements and service operations. The first type involves the loading or discharging of a container. The movement is defined by a detailed description of the container (including its size, weight, port-of-discharge, and serial number), the initial container location (ship or dock), and the desired final location (dock or ship).

The second type of operation does not involve containers. These operations are the removal or replacement of hatch covers on a given hold and the movement of the crane to a new hold.

In addition to the loading/discharge sequence, the following additional information is required: the attitude of the ship after each operation (heel, trim, transverse stability); a final loading summary stating the final ship attitude, the still-water, longitudinal bending moment, and a schedule of the fueling and ballasting required during the next leg of the voyage; a dynamic inventory of the containers on the ship and dock so that the exact status of both can be verified at any point in the loading/discharge process.

The crane operations schedule, final loading, and reports are to conform to the constraints, and the overall operation is to be optimal in terms of the general criteria described in this chapter.

ELEMENTS

The components presented here represent those of a representative shipping company operation plying the U.S.–Europe container trade. These are:

Containers: Several different container types are used and are characterized by length, width, height, and types—closed-top, open-top, refrigerated, tank containers, and specialized containers. In general, several combinations can be formed from these characteristics. For instance, 8 ft. $\times$ 8 ft. $\times$ 20 ft., 8 ft. $\times$ 8 ft. $\times$ 40 ft., and 8 ft. $\times$ 8 ft. 6 in. $\times$ 40 ft. are all popular sizes.

Containerships: The important attributes of containerships are holds with a length sufficient to hold specified-size containers divided into above- and below-deck areas. The deck level serves to divide all holds at the same level; there are six below-deck levels and two above-deck levels in the schematic drawing. A cell is a vertical stack of containers. Below-deck cells have fixed positions, while above-deck cells vary, depending on the length of containers they are made up of. Hatch covers are assumed to extend the full width of the holds, although a hold may be divided into several hatches. (See Fig. 16-5)

Cranes: Many terminals have two or more cranes working the holds simultaneously. Each crane is specially constructed to lift the containers one at a time (one 40-ft. or two 20-ft.) and place them in the various cells. At any one hold the crane can assume different positions corresponding to operations with different-size containers. Current cranes require about 3–5 minutes for one cycle; that is, one traverse from the dock to the ship and back. The cycle consists of the loading of a container, the discharge of a container, or a combined load/discharge operation. It takes approximately 15 minutes to either remove the hatch covers or replace them. To move the crane from one hold to another takes, on the average, 15 minutes. However, to move the crane from a hold aft of the deckhouse to forward of the deckhouse, a time of one hour is required. This occurs because the boom of the crane must be raised in order to clear the deckhouse.

Dock: Containers are stored on the dock in several parking areas. One area is generally set aside for outgoing containers, another for arriving containers. A third may be set aside for containers which were discharged from the ship but have to be reloaded.

The containers are parked in the outbound area in a rough two-di-

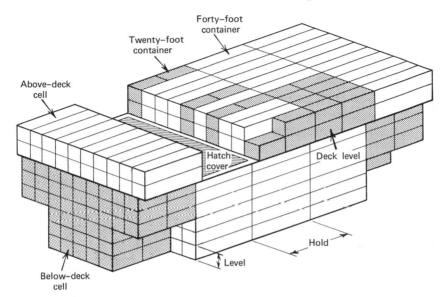

FIGURE 16-5. SCHEMATIC REPRESENTATION OF LOADED CONTAIN-
ERS ON VESSEL ABOVE AND BELOW DECK (SOURCE: HYDRONAUTICS,
INC.).

mensional array. That is, they are segregated according to port-of-discharge and approximate weight (light, medium, and heavy). The 40-foot
containers can be stacked two high and the 20-foot containers, three high.
When the containership arrives in port, not all of the outbound containers are on the dock; rather, usually only about 40 percent of them.
As a result, some containers are constantly flowing into the outgoing
parking area while others are removed for placement aboard ship.

Route: The route and traffic affects the load planning.

CONSTRAINTS ON LOAD/UNLOAD OPERATION

Rules exist which affect the loading/discharge operation of the ship.
These rules reflect safety considerations, regulations by various concerned agencies (the U.S. Coast Guard, ABS, etc.), union rules, and standard shipping-line operating procedures. For the definition of constraints,
it is convenient to define two general systems: the "ship" system, including the crane, dock, and route components; and the "container" system,
which is the containers individually and in aggregate.

The constraints on the container system consist of (1) the total number of containers that can be carried; (2) limiting weights of individual containers; (3) placement restrictions for types of containers on the ship; and (4) dockside availability constraints. The types of containers considered might include regular, reefer, and above-deck (red-label) containers of various lengths. Certain holds in the ship might accept only one container of one length below decks, while the others accept only another-length container. Most above-deck space may be filled by different-length containers as long as a given stack is consistently one or the other. Thus, an above-deck cell might be either 20- or 40-foot length.

Limitation of storage and parking facilities on the dock might cause only a top container in any stack (where one end is open if the container is on the top level) to be available for loading. That is, shuffling of the containers on the dock is not desirable. The end-open restriction reflects the present inability of the usual dock handling equipment to raise a 40-foot container over a two-high stack or a 20-foot container over a three-high stack.

The constraints on the ship system are more numerous, and can be divided into ship attitude, ship stability, and crane operation constraints. The ship attitude constraints state that (1) the draft forward is restricted to a given range; (2) the draft aft must fall within a certain range (the maximum and minimum ship displacements may be derived from these restrictions); (3) the difference between the drafts forward and aft (trim) must be less than a specified amount, depending on whether the ship is loading or completely loaded; and (4) the heel must be as close to zero as possible when loaded, and at no time can it exceed a specified amount (to ensure that containers will not bind in the below-deck guides when being loaded).

The ship stability constraints are defined in terms of the metacentric height (GM). Acceptable values of the GM are divided into two areas: permissible and desirable GM. The desirable range is determined from damage-stability considerations, while the upper range is specified as a result of consideration of the roll-stabilization capabilities of the ship. The stability constraint requires the GM to fall in either of the two areas, with the desirable area more favorable. A representative GM limit area and a representative ship envelope of permissible drafts, wherein the first three constraints above are satisfied, are shown in Figs. 16-6 and 16-7, respectively.

The usual crane operation constraints are simply (1) two cranes cannot work on adjacent holds simultaneously; (2) lateral movement of the crane is such that working priorities within a given hold are in a given sequence, such as forward 20-foot containers, aft 20-foot containers, and then 40-foot

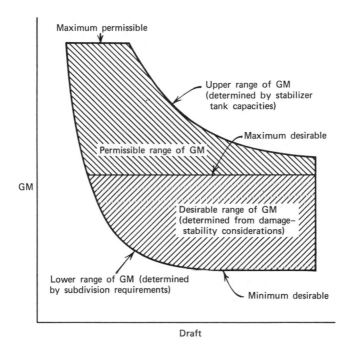

FIGURE 16-6.   METACENTRIC HEIGHT LIMITATIONS (SOURCE: HYDRONAUTICS, INC.).

containers; (3) above-deck levels must be entirely unloaded before any unloading of under-deck levels can commence; (4) the entire above-deck area in a hold must be unloaded before below-deck loading and/or unloading begins; and (5) deck loading and unloading must be carried out in an orderly side-to-side progression at each level.

OBJECTIVES OF LOAD/UNLOAD PLANNING

The objective of load/unload planning is to optimize the operation of the ship and container system. To achieve this, it is again convenient to divide the overall system into the two component systems, the "ship" and the "containers." For purposes of this classification, the ship comprises the ship itself, the dock, and all cargo-handling gear, which includes dockside cranes; the containers are the containers themselves, either individually or in aggregate.

Optimum for the ship then consists of (1) having desirable longitudinal,

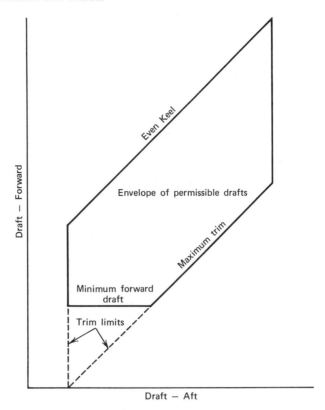

FIGURE 16-7.   ENVELOPE OF PERMISSIBLE DRAFTS (SOURCE: HY-
DRONAUTICS, INC.).

transverse, and vertical centers of gravity when loaded with a given cargo, for reasons of either stability or trim; (2) carrying the minimum amount of ballast necessary to achieve this condition either while loading or unloading; and (3) utilizing consumables while underway to maintain this desirable condition.

Optimum for the containers implies (1) minimization of handling of any container between its origin and destination; (2) utilization of combined load/unload operations for minimum total container handling time; and (3) maximum utilization of available cargo space within the limitations of container placement restrictions.

It is clear that consideration of only the immediate factors which are present in the ship and container systems, which would be used in determining a single optimum loading, is not sufficient to determine a consistently optimum loading. It is necessary to consider the factors which will be present in subsequent ports in determining a given loading so that continued optimum loading may be achieved. Thus, the ship system should be divided into current port and full-cycle ports (a cycle being the return of the ship to its current position by passage to specified ports of call), and the ship optimum is considered in terms of, for instance, minimizing ballast required while loading in the current port as well as minimizing ballast required during the voyage through an entire cycle.

Likewise, the container system is divided into current port and full-cycle ports; minimizing container handling thus involves combining as many load/unload operations as possible in the current port while producing a loading which will not require excessive handling of containers at subsequent ports. The resulting system is to be flexible enough to cope with special situations which require human intervention. For instance, if a container is damaged or a crane breaks down, the resulting consequence must be handled with a minimum of penalty to the overall system.

COMPUTERIZED LOAD PLANNING

At present, much or all of the load planning is done manually, sometimes with the aid of specialized slide rules or nomograms. The complexity of the situation, as well as the requirement for higher efficiency, has led to the development of computerized load planning. Two example programs are the "Container Allocation Program" by Ocean Transport Consulting Services, 555 Fifth Avenue, New York City, and a program described in "Automated Procedures for the Allocation of Containers on Shipboard" by W. C. Webster, P. Van Dyke, and H. P. Cojeen, Hydronautics, Inc., Laurel, Maryland, October 1969.

The "Container Allocation Program" was written (in BASIC FORTRAN IV language) in order to provide a minimum-cost scheduling of container loadings for a containership. The logic of the program is divided into two parts:

1. Load the given ship matrix for containers with the containers scheduled for a voyage at a point in time. Determine the acceptable matrix configurations, given the following noneconomic constraints:
   a. Acceptable ship stability;
   b. Acceptable ship trim and draft;
   c. Acceptable ship heel (0 in most cases);
   d. Container label compatibility;
   e. Satisfactory containerport segregation;

    f.   Acceptable container stack loading;

    g. No rehandling.

2. For the acceptable technical configurations computed, using the logic above, determine the least-cost configuration (or configurations falling within a set cost range from the least cost). This would be done by a simulation of the vessel's loading/discharge procedure, using the technically acceptable configurations. Constraints of this section of the program are as follows:

    a.   No negative or low stability during simulation;

    b.   No excessive trim/draft during simulation;

    c.   No excessive heel during simulation.

Nominal trims and heeling correctable by ballasting will be allowed and the economic penalty calculated thereon.

The input-file data for this program include ship characteristics, terminal characteristics, current ship loading, and the current terminal inventory for loading. The program size is about 8,000 bytes equivalent and the file size depends on number of ships and terminals. As an indication, 1,000 bytes are required for 5 ships, 10,000 bytes for 5 terminals, plus a 5,000-byte working file. The actual applications of this computer program are not known to the author.

The Hydronautics, Inc. computer program was designed to accomplish a logical loading/unloading sequence for individual containers on a containership. The program develops an optimum loading of the ship as one which achieves desired ship characteristics, implying minimum ballasting, and requires minimum cargo handling; this is achieved through consideration of both detailed current-port information and complete cycle estimates of expected trade. Practical constraints include consideration of exceptions and modifications to cargo, specific locations for given cargo, time dependence of cargo availability, crane movement restrictions, and achievement of desirable ship trim and stability characteristics. The input and output of each program within the system is designed to be in a form readily obtained from, and suitable for immediate use by, ship and dock operations personnel.

The program was developed, considering the basic factors affecting the loading of a containership which are discussed in the previous paragraphs. The program was initially based on parameters specifically representing those of United States Lines plying the United States–Europe container trade. The ships of the first applications were of the Lancer class. The containers were of the variety and size actually used. The first route selected for study consisted of two U.S. ports and three in Europe. Most U.S. containers were expected to be for European ports and vice versa; little intracoastal trade was expected.

The computer program distinguishes between fixed and variable inputs, and those that are part of the ship system or of the container system. This breakdown is shown in Tables 16-2 and 16-3 and in Fig. 16-8.

An instrument to compute safe loads for containerships was recently put into operation by the Johnson Line for the Axel Johnson class of containerships. This is called the Stalodicator and is simply an electric

TABLE 16-2.   INPUTS TO SHIP AND CONTAINER SYSTEMS

	Ship System	Container System	
Fixed	Ship characteristics, including curves of form, bonjean curves, fuel rate, and light-ship displacement	Location of container storage positions, including allowable container types.	
	Locations and capacities of fuel and ballast tanks	Admissible container types	Current Port
	Ports in cycle with distances	Additional container constraints	and
	Crane cycle times for load/ unload, lateral movement, hatch removal		Full Cycle
	Additional ship constraints		
Variable	Fuel, ballast conditions in port	Individual containers on board	
	Number of cranes and availability	Individual containers to be loaded, including destination, type, and storage and arrival availability	Current Port
		Aggregate of containers expected to be loaded by destination and type	
	Fuel burning and bunkering sequences	Aggregate of containers on board by destination and type	
		Aggregate of containers to be loaded by origin, destination, and type	Full Cycle

TABLE 16-3. OUTPUTS OF SHIP AND CONTAINER SYSTEMS

Ship System	Container System	
Report of cargo, ballast, fuel, lightship, and total weights and centers Stability information of vertical and horizontal centers of buoyancy, metacentric height, and moment to trim. Trim information of heel, drafts forward and aft Similar report considering only remaining cargo	Summary report of aggregate of containers on board by destination and hold Detailed report of individual container positions on ship by hold Summary and detail of containers to be unloaded, and containers which will remain Summary of aggregate of containers to be loaded by destination and hold Comparison of desired, achieved, and limits of vertical and horizontal centers of gravity Detailed report of desired loaded condition of ship based on loading estimates Detailed report of individual containers to be loaded.	Current Port
Detailed loading/unloading instructions for individual containers, including dock and ship locations, ship attitude at each step, crane instructions as to hold and hatch-cover positions		
Report of cargo, ballast, fuel, lightship, and total weights and centers, stability and trim information as loaded. Also fuel conditions by tank, ballasting instructions by tank as required, and bending moment Continued reports during voyage as fuel and ballast conditions change	Summary report of aggregate of containers on ship at completion of load/unload by destination and hold Detailed list of containers on board by hold	
Summary of ship condition expected during next cycle, including itinerary, cargo weight, ballast required, fuel weight, total displacement, and desired centers of gravity for cargo	Summary of aggregate of trade expected on next complete cycle by port of origin, destination, and type Summary of aggregate of containers as loaded by port of origin, destination, type, and hold, including longitudinal centers of gravity achieved for the total	Full Cycle

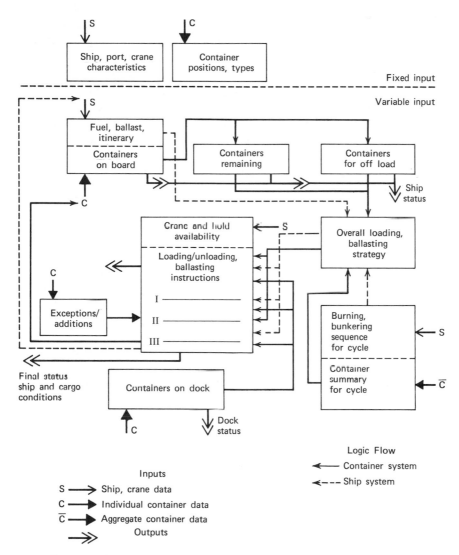

FIGURE 16-8. PROGRAM LOGIC OF HYDRONAUTICS, INC. COMPUTER PROGRAM FOR LOADING AND UNLOADING INDIVIDUAL CONTAINERS ON A CONTAINERSHIP.

calculator. The instrument has no connections to the ship's hull and does not measure actual stresses. Instead, the instrument is fed data concerning the loads in the cargo holds and the Stalodicator gives a reading that indicates how the given cargo distribution will affect the hull. The instrument is based on the Wheatstone bridge principle, and the components consist mainly of fixed and variable resistances. (It is, then, a special-purpose analog computer.) Thus, there are no moving parts except the setting knobs. Very little instruction and no previous experience are needed to operate it. Each Stalodicator S5, however, is tailored to a specific containership.

CONTROL

Once the loading or unloading operation is planned, the actual operation can take place. The crane operators and other personnel must be given the loading schedule and load locations. The load master must monitor operations to assure that the planned procedure is being carried out. Provision must be made for last-minute changes.

AIRPLANE LOADING AND LOAD PLANNING

Airplane loading and load planning for airplanes must consider essentially the same factors as for ships as discussed earlier; but, usually, the problem is much less complex. The containers must be loaded so as to maintain the airplane center-of-gravity within limits; the total weight must be within the maximum allowable airplane operating weight; and the containers should be loaded and moved at the terminal, so as to minimize handling. The factors that make the airplane load problem simpler are the comparatively few containers on a given airplane (even the largest now in use) and the fact that the airplanes are designed to have a rather large allowable center-of-gravity range.

TERMINAL OPERATION AND PLANNING

The majority of this chapter was devoted to the ship–port interface, concentrating on the efficient loading and unloading of the ship. As briefly discussed, to maximize the efficiency of the ship–land transportation system mode, one must consider also the port–land transportation interface and the operation of the terminal itself. The ship loading programs consider the terminal operation to a certain extent; the terminal movement and storage of containers are minimized to obtain a minimum-cost loading.

The problems of developing standard systems for optimal stowage and related port and ship control will continue to be present with containerization as long as new types of ships, containers, and handling systems are introduced. At every junction of new technologies there will arise a need to review the data systems. In this respect, the material shown in this chapter should be considered only as a typical indication of the developments to be watched.

Panel 0-31 of the Society of Naval Architects and Marine Engineers has, over the years, considered many of those ideas. Some of the conclusions which apply to one system do not apply to others. The particular problem results from long-line hauls where 12 or more ports of call may produce overstowage. The problem of carrying deck containers in the single-compartment ship varies with many design characteristics. The location of heavier vans deep below deck may allow more containers to be carried on deck, but the realities of the container terminal operation often do not permit this sequence of loading, due to the late arrival of the cargo on the pier. Ballasting is not a sufficient answer for deck weight as a ship's ballast capacity may be reached before the deck space is filled. United States Lines, after detailed and lengthy exercises in selective stowage methodology similar to the one described here, decided to use fixed ballast, due to the requirements for simplicity imposed by the personnel in charge of prestowage arrangements. Finally, the need to aid all users of a certain port, including the smaller ones, may lead to the development of stowage computer systems by the larger port administrations for the benefit of attracting a greater variety and number of shipowners.

Analysis, Assessment, and Forecasting

PLANNING IN SPURTS

In mid-1969, the shipping world appeared to have solved the problems of containerization. The decision to change from break-bulk ships to cellular container vessels brought about a spending spree in ports and equipment fleets. Everybody appeared happy, and anyone voicing the slightest reservation by mentioning the problems yet to be overcome, appeared to be a forecaster of gloom and doom. Yet the problems of implementation of containers as a medium of transport integration had not even been explored. Some lines, such as United States Line, swung to far-advanced computer methods dealing with their entire system, while the system was not yet completely conceived or partially tested. As a result, two years later, the awakening was so profound that United States Line abandoned computerized selected ship stow and went back to fixed ballast in ships, which allowed them conventional load planning methods. This remark is not intended to be pejorative, however, since the apparent development of containerization, like all of transportation history, proceeds in a graduated scale from low- to high-level automation with many plateaus in between. Any time a developmental plateau is reached, it appears that no further development is needed. The interest in progressive implementation, analysis, and planning wanes. Yet since the general trend to integrated transport automation (I/TA) continues along with economy's growth and expansion of population, new spurts upwards are, at such times, in the minds of planners and pioneers. Then, like the unforeseen eruption of a volcano, as the conclusions reached by the thinkers meet at a given moment with the pressure of further requirements, new steps in the direction of integration/automation of transport become visible. The parametric overview of the I/TA picture indicates container systems as the medium of our era; these developmental moves are all in this direction. The most likely candidates for the next important development, thus, lie in the opening up of new conventional transport systems to containerization. Any transportation today is susceptible to integration, to automation, and, consequently, to containerization. The entire field of supermarket developments will be affected by new meat-delivery systems in through-the-load cooling, which will eliminate meat processing in stores and, instead, provide for centralized plant operation. Paper and chipboard deliveries, as well as bulk steel products and prefabricated housing, are certain to be drawn into the cycle of I/TA developments and containers.

TRANSFER OF TECHNOLOGY

We have reviewed the impending changeover in the transportation of fresh agricultural farm products, fresh meats, and bananas in Chapter 6. Since the vast fleet and many port facilities serving the banana trade are almost as significant to containerization as the general cargo trade, this segment of the industry has been subjected to considerable systems analysis and forecasting. United Fruit Company employed Arthur D. Little, Inc. in an early stage of study to indicate future changes. The comparison between air shipments and surface transport was included. I myself did not concur with the technological forecasting developed by A. D. Little, Inc. Of the many systems used for containerization forecasting, I feel that only a combination of technology development related to a study of both conventional and possible systems has a relevance to the outcome. The six best-known forecasting methods, to be discussed later, must be evaluated in the light of three effects. These are:

1. Technological competency;
2. Profitability of investment and obsolescence analysis;
3. Sociological impact of the changeover on the structure of the man–service interface.

Harald Burmeister has made a study dealing with the economic analysis of new methods to transfer perishable goods in bulk from the producer, via the ocean, to the consumer, which deals with the question of whether containers can handle bananas in this manner. The transportation analyst concerned with further impact of containerization has no choice whether or not to forecast, since he must find tools to make business decisions. Technological forecasting is a dangerous but necessary method when containerization is involved. It is dangerous because investment decisions deal with present funding, while cost forecasting deals with future payoffs or failure. However, since it is the only planning method available, we must analyze it.

TERMS AND TOOLS

There are some terms which need defining to readers confronting them for the first time:

Technology refers to knowledge of engineering and the technical application to software and behavioral sciences when they interact to human activity.

Forecasting is generally the probabilistic assessment of the future.

Technological forecasting predicts in general probabilistic terms the how and when of spreading of technology to containerization. Usually, such transfer is imagined as evolutionary, passing through a ladder of steps (levels) from the most abstract fundamental research results to a commercially applied form.

Normative technological forecasting, in evaluating today's state of the art, selects future desirable and achievable goals, and then works backwards toward today, in order to establish the chain of actions needed to cause the desired development.

Technology transfer: Technological progress takes the form of an upward movement from one floor to the next. A further effect is on each floor where, for example, diffusion of one technology (and/or mergers of two or more technologies) takes place before, or at the same time as, the next step toward a higher floor is made. One possible "8-floor plan" would be, for example, from lowest to highest, as applied to containerization (see Table 17-1). Each floor may have sublevels, etc., but as the whole scheme is no more than an aid to understanding sporadic systems development. It represents technology transfer. It should be added that the two

TABLE 17-1. CONTAINER TECHNOLOGY TRANSFER LEVELS

Development Direction of Progress

	Primary Development Levels				Secondary Impact Levels			
	1	2	3	4	5	6	7	8
Level	Recognition of Basic Principle	Critical Analysis of Operational Resources Availability	Elementary Systems Technology (Ship Systems Improvements)	Functional Accomplishment (Intermodal Interface Planning and Systems Integration)	Application of Established Systems Technology	Environment	Implementation	Effects on Society Implication of new methods for social systems, ecology, environment and human life
Example	Automation	Marketing of new methods	Pioneer entry modes	Implementation of combined transport operations	Implementation of international containerization on three continents	Container implementation in production system of new industries	New agricultural developments in nutrition	
	Economy of scale	Innovations	Ro-Ro services	Interface Sea-rail	Logistics and support facilities	Technology out-growth (national defense, solid waste disposal, household goods movements)	Opening new resources—timber, minerals	
	Mechanization	New relations between physical distribution and delivery	On deck semi-containerships	Sea-road			New feeds for cattle	
	Growth			Air-road			Container bulk methods	
	Bulking						Inland containerization	

dimensions so far explained are complemented by a third, the nontechno-
logical environment, which interacts with the technological one and
exerts a great selective influence on the choice from among technological
alternatives. A time dimension is an implicit and obvious factor.

SCOPE OF FORECASTING

To be of operational value to container decision makers, the basic questions would have to be answered by any technological forecasting technique:

1. Given the existence of the present state of the art, how long will it take
   to introduce features of existing or new products, services, systems? This
   question requires an analysis of the time span needed between each level
   or floor.
2. In order to answer question one, a cost analysis is necessary for alternative
   ways of reaching the highest floor. Obviously, there are trade-offs between
   time and money and technological perfection.
3. Given time and cost, what will be the form of the new products, services,
   systems: performance characteristics, functional capabilities, social acceptability, etc.? There are obvious trade-offs among time, money, and
   form, so that all these questions are interacting ones, and the formulation
   given here as a sequence is too rigid.
4. How will the future development as forecasted influence the position of
   my transport business? Figure 17-1 illustrates the relationship between
   ship size, ship speed, and annual container throughput.

According to his choice of calling it either an opportunity or a threat,
the answer to this last question will cause one action or another.

Container forecasting is functional only if the basic uncertainties can
be resolved as follows:

1. Identify economic potential of container technological progress and opportunities and threats coming from the technological environment and
   obsolescence.
2. Establish potential timing for introduction of container technology by
   others; plan one's own research programs to acquire knowledge from outside sources, in such a way that major threats are obviated and necessary
   inputs for development are available when needed.
3. Gear planning programs toward application of container technology.
4. Establish performance criteria for new systems implementation.

Considering the impact that I/TA has on transport, a reformulation of
objectives for the total undertaking is necessary.

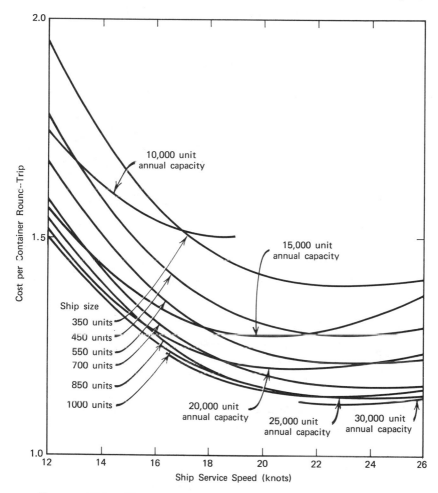

FIGURE 17-1. COST PER CONTAINER-ROUND-TRIP VERSUS SHIP SIZE AND SPEED, AND ANNUAL THROUGHPUT (SOURCE: U.S. GOVT. III).

EVALUATION PROCEDURE

The state of the art of container forecasting must evaluate the following relevant terms:

1. What *time horizon* is covered?
2. Is time a point in the future or a line into it; for example, does the technique—explicitly or implicitly—indicate the way (how and why) to the horizon, or does it try to forecast only the final point in time?

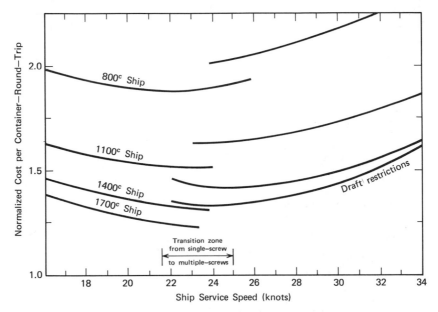

FIGURE 17-2. UNIT COST PER CONTAINER-ROUND-TRIP VERSUS SHIP SIZE AND SPEED—ALL SHIPS AT 65-PERCENT LOAD FACTOR (SOURCE: U.S. GOVT. III).

3. Where does the technique find its major field of application?

4. Is it normative in character and tendency, or potentially so; or is it definitive?

5. What is the overall importance of the technique, now and in the next decade, among the tools developed for transport forecasting? Figure 17-2 illustrates the relationship between ships, ship service speed and other technical conditions, and the container cost per round trip.

DANGER OF OVERSIMPLIFICATION

Goal-setting, plus methods to optimize the process of getting there, is necessary. The optimization may be in terms of time, or cost, or least risk, or a combination of these and other parameters. Which optimization to achieve is a matter of subjective need, choice, or judgment. Quantitative methods are no more than tools to penetrate, order, and make transparent the many dimensions with which our memory and judgment have to cope. They can no more than help us handle more than the customary one or two dimensions at the same time. Danger exists that the oversimplification necessary, in order to express complex contexts in the relatively primitive language of mathematics, leads to serious practical mistakes. It is difficult to draw an exact line between the one kind of functions and the other; however, it is a most important task.

Harald Burmeister presents methods for normative techniques of forecasting technology applicable to critical container analysis. The following categories are treated by him:

1. Matrices;
2. Programming techniques;
3. Decision-theoretical techniques;
4. Simulation;
5. Network techniques;
6. Relevance trees.

Since decision matrices and relevance trees are the most common forms of forecasting techniques, and serve at the same time as planning tools, I include those shown by Burmeister as an example (see Tables 17-2 and 17-3).

UNCERTAINTY AND RISK

Uncertainty is usually defined as partial or total ignorance of an outcome or development. Risk means that a random event's probability distribution of occurrence is known.

Investment analysis for containerization must be treated under conditions of risk; for example, the outcomes are known together with their probability of occurrence. This is an oversimplification, of course; but unavoidable, as complicated mathematical methods must be applied. A link between uncertainty and risk can be established through estimates of outcome. Analysis applying estimating procedures can use a mix of uncertainty and risk elements. Past performance and present characteristics of a service or its decision tools yield some information in the statistical sense, and subjective estimates must do the rest. This often shakes the confidence of an objective observer, as to the validity of the results. The only justification is that no better tools are available.

Everything lying in the future is uncertain or risky. The treatment of this problem in advanced investment analysis is extremely popular. Before the various methods are described, it is useful to state in operational terms what we consider uncertain or risky in the terms of investment eval

TABLE 17-2.   DECISION MATRIX*

Inputs available / Outputs desired	Finance cost and availability	Techn. skill for conceiving and maintaining	Management for planning and operation	Result
Self-contained reefer container, multipurpose				
Containers in present reefer ships				
Reefer container carried on deck any ship				
New system of container/special purpose ship for bananas				
Improvement of presently used transport methods				
Open full liner service of which banana transport only one part				

Source: Burmeister

* Example: Reefer-ship/container combinations.

uation. In practice, all inputs on which the future has a bearing contain this risk. On the one side, it is the cost of capital used as cutoff rate, on the other, the cash flow. Behind the cutoff rate lie other variables, such as market interest rate, stock market movements, public preferences, and the environment (including general economic and political conditions), until we arrive at the physical laws. Cash flow starts with price movements of investment, wages, and raw materials.

Substitution and new technology affect outflows; the size of market, competitors' actions, and service of a product affect inflows; also, these variables can be considered to depend on general economic conditions and political conditions, until the workings of the transport integration

TABLE 17-3.   RELEVANCE TREE

Example: Development of a temperature-control method for perishable goods.

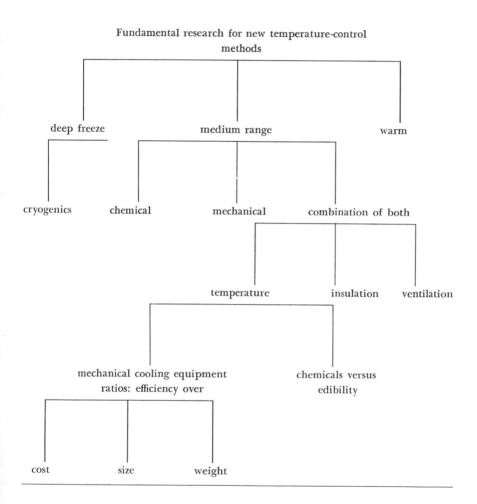

(Source: Burmeister.)

and automation trend are perhaps the only variable. A chain of events is usually traceable only after the facts have been analyzed. Predictions or measurements of possible dispersion of alternative developments become an impossibility even with the largest computer systems. Full knowledge of all distribution patterns link the variables. Therefore, the container analyst must lean toward operational analysis.

Scientific papers are produced at an increasing rate on the possible application of one or more or all of the following techniques applicable to investment analysis uncertainty aspect, and the effects on obsolescence:

1. Subjective probability distributions;
2. Utility theory;
3. Decision trees;
4. Game theory;
5. Heuristic programs;
6. Simulation;
7. Reducing uncertainty by further research;
8. Uncertainty and the cutoff rate.

IMPORTANCE OF LIFE-CYCLE EVALUATION

The container analyst may or may not convince the business management of his railroad, shipline, truckline, port, and leasing company that a particular new development in I/TA systems is about to become reality with the previously cited technological forecast systems. It may be easier to work with these types of tools when dealing with a transport system for the People's Republic of China than for the United States. The very exact outcome of the forecast may be more effective when progress is apparent. In a complicated, competitive system, the recognition is more difficult. The key to any container system calls for improved interfacing; and subsystems must be introduced as part of the overall systems planning. One of the most important substitutions, as such, deals with the change of gauge of ships, or simply with the implementation of feedership systems into the overall container-route geography. Therefore, the methodology mandatory to the basic system development is the careful selection of the optimal subsystem which mostly requires new tool selection and capital investments. This again makes for the urgency of developing the life-cycle cost analysis for such a subsystem, in light of its position in the overall systems investment policy.

EVALUATION CRITERIA OF LIFE-CYCLE COSTS

Several kinds of criteria can be used in a cost-effectiveness analysis of a containership. Our primary approach is to define specific missions and to calculate the number of ships of each type that would be required in order to accomplish each of the specified missions at some specified productivity level. We define productivity requirements for each of the missions consistent with the tonnages currently being moved in the existing operation. Given a productivity requirement, we determine the number of ships required to achieve the productivity goal, and we make cost comparisons on a fleet basis rather than on an individual-ship basis. The objective here is to reflect not only the cost differences of ship systems involved, but also the effectiveness differences as well. Having thus defined a constant effectiveness level, we are able to make consistent cost comparisons. We present a summary of three Small Port Vessels (SPV)-base cases for ten-year undiscounted acquisition and operating costs to give equivalent effectiveness on the separate hypothetical missions or modes of operation and for all the cargo productivity assumptions. In all cases, it shows that the SPV has, by far, the lowest life-cycle cost of any similar vessel.

An alternative approach for cost-effectiveness comparison is to define a figure of merit for each ship which reflects both cost and performance parameters. The typical figure of merit would be an effectiveness-over-cost ratio; that is, effectiveness units per dollar of cost. One such figure of merit is represented by the product of ship speed and ship capacity divided by total life-cycle cost. Comparing all potential containership configurations on the basis of this second criterion, using the other figure of merit for one-deck ships—

$$\frac{\text{speed} \times \text{square footage}}{\text{life-cycle cost}},$$

shows which ship yields the greatest speed and cargo capacity per dollar of acquisition and operation cost.

It is our belief that the first of these criteria is the more meaningful and, therefore, the remaining comparisons are life-cycle comparisons for a specified cost-effectiveness level.

COST DATA SOURCES

As a basis for cost comparison, we define a life-cycle cost structure which considers operating cost elements, such as crew costs, fuel costs, maintenance and repair costs, overhaul costs, insurance costs, regulatory-body survey costs, and administrative costs (Figs. 17-3 and 17-4). Costs for the SPV are based on designer's estimates and specification information provided by the engine manufacturer. As a detailed breakdown of operating costs for the purposes of comparison, we have used an assumed per diem charter rate assessed in the Far East. It is assumed that this per diem figure will reflect operating costs, administrative costs, and possibly a prorata share of original acquisition costs. Because the comparison ships are obsolete and newer ones are considerably more expensive, and because the per diem rates probably do not reflect acquisition costs, the cost estimate is undoubtedly low.

GROUND RULES FOR THE COST COMPARISON

The comparisons to be presented have been made on the basis of ten-year undiscounted operating and support costs plus acquisition costs. These are approximately equal to twenty-year discounted life-cycle costs, using a discount rate of 7.75 percent. The relative position of each of the ship types in the evaluation does not change, regardless of whether we use discounted or undiscounted costs, ten-year or twenty-year costs, or any of a broad range of discount factors. Our cost analysis is presented as a base case, with the estimate for each of the cost elements based on data and best judgment. It is recognized, however, that there may be differences of opinion with respect to the size of specific costs. We have tested the results of our cost-effectiveness analysis for sensitivity to changes in the basic cost assumptions by assuming the worst possible case with respect to our estimates for the SPV, and the best possible case with respect to our estimates for the other ship. The details of the sensitivity analysis are discussed later in this chapter. The results of the analysis do not change, however, and the SPV is still clearly the lowest-cost system for each of the three postulated missions.

ECONOMIC ANALYSIS

We have heretofore discussed the facts which form the conditions, possibilities, and constraints under which the container service must exist. In this respect, much coverage has been devoted to the key conveyance system—in particular, ocean ships systems and railroad service—which form the backbone of any intermodal integration.

Now it is necessary that we show a typical approach to the planning of

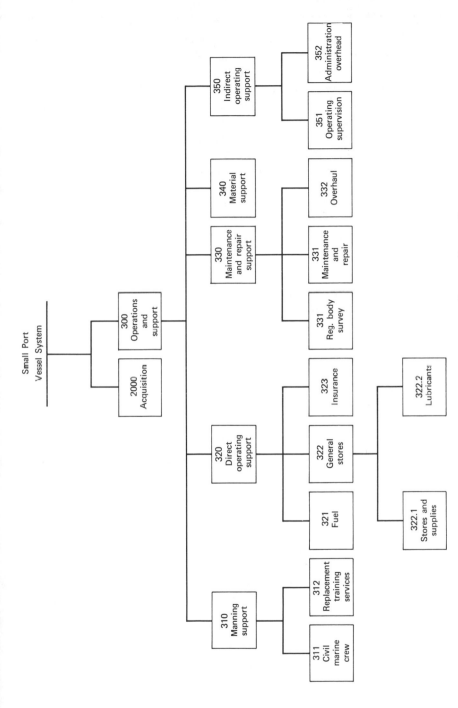

FIGURE 17-3. LIFE-CYCLE COST STRUCTURE OF SMALL PORT VESSEL SYSTEM.

tools for container transportation. This planning deals with the selection of the ship system. The reverse is also true. This chapter outlines the factors to be considered in the containerization selection requirements and the container system analysis.

The evaluation and refinement of a prototype framework for any container transportation system analysis requires a conceptual definition of a container systems model. Also, a synthesis of available alternative candidate models and testing of these alternative models to determine cost and service benefits is needed for the decision making. Estimation of development costs and tentative framework for a proposed model system of integrated container transportation are explained. This requires eight stage studies, identified as follows:

1. A transportation requirement demand model;
2. An intermodal constraints identification routine;
3. An analysis of international service limitations;
4. A technology design basis;
5. A mission performance evaluation of equipment and systems;
6. An integrated system performance model;
7. A time-period feasibility routine for transfer facilities and interchange;
8. An overall program design integration routine.

This framework must be used to evaluate structure and logic of each of the above components and for integration into one container systems framework. The applicability of key mathematical techniques formulated for carrying out the research necessary to implement a typical conceptual container system structure leads first to the system of life-cycle cost evaluation. Development of a model design suggestion and continuing guidance will be fully appreciated as prerequisites of adequate understanding of "real world" complexity. All relevant consequences of a systematic program are to be considered from viewpoint of shipper and consignee, container system operator, steamship service, inland carrier, equipment manufacturer, and governmental agencies.

This analysis is quite different from the customary mechanical or simulation methods used as planning tools in ocean transportation. The reader is referred to Datz, *Planning Tools for Ocean Transportation*. Instead of this, we will develop here a typical economic analysis as an example of how such a study is to be conducted.

MISSION ASSUMPTIONS

In order to compare the Small Port Vessel with the other ships properly, we will define three basic missions which the SPV might be called upon to perform, and we will determine the number of each of these ship types that would be required to accomplish each mission. The basic missions assumed for the purposes of comparison are:

Case 1.   The ships will engage solely in coastal operations with an average voyage distance of 200 miles between ports.

Case 2.   The ships will operate on a point-to-point basis in ocean-going cargo traffic between ports with the average voyage distance of 1,350 miles point to point.

Case 3.   This assumes a mixed deployment comparable to the typical itinerary of a ship now operating in the Far East feeder service. The delays in port and the varying load factors assumed for the SPV are comparable to those currently being experienced.

PRODUCTIVITY COMPARISON

Because of its higher speed, the Small Port Vessel will obviously cycle faster for any given voyage length than any of the competitive ships. In any given time period, then, the SPV will complete most round-trip voyages and deliver most cargo. If we assume that the ships will have to move an average of 117,750 measurement tons per month, Case 1 requires five SPVs, or six to nine competitive ships. This requirement is based on the assumption that the ships would be operating at virtually 100-percent load factor throughout their stay in the coastal area.

A more realistic assumption is presented in Case 3. The typical itinerary for that case includes assumptions of partial loads in most instances and of occasional delays in port waiting for cargo. For Case 3, we have assumed two different comparisons. Case 3-A is based on an assumption of five SPVs, and it compares costs for the other two ship types which are based on the number of ships required for productivity as compared with five SPVs. Case 3-B compares the number of ships of each type that would be necessary in order to move 77,000 measurement tons per month, which was the average moved per month by competitive ships in intratheater operations between January and June 1967. In this case, we are comparing 9 SPVs with 11 to 17 other feederships.

Ship costs can be compared on a per diem basis. The SPV ship per diem rate is based on daily operating cost plus amortization and interest charges per day at a six percent per annum interest rate with uniform annual payments. The assumption of a slow write-off of the SPV investment through uniform annual payments permits a conservative comparison of SPV and competitive rates, since it leads to a higher-than-likely per diem rate for the SPV. Due to the interest and amortization charges, the SPV ship per diem rate is higher than the rates for the other ships. But taking

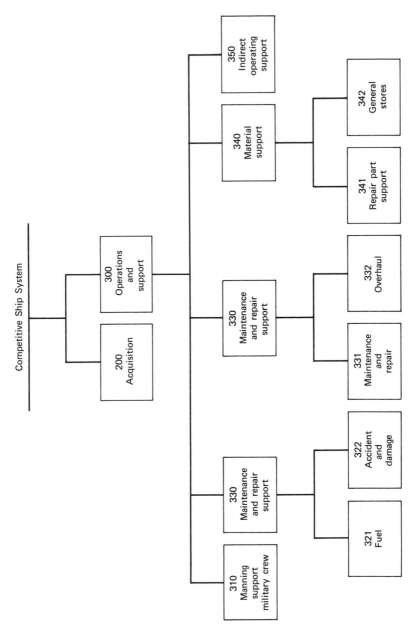

FIGURE 17-4. LIFE-CYCLE COST STRUCTURE OF COMPETITIVE SHIP SYSTEM.

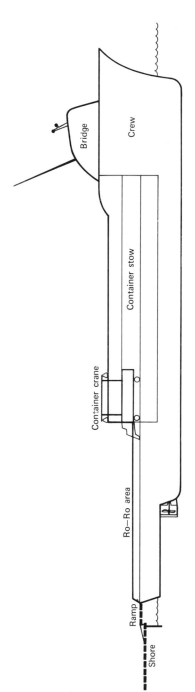

FIGURE 17-5. SPV Ro-Ro/containership (Source: The Rath Company).

into account the number of ships required for each mission, the SPV fleet per diem rate is lower by 15 to 30 percent in every case than the other fleet rate.

BASIC COSTS AND ASSUMPTIONS

Tables 17-4 and 17-5 present, by individual cost element, SPV and the other per-ship annual operation and support costs from which the preceding cost comparisons were developed. Only crew and fuel costs differ by operating mode for the SPV, while only fuel costs vary for the other ship. An attempt was made wherever possible to assure that the cost cate-

TABLE 17-4. SMALL PORT VESSEL ANNUAL PER-SHIP
OPERATION AND SUPPORT COSTS
(COSTS IN 1967 DOLLARS)

		Constant Costs (Over 10 Years)
	Case I	235,383
Crew	Case II	177,828
	Case III	289,936
	(A & B)	
Replacement Training Services		121
	Case I	113,434
Fuel	Case II	128,022
	Case III	106,755
	(A & B)	
General Stores		15,624
Insurance		36,000
Regulatory-Body Survey		2,000
Maintenance & Repair		36,000
Overhaul		18,000
Material Support		36,000
Operating Supervisor		96,000
	Case I	5,561,620
TOTAL (10 years' Operation & Support)	Case II	5,131,950
	Case III	5,430,360
	(A & B)	

TABLE 17-5. COMPETITIVE SHIP—ANNUAL PER-SHIP OPERATION & SUPPORT COSTS
(ALL COSTS IN 1967 DOLLARS)

		Constant Costs (Over 10 Years)	Variable Costs									
			YR 1	YR 2	YR 3	YR 4	YR 5	YR 6	YR 7	YR 8	YR 9	YR 10
Crew		331,523										
Fuel	Case I	147,781										
	Case II	149,544										
	Case III (A & B)	131,846										
Accident & Damage		6,300										
Maintenance & Repair		35,000										
Overhaul				135,000	135,000		135,000	135,000		135,000	135,000	
Material Support		70,000										
Total Administrative Expenses (Over 10 Years)	Case I	671,604										
	Case II	673,367										
	Case III (A & B)	655,669										
TOTAL (10 Years' Operation & Support)	Case I	7,253,320										
	Case II	7,272,360										
	Case III (A & B)	7,081,230										

gories for both ships correspond to each other, so that the comparisons of per-ship totals have meaning. The SPV insurance cost element corresponds to the accident and damage category of the competitive ship, and SPV operating supervision corresponds in concept to administrative expenses of the other ship. It was assumed that the material-support-cost element of the competitive ship includes costs that are grouped under general stores for the SPV.

SPV COST ASSUMPTIONS AND SOURCES

These annual per-ship cost computations were based on the assumptions presented in Table 17-6. For the SPV, the insurance, maintenance and repair, material support, and operating supervision costs, as well as stores and supplies costs, are designer estimates. Fuel and lubricants costs were calculated from the typical General Motors marine diesel engine data on typical ship supplies for 645E5 12-cylinder turbocharged engines and accessories. Annual regulatory-body survey charges were estimated from those for commercial ships of similar physical characteristics. As an approximation, we have averaged total life-cycle survey costs and applied a constant annual cost. The assumption does not affect the results.

Total annual SPV crew costs per ship are the sum of base pay plus pension and welfare costs for a civilian crew plus repatriation costs. Table 17-7 gives a detailed breakdown of base pay and benefits. Transportation costs included here are those in addition to annual repatriation costs.

Annual fuel costs were developed for each of the three operating profiles based on the total fuel consumption per typical voyage or scenario and on the number of voyages per operating year of 330 days. Fuel consumption differs for time spent at sea, in port, and at the beach. The number of hours spent at sea per voyage depends on the round-trip distance for the operation and on the ship speed. The number of hours spent in port and on the beach were assumed to be the same for the SPV as for all modes. This estimate is a conservative one for the SPV, since it does not take into account any possible increases in efficiency in loading or discharging cargo which might occur because of its unique ramp design and its exceptional stability while beached. Nor does it take into account the quicker departures made possible by the SPV's shallow draft and its independence of the tide.

TABLE 17-6. VESSEL ANNUAL OPERATION AND SUPPORT COSTS

SPV Cost Element	Conversion Formula	Physical & Cost Factors	Sources
Crew	$C_{li} = (P_t \times M) + (S \times D_s \times K)$ $+ (B \times P_b \times D_{bi}) + (R \times K)$	$P_t = \$11,804.67$—total monthly pay + pension and welfare	estimate based on commercial rates for twin-screw ship
		$M = 12$—months/year	
		$S = \$2.00$—subsistence cost/day/man (overseas)	
		$D_s = 365$—days/yr. overseas	assumption that overhauls take place overseas
		$K = 11$—total crew members/ship	designer estimate
		$B = 100\%$—base pay percent increase bonus per day in bonus area	
		$P_b = \$230.22$—Total crew base pay/day	estimate based on commercial rates for Class D, twin-screw ship
		$D_b = \left\{\begin{array}{l} \text{CASE I} = 330 \\ \text{CASE II} = 80 \\ \text{CASE III} = 302 \end{array}\right\}$—days/ year in bonus area	estimate based on speed (17.5 kn) and operating profile; assume ship in bonus area within 50 miles of coast
		$R = \$884$—repatriation cost/man	
		$i = 1,2,3$—case index	
		$\left.\begin{array}{l} 1 = \text{CASE I} \\ 2 = \text{CASE II} \\ 3 = \text{CASE III} \end{array}\right\}$	

TABLE 17-6. (Continued)

SPV Cost Element	Conversion Formula	Physical & Cost Factors	Sources
Replacement (services only)	$C_2 = (T \times K \times A) \times D_t$	$T = \$44.$—civil marine training cost/man/day	Navy estimate for FDLS cost analysis
		$K = 11$—total crew members/ship	designer estimate
		$A = .25$—civil marine turnover rate/year	
		$D_t = 1$—days required for training	estimate based on assumption that crew does not participate in loading and discharging of cargo
General stores	$C_3 = (S \times M) + (H_y/H_l \times L \times C_1 \times E)$	$S = \$10,000$—stores and supplies cost/month	designer estimate
		$M = 12$—months/year	
		$H_y = 7,920$—operating hours/year	assumption of 330 operating days/year
		$H_l = 750$—hours between lubricant changes	
		$L = 312$—ship lubricant capacity (gal.)	General Motors Electro-Motive Marine Application Data EMD645 Diesels
		$C_t = \$.55$—lub. oil cost/gal.	designer estimate of commercial costs
		$E = 2$—number of engines	

TABLE 17-6. (Continued)

SPV Cost Element	Conversion Formula	Physical & Cost Factors	Sources
Fuel	$$C_{4i} = \sum_{j=1}^{3} \left(F_{e_{i,j}} \times E_{i,j} \right) \\ \times H_{v_{i,j}} \times V_i \times C_{fi}$$	$i = 1,2,3$—case index $1 = \begin{cases} \text{Case I} \\ \text{Case II} \\ \text{Case III} \end{cases}$ $2 =$ $3 =$ $j = 1,2,3$—steaming profile location index $\begin{cases} 1 = \text{at sea} \\ 2 = \text{in port} \\ 3 = \text{at beach} \end{cases}$ for all i $F_{e_{i,j}} \& = \begin{cases} 1 = 104 \\ 2 = 13 \\ 3 = 48.87 \end{cases}$ for j —engine fuel consumption rate in gal./hr./engine	assumption that diesels operate at sea, generator operates in port, and 3 thrusters operate at the beach Fuel consumption data for a) diesels—General Motors *Electro-Motive Marine Application Data EMD645 Diesel Engines* b) generator—designor estimate c) thrusters
		for all i $E_{i,j} \& = \begin{cases} 1 = 2 \\ 2 = 1 \\ 3 = 3 \end{cases}$ for j —number of engines or generators operating	SPV design

479

TABLE 17-6. (Continued)

SPV Cost Element	Conversion Formula	Physical & Cost Factors	Sources
Fuel (cont.)		$H_{v_{i,j}}$ for $i = 1$, $j =$ $\begin{cases} 1 = 22.86 \\ 2 = 24 \\ 3 = 24 \end{cases}$ for $i = 2$, $j =$ $\begin{cases} 1 = 154.29 \\ 2 = 48 \\ 3 = 48 \end{cases}$ for $i = 3$, $j =$ $\begin{cases} 1 = 432 \\ 2 = 528 \\ 3 = 216 \end{cases}$ —hours per voyage in location for each case	based on operating profile: distances and assumptions of hours spent in port or on beach, and on SPV speed (17.5 kn) **CASE I** Round-trip distance 400 n mi; 24 hours in port; 24 hours at beach **CASE II** Round-trip distance 2,700 n mi; 48 hours in port at each end **CASE III** 18 days at sea; 22 days in port; 9 days at beach
		V_i, for $i =$ $\begin{cases} 1 = 112 \\ 2 = 32 \\ 3 = 7 \end{cases}$ —number of voyages/year for each case	based on 7,920 operating hours per year and total hours computed per voyage
		C_{fv} for all $i = \$.12$—cost diesel fuel/gal.	

TABLE 17-6. (Continued)

SPV Cost Element	Conversion Formula	Physical & Cost Factors	Sources
Insurance	$C_5 = I \times M_y$	$I = \$3,000$—monthly insurance cost/ship $M_y = 12$—month/year	designer estimate
Regulatory-body survey	$C_6 = C_6$	$C_6 = \$2,000$	American Bureau of Shipping, *Rate Schedule of Charges for Inspections*
Maintenance and repair	$C_7 = R \times M_y$	$R = \$3,000$—maintenance & repair cost/month $M_y = 12$—months/year	designer estimate
Overhaul	$C_8 = O_m \times M_y$	$O_m = \$1,500$—overhaul cost/month $M_y = 12$—months/year	designer estimate
Material support	$C_9 = G \times M_y$	$G = \$300$—gear replacement cost/month $M_y = 12$—months/year	designer estimate
Operating supervision	$C_{10} = S_o \times M_y$	$S_o = \$8,000$—marine superintendence per month $M_y = 12$—months per year	designer estimate

TABLE 17-7. SMALL PORT VESSEL—MANNING COST

Rating	Number	Monthly Pay	Per Day
Master	1	1,230.02	+ P&W* $6.02
Chief Mate	1	730.06	+ P&W* $6.02
2nd Mate	1	645.50	+ P&W* $6.02
Chief Engineer	1	1,067.00	+ P&W $7.17
1st Asst. Engineer	1	705.37	+ P&W $7.17
2nd Asst. Engineer	1	623.67	+ P&W $7.17
Able Seamen	3 @392.58	1,177.74	+ P&W $4.25 (Approx.)
Chief Cook/Steward	1	525.27	+ P&W $4.25 (Approx.)
Messman	1	302.56	+ P&W $4.25 (Approx.)
TOTAL	11	7,007.19	

Total Monthly Pay		7,007.19
Est. 40% O.T.		2,802.88
M.M.P. P&W Plan	541.80	
M.E.B.A. P&W Plan	645.30	
N.M.U. P&W Plan	637.50	
Total Pension & Welfare	1,824.60	1,824.60
Est. of Transportation		170.00
Est. Monthly Crew Costs 5/2167		11,804.67

* Pension and Welfare.

SENSITIVITY ANALYSIS

An analysis of the sensitivity conclusions to changes in the above assumptions for individual cost elements was made in order to determine whether the SPV would remain the least-cost ship. A worst high-cost case was chosen for the SPV by:

1. Adding a management fee of $33,000 per ship per year ($100 per operating day ;
2. Escalating crew base pay and benefits by five percent for each succeeding year ;
3. Increasing regulatory-body survey charges from $2,000 per year to $5,000 per year.

It is clear that the worst-case SPV fleet has the least cost in life-cycle terms for all the mission-cargo productivity cases analyzed. Each ship type has characteristics which affect its use in small ports, in certain feeder areas or under certain trading conditions. Table 17-8 compares 25 proposed feederships, as far as technical characteristics are concerned.

TABLE 17-8. COMPARISON OF SMALL CONTAINERSHIPS

Ship Name	Overall Length L.O.A. (ft.)	Length B.P. L.B.P. (ft.)	Moulded Beam B (ft.)	Moulded Depth D (ft.)	Draught H (ft.)	D.splt. Tons (tons)	Total DWT. (tons)	Service SPEED (knots)	Rated B.H.P.	Gross Tonnage	Capacity in terms of 20 × 8 × 8 I.S.O. Containers	Container Capacity Rating 4X = 125 16X = 500	Basic Type
1 "DEER" CLASS 3 Vessels e.g. "IMPALA"	250.0	222.0	35.5	20.0	13.0		1,500	12.5	1,320		63	2X	C.C.V.
2 "HUSTLER" CLASS 19 Vessels e.g. "MINHO"	279.8	258.3	44.9	19.8	15.4		2,100	15/16	3,200	430	124	4X (3X)	C.C.V.
3 SEAFREIGHT-LINER I & II	388.5	366.0	53.0	28.0	14.5	5,470	3,213	13.5	3,780	4,034	218	7X	C.C.V.
4 "GREYHOUND"		317.0	61.5	25.0	12.95		4,180	14.5	6,000		(320) 211 × 35 ft.	6X	C.C.V.
5 VUYK & ZONEN 1971	366.0	366.0	56.0		20.4		4,820	17 TRIAL	6,600	3,200	329	10X (7X)	C.C.V.
6 "ANTARES"	250.7	223.1	42.7	32.4	13.75		1,123	14.6	2,200	499.9	70	2X	R-O-R-O
7 "SCANDIC"	248.0	222.0	46.0	35.0			1,100	17.0		844 (313)	85	2X	R-O-R-O
8 "HAWEA"	366.3	338.0	56.0	35.0	16.2	5,490	2,610	16.5	8,000	2,926 (801)		(4X)	R-O-R-O
9 Olsen's "BOMMA" (R-O-R-O, side-ports, crane derricks)	285.0		49.2	35.6			2,700	15.0	4,000	1,600		4X (3X)	R-O-R-O

TABLE 17-8. (Continued)

Ship Name	Overall Length L.O.A. (ft.)	Length B.P. L.B.P. (ft.)	Moulded Beam B (ft.)	Moulded Depth D (ft.)	Draught H (ft.)	Displt. Tons (tons)	Total DWT. (tons)	Service SPEED (knots)	Rated B.H.P.	Gross Tonnage	Capacity in terms of 20 × 8 × 8 I.S.O. Containers	Container Capacity Rating 4X = 125 16X = 500	Basic Type
10 "TRANSCON-TAINER I"	342.6	315.0	61.3	21.33	15.35		1,800	15.0	4,400		192	6X (3X)	R-O-R-O
11 "DESTRO"	360.3	328.0	63.0	42.6	16.25	5,260	2,820	17.5	8,000 B.H.P.	1,599	186	6X (4X)	R-O-R-O
12 "MAHENO"	429.5	400.0	63.0	40.0	19.58	9,150	5,050	18.0	13,000	4,510 (1,660)		(8X)	R-O-R-O
13 AEROMAR "M.S.S."	178.0	175.0	28	12.0	8.0	714	253	12.5	900	300	14		F.F.V.
14 "ATLANTIC SHORE"	155.0	130.0	33.5	12.95	11.4		810	13.0	2,400	499	(30)	X	F.F.V.
15 MOK & HILL Feeder Vessel	176.0	167.3	38.0	13.0	11.0	1,360	590	11.75	2,250	193	(22)	X	F.F.V.
16 Erio Rath's S.P.V.	286.0	261.0	49.25	20.5	12.33	2,415	1,400	14.5	3,200	192	112	4X	F.F.V.
17 TUG "CABO ROJO" BARGE	95.0	—	—	—	Equitable Equipment Co. standard tug						—		T. & B.
"ST. CROIX"	200.0		56.0	13.3	Puerto Rico Lighterage (1,500 cargo dwt.)				(1,900) —	1,200	(60) 30 × 40 ft. trailers	2X	
18 "HYDROCONIC" TUG "CASTLE COVE"	98.75	89.25	26.5	15.0	12.5	400.0		12.3 (FREE RUNNING)	1,230	22.5 TON BOLLARD PULL			T.
19 OLSEN BARGE	275.0	68.0	19.5				2,000				337	(3X)	B.

TABLE 17-8. (Continued)

Ship Name	Overall Length L.O.A. (ft.)	Length B.P. L.B.P. (ft.)	Moulded Beam B (ft.)	Moulded Depth D (ft.)	Draught H (ft.)	Displt. Tons (tons)	Total DWT. (tons)	Service SPEED (knots)	Rated B.H.P.	Gross Tonnage	Capacity in terms of 20 × 8 × 8 I.S.O. Containers	Container Capacity Rating 4X = 125 16X = 500	Basic Type
20 TUG "DIANA L. MORAN" V-NOTCH STERN BARGE	— 290					6,000			1,750				T. & B.
21 "SEA-LINK" TUG BARGE NO. 69 "RELIANCE"		85 —					— 1,500	(12)	500.0 —				T. & B.
22 Hakker's Multi-purpose standard coaster.	165.0	150.0	—				800	8.0	800		28	X	Cargo
23 "BAPBEL BOLTEN"	284.6	259.0	47.8	24.75	12.5		1,442 cargo	14.6	2,500		88	2X	Cargo
24 "ORWELL FISHER"	295.6	274.0	49.25	24.9	15.2	3,750	2,523	14.0	2,450	1,733	116	3X	Cargo
25 "COLCHESTER": Before	226.0		37.0	23.0	13.25		935.			866.0	86	2X	Cargo
Conversion: After	280.0		37.0	23.0	14.60		1,810.0			1,946.0			C.C.V.
26 REMARKS								Figures in brackets estimated		Net tonnage in brackets	Figures in brackets estimated	Figure in brackets based on cargo deadweight	

SOURCE: New Zealand Institution of Engineers.

485

Table 17-9 compares the four groups of those ships in their cargo handling methods and effectiveness. Table 17-10 then establishes, as a result of these two tables, required freight rate structure, which affects the economics of the ship operation.

TABLE 17-9.   CARGO HANDLING METHODS COMPARISON

	Barge Carrier	Containers Carrier	Pallet Carrier	Conventional Cargo Vessel
Bale Capacity (million c. ft.)	1.2	1.2	1.2	0.8
No. of barges/containers	62 barges	1,130 cont'rs.	—	—
Cargo carried p.a. (million tons)	1.04	1.09	1.0	0.8
Cargo handling rate	4 barges per hour	40 cont'- per hour	250 tons per hour	110 tons per hour
RCMR. (Bale cap.)	7.0	3.9	2.7	1.0
Total Time per R.T. (days)	abt 21	abt 21	abt 28	abt 42
Ships in service (weekly service)	3	3	4	6
Building price per ship ($m.)	8.4	10.5	9.2	5.3
Total investment ($m.)	42.46	38.3	37.15	31.8
Total yearly ship related costs ($m.)	9.21	10.42	10.06	9.57
Ships cost per ton cargo transported	8.85	9.60	10.05	12.00
Handling cost per ton transported	14.00	11.50	8.60	20.00
Total transported cost per ton cargo ($U.S.)	22.85 (108%)	21.10 (100%)	18.65 (82%)	32.00 (152%)

Source: New Zealand Institution of Engineers.

TABLE 17-10. REQUIRED FREIGHT RATE

A comparison of four ship types able to carry 125 standard 20 ft. × 8 ft. I.S.O. containers.

Ships assumed in operation 330 days per year.
Length of Voyage = 520 nautical miles per round trip. (Round Trip = 1,040 miles).
Fuel consumption (all purposes) = 0.4 lbs/SHP/Hour.

BASIC type (4X rating)	Cellular container vessel "IMPALA"	Fast "feeder" vessel Rath's "SPV"	Roll-on roll-off vessel "ANTARES"	Container Barge (US) Puerto-Rico Lighterage Company "ST. CROIX"	Tug "CABO ROJO"	REMARKS
1 Type ship	"IMPALA"	Rath's "SPV"	"ANTARES"	"ST. CROIX"	"CABO ROJO"	
2 Displacement (tons)	2,560	2,515	3,080	1,950		Estimated
3 Total dwt. (tons)	1,500	1,500	1,500	1,250		
4 Cargo dwt. (tons)	1,250	1,250	1,250	1,250		Basis
5 Service speed V (knots)	13.0	16.5	14.5	8.0 towed	8.0 towing	
6 Length between perps. L.B.P. (ft.)	222	270	223.1	200.0	95.0	
7 Beam B. (ft.)	35.5	49.25	42.66	56.0		
8 Depth D. (ft.)	20.0	20.5	32.42	13.3		To Upper Dk.
9 Draught H. (ft.)	13.0	12.33	13.75			
10 Power (B.H.P.)	1,350	3,200	2,200		1700/1900	
11 Cubic No.	158	272	309	149		1000
12 Block Coeff.	0.873	0.512	0.748	0.900		$L \times B \times D$ Derived
13 Stell Wt. (tons)	616	685	1,130	660		Estimated

TABLE 17-10. (Continued)

BASIC type (4X rating)	Cellular container vessel	Fast "feeder" vessel	Roll-on roll-off vessel	Container Barge (US) Puerto-Rico Lighterage Company	Tug	REMARKS
14 Outfit Wt. (tons)	238	120	277	40		Estimated
15 Container guides	70	—	—	—		Estimated
16 Machinery Wt. (tons)	136.0	210	173	—		Estimated
17 Light Ship. (tons)	1,060	1,015	1,580	700		Estimated
				TUG & BARGE AS A UNIT		
18 Sea days per R.T.	1.67	1.31	1.49	2.70		520/24xV
19 Port days per R.T.	1.75	1.42	1.58	1.42		Estimated
20 Total days per R.T.	3.42	2.73	3.07	4.12		
21 R.T. per year	96.6	121.0	109.7	80.2		330 p.a. ÷ (20)
22 Sea days per year	160	159	164	217		(18) × (21)
23 Port days per year	170	171	166	113		(19) × (21)
24 Total crew (actual)	11 (G)	8 (US)	10 (UK)	—		
25 Total crew (assumed)	10	10	10	6		
Crew plus relief	12	12	12	8		Including 2 on leave
26 Cost of ship (US$) = Owners Investment = P	1.515 m	2.00 m	2.15 m	1.39 m	0.402 m	Estimated
27 Crew cost %	64.0	64.0	64.0	48.0		
28 Maintenance and repairs %	9.4	16.3	9.4	9.9		

TABLE 17-10. (Continued)

BASIC type (4X rating)	Cellular container vessel	Fast "feeder" vessel	Roll-on roll-off vessel	Container Barge (US) Porto Rico Lighterage Company	Tug	REMARKS
29 Stores and supplies %	4.5	4.5	4.50	2.7		
30 P. & I. %	4.3	4.3	4.3	2.6		
31 Hull and Machinery						
Insurance %	6.3	8.0	8.0	3.6		
32 Overhead %	2.7	3.2	2.8	2.5		
33 Fuel Costs %	8.8	19.7	14.0	15.2		
34 Effective Rate	100.0%	120.0%	135.0%	84.5%		Excluding "in-port" costs

"Deciding on a Feeder Service," Peter L. Dawson.

For the net revenue to increase with the inclusion of transshipment traffic $(K_3 + K_4)R$ must exceed K_3C/V, i.e., K_4/K_3 must exceed $(C - RV)/RV$,

where K_3 = number of loaded containers (per year) discharged and then transshipped
K_4 = number of loaded containers (per year) put aboard to be transshipped
C = ship operators cost per round trip
R = gross revenue per container carried
V = maximum number of containers a ship can carry.

The above amplifies the quotation given in the main text.

489

TABLE 17-10. (Continued)

	BASIC type	C.C.V.	F.F.V.	R.O.R.O.	TUG & BARGE	REMARKS
35	(CRF) P.	34.7%	45.9%	49.20%	22.8%	i = 20% before tax
						n = 15 years.
36	Operating costs	24.1%	28.8%	25.8%	19.1%	Same as 34.
37	In port costs	41.2%	50.8%	23.5%	33.7%	Port dues + cargo handling
38	Total Average Average Annual Operating Costs	100.0% (3)	125.5% (4)	98.5% (2)	75.6% (1)	35 + 36 + 37
21	Round Trips p.a.	96.6	121.0	109.7	80.2	
39	Cargo p.a. (tons) ÷ 10,000	24.15	30.25	27.43	20.05	(4) × (21)
40	Containers p.a. (min.) ÷ 1,000	12.075	15.125	13.715	10.025	(22) = 20 tons
41	(RFR per ton) (RFR Per container)	100.0% (3)	100.2% (3)	86.5% (1)	91.2% (2)	Including "in-port" costs
42	(RFR per ton) (RFR per container)	100.0 (2)	102.0% (3)	112.4% (4)	77.8% (1)	Excluding "in-port" costs

TABLE 17-10. (Continued)

BASIC type	C.C.V.	F.F.V.	R.O.R.O.	TUG & BARGE	REMARKS
43 Modified "Figure of Merit"	1.16	1.17	1.31	0.94	Marine Tech. July 1968.
	(2)	(2)	(1)	(4)	
44 Transport Efficiency, E	12.0	6.5	8.0	5.6	Mar. Rep. Feb. 1, 1970.
	(1)	(3)	(2)	(4)	

MEASURES OF MERIT

Apart from those methods which bring in AAC, PW and DCF there is a variety of formulae, simple and complicated, used as "yardsticks."

Applied consistently over a period of time to one ship, or one type of ship, they will service their purpose. Two have been shown in Table 2 (above).

The majority do not consider operating costs and are therefore "hydrodynamic" rather than economic "efficiencies."

$$\text{Modified "Figure of Merit"} = \frac{\text{Payload} \times \text{Speed} \times 1{,}000}{\text{AAC} \times (15 \text{ years})}$$

$$\text{Transport Efficiency, E} = \frac{\text{Payload} \times \text{Speed}}{\text{Power}}$$

Source: New Zealand Institution of Engineers.

491

INTERDISCIPLINARY ENVIRONMENT

Rapid and unpredictable changes in our post-industrial society have made the techniques of business management taught in textbooks no longer valid. To find new approaches we must identify and explore our needs.

Dr. Kazuo Noda
Japan Research Institute, 1971

18

Man–Container Interface

DIVISION OF LABOR

Conventional ocean transportation functioned with a simple separation of labor and management. The shipowner provided the sea-going labor to handle the ship. The stevedore handled the cargo ashore, and from the shore onto the vessel or vice versa with longshoremen labor. But containerization means integration of both into an intermodal, unified ship operation with land–cargo interface. The ship is now merely a sea-going tractor to move the container over the water, just as the truck tractor moves its trailer on land. The new containerization systems operator, thus, is an employer of both seamen and longshoremen. For good measure, truck drivers and clerks are added to it. Railroads will also be affected soon. Even ship operations which still use independent agents instead of their own shore operations provide labor force integration. True intermodal systems, such as Sea-Land, Matson, and CTO operators, involve land handling forces beyond the port zone and often hundreds of miles from the interface of land and sea. Seatrain Line's parent company owns a railroad line and has arranged through-land bridge services based on the Inter-Change Regulations of the Interstate Commerce Act.

ONE FOR ALL

Since the maritime phase of containerization is the key element at this time, this discussion will deal primarily with the man–container interface in this field. At the time of writing this book, the United States was involved in two dock strikes. Also, a major strike had just occurred in the railroads. There is a tendency among labor to unify. Even if unification does not take place, the bargaining method displayed by the longshore labor may offer a dangerously inviting pattern for the rest of transportation labor. Therefore, the labor solutions suggested for an integrated interface at the waterfront should as well be applied for methods which affect other types of coordinated, integrated transportation.

HAMBURG PRINCIPLES

Since 1934, the International Transport Workers Federation (ITWF) studied transport coordination and its effects on the labor market at its headquarters in Amsterdam. Both studies ran parallel with an extensive analysis conducted by the International Chamber of Commerce in Paris dealing with segmented transportation and competition between the media. The author had the privilege to cooperate with both these studies and therefore gained knowledge of the hopes and fears of both labor and management.

As a result of these activities, the Inland Transport Committee of the International Labor Organization (ILO) presented a study entitled, "Methods of Improving Organization of Work and Output in Ports." After discussion, this study resulted in the preparation of Resolution No. 66, adopted by the ILO Conference in Hamburg, Germany, which therefore came to be known as "The Hamburg Guidelines." The principles were developed to protect port output from continued labor stoppages. Although containerization was in its mere infancy, it was recognized by labor for its dual effect, namely, the economy of scale and the displacement of manpower by capital-furnished machinery. Ever since the Hamburg Resolution, labor has developed its case for the protection of its diminishing job offerings. Since the days of the replacement of weavers by textile machinery in England, there has never been as great a tool for labor union leaders to exercise their rule over their membership than containerization. The fear of losing employment and the concurrent problems of middle aged, untrained men to make a living in our highly technical society comprise the spectrum that haunts the transfer from old-fashioned transportation methods to productivity. However, this problem demands a solution if containerization is to be allowed to serve the world community and retain the character of free enterprise.

RESOLUTION 66

The lengthy Resolution 66 can be summarized in the 12 important criteria which manpower solidification in the container age is suggested to accomplish.

1. **Labor organization:** The cooperation of labor to improve productivity in the ports is also dependent on psychological factors which are often not sufficiently appreciated and somewhat difficult to assess. Since labor sees in the union the representatives of its own rights toward the employer there must be recognition of the rights of the union to analyze the problems with its members and to carry forward the legitimate demands to management.

2. **Fear factor:** With the admitted tendency of ever fuller automation and further elimination of human labor as links in the container-transport chain, labor is at all times rightfully fearful of being replaced, substituted, or otherwise made redundant.

3. **Adjustment of work rules:** Since the relations between labor and management are developed while the technology changes, there must be the right to adjust work rules and increase human effectiveness accordingly.

4. **Divisions of work:** Containerization is particularly exposed to the link system in the door-to-door delivery chain. Since each mode has its own trade union, the line-up of the divisions and responsibility gives cause to jurisdictional frictions.

5. **Sharing benefits:** In order to insure the highest productivity leading to high standards of living, the benefits of higher productivity should be equitably distributed among management, labor, and users of containerization. It is difficult to decide how these benefits are to be shared. Productivity analysis is required to study the contribution of labor and management in light of further mechanization and automation.

6. **Guaranteed wage and steady men:** Labor, more and more, is coming to demand a pattern that requires a guaranteed, annual minimum wage. With the regularity of containership services, such an arrangement can be good for both management and labor.

7. **Grievances and disputes:** Since a free society cannot coerce any section of its population to work under conditions which are not freely and generally acceptable, the machinery for relief of grievances must be adjusted to the promotion of work integration. Suitable machinery must be established at all appropriate levels for the observation of and application of agreements which deal with the grievances of individuals or groups of union members.

8. **Safety and welfare:** Safety measures are often developed from experiences made during the operation. In many countries, including the United States, safety enforcement is part of government control duties.

9. **Discipline and supervision:** The more mechanized an interface operation becomes, the more important is the discipline among the workers as related to their jobs. The lack of discipline may show itself in a number of ways, such as loafing on the job, taking unauthorized rest periods during work, starting late, knocking off early, and adopting turn-taking or go-slow tactics.

10. **Organization of work:** Port work requires an intimate relationship between many different crafts often having divergent interests. Containerization, which is nothing but planned interfacing made easy, must count on close cooperation of all the sectors employing these crafts.

11. **Resistance to change:** Many of the problems in implementation of containerization are the results of psychological impacts on men as well as management. From a psychological point of view, the container transport worker must feel that he is essential to the success, that his skills are important to the mission, and that he has a regarded, honorable profession.

12. **New equipment and techniques:** Without prejudice to any legislation or practice regarding retrenchment benefits or similar measures, the competent authorities or employers, or both, should take all practicable steps to ensure that methods of improving organization of work or the introduction of new equipment do not lead to sudden or arbitrary dismissals from the industry nor to a permanent accentuation of the casual character of the employment.

New types of mechanical equipment, whether they are for use on board ship or on the shore, and new methods of work, when they are efficient, economic, and safe are also desirable. They should contribute to easing the work of the dockworker and to speeding up the turnaround of ships. Figure 18-1 shows the assessment of the effects of labor intensity vs. capital intensity in the development of a typical containerization case.

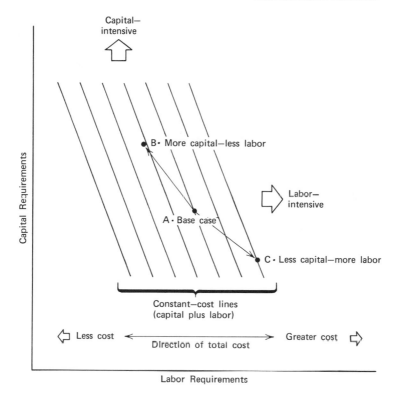

FIGURE 18-1.   CAPITAL–LABOR REQUIREMENT SHIFTS FOR FIXED OUTPUT.

EQUITABLE DEMANDS

The Hamburg meeting and the guidelines described above were re-confirmed by a "Tripartite Technical Meeting on Dock Labour in Rotterdam," April 1969, at which Mr. T. W. Gleason, President of the International Longshoremen's Association (ILA), represented the United States labor group. By this time the important changes in cargo handling were reflected in a document entitled "Conclusion Concerning the Social Repercussions of the Introduction of Unit Load Systems." Item No. 32, the most important one of this document for labor, states:

> *CONDITIONS OF WORK AND LIFE*—Dock workers should share in the benefits secured by the introduction of new methods of cargo handling.

Item 26 appears to be the most important one for management; it states:

> *LABOR-MANAGEMENT RELATIONS*—Where it does not already exist, appropriate joint industrial machinery should be set up with the view to

creating a climate of confidence and cooperation between dock workers and port operators or employers in which social and technical change can be brought about without tension or conflict and grievances promptly settled in accordance with the Examination of Grievances Recommendation, 1967 (#130).

One must always remember that the International Labor Organization is made up of representatives of the governments, employers, and labor. Therefore, the outcome of discussions leading to the guidelines are tempered with the realities of transportation's life.

WORLD REALITIES

In the extreme, labor's greatest fear is to become redundant. On the side of management, continued strife with work interruptions can mean to the corporate structure what the layoff means to labor. In other words, both groups fear not a loss of profit, a loss of opportunity, or a squeeze between spiraling cost and traffic limitations, but both actually fear the end of their "way of life"—the end of participating in the transportation industry.

The effects of the changeover personified by containerization have come to the whole world. A ship line servicing a country which prohibits the use of containers and the country which is no longer prepared for break-bulk cargo cannot give efficient integrated service. The theory of labor's participation in containerization requires at least a minimum of acceptable conditions for both ends of the line. Therefore, a review of the outstanding examples of labor on the waterfronts of the world is indicated. We select the countries which have significant, unique positions with regard to the operation of containers. This does not include other types of unitized cargo—such as roll-on, roll-off ships, palletization, or the LASH-type vessels—as they may be subject to more specialized jurisdiction.

Japan

The Japanese labor position is in accordance with the general paternal system. Longshore labor is normally employed as long as the enterprise remains active. Conditions in Japan's ports have been changing toward containerization, but since there is a great demand for labor there have been no layoffs to speak of. The entire picture is harmonious, and Japan's labor unions are advocates of the implementation of mechanized methods in the port.

USSR

Under the Russian labor regulations, the state enterprises have the right to relocate labor. Russia is right now entering the container age and one cannot find any special considerations exceeding the Hamburg guidelines.

Venezuela

Venezuela has been the battlefront of the first attempts by Grace Line to implement containerization in the early '50s. Since the political body took sides with labor unions in the Port of La Guaira, Grace Line was forced to abandon its service there. Laws were passed which prohibited the use of containers, and to date Venezuela is the only country strongly opposed to any use of containerization. The local national steamship companies of Venezuela and Colombia (partners in Grancolombiana Steamship Lines) first used small nonstandard boxes for shipside package service, but now have 750 standard 20-ft. units.

Venezuela became the outstanding example of the false promise that stopping containerization would hold up labor's prosperity. Conditions brought about by intermodal transportation, if properly planned, do just the opposite. Increased opportunities to enlarge trade will benefit the labor force. Even if a government develops a productivity standard, the growth can be used to indemnify the redundant labor.

Great Britain & Europe

The European management attitude is best characterized by the statement of Dr. J. P. Backx, President of ICHCA and of the Rotterdam Port Employers Association: "Containerization will bring about a reduction of labor. How big this reduction will be cannot be said at the present moment." Europe has had many problems adjusting to the new revolutions in transportation. Uncertainty and fear of unemployment have played havoc with the work force. There have been two important trends, one to assure permanent labor opportunities for certain numbers of steady men and the other to develop a training program. This training program is a three-year apprenticeship leading to a certificated position. Specialization courses for crane operators, signal men, mechanics, and similar skills follow for those who appear qualified.

Mexico

Mexico, which has a gradually developing transportation network, has had excellent labor relations in its ports. Mexican longshore labor unions resemble guilds which were common during the Middle Ages. The union contracts with the ship operator as agent for handling on a per-ton basis or on a ship basis. The experiences made in Ensenada during the West Coast dock strike included use of containers. This Mexican attitude provides a valid possibility for many developing nations, and it is understood that the governments of Thailand, the Philippines, and Indonesia are thinking along similar terms.

United States—East Coast and Gulf

The International Longshoremen's Association is directed by Thomas W. Gleason, who participated in the guideline developments during the Rotterdam meeting. Gleason's expressed attitude is that his union is fully aware of the diminishing job picture. Therefore, he wants to get the most out of the shipping industry while the picture still allows him to exercise the role of power.

In October 1969, Gleason spoke at the Baltimore Container meeting, at which time he said:

We of the ILA are resolved to save the economic life of the dock worker. We will not see him consigned to a slow economic death which the shipping industry has in mind for him. We intend to see to it that containers or no containers, the traditional work of the dock worker shall not be taken from him and, furthermore, he will have employment in all new work categories which substitute for his traditional functions.

ILA pattern: Since that time the ILA has won two very significant measures:

1. The container stuffing rules, calling for a 50-mile circle with its radius extending out from the center of each port;
2. The guaranteed annual income (GAI), which went into effect October 1, 1965, and assured 2,080 hours of pay (40 hours a week for 52 weeks/year) whether they work or not. This amounts to $9,568.00 per man per year.

Although all unions on the United States East Coast and Gulf Coast, with the exception of Fort Pierce, Florida (no local labor union), are under the jurisdiction of Teddy Gleason (as he is commonly known), not all labor unions have enjoyed the same benefits.

The New York employers agreed to GAI in anticipation of a large freight movement in containers. This did not come about as planned. On the busiest days, according to the Wall Street Journal, 13,000 men were working cargo, 4,000 more were collecting GAI and 1,000 were sick, on vacation, or absent for some other reason. Employers claim that 2,000 men averaged about one work day per week the past year. The latter figure is prevalent among the workers on banana docks in Wehawken, New Jersey.

Another unique regulation which protects longshore labor in the Port of New York, even if they do not work, is the "inverse seniority principle." This system permits longshoremen to pass up a job and let it go to a man with lower seniority without losing a day's pay for refusing work. If there were shortages of 50 men to work shifts, the debiting for job refusal would begin with the lowest man and proceed upward. Otherwise, the union claims older men would be overworked while younger men would sit about collecting GAI.

Other Ports

South Atlantic and Gulf of Mexico ports do not have the GAI benefits. Baltimore and Philadelphia guarantee only 1,800 hours and Hampton Roads 1,600 hours. The Port of Boston guarantees 2,080 hours as does New York, but employs only 1,200 workers, and this small number is kept busy every day.

MANAGEMENT ATTITUDE IN NEW YORK

The cost of the settlement in New York was accepted by the shipping industry because there are divergent views among their management, who are members of the negotiating NYSA. The container lines are typified by Michael R. McEvoy, Chairman of Sea-Land. A former school teacher, he has the attitude which any humanitarian would have, that it is best to get along with labor by making them part of the team. But Mr. McEvoy expressed the resultant problems on the seventh day after the ILA strike by stating, "There is enough work in the port. The problem is getting the workers to their work." Sea-Land and the other lines would like to be able to shift the labor from the places where there is no work to the logical place where there is work. However, under the complicated inverse seniority agreement, this is not possible. Many longshoremen have learned to handle the controlling computer and make the computer react in a method called "badging," which allows them to collect their GAI. While the computer transmits the man's information to the central headquarters in downtown New York, thus recording his availability to work, the man

TABLE 18-1. NEW LABOR REQUIRED OF MEDIUM-SIZE
CONTAINER REPAIR STATION

Metal workers, general mechanics, shipbuilders	9
Welders	3
Carpenters	2
Engine mechanics	1
Refrigeration mechanics	1

himself rushes away to another job, such as construction worker, truck driver, or bartender. He also draws his GAI pay. The GAI agreement was not renewed by management on October 1, 1971. Instead of the well-known longshoremen with the cargo hook, a container operation requires specialists. Table 18-1 shows the typical makeup of a medium-sized container repair station.

ILWU PATTERN

On the West Coast of the United States, the labor situation is different from the scene described for the East Coast and Gulf. The International Longshoremen's and Warehousemen's Union (ILWU) represents all ports and negotiates its contracts with the Pacific Maritime Association (PMA).

The position of the shore labor, including the drivers of container chassis, has been summarized in a statement by Harry Bridges, ILWU:

> Speaking from a broad perspective, certain traditional types of jobs are going to be eliminated, others will change in content, and certain new kinds of jobs will emerge. Given the rapid spread of containerization, it is immediately apparent that labor will face some serious challenges. Some workers are sure to be displaced from jobs they are now holding. The jurisdictional boundaries between various jobs and unions will become clouded. Many workers will have to learn new skills to replace those no longer required. New companies will come into being and others will cease to exist. Productivity increases of this magnitude mean tens of millions of dollars in labor cost savings to the employers. We intend to get some of these savings.

To permit understanding of the analysis of the West Coast labor situation, we find that the two most significant measures gained by labor in its agreements are:

1.   Management has agreed to payments on mechanization and modernization of cargo handling by paying a bonus for container handling into a special fund which allows the unions to establish (subject to Treasury

Department approval) payments of benefits for retirement, death, or disability.

2. Container freight stations must have a basic complement of "steady men" who shall perform all types of cargo work in vanning and de-vanning containers (equivalent to stuffing and stripping). This means that all assembled cargo must be physically handled by ILWU labor at the container freight station. The only exceptions are containers in service to points beyond the 50-mile zone from the port and all inland points where they go directly to by rail or by truck. Sea-Land's U.S. internal containers, which are considered store-to-door, are also exempted.

Under the ILWU agreement, containerization grew in size and importance. Harry Bridges, President of ILWU, at the Containerization meeting in Los Angeles in November 1969, stated that productivity had increased at the piers under the agreement in excess of 26 percent and that the union expected full implementation of the container freight station supplement at the earliest date. Since this supplement entails displacement of teamster labor which presently handles some of the functions of the longshoremen, the ILWU offered a pattern of patient adjustment and promised avoidance of jurisdictional strife. In all, the ILWU had taken a very conciliatory attitude in the development of containerization until June 1971.

STRIKE PATTERN

The Pacific Coast longshore contract expired July 1, 1971, and the ILWU walked out. Amazingly, for 60 days there was not even any discussion of the problem. It became apparent that there was an internal fight within the union and that some locals, such as Los Angeles–Long Beach, had developed a very difficult attitude. When the government announced the new wage and price freeze program in August 1971, the possibilities of settling the strike by agreeing to higher compensation disappeared. Of course, it will be noted that until this time, the West Coast labor did not work under the GAI coverage of the ILA.

MAGNA CHARTA FOR MANAGEMENT

Never has containerization faced such a tremendous problem. The settlement of all segments of the entire manpower situation cannot be expected to be simple. Management in the first container decade had great hopes for the development of a cost-benefit development from economy of scale, large investments, and a good labor relations situation. Management has read into the Hamburg spirit that this was good for both parties. The attitude of one of the container industry leaders, Michael McEvoy of Sea-Land, indicates the willingness:

> There are many ways to improve relations between management and labor and head off future clashes. On the management side, for instance, there should be no differentiating between non-union and unionized workers. The longshoremen should not be looked upon primarily as union members, but should, rather, be treated as employees of the company, the same as anybody else. This would instill in them a sense of belonging. They could consider themselves as part of an undertaking and be proud of its achievements to which they contributed with their own work.

LABOR PROGRESS AT THE JUNCTION

What has happened to the labor situation since the progress of mechanization in cargo handling is the result of a lack of anticipated effects by management on the manpower relationship. With the economy of scale, labor has acquired an overpowering position at the controls of the machinery. The tools of economy of scale have reduced the number of employees, but have placed in the hands of the remaining transport workers an immense increase in power. Human effects, consequently, have been completely changed. While any compassion in the early days of containerization would require provisions against the loss of livelihood and protection for the diminishing jobs of labor, the roles have now been reversed. It is the public that is primarily suffering from excess of labor's control of the transportation machinery. Chicago labor attorney Henry Seyfarth, in a speech before the New York Traffic Club in June 1971, stated:

> As a whole, how do we reverse this trend from which we are now suffering that has developed over a period of some 30 to 35 years? How do we stabilize our economy so that we no longer have imposed upon us these continuous increases in labor costs which cannot be recovered through increased efficiencies and which must be passed on partially or wholly to the consumer through price increases, thereby contributing to inflation with all of its inequities and destructive characteristics. . . . Our business community, once known for its great leaders, is now paralyzed by the number and immensity of the problems confronting it; none of them capable of quick or easy solution. But the problem is not one alone for the businessman; its solution will be achieved when those who have a stake in society, when those who find pleasure and satisfaction in working and achieving to build a responsible society become as articulate and influential with elected of-

ficials as are those who desire more pay, less work, more relief payments and less responsibility. . . . A gigantic task faces all such people who value the right to acquire and to enjoy the fruits of their labor. It involves the process of education, counter-organization, and intense participation in government and political circles. It involves the willingness of each of us to work toward a broader base of knowledge and information on labor economics, and to find the ways and means of relating this knowledge and information to the common problem of price inflation. It is obvious that the fires of inflation are fed every time a wage increase exceeds a productivity gain.

SEA-GOING LABOR

Sea-going labor faces a serious threat to job existence. Highly sophisticated cargo ships used in containerization require fewer men but adequately trained ones. The problem of the American Merchant Marine is quite serious. Unions, such as the Masters Mates and Pilots Union, which provides officers for the cargo ships, have long used very strict seniority systems. Such a system provides for three groups and for slow advancement from one to the other. Therefore, the youngest members of the shipping fraternity who have the best experience to handle modern ships with highly sophisticated machinery are being held back by people who have been going to sea for 20 years or more on conventional ships but have little knowledge of the new methods. The Maritime Administration since 1959 has been thinking in terms of an ocean going cargo vessel carrying no crew. It would be controlled and navigated automatically by shipborne instrumentation. A shore-based human operator could monitor the ship's operation via telemeter information, and he could override the ship-borne control, if necessary, and control the ship remotely by radio length. There is also the idea of a similar mechanized ship which is manned by a very small riding skeleton crew, perhaps of 7 to 11 men. Again, this crew is there only to supervise and direct navigation and take minimum emergency measures, besides guiding the ship out of and into ports. There is no doubt that ideas like this will come to bear, most likely with the manning of a ship by crewing from helicopters near the shoreline. The union's position in face of these prospects is expressed by Rick Miller, Vice President of the National Maritime Union: "People who work on the ships, the docks, in the offices and shipyards all have a stake in the container revolution with the largest stake of all coming to those for whom it means a whole new way of life."

This, then, leads also to a new field of naval architecture related to the human factors. Unions look forward to provisions of recreation and leisure time on board the ship. For the off-watch hours, elaborate provisions for relaxation—including pianos, swimming pools, gymnasiums, films, tape decks, and extensive libraries—will be coupled with facilities for additional professional training and reeducation. The question of providing facilities for female members of the crew has been solved in many Scandinavian and European countries to the apparent satisfaction of labor. It is most likely that this, too, will have to be considered. Therefore, instead of the Spartan conventional cargo ship, we may expect productive containerships with much expanded labor facilities somehow equivalent to or better than passenger quarters.

SPLIT CREWS

Tow boats on the Mississippi River and the roll-on, roll-off ferries across the English Channel have long operated with a never-stop operation system. This led to the creation of the rule that the men were to be paid for a day's work with a day's leave. Limitation of cockpit time on flight crews has provided the precedent of the split crew. This crew exchange works well when highly technical equipment is involved. A particular analysis of the working conditions of the nonstop, turnaround containership, similar to the semimechanized ship systems planned, would allow the crew only a certain number of days on board. Then the crew would rest ashore until the next vessel arrives.

With the increase in ship sizes, ship collisions have dangerously multiplied. Most noticeable of this development has been the number of tanker accidents and sinkings. However, with the increase of super containerships, the safety factor would be a more important element, especially if further reduction in crew size should occur. Manning of the ships in the United States is based on the safety regulations prescribed by the United States Coast Guard. The union usually adds a number of men whom they consider indispensable to alleviate the work load on the crew. The possibility of reduction in vessels' crews is being considered by all seafaring nations. The entire matter will sooner or later lead to some safety rules for ocean manning similar to such rules in commercial aviation.

WORK TOGETHERNESS

The railroad industry can be considered as the link of containerization. Rails have recognized that they are caught up in the critical fight for survival as a private enterprise. To bring about a blueprint of self-help, the publication *Modern Railroads,* in Fall 1971, organized a conference to discuss the industry's problem with a team of the most brilliant people of the industry. It became clear from the discussion that there was no rail future without labor-management teamwork. The application of this principle is so significant for containerization that this Rail Management Labor Conference of 1971 provides a corollary to the pragmatics of container-labor relations. Through these discussions, the panel group decided that there would be common ground on which an industry task force could face productive probing into the structure of manpower cost and pay on the railroads. The labor components indicated that their people would not be interested in any proposal for profit sharing, but that a new approach would have to be developed. A statement of the labor members of the group was cited by *Modern Railroads.* Protection of existing wages and job security must be the goal of the union, while the carriers will try to eliminate certain prerogatives in the interest of their work effectiveness. It deals with the weak spot in the present system of labor relations. To increase business, the industry must innovate. That usually means changes in the work rules. Labor relations people are not equipped to deal in transport systems technology.

A labor union official, who had been active in his local for twenty-five years and had been dealing with labor relations people about all issues, including claims, stated:

> I have not talked for years with anyone who can say to me, "now look, if we do this we can get more business and that means more jobs." What do we really stand to lose by bringing a labor representative to the design board about a new work system? Why do we fear doing this?

HUMAN RESOURCES ENGINEERING

Enough has been stated on how the two sides act. The impasse sooner or later affects all segments and transmits its destructive force to the economy of the nation. While labor has now gained a surprising advantage over management on the waterfront, the political balance will require readjustment. The public ignorance of the impact of the transportation workpower conditions has allowed these conditions to occur. With strife and a continued uncertainty in the transport modes, the community can never be expected to stabilize the economy, much less to fight against inflation effectively. In longshoremen's eyes, the management wants labor to carry the burden of the load. AFL-CIO President George Meany spoke in late October 1971 of "sharing the sacrifices."

On March 13, 1972, the Pay Board presented a study to its members which notes that the ILWU and Pacific Maritime Association have been working through collective bargaining since 1958 to permit "mechanization and modernization" on the docks and elimination of restrictive work rules. Part of this effort was the employers' pledge that the longshoremen were entitled to "share" in the benefits. But this hasn't happened, the Pay Board study suggests. It shows that while unit labor costs in the private nonfarm economy have risen about 30 percent since 1960, the cost of handling a ton of cargo has dropped by over 30 percent. The study estimates that PMA members have saved between $900 million and $1 billion since 1960. But only about $62 million has been shared with the longshoremen in the form of improved retirement and pay-guarantee benefits, the study says.

SHARING THE SACRIFICES

Manpower stability is the main ingredient of transportation economy. With the good intentions of Meany and Bridges on one side, and with the understanding in management shown by Mike McEvoy, a solution to the pressing stability problem must be found before the dimensions of the excess overwhelm the entire system. I know that many people advocate political solutions. The human condition of the world is moving in the opposite direction. Democracy implies a free labor market and thus strike elimination will be hard to establish. The answer to our problems must deal with the facts of the labor-management relationship in the age of mechanization of transport. This leads to the urgent need for the establishment of a systematic approach to this part of the container system.

MANPOWER ENGINEERING

In Chapters 1 and 3, we have shown that container systems engineering is unique in that it interfaces between manpower, physical things, and institutional organizations. No better proof of this theory can exist than the fact that containerization would be unable to fulfill its mission of transport integration unless it would develop pragmatic guidelines to pass along the benefits of the system to both management and labor. Harmony and efficiency of work in the port which has been considered by ILO at Hamburg and Rotterdam, as discussed in this chapter, has has never been implemented to provide the public their due share.

My thinking is that the implementation of the man–container interface calls for the employment of a third party, the "behavioral engineer," as moderator in container disputes. Complexities of the container industry are so deeply rooted that decision making should not be left to the judgment or bargaining of management and labor alone. Limitation of control is required to adjust world container transport problems in the manual fields.

A new look must be taken at the interface between labor and management in container transportation. I can identify eight stages at which an approach by behavioral engineering can use certain logical rules to produce equitable conditions:

Professional treatment of manpower: The common interests between the four parties—labor, management, government, and the public—should be treated in a professional, equitable fashion by qualified members.

Productivity measurement: The economy of scale in transportation must be measured by pragmatic methods, and the contributions of labor, capital, and institutions (such as port authorities) must be developed to provide a key for fair competition.

Living standards and cost of living: Inflationary trends inherent in our economic system must be analyzed to provide for stability in living standards and, consequently, in cost of living of transportation labor.

Guild organizations or permanent employment: Labor should be allowed the alternative of decision whether to act as a guild providing services for a fixed fee while the labor union internally develops its seniority and pay scale or to be guaranteed an annual wage by being a permanent employee of the carrier company with the company exercising discretion where to use the worker to the benefit of the company.

Human development, skill, and training: This would deal with profession proficiency and adequacy of the men in charge of the more complicated technologies and equipment in the field of transportation. It is a basic principle without which highly sophisticated machinery cannot be expected to function.

Retirement funding and procedures: The principle of mechanization and modernization should be used to establish a national fund providing job security, compensatory payments, and retirement benefits to all transport workers endangered by these developments.

Jurisdictional unity: Treatment of all transport workers connected with the integrated transport process must be unified in the interest of the community as well as the worker himself. However, local conditions must be guidelines for the possible level of employment and level of compensation. The protection of the less developed areas is important in order to maintain the national economy.

Open agreements and adjustment machinery: All labor agreements in the transportation field should be without a cancellation date, yet should allow for continuous supervised adjustments of the content. To be fair to both labor and management requires translation of the above seven guidelines in light of the constant pattern of change. In exchange for that, strikes, work stoppages, slow-downs, and other methods of refusal to fulfill labor's mission must be renounced as bargaining tools by labor.

FIVE MIAMI POINTS

The Executive Council of the AFL-CIO, as a result of their meetings in Miami in February 1972, announced a five-point policy program which does, in effect, reflect a step toward a needed readjustment of the man–container relationship here developed. The five points include:

1. No strike during the period of contract negotiations;
2. Three-to-five-year contracts to provide assurance with respect to continuity of operations;
3. Uniform contract expiration dates;
4. Provision for automatic wage adjustments annually;
5. Establishment of a mechanism or procedure for the resolution of disputes without stoppages.

The Widening Technology

TECHNOLOGY TRANSFER

As containerization acquires more status as a science in itself, it permits the transfer of its own technological achievement to more applications in life. We know that our land, air, and water are finite. There is just so much of each and no more. We have to learn a philosophy to employ the available resources in a sensible fashion. This rejection of excessive growth applies to means of transport, too. Thinking people evidenced this in the opposition to the trans-Alaska pipeline and the SST (supersonic transport). If any valid significance can be attached to this, it is that people are willing to learn to live with what they have. This course refers to the problems—better use of available transport service rather than construction of new ones. Further mechanization of ocean shipping and the construction of further rail systems, such as Archdeacon's TRT, GATX, RRollway, and other major uses, are hard to realize until all transport media are optimized. The best proof of this trend can be seen in the decision of San Francisco, asking for the removal of the Embarcadero Freeway, and the scuttling of the plans for the Beverly Hills Freeway in Los Angeles. The systems under pressure turn inward to find better solutions for present needs in existing technology.

"Technology transfer" was first developed by the United States Navy during the McNamara attempt to procure Naval vessels under the "TPC" (Total Package Contract) system. With three competitors working on the Fast Deployment Logistics Ship (FDL) for the Navy, the plan was developed to make the winner use the best technological features of all three proponents in the final version. Similar methods had been applied, in part, by the United States Air Force. With this system, unification of a systems technology can be obtained by selection of the best components and subsystems, and integration of these into a better optimal unified answer. Here it becomes evident that containerization is turning into a cargo systems science in itself. Until now, the success was purely based on marketing which, too often, is simply the result of advertising and public relations. How many harmful drugs, cigarettes, and foods have been turned into phenomenal successes and then, eventually, had to be banned? The specter of such developments also may haunt the container systems designers. The list of pragmatic inquiries into the overall validity of a certain concept for the nation, and the world as a whole, requires, indeed, methods far removed from repetition of the Madison Avenue slogans implanted by some good carrier salesman. Just like the producers of consumables that were found to be bad for our health, the super sales ideas can fall by the side of the road of progress. Basic, fundamental, systematic analysis of the meaning and effects of a concept give it assurance of survival.

FEAR OF OBSOLESCENCE

Our user/buyer public in all walks of life becomes more sophisticated about the true viability of a transport system. We also have to recognize that the producer of equipment, the financier, and the carriers who decide on the implementation today are faced with a completely new set of circumstances. During the '50s and '60s, manufacturers of highway vehicles, such as trailers, saw their market in a way similar to the one developed by the automobile industry. From year to year, new models were offered to the motor carrier. Almost every four years, all major trailer fleets of American motor carriers had to be renewed. The continuous trend of change in the highway size and weight limitations helped the manufacturer sell his wares. How could a motor carrier survive with heavy, 35-ft. long, 8½-ft. high trailers when his competitor used 40-ft. long, 9-ft. high vans, offering his trade a better rate as the result of this? The modal competition between road and rail was stimulated with a pressure to increase trailer sizes all the way up to 45-ft. long and 9-ft. high—true boxcars on the road! When one trailer was not enough, pressure was placed on the toll road authorities to permit 2 or 3 trailer trains against a slightly higher user charge. I do not claim that this pressure system has yet been ended. But the day of reckoning came closer with the advent of piggyback (TOFC) and containerization. In other words, when the media of transport can grow no longer in height, length, weight, and size, they must find new means to become better. And to become better in the market place means better to their customers and to the public they are intended to serve.

It is this trend toward greater economy and systems effectiveness that offers the true new danger of early obsolescence. If it is accepted that the continuous trend of inflation in the economy will continuously produce greater demands of labor on operating cost levels, further mechanization will be self-imposed. Most containerization still is largely related to ocean transportation. For true effectiveness, the intermodal door-to-door through service must be developed and implemented for the benefit of new shippers.

This leaves fields for further pressure on the systems to change. Changeover with implementation of not more, but different containerization aspects will result in better adaptation of inland containerization. A financial analyst, called upon to determine the life cycle validity and obsolescence of an investment in container facilities, must seek the value analysis of this particular concept. Will it remain viable under the pressure of the onslaught of further trends to automation? Containerization is a process, not a finite system, and, therefore, will continue to go on to improvement, giving better service at a relatively lower cost. If the cost cannot be reduced, it must at least maintain a significant profit share, which will allow fighting off inflation, increased labor cost, and the replacement value of certain parts of the facilities.

WHERE IS MY TENANT?

Such analysis of the coming intensification of the containerization process through implementation of computers, data processing, automated mechanization, and closer cooperation, forces the consideration of the continued growth of intermodality. Methods can be found to cope with more than one set of standards. In Chapter 3, we talked about systems tolerance. The survival expectancy of any tolerant standard container system is greater than a closed circuit system. To convert a system by implementation of minor changes into a tolerant system can be done. But a monolithic, closed system using a certain type of noninterchangeable equipment will find itself facing a more automated, standardized competing carrier. On that day the landlord port authority may endanger its investment because the nonstandard carrier tenant may some day be unable to continue his own lease. Containerization would, in short, be spiked with the same management decision complex that eliminated many of the break-bulk steamship companies, giants at one time in their own field. When we see stacks of thousands of containers unusable for present operations in the Port of Los Angeles, we wonder how much promise the future holds for those who have not learned that systems engineering is required in the planning stage of containerization.

SPREADING THE GOSPEL

While ingenuity of the new generation of container engineers will bring about internal improvement within containerization, the development of new intersystems solutions must focus on an expansion of the container idea to the public life and commerce of our world. The Great Wall of China is the greatest construction accomplishment of the human race and one of the most foolish ones. It is 1,684 miles long, separating one system from another. It was penetrated not by military force climbing over it, but by the simple Chinese expedient of paying off the gate people. The relationship between intermodal containerization on the sea and an unintegrated transportation economy requires new methods to spread the gospel where it will do the most good for human life.

Many of the problems of limitation of container application today are not physical. The institutional resistance to change and the conventional habit to permeate obsolete conveyances can last only as long as the state of the economy and the condition of the world trade tolerates it. To overcome this apathy and lethargy, interrelations between existing conveyances, new facilities, and a competitive new marketing in the field of transportation will come about, as a result of systematic thinking. When we analyze what went wrong as containerization became stalled, due to overtonnage on the North Atlantic in 1971, we develop a new modesty and a new understanding that there are no simple answers for the benefits of the system to become accessible to those who can use it. Never before the '60s and '70s has there been such an explicit concentration on the methods of the expansion of knowledge. It was the conspicuous feature of the decade to develop systems analysis, systems engineering, and the cross-fertilization of pragmatic ideas. It was found that much information had to be collected and logically arranged. The ultimate value of the intuitive element which comes to the analyst from experience in the field and in the market is the final ingredient in technological processes. Transportation has suffered patiently with wasteful methods for a long time. Innovation crosses the minds of men when it becomes apparent that better processes are available. This leads to a rational discovery of a scientific analysis. The outcome of such analysis is a new order of cooperative measures, turning the chaos in transportation into a new process of coordination, cooperation, and accommodation.

NATIONAL DEFENSE

As long as the world situation requires of the United States the maintenance of a defense posture, the mobility of the Armed Forces is of importance. General Frank Besson was the courageous implementor of mobility. After World War II, he would tell his audience the result of his studies on logistic movements during the Revolutionary War and World War II. According to Besson, artillery supplies moved to the front during the Revolutionary War with an average speed of 1.4 miles per hour. All the improvements in technology in World War II barely more than doubled this speed to 3.2 miles per hour. Questioning the reasons behind such factors, Besson found the answers to be in the lack of mobility at transfer points. A standard American boxcar moves approximately 9,000 miles per year, spending the rest of its life standing at the siding, waiting for cargo transfer. The piggyback cars, however, produced mileages of over 200,000 miles per year in contrast, because they are designed for cargo-transfer ease.

General Besson accomplished the introduction of the U.S. Army's CONEX container into the armed forces. The unique design made this container transportable inside the famous "Deuce/and/half" standard 6 × 6 army truck. The CONEX, of course, is not designed as an intermodal container, but serves to ease the methods of transfer plus preservation of stored goods. A later improvement developed by General Besson was the implementation of the first container bridge to Europe, using three ships. The SS *Carib Queen* (renamed *USNS Taurus*), the Marine Corps Attack Ship, the *Comet*, and the converted *Trans-Globe* (the first entry of Peck and Kahn) started the military containership business. This service was operated, using odd-size Army "standard" vans between 28 and 32 feet in length. Speed and convenience were a result of excellent systems engineering, even with poor equipment. The goal was to use this container system to reduce the Army inventory in the supply pipeline. The *Comet-Challenger* test (which I conducted for General Besson) established the possibility of using containers as the main element in modern Army logistics.

After completion of these tests off the shores of Bremerhaven, General Besson turned to me while on the motorboat riding back to shore and said, "If you can now put containerization into the ammunition supply, we finally have an improvement over the Revolutionary War." It was not until very late in the Viet Nam conflict that this finally was implemented into logistic support.

It is remarkable to see how the institutional establishment of the military has resisted the challenge of containerization. The cause of the resistance is the institutional desire to defend a personnel setup and a large command. But times of economy finally brought about some long-needed changes. Excuses are stated against full orderly implementation of this process in the military forces at the meetings of military with civilian carriers. Much "lip service" is paid to containerization, yet military ships are still being planned with an expected life cycle of 20 years without consideration of full containerization.

MOBILITY REQUIREMENTS

We feel a need to study the military container program for several reasons:

1. The volume importance of the military in the total cargo distribution picture;
2. The similarity of problems between certain military and commercial constraints;
3. The resulting cross-fertilization of van-use technology as a systems outgrowth.

The major need of military transport occurs during the introduction of military forces into a new area, whether hostile or friendly. The transportation capability of airlift for personnel and some first-moment supplies will never replace the large-equipment support a modern force of any type requires to maintain its standing. Commonly, such a deployment occurs during a landing on a foreign shore. In Chapter 11, we have explained the need for protected harbors for cargo transfer. But when these port facilities are destroyed or not available for containership use, the military must resort to landing over the shoreline. Of course, shipping to underdeveloped areas frequently faces the same requirement.

The maintenance of a specialized ship fleet dedicated to large-scale landings was envisioned by former Secretary of Defense Robert S. McNamara. But Congress and the American public could not be convinced to support this measure. As a result, by and large, the military must plan to use merchant vessels available for its transport. Most of the general-cargo vessels, however, in our era are containerships or LASH-type vessels. Since the surf condition would be dangerous to the barges used by LASH, SEABEE, or similar floating container systems, the weight of the support system will have to rely on the military use of containers. This leads us to inquire into the application of civilian containers as an outgrowth of the systems technology, and the adaptability of these vans to the military constraints.

In the over-shore panorama, we must deal with problems ashore and problems in the surf zone which the cargo must transverse. Shoreside constraints, such as sandy beaches, cliffs, poor roads, and port area congestion, are solvable with military transport systems. These same problems have now been with the Defense establishment since World War II, and a great deal of experimentation has gone into the development of several systems standards. An idea set forth by Lanciano in "Containers and Contingencies" (article in *Proceedings of the U.S. Naval Institute,* September 1971) is not to use containers for the first 60 days of landing. But this appears to be a costly and ineffective method. If 58 percent of all military supplies today were loaded into container vans as a distribution-line subsystem, it would require the military to take this cargo out of containers, repackage it, and then move it to the front in conventional break-bulk ships. It is evident that the answer must be to find a better solution, to move containers to the shore rather than to de-van the cargo.

SURF DELIVERY SYSTEMS

Continued studies are being conducted in military science with the LOTS (landing over the shore) system to find ways to overcome the motion danger of the surf. We list three systems contenders:

1. Special nonbroaching shallow-draft ships for containers from "gateway ports" about 500 miles away;
2. Cargo helicopter service;
3. Hovercraft landing over the surf.

The application of small vessels for landing military cargo requires very much the same kind as those serving coastal zones in Malaysia, Indonesia, the Caribbean, the African coast, and Samoa in commercial service. Such a ship must be able to handle all kinds and sizes of containers, on wheels, as well as vehicles, machinery, and similar supplies. Since we have used this type of vessel as typical model for a critical analysis of the life-cycle cost, we provide sketchy details of this vessel. The development of this new ship coordinating ocean-going and over-the-beach discharge capabilities is consistent with advanced forms of container cargo operations.

BROACHING PREVENTION

Dual-purpose ships for deep-sea transportation and over-the-beach discharge face the problem of the beach currents to hold themselves in position while handling cargo. Since anchoring becomes impossible in the shallow water, the conventional vessel must "beach" itself by impact on the beach bottom. This "stranding" has severe damaging effects on the ship structure and bottom, but has in the past been the only way of holding a ship steady at the beach. This beaching method was the way to prevent broaching.

Broaching is the tendency of a vessel to turn from its steerageway to a position parallel to the beach, broadside to the incoming wave front. This phenomena is caused by the interplay of forces taking place in the surf zone environment. If a floating object is exactly perpendicular to the incoming waves and there are no other forces acting on the object, then that object goes temporarily into a state of "unsettled dynamical sensitivity" similar to a ball balanced on the top of a needle. Even the slightest angular force or side thrust creates offset power, instantly rotating the object about its center bow-to-stern axle. This force increments in magnitude in seconds by additional transverse drag due to the sea currents along the shore. Rotational motion is being highly accelerated as the angle of the vessel to the wave front increases. As more of the ship's area becomes available to the drag forces, rotation increases both in speed and intensity second by second. As more forces find more surfaces on the sides of the vessel to press upon, the movement races out of control and continues until finally the object reaches a state of "settled dynamic stability" in the fully broached position parallel to the incoming waves.

Steerage in this broached condition is absolutely impossible. Once broaching has occurred, a ship is helpless and will founder soon, capsize, and sink. Unless constant dynamic adjustments are made to compensate for the always present but variable longshore currents, rip currents, and differential wave fronts, and to maintain the desired center axle, broaching cannot be prevented by a ship.

In the surf environment, the length of the ship hull and its relationship with power distribution is an intricate matter. No single location for propulsion could offset the broaching forces; the Small Port Vessel, however, holds itself in water deep enough to exercise power against variable currents, and this power is distributed along the entire length of the vessel.

POWERED BARGES

The proposed vessels are essentially powered barges with a ship-type fo'c's'le and bridge equipped with twin screws powered by two diesel engines which are remotely controlled from the wheelhouse. In addition, the vessels are equipped with two 360°-steerable drive-power units which are designed to assist in close maneuvering. The vessel is designed for extreme maneuverability under low-speed or zero-speed conditions and sensitive astern operations. The vessel is basically designed with the main (weather) deck as working and cargo area. All under-deck spaces, with the sole exception of the engine-room space, are tanks. Primary use of these tanks is as ballast. However, in military service these tanks can and may be used as fuel tanks. This also allows the vessels to position themselves across the ocean without outside assistance.

The development of the SPV ship system by the proponent took over 10 years of mission analysis, engineering, and field testing with different vessel types. As outgrowth of the first United States commercial Ro-Ro operation between Florida and Puerto Rico, a small ocean-going craft of 65-ft. length under the name of *MV Seatruck Lloyd* was launched at Merril Stevens Drydock Company in Jacksonville, Florida, in 1956. This vessel has been operating in the open ocean between Puerto Rico (San Juan harbor) and St. Thomas and St. Croix, Virgin Islands, to date. The experiences gained from this ship were incorporated in a design patent.

The first ship to incorporate some of the design features for small, ocean-going ships was the *MV Salvador Run,* built by converting the hull of an LSM(R) into this vessel in 1960. Followed by two similar conversions, this fleet has operated 'til now in the Caribbean in very shallow waters and into unimproved ports. Landing-type operations were started and conducted with two Ro-Ro barges in 1962, and the off-shore holding experiences led to the design of the first SPV in 1963. Model tests were conducted, and a continuous programmed development followed. The preliminary design incorporating the novel type of air-cushion-supported stern ramp was started in 1966. The entire proprietary development is presently subject to pending patents. Finally, the incorporation of the proprietary "Delta Hull" and the "Task Deck" completed the design integration.

HELICOPTER DELIVERY

While the SPV method uses a new type of ship in the water medium, innovators have been working on systems to deliver containers by helicopter from ships to the beach. The logistical problems encountered in undeveloped ports produced the interest in this development. After a thorough analysis of the logistical problems, it was decided that the need for a heavy-lift helicopter capable of merging with seaboard containerized transport was required. Development of such a system was initiated by Boeing in June 1971 with operational availability anticipated by the end of 1980. The aircraft, designed with a capability of aerial transport of containers with 22½-ton-and-above weights, will be able to offload containerized shipping in Sea States up to 5 (Beaufort scale) and under all weather conditions, day or night.

Helicopter manufacturers began demonstrating the feasibility of offloading ships at sea in 1968. Sikorsky Division of United Aircraft demonstrated such capability in the Long Island Sound. Vertol Division of the Boeing Company demonstrated such an operation at San Francisco Bay. By 1970, the military made a feasibility study under full operational conditions. In December of 1970, a test was conducted jointly by the Army and the Navy at Fort Story, Virginia. An American Export–Isbrandtsen containership was anchored four miles off shore and was offloaded aerially, using both Sikorsky CH-54 and Boeing CH-47 helicopters. In addition, offloading by barge was attempted. The ship was loaded with the Army 8 × 8 × 20-foot MILVAN container. Sea states of 3 (up to 8½-foot waves) were encountered. Helicopters were able to achieve offload over the entire five-day operation. Because of the high winds and sea states, barge transportation was inoperative for two of the five days. It must be recognized that helicopter feasibility was clearly established even though the operation was accomplished by existing equipment not designed to perform the mission. Container weights are limited to those achievable by currently existing systems (in the 10-to-12-ton area).

CANADIAN COMMERCIAL EXPERIENCE

The first commercial application of containerized sky lift started in the summer of 1970. Canadian Steamship Lines, Ltd. (CSL) equipped their vessel, the SS Fort St. Louis, with special hatches and removed all conventional cargo gear from the upper deck. This allowed the use of helicopters instead of container cranes in ports of Eastern Canada, approximately

1,000 miles south of the North Pole. In the presence of 30-ft. tides and ice flows blocking the Bay entrances, the operation used containers of all varieties. During a 32-day trial, almost 3,000 tons of cargo of every description was flown from the ship approximately 6 miles across the shore to an inland depot.

CONTAINERS BY HOVERCRAFT

Hovercraft only recently has been actually built to great capacities. In 1970, we directed the attention of Global Marine, Inc., one of the largest offshore drilling contractors of the world petroleum industry, to the capabilities of the hoverskirt invented first by Sir Christopher Cockerill in England. Later developments in Great Britain under the financial sponsorship of the National Research Development Corporation produced indication that loads of over 4,000 tons could be successfully lifted by air-cushion methods. The first large drilling platform was placed in service in mid-1971, and many more will follow.

Hovercraft overcomes the friction with the surface of land or sea by creating a slight air film between the air-containing skirt and the supporting mass. The use of hovercraft to transport passengers over water at speeds of 40 knots and better makes the hovercraft an interesting novelty in the water-transport field. But the real significance of hovercraft systems is in the craft's ability to use unimproved beaches, swampland, and just about any available surface to hover over and to deliver its cargo. For this reason, the development of the first American twin-engine hovercraft in 1972 leads to a new ship-to-shore system.

FLOATING CONTAINERPORT

Eness has developed a portable crane facility for unloading and loading containerized cargo. (See Fig. 19-1.) It was primarily developed for use in commercial applications in underdeveloped ports. The Barge Crane consists of two longitudinally separable hulls which support a structural frame on their kingposts. The frame serves as a means of achieving and maintaining separation, as well as a means for supporting a boom-type crane. The hull separation provides a catamaran reaction, having excellent resistance to list from off-center load as well as action of the sea. A detailed study indicates that at midway between sea states 4 and 5, the maximum list is only 2½ degrees. The crane is capable of lifting containers of 44,000 lbs. at an outreach of 96 feet. The potential is as high as 24 containers per

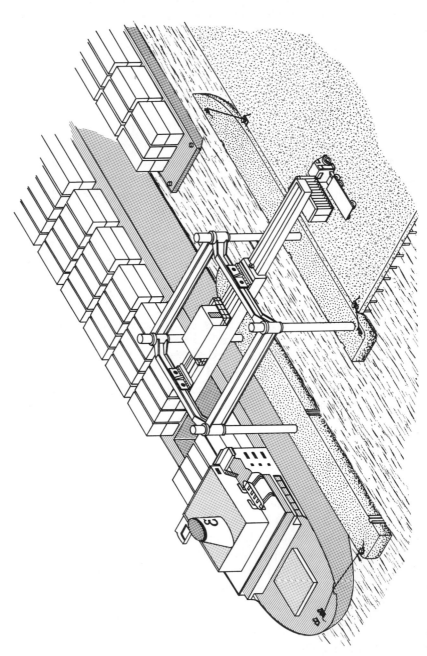

FIGURE 19-1. FLOATING CONTAINER CRANE CAPABLE OF UNLOADING CONTAINERS WITHOUT PREPARED CONTAINER PIERS. (PATENTED BY ENESS RESEARCH & DEVELOPMENT.)

hour. The crane is also capable of 70,000 lbs. at an outreach of 70 feet. The capability will permit unloading a containership having a beam of 106 feet.

In a study to determine a preliminary design, it was found that while the crane has an operational capability of a sea state greater than 4, its use with conventional landing craft is difficult because of the motion of the boats; and, of course, these crafts are too small to carry containers. Using these existing means for off-loading presents a major problem. In a search to improve the operation, we looked to other types of craft. The Bell Aerospace Company has been good enough to provide Eness with information on their Model 7380 hovercraft. The extent of our investigation indicates that this craft is a feasible solution in an operation with the Eness barge crane at the higher sea states. Based upon the hovercraft maintaining a cushion height of approximately four feet, it appears as though operation in a sea state of 3 is possible. To achieve the operation, the hovercraft will be supplied with pads while the crane barge will be provided with cross trusses similar to those anticipated for normal crane operation, except that these trusses will be suitable to receive and maintain the hovercraft stationary against motion of the sea. These trusses can be stowed on the deck of the barge and installed in place, using the crane. This arrangement assures us that there will be no relative vertical motion between the container and the loading area on the hovercraft, thus simplifying loading of containers. The motion from the sea on the system will be but a small motion, probably less than encountered in loading conventional containerships when tied up to a pier.

NO PORTS AVAILABLE

Operations are feasible whereby a containership is loaded with hovercraft, fork lifts, and a number of containers, which would be delivered directly to shore. The Eness barge crane is capable of lifting the hovercraft from an outreach position of 55 feet. A fork-lift truck of 35,000 lbs. capacity will weigh close to 50,000 lbs., which is the capacity of the 7,380 hovercraft and is less than the capacity of the crane; so it can be landed onto the hovercraft. Combining these elements, it can be illustrated that a containership can be used to unload containers in an underdeveloped port while at anchor in a sea state up to approximately 3 or possibly better.

AREA APPLICATION

It is possible to handle twenty containers per hour by hovercraft since there is no vertical motion between the container and its landing area such as with other floating equipment. The concept presented herein is close to reality. The basic design of the crane has been prepared for the Navy, and hovercrafts are operational. We are not fully aware of all the aspects of the operations but it is sufficiently flexible in many respects. In areas without adequate ports, this concept as presented may fill some of the missing links. Larger loads may be distributed (when needed) by smaller containerships. The essential fact is that the concept eliminates the vertical motion between the craft and the container which, heretofore, could not be accomplished, and, as such, makes the operation feasible in the higher sea states.

AMPHIBIANS OVER THE SURF

The flow of cargo inbound to the shore delivery station is greatly expedited by using the Eness Crane/Bell Hovercraft combination. Fixed-sidewall hovercraft which use the design of an air-filled center channel to obtain lift, but, otherwise, resemble a catamaran hull, would not be able to deliver the cargo to shore since they are not amphibious and, therefore, would be subject to the same broaching forces described heretofore for hull-displacement vessels. The design effort of the Navy and Marine Corps is directed toward the amphibious type of hovercraft. However, the joint program of the Maritime Administration and the Navy on surface-effect crafts is intended to develop high-speed, deep-water vessels which use air primarily as a design expedient to obtain greater speeds of travel.

SPUD PIERS

In line with more conventional ideas, the Defense establishment has also looked into the possibility of building offshore container terminals using the bottom implantation of spuds. Spuds mentioned here are steel towers equipped with a sharp end. These spuds are frequently used in offshore oil operation in depths up to 80 feet of water. The spuds are attached to a barge which is first floated into position. Then the spuds are lowered to the bottom of the sea at this location. This lowering process can be accomplished either by progressive mechanical clamping or by hydraulic cylinders. A simple, readily available system even consists of segmented barge sections which fit together, using a locking device similar to the chassis-tractor attachment commonly referred to as "Fifth Wheel Kingpin." These portable spuds have been well tested in all types of offshore port construction and are a proprietary development of Robishaw Engineering Company.

As soon as the spud bottom drives itself firmly in the sea bottom, the further spudding action raises the barge up to any desired height over the wave structure. Thus, the resultant pier can be equipped with a container crane. Then installation of a bridge or roadway to shore will produce a container port facility which may be used for one or two container-ships at a time.

MILITARY-CIVILIAN CROSSFEEDS

Again we recognize the close relationship of the ideas between the military and civilian applications. Transport mobility has been the guiding light of the military throughout history. Even if we feel opposed to all war and militaristic development, we cannot deny this powerful drive. During the pre-railroad days, military activities had to cease during the snow or rainy seasons. The troops would be quartered for the winter. When the railroad bed created improved and "winterized" roadbeds for all-weather transportation, the need for winter quarters ceased. At the same time, the availability of high-volume ammunition supplies all year around allowed use of high-speed weapons. The large consumption of ammunition of the machine guns could not be supplied otherwise. In line with this, the artillery demands for more shells led to the use of the first motor trucks by the German army during the siege of Paris in 1870. But the forward move of integrated transport technology via the military/civilian interchange of ideas does not go in a single, much less gradual, line of growth. Civilian cargo science must first produce and develop the next level of higher technology advance. The military will be reluctant to make further use of this development until the urgency arises. Then, and only then, will the military respond to the development and the constraints. Therefore, we can readily see the significance of the creation of such an organization as the National Defense Transportation Association (NDTA) to stimulate the level of knowledge needed to bridge the gap between the civilian progress in this field and its military acceptance.

THE MIL-VAN PLAN

The military sector has purchased many thousands of large, intermodal 20-ft. containers. Analysis of their validity and application contradicts intermodal container aspects. Too much strength is built into the MILVAN for highway use. It could well be understood that the military establishment would need to have a fleet of vans available for use in emergency. But with true overzeal, the military has gone into the design of their own container and has markedly avoided purchase of the standard ISO type of van. No doubt one could design more and more strength into the van. But strength is translated into metal, and metal into weights. The outcome is that in the event of the emergency, the Defense establishment will have some 8,000 "military" vans available. After they are all in use and moving to the front, where they are needed, they will have to be followed by hundreds of thousands of common standard containers. If the best defense resides in a ready, available container transport economy, it would be better to expand the systems of assembly and distribution of containers than to engage in the construction of special MILVANS.

HOUSEHOLD GOODS IN VANS

The action of the Defense establishment in relation to the transportation of household goods for military dependents goes in exactly the opposite direction from the MILVAN program. It has become a custom of the military to transfer their dependents by moving all their belongings to whatever place in the world the military man is assigned. Since relocation and reassignment are frequently necessary to accomplish defense planning, there is an enormous amount of household goods being shipped from one place of the globe to another. The tonnages involved are staggering, and General Otis Winn estimates that these moving services produce gross cost for the military of approximately half a billion dollars per year. Delivery of the serviceman's household goods and other personal property has developed into a world-wide property transportation program. However, with all the technological advances applied to this system, the military has yet to use this program in support of the container systems integration. The household moving industry still uses hundreds of thousands of small plywood crates which are hand-made from milled lumber either at the shipper's premises or at the carrier's warehouse. Once in a while, these crates are assembled from pre-cut components.

Sooner or later, of course, this industry is going to be containerized.

There would be no problem in the military's reorganizing their transportation service so that, in accordance with rank and grade or with some other significant criteria, each household shipper would be permitted one or more containers for each shipment. These containers could vary in size from the smallest ISO standard to a larger van. But in any event, the military must do away with the plywood boxes, called packing crates, in order to have a significant position in the container transportation field. The relationship between too few specialized containers handled in the MILVAN program and no containers in the household goods movement is too much of a contradiction for the progressive thinkers in the military to overlook. On the other hand, the largest shipper in the United States is the United States Government. If the government will enter the field, based on military requirements, it will help ease the full acceptance of containerization in inland transportation.

DISTRIBUTION CENTER NETWORK

The search for a broader role of containerization in the physical distribution service of the United States has led D. H. Overmyer, a storage-in-transit leader, to consider the implementation of vans into the chain warehouses operation. The analysis of the shipper's interest in transportation has led Overmyer to three simple answers. What the shippers want are:

1. Lower freight rates;
2. Faster, more reliable delivery service;
3. Loss and damage reduction.

A system under which a container train would move as a unit one night a week in both directions between New York, Cleveland, Detroit, Chicago, Dallas, Los Angeles, and San Francisco would provide the backbone of such a distribution system. Consolidations in these container trains would reduce railroad switching cost, handling, and paper work. It would also allow the use of the skeletal cars, such as the Portager Car. It would allow the lowering of freight rates due to lightweight trains and economy of scale, as a result of train efficiency. Direct, point-to-point, scheduled container trains would evade freight-yard delays. Transfer from flatcar to delivery tractor would be handled in a fashion similar to port procedures. Finally, minimized cargo handling with goods sealed from shipping dock to unloading point reduces the possibility of misrouting, lot splitting, improper stowage, and pilferage. This plan, which was developed for Overmyer by A. T. Kearney, deals with COFC unit trains and allows commingling of import/export cargo with domestic container traffic. Kearney also envisions for these seven centers true "inland ports" equipped with:

1. Rail facilities capable of handling full container trains;
2. Central container storage area with selecto-matic storage and retrievable procedures for full van loads of standard items, such as soap, paper products, and cosmetics;
3. Unitizing and break-bulk facilities with local delivery truck and container capacity;
4. Fully equipped automated warehouse facilities for distribution of container loads of parts and components;
5. Computer control center tuned in with the other area centers;
6. Tributary facilities dealing with fresh and frozen perishables, household goods, and similar special commodities.

CARAVANS AND CONTAINERS

In the history of transportation, caravans united travelers for mutual assistance and defense on their long journey through dangerous desert countries. Caravan trade preceded maritime commerce in the Near East, existing from earliest recorded history. Later in American history, wagon trains over the Santa Fe trails developed in a similar fashion. Recently, the construction of motor truck terminals along the interstate highway system provides for the stronghold of modern trucking by unitized facilities. The accomplishment of in-transit storage and distribution in containers will follow the route of the modern caravan, the unit container trains, to their interchange points. Inland port planning will write a new chapter in cost-effective physical distribution in the United States. This development will be greatly supported by the state tax laws affecting goods in storage. A full study of the tangible personal property taxes, as they affect inventories of manufacturers, producers, and distributors, reveals that in many locations, goods stowed in transit are exempt while in public or private warehouses or en route to destinations within or outside the state, regardless of origin.

SOLID-WASTE MANAGEMENT

No one will doubt that the largest tonnage offered to transportation comes from our waste-making society. The mountains of all types of solid waste which surround our cities demand immediate attention. Not only environmentalists and ecologists search for answers, but transportation men cannot overlook the close affinity between the systems which would best serve the industry and the most cost-effective techniques. Containers are being used to collect solid waste from households and commercial locations. This waste is then compacted and transferred to other containers and finally reaches the garbage disposal areas close to our cities and centers of population. There is a belief that solid waste should be further removed from suburban locations and either be moved to distant collection and treatment areas or disposed of at sea along the continental shelf at one point or another. Whichever the solution, containerization will be the most effective technology to cope with the growth required and the economy of scale necessary to produce a low-cost collection system.

PHYSICAL COLLECTION AND PRODUCTION

Every large cargo movement which cannot be moved through pipelines or conveyors at the transfer points will end up in containers eventually. The key to these developments is the tolerant uniform system which allows this type of handling in unit size everywhere. The transport economy's greatest success will consist of cost reduction in the production machinery and function. An examination of the many phases of this system exceeds the space available in this book. The approach, however, is container systems engineering, which provides dynamic integration.

Chapter

20

Status and Trends

STATUS REPORT

The book until now has developed the theory of transportation optimization by a methodical demonstration of individual systems and processes. Significant present developments and future trends should be singled out before concluding this study. The value of these developments and trends to the environment of transportation and the economy will be shown. Quantification of the variables is the preferred measuring device and discloses the effectiveness of certain activities (present, planned, or in progress).

SIGNIFICANT DEVELOPMENTS

By the end of 1971, there were clear signs of changes in the progress of containerization: overtonnage on the ocean, significant labor difficulties, and retardation of intermodal and institutional coordination. Since these difficulties occurred simultaneously with the economic recess of 1971, some economists ascribe it to the cyclic movement of our economic order. There is, however, an inherent explanation in the philosophy of cargo systems science. It deals with setting a new course, looking for new goals, and shifting emphasis within the development.

Production process is to industrialization what containerization is to transportation. The distribution processes have not kept pace with the efficiency of the production process. It costs more to distribute goods than to make the goods. To unclog this inefficiency, industrialization could have moved in two directions. In one direction, existing transport systems found to be inefficient could have been replaced by super-systems with jumbo capacity. In contrast, containerization is moving toward improvement through the use of coordination between existing methods. The reader has seen indications of this trend throughout the text.

ADVANCE ADJUSTMENTS

It is universally agreed that the effects of industrialization on an ever-increasing number of people, corporations, and institutions became noticeable over the last hundred years. At first, the benefit of the advance was concentrated. Slowly and as the means of production and distribution multiplied, more and more recipients of benefits replaced those who suffered directly from the changeover. The term "advanced nation" came to be generally understood as dealing with a country equipped with highly efficient transport facilities for the interchange of goods. The system of the transport developed the nation. Intensification of transportation produced the shift-over from labor control to capital power.

From the practical standpoint, all of this deals with capital growth. Jay W. Forrester, Professor at MIT, has become known for the development of methods for systems engineering to solve world problems. Back in his engineering days of the '40s, Forrester invented the coincident-current addressed magnetic memory systems, now widely used in computers. In 1961, Forrester began to deal with the dynamics resulting from the complexities of human life. Recently, he presented a very significant analysis of the relationship between five controlling factors:

1. Population growth;
2. Capital investment;
3. Pollution;
4. Natural resources;
5. Quality of life.

His conclusion is a suggestion that industrial expansion should be slowed down. Forrester's "zero growth" idea also applies to transportation, as part of the overall industrial process. Two coexistent trends move today in opposite directions:

1. Size growth;
2. Penetration in depth.

SIZE VS. DEPTH

Certainly, both developments are going on at the same time. But in the same line of thought developed by Forrester, the change of emphasis from the first to the second development now begins to appear. The U.S. Coast Guard and IMCO begin to think of limiting further growth of the bulkers over the 350,000-ton size, while engineers in Japan, Holland, Great Britain, and the United States have plans for up to one million tons on their drawing boards.

Containerization is definitely growing in depth. The cause-and-effect relationship of containerization stimulates certain developments in the segments which, in turn, will produce new impetus in transport integration:

1. Railroading;
    a. Expansion of container use in domestic transportation to develop genuine interest among the operators;
    b. Development of container standards more adequate for railroad utilization and rate making;
    c. Acceptance of maritime containers, not on a special-service basis, but as tolerant accommodation;
2. Highway trucking;
    a. De-regulation, giving greater flexibility to accommodate both rail and maritime containers to the demands of the economy;
    b. Development of simple, lightweight adjustable chassis which facilitate transfer for intermode and shipper portal;
    c. Opening of the field for innovative operators to enter the container hauling of special commodities both nationwide and international (open container service to Canada, Mexico, and Central America on a national interchange basis);
3. Institutional;
    a. Simplification of trade documentations;
    b. Development of uniform code for commodities and containers;
    c. Development of common-use electronic data systems;
    d. Re-evaluation of the port segment and establishment of a nationwide "port authority" capable of protecting ports from the results of continuing port concentration. Benefits obtained from remaining ports would be used to offset the adverse effects of change.

4. Production management;
   a. Integration of containerization into production;
   b. Concentration of terminal activities related to territorial expansion requirements of the population;
   c. Dedication of containerization to an inventory and marketing strategy;
   d. Establishment of physical distribution on all-weather reliability and total services in transit;
5. Government;
   a. Final acceptance of containerization as the basis of national transportation policy as related to other than bulk transportation modes;
   b. Consideration of nationwide, mandatory pooling of all standard-size containers concurrent with objection to new proliferation of sizes;
   c. Application of these principles to international relations.

Among the many developments which are presently in progress, the ones shown above are those which I consider to hold most influence over the future scenario of containerization.

POSSIBLE TRENDS

In contrast to above developments, the following future trends are highlighted:

1. Barge-Aboard-Vessel (BAV);
2. Land bridge automation;
3. Replacement of reefer fleets.

BAV SYSTEM

A special subsystem of containerization uses barges instead of containers. These barges are lifted, hoisted, or floated into the hull of the vessel which effects the ocean transportation and gives this system the generic name "Barge-Aboard-Vessel" (BAV) System. Without doubt, the largest user of the BAV System is the LASH (Lighter-Aboard-Ship) design group which was invented by Friede & Goldman, naval architects in New Orleans, Louisiana. There are 22 of these ships presently operating, planned, or under construction, both in the United States and in Japan. Impact of the idea on United States' container shipping is well demonstrated by the fact that almost one-fifth of the present and projected American containership tonnage is made up of LASH-type vessels. Another naval architect, J. J. Henry, developed a competing system called the SEABEE (Sea-Barge-Clipper), which differs slightly in barge size and lifting mechanism. But since the large group follows the LASH design, the explanation given for this type of vessel applies, in effect, to the SEABEE and similar systems, as well. Here are the general systems criteria:

Barge subsystem: The barges used are the same as those listed below under the LASH barge system and consist of one compartment. It has one hatch cover installed on an elevated combing. Both ends of the barge are 18 inches lower than the hatch cover. The barge ends serve as base for installation of the corner-post structure when barges are stowed on the transporter vessel. Prior to loading, the four corner-post extensions are installed at the two barge ends. The bottom of each barge is equipped with a recessed structure. The upper ends of the portable corner posts fit into the recessed structure in a very similar fashion to that used by interconnecting containers at the corner. Details of the design specification of a LASH barge are as follows.

LASH lighter: The lighter is essentially a floating container, box-shape in configuration, and fitted with large multisection pontoon-type hatch covers and four substantial lifting and stacking posts. The principal characteristics are as follows:

Length (outside to outside)	61'6"
Beam (outside to outside) at midship	31'2"
Depth of hull (outside to outside) at midship	13'0"
Draft (salt water)	8'3"
Displacement (loaded)	500 short tons
Capacity	17,750 cu. ft. (8 containers)

The lighter shall be constructed of American Bureau of Shipping certified steel; and all material, scantlings, welding, and workmanship shall comply with the requirements of the American Bureau of Shipping. All plating and shapes shall be free of waviness, indents, and buckles, and shall be properly fitted before welding.

The lighter is designed on a transverse system of framing with sufficient longitudinal strength in the sides and deck to permit lifting of the loaded lighter by the LASH crane. The design is based on a weight of structure resulting from the scantlings indicated. The lighter shall be compartmented to provide watertight double-bottom and side sections and end compartments. Deck fittings consisting of four 24-in. cast-steel kevels for the purpose of handling lighters alongside the mother vessel or at dock shall be provided and located near the corners of the lighter. Recessed cargo-lashing eyes shall be provided in the hold, consisting of two rows, approximately 2 ft. and 7 ft. above the double-bottom and spaced approximately 10 ft. apart along the sides. Provision shall be made, by means of four extra-heavy pipe sockets, to accommodate portable, owner-furnished, kerosene running lights. Chafing bars shall be located on all four corners as of mooring cleats and extending approximately 4 ft. on the sides and ends. Four towing pads shall be provided, one at each wedge support casting. Pads shall have a $2\frac{1}{4}$-in. hole.

Intermodality of barge system: The primary application of the LASH system is in its use related to inland waterway systems. The use of small barges to discharge ocean-going ships in the stream was first tried by Hansa Lines, Bremen, Germany. They carried as many as four loaded lighters, deck-loaded like containers, on their combination vessels. The discharge consisted of lifting the loaded lighters with the ship's gear over the side and lowering them into the water. Jerome Goldman, President of Friede and Goldman, improved the system by applying two principles arrived at as a result of system analysis:

1. Lifting from the stern to prevent side motions of the ship;
2. Corner-post stacking to improve load stacking.

Originally, the idea appeared to have most merit as an intermodal facility between the river and canal systems which carry much of the freight in the United States and Europe. The expansion of the Mississippi River and inland waterway systems is equivalent to the European inland navigation system which connects most of Europe with the sea. Expansion of this segment of the idea to the great river systems of Africa, Asia, and Latin America will stand out as the important intermodal future between inland and ocean transportation in these countries.

Port handling facilities: The LASH system has also been advocated to expedite cargo handling in ports. The generic idea is that the ship will not come to the pier at all, but will discharge the lighters in the stream, in the bay, in the estuary, and in the turning basin. From there, the lighters are then taken to individual berths where the hatches are open and the cargo is discharged or loaded. With the use of pallet units, the cargo handling can be expedited with the application of fork trucks equipped with specially long lifting arms, so that they can place or recover pallets directly out of the hold of the barge. The advocates of this system point to the fact that much dry cargo in containers is handled by pallet units anyway. Each barge is equivalent in size to approximately six 40-ft. containers.

BAV VS. CONTAINER

The BAV system is not designed to be effective in handling physical distribution between land-based shipper/consignee facilities. In this respect, the additional handling of the cargo in and out of the barges to attain this could not compare in cost effectiveness to the container system and Ro-Ro system.

There are large economical systems based on the efficient method of using waterways and relating them to production and distribution facilities. Japan, for example, is proud of its water access to its iron and steel industries. These plants are either located on the water's edge or can be made accessible to water. Much of Japan's stride to increase its gross national product is ascribed by Japanese economists to this factor.

EUROPEAN EXAMPLE

There are facilities in use on the European waterways which have been historically water-transport oriented. Steel and other materials arrive by barge; they are picked up by an overhead conveyor system and conveyed directly into the plant. Machinery is then produced from these raw materials. Ideally, at the end of the production line, the overhead lift again picks up the final product and takes it back to the water's edge to provide direct shipping by barge. Many such factories or warehouses are equipped with areas over the water, which are covered so that the loading and unloading is not hampered by weather conditions. The same cover structure contains the overhead lift track. If the popularity of the LASH system increases and standard sizes for barges and ships can be accepted world-wide, the intermodality of the LASH system can be enhanced. Of course, presently, most conventional barges used on the waterways of the world are not capable of being carried on the LASH-type ships because of size and lack of stacking facilities.

COMMODITY RANGE

The purpose of the LASH barge system for the steamship operator is to provide larger lots per shipment and to reduce the number of lifts. In keeping with this idea, the first successful operation of LASH vessels was in the Gulf-to-Europe trade route by Independent Gulf Lines (IGL) for the International Paper Company of Mobile, Alabama. The first two ships were the *Arcadia Forest* and the *Atlantic Forest*. These ships handled paper products from the United States to Europe and steel products on the return voyage. These products have several considerations in common:

1. They are shipped in very large lots which would require excessive stuffing and stripping procedures for containers.
2. Storage-in-transit facilitates the sales policy of the producer.
3. Shipment period can be geared to distribution requirements, as cargo can be left in the barges for ultimate delivery. One LASH shipload will serve an area distribution point.

It, therefore, appears that the greatest application of the LASH system is in the method of unitized bulk (uni-bulk). The loads can be up to 500 tons for each barge. The ship is equivalent to a large floating railroad train carrying many commodities, each in its own container.

All BAV systems offer the opportunity to provide an intermediate step between bulk shipping of solids and/or liquids and the containership. Innumerable variables of this hull use will appear. The large BAV ships can handle containers and even Ro-Ro cargo. The Substitution of present-day barges by air cushion propelled deliveries to marshy and shallow-draft areas may offer many additions to the BAV technology. The most important design improvement would be a large lifting device which would handle the entire cargo content of a barge with unit lifting instead of the piecemeal method presently used. America's latest addition of waterways, reaching all the way from the mouth of the Mississippi to Oklahoma City, opens up another area for the use of the BAV system.

LAND BRIDGE VS. CANALS

The second of the future trends concerns itself with the "land bridge" principle. Originally, containerization and Ro-Ro were developed with the thought that the cargo would move from land origin to sea transport and again to land destination. The thought of moving cargo in transit over land areas is as old as transportation itself. Before the opening of the Panama Canal, all supplies from the eastern shores of the United States to California were transferred across the Isthmus of Central America either in the territory of Mexico or Panama. The digging of the "big ditches," as the Suez Canal and the Panama Canal came to be known, was an important step in the coordination of transportation by water— the most effective means during the Industrial Revolution. These were the first visible effects of economy of scale. Today, the great value of the interoceanic canals is mostly in the field of bulk cargo. For this reason, they must be deep and wide, if they are to be effective. Even with the ship growth limitation discussed before, the canals must be able to carry larger ships than they have been carrying. The canals have lost their attraction in the container trade. Present canal sizes produce restraints to the development of maximum containership sizes.

Possibilities and Types

There are presently three land bridge possibilities: across the North American continent, across the Russian land mass, and across the Central American Isthmus. Examination of the land bridges reveal two types of system possibilities which require analysis:

1. Intermodal land bridges—These cover the long land haul of the United States, Canada, and Russia.
2. Potentially automated mini-land bridges—There are five possible land bridges of this type to be examined for Central America.

The recently completed railroad from Sidney to Western Australia may be considered another potential for a long land bridge, and transit through Israel from the Mediterranean to the Gulf of Akaba may be considered a potential short land bridge competing with the Suez Canal.

Land bridge concepts must be examined for their systems value. Economic quantifications bearing on decision making must deal with the ship type and the overall container system related to the land bridge operation, since the land bridge is only a subsystem and has no value to containerization, except under these conditions.

Much has been said and written about the land bridges across the United States and Canada. Although the theory of transferring containers in the trade between Europe and Japan, via the United States and Canada, seems to be appealing, I found it to be an ineffective system. The rejections are based on the following:

1. Cost consideration—The cost of direct through service by containerships which can pass through the Panama Canal is less than transferring the cargo twice (from and to rails), even considering that the transfer takes a shorter geographical route into account.
2. System consideration—No train has been invented that could carry the exact load of a large containership even as a unit train. This would mean a delay factor and would often produce dissimilarity among the ship links spanning the Atlantic and the Pacific.

The trans-Siberian land bridge works on a different principle. Trains running from Western Europe to Japan via Russia are mostly railroad services. At the end of the Siberian land bridge, there is ship service between the ports of Nakhodka, Russia, and Niigata, Japan. This service has the flexibility of providing as much gradual growth as the trade seems to require. No precise interface seems to be required, since the railroad operators in Russia have agreed to supply as many flatcars as the service demands. The service began after an agreement was concluded between the All-Soviet External Transport Corporation; Container Transport International (CTI), Japan; and MAT Transport, Switzerland. A capacity of 24,000 containers per year is presently anticipated for this land bridge route, which has adopted the name "JEURO."

Economy of Short Land Bridges

To quantify the potential profitability of short land bridges, we must first reach out and identify the stages with which we are concerned:

Stage   I: Spanning the land area;

Stage   II: The containerport system at either end;

Stage III: Main route ship systems;

Stage IV: Cross-feed of additional container traffic;

Stage   V: Automation systems.

Spanning the land area—Stage I: Although Central America is not the only place where short land bridge technology could be applied, it is the best example. Firstly, I am personally familiar with the area, having been engaged in several phases of this development during the last decade. Secondly, there are six alternative solutions which can be considered.

In the Central American continent, there are six possible land bridges, some of which are presently functional for small-scale container operations. These are:

1. Cross Mexico (Salina Cruz–Coatzacoalcos);
2. Cross Guatemala (Matias de Galvex–Champerico);
3. Cross Honduras by train and rail (Puerto Cortez–Gulf of Fonseca);
4. Cross Nicaragua (Blue Field–Puerto Samosa and Corinto);
5. Cross Costa Rica (Puerto Limon–the Pacific);
6. Parallel to the Panama Canal, there are both a highway and a railroad line.

Considerations for land bridges across the Isthmus: Generally speaking, the following considerations of five pragmatic program points could serve to illustrate the feasibility:

1. The congestion and traffic condition in the Panama Canal are increasing. Canal tolls are rising and the Canal becomes more restrictive to container traffic as time goes on.

2. Costs of transferring containers (20 ft., 35 ft., and 40 ft.) have become a well-accepted fact among steamship companies. Mechanization of transfer allows very low-cost automated transfer today.

3. Creating containerports on both sides of the Isthmus is desirable. This will allow the development of transfer ports from the Atlantic to the Pacific and also allow feedership operation from the Orient to Latin America and the Caribbean.

4. The railroad conditions are better now than ever before; however, they may still have to be improved to shorten the rail distance and to expedite service.

5. The operation could be started with floating container cranes in approximately two years after permission has been granted and financing has been arranged for the facilities.

The land bridge of Mexico—Stage II: The feasibility of handling containerized intercoastal cargo across the Mexican Isthmus of Tehuantepec, instead of by the usual route through the Panama Canal, has been investigated by W. B. Saunders, Inc., and by the United Nations Commission. Containerships could dock at the Port of Coatzacoalcos on the Gulf of Mexico, where westbound containers would be unloaded for the rail movement across the Isthmus. This movement would be over the 189-mile route of the National Railways of Mexico, traveling south into the port of Salina Cruz. There the containers would be reloaded into another ship, which would complete the voyage to Los Angeles, San Francisco, Japan, or other Far East destinations. It is the most important trade route between Europe and Japan, because it is the shortest with good rail connections.

The Port of Coatzacoalcos on the Atlantic lies along one side of the Coatzacoalcos River, the narrow mouth of which contributes to the calm waters at the harbor. Although the river is rather narrow, it is wide enough to permit the average vessel to turn around. In any case, it would not be a matter of much difficulty for a vessel to back out into the Gulf, rather than turn around in the harbor with help of tugs or thrusters. There is at least 28 ft. of water in the harbor, with a rise of 1½ ft. at high tide.

The outer harbor is protected by breakwaters, but occasional dredging is necessary to keep it navigable. Present practice is to load and unload in the inner harbor. The narrow channel that connects the outer with the inner harbor is only 89 ft. wide and an average of 30 ft. deep, depending on the tide. Ships which are now being used for intercoastal

U.S. containerized cargo would have a tight squeeze to pass through this channel.

The route of the National Railways of Mexico from Coatzacoalcos to Salina Cruz spans 189 miles of both marshy and mountainous terrain. The marshy condition of the lowlands makes it difficult to maintain the ballast, ties, and alignment of the rail. Whereas Coatzacoalcos lies in the mouth of a river and, therefore, has calm waters, the port of Salina Cruz directly faces the Pacific Ocean. Because of high surf conditions, waves bring in a great deal of sand. The port, thus, has been divided into outer and inner side harbors.

Panama land link—Stage II: Parallel to the Panama Canal is a well developed railroad line and a good highway extending between the Atlantic port of Cristobal/Colon and the Pacific port of Balboa/Panama. There are deep-water facilities in the Canal Zone, developed by the United States under the Panama Canal Treaty. The Republic of Panama is interested in developing (outside of the American jurisdiction) the land bridge system facilities on both sides of the oceans to attract revenue for the Republic of Panama and to participate in world trade. The distance between the two facilities would be well under 100 miles. The containerport facilities required for land bridges would be those described in Chapter 11, with a modification toward automation which will be discussed later.

Ship economy of scale—Stage III: The development of land bridge facilities must be integrated with the levels of technology of containership systems. Today, most containerships range in size from 15,000 to 30,000 gross tons. The efficiency increase, described by Professor Harry Benford of the University of Michigan, for large bulk vessels can be applied to the size of the containership as well. Containerships today, as we have shown, are very small compared to the present size of bulk carriers. Therefore, if our containership size were to double or triple, they would still result in relatively small ships compared to the mammoth tankers or OBOSs (Ore-Bulk-Oil Ships), which are underway today. But the size increase of the ships would make the cost of carriage per container on a maritime route more cost-effective. If the technology of the containerports can keep pace with the economy of scale of the ship, future trends are to go in this direction. Therefore, the investigation of the importance of small land bridges must, at this stage, look to the phases of development in the containership system. (See Fig. 20-1.)

Meeusen, the consultant to the Port of Rotterdam, predicts that development of containerships will move through ten levels of technology. These ten levels are:

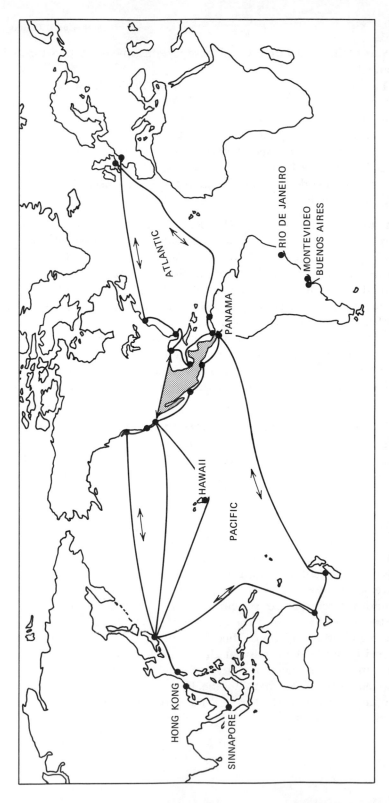

FIGURE 20-1. CIRCLE PATTERN OF GIANT CONTAINERSHIP ROUTES WITH LAND BRIDGE CONNECTIONS.

Level   I: After container vessels have exceeded the 36,000-ton mark, fully automated port areas, including computerized stowage and retrieval, become mandatory.

Level   II: The introduction of automated transfer will reduce the cost of container handling so that, consequently, the remaining conventional cargo systems will disappear from the main trade routes.

Level III: All cargo being containerized, a much larger number of containers will have to be handled.

Level   IV: This will lead to further demand for application of economy of scale by means of giant container vessels and better inland interface.

Level   V: Giant vessel dimensions may be of the same order of magnitude as tankers.

Level   VI: Giant container vessels will, in turn, lead to new trade routes.

Level VII: New trade routes will require automated container terminals, at which the container will be transferred.

Level VIII: New land bridges—such as Panama, Tehuantepec, and Israel—will, therefore, become feasible.

Level   IX: Transfer ports will be important instruments for international trade.

Level   X: Giant container vessels, finally, will operate between a few automated transfer terminals at both sides of the narrow land bridges and in major ports of the industrial nations.

To support the main ship route systems demonstrated in Stage III, containerports at land bridge terminals could also serve as change-of-gauge facilities, where ship container traffic can be exchanged with other ship container traffic and, potentially, with large barges. The possibility of developing giant ships which could carry both containers and BAV barges finds no problem in ship design technology. The only developments necessary are those dealing with port facilities.

In this stage, where cross-feed of additional traffic motivates a further growth in ships and facilities, we must look at the change of gauge as a system to complement overall cost effectiveness.

Change of gauge—Stage IV: In my discussion of the Isothermic Unitized Cargo System before the Society of Naval Architects and Marine Engineers (SNAME) on November 13, 1964, I stated that the maintenance of adequate transit environment would lead to the coordination of several general-cargo-ship services into one single distribution system made up of several, independent containership services. In other words, what existed in the world in the early days of rail transportation in feeder, branch, and main lines will come to be seen as well in the container service system, yet on a much larger world-wide scale. The advent of this idea provides the understanding of how the many small islands of the Pacific will just as well participate in the production-to-distribution chain as suburbs of the most advanced containerport towns.

W. Waters discussed this in his paper presented in October 1971 before the New Zealand Institution of Engineers. Along the same lines, the self-propelled services of Coordinated Caribbean Transport (CCT), a Division of the U.S. Freight Company, between Florida and Central America were coordinated in the fall of 1971 with the barge services of Trans-Carib Hydro, a Division of the Crowley interest. The purpose of this coordination was to provide refrigerated container through services between Puerto Rico and the Virgin Islands on one hand, and the Central American Republics of Guatemala, Salvador, Nicaragua, and Costa Rica on the other hand, connecting via Miami, Florida. These are the significant signs of the penetration of the interchange of containers into the root system of world trade. The accrual of container traffic produced by many feeder systems will further enhance the concentration of major traffic at the containerports located along land bridge areas. Figure 20-2 shows the cradle of containerization in the Americas. Door-to-door transportation to these areas will typically work as change of gauge by transferring containers from one type of ship to another.

Automation systems—Stage V: For the containerports which would serve as land terminals for the ship systems, the reader will find details in Chapter 11. We are now dealing with the correlation of two containerports separated by a variable distance. Analysis applied to the Mexican land bridge by W. B. Saunders demonstrated the superiority of rail-connected service over truck service. The rail service, in turn, can be optimized to unit train operation. Electrification of such a railroad would produce high, consistent train speeds between two containerports. Accomplishment of this would be facilitated by fully automated train operation, which is already customary in many high-speed railroads.

If the volume warrants, the ideal operation uses continuous conveyor belts to move the containers from port to port and to feed directly into the container through-port. The technology of container conveyor systems has been described in detail by Meeusen. He applies it to port complexes and within ships. There is no reason why the system cannot be expanded to distances of several hundred miles in length. High-capacity conveyor belts have been in use for a long time between coal mines and ports approximately 100 miles in distance. Litton Industries developed an idea which had been proposed over 20 years ago. The Munitions Board considered the use of conveyor belts between the Great Lakes, to

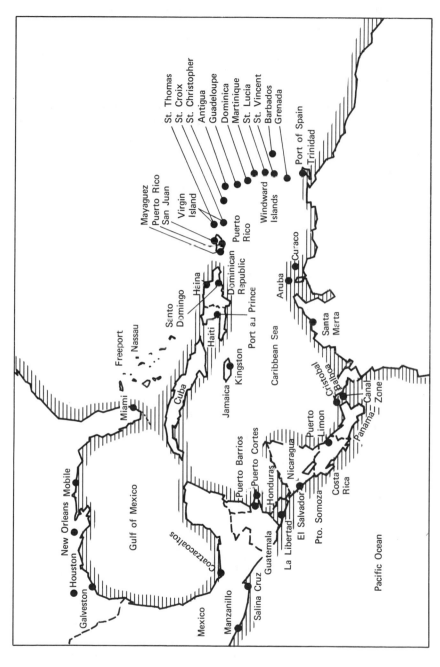

FIGURE 20-2. THE CARIBBEAN AREA WAS THE CRADLE OF CONTAINERIZATION BETWEEN THE U. S. EAST COAST AND PUERTO RICO.

allow for continuance of maximum-size ships on both lakes. Litton Industries wanted to use this system to cut the cost of hauling iron ore on the Great Lakes. Since the ship size is limited by the locks between the lakes, an alternative span was called for. Litton considered the application (which was successfully designed by the Hewitt Robbins Division of Litton Industries) of the idea of the Munitions Board to automate transfer from "Laker to Laker." The technology was tested out on a 70-mile-long conveyor belt for the transportation of copper ore in North Africa. Conveyor systems of that size can be equipped to alternately carry bulk cargo or containers. Litton abandoned the idea in 1971. The technology, however, remains valid.

Today, the technology of long-distance conveyor systems has been advanced by these studies. The formula of combining giant containerships with automated containerports and long-distance conveyor systems may provide a most effective world transport system for the future.

Land Bridges and Developing Nations

Automated land bridge systems will allow further growth of deep-sea containerships, leading to further load concentration and increased economy of scale. Before completing the review of the second future trend on "land bridge automation," we should consider locating these land bridges in developing areas. This could have multiple effects.

The location of highly automated facilities in developing countries establishes an important link of technology, and as we will see later, refers back to Forrester's idea of the "growth of the capital investment in agriculture." M. K. J. Rynish, in the October 1971 issue of the *ICHCA Monthly Journal,* describes the orientation of highly sophisticated cargo systems to the so-called "Third World Countries":

> The greatest problem facing the world today, and the one which all thinking people must be concerned with, is the growing gulf between the rich countries, the manufacturing nations and the poor countries, the underdeveloped nations.
>
> I maintain it is primarily a transportation problem. The rich countries are suffering from an excess of surface transport, and the poorer countries are suffering from a lack of it.

The lack of automated short land bridges on the Isthmus of Central America would require very large capital investment. This capital should come from international bodies, with participation of all nations who would benefit from such a transport link. The operation of such facilities should be under the United Nations, and the profit from these operations could support general activities of the United Nations.

Second Panama Canal

Such a land bridge would eliminate the need for a second Panama Canal which could be built effectively only with the use of atomic explosives. The pollution danger also makes such an application undesirable today. The military value of the present Canal to the United States does not affect the defense posture of this country. Since present-size ships can pass through the Canal, there would be no need for change in strategy. If warships are to be built larger than the present Canal limitations, the decision does not come from the Canal, but from two other considerations:

1. Cost effectiveness of such jumbo ships;
2. Value of any jumbo ships facing up to atomic missiles.

If the Canal is to remain as an artery of commerce, international cooperation should provide the means to build and operate such a facility. The benefits to the American taxpayer will be no greater than those to the rest of the world. The principle of self-liquidation must apply to containerized facilities of the future.

VANNING OF PERISHABLES

Turning now to the last of the significant trends, we must study a range of commodities heretofore not applied to containerization. Large cargoes are still carried by a fleet of several hundred medium-sized refrigerated ships. The so-called meat-and-fruit trades operate between Australia, Latin America, Africa, and the consumer nations of Asia, Europe, and North America. High-speed ships carry only a limited range of commodities, which are regularly shipped in ship-size lots. Regularity of call does not extend to starting ports. The ships always call at the same delivery ports, equipped with special handling facilities. Starting ports may vary according to seasons or to the occurrence of a sudden tropical storm which could destroy bananas planted in a certain producing region.

Historically, perishable foods have often been an incentive for improvements in commercial transportation. American apples, for example, made up the first cargo for steamers between England and the New World.

We have described the technology now available for the containerization of fresh and frozen perishables in Chapter 13. It would appear that with this technical possibility, the investment aspect of the present conventional refrigerated ship fleet will change. Harald Burmeister developed an extensive study dealing with the potential of this changeover. In his summary, referring to containerization, Burmeister states: "There are sufficiently strong indications that such a system could work, and it may not detain one competitor whose survival depends, on a lesser degree, on its success or failure."

The changeover to containers has been delayed due to the unique structure of the reefer fleet. Most of the world's ships are owned by Europeans and Israelis. Ships sail to pick up certain contracted refrigerated loads. On this outbound voyage to the pickup, the ships handle mostly simple commodities, such as small European and Japanese automobiles. On the return voyage, the ships are fully loaded for their consumer destination. The ships involved are relatively new. There is an active market in such second-hand ships because many developing nations, such as Taiwan and the Philippines, acquire these ships for their incipient trade in perishables. For the shipowners that specialize in this type of tonnage, Burmeister concluded that no change would occur until a large competitor would take the first step.

This first step is now being taken. The transportation of frozen meats by the ACT fleets from Australia to Europe and by Hamburg-Sud's Columbus Line from Australia to the United States has been in effect for some time. Now the United Fruit Company, ZIM line, and some U.S.–European carriers have started to use high-capacity reefer containers. These containers, like the COOLTAINER by Frigitemp Corporation, allow initial cooling in transit. Initial cooling for certain commodities can replace precooling and allow cargoes to be shipped from the field directly to their destination. All fresh commodities require effective internal environmental stabilization, so that the product's heat is removed while the cargo is in transit. This equipment is quite different from the conventional refrigeration system and uses high-pressurized humid air to do the work in transit.

With the advent of this equipment, the world-wide transportation of fresh foods will change radically. New life will be added to containerization, and the true meaning of intermodal through-transport will be strengthened by the introduction of containers which fulfill a mission in transit to improve the cargo transported in the container. At the intersection of new cargo treatment technologies with such containerization as the COOLTAINER lies the promise of the future validity of the method.

As the new method is accepted by the trade as the effective intermodal system, a new chain of events will be set in motion. The technology level of this change can be described on a phasic progress:

Phase   I: Perishable services gradually shift to mechanically refrigerated containers.

Phase   II: Integration of vanned perishables into general-cargo service becomes possible.

Phase III: LASH and container vessels compete for the reefer trade.

Phase IV: Feederships to automated land bridge containerports feed reefer containers or LASH barges into the system.

Phase   V: Jumbo containerships move on regular routes at regularly scheduled intervals.

On September 25, 1972, Robert S. McNamara, now President of the World Bank revealed disturbing findings of his bank to the International Monetary Fund. The development of the World Bank's loans appear to widen the gap between the developed and the poor, underdeveloped nations. His conclusions are that human degradation reaching 30% to 40% of the citizens cannot be tolerated for too long. His remarks deal with feeding, health and employment factors, all of which can be ascribed to deficient transport mobility in the underdeveloped nations. The experience of those concerned with the widening gap in transport systems forces us to face up to the urgency of intermodal needs as the answer to bring the poorer nations out of the depth of this gap and into a tolerable relationship with the rest of the world. Of the great many varieties in the container systems world, some simple forms can be adapted pragmatically in all parts of the world. Containerization has developed transportation from a fragmented system into the tool for essential progress. Interdisciplinary assessment of each individual area problem must be used to propose new, even radical solutions which can be implemented with local means and a minimum of international support.

The ultimate effect of all future trends is to unify and internationally integrate deep-sea jumbo ship service with the land modes. An encounter will take place at ports equipped to interface several systems of long-distance mobility and to interconnect with feeder services. Opportune locations of such system terminals in poor, developing countries allow the opening of new areas of tropical agriculture, meat production and, in turn, interchanges cargo with the products of the advanced areas of mass production on the North Atlantic and the North Pacific. These developments expand opportunities to reduce the widening gap of transport technology in the world economy.

QUANTIFICATION OF DEVELOPMENT

This indication of trends and developments may appear futuristic. Everything which is not presently tangible exists only as a vision. To make a sophisticated approach to such systems requires value analysis. According to Lawrence D. Miles, in his book, *Techniques of Analysis and Value Engineering,* a "value analysis" is a "superior problem-solving system." To use this method in technological forecasting requires quantification of the variables. Harald Burmeister, in his book, shows how difficult it is to quantify *all* variables. Without quantification, we cannot determine the order of importance and the precedent within the system. This is very important for decision in investments and, particularly, in predetermination of the possible obsolescence of facilities and equipment.

The cargo systems engineer must reduce the realm of the nonquantifiable variables to a minimum. He must do so by continuously expanding the technology of quantification. As far as I am concerned, nothing in the field of transportation is nonquantifiable.

Elliot Schrier, President of Manalytics, Inc., in his paper, "Too Much and Too Little," presented at the Oakland Containerization Conference in September 1971, states:

> We have used linear programming and computer simulation models to select optimum routes from inland origins to inland destinations, to minimize shippers' costs. We have developed financial planning models to calculate the effects of alternative investment, operating and marketing decisions on carrier unit cost and profits. We even have the beginning of a unique, flexible and comprehensive capacity-demand data base for containerizable cargo, which we are developing further with industry on a multi-participant basis. These and other elements of management technology can and will be applied to improve the container system.

Format of Thinking

THE UNKNOWN AND THE UNCERTAIN

Having identified the pattern of relationships between the expanding container systems and the transportation segments throughout the book, we find that we have a range of choices which allows the free play necessary to arrive at the best combination. There are no two identical container systems. With each system goes certain benefits and a number of unique constraints. Eventually, however, the entire structure must emerge with small tolerance at the interface.

The center of gravity of the development of all present containerization lies in the juxtaposition of two problems in systems engineering:

1. Coping with the unknown—The level of knowledge required by the systems engineer in the great variety of fields is very large and requires apprenticeship in all major phases of transport.
2. Preparing for the uncertain—The final goal of containerization is full mechanization and automation of transfer. This attainment may be slowed down by institutional resistance. The tenet of the systems ideology, however, remains constant.

I have also attempted to analyze the institutional motivations behind the resistance to container implementation. The trend becomes somewhat clear as we learn more. My inclusion of "trends" in the section, "Conveyance Systems," may be considered futuristic. But how can we expect this system to be "static" in a field of technology which is just coming out of the first decade?

I have shown the often opposing tendencies among the segments. These tendencies must be reconciled by a "Code of the Container" which, like all basic laws, provides the constitution for the container community. There are those who expect to find monolithic structures in any endeavor. The nature of containerization development is fluid and not firmed up. The only permanent tendency is toward change.

THE INHERITANCE OF TECHNOLOGY

For generations, transportation has acquired an increasing significance in the life and functioning of modern society. Yet very few people have ever developed an overall scientific approach to this segment, which constitutes almost one-third of the gross national product of the industrial nations. Most studies of transportation have taken the parochial form. The teachings have dealt with many particular phases of the segmented transportation economy; but very seldom has there been an overall combination of the approach to all segments at the same time. I refer to the studies of transportation from the technical, organizational, and economic points of view.

Much has been said about the side benefits which have developed from the methodology used in the aerospace industry. Systems analysis and systems engineering have become the significant tools with which man has been able to develop a piece of machinery that would fly from Earth to the face of the moon, work there, and return to Earth. It is the masterful expression of coordination and combination of technologies in many fields.

PLANNING PATTERN

The secret is to develop a plan or design to move from the certain and known to the unknown and uncertain. For instance, after many years of consideration, the Citrus Marketing Board of Israel decided to switch from conventional cargo-handling methods to containers. Frigitemp Corporation of New York was asked to develop a refrigerated container system for ZIM lines. At this intersection, Frigitemp applied systems analysis and engineering to solve the problem. First, the stages in the development of the technology were carefully identified. Selection of the through-the-load refrigeration method, the air pressure and the velocity requirements were matched with the thermal rating of the container, and the delivery profile involved. In other stages, Frigitemp identified the best experiences obtained in carrying citrus from the United States to Europe and the experimental work of the United States Department of Agriculture. Plant behavior was studied in terms of agricultural pathology and physiology. All these stage results were fed back to the design group, which had the experience of containerization in general, inland transportation in Israel, and delivery in Europe, as well as in the United States.

After the stage of analysis was completed, the parameters of the equipment design and operation were related to each other. In several go-arounds, the significant elements were singled out and optimized. The process led to value analysis and recognition of the design elements. Thereafter, the first design integration took place. After further analysis and review of the probable results, the system was developed.

Systems designers and cargo scientists in New York and California were thus able to develop an operational container system. In effect, the actual activity took place almost 10,000 miles from the "drawing board" at which the system was conceived.

ACCEPTING FLUIDITY

All this amounts to the fact that opposing and disturbing pressures become apparent as containerization becomes further implemented. The fluidity of the changeover and the pressure of getting the job done, however, relentlessly push forward toward mechanization automation. Containerization has grown too much and too fast in certain segments, particularly the ship sector. To take advantage of this advance will require consolidation of these gains in the marine segments while implementation in other segments remains incomplete. In the course of these developments, people will be faced with many uncertainties. These uncertainties arise as a result of the numerous alternatives which are open for the implementation of containerization in certain fields. Questions arise as to the direction in which to move forward. The systems engineer must have a grasp of many unknown factors, in order to deal with the many alternatives.

BASIC ENCOUNTER

The remaining great problems of containerization are those in the attitudes of the segments of the transportation industry. Containerization will reduce the individual freedom of action of a transport segment by transforming it into a subsystem of a unified new industry. The new industry seeks to avoid duplication of efforts and looks for the best possible combination to provide the most effective integrated transportation service. This takes reconciliation among the elements of industry. This is not a purely technical matter, but one which deals with human behavior and attitude. We have seen a very good example in the analysis, "Man–Container Interface," in Chapter 18.

What makes this matter more complicated is that containerization is a polysystem interface. Many problems of many segments come to the surface at the same time. All have importance, but all must be placed in a single perspective, namely, a more effective, coordinated transportation system. This leads to a basic free-for-all when carrier groups meet with shipper groups, representatives of port facilities, forwarders, and equipment manufacturers. Such encounters often take place at public meetings; these meetings have been held for the past decade under the auspices of The Containerization Institute, the National Defense Transportation Association, the University of California, and the International Cargo Handling Coordination Association (ICHCA), to name just a few. Ports, such as those in New Orleans and Baltimore, have sponsored similar workshop sessions. At these technical meetings, several hundred interested persons from the industries confront a rostrum of 20 to 30 participants. The ensuing discussions produce many valid alternatives to the medium of containerization as it now exists. Many opinions expressed by the participants must be analyzed for their overall validity, in order to avoid application of a parochial view which, in the long run, would be detrimental to the entire system. Therefore, in order to be effective, these meetings need a summary expression. The good ideas must be put into practice; the others must be discarded. This is a very valid systems approach.

TOWARD A CARGO SYSTEMS SCIENCE

But who is to say what is right and wrong? Many have been trained in their particular technological field and have been active in their particular segment of the industry for many years. Each segment has developed its own particular view as to how the transportation industry should work and what its own place within it should be. Many valid attempts have been made to develop a scientific doctrine, and the list of organizations, universities, and private institutions which have attempted practical solutions would be too long to enumerate.

In this connection, there is a noteworthy organization in Great Britain called the "Institute of Transport"; it is not confined to containerization. The record of the Institute over its fifty years' existence is impressive in the development of the study and advancement of the science and art of transportation in all world-wide segments. Today, the Institute holds roughly 250 meetings a year all over the world and has members in over 60 countries. It deals with the study of the coordination of transportation and initiates investigation and research into the best means, methods, and applications for the solution of transportation problems. The Institute has also played an important part in the development of the study of transportation at universities, with significant emphasis at Oxford University, where it has obtained the establishment of a professorship.

Typical is the influence of the Institute of Transport on the transportation industry in New Zealand. A work-study group has been supported by the Auckland Harbor Board and has brought together at the Institute all segments of the transportation industry of New Zealand. Also, ICHCA has developed a very effective committee in New Zealand. In this book, we have made use of three outstanding studies prepared in New Zealand, dealing with ports, vessel selection, and tariff rates. This is an indication of the high level of transport science developed in that area. Containerization needs its own "Institute" because of the need to create cross-fertilization.

FORMAT OF FUTURE THINKING

Containerization, like any other human endeavor, faces the generation gap. Besides the generation gap between conventional and unitized ships, there are also generations of containerships competing with each other. The difficulty is that the facilities for each generation must be rejuvenated to keep abreast of the latest developments.

The uncertainty syndrome faces the container industry. Fluid adaptation of new facilities must be made to recoup investments. Heretofore, research and development have been used by generalists with a good knowledge of mathematics; but the truth is that the nature of cargo systems science needs its own special analysis.

Alice M. Rivlin, in her book, *Systematic Thinking for Social Action,* states that rigorous rational analysis can strip away illusions. But if ultimately intuitive judgment is overlooked or obscured, the general analysis can create new illusions of their own. A prerequisite to developing such intuition is to fully comprehend the format of the future. As an example, let us look at what happened with United States Lines. A considerable amount of effort was spent there in developing automated selection procedures for the location and stowage of containers on their tri-continental bridge service. Since this system was too complicated for the man–control interface, it had to be discarded after six months' use because it was found to be unmanageable. This, then, required United States Lines to place 3,000 tons of fixed ballast in each ship to make the calculation easier. This, in turn, meant that with approximately 40 ships operating in the fleet daily, 120,000 tons of ballast was being moved just to keep the containerships stable.

CURRICULUM REFERENCE

A task confronting cargo systems science is to bring up a new generation of qualified "cross-section" engineers. The multisystem interface, which containerization is, demands apprenticeship in the various fields, in addition to academic training in systems engineering. Multinational experience is required to provide ample understanding to fit components together. Men must learn to use comparative study methods.

Among other things, the curriculum should include:

1. Physical distribution method of goods in containers;
2. Container transportation market and traffic forecasting;
3. Planning and design of integrated transport systems and subsystems;
4. Optimization of container system management and operations;
5. Container and related transportation equipment and component design;
6. Investment appraisals of container transport systems;
7. Performance, reliability, and safety of container systems and equipment.

FURTHER MATURING OF TECHNOLOGY

Systems engineers are usually a realistic group. Yet on occasion, technology far outpaces the theoretical understanding of the intricacies of the system and its place in the world. There is a frequent tendency to create euphoria by overemphasizing what is favorable and overlooking the real problems. It is a sign of maturity in a branch of science when major innovations lose their glamor, once the industry takes a real accounting of how the system itself will work. Throughout this text we have dealt with the compromise between many disciplines and a multi-systems integration problem.

There is hardly anyone in the community who, sooner or later, will not come into contact with containerization. For example, to house our people, prefabricated or mobile homes become prominent. Modern prefabricated homes use the technique of container structure and handling method.

Then we have an example of an entirely different nature. Since the beginning of the Interstate Commerce Commission, it had to deal with the yearly problems incurred with the temporary storage and availability of railroad cars to haul the grain from the wheat states. James Warwick, Vice President of Transport Systems, developed a technology in which containers would be used as temporary storage. A new port technique would interface containerized inland transport of grain with bulk grain ships, discharging the container's contents directly into the hold of bulk ships, because ocean transportation of grain in containers would not be economical.

Transportation of heavy steel products and such low-rated commodities as barbed wire and concrete reinforcing bars will change, too. Mechanization of discharge from BAV barges to intermodal service is an open requirement. When it comes to pass, it will afford a new phase of economy of scale in an unprecedented development.

HOVER SHIPS AND ATOMIC POWER

Navy planners, after decades of building larger warships, are beginning to think small and bold. Admiral Elmo Zumwalt, the forward-looking Chief of Naval Operations, is radically reshaping the thinking of surface ships. Zumwalt's emphasis is on smaller and faster ships. These ships are generally less expensive than those which the Navy is presently building. Among the ships projected are surface-effect ships in the range of 100 knots with capacities of 2,000 to 10,000 tons.

Almost simultaneous with this, in October 1971, the Maritime Administration presented a briefing to the shipping-industry executives to propose the use of nuclear power. Samuel H. Esleeck of Babcock and Wilcox explained that a nuclear-powered ship with 120,000 shaft horsepower designed as a containership would cost about 1.5 million dollars per year, compared with an oil-fuel ship. Operational costs also would be higher. However, the annual fuel cost would run only about one-fourth of an oil-fuel ship. This would result in a net saving of approximately 1.1 million in favor of the atomic-powered ship. In addition, Mr. Esleeck contended that the nuclear ship does not have to devote any of its cargo space or weight for the carriage of fuel. This fact alone enables it to go faster and make more frequent voyages per year. The economy of scale can make five nuclear-powered ships do the work of eight fuel-powered ships, bringing about a savings in fuel cost alone of six million dollars per year.

I have shown at the outset of this book that much progress in transportation has come about as the outgrowth of government-supported military development. Remember that modern warfare, modern machine guns, and modern artillery came about as a result of railroad technology and the first trucks. Carlos Fallon ascribes to Emanuel Kant the statement: "I can because I must." The use of atomic power developed by Maritime interests, and hovercraft technology inspired by the Navy, can produce 100-knot medium-sized vessels. Containerization of the next decade must be prepared for this event with new automated technology. Imagine connecting the mainland with Hawaii by a ship in 24 hours! This makes automated transfer of containers from such a ship to the connecting carriers mandatory. Integrated methods and real-time control become required instead of just desirable. A ship that goes to Hawaii in 24 hours cannot afford to spend more than 2 hours in port at each end. This also calls for a new type of manpower. It also needs uncongested ports. Places such as San Diego may have a new field open to them in the application of fully automated port facilities.

Throughout this text I have used the approach of a new development in the field of transportation. Since it deals specifically with freight transportation and with a systematic integration, we truthfully can call it "Cargo Systems Science." Science generally finds inspiration in the rewards of discovery. In contrast, the engineer's approach is creation. In the field of unifying our methods and facilities of transportation, it appears that it requires both discovery and creation. All this goes along quite well until the question of forecasting arises. My friend, Harald Burmeister, has proven in his book that the structure of transportation is far too complicated to accommodate the known forecasting methods. Time-event prediction, which many readers may have hoped to find related as a method applicable to containerization, is not equipped with enough background data to draw conclusions for the future. The scientific method applying to containerization must be ready to serve all branches of technology; because each, by reason of its proven insufficiency, has need of support from the others. Cargo systems science is the tool of western man; and with it, more doors can be opened than with bare hands.

THE CONSERVATIONIST APPROACH

There is growing concern with conservation in our society. We are now conscious of our possibly diminishing resources. We are no longer interested in adding monster facilities to the existing network of highways, railroads, airports, and terminal areas. Now, we begin to think in terms of land-use control and the limitations on industry. We begin to understand that the quality of life can no longer afford to use the environment carelessly. To develop methods which apply this type of thinking to the field of transportation is part of the cargo systems science transport response to environmenal thinking. The polysystems interface of containerization provides the possibility of transportation resources economy.

E PLURIBUS UNUM

As I come to the conclusion of my book, I fear that some readers may be disappointed because of the lack of "instant solutions" to the container problems. Many of the major problems dealing with work rules, further automation, opening of new routes and trading areas, and the answer to port limitation have been discussed to the extent that they can be developed today. We still live in the period where containerization is novel and lives side by side with some remaining conventional shipping and some unit load handling of palletized cargo. How soon these methods will fade depends largely on other developments in the field. Systems unitization, like the inclusion of refrigerated meat and fruit services in general-cargo shipping, will result in a new wave of technology which is on the drawing board today. What appears futuristic may well be the operating basis of tomorrow!

In our daily life we are getting accustomed to many instant solutions. We are impatient with continued, lengthy developments. Looking at the magnitude of investments needed to containerize, one should be grateful that the changeover is as slow as it is. But let there be no doubt about it, containerization acts like a glacier. It is moving slowly forward, but always on the move.

If there is any lesson to be learned of this technology, it is that multidisciplinary understanding is required. These qualifications are needed today by all segments of transport. The art of creative integration has always been desired by man. For containerization, it is the way of life. The Romans already had a phrase for it: "E Pluribus Unum."

Bibliography

BOOKS

Armand, Louis and Drancourt, Michel, *The European Challenge*, Dover Publications, 1967.

Barker, James R. and Brandwein, Robert, *The United States Merchant Marine in National Perspective*, Heath Lexington Books, 1970.

Burmeister, Harald, *The International Banana Transport: Can Containers Handle It?*, University of Lausanne, 1969.

Datz, I. M., *Planning Tools for Ocean Transportation*, Cornell Maritime Press, Inc., 1971.

Fallon, Carlos, *Value Analysis to Improve Productivity*, Wiley Interscience, 1971.

Immer, John, *Container Services of the Atlantic*, 1970, Work Saving International, 1970.

Institution of Civil Engineers, *Telecommunications in Ports*, 1971.

Machol, Robert E., *Systems Engineering Handbook*, McGraw-Hill, 1965.

Makower, M. S. and Williamson, E., *Operational Research*, Dover Publications, 1967.

Marshall, Alfred, *Principles of Economics*, MacMillan, 1961.

Miles, Lawrence, *Techniques of Value Analysis and Engineering*, McGraw-Hill, 1961.

Oram, R. B. and Baker, C.C.R., *The Efficient Port*, Pergamon Press, 1971.

Sauerbier, Charles L., *Marine Cargo Operation*, John Wiley & Sons, 1956.

Tabak, Herman D., *Cargo Containers, Their Stowage, Handling and Movement*, Cornell Maritime Press, Inc., 1970.

Ullman, Gerald H., *The Ocean Freight Forwarder, the Exporter and the Law*, Cornell Maritime Press, 1967.

Van Metre, Thurman, *Industrial Traffic Management*, McGraw-Hill, 1953.

Wiener, Norbert, *Cybernetics*, MIT Press, 1961.

Wolfe, Roy I., *Transportation and Politics*, D. Van Norstrand Co., Inc., 1963.

PAPERS

Archdeacon, Gerald D., "The T.R.T. System, A Transcontinental Rapid Transit System," 1968.

Armand, Louis, Paper Presented at the IRCA-UIC Congress, London, May 18, 1971.

Baker, John J., "Warehousing in Motion," paper presented to the Transportation Research Forum of New York, November 12, 1968.

Benjamin, James F., "An Objective Look at Intermodal Transportation," paper presented at The Containerization Institute Conference, New York, March 24, 1971.

Black, Alexander, "Unitization and Intermodal Transport Compatability," paper presented at the Transportation in the 70's Conference, University of California, San Diego, April 1970.

Breakiron, P. L., "Improving the Transport of Perishables Through Better Equipment and Methods," paper presented at the International Conference on Handling Perishable Agricultural Commodities, March 1971.

Bridges, Harry, "Containers and Their Effect on Waterfront Workers," paper presented before The Containerization Institute, November 13, 1969.

Broido, J. A., "Critical Cost Factors in Container Systems," paper presented at the Transportation in the 70's Conference, University of California, San Diego, April 1970.

Budorick, Robert E., Remarks presented at the Technical Congress, 4th International Shipping and Containerization Exposition, Oakland, September 14, 1971.

Bussel, Dr. Joseph, "Cooling and Shipping of Oranges in Refrigerated Containers under Quarantine Regulations, Department of Food Engineering and Biotechnology, Technion-Israel Institute of Technology, Haifa, Israel.

Caiazza, T. M., "Rails are Better," paper presented at the Second Annual Meeting of the Pacific Institute of Transportation, Honolulu, April 1968.

Carrabino, Joseph D., "Determining the Port's Role in Containerization," paper presented at the Transportation in the 70's Conference, San Diego, April 1970.

Collins, David, "Vehicle Control as a Basis for the Efficient Use of Transportation Networks," paper prepared for the Railway Systems and Management Association.

Cushing, Charles R., "Protection and Securing of Deck Stowed Containers," paper presented before the New York Metropolitan Section of the Society of Naval Architects and Marine Engineers, March 13, 1969.

Danagher, J. H., "Automatic Supervision and Recording of Temperatures and Pressures in Refrigerated Containerships," paper presented at the International Institute of Refrigeration Congress, Washington, D.C., 1971.

Day, James V., "Impact of Containerization on Regulatory Policy," paper presented at the Second International Container Services & Equipment Exposition, Baltimore, October 30, 1968.

Dilloway, Philip, "Human Factors Affecting Merchant Ship Navigation Safety," paper presented at the Institute of Navigation's National Marine Meeting, King's Point, N.Y., October 13, 1966.

East African Railways, "Wagon Load and High Capacity Loading of Wagons—Block Trains, Containers," paper presented at the 20th Session of the IRCA-UIC Congress, London, May 1971.

Fabiano, Luigi, "L'Impiego Dei Containers in Agricoltura," Societa Parmense di Lettura e Conversazione, Dicembre 11, 1968.

————, "Concetti Base Per La Scelta Dell 'Ubicazione di un Terminal per Containers," 17 Maggio, 1970.

————, "Porque Tenemos Que Adoptar el Sistema de los Containers," Feria Muestrario Internacional, Mayo 1970.

————, "Il Trasporto Dei Prodotti Deperibili Ortofruitticoli Dal Bacino Del Mediterraneo all Europa Continentale di Fronte Alla Nuova Tecnologia Del Container," paper prepared for the ICHCA Seminar, Oakland, April 1972.

Feiler, A. M., "Modeling Transportation and Distribution System," AIIE Transportation and Distribution Division Conference, Pittsburgh, January 27, 1971.

————, "Project Risk Management," Delivered at INTERNET 72 Congress, Stockholm, May 17, 1972.

Fixman, C. M., "Operations Research and Ship Design," paper prepared for the American University 15th Ocean Shipping Management Institute, April 1962, Washington, D.C.

Geddes, P. O., "Containerisation in New Zealand Being Some Economic Aspects of the Impact of Containerisation on the Transport Market in New Zealand, with Special Refernce to Rail Freight," paper presented at the IRCA-UIC Congress, London, May 1971.

El-Ghorfi, N., "Cultivation of Legumes, Fruits and Vegetables in Developing Countries," paper presented at the World Food Congress, Washington, D.C., June 1963.

Gibb, T. G., "The Carriage of Goods by Road in Europe," paper presented at the 20th Henry Spurrier Memorial Lecture, London, December 14, 1964.

Gibson, A. E., Remarks at the 4th International Shipping and Container Exposition, Oakland, September 14, 1971.

————, "New England's Stake in the New Maritime Program," paper presented at the Second Annual Port of Boston Night Program, sponsored by the International Center of New England and the Massachusetts Port Authority, Boston, March 11, 1971.

Grant, Terry (Lt. Cmdr.), "American Participation in IMCO," paper presented at the Transportation in the 70's Conference, University of California, San Diego, April 1970.

Grayson, Richard C., "Cooperation, Accommodation and Coordination," paper presented at the 45th National Convention of the Propeller Club of the U.S. and American Merchant Marine Conference, Tulsa, October 15, 1971.

Griffith, John H., "Trans-Modalist Steamship Service," paper presented at the State University of New York, Maritime College, Fort Schuyler, N.Y., 1968.

Grygiel, John, "Container Trains Today," paper presented at the Transportation in the 70's Conference, University of California, San Diego, April 1970.

Guilbert, Edward A. (Col.), Remarks presented before the Second Annual Pacific Institute of Transportation, Honolulu, April 8, 1968.

Harlander, Leslie A., "Further Developments of a Container System for the West Coast–Hawaiian Trade," paper presented at the Spring Meeting of the Society of Naval Architects and Marine Engineers, San Francisco, April 1961.

Hashimoto, Masashi and Tamaki, Mitsuo, "Freight Transport Policies of the Japanese National Railways with Particular Reference to Container Traffic," paper presented at the IRCA-UIC Congress, London, May 1971.

Healy, Joseph J., "A New Frontier: Inter-Modal Containerization," paper prepared

for the Connecticut General Life Insurance Conference, December 7, 1966, Hartford, Conn.

Henry, James J., "Container Ships," paper presented at the Annual Meeting of the Society of Naval Architects and Marine Engineers, New York, November 1966.

Hiltzheimer, C. I., "Second Generation Containerships," presented at the Second Annual Meeting of the Pacific Institute of Transportation, Honolulu, April 1968.

Hitchcock, J. D., "Communications: Telephones, Telex and Data," paper presented at the Institution of Civil Engineers, January 14, 1971, London.

Honsinger, Vernon C., "An Engineer's Introduction to PERT Scheduling and Control," paper presented at the Meeting of the Hawaii Section of the Society of Naval Architects and Marine Engineers, September 14, 1965.

Hunter, Peter, Remarks presented before the Second Annual Meeting of the Pacific Institute of Transportation, Honolulu, April 1968.

Ike, K., "Containerization One Year Later in Japan," paper presented at the Second Annual Pacific Institute of Transportation Conference, Honolulu, April 1968.

Illes, Joseph A., "Leisure Products," paper presented at the 11th Annual Conference and Shippers' Dialogue, The Containerization Institute, New York, March 1971.

Immer, John, "Far East Developments," paper presented at the Transportation in the 70's Conference, University of California, San Diego, April 1970.

Ingram, Robert A., Remarks before the 11th Annual Conference and Shippers' Dialogue of the Containerization Institute, New York, March 1971.

Johnson, Williard, "Current Innovation in World Food Production," reprinted from the *Journal of Law and Economic Development*, Vol. II, No. 2, 1968.

Jul, Mogens, "Food Preservation and Processing," paper presented before the World Food Congress, Washington, D.C., June 1963.

Jurgensen, Harald, "World Trade and Transport," paper presented at the 10th Biennial International Conference, Madrid, June 1971.

Kee, Loh Heng, "Developments in Singapore the Shipping Hub of South East Asia," paper presented at the 10th ICHCA Biennial Conference, Madrid, June 1971.

Kefauver, Russell (Rear Admiral), "Military Sealift and Containers," paper presented at the National Defense Transportation Association Regional Meeting, Honolulu, April 8, 1968.

Kieft, M. C., "The Effect of Ports on Ships," paper presented before the 10th Biennial International Conference of the International Cargo Handling Coordination Assn., Madrid, June 1971.

Klaassen, L. G. and Strazewski, J. A., "The Market for the Transport of Containers under Controlled Temperature," paper presented at the IRCA-UIC Congress, London, May 1971.

Kolaric, Vojislav, "The Effect of Containerisation on General Transport Economies," paper presented at the IRCA-UIC Congress, London, May 1971.

Kriebel, F. E., "Insights on Where We Go From Here in Shipping and Containerization," paper presented at the Fourth International Container Exposition and Technical Congress, Oakland, September 15, 1971.

Laemmerhold, Herr, Closing Address at the IRCA-UIC Congress, London, May 1971.

Laugier, Henri, "The Role of Long-Range Research in the Freedom from Hunger Campaign," paper presented at the World Food Congress, Washington, D.C., June 1963.

Leach, Rodney, "Significance and Implications of Containerization—A European View," paper presented at 2nd Annual Conference of Pacific Inst. of Transportation, Hawaii, April 1968.

Leblanc, Jacques, "Containerization: A European Perspective," paper presented before the Oakland Technical Conference, September 15, 1971.

Lewis, T. L. (Capt.), "Canals and Channels—A Look Ahead," paper prepared for the U.S. Naval Institute PROCEEDINGS, August 1967.

Macomber, F. S., "Japan to Europe by Land Bridge—Some Economic Comparisons," paper presented at the Fall Meeting of The Containerization Institute, San Francisco, October 1968.

Magee, John F., "Decision Trees for Decision Making," paper prepared for *Harvard Business Review*, July 1964.

Martin, Ray A., "Rail Transport," paper presented at the Transportation in the 70's Conference, University of California, San Diego, April 1970.

Mather, Glenn, "Containerization," an advance copy from section prepared for the *World Book Encyclopedia*, 1971.

May, Paul, "Cooperation between Food Processing Establishments in the Developed Countries with Those in the Developing Countries," paper presented before the World Food Congress, Washington, D.C., June 1963.

Meeusen, P., "Container Trade Development During and After the Third Generation Container Vessels," lecture at the Rotterdam Port Seminar, 1971.

Miller, C. D., "Economics of Super Barge Operation," paper presented before the Society of Naval Architects & Marine Engineers, Houston, February 12, 1965.

Miller, Dave S., "The Economics of the Containership Subsystem," paper presented at the October 1968 Meeting of the Philadelphia Section of the Society of Naval Architects and Marine Engineers.

Norris, John, "Facilitation and Its Role in the Container Age," paper presented at the Transportation in the 70's Conference, University of California, San Diego, April 1970.

O'Meara, John F., Speech presented before the 11th Annual Conference of the Containerization Institute, New York, March 1971.

Ordman, N. N. B., "The Effect of Ships on Ports," paper presented at the 10th Biennial International Conference of ICHCA, Madrid, June 1971.

Parsons, M. S., "Customs, door-to-door," paper presented at IRCA-UIC Congress, London, May 1971.

Perl, Guenter, "The Merits and Demerits of Containerization and Unitization," paper presented at the 11th Annual Conference of The Containerization Institute, New York, March 1971.

Porton, O. I. M., "A Look at Labor and Containers in Europe," paper presented at the 5th International Container Services & Equipment Exposition, Chicago, April 1970.

Querleux, J., "The Door-to-Door Tariff for Transcontainers in French Internal Traffic," paper presented at the IRCA-UIC Congress, London, May 1971.

Rath, Eric, "Kleinbehalter im Transportwesen per Achse und Schiff," May 1, 1934.

———, "What's New in Fishyback," 1956.

———, "Iso-Thermic Unitized Cargo System," paper presented at the Annual Meeting of the Society of Naval Architects and Marine Engineers, New York, November 1964.

———, "Second Generation Containerships," paper presented before the 2nd Pacific Institute of Transportation Conference, Honolulu, April 8, 1968.

———, "U.S. Containerization in the Crunch," paper presented at The Containerization Institute Conference, Oakland, September 1971.

Reese, Aaron W., "The Federal Maritime Commission's Role in Containerization," paper presented at the Transportation in the 70's Conference, University of California, San Diego, April 1970.

Reistrup, Paul H., Summary Remarks of Section IV of the IRCA-UIC Congress, London, May 1971.

Richards, D. H. (Brig. General), "Compatability in Containerization," paper presented at the Transportation in the 70's Conference, University of California, San Diego, April 1970.

Robert, J., "Wagons Used by the SNCF for the Transport of Large Containers and Semi-Trailer Road Vehicles," paper presented at the IRCA-UIC Congress, London, May 1971.

St. Jeor, C. E., "Where Do We Go from Here in Shipping and Containerization," paper presented at the 4th International Shipping & Containerization Exposition & Congress, Oakland, September 1971.

Saunders, William B., "The Outlook for Unit Trains," paper presented to the XI Pan American Railway Congress, Mexico City, October 1963.

Schrier, Elliot, "Too Much and Too Little," paper presented at The Containerization Institute Technical Congress, Oakland, September 1971.

Scott-Malden, C. P., and Price, E. H. M., "The Transport of Freight in Great Britain," paper presented at the IRCA-UIC Congress, London, May 1971.

Seeger, Ing. Friedrich (Dr.), "The Container Traffic as a Problem Affecting the Goods Train Schedules," paper presented at the IRCA-UIC Congress, London, May 1971.

Senizergues, P., "Study of the Market Open to the Different Modes of Goods Transport," paper presented at the IRCA-UIC Congress, London, May 1971.

Seyfarth, Henry E., Remarks before the New York Traffic Club, May 18, 1971.

Sheronas, Victor F., "Cleaning and Sanitizing of Containers," paper presented at the 2nd International Container Services & Equipment Exposition, Baltimore, October 30, 1968.

Silverman, Maxwell and Gaul, Roy D., "The Concept of Portability Applied to Future Oceanographic Ship Operation," reprinted from *Ocean Science and Ocean Engineering,* June 1965.

Sinclare, P. H. and Parker, J. D., "Cargo Handling and Communications," paper prepared for the Institution of Civil Engineers, January 14, 1971, London.

Smith, R. G., "Data and Data Systems for Cargo Handling," paper prepared for the Institution of Civil Engineers, January 14, 1971.

Stoessel, Robert F., "Adding Air to Intermodal Distribution," paper presented at the Transportation in the 70's Conference, University of California, San Diego, April 1970.

Sturmey, S. G., "The Structure of Commerce," paper presented at the 10th ICHCA Biennial Conference, Madrid, June 1971.

Traut, Robert, "A New Departure for Containerization," paper presented at the Transportation in the 70's Conference, University of California, San Diego, April 1970.

Turner, C. A., "Australia Containerization and Railways," IRCA-UIC Congress, London, May 1971.

Van Leeuw, J., "Load Unit and Complementary Character of the Modes of Transport," paper presented at the IRCA-UIC Congress, London, May 1971.

Verdon, L. and Rousse, R., "Equipment of Container Terminals and Handling Gear," paper presented at the IRCA-UIC Congress, London, May 1971.

Voges, George R., Speech presented before the 11th Annual Conference on Containerization, March 1971.

Ward, Montigue, "The Container Age in Shipbuilding," paper presented at the Transportation in the 70's Conference, University of California, San Diego, April 1970.

Water, W., "Coastal Container Shipping," paper prepared for the New Zealand Institution of Engineers, Wellington Branch, October 7, 1971.

Wax, Charles M., and Tencer, Ben, "Port Congestion By-Pass Possibilities," paper presented at the Containerization Institute Meeting, Oakland, September 1971.

Webster, W. C., Van Dyke, P., and Cojeen, H. P., "Automated Procedures for the Allocation of Containers on Shipboard," paper presented at the Meeting of the Chesapeake Section of the Society of Naval Architects and Marine Engineers, October 1969.

Wiersema, Ray, "Facilitating Integration," paper presented at the Transportation in the 70's Conference, University of California, San Diego, April 1970.

Wills, Arthur E., "The Cargo Container," paper prepared for the Insurance Company of North America, May 1968.

REPORTS

American Association of Port Authorities, Annual Report on Committee VII, "Port Practices, Rules and Terminal Rates, 1953."

American Plywood Association, Tacoma, Laboratory Report 114, "Design Data on Plywood for Transportation Equipment," by Jo Bonney.

Bigler, Allen R., Vancouver, Wash., Bigler Parking Systems, Part II, June 30, 1970.

———, Index Container Systems, Part III.

———, "Description of Index-O-Systems for Multilevel Storage (Bigler Container System)."

Browne, Ralph, "A Preliminary Report on Multilevel Container Handling Systems," International Research Associates, Renton, Wash., May 18, 1970.

Douglas Aircraft Co., Inc., "Index-O-Multi Level Storage," Report No. D.A.C. 56071, Volume IV, Part 8, March 16, 1969.

Eastman Dillon, New York, "Report for Institutional Investors," Maritime Fruit Carriers, Ltd.

Ecocentre, MacGregor-Comarain, "El Desarrollo del Transporte Maritimo y su Medio Ambiente," reports presented by R. H. Jacquinet, N. Tien Phuc and A. Piatier. Madrid, December 5, 1972.

Evans, Edward S., Transportation Research, Washington, D.C., "The Use of Surplus War Cargo Planes to Transport Agricultural Perishables," January 1945.

Henry, J. J., Co., Inc., "Study of Tipping Moments for Containers," by F. D. Chu for American Mail Line, August 1967.

Hewitt-Robbins, Div. of Litton Industries, "Trailer-Container Terminal Handling Operations," prepared for Trailer Train Co., November 1966.

Hilliard, Arthur, Griffith John H., and Rath, Eric, "Cargo Systems '68—Reports on Current Status of Integrated Ship Cargo Systems," prepared for the American Merchant Marine by The Propeller Club of the U.S. Port of State University of New York—Maritime College, Fort Schuyler, N.Y., 1968.

Insurance Institute of London, Report by Advanced Study Group No. 188, London, "An Examination of the Changing Nature of Cargo Insurance Following the Introduction of Containers," 1969.

Kouffeld, R. W. J. and Knobbout, J. A., "Comparative Tests of the Thermal Performance of an Insulated Vehicle," prepared for the International Institute of Refrigeration, 1970.

Litton Industries, "Economic Analysis of the Small Port Vessel," Culver City, Calif., October 1967.

Maritime Transport Committee, "Developments and Problems of Seaborne Container Transport, 1970," published by OECD Environment Directorate, Paris, April 1971.

Maritime Transportation Research Board, Division of Engineering—National Research Council, "Legal Impediments to International Intermodal Transportation," National Academy of Sciences, Washington, D.C., 1971.

McKinsey & Company, Inc., London, England, "Containerization: The Key to Low-Cost Transport," prepared for the British Transport Docks Board, June 1967.

Meeusen Consultants, "Rotterdam Studies Containerisation Beyond the 3rd Generation Containervessels," Barendrecht, Holland.

Nielsen, H. & Son Engineering Works Ltd., Herkaer, Herlev, Denmark, Internal Report, November 1970.

Ocean Transport Consulting Services, New York, "Container Allocation Program."

Rath Company, The, La Jolla, Calif., "Cost Study—Small Port Vessel," prepared for the Military Sea Transportation Service.

Rath, Eric, "The TASK Ship, The Integrated Ro/Ro Container System."

Saunders, W.B. & Company, Washington, D.C., "Trans-Isthmus Corporation, An Appraisal," report describing prospects of proposed new container transportation system between the U.S., Mexico and Central America, April 1964.

——, Washington, D.C., "Prospects for Transportation of Containers Across the Mexican Isthmus," December 1963.

Stanwick Corporation, "Design Work Study."

Steadman Industries Ltd., Rexdale (Toronto) Canada, Report to Shareholders Annual Meeting of Interpool International Ltd., June 1971, by I. Gould.

Truck Trailer Manufacturers Assn., Washington, D.C., TTMA Recommended Practice, "Intermodal Bulk Liquid Containers," by Charles J. Calvin, July 1970.

United Nations, "Coastal Shipping, Feeder and Ferry Services, Department of Economic and social Affairs," New York, 1970.

——, "Unitization of Cargo," Report by the Secretariat of UNCTAD, New York, 1970.

——, Conference on Trade and Development, UNCTAD, Committee on Shipping,

Report by the Secretariat "Converting General Cargo Ships to handle Unitized Cargo," September 1972.

United States Steel, Pittsburgh, "Market Report—Containerization—A Growth Market in Transportation," May 1966.

University of California, Los Angeles, Dept. of Engineering, "Simulation Analysis of Military Ocean Terminal, Bay Area," Report No. 68-16, March 1968.

———, Dept. of Engineering, "Systems Analysis of Port of Los Angeles, California," Report No. 69-40, July 1969.

———, School of Engineering & Applied Science, "Systems Analysis of the Port of Long Beach, California," Report No. 70-3, January 1970.

OFFICIAL PUBLICATIONS

American Bureau of Shipping, "Guide for the Certification of Cargo Containers," New York, 1969.

British Standards Institution, London, "Specification for Freight Containers," BS3951, 1967.

Federal Maritime Commission, Washington, D.C., "Quarterly Report of Freight Loss and Damage Claims," Notice of Proposed Rulemaking, 46CFR Part 546, Docket No. 71-74, August 1971.

———, Preliminary Staff Report on "Non-Vessel Operating Common Carriers by Water," December 1970.

International Labour Organisation, Inland Transport Committee, Geneva, "Summary Record of the Sixth Session," Hamburg, March 1957.

———, "Introduction to Work Study," Geneva, 1957.

———, "Methods of Improving Organisation of Work and Output in Ports," Second Item on the Agenda for the Sixth Session of the Inland Transport Committee, Hamburg, 1957.

———, Tripartite Technical Meeting on Dock Labour, Rotterdam, April 1969.

International Road Transport Union, Geneva, 1970.

Lloyd's Register of Shipping, "Freight Container Certification Scheme," London, 1968.

———, "Longitudinal Bending Moments," by J. M. Murray, London, 1947.

———, "Wave Excited Main Hull Vibration in Large Tankers & Bulk Carriers," by R. A. Goodman, London, April 1970.

———, "Strength of Large Tankers," by W. J. Roberts, London, 1970.

Statutory Instruments, "The Motor Vehicles (Construction and Use) Regulations," Her Majesty's Stationery Office, London, 1955.

U.S. Air Force, "Cargo Handling System for a Military Air Freight Terminal," Emmett B. Cassady, Brigadier General, USAF, Director, Transportation & Services.

U.S. Army Mobility Equipment, Research & Development Center, Ft. Belvoir, Va., "A Critical Analysis of the State of the Art in Containerization," by S. Berger, et al., November 1970.

U.S. Dept. of Agriculture, Agricultural Marketing Service, Washington, D.C., "Protecting Perishable Foods During Transportation by Truck," December 1956.

——, ARS, "Impending European Standards for Vehicles Used to Transport Perishable Foods," by Robert F. Guilfoy, Report ARS 52-59, December 1970.

U.S. Dept. of Commerce, Washington, D.C., *Modern Ship Stowage*, by Joseph Leeming, 1942.

——, Maritime Administration, Washington, D.C., "Guidelines for Deck Stowage of Containers," by J.J. Henry Co., Inc., July 1970, Report No. MA-RD-71-4.

——, "Guidelines for Deck Stowage of Containers," by J.J. Henry Co., July 1970, Report No. MA-RD-71-5.

——, "The Impact of Containerization on the U.S. Economy," Vol. 1, by Follet, et al., September 1970.

——, "An Evaluation of Alternative Railroad Terminal Container Handling Systems," by Donald P. Ainsworth, et al., Robert Reebie & Associates, Inc., Greenwich, Conn., March 1971.

——, "Transocean Tug-Barge Systems," by Ernest Koenigsberg, et al., Matson Research Corp., San Francisco, July 1970.

——, "Proposal to Assist in the Conduct of Studies and Program Planning in Concept Formulation," prepared by Peat, Marwick, Livingston & Co., Boston, February 1968.

U.S. Department of Transportation, "Domestic and International Facilitation Program," 1971.

——, "Study of Container Interchange and Pooling Arrangements," prepared by Booz, Allen & Hamilton, Inc., June 1970.

U.S. Navy Mine Defense Laboratory, Panama City, Fla., "The Ship Design Process," by Richards T. Miller, January 1965.

U.S. War Dept., Washington, D.C., "Military Pipe-Line Systems," Technical Manual TM5-350, November 15, 1943.

CATALOGS

Aeroquip Corporation, Industrial Division, Jackson, Mich.

Aluminum Company of America, Commercial Development Div., Pittsburgh, Pa.

American Association of Port Authorities, Inc.

American Export Isbrandtsen, 26 Broadway, New York, N.Y. 10004.

ATC Leasing Corp., 4346 Sheila Street, Los Angeles, Calif. 90023.

Auckland Harbour Board, Auckland Harbour, New Zealand.

Boyd Brothers Steamship Agencies, Ltd., Balboa, Canal Zone.

Breco Materials Handling, Tubs Hill House, London Road, Sevenoaks, Kent, England.

Canadian National, Montreal, Quebec, Canada.

Central Steel Tube Company, Clinton, Iowa.

Colt Industries, Fairbanks Morse Weighing Systems Division, 1901 Route 208, Fair Lawn, N.J. 07410.

Columbia Export Packers, Inc., 19032 So. Vermont Avenue, Torrance, Calif. 90502.

Comanco, Inc., Box 9, Berwick, Pa.

Computer Identics Corp., Southwest Park, Westwood, Mass. 02090.

Containair Systems Corp., 145–80 228th Street, Springfield Gardens, N.Y. 11413.

Continental Trailer Corp., 13231 Lakeland Road, Santa Fe Springs, Calif. 90670.

Dorsey Trailers, Elba, Ala. 36323.

Duramin Engineering Co., Ltd., Harbour Road, Lydney, Glouchestershire, England.

Eness Research & Development Corp., 75 Carver Avenue, Westwood, N.J. 07675.

Evans Products Company, Transportation Equipment Div., Plymouth, Mich.

Carl F. Ewig, Inc., 44 Whitehall Street, New York, N.Y.

First National Bank of Boston, Automated Corporate Services Dept., 40 Morrissey Blvd., Dorchester, Mass. 02125.

Frigitemp Corporation, 121 E. 18th Street, New York, N.Y. 10003.

Fruehauf Trailer Company, Detroit, Mich.

FWD Wagner, Inc., 4427 N.E. 158th Avenue, Portland, Ore. 97220.

General American Transportation Corporation, 120 S. Riverside Plaza, Chicago, Ill. 60690.

General Steamship Corporation, Ltd., 400 California Street, San Francisco, Calif. 94119.

German Federal Railroads, 11 W. 42nd Street, New York, N.Y. 10036.

Hans H. Grosse & Co., 2000 Hamburg 11, Germany.

International Chemical Corporation, 25 Almeria Avenue, Coral Gables, Fla.

International Minerals & Chemical Corporation, Skokie, Ill.

Interpool, 630 Third Avenue, New York, N.Y. 10017.

Japan Container Association, 8th Floor, Yaesu-Mitsui Bldg. 7, 5-Chome, Yaesu, Chuo-ku, Tokyo, Japan.

R. G. LeTourneau, Longview, Texas 75601.

Litewate Transport Equipment Corporation, 4220 So. 13th Street, Milwaukee, Wis. 53221.

Litton Systems, Ingalls Shipbuilding Corp., 9220 W. Jefferson Blvd., Culver City, Calif. 90230.

Lockheed Shipbuilding & Construction Co., 2929 Sixteenth Ave., S.W., Seattle, Wash. 98134.

Matson Navigation Company, 100 Mission Street, San Francisco, Calif. 94105.

Meeusen Consultants, n.v., le Barendrechtseweg 30, Barendrecht, Holland.

Mitsubishi Heavy Industries, Ltd., 10, Marunouchi, 2-Chome, Chiyodaku, Tokyo, Japan.

Mitsui Shipbuilding & Engineering Co., Ltd., 6-4, Tsukiji, 5-Chome, Chuo-ku, Tokyo, Japan.

National Castings Group, Midland-Ross Corporation, 10600 Quincy Avenue, Cleveland, Ohio 44106.

Paceco, Div. of Fruehauf Corp., Alameda, Calif.

Package Research Laboratory, Rockaway, N.J.

Panama Agencies Company, Balboa, Canal Zone.

Pan American World Airways, New York, N.Y.

PDQ Plastics, Inc., 245 Frelinghuysen Avenue, Newark, N.J. 07114.

Pennsylvania Box & Lumber Co., John Fitch Industrial Park, Warminster, Pa. 18974.

Port of Hamburg, Hamburg, Germany.

Port of Long Beach, Long Beach, Calif.

Port of New York Authority, 111 Eighth Avenue, New York, N.Y. 10011.

Reynolds Metal Company, Richmond, Va. 23218.

Santa Fe Railway, 80 E. Jackson Blvd., Chicago, Ill. 60604.

Sea-Land Service, Inc., Elizabeth, N.J.

Signode Corporation, Strapping Division, 2600 N. Western Avenue, Chicago, Ill. 60647.

Societe Intercontinentale Des Containers, 6, Rue Daru, 75 Paris 8e, France.

Carl Spaeter, Hamburg 33, Saarlandstrasse 2-30, Hamburg, Germany.

Steadman Industries, Ltd., 280 Belfield Road, Rexdale 605, Ontario, Canada.

Strick Trailer Corporation, Container Division, Fairless Hills, Pa.

Sylvania Electric Products, Inc., Transportation Control Systems, 100 First Avenue, Waltham, Mass.

Taiben Trading Corporation, Taipei, Taiwan.

3M Company, 3M Center, Saint Paul, Minn. 55101.

Trailmobile, Div. of Pullman, Inc., 200 S. Michigan Avenue, Chicago, Ill. 60604.

Transcontainer, 3 Hannover, Joachimstrabe 8, Bremen, Germany.

United Airlines, Chicago, Ill.

United States Lines, One Broadway, New York, N.Y.

United States Steel, Transportation Industry Marketing, Pittsburgh, Pa. 15230.

University of California-Los Angeles, Dept. of Engineering, Los Angeles, Calif.

Weyerhaeuser Company, Tacoma, Wash. 98401.

MAGAZINES

Agricultural Engineering, published by ASAE, 2950 Niles Road, St. Joseph, Mich. 49085.

Air Transportation, 26 Beaver St., New York, N.Y. 10004.

Ashrae Journal, published by ASHRAE, Headquarters, 345 E. 47th Street, New York, N.Y. 10017.

Brandon's Container World, Suite 1927, One World Trade Center, New York, N.Y. 10048.

Business Week, 330 W. 42nd Street, New York, N.Y. 10036.

Cargo Airlift, P.O. Box 6710, Chicago, Ill. 60680.

Commercial Car Journal, Chestnut and 56th Streets, Philadelphia, Pa. 19139.

Containerisation International, The National Magazine Co., Ltd., 680 Garratt Lane, London SW17, England.

Container News, 150 East 52nd Street, New York, N.Y. 10022.

CTD, published by Centro Italiano Studi Containers, Via Montefeltro 4/6, 20156 Milano, Italy.

Defense Transportation Journal, published by NDTA, 1612 K St., N.W., Washington, D.C.

Design News, 221 Columbus Avenue, Boston, Mass. 02116.

Fairplay, Palmerston House, Bishopsgate, London, E.C.2, England.

Fairwind, published by the National Maritime Development Inst., 240, Tun-Hua N. Road, Taipei, Taiwan, Republic of China.

Food Engineering, Chestnut & 56th Streets, Philadelphia, Pa. 19139.

Fortune, Time, Inc., 541 N. Fairbanks Court, Chicago, Ill. 60611.

Handling & Shipping, 812 Huron Road, Cleveland, Ohio 44115.

ICHCA Monthly Journal, Abford House, 15 Wilton Road, London, SWIV, England.

Marine Engineering/Log, 350 Broadway, New York, N.Y. 10013.

Marine Technology, published by SNAME, 20th & Northampton Sts., Easton, Pa. 18042.

Maritime Reporter & Engineering News, 107 E. 31st Street, New York, N.Y. 10016.

Modern Railroads, 5 South Wabash Avenue, Chicago, Ill. 60603.

Proceedings, U.S. Naval Institute, Annapolis, Md. 21402.

Refrigerated Transporter, 1602 Harold Street, Houston, Texas 77006.

Shell Aviation News, Shell Oil Company, 50 W. 50th St., New York, N.Y. 10020.

Tow Line, published by Moran Towing & Transportation Co., Inc., 17 Battery Place, New York, N.Y. 10004.

Traffic Management, 205 E. 42nd Street, New York, N.Y. 10017.

Traffic World, Washington Bldg., Washington, D.C. 20005.

Trailer/Body Builders, 1602 Harold Street, Houston, Texas 77006.

Transportation & Distribution Management, Washington Bldg., Washington, D.C. 20005.

Via Port of New York, published by Port of N.Y. Authority, 111 Eighth Avenue, New York, N.Y. 10011.

World Ports, 1612 K Street, N.W., Washington, D.C. 20006.

NEWSPAPERS AND NEWSLETTERS

Ferinfor, Paris
Financial Post
Freight News, London
International Freighting Weekly/Ports and Terminals
Los Angeles Times
Todd Daily News
Transport Topics
Wall Street Journal

Containerization Institute Newsletter
"Perishables Handling," University of California, Davis Newsletter

YEARBOOKS

Containerization International Annual Container Guide 1968–69
Containerization International 1970 Yearbook
Containerization International 1971 Yearbook

U.S. GOVERNMENT SOURCE CODES

U.S. Govt. I—*A Critical Analysis of the State of the Art of Containerization*, S. Berger, et al., Control Systems Research, Inc., Arlington, Virginia, November 1970.

U.S. Govt. II—*The Impact of Containerization on the U.S. Economy, Vol. II*, Earl Follette, et al., Matson Research Corporation, San Francisco, September 1970.

U.S. Govt. III—*The Impact of Containerization on the U.S. Economy: Vol. I*, September 1970.

U.S. Govt. IV—*Transocean Tug-Barge Systems. A Conceptual Study, Vol. I, The Executive Summary*, Ernst Koenigsberg, et al., Matson Research Corporation, San Francisco, July 1970.

U.S. Govt. V—*An Evaluation of Alternative Railroad Terminal Container Handling Systems*, Donald P. Ainsworth, et al., Robert Reebie and Associates, Inc., Greenwich, Connecticut, March 1971.

U.S. Govt. VI—*Inland and Maritime Transportation of Unitized Cargo, National Academy of Sciences*, National Research Council, Publication 1135, July 1963.

U.S. Govt. VII—*Guidelines for Deck Stowage of Containers*, Prepared for the U.S. Dept. of Commerce, Maritime Administration, by J. J. Henry Co., New York, July 1970.

UN/IMCO 1972 CONFERENCE

United Nations/Inter-Governmental Maritime Consultative Organization—Conference on International Container Traffic 1972 Documents

Final Act UN/IMCO 1972
Customs Convention on Containers 1972, UN/IMCO 1972
International Convention for Safe Containers (CSC) UN/IMCO 1972

Report of the Third Committee, 1 December 1972, UN/IMCO 1972

Oct 1 Memorandum "Exchange of Views Between Representatives of Governmental and Non-Governmental Organizations" 21 November 1972

Index